Understanding Voter Behavior With Predictive Modeling

Georgia Panagiotidou
Aristotle University of Thessaloniki, Greece

IGI Global
Scientific Publishing
Publishing Tomorrow's Research Today

Vice President of Editorial Melissa Wagner
Director of Acquisitions Mikaela Felty
Director of Book Development Jocelynn Hessler
Production Manager Mike Brehm
Cover Design Jose Rosado

Published in the United States of America by
IGI Global Scientific Publishing
701 East Chocolate Avenue
Hershey, PA, 17033, USA
Tel: 717-533-8845
Fax: 717-533-7115
Website: https://www.igi-global.com E-mail: cust@igi-global.com

Library of Congress Cataloging-in-Publication Data

Names: Panagiotidou, Georgia, 1984- editor
Title: Understanding voter behavior with predictive modeling / Edited by Georgia Panagiotidou.
Description: Hershey, PA : IGI Global Scientific Publishing, [2026] | Includes bibliographical references and index. | Summary: "This book aims to advance the study of electoral behavior by showcasing innovative approaches that leverage predictive models, artificial intelligence, polling methodologies, and advanced research techniques"-- Provided by publisher.
Identifiers: LCCN 2025012306 (print) | LCCN 2025012307 (ebook) | ISBN 9798337310374 hardcover | ISBN 9798337310381 paperback | ISBN 9798337310398 ebook
Subjects: LCSH: Voting research | Election forecasting | Elections--Technological innovations | Artificial intelligence--Political aspects | Polling places
Classification: LCC JF1001 .U43 2025 (print) | LCC JF1001 (ebook) | DDC 324.6/50285--dc23/eng/20250708
LC record available at https://lccn.loc.gov/2025012306
LC ebook record available at https://lccn.loc.gov/2025012307

British Cataloguing in Publication Data
A Cataloguing in Publication record for this book is available from the British Library.

Table of Contents

Detailed Table of Contents

The prediction of election outcomes is a prominent subject of research in a multidisciplinary field of science. This study aims to examine the evolution of trends, methodologies, and key factors that shape the framework of election forecasting. To achieve this, we used the method of bibliometric analysis on the available literature of Scopus platform. The data collected from 2000 to 2025 were analyzed by the VOSviewer software. Our research concluded that there are three main trends in the field of election prediction. The traditional school which focuses on econometric and advanced statistical models, the decision-making method grounded in social sciences and computational methods, finally and more recently, the data-driven models which use sophisticated machine learning algorithms, neural networks, and Natural Language Processing (NLP). In addition, Tumasjan's seminal work on predicting election results through Twitter platform was the most influential research, and Lewis-Beck is the most cited and significant author with the most collaborations across the academic community.

The ability to vote is one of the most valuable rights and privileges afforded by the Constitution of the United States to its citizens. For many, voting is not just a civic duty; it is also a choice. Voting is crucial to our democracy, and any changes to it may affect the efficiency of the democratic process. The bigger question is whether voters behave rationally by engaging in a cost-benefit calculus in deciding whether or not to vote. Using data science, this paper will examine the probability of voting and investigate its impact via cost and benefit among other variables using the 2020 American National Election Studies (ANES) dataset. In addition, the study will also assess the impact voter perceptions of "a sense of duty" have on voter turnout. Empirical work provides additional evidence that feelings of civic duty truly do motivate voter turnout. Using the latest methods of statistical analyses, we identify and understand the factors that benefited and hindered voting in the ANES 2020 data and the impact of voter benefits and costs on turnout.

This chapter examines issue voting in political competition and voter behaviour in Greece during the two parliamentary elections of 2015. Drawing on data from the HelpMeVote platform, the analysis employs Principal Component Analysis (PCA) and fuzzy clustering to position parties and voters on key issue dimensions and trace their shifts between January and September. The January election was dominated by the memorandum–anti-memorandum divide, which largely determined party agendas and voter alignments. By September, this central cleavage had weakened, as SYRIZA and ANEL, despite their prior anti-memorandum stance, revised their thematic agendas, prompting varying degrees of voter realignment. Results indicate that while some parties and voters displayed significant thematic repositioning, others remained stable, highlighting both the persistence of ideological identities and the capacity of party strategies to reshape electoral competition. The findings contribute to understanding issue-driven voting, party–voter congruence and the dynamics of political change in crisis contexts.

Quantitative methods in election studies are of extreme importance as they are of greatest importance for generalization of voter behavior and election result. The interpretative use of a set of statistical techniques: regression analysis, correspondence analysis, and hierarchical clustering, is applied in this research work for interpretation and analysis of the 2024 Andhra Pradesh election data. Regression is utilized to model connections between voting and socio-demographic determinants, while correspondence analysis aims to locate interactions between categories of variables, for example, between parties and the demographics of voters. Regions are grouped based on regions that share similar patterns of elections via hierarchical clustering, while regional trends, regional discrepancies and differences are determined. Through the use of these quantitative methods, analysis seeks to identify voting patterns, local voting patterns, and socio-economic influence on party performance.

This study conducts a systematic bibliometric analysis of predictive modeling in electoral research, situating computational methods within the study of voter behavior. Drawing on a broad corpus of scholarly literature, it identifies key research trajectories, thematic patterns, and leading contributors. Findings show a shift from traditional statistical approaches to advanced applications of machine learning, artificial intelligence, and sentiment analysis in election forecasting. Citation networks highlight the United States, India, and China as major centers of academic activity. Thematic and co-occurrence analyses reveal strong associations among artificial intelligence, decision trees, social media engagement, supervised learning, and electoral prediction. A conceptual map from Multiple Correspondence Analysis shows how computational tools complement, rather than replace, classical paradigms. Collaboration networks demonstrate global linkages, while ethical concerns regarding privacy, bias, and transparency underscore the importance of balancing interpretability with fairness.

Electoral behaviour research evolves through digital transformation, using big data for predictive analysis and data-driven methods. This paper explores how political science benefits from evaluating large datasets to detect voter behaviour patterns. Researchers now use voter registration, social media analytics, polls, and economic indicators, supported by data science and geographic visualization tools. The integration of natural language processing and machine learning enhances accuracy in sentiment analysis, voter forecasting, and population comparisons. The chapter also discusses challenges in managing vast electoral data, including privacy risks, real-time processing issues, and data bias. Big data applications improve election forecasting, campaign strategies, and voter survey precision. This work highlights how political science aligns with AI and data science to build accurate, technology-enabled election prediction models. It offers essential tools and methods for researchers, strategists, and policymakers to analyze modern voting behaviour.

This chapter addresses the persistent underestimation of Republican vote shares in U.S. presidential election forecasts, with a focus on the 2024 cycle. Despite methodological refinements, polling errors remain systematic. The chapter proposes a theory-driven, voter-level modelling strategy using logistic and Bayesian logistic regression applied to 2024 ANES data. Moving beyond poll aggregates and structural indicators, the models incorporate predictors such as ideological orientation, economic dissatisfaction, and sociodemographic traits. Results confirm that these factors substantially improve predictive accuracy, reducing the gap between estimated and actual vote shares. The weighted Bayesian model predicted Trump's national vote share within 1.6 percentage points—outperforming many major polling organisations. Overall, this approach demonstrates the empirical and diagnostic value of behavioural modeling in electoral forecasting and contributes to a broader methodological shift that centres voters' individual characteristics as key to understanding electoral outcomes.

This chapter presents a framework for predicting the vote choice of undecided voters, integrating Fuzzy Clustering, stacked data analysis and binary logistic regression on the 2010 Greek regional elections. Drawing on the evolution of electoral behavior research -from Siegfried's electoral geography and the Columbia and Michigan schools to ideological polarization, rational choice and issue voting- the study addresses earlier limitations by capturing the probabilistic, multidimensional nature of voter preferences. Analysis of Voter Advice Application (HelpMeVote) data shows that party identification strongly predicts choices for the two major parties, while smaller parties are better explained by issue salience, candidate attributes and demographics. Fuzzy Clustering reveals overlapping thematic voter groups, while stacked data and logistic regression estimate their effect on stated and predicted vote choice. The findings demonstrate the value of probabilistic models for forecasting undecided voters and the need for adaptable, data-driven tools in the era of digital campaigns and AI.

This chapter examines the transformative impact of Artificial Intelligence (AI) on political decision-making, marketing, and electoral forecasting. AI's integration into politics reshapes how campaigns are conducted and how decisions are made, but it also raises significant ethical concerns.AI-driven tools are increasingly used to analyse voter behaviour, craft political messages, and predict election outcomes. From targeted advertisements to sentiment analysis on social media, AI enables more precise campaign strategies. However, it also introduces risks like misinformation, deepfakes, and algorithmic bias, which can undermine democratic processes and public trust. Case studies illustrate how AI's role in politics varies by context—democracies focus on transparency and public engagement, while authoritarian regimes use AI for control and surveillance. Predictive models powered by machine learning have shown success, where AI models outperformed traditional polling.

This study is aimed at examining how political audiences of a documentary titled Gold Mafia received it. Drawing from reception theory as a theoretical frame work it answers the questions how did the audiences receive the documentary and how did the documentary influence their political attitudes and behavior towards ZANU PF. To achieve its goals this qualitative study utilizes in-depth interviews with purposively selected ZANU PF supporters who watched the documentary. The study fleshes out that the audiences were angered by the documentary and resultantly a majority opted out of ZANU PF while others expressed that they will never vote for the political party again. This therefore shows that documentaries carrying discourses of corruption done by the elite has the power to alter political attitudes and behaviors of audiences.

The integration of artificial intelligence (AI) into the 2024 European Parliament elections redefined the dynamics of political campaigning, voter behavior, and democratic integrity. This chapter examines the dual role of AI as both an enabler of participatory democracy and a catalyst for electoral manipulation, focusing on populist movements in Estonia, the Netherlands, Greece, and Italy. Through a comparative analysis of AI-driven microtargeting strategies and an evaluation of EU regulatory frameworks such as the Digital Services Act and the Artificial Intelligence Act, the study reveals critical vulnerabilities in safeguarding electoral processes. It argues for an adaptive, multi-scalar regulatory approach to mitigate the epistemic and structural risks posed by algorithmic political persuasion, ensuring democratic resilience in the age of digital transformation.

Preface

SCOPE AND FOCUS OF THE BOOK

The study of voter behavior has long been central to political science, offering insight into how citizens decide at the ballot box and into the functioning of representative democracy. From the mid-20th-century sociological analyses of the Columbia School and the psychological models of the Michigan School to modern statistical forecasting, researchers have sought to explain and predict electoral choice. These foundations shaped decades of research but left unanswered questions, especially as political systems, media, and demographics evolve.

In the past two decades, the rise of big data, artificial intelligence, and digital analytics has transformed electoral studies. Where traditional polling once dominated, today's research integrates social media data, geospatial mapping, large-scale experiments, and complex predictive models. This diversification enables more nuanced analyses, capturing subtle shifts in voter preferences, emerging issues, and campaign effects in real time.

My engagement with electoral analysis began over twenty years ago with a focus on Greek politics, later expanding to comparative studies and new analytical techniques. I soon recognized the limits of static models that assumed stable political systems, fixed loyalties, and predictable alignments. In Greece, as in many democracies, party fragmentation, anti-establishment movements, and volatile public opinion have challenged those assumptions.

This is a global story. Around the world, declining trust in institutions, the spread of misinformation, and the rapid emergence of new issues have made voter behavior more fluid than ever. Campaigns now unfold across multiple channels, from traditional media to microtargeted digital ads, each shaping voter information in distinct ways. Understanding decision-making in this environment requires combining theory, rigorous statistical modeling, and attention to social and cultural contexts.

Predictive modeling has become a powerful tool for detecting hidden patterns, simulating scenarios, and tracking shifts in voter sentiment. But it also raises challenges: data quality, representativeness, transparency, accountability, and algorithmic bias are now central concerns in electoral research. Against this backdrop, *Understanding Voter Behavior with Predictive Modeling* gathers global contributions offering theoretical insights, methodological innovations, and applied case studies on political marketing, digital media, and campaign strategy. Together, they form a narrative moving from conceptual foundations to applied analysis, showing both the promise and complexity of studying elections today.

The unifying theme is that the study of voter behavior must evolve with contemporary politics. It is no longer enough to examine voter intentions or past trends; we must use dynamic data, respond to shifting agendas, and account for cultural context. This applies equally to established and emerging democracies, where forecasting and interpreting voter behavior is both a scientific challenge and a civic duty.

This preface reflects my own journey in electoral research, shaped by respect for both the art and science of political analysis. I hope the work presented here will serve as a reference for election scholars and as an invitation to think critically and creatively about the tools we use to understand democracy.

POSITIONING THE TOPIC IN TODAY'S WORLD

In today's interconnected political landscape, voter behavior analysis is not merely academic, it is essential for understanding the health and direction of democracy. Electoral competition has grown more complex, shaped by technological advances, socio-economic shifts, cultural change, and geopolitical pressures. Elections remain moments of decision, but now unfold in a fragmented, fast-moving, and contested information environment.

Digital communication has transformed both campaigning and how voters process information. Social media, online news, and targeted digital ads allow political messages to reach specific audiences instantly. These tools create new opportunities for engagement but also raise challenges for transparency, fact-checking, and combating misinformation. Campaigns now focus as much on shaping the information space as on persuading or mobilizing voters.

In this environment, predictive modeling and advanced analytics have become indispensable. Machine learning, natural language processing, and other AI-driven tools help detect patterns in vast datasets, uncover subtle shifts in public sentiment, and forecast electoral outcomes. Such methods reveal insights beyond the reach of traditional approaches, highlighting the growing influence of specific issues or voter segments.

Yet these tools carry risks. Models depend on data quality and underlying assumptions; incomplete or biased datasets can distort conclusions. Their use raises ethical questions about voter privacy, the influence of microtargeting, and the responsibility of researchers to ensure analytics strengthen, rather than weaken, democratic participation.

The COVID-19 pandemic reinforced the need for adaptive, data-driven electoral analysis. Elections worldwide faced delays, changes in voting methods, and heightened polarization. Traditional campaign and polling practices were disrupted, accelerating reliance on digital tools and intensifying debates about integrity and access. The ability to integrate diverse data sources and adapt models quickly became essential for campaigns, observers, and policymakers alike.

Beyond crises, structural shifts are reshaping politics. Party systems are fragmenting, elections are more competitive, and long-standing voter alignments are giving way to fluid patterns influenced by generational change, identity politics, and issues such as climate change, migration, and inequality. In the digital age, these forces interact with personalized, issue-driven politics to create an increasingly unpredictable electoral landscape.

In this context, *Understanding Voter Behavior with Predictive Modeling* offers a multidisciplinary response to the challenges and opportunities of modern electoral research. Drawing from diverse national and methodological perspectives, its chapters show that predictive modeling is not a single solution but a broad, evolving set of tools, each with distinct strengths, limitations, and ethical implications.

What unites them is a shared aim: to combine quantitative rigor with qualitative insight, merge computational power with contextual understanding, and ensure that innovation serves the public interest. In doing so, electoral research can remain relevant, responsible, and responsive to the rapidly changing realities of 21st-century politics.

WHO THIS BOOK IS FOR

The scope and structure of *Understanding Voter Behavior with Predictive Modeling* are designed to engage a broad, interconnected audience across disciplines, professions, and regions. Electoral behavior intersects with political science, sociology, economics, computer science, and communication studies, making the book relevant to all who seek to understand and anticipate the forces shaping democratic decision-making.

Academics and researchers will find empirical insights, methodological innovations, and theoretical perspectives that support comparative and interdisciplinary inquiry. Data scientists and AI specialists can draw on the volume's methodological discussions and ethical considerations to develop transparent, contextually grounded tools. Pollsters and survey methodologists will gain strategies for integrating predictive modeling with traditional polling to better interpret voter sentiment and adapt to modern challenges. Political strategists and campaign professionals can refine planning and targeting by understanding the interplay between preferences, communication, and messaging. Policymakers, election commissions, and NGOs will find approaches for monitoring electoral processes, detecting suppression or disinformation, and strengthening transparency. For graduate students, the book offers a rich foundation for coursework and research, while informed citizens and democracy advocates will benefit from accessible explanations and global perspectives.

For all these diverse audiences, the book aspires to foster a shared language between disciplines and professions, creating a space where methodological rigor meets practical application. In doing so, it reflects the conviction that understanding voter behavior is not solely the domain of any single group but rather a collaborative endeavor that benefits from and requires the insights of many.

STRUCTURE AND CONTENT OF THE VOLUME

This volume comprises fifteen chapters, carefully organized into three thematic sections that together provide a comprehensive exploration of voter behavior and electoral analysis in the age of predictive modeling. The first section, *Theoretical Foundations and Analytical Approaches to Voter Behavior*, establishes the conceptual and methodological groundwork for understanding electoral dynamics. The second section, *Predictive Models, Statistical Applications, and Data-Driven Forecasting*, focuses on the use of advanced computational tools, big data, and statistical modeling to forecast electoral outcomes. The third section, *Communication, Campaign Strategies, and Digital Influence on Electoral Outcomes*, examines how political messaging, digital platforms, and emerging technologies shape voter perceptions and campaign effectiveness.

The first section opens the first chapter which introduces us to a comprehensive bibliometric analysis of the election forecasting literature, offering readers a panoramic view of how scholarly approaches to predicting electoral outcomes have evolved over the past quarter century. Drawing on the Scopus database and advanced visualization tools, the authors map three major trends in the field: the traditional econometric and statistical models, decision-making frameworks rooted in social sciences, and, more recently, sophisticated data-driven techniques powered by machine learning, neural networks, and natural language processing. By identifying seminal works, such as Tumasjan's pioneering Twitter-based prediction study, and spotlighting key scholars like Lewis-Beck, this chapter equips the reader with a deep understanding of the intellectual genealogy of election forecasting, setting the stage for the empirical and applied chapters that follow.

The second chapter moves from the meta-analysis of the literature to a focused investigation of voter rationality in the context of the 2020 U.S. Presidential Election. Using the American National Election Studies dataset, the authors examine whether voter turnout can be explained through a cost–benefit calculus, while also exploring the often-overlooked motivational role of civic duty. Through sophisticated statistical modeling, the study uncovers how perceptions of voting costs, perceived benefits, and moral obligation interact to influence electoral participation. This analysis not only refines our understanding of the rational choice paradigm in political behavior but also highlights practical levers for increasing democratic engagement in the United States.

The third chapter applies advanced statistical methods to examine thematic realignment in Greece's two parliamentary elections of 2015. Using HelpMeVote platform data, the analysis employs principal component analysis and fuzzy clustering to map shifts in voter–party congruence as the political agenda moved from a dominant memorandum–anti-memorandum divide in January to a more diffuse thematic landscape in September. The findings illuminate the interplay between enduring ideological loyalties and the strategic repositioning of parties in times of crisis, contributing to comparative studies of electoral volatility.

The first section closes with the fourth chapter which offers a clear, methodologically rigorous example of how statistical tools can be applied to electoral data to uncover patterns and regional differences. Through regression, correspondence analysis, and hierarchical clustering, the authors dissect the results of the 2024 Andhra Pradesh election, revealing how socio-demographic variables, party alignments, and geographical factors interact to shape voting outcomes. This final chapter of the section reinforces the crucial role of quantitative methods in drawing generalizable insights from electoral data while also providing a methodological bridge to the more predictive and applied studies in the following section.

The second section begins with chapter five, a systematic bibliometric analysis that maps the intellectual terrain of predictive modeling in electoral research. By tracing the evolution from traditional statistics to machine learning and artificial intelligence, the authors highlight the growing integration of decision trees, supervised learning, sentiment analysis, and social media metrics into forecasting practice. Their conceptual mapping demonstrates how computational methods complement rather than replace classical approaches, while collaboration network analysis reveals a globally connected research community. Importantly, the chapter also brings ethical considerations to the forefront, emphasizing the need to balance predictive power with transparency and fairness in electoral analytics.

The discussion moves next to chapter six and the world of big data, exploring how the unprecedented scale and diversity of modern datasets are transforming electoral studies. Leveraging information from voter registration records, social media streams, polling data, and economic indicators, the chapter illustrates how natural language processing and machine learning enhance the precision of sentiment analysis and voter forecasting. It also addresses the practical and ethical challenges of managing vast electoral datasets, from privacy protection to real-time data processing and the mitigation of bias. By integrating political science with cutting-edge data science, the authors demonstrate the potential for big data to improve election forecasting, optimize campaign strategies, and refine voter survey methods, making this contribution essential for scholars and practitioners navigating today's data-rich environment.

Building on this data-centric perspective, the next seventh chapter addresses one of the most persistent challenges in electoral forecasting: predicting the behaviour of undecided voters. Using issue-based statistical modelling, specifically fuzzy clustering and discriminant analysis, the author offers a framework for identifying latent patterns in voter preferences and mapping the pathways by which undecided individuals align with particular parties. The methodology not only refines pre-election predictions but also sheds light on the thematic issues most influential in swaying this critical segment of the electorate. This approach is particularly valuable in multiparty systems or closely contested races, where a small shift among the undecided can decisively alter the outcome.

Chapter eight turns to the application of voter-level behavioral modeling to the high-stakes context of the U.S. presidential election. Confronting the recurring issue of underestimated Republican vote shares, the authors employ both logistic and Bayesian logistic regression on 2024 ANES data, integrating ideological orientation, economic dissatisfaction, and sociodemographic characteristics. The resulting models achieve exceptional predictive accuracy, with the Bayesian approach estimating Donald Trump's vote share within 1.6 percentage points of the actual result. Beyond the empirical success, this work signals a methodological shift toward centring individual-level variables rather than relying solely on aggregated polling or structural indicators, marking an important advance in the predictive toolkit of electoral research.

The ninth and closing chapter for this second section widens the lens to consider the strategic uses of predictive modeling and AI within political marketing campaigns. Drawing on diverse case studies, the authors show how AI-driven tools, from targeted advertising and sentiment analysis to real-time message optimization, are reshaping the way political actors engage with voters. They underscore AI's capacity to outperform traditional polling in certain contexts, while also warning of its darker applications, such as misinformation campaigns, deepfakes, and algorithmic bias. The comparative perspective, contrasting democratic contexts that prioritize transparency with authoritarian settings that deploy AI for surveillance, offers a nuanced understanding of both the potential and the perils of these technologies. This chapter thus serves as a bridge between the technical discussions of modeling and the broader questions of democratic integrity that run throughout the volume.

The third section opens with chapter ten, an exploration of disinformation and its corrosive impact on electoral integrity in both the European Union and the United States. By framing the issue within the broader context of foreign information manipulation and disinformation (FIMI), the authors reveal how coordinated, often foreign-sponsored, campaigns strategically exploit the vulnerabilities of democratic systems. Their analysis underscores that the challenge is not merely technological but deeply political, as disinformation can erode trust, distort public discourse, and weaken the resilience of democratic institutions.

From here, the volume moves into the mechanics of political marketing, with chapter eleven offering a critical examination of how U.S. presidential campaigns have harnessed audience segmentation, emotional framing, and targeted messaging to construct candidate identities. The chapter situates these strategies within the broader digital transformation of campaigning, where big data analytics and social media metrics guide nearly every communicative choice. While acknowledging the efficiency and outreach benefits of marketing-driven politics, the author also warns of the risks, especially the replacement of substantive political debate with emotionally manipulative appeals, thereby shifting the electoral process toward a market-like competition for attention rather than an informed contest of ideas.

A different perspective on voter engagement emerges in chapter twelve on political brand hate, which introduces this concept to the study of electoral behavior for the first time in the MENA region. Drawing from psychology and marketing, the authors analyze how negative experiences, ideological incompatibility, and symbolic incongruence can produce deep-seated political aversion. The research, based on quantitative data from Moroccan voters, reveals that such brand hate significantly reduces re-vote intention, but that performance tolerance, or the ability of a political brand to meet voter expectations, can mitigate these effects. This insight offers valuable guidance for political actors seeking to repair damaged relationships with their electorates.

In Chapter thirteen, the theme of digital transformation returns in a subsequent study of social media's global impact on political communication and election outcomes. Using case studies from Brazil, the Philippines, and Romania, the authors demonstrate how platforms such as TikTok, Facebook, and Instagram enable both mass outreach and microtargeting, creating unprecedented opportunities for voter engagement. Yet the same tools also facilitate polarization, disinformation, and the erosion of trust. By incorporating emerging technologies like artificial intelligence, augmented reality, and blockchain into their analysis, the authors present a forward-looking assessment of both the opportunities and the ethical hazards inherent in digital campaigning.

The fourteenth chapter offers a rare examination of political persuasion through documentary media, analyzing how the film Gold Mafia reshaped political attitudes toward Zimbabwe's ruling party, ZANU PF. Drawing on reception theory and qualitative interviews with party supporters, the study finds that exposure to corruption narratives can prompt strong emotional reactions, leading some voters to abandon long-held partisan loyalties. This case study demonstrates that political communication is not limited to campaign messaging or news coverage; cultural and media products can also play a decisive role in reshaping voter perceptions.

Chapter fifteen closes this final section with an investigation into AI-driven electoral strategies during the 2024 European Parliament elections, focusing on their use by populist movements in Estonia, the Netherlands, Greece, and Italy. The chapter presents a dual narrative: on one hand, AI-enabled microtargeting can enhance participation and tailor messages to diverse constituencies; on the other, it can be weaponized for manipulation, raising profound concerns for democratic integrity. By evaluating existing EU regulations such as the Digital Services Act and the Artificial Intelligence Act, the authors identify both strengths and gaps in the current governance framework. Their argument for adaptive, multi-scalar regulatory approaches reinforces the central lesson of this section, that technological innovation in political communication must be matched by equally innovative safeguards to preserve the democratic process.

CONCLUSION: ADVANCING THE STUDY AND PRACTICE OF ELECTORAL ANALYSIS

Bringing together the work of scholars from across the globe, this volume offers a wide-ranging yet coherent exploration of how elections are studied, understood, and anticipated in the twenty-first century. Across its three sections, the chapters speak to one another, moving from theoretical foundations to methodological innovation and, finally, to the communicative and strategic dimensions that shape electoral outcomes. This progression reflects the reality of electoral analysis itself: theory and data are not separate worlds, but parts of a single, evolving conversation about how citizens make choices and how those choices can be understood in an age of rapid technological and political change.

The collective impact of these contributions lies in their ability to connect local case studies with global patterns, to blend statistical precision with an awareness of the cultural and political contexts in which voting takes place, and to look ahead to the challenges and opportunities that new technologies bring. Whether through the refinement of predictive models, the application of big data and AI, or the careful study of campaign strategies in both physical and digital arenas, the chapters in this book demonstrate that electoral research remains both an essential scholarly pursuit and a practical tool for those engaged in the democratic process.

In this way, the volume does more than document current knowledge, it helps shape the future of the field. By presenting new evidence, proposing innovative approaches, and raising critical questions about ethics, transparency, and trust, it invites ongoing dialogue between academics, practitioners, and citizens. The hope is that these pages will not only inform but also inspire further inquiry, encouraging readers to think more deeply about the forces that influence elections and the ways in which democratic societies can better understand themselves.

Acknowledgments

I would like to express my deepest gratitude to all contributing authors for their dedication, expertise, and commitment to this project. Their work has brought to life the vision behind this volume. My sincere appreciation goes to the political science associations, academics and colleagues worldwide who helped disseminate the call for chapters, enabling this project to bring together voices and research from across the globe.

I am equally grateful to IGI Global for their guidance, support, and trust throughout this endeavor.

Finally, I wish to thank my family, close friends and mentors for their unwavering encouragement during the many months of editing and coordination.

Section 1
Theoretical Foundations and Analytical Approaches to Voter Behavior

Chapter 1

Forecasting Election Outcomes: A Bibliometric Analysis

Grigorios Charalampos Tsiligkaridis
https://orcid.org/0009-0005-0875-3394
University of Western Macedonia, Greece

Ioannis Nikolaos Mallidis
https://orcid.org/0000-0002-1207-8564
University of Western Macedonia, Greece

Grigorios Petros Giannarakis
https://orcid.org/0000-0002-5283-1071
University of Western Macedonia, Greece

ABSTRACT

The prediction of election outcomes is a prominent subject of research in a multidisciplinary field of science. This study aims to examine the evolution of trends, methodologies, and key factors that shape the framework of election forecasting. To achieve this, we used the method of bibliometric analysis on the available literature of Scopus platform. The data collected from 2000 to 2025 were analyzed by the VOSviewer software. Our research concluded that there are three main trends in the field of election prediction. The traditional school which focuses on econometric and advanced statistical models, the decision-making method grounded in social sciences and computational methods, finally and more recently, the data-driven models which use sophisticated machine learning algorithms, neural networks, and Natural Language Processing (NLP). In addition, Tumasjan's seminal work

DOI: 10.4018/979-8-3373-1037-4.ch001

on predicting election results through Twitter platform was the most influential research, and Lewis-Beck is the most cited and significant author with the most collaborations across the academic community.

INTRODUCTION

By studying election forecasts, political parties and candidates can effectively target certain categories of voters and properly generate their political manifestos. Furthermore, election forecasting gives useful information about the elements that shape public opinion and may influence voter behavior. That is why the prediction of election outcomes has become a prominent subject of research in a multidisciplinary field of science. Moreover, both the quantitative and the qualitative development of data-gathering methodologies have the potential to focus more on data-driven forecasting techniques. From this point of view, bibliometric analysis has emerged as a thorough approach for examining and investigating huge numbers of data and simultaneously understanding the evolution of a scientific field and its rising domains (Donthu et al., 2021). Also, it appears collaborations among authors and organizational connections, helping to identify the significant contributors and networks in the scientific field (Van Eck & Waltman, 2010). Because bibliometric analysis employs quantitative metrics, it provides less biased outcomes than other methods (Ellegaard & Wallin, 2015). In the field of election research, we implemented bibliometric analysis to investigate important concepts. For example, Widayat et al. (2022) used bibliometric analysis to investigate the Indonesian Presidential election in social media, Subekti et al. (2023) on political campaigns, and Perannagari & Chakrabarti (2020) on political marketing. However, there is a noticeable lack of bibliometric analysis focused on the models that forecast election results. The purpose of this study is to designate the intellectual conception, the key contributors, and the contemporary trends in this discipline.

Research Questions

1. What are the most prevalent models used for election forecasting, and how have they evolved over time?
2. Who are the key contributors, and what are the main collaborations in this field?

Literature Review

Reviewing electoral forecasting literature we demonstrated eight main categories of models. At the first part of this section we present the most important models that were reported in the literature until February of 2025. At the second part of this unit, we will address the challenges these models face in their implementation, as well as emerging ethical issues related to public trust and the transparency of their processes.

Forecasting Models

Opinion Polls

Opinion poll techniques collect data to measure public opinion and voter preferences, providing a snapshot of voters' preferences during pre-election periods (Witzenberger & Diakopoulos, 2023). This technique provides forecasts by analyzing people's choices among different candidates (Traugott & Lavrakas, 2008). However, even though data from polls can contribute to the accuracy of forecasts, they face issues such as sampling errors and systematic biases which may distort the results.

Polls Aggregation

The *poll of polls* or polls aggregation is the method of integrating each individual poll to create a unified set of all polls. This approach is especially useful because it can mitigate random errors by reducing the variability of each individual poll, minimize systematic biases, and improve accuracy (Pasek, 2015). It also provides on-going updated data on voting behavior and public opinion trends throughout the pre-election period (Pasek, 2015). However, accuracy problems arise when many individual polls suffer from similar biases, particularly due to the house effect, resulting in survey techniques or companies producing different conclusions (Silver, 2016). Moreover, the results derived exclusively from public opinion polls, excluding other factors that influence the election result, such as economic indicators and the electoral advantage of already elected politicians and their recognition (Silver, 2016). To solve this problem, poll aggregators should weigh outcomes relative to sample size and representativeness (Silver, 2016). Managing multiple estimates can improve accuracy. However, blindly aggregating surveys without considering differences in sample size and data quality can lead to misleading conclusions (Pasek, 2015). Ignoring potential biases during aggregation can also produce artificially accurate results, since the actual error in surveys is higher from the reported sampling error (Silver, 2016).

It is important to realize that this strategy is particularly susceptible, especially dealing with surveys of varying quality and error types. Aggregating polls involves integrating data from various sources which had used diverse methods (Armstrong, 2001). Aggregators can enhance accuracy by considering sample sizes and the precision of similar polls. Larger samples lead to more precise estimations, and weighting results based on the square root of sample size reduces errors (Armstrong, 2001). For example, in case of USA Presidential election, deciding which polls to include requires careful assessment of accuracy, representativeness, and bias at both state and national levels (Silver, 2016). Poll aggregators used various methodologies, as there is not a merely efficient approach (Pasek, 2015). In conclusion, aggregations provide a snapshot of the current election status and assume that errors will be balanced across multiple polls. Thus, for an aggregating model to be advantageous, it requires careful consideration of these factors to avoid misleading results. Moreover, traditional poll aggregation methods fall short to integrate new information and assessments into the understanding of the evolving election atmosphere and conditions, because they focus on a narrow time frame and lack mechanisms to incorporate additional data (Pasek, 2015).

Economic Voting

Economic Voting relies on rational choice theory, incorporating political science and economics aspects. This approach examines how economic indices such as GDP, unemployment rate and disposal income, and political factors such as the performance of the incumbency, historical election data, and opinion polls impact voter behavior and election outcomes (Lewis-Beck & Stegmaier, 2009). This model is also known as *Economic voting*, because the voter traditionally rewards the government for good economic performance and blames it for bad (Lewis-Beck & Stegmaier, 2000). The analysis is usually national, analyzing aggregate historical data, and the estimation is carried out using ordinary least squares (OLS) on single equations (Lewis-Beck & Dassonneville, 2015). Furthermore, the final prediction is unique because this estimation is static rather than dynamic (Lewis-Beck & Dassonneville, 2015). This model offers early and accurate insights into election outcomes by analyzing economic and political factors. It provides valuable information about the underlying mechanisms of the electoral and political landscape and contributes to our understanding of the complex interplay between the economy, politics, and voting behavior (Hummel & Rothschild, 2014). However, like the traditional aggregating polls, the economic voting model is inadequate for integrating additional information of the pre-election atmosphere and conditions because of its reliance on a small set of predictors, and a small number of available historical data derived from past elections results. In addition, the strength of economic voting is found to vary across countries and over time due to political and economic contexts (Dassonneville & Lewis-Beck, 2014). Factors such as the diversity of political and electoral systems, particularly in the member states of the European Union, the blame-shift of responsibilities to accountability under coalition governments, and the instability of economic conditions that prevailed during the post-communist transition in Eastern European countries, mitigate our ability to use a generalized standard model to predict election outcomes. (Dassonneville & Lewis-Beck, 2014).

Election Markets

Prediction markets like Iowa Electronic Markets, enable participants gamble on the winners of political elections by buying future contracts (Erikson & Wlezien, 2008). Grounded in the Hayek hypothesis, these markets efficiently aggregate diverse information from participants, producing equilibrium prices that reflect accurate estimations of election probabilities (Berg et al., 2008). Ideally, election markets incorporate all relevant information—including polls, economic indicators, policy announcements, and aggregated trader expectations—into contract prices (Wolfers & Leigh, 2002).

Moreover, this approach also confronts limitations to predict validated election results. The people who engage in election markets are not a representative sample of the entire population of the voters (Berg et al., 2008). Besides, the nature of gambling in prediction markets frequently tends to be more speculative than rational. Just a minor number of participants may manipulate the trading trend with the aim of causing price volatility to achieve short-term profits having as result the failure of a precise electoral result prediction (Berg et al., 2008). Additionally, the average trader reveals "wishful thinking bias" resulting in being long on his desired candidate and short to his opponent (Forsythe et al., 1999).

Experts' Judgments

A pundits-based approach refers to the practice of forecasting election results relying on pundits' expertise and experience. The Delphi technique is a structured method in which forecasts are generated based on the consensus among experts (Graefe et al., 2014). In this approach, pundits possess up-to-date information such polls and are aware of the impact of pre-election events such as debates and party conventions (Cuzán et al., 2005). Even so, not all experts are equally capable of correctly predicting election results despite their specialized knowledge and experience. Especially those who are overconfident, or try to please party machinery, or are dogmatically attached to a particular party or political ideology cannot overcome their biases and fail to predict election results accurately (Tschoegl & Armstrong, 2008).

Synthesized Models

Synthesized models are techniques that combine multiple predictive models. There are two types of synthesized approaches, the "Standard" and the "Bayesian" (Pasek, 2015). Standard approach such "Pollyvote" (Cuzán et al., 2005) and the "FiveThirtyEight" (Silver, 2016) combines predictions from polls, aggregated polls, pundits' opinions, quantitative models, and prediction markets, to produce a final forecast (Pasek, 2015). The "Bayesian" approach differs from the "Standard" because it bases its predictions on employing the most recent data that is available during the pre-election period until the day of the election (Pasek, 2015). Any added information instantly updates the prediction (Pasek, 2015). Linzer's seminal study (2013) depicts the success of the Bayesian model, particularly with its effectiveness in associating the state-level election poll results with the national in a comprehensive manner (Linzer, 2013). Empirically, synthesized models have proven to be more effective than methods relying on a single forecasting model (Graefe et al., 2014).

Despite their effectiveness, synthetic models also face significant challenges. Firstly, the use of synthetic models, and especially Bayesian models, requires advanced skills and computational resources, which limit their accessibility to researchers lacking expertise in these technologies (Pasek, 2015). Bayesian models rely their accuracy on prior assumptions. In case they are incorrect or incorrectly weighted, it is difficult to achieve an accurate result (Pasek, 2015). Further, the complexity involved in producing accurate and valid forecasts may lead these models to overlook the quality and impartiality of individual components, especially polls (Pasek, 2015). Finally, these models place greater emphasis on the computational aspect and largely ignore the theoretical basis of political and electoral analysis, making it hard to comprehend the underlying political phenomena behind election outcomes (Pasek, 2015).

Social Media Data / Data-Driven Forecasting / Predictive Analytics

Direct access to vast volumes of data, at a very low cost, and the ability to analyze them using artificial intelligence tools have opened an entirely new field for predicting electoral outcomes (Brito et al., 2021). Social media, especially Twitter (X) and Facebook, were an unexplored field to contemplate public sentiment. Natural Language Processing (NLP) and machine learning algorithms (ML) are the most applicable techniques for sentiment analysis. However, social media analysis confronts serious methodological limitations. Brito et al. (2021) argue that there is no fixed and replicable procedure for replication and generalization across different electoral contexts. Moreover, until now, which contradicts the primary purpose of prediction, that is, to forecast an event beforehand (Kwak & Cho, 2018). Also, bots, spammers, propaganda messages, and variations in users' attitudes may produce unreliable data (Chauhan et al., 2021). Relying only on social media for forecasts is inadequate in countries with diverse social, economic, and cultural characteristics across their regions. Ignoring other factors such as GDP, religion, literacy levels, and health indicators limits the accuracy of predictions (Koli & Ahmed, 2019).

Computational Forecasting

Simulation-based approaches implement stochastic models like Markov Chain Monte Carlo (MCMC) and Monte Carlo simulation, to forecast election outcomes. MCMC is a statistical method that can estimate complex models and make predictions by running many random trials constructing synthesized scenarios, making them applicable to election forecasting (Çetin & Bentli, 2013). Agent-based modeling (ABM) is a simulation-based approach that implements historical data based on previous voters' behavior to predict future election outcomes (Gao et al., 2022). Other models base their predictions on utilizing Geographic Information Systems (GIS). However, this electoral forecasting method confronts challenges because of its computational complexity (Çetin & Bentli, 2013), the reliance on historical data, the occurrence of probable biases, and the huge amount of resources that are required to conduct large-scale analyses (Gao et al., 2022).

Table 1. Comparative Analysis of Electoral Forecasting Models

Models	Data source	Strengths	Limitations
Opinion Polls	Survey data of voter preferences	Measurement of voter preferences	Sampling errors, False response or nonresponse, uses data from only one source excluding others
Aggregating Polls	Integration of multiple opinion-polls	Mitigates random errors, Use of updated data, Smooths variations	Susceptible to favoritism (house effect), uses data from only one source excluding others, quality variation
Economic Voting	Economic indicators and political factors, historical data	Capacity of early predictions, Techniques based on theory framework	Static, restricted and targeted forecasting set, limitation of country's political, economic and cultural context
Prediction Markets	Market and contract prices on election results	Encompasses information of different sources	Not representative sample of voters, wishful thinking bias, Speculative trading

continued on following page

Table 1. Continued

Models	Data source	Strengths	Limitations
Expert Judgments	Pundits' evaluations, Delphi technique	Integrates nuanced and sophisticated knowledge	Overconfidence, prejudice, limited replicability
Synthesized Models	Combination of multiple methods ("Standard" and "Bayesian")	Broadly the most accurate models, dynamic, effective balance of multiple sources' inputs	High skills and computational resources, high dependence on prior assumptions,
Social Media Data-Driven	Social media, Web sources, NLP	Direct access to large scale of real-time data, low cost, opinion mining and real-time sentiment analysis	Bots, misinformation, generalization and replicability issues, transparency
Computational/Simulation-Based	Historical data, Simulated and synthetic scenarios	Handles and tests intricate scenarios	Data-centric, high skills and computational demands

Note. Comparative analysis of different electoral forecasting models. Data sources, Strengths, and limitations

Applications, Challenges, and Conceptual Topics in Election Predictions

Transparency and Ethical Considerations for Democratic Elections

Although these models are sophisticated and based on thorough computational and theoretical background, the accuracy of their predictions faces serious challenges. The 2016 US Presidential Election was a characteristic example. Even though most of the opinion polls predicted that Clinton was the favorite to win the election race, ultimately, they failed to predict the winner because they underestimated the late shifts among undecided voters, and forecast errors in swing states such as Pennsylvania, Michigan, and Wisconsin (Kennedy et al., 2018). Similarly, the same phenomenon happened in 2019 Australian elections, all polls and expert evaluations also failed to predict the winner (Goot, 2021). Diverse forecasting models, including, opinion polls, aggregated polls, synthesized models, pundits' evaluations, election markets, social media-data-driven predictions and economic models, all failed the Brexit as result in UK's referendum on EU membership (Fisher & Shorrocks, 2018).

These forecasting failures identify the limitations of the existing models. For this reason, questions arise regarding public confidence in the reliability of the electoral forecasting methods used and whether these failures were due to real weaknesses of the methods or attempts to deceive and manipulate the voters. Thus, honest communication between researchers and the public about the capabilities, limitations, and transparency of the models used is an ethical imperative.

Many studies have identified that there are crucial ethical problems related to the election forecast models. Issues such as data privacy, algorithmic bias, and manipulation of public opinion all constitute topics that need deep consideration (Mittelstad et al., 2016). Therefore, social media-driven election predictions models may fail to filter out unreliable data, which can lead to the spread of fake news and disinformation (Tenove, 2020). Moreover, When computational methods lack transparency in their parameters, assumptions, and limitations, this creates skepticism about the reliability and validity of the forecasting outputs (Brito et al., 2021; Mittelstad et al., 2016)

Thus, despite the belief that social media would enhance and democratize public discourse and communication, in many cases these networks have been exploited by opportunists to manipulate public opinion by organizing propaganda (Tenove, 2020). In India's 2019 election race, political parties utilized big data analytics to target specific groups of voters, while at the same time propaganda and fake news were spread to strengthen the candidates' profile (Neyazi & Schroeder, 2021). This practice created intense questions about the privacy and transparency of the electoral process (Neyazi & Schroeder, 2021). Similarly, the great scandal of Cambridge Analytica, which used data without the consent of millions of social media users to analyze their psychological profiles for use in targeted political advertising in both the 2020 Brexit referendum and the 2016 US presidential election (Isaak & Hanna, 2018).Furthermore, unfair practices were also utilized online to influence the electoral base were also presented in the elections in France in 2017 (Ferrara, 2017), and Kenya in the same year (Mutahi & Kimari, 2020).

The aforementioned examples identify the necessity for more transparency, ethical considerations, and digital defense against fake news and disinformation to protect the democratic integrity of electoral institutions (Tenove, 2020). Consequently, beyond technical issues, it is essential that the presentation of these predictive methods be effectively communicated so that the public can understand and trust them (Tenove, 2020). This could be accomplished if each forecast clearly highlights the potential, limitations, and biases may have taken place (Tenove, 2020). The coverage of the forecasts by the mass media may craft the public's perception of the electoral and political landscape, impact voters' turnout, and even affect people's preference (Strömbäck & Kiousis, 2011). These issues are substantial for a meritocratic electoral process.

A notable example of successfully countering digital threats was Taiwan's 2020 Presidential Elections when institutions cooperated with fact checkers and civilians based on a four-pillar structure (Kao, 2021).

Cross-National Variability in Election Forecasting

Until a decade ago, most work focused on forecasting election results on Western democracies. Countries such as India, Brazil, and Indonesia have been understudied and only in the last decade has there been growing interest in applying, especially social media-driven models, to these countries. More and more studies are being published drawing attention to apply models to an electoral landscape which is challenging because of its unique features including the electoral system, multipartism, coalition politics, and cultural, social and economic heterogeneity (Tillin & Pereira, 2017; Adeney & Swenden, 2024; Koli & Ahmed, 2019). In a very unstable political environment with weakly institutionalized parties, clientelism, political intrigues, numerous parties competing for victory, and ongoing party negotiations to reach a consensus, it is hard to predict the final winner, and more difficult to link votes to seats (Aspinall & Mietzner, 2014; Adeney & Swenden, 2024; Power, 2010). In addition, the forecasting becomes even more complicated due to religious, linguistic, economic, and identity diversifications that can cause unpredictable shifts in voters' viewpoints in response to regional dynamics or local events (Pepinsky, 2025; Adeney & Swenden, 2024).

To tackle this challenge, researchers should collect locally grounded data (Tillin & Pereira, 2017), to recognize the cultural, economic and institutional factors that impact the political landscape and electoral volatility of each nested geographic pattern (Koli & Ahmed, 2019; Norris, 2014). They should also collaborate with local institutions and pundits to heighten data quality in order to construct a model that reflects the local dynamics rather than trying to develop a one-size-fits-all model for all Eastern democracies (Koli & Ahmed, 2019; Norris, 2014).

Evolution of Forecasting Approaches Over Time

The transition from traditional econometric models to decision science and machine learning models indicates a methodological shift from approaches based on theoretical frameworks to data-driven models. In recent years, computers have become robust and faster, resulting in a shift to more sophisticated and technical approaches such as Bayesian and computer simulation models. Furthermore, in the last decade, machine learning algorithms, big data, and real-time social media have transformed forecasting into data-driven approaches. However, despite the general trend of researchers approaching their forecasts based on data, none of the eight forecasting models has managed to establish itself as dominant, as each one faces its own limitations. For this reason, there are increasing attempts to synthesize different models in order to add more dynamics to the quality of predictions.

Data-driven models can amplify the forecasting accuracy of election outcomes, especially in intricate and multifactor political landscapes. Yet, the inner process of these models is like a black box and bring up inquiries about transparency, generalization and interpretability (Guidotti et al., 2018; Mittelstad et al., 2016; Brito et al., 2021). Moreover, they are high technical approaches without theoretical background that lack explanatory logic about the results, restricting their helpfulness to explain voter behavior (Guidotti et al., 2018).

Interpreting VOSviewer Clusters and Trends in Election Forecasting

The previous review of forecasting models of election outcomes offered the theoretical framework to examine more systematically the evolution of these models across literature by using bibliometric analysis. The bibliometric analysis was conducted by using VOSviewer software. VOSviewer is a sophisticated tool which provides a visual approach to academic research, indicating influential studies, mapping the collaboration networks, showing off opportunities for interdisciplinary cooperations, and highlighting emerging clusters of research on the emergence of forecasting models (Van Eck & Waltman, 2010).

To make sense of the bibliometric maps we produced, let explain some examples of clusters and trends that were revealed by VOSviewer analysis. These clusters are not only a group of keywords and authors names, but they illustrate the shifting methodological evolution in this scientific field. For example, *Traditional forecasting models* form a well-defined cluster with keywords such as econometric model, structural model, probability model, Pollyvote, and pre-election polls presenting a community of well-grounded forecasting models, with validated practices. Another well-defined cluster is social media data-based forecasting. Key terms such as lexicon, social media analysis, twitter sentiment analysis, python, decision trees, bots, and the pioneering author Tumasjan indicates links to sentiment analysis, machine learning algorithms and social media. Moreover, the light green to yellow color on *VOSviewer Overlay Visualization map* highlights that this is the newest methodological approach. Additionally, the looser co-authorship ties on *VOSviewer Network Visualization map*, also shows that it is the youngest and most scattered field of research that is still growing.

METHODOLOGY

We chose Scopus database as the source for bibliometric data since it provides exceptional accessibility to scholarly studies. The collected studies are articles, review articles, conference papers, and book chapters published between 2000 and 17 February of 2025 in English language to cover the contemporary trends. The search strategy comprises keywords:

("election*forecast* OR "election*predict* OR "forecast* OR «predict*election*)

Then, we exported a CSV file including data from the categories: Citation Information, Bibliographical Information, and Abstract & Keywords, specifically the fields Year, Source Title, Cited By, Link, Affiliations Index, Keywords References, and Document Type. Initially, we retrieved 659 articles of which 132 were not related to predicting the election outcomes or did not present any forecasting election models. Thus, 527 papers were relevant for the scope of our research.

First, an overview of our research presented using descriptive statistics extracted from the Scopus Database. This included the types of studies done on the topic, trends over the years, how popular the topic has been in the last 25 years, the countries most studied, the journals that published on it, and the scientific fields with the most publications.

Afterwards, we utilized VOSviewer software to illustrate co-authorships, co-occurrences, keywords, citations, and time trend analyses for the most popular models over the years. Bibliometric networks constructed and visualized from the exported data. Specifically, the network construction involved creating visual and analytical representations of the relationships among authors, publications, and research topics. This method studies collaboration patterns among authors and organizations, highlights significant publications and foundational papers, and maps thematic clusters to indicate research trends and focus fields. This process identifies the most notable contributors, significant journals, the evolving advancements in the scientific area overtime, and potentially may reveal gaps in the existing literature.

We answered the first research question by using *VOSviewer Overlay Visualization* map. *VOSviewer Overlay Visualization* map plots a gradient color timeline that represents the evolution of a condition overtime (Van Eck & Waltman, 2023). In our case, this map was employed to show the emergence of scientific areas of forecasting models over the last 25 years. The map has been interpreted through the nodes and the gradation of their colors. According to the official VOSviewer manual (Van Eck & Waltman, 2023), nodes represent items which, depending on the options recommended by the software, can be authors, documents, organizations, countries, keywords, or sources, while the colors provide a chronological perspective. The darker the color the older the period and vice versa. To answer our first question, we imported to VOSviewer our bibliographic data to create a co-occurrence map based on text data, *Title*, and *Abstract* field. Afterwards, before constructing the final co-occurrence maps and letting VOSviewer to generate clusters, we cleaned and reviewed all the extracted term. Using VOSviewer's term list view, unrelated or repeated words that did not add value to our study removed, and similar terms and synonyms grouped into unified entries. After the previous step, all the input terms for VOSviewer's clustering function were clear and meaningful. As a result, the generated clusters were interpretable and well aligned with the literature topics.

Each node is represented by a keyword. We chose Binary counting as the counting method, with a threshold of ten set for the minimum number of occurrences of three. We select a total number of six hundred items. Finally, we applied the Association Strength method to normalize the co-occurrence data. Van Eck and Waltman (2009) argued that association strength is a robust method that offers a meaningful and clear visualization of perceived networks and conceptual connections within co-occurrence data in bibliometric analyses. Specifically, their empirical findings proved that this method discloses research trends, provides distinct thematic clusters and a sound network connection, with eliminated bias (Van Eck & Waltman, 2009).

To answer our second research question, we first created a map based on bibliographic data using citations and documents. All documents with fifty or more citations from our Scopus Database were used. A VOSviewer Density Visualization map was produced, based on this bibliographic data. The analysis focused on citations and documents, with a minimum citation threshold set at one hundred. Forty-one documents met this criterion. Each point on the plot represents the year and the first author's name of a document on the VOSviewer Density Visualization map. This type of map presents how often the items we examine appear in our study (Van Eck & Waltman, 2023). The colors on this map form a gradient from blue presenting area with the fewest citations, to green showing moderately cited areas, to yellow which indicates most cited areas (Van Eck & Waltman, 2023). The more vivid the color in an area, the higher the number of citations it corresponds (Van Eck & Waltman, 2023). Afterwards, we constructed a table with *the most cited documents in the last 25 years (50 citations or more)* to provide a clearer insight into the cited studies, their publication dates, and their authors. Then, we extracted a figure from the Scopus Database platform showing the authors with the highest number of publications. Finally, a VOSviewer Network Visualization map was created to illustrate the main collaborations among authors. Thus, a map was generated using the Scopus Database. The analysis focused on co-authorships and authors, applying Full Counting as the counting method. The minimum number of documents per author was set to two. Out of 1,056 authors, 129 met this threshold. Only thirty-five authors were included to ensure a central network; otherwise, most clusters would remain isolated without links to other clusters. The map uses nodes, edges, and colors with the same meanings as those in the VOSviewer Overlay Visualization map.

Limitations of the Study

This study, like any other study, faces bibliographic limitations. We selected studies only in English language, excluding non-English works. Furthermore, we used only the Scopus database for bibliometric analysis excluding publications from other platforms. Furthermore, the precision of the findings relies on the quality of indexing inside Scopus, so inaccuracies in the search strategy may affect the credibility of analysis.

RESULTS

First, we extracted figures from the Scopus Database platform to present introductory data for our research. Specifically, descriptive statistics were provided for document types, annual trends in documents related to forecasting election outcomes, documents by subject area, and documents by country or territory. After presenting these figures, the results of the research questions (RQs) were analyzed.

Figure 1. Descriptive statistics for document types

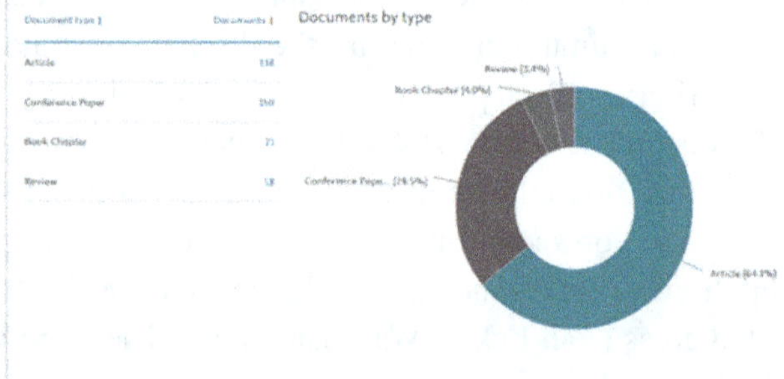

As shown in Figure 1, the allocation of the four diverse types of documents is: 338 (64%) articles, 150 (28.5%) conference papers, 21 (4%) book chapters, and 18 (3.5%) review articles.

Figure 2. Analysis of annual trend documents on forecasting election outcomes

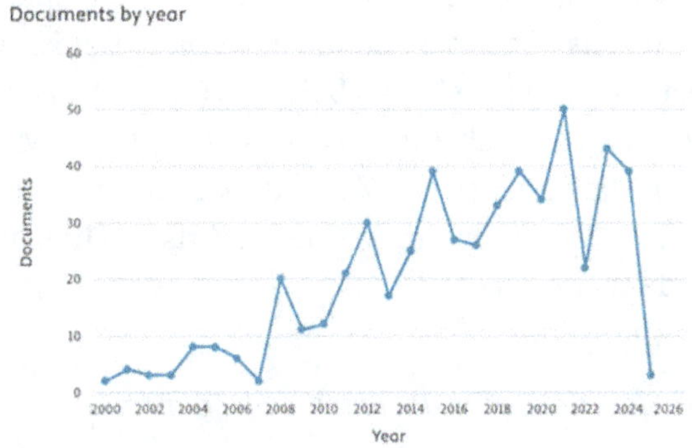

Note. **Copyright ©2025 Elsevier B.V. Scopus© is a registered trademark of Elsevier B.V.**

As shown in Figure 2, the volume of published documents displays stable growth over time. However, there were periods when publications were steady or presented a slight decrease. Until 2006, publishing trends were at low levels. In 2007 there was a sharp increase in publications followed by a steady growth of publications despite fluctuations that observed until 2021 when the peak was measuring fifty publications. However, the following year a sudden decrease in publications appeared falling to half the amount in 2022. The last two years observed a sharp increase in publication reaching closely to forty in the years 2023 and 2024. Publications for 2025 could not be measured, as we are only in early March. Yet, three publications have already been published designating that the interest in this scientific field remains intense.

Figure 3. Descriptive statistics for documents by subject area

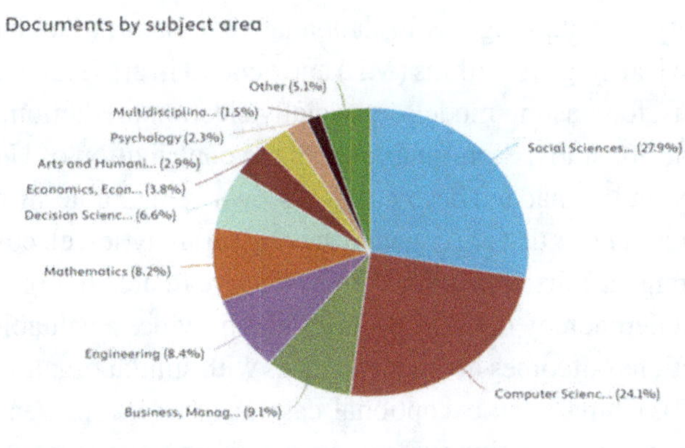

Note. *Copyright ©2025 Elsevier B.V. Scopus© is a registered trademark of Elsevier B.V.*

As shown in the pie chart in Figure 3, the scientific field of forecasting election outcomes is multidisciplinary. There are at least nine distinct topic areas that produce studies on election results. The most dominant subject fields, with a worthwhile contribution to election results are Social Sciences (27.9%), and Computer Science (24.1%). Modest but still remarkable areas are Business (9.1%), Management, (8.4%) Engineering, (8.2%) Mathematics (8.2%), and Decision Science (6.6%). Smaller representations have (3.8%) Economics, (2.9%), Arts & Humanities (2.9%), Psychology (2.3%), and other sciences.

Figure 4. Descriptive statistics for documents by country or territory

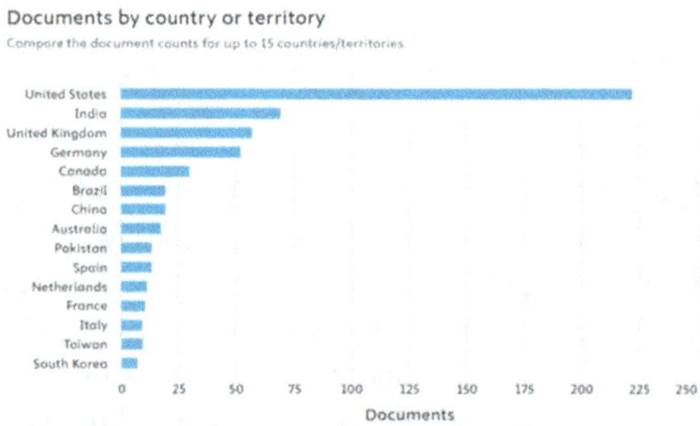

This figure depicts the ten most studied countries in election prediction outcomes. The United States is by far the most studied country in this scientific field with nearly 225 documents. As the most powerful western democratic nation logically attracted the world's interest. India ranks the second place, presenting an intense scientific activity, due its progress in data analytics, natural language processing (NLP), machine learning algorithms (ML) and general in artificial intelligence (AI) disciplines. Thus, forecasting models, especially election prediction, involve multidisciplinary fields of study. Significant is also the contribution of United Kingdom (UK), Germany and Canada. These countries own remarkable institutions, think tanks and research centers that are engaged in political analytics, election predictions, governance, foreign affairs, and other themes that are related to policy. Brazil is the most significant democracy in Latin America and provides a valuable paradigm for electoral predictions outcomes in other countries with similar organization (Turgeon & Rennó, 2012). China is an exceptional case such as it represents a *One-party political system,* making election forecast seem unnecessary. However, China is the seventh most studied country not for national elections but for local ones. China's provincial rural elections have remarkably higher turnout compared to municipal elections (Wu et al., 2023). Also, Spain, is a country with complicated political environment, containing autonomous movements, such as Catalan independence movement (Crameri, 2015), offers urgent reasons for further research. Australia, Pakistan the Netherlands, France, Italy, Taiwan, and South Korea have not yet received high attention.

RQ1: What are the most prevalent methods implemented in forecasting election models, and how have they evolved?

We created a *VOSviewer Overlay Visualization* map to designate the evolution of the most prevalent methods in forecasting election models.

Figure 5. VOSviewer overlay visualization map

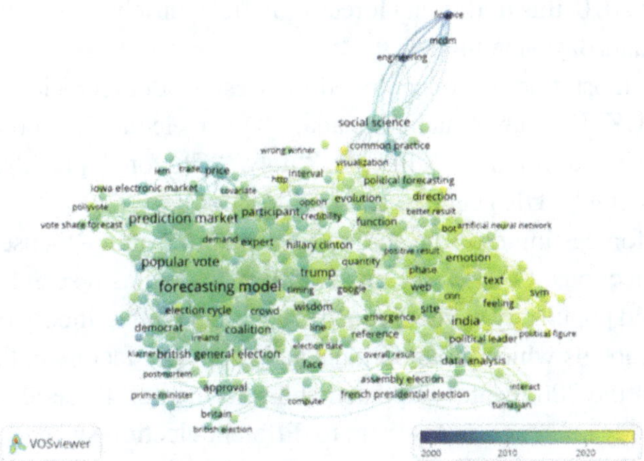

The map displays the evolution of electoral forecasting models over the last 25 years. The colored gradient timeline, at the bottom of the figure, denotes the emergence of scientific areas connected to forecasting models over this period. Each scientific area is visualized as a colored cluster on the plot. Initially, the software distinguished ten clusters. After checking the items of each cluster, we concluded that there were clusters which contained similar terms to others, so we integrated them. Three distinctive clusters represent the main three scientific areas of forecasting models.

Econometric and Statistical Forecasting (Traditional Forecasting Models) (2000-2010, 2010-2020)

Cluster one is located on the left side of the map in the dense, blue green area.

Key items such as "econometric model," "economic growth," "economic indicator," "probability model," "pollyvote," "election market," "fundamental," "incumbent," "lewis beck," "political science," "pollster" "pre-election poll," "quantitative model," "regression model," "historical data," "social science," "trial heat poll" "statistical model" "prediction market," "structural model," "Iowa electronic market," "expert judgment," "citizen forecasting," reveal that this cluster encompasses forecasting models such as economic vote, election markets, econometric and regression techniques, polls, pundits' opinions and synthesized (or combined) models. After 2010, this traditional forecasting field enriched its methodology with probabilistic and Bayesian models.

Moreover, most studies concentrated on western democracies, especially the USA and the UK. Key items such "Canada," "Dutch election" "Europe," "France," "Germany," "United Kingdom," "Ireland," "Italy," "Clinton," "presidential election." "Liberal democrat," "UK general elections," "labor party."

The most forecasting election studies on the 20th century focused on the USA presidential elections. On these seminal studies, known as research on "VP functions" (vote and popularity studies) constructed all the future theory on structural or fundamental models which input political and economic factors in their equations. The studies in the 20th century updated and reformed all these ideas into a more methodical study and encompass them to different election systems except for the USA presidential elections. Key terms that manifest this research are "federal election," "German Bundestag elections," "multiparty system," "parliament," "party system," "prime minister," "electoral college," "coalition," "us senate election," "us congressional election," "senate race" "midterm election forecast."

In addition, its contribution was significant in improving the accuracy and validity of statistical models. Key items for this contribution are "poststratification," "estimator," "coefficient," "cross validation" "confidence," "determinant," "percentage point," "prediction error," "predictive accuracy," "variance," "systematic bias."

Decision Science and Computational Forecasting (2005- 2015, 2015-present)

Cluster two is located at the top-center and mid-right to the green-blue area of the map.

Key items such as "mcdm," "finance," "social science," "computer science," "data mining," "engineering," "decision making," "utilization," "network analysis," "visualization," "political forecasting," denote that this cluster is the crossroads of social science, decision-making models and computational analysis. In 2005, decision-sciences were first introduced to predict election results. Gradually, more sophisticated methods were introduced, and after 2015, innovative models based on financial, engineering, and advanced computational decision-making models get incorporated.

This interdisciplinary field of election forecasting improved prediction accuracy by using forecasting methods different from traditional polls.

Social Media Data-Based Forecasting (2015–present)

Cluster three is located on the right side of the green-yellow area of the map.

Key terms such as "artificial intelligence," "bert," "decision tree," "deep learning," "emotion," "knn," "lexicon," "naïve bayes classifier," "network analysis," "opinion mining," "public sentiment," "python," "retweet," "sentiment analysis technique," "sentiment score," "sentiment analysis," "social media analysis," "big data analysis," "sm platform," "google," "you tube," "Wikipedia," "social media content," "support vector machine," "twitter api," "twitter sentiment analysis," "tumasjan," "online social network," "online user," show that in this cluster involves social media-driven forecasting models based on sentiment analysis. Key concepts comprise Machine learning algorithms, NLP, and deep learning.

These social-driven forecasting models confront significant challenges due to the data quality. Propaganda, fake news, bots, and user activity may distort the data quality. Researchers try to validate their results using methods such as mean absolute error, mean squared error and F1 score. Key items aligned to these challenges involves "fake news," "bots," "reliability," "validation," "mean absolute error," "limit," and "sensitivity."

Nowadays, this type of election prediction model has spread to other countries in the world, including Asia and South America and is not only limited to Western democracies. Key items are "India," "Indonesia," "Brazil," "Colombia," "Pakistan," "Australian election" "latin America,"

RQ2: Who are the key contributors and what are the main collaborations in this field?

We created a *VOSviewer Density Visualization map* to designate the evolution of the most prevalent methods in forecasting election models.

Figure 6. VOSviewer density visualization map

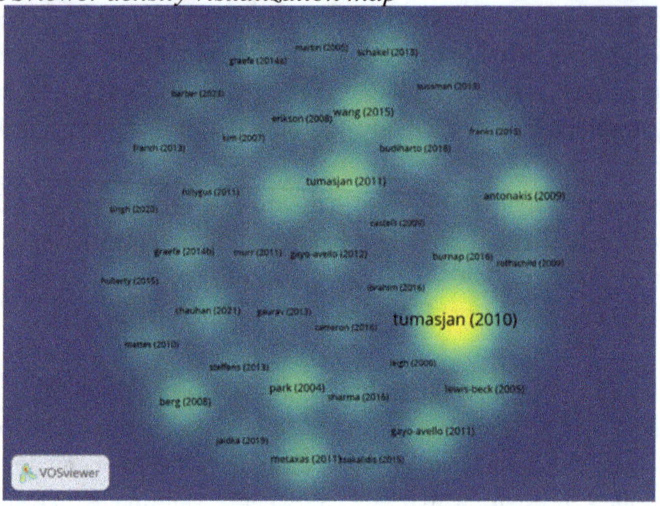

The most vivid yellow item on the map is "tumasjan (2010)", that signifies that Tumasjan's study *Predicting elections with Twitter: What 140 characters reveal about political sentiment* had a huge influence in electoral forecasting. This is true, as it is considered a seminal study relevant to forecasting election outcomes by examining the volume of posts on Twitter (Brito et al., 2021). Other authors who have used social media data to predict election results or to controvert the validity of this approach such as Gayo-Avello (2011, 2012) have cited this study. Other important studies belong to Tumasjan (2011), Antonakis (2009), Park (2004), Wang (2015), Gayo-Avello (2011, 2012), Berg (2008), Lewis-Beck (2005), Graefe (2014) and others. Below is a table presenting 41 documents which have gained more than 100 citations on Scopus platform. The table contains the authors' names, the document titles, the year of publication, and the number of citations.

Table 2. The Most Cited Documents in the last 25 years (one hundred citations or more)

A/A	Authors	Title	Year	Cited
1	(Tumasjan et al., 2010)	Predicting elections with Twitter: What 140 characters reveal about political sentiment.	2010	1905
2	(Tumasjan et al., 2011)	Election forecasts with Twitter: How 140 characters reflect the political landscape	2011	332
3	(Antonakis & Dalgas, 2009)	Predicting elections: Child's play!	2009	305

continued on following page

Table 2. Continued

A/A	Authors	Title	Year	Cited
4	(Park et al., 2004)	Bayesian multilevel estimation with poststratification: State-level estimates from national polls	2004	266
5	(Wang et al., 2015)	Forecasting elections with non-representative polls	2015	259
6	(Jungherr et al., 2012)	Why the pirate party won the german election of 2009 or the trouble with predictions: A response to tumasjan, A., sprenger, T. O., sander, P. G., & welpe, I. M. "predicting elections with twitter: What 140 characters reveal about political sentiment	2012	223
7	(Metaxas et al., 2011)	How (Not) to predict elections	2011	203
8	(Gayo-Avello et al., 2011)	Limits of Electoral Predictions Using Twitter	2011	199
9	(Berg et al., 2008)	Prediction market accuracy in the long run	2008	196
10	(Lewis-Beck M. S., Election forecasting: Principles and practice, 2005)	Election forecasting: Principles and practice	2005	160
11	(Budiharto & Meiliana, 2018)	Prediction and analysis of Indonesia Presidential election from Twitter using sentiment analysis	2018	159
12	(Burnap et al., 2016)	140 characters to victory? Using Twitter to predict the UK 2015 General Election	2016	153
13	(Schakel & Jeffery, 2013)	Are regional elections really 'Second-Order' elections? [Les élections régionales, sont-elles vraiment des élections de second ordre?]	2013	129
14	(Chauhan P.; Sharma N.; Sikka G., 2021)	The emergence of social media data and sentiment analysis in election prediction	2021	120
15	(Sharma & Moh, 2016)	Prediction of Indian election using sentiment analysis on Hindi Twitter	2016	116
16	(Graefe et al., 2014)	Combining forecasts: An application to elections	2014	112
17	(Gayo-Avello, 2012)	No, you cannot predict elections with twitter	2012	103

By studying the documents in Table 1 we identify the three scientific fields of electoral forecasting models as we have seen before. For example, Tumasjan's, Metaxas, Gayo-Avello's, Jaidka's studies represent *Social Media data-based forecasting,* Lewis-Beck' s, Graefe's, Berg's, Rothschild's' works indicate *Econometric and Statistical Forecasting,* and Antonakis, Park's research portrays *Decision Science and Computational forecasting*.

Figure 7. Authors with the most noticeable number of publications

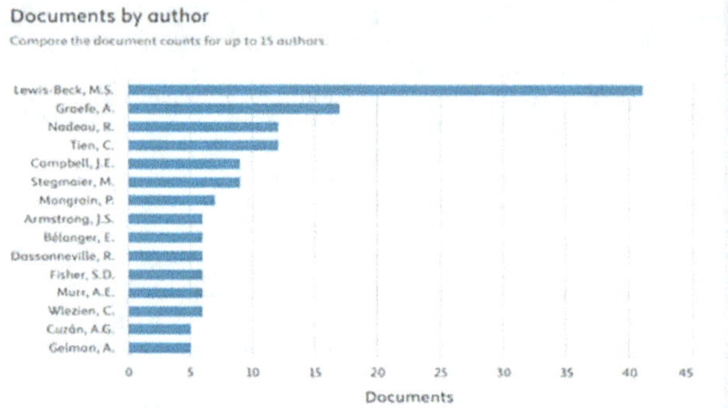

Note. *Copyright ©2025 Elsevier B.V. Scopus© is a registered trademark of Elsevier B.V*

M.S. Lewis-Beck is the author with over forty publications, making him the most influential researcher in electoral predicting models. A. Graefe, R. Nadeau, and C. Tien have published around fifteen publications and have significant participation in this scientific field. J.E. Campbell and M. Stegmaier have also made important contributions, providing about nine publications. Although P. Mongrain, J.S. Armstrong, E. Bélanger R. Dassonneville, S.D. Fisher, A.E. Murr, C. Wlezien, A.G. Cuzán, and A. Gelman have a smaller number of publications, all are noted for their statistical methods in election forecasting and especially because created the fundamentals for "economic voting" or "VP function" and the combining methods. We could say that they represent the previous era before the technological boom of social media sentiment analysis, machine learning algorithms, deep learning methods, and computational simulation.

Figure 8. VOSviewer network visualization map

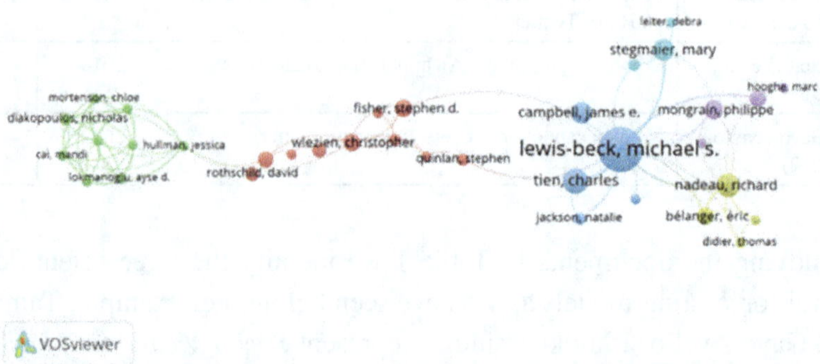

As shown in Figure 8, there are six separate clusters. The most prevalent among them appears to be the blue cluster. The key author (the central and largest node) with the most collaborations is Lewis-Beck. Other significant co-authors include Tien and Campbell. This cluster represents the traditional school of forecasting methods based on the economic voting approach and other econometric models. The key author of the light blue cluster is Stegmaier. Stegmaier also belongs to the traditional school of forecasting methods, with her main studies focusing on the US presidential elections. Nadeau, Bélanger, and Didier are also involved in economic voting models. However, they focused their studies except of the USA election and on Canadian elections. They also maintain a close connection with the blue cluster and especially with Lewis-Beck. Morgain and Dassonneville also represent the traditional approach. In collaboration with Lewis-Beck, they have focused on European election studies.

Wlezien, Fisher, Rothschild, and Gelman are representative authors of the red cluster. Decision-making models and synthesized models (Bayesian and polling aggregation) are the most employed approaches. This cluster is more connected with traditional models and less connected with the green cluster which represents the new age of data-driven forecasting models.

DISCUSSION

The discussion summarizes the chapter's main points and explores their implications for future research and practice. The purpose of this work was to investigate the scientific field of election result prediction. Specifically, to identify which models exist, how they have evolved over time, and the main factors influencing their development. Through an extensive literature review using the Scopus platform, we collected the main studies to present a comprehensive literature review. For data visualization, we used the software VOSviewer. Thus, we divide our study into two parts aiming to respond to the research questions.

1. What are the most prevalent models implemented in forecasting election models, and how have they evolved?
2. Who are the key contributors and what are the main collaborations in this field?

Our conclusions for the first research question are as follows. Publications on election result prediction were limited until 2006. Since then, there has been a steady increase in publications, with few fluctuations during the period 2021–2022. The main trends in election forecasting are distinguished both in terms of the models and their gradual evolution over time. Econometric and statistical models constitute a method of longitudinal forecasting that, after 2010, incorporated probabilistic and Bayesian models as well. Although most studies initially focused on the United States, research gradually expanded to other countries in the Western world with different electoral contexts and characteristics. A separate category of election forecasting involves decision-making and computational models. Decision-making models used mixed forecasting methods until 2015, combining ideas from social sciences and statistics, while after 2015 they also incorporated new web-based techniques. Computational models used stochastic processes based on historical data and social behaviors. Technological advancements and the easy accessibility of social networks revolutionized the field of forecasting. Data-driven models based on social networks came to dominate. Sentiment analysis, processed with machine learning algorithms, natural language processing models, and more recently deep learning, has dominated the field of forecasting. Now, new countries have begun to enter the field of election prediction, and research has expanded globally, beyond the electoral landscape of Western countries. However, all models face challenges such as data validity, the inability to create an ideal model that ensures reproducibility of prediction processes, and the difficulty in generalizing methods across diverse electoral and political environments. This creates the need for more sophisticated or synthesized models that can combine multiple approaches.

In our search, we first examined which works have most influenced researchers in the field, which authors published the most influential studies, and which collaborations have dominated the scientific community. The most influential works were the seminal studies by Tumasjan (2010, 2011), which pioneered electoral forecasting through the social platform of Twitter. Upon these basic researchers, many researchers have delved into this methodology and further developed it. Criticism regarding the reliability of this methodology and suggestions for improvement were presented in the publications of Gayo-Avello (2011, 2012). His remarks challenged many researchers who tried to overcome the limitations he pointed out, which led to the evolution of existing methodologies and models. Other important works include Antonakis (2009) on decision-making models, Park (2004) on Bayesian models, Berg (2008) on prediction markets, Graefe (2014), Wang (2015) on predicting election results without using representative samples, and Lewis-Beck (2005), who incorporated the fundamental principles and methodologies of traditional election prediction models. Lewis-Beck is also the most influential author, having published the highest number of studies and collaborated extensively with other researchers. He is the key author in the field of traditional predictions.

A long-time span of twenty-five years was used for bibliometric analysis. However, technological developments in the field of electoral forecasting rapidly developed in recent years, contrasting to what was happening until the beginning of the twentieth century. As a result, the findings of this study may become outdated within a brief period. For example, the traditional school of forecasting has been present in this scientific field since the mid-twentieth century, commonly known then as the VP function model. However, new methods have now entered the field of election forecasting and are evolving rapidly, at a time when traditional methods have reached the limits of their capabilities.

CONCLUSIONS

In this study, we examined how election forecasting has changed over the past 25 years. We depicted the most significant contributors, the key networks of collaboration, and the most popular forecasting models. Our analysis shows that the field has shifted away from the traditional school to the more sophisticated models of decision-science, computational models, and recently to data driven based forecasting. The earliest works were more focused on the USA and other Western countries. But over time, more research was directed to other countries like Brazil, India, and Indonesia, each with its own political and electoral landscape.

Researchers in recent years caught up in their attempt to optimize their models only in terms of the technical part, neglecting the other arm of the research that has to do with interpreting the political landscape and voter behavior. At the same time, the global political landscape is changing fast. New democracies have been established with characteristics that differ substantially from those of western democracies. Not only because of their different political environments but also because of their specific economic, linguistic, and cultural features and the restricted access to quality data.

A challenging area in forecasting has just arrived. On the one hand scholars need to evolve their methodologies in a transparent, and ethical way accomplishing the replicability and generalization of their methods. On the other hand, they must be able to identify the specificities of diverse electoral and political landscape in order to be able to understand voters' behavior by collecting data from the right sources.

The new technological era opens avenues for more collaboration across different fields offering more validity to predictions, while enriching with empirical insights the theoretical framework the voting behavior.

REFERENCES

Adeney, K., & Swenden, W. (2024). Multinational democratic federations: Comparing India with multi-level systems from the global north. *Studies in Indian politics, 12*(2), 164-182. DOI: 10.1177/23210230241291357

Antonakis, J., & Dalgas, O. (2009). Predicting elections: Child's play! *Science, 323*(5918), 1183–1183. DOI: 10.1126/science.1167748

Armstrong, J. S. (2001). Combining forecasts. In J. S. Armstrong (Ed.), *Principles of forecasting: A handbook for researchers and practitioners.* https://books.google.gr/books?hl=en&lr=&id=ezTaBwAAQBAJ&oi=fnd&pg=PR7&dq=%22Combining+forecasts%22+In+Principles+of+Forecasting:+A+Handbook+for+Researchers+and+Practitioners&ots=7GjlW9nxf3&sig=BlsxRBKSI-yUy5c57VrE0wYtBZ4&redir_esc=y#v=onepage&q=%22Combini

Aspinall, E., & Mietzner, M. (2014). Indonesian politics in 2014: Democracy's close call. *Bulletin of Indonesian Economic Studies, 50*(3), 347–369. DOI: 10.1080/00074918.2014.980375

Berg, J., Forsythe, R., Nelson, F., & Rietz, T. (2008). Results from a dozen years of election futures markets research. *Handbook of experimental economics results, 1*, 742-751. DOI: 10.1016/S1574-0722(07)00080-7

Berg, J. E., Nelson, F. D., & Rietz, T. A. (2008). Prediction market accuracy in the long run. *International Journal of Forecasting, 24*(2), 285–300. DOI: 10.1016/j.ijforecast.2008.03.007

Brito, K. D., Silva Filho, R. L., & Adeodato, P. J. (2021). A systematic review of predicting elections based on social media data: Research challenges and future directions. *IEEE Transactions on Computational Social Systems, 8*(4), 819–843. DOI: 10.1109/TCSS.2021.3063660

Budiharto, W., & Meiliana, M. (2018). Prediction and analysis of Indonesia Presidential election from Twitter using sentiment analysis. *Journal of Big Data, 5*(1), 1–10. DOI: 10.1186/s40537-018-0164-1

Burnap, P., Gibson, R., Sloan, L., Southern, R., & Williams, M. (2016). 140 characters to victory?: Using Twitter to predict the UK 2015 general election. *Electoral Studies, 41*, 230–233. DOI: 10.1016/j.electstud.2015.11.017

Çetin, N., & Bentli, İ. (2013, June). Application of Markov process to forecast elections outcomes by computer simulation. *In First International Conference on Management and Economics.* https://www.researchgate.net/profile/Ismail-Bentli/publication/266334248_APPLICATION_OF_MARKOV_PROCESS_TO_FORECAST_ELECTIONS_OUTCOMES_BY_COMPUTER_SIMULATION/links/5562f64708ae9963a11b5b4d/APPLICATION-OF-MARKOV-PROCESS-TO-FORECAST-ELECTIONS-OUTCOMES-BY-COMPUTER-SIMULATION.pdf

Chauhan, P., Sharma, N., & Sikka, G. (2021). The emergence of social media data and sentiment analysis in election prediction. *Journal of Ambient Intelligence and Humanized Computing, 12*(2), 2601–2627. DOI: 10.1007/s12652-020-02423-y

Crameri, K. (2015). *Political power and civil counterpower: The complex dynamics of the Catalan independence movement. In contesting Spain? The dynamics of nationalist movements in Catalonia and the Basque Country.* Routledge., https://www.taylorfrancis.com/chapters/edit/10.4324/9781315684543-6/political-power-civil-counterpower-kathryn-crameri

Cuzán, A., Armstrong, J., & Jones, J. (2005). The Pollyvote: Applying the combination principle in forecasting to the 2004 Presidential Election. *In International Symposium on Forecasting,* San Antonio.

Cuzán, A., Armstrong, J., & Jones, R. (2005). Combining methods to forecast the 2004 presidential election. *The Pollyvote. In Annual Meeting of the Southern Political Science Association. New Orleans. January.* https://d1wqtxts1xzle7.cloudfront.net/78209494/combiningmethodstoforecastthe2004presidentialelection.pdf?1641472222=&response-content-disposition=inline%3B+filename%3DCombining_Methods_to_Forecast_the_2004_P.pdf&Expires=1694804221&Signature=eJ7q7ztsjLyx2w

Dassonneville, R., & Lewis-Beck, M. (2014). Comparative election forecasting. synthetic models for europe. *In Annual Meeting of the American Political Science Association, Date: 2014/08/28-2014/08/31*, 1-29.

Donthu, N., Kumar, S., Mukherjee, D., Pandey, N., & Lim, W. M. (2021). How to conduct a bibliometric analysis: An overview and guidelines. *Journal of Business Research, 133*, 285–296. DOI: 10.1016/j.jbusres.2021.04.070

Ellegaard, O., & Wallin, J. A. (2015). The bibliometric analysis of scholarly production: How great is the impact. *Scientometrics, 105*(3), 1809–1831. DOI: 10.1007/s11192-015-1645-z

Erikson, R., & Wlezien, C. (2008). Are political markets really superior to polls as election predictors? *Public Opinion Quarterly*, *72*(2), 190–215. https://doi.org/https://doi.org/10.1093/poq/nfn010. DOI: 10.1093/poq/nfn010

Ferrara, E. (2017). Disinformation and social bot operations in the run up to the 2017 French presidential election. *First Monday*, *22*(8). Advance online publication. DOI: 10.5210/fm.v22i8.8005

Fisher, S., & Shorrocks, R. (2018). Collective failure? Lessons from combining forecasts for the UK's referendum on EU membership. *Journal of Elections, Public Opinion, and Parties*, *28*(1), 59–77. DOI: 10.1080/17457289.2017.1380656

Forsythe, R., Rietz, T. A., & Ross, T. (1999). Wishes, expectations and actions: A survey on price formation in election stock markets. *Journal of Economic Behavior & Organization*, *39*(1), 83–110. DOI: 10.1016/S0167-2681(99)00027-X

Gao, M., Wang, Z., Wang, K., Liu, C., & Tang, S. (2022). Forecasting elections with agent-based modeling: Two live experiments. *PLoS One*, *17*(6), e0270194. DOI: 10.1371/journal.pone.0270194

Gayo-Avello, D. (2012). No, you cannot predict elections with Twitter. *IEEE Internet Computing*, *16*(6), 91–94. DOI: 10.1109/MIC.2012.137

Gayo-Avello, D., Metaxas, P., & Mustafaraj, E. (2011). *Limits of electoral predictions using twitter, 5*(1), 490-493. DOI: 10.1609/icwsm.v5i1.14189

Goot, M. (2021). How good are the polls? Australian election predictions, 1993–2019. *Australian Journal of Political Science*, *56*(1), 35–55. DOI: 10.1080/10361146.2020.1825616

Graefe, A., Armstrong, J., Jones, J.Jr, & Cuzán, A. (2014). Combining forecasts: An application to elections. *International Journal of Forecasting*, *30*(1), 43–54. DOI: 10.1016/j.ijforecast.2013.02.005

Guidotti, R., Monreale, A., Ruggieri, S., Turini, F., Giannotti, F., & Pedreschi, D. (2018). A survey of methods for explaining black box models. *ACM Computing Surveys*, *51*(5), 1–42. DOI: 10.1145/3236009

Hummel, P., & Rothschild, D. (2014). Fundamental models for forecasting elections at the state level. *Electoral Studies*, *35*, 123–139. DOI: 10.1016/j.electstud.2014.05.002

Isaak, J., & Hanna, M. (2018). User data privacy: Facebook, Cambridge Analytica, and privacy protection. Computer, 51(8), *51*(58), 56-59. DOI: 10.1109/MC.2018.3191268

Jungherr, A., Jürgens, P., & Schoen, H. (2012). Why the pirate party won the german election of 2009 or the trouble with predictions: A response to tumasjan, a., sprenger, to, sander, pg, & welpe, im "predicting elections with twitter: What 140 characters reveal about political sentiment". *Social Science Computer Review, 30*(2), 229–234. DOI: 10.1177/0894439311404119

Kao, S. S. (2021). Taiwan's response to disinformation: A Model for Coordination to Counter a Complicated Threat. *National Bureau of Asian Research.* https://www.nbr.org/wp-content/uploads/pdfs/publications/sr93_taiwan_sep2021.pdf

Kennedy, C., Blumenthal, M., Clement, S., Clinton, J., Durand, C., Franklin, C., McGeeney, K., Miringoff, L., Olson, K., Rivers, D., Saad, L., Witt, G. E., & Wlezien, C. (2018). An evaluation of the 2016 election polls in the United States. *Public Opinion Quarterly, 82*(1), 1–33. DOI: 10.1093/poq/nfx047

Koli, A., & Ahmed, M. (2019). Exploring the power of social media in election predictions. *International journal of recent technology and engineering, 8*(2), 4539-4549. DOI: 10.35940/ijrte.A9192.078219

Kwak, J., & Cho, S. (2018). Analyzing public opinion With social media data during election periods: A selective literature review. *Asian journal for public opinion research, 5*(4), 285–301. DOI: 10.15206/ajpor.2018.5.4.285

Lewis-Beck, M., & Stegmaier, M. (2009). American voter to economic voter: Evolution of an idea. *Electoral Studies, 28*(4), 625–631. DOI: 10.1016/j.electstud.2009.05.023

Lewis-Beck, M. S. (2005). Election forecasting: Principles and practice. *British Journal of Politics and International Relations, 7*(2), 145–164. DOI: 10.1111/j.1467-856X.2005.00178.x

Lewis-Beck, M. S., & Dassonneville, R. (2015). Forecasting elections in Europe: Synthetic models. *Research & politics, 2*(1). DOI: 10.1177/2053168014565128

Lewis-Beck, M. S., & Stegmaier, M. (2000). Economic determinants of electoral outcomes. *Annual Review of Political Science, 3*(1), 183–219. DOI: 10.1146/annurev.polisci.3.1.183

Linzer, D. A. (2013). Dynamic Bayesian forecasting of presidential elections in the states. *Journal of the American Statistical Association, 108*(501), 124–134. DOI: 10.1080/01621459.2012.737735

Metaxas, P., Mustafaraj, E., & Gayo-Avello, D. (2011). How (not) to predict elections. *In 2011 Ieee Third International Conference on Privacy, Security, Risk and Trust and 2011 Ieee Third International Conference on Social Computing* (165-171). IEEE. DOI: 10.1109/PASSAT/SocialCom.2011.98

Mittelstad, B., Allo, P., Taddeo, M., Wachter, S., & Floridi, S. (2016). The ethics of algorithms: Mapping the debate. *Big Data & Society, 3*(2), 2053951716679679. https://doi.org/https://doi.org/10.1177/2053951716679679. DOI: 10.1177/2053951716679679

Mutahi, P., & Kimari, B. (2020). Fake news and the 2017 Kenyan elections. *Communicatio: South African journal of communication theory and research, 46*(4), 31-49. DOI: 10.1080/02500167.2020.1723662

Neyazi, T., & Schroeder, R. (2021). Was the 2019 Indian election won by digital media? *Communication Review, 24*(2), 87–106. DOI: 10.1080/10714421.2021.1933311

Norris, P. (2014). *Why electoral integrity matters*. Cambridge University Press. DOI: 10.1017/CBO9781107280861

Park, D., Gelman, A., & Bafumi, J. (2004). Bayesian multilevel estimation with poststratification: State-level estimates from national polls. *Political Analysis, 12*(4), 375–385. DOI: 10.1093/pan/mph024

Pasek, J. (2015). Predicting elections: Considering tools to pool the polls. *Public Opinion Quarterly, 79*(2), 594–619. DOI: 10.1093/poq/nfu060

Pepinsky, T. B. (2025). Cleavages, institutions, and democracy in Indonesia: The 2024 elections in comparative perspective. *Journal of Current Southeast Asian Affairs, 18681034251349467*, 18681034251349467. Advance online publication. DOI: 10.1177/18681034251349467

Power, T. J. (2010). Optimism, pessimism, and coalitional presidentialism: Debating the institutional design of Brazilian democracy. *Bulletin of Latin American Research, 29*(1), 18–33. DOI: 10.1111/j.1470-9856.2009.00304.x

Schakel, A., & Jeffery, C. (2013). Are regional elections really 'second-order' elections? *Regional Studies, 47*(3), 323–341. DOI: 10.1080/00343404.2012.690069

Sharma, p., & Moh, T. (2016, December). Prediction of Indian election using sentiment analysis on Hindi Twitter. *In 2016 IEEE International Conference on Big Data (big data)*, 1966-1971. DOI: 10.1109/BigData.2016.7840818

Silver, N. (2016). A user's guide to FiveThirtyEight's 2016 general election forecast. *Fivethirtyeight Blog*. https://fivethirtyeight.com/features/a-users-guide-to-fivethirtyeights-2016-general-election-forecast/

Strömbäck, J., & Kiousis, S. (2011). *Political public relations*. Taylor & Francis. DOI: 10.4324/9780203864173

Tenove, C. (2020). Protecting democracy from disinformation: Normative threats and policy responses. *The International Journal of Press/Politics*, *25*(3), 517–537. DOI: 10.1177/1940161220918740

Tillin, L., & Pereira, A. (2017). Federalism, multi-level elections and social policy in Brazil and India. *Commonwealth and Comparative Politics*, *55*(3), 328–352. DOI: 10.1080/14662043.2017.1327928

Traugott, M., & Lavrakas, P. (2008). *Voter's guide to election polls* (4th ed., Vol. 1). Rowman and Littlefield., https://books.google.gr/books?hl=en&lr=&id=aSOSDQAAQBAJ&oi=fnd&pg=PR9&dq=Voter%27s+Guide+to+Election+Polls&ots=DCHX7sRbo1&sig=nEnvoWmn986B9Whl6Qghxb0Bl6Y&redir_esc=y#v=onepage&q=Voter's%20Guide%20to%20Election%20Polls&f=false

Tschoegl, A., & Armstrong, J. (2008). Review of Philip E. Tetlock (2005), Expert political judgment: How good is it? How can we know? SSRN *Electronic journal*. DOI: 10.2139/ssrn.1153126

Tumasjan, A., Sprenger, T., Sandner, P., & Welpe, I. (2010). Predicting elections with twitter: What 140 characters reveal about political sentiment. *In Proceedings of the International AAAI Conference on Web and Social Media, 4*(1), 178-185. DOI: 10.1609/icwsm.v4i1.14009

Tumasjan, A., Sprenger, T., Sandner, P., & Welpe, I. (2011). Election forecasts with Twitter: How 140 characters reflect the political landscape. *Social Science Computer Review*, *29*(4), 402–418. DOI: 10.1177/0894439310386557

Turgeon, M., & Rennó, L. (2012). Forecasting Brazilian presidential elections: Solving the problem. *International Journal of Forecasting*, *28*(4), 804–812. DOI: 10.1016/j.ijforecast.2012.04.003

Van Eck, N., & Waltman, L. (2009). How to normalize cooccurrence data? An analysis of some well-known similarity measures. *Journal of the American Society for Information Science and Technology*, *60*(8), 1635–1651. DOI: 10.1002/asi.21075

Van Eck, N., & Waltman, L. (2010). Software survey: VOSviewer, a computer program for bibliometric mapping. *Scientometrics*, *84*(2), 523–538. DOI: 10.1007/s11192-009-0146-3

Van Eck, N., & Waltman, L. (2023). VOSviewer manual. *Leiden: Univeristeit Leiden, 1*(1), 1-53. https://www.vosviewer.com/documentation/Manual_VOSviewer_1.6.18.pdf

Wang, W., Rothschild, D., Goel, S., & Gelman, A. (2015). Forecasting elections with non-representative polls. *International Journal of Forecasting*, *3*(1), 980–991. DOI: 10.1016/j.ijforecast.2014.06.001

Witzenberger, B., & Diakopoulos, N. (2023). Election predictions in the news: How users perceive and respond to visual election forecasts. *Information Communication and Society*, •••, 1–22. DOI: 10.1080/1369118X.2023.2230267

Wolfers, J., & Leigh, A. (2002). Three tools for forecasting federal elections: Lessons from 2001. *Australian Journal of Political Science*, *37*(2), 223–240. DOI: 10.1080/10361140220148115

Wu, L., Rogers, B., & Wang, G. (2023). Explaining voting participation gaps in local government elections in rural China. *Asian journal of comparative politics,*, *8*(1), 307-330. DOI: 10.1177/20578911221125510

ADDITIONAL READING

Azizah, N., Putra, N. R. E., & Ramadhan, N. A. S. (2024). Social Media and Elections: Reviewing the Use of Social Media in Election Contests during 2016-2022–A Systematic Review and Bibliometric Analysis. *INDONESIAN GOVERNANCE JOURNAL: KAJIAN POLITIK-PEMERINTAHAN*, *7*(1), 59–68. DOI: 10.24905/igj.v7i1.149

Franch, F. (2013). (Wisdom of the Crowds) 2: 2010 UK election prediction with social media. *Journal of Information Technology & Politics*, *10*(1), 57–71. DOI: 10.1080/19331681.2012.705080

Kenett, R. S., Pfeffermann, D., & Steinberg, D. M. (2018). Election polls survey, a critique, and proposals. *Annual Review of Statistics and Its Application*, *5*(1), 1–24. DOI: 10.1146/annurev-statistics-031017-100204

Lewis-Beck, M. S. (2005). Election forecasting: Principles and practice. *British Journal of Politics and International Relations*, *7*(2), 145–164. DOI: 10.1111/j.1467-856X.2005.00178.x

Mueller, J. E. (1970). Presidential popularity from Truman to Johnson1. *The American Political Science Review*, *64*(1), 18–34. DOI: 10.2307/1955610

Nannestad, P., & Paldam, M. (1994). The VP-function: A survey of the literature on vote and popularity functions after 25 years. *Public Choice*, *79*(3), 213–245. DOI: 10.1007/BF01047771

O'Connor, B., Balasubramanyan, R., Routledge, B., & Smith, N. (2010, May). From tweets to polls: Linking text sentiment to public opinion time series. In *Proceedings of the International AAAI Conference on Web and Social Media* (Vol. 4, No. 1, pp. 122-129). DOI: 10.1609/icwsm.v4i1.14031

Skoric, M. M., Liu, J., & Jaidka, K. (2020). Electoral and public opinion forecasts with social media data: A meta-analysis. *Information (Basel)*, *11*(4), 187. DOI: 10.3390/info11040187

Stoetzer, L. F., Erfort, C., Rajski, H., Gschwend, T., Munzert, S., & Koch, E. (2025). An election forecasting model for subnational elections. *Electoral Studies*, *95*, 102939. DOI: 10.1016/j.electstud.2025.102939

KEY TERMS AND DEFINITIONS

Bibliometric Analysis: Method for studying academic research frameworks and trends by examining authorship, citations, and collaborations.

Data-Driven Forecast: Model that analyzes actual data to assess future results in a systematic way.

Delphi technique: A structured method in which forecasts are generated based on the consensus among experts.

Economic Voting: The idea that the voter's behavior is based on economic conditions.

Election Markets: Markets where people bet and trade contracts on election outcomes.

Opinion Polls: Surveys that ask people about their voting intentions or preferences.

Sentiment analysis: A natural language processing (NLP) method that analyzes text or emojis to detect writer's emotions.

Social Media: Online platforms where people communicate, create content and share information.

VOSviewer: Software tool that creates visual maps that show connections between studies, authors, or keywords.

Chapter 2

In Search of the Rational Voter in the 2020 Presidential Election:

Understanding the Impact of Voter Costs and Benefits on Turnout

Norou Diawara
https://orcid.org/0000-0002-8403-6793
Old Dominion University, USA

Tiffany Henley
https://orcid.org/0000-0002-1332-1781
Pace University, USA

Samuel L. Brown
Old Dominion University, USA

Md Iqbal Hossain
https://orcid.org/0009-0000-7297-4953
Old Dominion University, USA

ABSTRACT

The ability to vote is one of the most valuable rights and privileges afforded by the Constitution of the United States to its citizens. For many, voting is not just a civic duty; it is also a choice. Voting is crucial to our democracy, and any changes to it may affect the efficiency of the democratic process. The bigger question is whether voters behave rationally by engaging in a cost-benefit calculus in deciding whether or

DOI: 10.4018/979-8-3373-1037-4.ch002

not to vote. Using data science, this paper will examine the probability of voting and investigate its impact via cost and benefit among other variables using the 2020 American National Election Studies (ANES) dataset. In addition, the study will also assess the impact voter perceptions of "a sense of duty" have on voter turnout. Empirical work provides additional evidence that feelings of civic duty truly do motivate voter turnout. Using the latest methods of statistical analyses, we identify and understand the factors that benefited and hindered voting in the ANES 2020 data and the impact of voter benefits and costs on turnout.

INTRODUCTION

In the realm of voter participation, understanding the complexity of voter behavior is crucial for predicting election outcomes. The rational choice model has long been a cornerstone in explaining how individuals make decisions based on maximizing their utility. However, in the context of voting behavior, this traditional model has been modified to incorporate a crucial element—the duty variable. This empirical paper models the modified rational choice model of voting, shedding light on how the sense of duty influences voter decision-making processes. By exploring the interplay between the Downs (1957) rational choice theory and the duty variable (Riker and Ordeshook, 1968), this study seeks to explain the process that people undergo in deciding whether or not to vote. The rational choice model can be expanded to integrate a sense of civic duty toward voting, serving as both a constraint and an incentive for voter turnout (Goldfarb et al. 2010). According to the Down's model, citizens use a simple calculation in the voting decision-making process: if the benefits of voting exceed the cost of voting, they vote; otherwise, they do not. In contrast to Down's utilitarian model, Baron (2012) examined voting as a duty concept and suggests that moral duty to a group comes at the cost of self-interests and the interests of outsiders. Individuals are more likely to push or press a close partner or friend to vote if they have a political preference, since increasing involvement from like-minded persons is thought to result in greater expected advantages. This idea is consistent with group theories of voter turnout, in which the motivation to vote stems from the possibility of accomplishing communal goals through increased group engagement (Feddersen et al. 2006). Research shows that advertising influences voting turnout and mobilizes partisans (Law 2021).

Understanding voter behavior is essential for accurately predicting election outcomes. The rational choice model, rooted in utility maximization, has long been a foundational framework for explaining individual decision-making. However, in the context of voting, this model has evolved to include an important addition: the sense of civic duty. This empirical study applies a modified rational choice model to explore how the duty variable influences voter decision-making. Building on Downs' (1957) rational choice theory and the extension by Riker and Ordeshook (1968), the analysis investigates the process individuals undergo when deciding whether to vote. According to the traditional model, voters assess whether the benefits of voting outweigh its costs; if so, they vote. Yet, incorporating a sense of duty can transform this calculation, acting as both a constraint and an incentive (Goldfarb et al., 2010). Further expanding on this idea, Baron (2012) argues that individuals who see voting as a duty are more likely to encourage close friends or partners with shared political views to vote, amplifying turnout through social influence. This aligns with group-based theories of voter participation, where motivation arises from achieving collective goals through coordinated engagement (Feddersen et al., 2006). Additionally, research suggests that political advertising plays a significant role in mobilizing partisans and increasing voter turnout (Law, 2021).

The rational choice model of voting, originally proposed by Downs (1957) and later refined by Riker and Ordeshook (1968), suggests that individuals decide to vote based on a calculated assessment of expected benefits versus costs. Specifically, voters consider the potential benefit of their preferred candidate winning, the likelihood that their vote will make a difference, and the opportunity costs associated with voting—such as registration, traveling to polling places, and acquiring information. Recent empirical evidence highlights how social and political events can influence this decision-making process. For instance, Holbein et al. (2023) find that the murder of George Floyd sparked a substantial rise in voter registration, as many Americans were galvanized to participate politically in response to racial injustice.

In large-scale elections—such as the 2020 U.S. presidential election—the rational choice model predicts that most individuals would opt not to vote. This is because, although the cost of voting may be relatively low, the perceived benefit is minimal due to the extremely low probability that a single vote will be decisive. Yet, in practice, many people do vote in major elections, a phenomenon known as the "paradox of voting." This paradox challenges the assumption of purely rational behavior in electoral participation. Research shows that individuals facing higher opportunity costs are less likely to vote, illustrating the cost effect (Faravelli et al., 2020). Furthermore, people tend to weigh their personal interest in the election outcome against the likelihood that their vote will influence the result (Heckelman et al., 2015).

The basic rational choice model often fails to account for actual voting behavior observed in real-world elections. However, rather than discarding the model entirely, scholars have sought to refine it to better reflect the motivations behind voter participation. One influential revision comes from Riker and Ordeshook (1968), who introduced the concept of satisfaction as a key factor in the voting decision. They argued that voting offers individuals a sense of fulfillment—such as complying with the civic ethic of voting, expressing allegiance to the political system, reinforcing partisan identity, and affirming one's political efficacy. Even the simple enjoyment of participating in an election can serve as a motivator. Riker and Ordeshook encapsulated these non-material benefits under the idea of citizen duty, which helps explain why people vote even when the probability of influencing the outcome is negligible.

In their seminal work on voter turnout, Wolfinger and Rosenstone (1980) analyzed data from the 1972 Current Population Survey, which included responses from 88,105 individuals. Their findings showed that education was the strongest predictor of voting behavior, followed by age, religiosity, wealth, and marital status. Building on the concept of voting as a rational decision, Gelman et al. (2012) investigated the probability that a single vote would be decisive in the 2008 presidential election. They incorporated cost-benefit considerations and evaluated three methods for estimating the likelihood of a decisive vote, using simulations to demonstrate how voting power varied across the 51 states. Their analysis showed that this probability could be explained by factors such as state partisanship, the need for an electoral college win, a state's national median level, and the presence of campaign efforts and organizers. This probabilistic view of voting supports the need for more sophisticated modeling approaches, such as deep learning algorithms, to capture complex, nonlinear dynamics. Lee (2021), for instance, proposed a voting model grounded in public choice economic theory. Meanwhile, Edlin et al. (2008) and Brennan and Freiman (2023) framed voting as an act of altruism, offering a normative alternative to purely self-interested models. Other research has linked information environments to voter participation. Hayes and Lawless (2015) found that areas with limited media coverage of congressional races experienced lower voter turnout and reduced political knowledge. Expanding the scope to Europe, Addeo et al. (2024) examined regional and national voter turnout trends over time using various statistical regression techniques.

Through meticulous analysis, the Schraufnagel (2020) study considered various factors such as voter registration restrictions, absentee voting laws, early voting availability, and other electoral practices. Notably, states like Oregon emerge as leaders in facilitating easier voting processes, while others, like Texas, lag behind due to limited reforms. The research underscores the significant disparities in voting accessibility among states and highlights the importance of ongoing legislative efforts to enhance voter participation. Citizens see voting as a moral obligation to support their country or as a way to protect their own interests, reflecting a larger cultural norm of responsibility and self-defense (Baron, 2012). In politics, social values seem to be more important than the old economic left/right division (Facchini et al., 2019). This is voter behavior showing strategic tendencies regardless of costs (Feddersen et al., 2006).

Research on civic responsibility is compelling in terms of its impact on behavior. Civic duty, which entails a sense of obligation towards society, has primarily been examined in relation to voting. Studies have shown that individuals who strongly identify with civic duty are more inclined to vote because they view voting as a moral responsibility necessary for good citizenship (Blais and Daoust, 2020). However, there is limited research on how civic duty influences behavior in other contexts. For instance, Blais, Galais, and Mayer (2019) discovered that the obligation to stay politically informed is not as prevalent, and for many who feel a duty to vote, their sense of civic duty does not extend to staying informed. Amid the recent pandemic, little is understood about whether civic duty encompasses adherence to behaviors like physical distancing.

Beyond institutional factors, the motivations behind voting are also shaped by individual beliefs and cultural norms. Many citizens view voting as a moral duty—either as an expression of patriotism or as a means of self-protection—reflecting broader societal values around responsibility and civic participation (Baron, 2012). Recent research suggests that social values increasingly influence political behavior, often surpassing traditional economic left-right distinctions (Facchini et al., 2019). This shift is consistent with theories of strategic voting behavior that emphasize motivations beyond simple cost-benefit calculations (Feddersen et al., 2006).

Voting behavior is often influenced by individuals' expectations of benefits from electing a preferred candidate, fulfilling a sense of civic duty, and weighing associated costs—whether in terms of money, time, or effort (Feddersen, 2004). People demonstrate their commitment to social responsibility in various ways. For example, many are willing to wait in long lines to vote during major elections, even when the likelihood of their single vote affecting the outcome is minimal (Feddersen et al., 2009). Among younger voters, civic duty often serves as a primary motivator. They view participation in elections not only as a right but also as a responsibility essential to their role as citizens in a democratic society (Whaley et al., 2021). This chapter will focus on the role of the duty variable in shaping both the decision to vote and the probability of doing so, analyzed within a cost-benefit framework. The behavior of a rational voter will be modeled using three statistical methods, allowing for a deeper understanding of how duty interacts with perceived costs and benefits in influencing turnout.

In this chapter, we will analyze presidential electoral data from the year 2020 from the American National Election Studies (ANES) because this year marks a pivotal moment in history in election administration and political behavior. Therefore, we seek to understand the impact of costs and benefits on voter turnout. This research looks at the impact of the voters and their sense of duty under a cost and benefit analysis.

DESCRIPTION OF DATA

The American National Election Studies (ANES) 2020 Time Series Study continues a longstanding tradition of examining public opinion and voting behavior in U.S. presidential elections, with origins dating back to 1948. This latest iteration incorporates reinterviews with 2020 ANES participants, a newly drawn cross-sectional sample, and post-election surveys with participants from the General Social Survey (GSS). Data collection occurred through three modes—web, video, and telephone—based on each respondent's assigned group. Phone and video interviews were conducted by trained interviewers using specialized software.

The dataset includes pre-election responses collected between August 18 and November 3, 2020, and post-election surveys conducted from November 8, 2020, to January 4, 2021. For the purposes of our study, we focus exclusively on the post-election data.

The ANES 2020 dataset comprises 8,280 individual observations, with each row representing a unique respondent. The dataset contains 1,771 variables, covering a wide range of information, including demographic characteristics (e.g., age, gender, race, education), political behavior (e.g., voting patterns, party affiliation), responses to survey questions, and other relevant attributes.

This rich dataset provides a comprehensive and detailed dataset for conducting analyses and investigations into public opinion and voting behavior during the 2020 U.S. presidential election.

Table 1 summarizes the demographic profile of participants based on the 2020 General Election, including key variables such as age, race, gender, education, marital status, occupation, and home ownership.

Table 1. Demographics of Voter Turnout for the 2020 General Election

Variables		Not Voted	Voted
Duty	Views voting as choice	154 (13.95%) (69.37%)	950 (86.05%) (34.12%)
	Views voting as duty	68 (3.58%) (30.63%)	1834 (96.42%) (65.88%)
Age	18-34	74 (12.80%) (33.33%)	504 (87.20%) (18.10%)
	35-49	71 (9.62%) (31.98%)	667 (90.38%) (23.95%)
	50-64	43 (5.26%) (19.36%)	775 (94.74%) (27.83%)

continued on following page

Table 1. Continued

Variables		Not Voted	Voted
	65+	34 (3.90%) (15.31%)	838 (96.10%) (30.10%)
Race	White	136 (6.08%) (61.26%)	2102 (93.92%) (75.50%)
	Black	27 (10.00%) (12.16%)	243 (90.00%) (8.73%)
	Hispanic	40 (16.19%) (18.02%)	207 (83.81%) (7.44%)
	Asian	7 (6.86%) (3.13%)	958 (93.14%)) (3.41%)
	Others	12 (8.05%) (5.41%)	137 (91.95%) (4.92%)
Gender	Male	116 (8.54%) (52.49%)	1242 (91.46%) (44.79%)
	Female	105 (6.41%) (47.51%)	1531 (93.59%) (55.21%)
Education	Less than high school	30 (31.91%) (13.51%)	64 (68.09%) (2.3%)
	High school graduate	67 (15.22%) (30.18%)	373 (84.78%) (13.4%)
	Some college or less than 4 years	72 (7.42%) (32.43%)	898 (92.58%) (32.26%)
	4-year college degree Or Postgraduate degree	53 (3.53%) (23.87%)	1449 (96.26%) (52.05%)
Marital Status	Partnered	90 (5.44%) (40.54%)	1565 (94.56%) (56.21%)
	Single	132 (9.78%) (59.46%)	1219 (90.23%) (43.79%)
Occupation	Full Time	140 (7.46%) (63.06%)	1736 (92.54%) (62.36%)
	Unemployed	73 (7.30%) (32.88%)	927 (92.7%) (33.3%)
	Part Time	9 (6.92%) (4.05%)	121 (93.08%) (4.35%)
Home Ownership	Inapplicable	111 (7.06%) (50.00%)	1462 (92.94%) (52.51%)
	Rent	49 (14.12%) (22.07%)	298 (85.88%) (10.70%)
	Own	51 (5.07%) (22.97%)	954 (94.93%) (34.27%)
	Others	11 (13.58%) (4.95%)	70 (86.42%) (2.51%)

REVIEW OF THE STATISTICAL MODELS

This section outlines the data analytic strategy, focusing on three distinct statistical modeling approaches: Conditional Inference Trees (CIT), Boruta models, and Generalized Linear Models (GLM). We begin with an exploration of CIT, proceed to the Boruta method, and conclude with an analysis of GLM. Each approach provides unique strengths and perspectives in predictive modeling, collectively enhancing our understanding of statistical analysis and machine learning techniques.

Conditional Inference Tree

Conditional Inference Trees (CIT) enhance traditional decision trees by combining interpretability with improved predictive accuracy. Unlike conventional decision trees, which are often prone to overfitting, CIT relies on a rigorous statistical framework that uses conditional permutation tests at each node to ensure splits are based on statistically significant differences. This approach effectively reduces overfitting, making CIT a robust and reliable tool for predictive modeling across diverse datasets. The careful conditional inference process strengthens its ability to balance accuracy with interpretability.

Choi (2017) addressed classification challenges by recursively partitioning the feature space—such as with vertical splits—and assigning class labels through majority voting within each region, ensuring accurate categorization of data points.

To thoroughly evaluate CIT's effectiveness, we conduct extensive experiments comparing its predictive performance against other prominent machine learning algorithms. Moreover, we investigate the interpretability of CIT models, aiming to understand how their statistically-driven structure enhances transparency and clarity in model decision-making.

For example, let X be the dataset with n observations and p features, and let y represent the target variable. The conventional recursive partitioning algorithm initiates tree construction by evaluating candidate splits based on impurity measures such as Gini index or information gain. However, CIT introduces a conditional inference framework, where the process of node splitting is contingent on the outcome of conditional permutation tests.

For a given node t in the tree, let R_t represent the region associated with that node. The null hypothesis H_0 posits that there is no significant difference in the distribution of the target variable y across the regions defined by the split. The conditional permutation test involves repeatedly permuting the target variable within each region, recomputing the test statistic, and assessing whether the observed statistic falls within the permuted distribution.

The conditional inference process ensures that splits occur only when statistically significant differences are detected. Mathematically, this can be expressed as:

$$p(Observed\ Test\ Statistic\ \geq\ Permuted\ Test\ Statistic | H_0)\ <\ \alpha$$

where α is the chosen significance level. This strict adherence to statistical significance at each decision node minimizes the likelihood of overfitting and fortifies CIT's predictive modeling capabilities.

In our empirical assessment, we conduct extensive experiments comparing CIT's predictive accuracy ($Accuracy_{CIT}$) with that of other machine learning algorithms. Additionally, the interpretability facet is explored through statistical analysis of the structural attributes influenced by statistical significance, contributing to a nuanced understanding of CIT's decision-making process. This mathematical underpinning of CIT's methodology not only enhances the robustness of the model but also provides a systematic framework for evaluating its efficacy in achieving the delicate balance between accuracy and interpretability in predictive modeling.

Boruta Models

Boruta is an innovative feature selection algorithm designed to improve the interpretability and efficiency of machine learning models by identifying and ranking relevant features within a dataset. As an extension of the Random Forest algorithm, Boruta works by comparing the importance of each real feature to that of randomized "shadow" features created by permuting the original data. This approach enables Boruta to effectively distinguish truly important variables from noise. Well-suited for complex datasets with many features, Boruta provides a transparent, data-driven method for feature selection, leveraging the strengths of Random Forests while optimizing overall model performance.

The Boruta feature selection process involves the following key steps:

- Boruta begins by creating shadow or "randomized" features based on the original dataset. This is achieved by permuting values within each column to generate a set of synthetic features.
- A Random Forest model is then trained on the combined set of actual and shadow features. The importance scores of each feature are calculated based on metrics such as Gini impurity or information gain.
- Boruta performs a statistical test to determine whether the importance score of each actual feature is significantly higher than the maximum importance score observed for its corresponding shadow features. Features with signifi-

cantly higher importance are labeled as “important,” while those failing the test are deemed “unimportant.”

- o The process is iteratively repeated until all features are either labeled as “important” or “unimportant” or until a predefined number of iterations are reached. This ensures a comprehensive evaluation of feature importance across multiple iterations.
- o Features marked as “important” contribute to the final subset of selected features. This refined feature set is then used for training machine learning models and promoting model efficiency and interpretability.

In our study, we apply Boruta feature selection to enhance the performance of our predictive models. Utilizing the Boruta algorithm in conjunction with machine learning techniques allows us to optimize model interpretability and accuracy by identifying and prioritizing the most relevant features in complex datasets. Our experimental setup involves comprehensive evaluations of Boruta's effectiveness, comparing model performance with and without feature selection, and examining the impact on predictive accuracy across various machine learning algorithms.

Generalized Linear Models

Relationships between categorical dependent (response) and independent variables (covariates) are modeled using logistic regressions. Logistic Regression (LR) is the frequently used model to predict categorical responses. Given the values of the covariates, binary logistic regressions calculate the likelihood that a property of a binary variable is present. Here we assume that the data $(Y_1,Y_2,\ldots,Y_n)$ are independent and that Y is a binary response variable with $Y_i=1$, $(i=1,2,3,\ldots,n)$ for the presence of the character and $Y_i=0$ for the absence of the character. We are concerned about participation in voting and non-participation in voting for our research study. Suppose π_i represent the success probability. Additionally, think of the collection of explanatory variables $x=(x_1,x_2,\ldots,x_p)$ inputs as being either discrete, continuous, or a combination of both. So, p is the number of independent variables in our dataset or model and n is the total number of observations. Now we can write the $P(Y_i=1|X=x)$ or π_i as,

$$P(Y_i = 1|X = x) = \pi_i = \frac{\exp\left(\beta_0 + \beta_1 x_{i1} + \beta_2 x_{i2} + \ldots + \beta_p x_{ip}\right)}{1 + \exp\left(\beta_0 + \beta_1 x_{i1} + \beta_2 x_{i2} + \ldots + \beta_p x_{ip}\right)},$$

where

β_0= intercept of the logistic model.

β_i= effect of variable x_i on π_i.

Y_i= binary response of ith individual (voting or not-voting of an individual)

x_{ij}= response of jth independent variable for i^{th} individual. Where j=1,2,…,p and i =1,2,…,n.

We can also write π_i as in the logistic function form as,

$$logit(\pi_i) = \log\left(\frac{\pi_i}{1-\pi_i}\right) = \beta_0 + \beta_1 x_{i1} + \beta_2 x_{i2} + \ldots + \beta_p x_{ip}.$$

Here, the ratio of π_i over 1-π_i with

π_i= success probability (probability of having voting for i^{th} individual).

shows the odds of being a voter, a measure that compares the two groups (voters and non-voters) with respect to the predictor variables selected.

Now, to use this model to predict if an individual voted, we need to estimate the parameters of the model. Although we can use the least-squares strategy, maximum likelihood is favored since it has better statistical properties for estimating *β’s* in the model. The number of *β’s* in the complete model and the reduced model are denoted by p and r, respectively. Then the likelihood ratio test statistic to test the model is,

$$\Lambda^* = -2\left\{l(\hat{\beta}') - l(\hat{\beta})\right\},$$

where $l(\hat{\beta})$ and $l(\hat{\beta}')$ are the complete model's and the reduced model's log likelihoods, respectively. Here, $\Lambda^* \sim \chi^2_{p-r}$; p and r being the number of parameters in the full and the reduced model, respectively.

Cost-Benefit Analysis

Cost-benefit analysis is a fundamental paradigm in political science and decision theory that is used to assess the rationality of human behaviors, especially when it comes to voting behavior. The cost-benefit model of voting, first introduced by Downs (1957) and expanded upon by Ordeshook (1968), clarifies the calculations people do while determining whether or not to engage in political processes. Mathematically, this can be expressed as:

$$R = pB - c + d,$$

where R = the net return from voting or reward,

p= the probability the voter will be decisive,

B= the utility differential that results when the act of voting is decisive,

c= positive costs of voting not associated with the outcome,

d= positive benefits of voting not associated with the outcome/Civic Duty.

Facchini and Jaeck (2019) and Addeo (2024) discussed the cost of electoral activism: if voting is easy, more voters should participate. However, they did not add the reward equation as formulated; they just explained facilitation rules.

ANALYSIS OF DATA AND DISCUSSION

We employed a stepwise variable selection method within the dataset to estimate voting behavior, resulting in the identification of approximately 50 variables. Subsequently, we utilized the Boruta approach to further refine the selection, ultimately reducing the number of variables to 21. This curated list includes variables that significantly contribute to explaining the voting behavior. However, upon examination, many of these variables appeared to lack practical relevance in real-life scenarios. Therefore, we supplemented this list by incorporating additional variables based on relevant literature, aiming to establish connections between our research findings and recent scholarly work. Numerous studies indicate that voter identification requirements decrease voter turnout, with certain studies highlighting particularly suppressive effects on minority voters (Alvarez et al. 2011).

Following the methodology outlined by Blais et al. (2015) or Gelman et al. (2010), we embarked on a study aimed at assessing the voting probability utilizing data from the American National Election Studies (ANES). We hypothesize that various factors influence voting behavior. The ANES dataset comprises a sample size of 8,280 respondents and does not encompass variables such as cost and benefit.

Beginning with a General Linear Model (GLM), our approach involves constructing a model that classifies Model voting behaviors based on learning behaviors, with these classes potentially associated with specific labels. Through evaluating the model's performance using metrics such as Adjusted R-squared or AIC (Akaike Information Criterion), we aim to elucidate the probability of voting.

The variables contributing to the voting probability are shown in Table 2.

Table 2. Variables contributing to voter turnout

Number	Variable	Values
V201510	Education***	1 = Less than high school, 2 = High school graduate, 3 = Some college or less than 4 years, 4 = 4-year college degree Or Postgraduate degree
V201508	Marital Status	1 = Partnered, 2 = Single
V201533x	Occupation	1= Full Time, 2 = Unemployed, 3 = Part Time,
V201549x	Race*	1 = White, 2 = Black, 3 = Hispanic, 4 = Asian, 5 = Others
V201581	Home ownership**	1 = Inapplicable, 2 = Rent, 3 = Own, 4 = Others
V202064	Party Registration	1 = Inapplicable, 2 = Democrate, 3 = Republican, 4 = Others
V202219	Votes Counted Fairly	1 = Never, 2 = Some of the time, 3 = About half of the time, 4 = Most of the time, 5 = All of the time
V202017	Monetary Contribution	1 = Yes, 0 = No
V202051	Registered to Vote	1 = Inapplicable, 2 =Yes, 3 = No
V202352	Social Class	1 = Lower class, 2 = Working class, 3 = Middle class, 4 = Upper class
V201244	Party better handling the COVID-19 (Voting Choice)	1 = R. would do a much better job, 2 = R. would do a somewhat better job, 3 = Not much difference between them, 4 = D. would do a somewhat better job, 5 = D. would do a much better job
COVI Index	Cost	*Scot Schraufnagel, Michael J. Pomante II, and Quan Li (2020)*
V201221	Duty***	1 = Mainly a duty, 0 = Mainly a choice
	Benefit	https://rockinst.org/issue-areas/fiscal-analysis/balance-of-payments -portal/
V202066	Vote	1 = Voted, 0 = Did not vote

These variables will be carefully examined and incorporated into the GLM to analyze their respective impacts on voting behavior.

Variables cost and benefit were retrieved from Schraufnagel et al. (2020) and the Rockefeller Institute of Government (https://rockinst.org/issue-areas/fiscal-analysis/balance-of-payments-portal/).

The map shown in Figure 1 indicates the cost of voting for each state. If the cost is higher, the color is darker red, and if the cost is lower, the color is light green.

Texas has taken the 50th rank, signifying the state with the most restricted electoral atmosphere. Texas has an in-person voter registration deadline 30 days before Election Day, has decreased the number of voting places by more than half in some areas, and has the most stringent pre-registration rule in the country.

Figure 1. Count of Voting by State

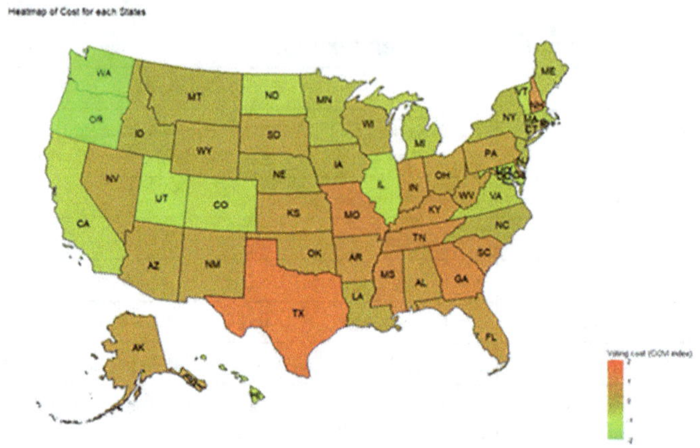

Figure 2. Standardized Benefit by State

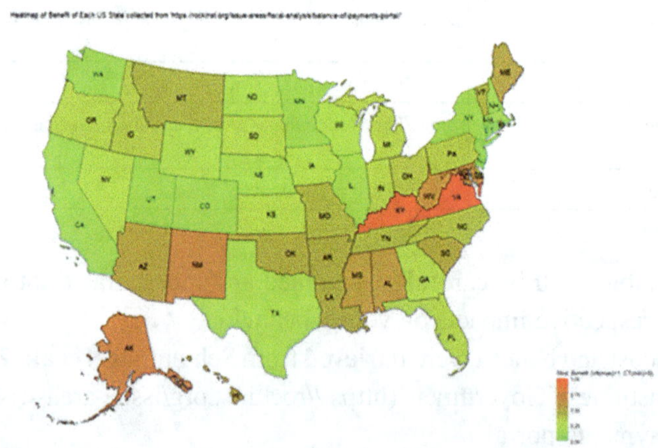

The map in Figure 2 indicates the standardized benefit for each state. If the benefit is higher, the color is darker red, and if the benefit is lower, the color is light green.

Virginia and Kentucky rank number one and two respectively in terms of Per Capita Balance of Payments in 2020 without COVID handling.

RESULTS

Using the selected variables, we initially applied Conditional Inference Tree (CIT) methodology to elucidate the patterns and factors influencing voting behavior. CIT extends traditional decision tree techniques by incorporating a strict statistical framework, thereby enhancing interpretability and predictive accuracy. By employing CIT methodology, researchers can gain valuable insights into the complex interplay of variables influencing voting behavior, thereby contributing to a deeper understanding of electoral dynamics and decision-making processes.

Interpretation of a CIT, terminal node with a high proportion of voters indicates a subgroup of respondents who are more likely to vote. The path from the root node to a terminal node represents the decision-making process, showing which variables and thresholds are most influential in predicting voting behavior. By examining the terminal nodes and their associated characteristics, we can gain insights into the demographic and attitudinal factors that drive voting behavior within different subgroups of the population.

The CIT with all the variables in the selected variable list is illustrated in Figure 3.

Figure 3. CIT Variables

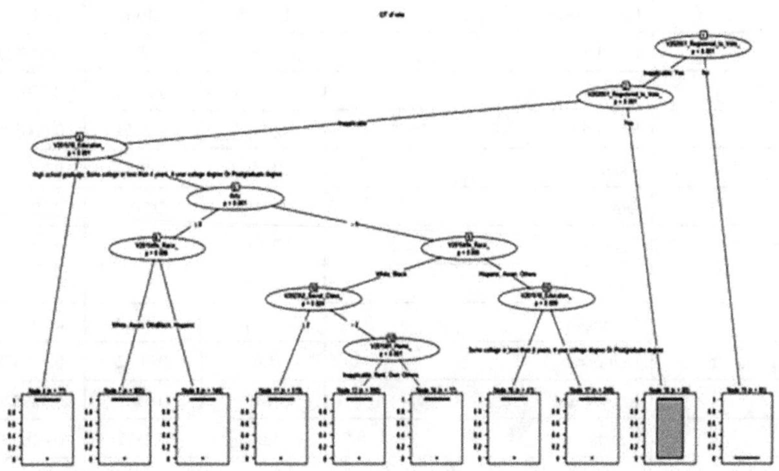

In summary, the CIT decision tree provides a visual and interpretable representation of the complex relationships between predictor variables and voting behavior, allowing researchers to identify patterns and make predictions based on the characteristics of individual respondents.

The estimated model from the GLM approach is based on the previous variable list.

Table 3 shows the results of the logistic regression analysis of the Cost/Benefit model of voting in the United States. The variables that were significant with a p-value less than .0.001 were education, Hispanic participants, votes counted fairly, and non-registered participants. These variables were very influential in determining whether an individual voted in the 2020 general election. The other variables that were significant with a p-value less than 0.05 were registered voters, social class, cost, monetary contributions, unemployment, Black participants, and party registration-Other. The variables that were not significant were marital status, part-time employment, Asian and Other participants, home ownership, Democrat and Republican party registration, voting choice, COVID-19, and Benefit.

Table 3. Cost/benefit model

Variables		Estimate	Std. Error	Pr(>|z|)	
	(Intercept)	-0.07203	0.5336	0.892622	
Education	High school graduate	0.9767	0.2796	0.000478	***
	Some college or less than 4 years	1.148	0.2602	0.000010	***
	4-year college degree or postgraduate degree	1.44	0.2793	0.000000	***
Marital Status	Single	-0.2024	0.1561	0.194813	
Occupation	Unemployed	0.3973	0.1664	0.016923	*
	Part Time	0.03135	0.3462	0.927853	
Race	Black	-0.5125	0.2366	0.030284	*
	Hispanic	-0.7793	0.2179	0.000349	***
	Asian	-0.08955	0.4873	0.854213	
	Others	-0.3193	0.303	0.291884	
Home	Rent	-0.193	0.2001	0.334891	
	Own	0.3093	0.1796	0.085134	.
	Others	-0.1249	0.3647	0.731934	
Party Registration	Democrat	-1.01	0.7072	0.153407	
	Republican	0.1378	0.6401	0.829524	
	Others	-1.099	0.5572	0.048607	*
Votes Count Fairly		0.2888	0.0641	0.000006	***
Monitory Contribution		0.514	0.2466	0.037137	*
Registered to Vote	Yes	-1.013	0.3594	0.004802	**
	No	-7.116	0.7224	< 0.000000	***
Social Class		0.3496	0.1103	0.001529	**
Voting Choice	Inapplicable	0.5941	0.3359	0.076978	.
	Moderately strongly	0.1762	0.3691	0.633076	

continued on following page

Table 3. Continued

Variables		Estimate	Std. Error	Pr(>|z|)	
	Very strongly	-0.2437	0.3486	0.484605	
Covid		-0.01712	0.06174	0.781538	
Cost		-0.2896	0.1089	0.007839	**
Benefit		-0.00003864	0.00002192	0.077959	.

.p < 0.1, *p < .05, **p < .01, ***p < .001

The Cost/Benefit model showed that participants with a high school diploma were 2.656 times more likely to vote than a participant who did not graduate from high school after controlling for all other variables in the model ($exp(0.977)=2.656$). Additionally, participants with some college and a 4-year college degree or more were 3.152 and 4.221 times more likely than participants without a high school degree to vote in the 2020 general election. These findings show that as the level of education grows, participants are more likely to vote.

Discriminatory practices based on race has traditionally negatively impacted the ability of minorities to vote in national elections (Henley et al., 2024). The Cost/Benefit model demonstrates that if an individual is Black, their odds of voting is decreased 41% of the time compared to white individuals ($exp(-0.513)=0.599), 1-0.599=0.410$). The outcome for Hispanic participants is worse. The odds of Hispanic participants voting decreases about 54.10% compared to White participants ($exp(-0.779)=0.459), 1-0.459=0.541$). Surprisingly, the variables Asian and Others were not significant.

Social Class and voting integrity have a positive effect on voting in the 2020 general election. The odds of voting increases 1.419 if an individual's social class increases one unit, if all other variables are constant ($exp(0.350)=1.419$). Similarly, the odds of voting increases 1.335 if the individual feels their vote will be counted fairly increases one unit with all other variables are constant ($exp(0.289)=1.335$). Baber et al. (2022) refer to this concept as political efficacy. Voter integrity allows citizens to see how government responds and addresses issues within the political system. Conversely, cost has a negative impact on voting. The odds of voting decreases 25.20% if an individual's voting cost increases by one unit ($exp(-0.116)=0.890$, $1-0.890=0.11$).

Table 4 displays results of the logistic regression analysis for the Duty model. The variables that are significant with a p-value of less than .001 are duty, some college education, and college degree or postgraduate degree. The variables that are significant with a p-value less than .05 are home-rent, high school graduate, Hispanic, and homeownership-Others.

Table 4. Duty Model

Variables		Estimate	Std. Error	Pr.(>|z|)	
	(Intercept)	0.750286	0.692661	0.278722	
Duty		0.977474	0.237736	3.93E-05	***
Education	High school graduate	1.03235	0.462034	0.02546	*
	Some college or less than 4 years	1.516267	0.44844	0.000722	***
	4-year college degree Or Postgraduate degree	1.521595	0.450853	0.000738	***
Marital Status	Single	-0.1522	0.250999	0.544267	
Occupation	Unemployed	0.145875	0.263636	0.580045	
	Part Time	-0.36271	0.504709	0.472361	
Race	Black	-0.32022	0.4019	0.425594	
	Hispanic	-0.81911	0.345101	0.017618	*
	Asian	0.117249	0.663521	0.859739	
	Others	-0.23948	0.546181	0.661048	
Home	Rent	-0.82618	0.308191	0.007346	**
	Own	0.013546	0.285243	0.962123	
	Others	-1.18811	0.521745	0.022776	*
Party Registration	Democrat	-1.7505	1.364323	0.199472	
	Republican	0.680638	1.248893	0.585758	
	Others	-1.50016	0.856503	0.079862	.
Votes Count Fairly		0.194254	0.108764	0.074098	.
Monitory Contribution		0.621206	0.39193	0.112968	
Registered to Vote	Yes	-0.91516	0.542745	0.091764	.
	No	-20.1501	532.3398	0.969806	
Social Class		-0.00698	0.177184	0.968593	
Covid		0.044846	0.097712	0.646265	

.p < 0.1,*p < .05, **p < .01, ***p < .001

The regression analysis shows that duty is very influential in determining voting behavior. The odds of voting are increased 2.656 if participants view voting as a duty compared to viewing voting a choice (*exp*(0. 977)=2.656). Education is also positively associated with voting. However, the level of significance is lower (.05 vs. 001) in this model for the variable some college education than the Cost/Benefit Model (Table 3). Another notable finding is the relationship between renting and voting. For participants that listed their homeownership status as rent, their odds of voting decreased 56.2% compared to participants that listed their homeownership status as inapplicable (*exp*(-0.826)=0.438),1−0.432=0.5622).

Table 5 provides the results of the logistic regression analysis of the model Duty vs. Cost/Benefit. The table shows that the variables that are significant at a p-value less than .001 are duty, some college education, and 4-year college degree or post-graduate degree. The variables that are significant with a p-value of less than .05 are rent, high school graduate, Hispanic, and home ownership-Others.

Table 5. Duty versus Cost/Benefit Model

Variables		Estimate	Std. Error	Pr.(>|z|)	
	(Intercept)	0.9565	0.7156	0.181377	
Duty		0.995	0.2386	0.0000303	***
Education	High school graduate	1.038	0.4612	0.024375	*
	Some college or less than 4 years	1.501	0.4471	0.000787	***
	4-year college degree Or Postgraduate degree	1.498	0.4495	0.000863	***
Marital Status	Single	-0.1692	0.2517	0.501495	
Occupation	Unemployed	0.163	0.264	0.537112	
	Part Time	-0.356	0.5049	0.480769	
Race	Black	-0.2603	0.4048	0.520158	
	Hispanic	-0.8251	0.3521	0.019112	*
	Asian	0.0893	0.6727	0.894397	
	Others	-0.2463	0.5451	0.651466	
Home	Rent	-0.8203	0.3086	0.007854	**
	Own	0.02517	0.2853	0.929716	
	Others	-1.173	0.5249	0.025416	*
Party Registration	Democrat	-1.757	1.37	0.199749	
	Republican	0.7439	1.255	0.553352	
	Others	-1.526	0.8613	0.076419	.
Votes Count Fairly		0.2077	0.1093	0.057385	.
Monitory Contribution		0.61	0.3927	0.120267	
Registered to Vote	Yes	-0.9545	0.5471	0.081073	.
	No	-20.19	531.5	0.969697	
Social Class		-0.003236	0.1773	0.985443	
Covid		0.02333	0.09928	0.814203	
Cost		-0.1157	0.1731	0.50382	
Benefit		-0.00004021	0.00003495	0.249965	

.p < 0.1, *p < .05, **p < .01, ***p < .001

The logistic regression analysis demonstrate that duty and education had a major impact on voting in the 2020 General Election. If an individual views voting as a duty, their odds of voting increases 2.604 times compared to individuals that view voting as a choice, conditional on all other variables fixed ($exp(0.957)=2.604$).

Education also positively affects voting. If an individual is a high school graduate, completed some college, or holds a bachelor or post graduate degree, then their odds of voting respectively increase 2.824 ($exp(1.038)=2.824$), 4.486 ($exp(1.501)=4.486$), and 4.473 ($exp(1.498)=4.473$) times compared to individuals with less than a high school degree.

Notably, the variables cost, benefit, social class, votes counted fairly, and Black were not significant. This finding suggests that the duty variable trumps factors that traditionally hinder voting. However, Hispanic participants are still negatively affected by obstacles that prevent them from voting. Their odds of voting are decreased 56.20% of the time compared to white participants ($exp(-0.825)=0.438$) ,$1-0.438=0.562$).

DISCUSSION

The practical importance of the cost and benefit variables can be challenged in the model with the ANES data. The model in ANES data directly builds the probability of voting based on characteristics and features such as duty, race, education, etc. Another study by Gelman et al. (2010) demonstrates how correlations in election forecasts facilitate conditional outcome inferences through Bayesian inference and simulations.

In the ANES dataset, voter behavior does not appear strongly linked to cost-benefit calculations, offering limited support for the traditional rational choice model of voting. However, there is considerable potential for future research to better capture this relationship. Improved data collection and subsequent surveys could aim to identify and measure the factors that contribute to the perceived costs and benefits of voting. Additionally, future studies might explore the role of emotions and feelings in voter turnout. For example, Srinivason and Paat (2024) analyzed tweets from the 2020 General Election expressing emotions such as joy, love, sadness, fear, anger, and disgust, suggesting that public sentiment could serve as a proxy indicator for voting behavior.

In this chapter, the focus on understanding how rational choice theory influences voting decisions, while emphasizing cost-benefit considerations, shows the role of duty. Our theoretical framework draws on the foundational work of Downs (1957) and Riker and Ordeshook (1968).

The variable 'duty' is more closely related to the decision and probability of voting than cost/benefit which demonstrates propensity for motivation. To determine this, we used Boruta and the random forest models. One can propose other models, but the suggested models relax the Gaussian assumptions by considering the classification based on the subclasses. Under these methods, the data are divided into testing and validation. Using the testing, some features are selected. Within a class, say level of education, if a feature has no significant effect on the voting, that feature is not selected and found to be irrelevant. Abramovich and Pensky (2019) discussed the challenges in classification with a small number of classes and small sample size. Building a simulation study would be almost impossible, as the duty associated with voting is more complex to describe. The latter would require a rational of voting, a rational that Blais (2015, page 55) called: "In its simplest formulation, the calculus of voting model appears unsatisfactory. Should we conclude that the model is basically flawed and should be dismissed?" On page 63, the author suggested that besides the cost and benefit, "the term p is probably the most problematic." We have proposed an attempt to rationalize the voting data.

There is a volatility in the reward recorded. This is to say that the subjectivity in the reward (or subjectivity in the benefit and cost) is highlighted here. Further exploration is needed to validate the benefit and cost. As mentioned in their research, the cost depends on many other factors that may be outside the scope of the ANES of course, and are spatio-temporal dependent. We were not surprised when the correlation between the cost and the average probability of voting was not significant. The same can be said between the benefit and the cost of voting.

Blais et al. (2019) stated that "little is known about the cost of voting" and the perception of voting, in five countries, USA not included. This is related to the probability of voting. In that paper, they described the cost of voting on a 0 to 1 scale, with 0 corresponding to maximally easy and 1 to maximally difficult, respectively. Perception of voting is related to turnout. However, they mention that the substantive impact of cost is fairly small. From Blais et al. (2019), "a huge majority of citizens do not think voting is costly," hence the variable duty seems a valuable determinant in capturing the probability of voting. Individuals tend to vote more frequently in elections with significant repercussions, when the results are expected to have a large influence on policy (Hansen et al. 1987). Voter turnout is based on membership to a certain group and assumes that the possibility of that group becoming decisive is high enough (Harsanyi 1977). Conventional game-theoretic models struggle to explain high participation in major elections due to the perceived low influence of an individual vote. However, a unique model in which ethical agents interact based on perceived moral responsibilities modified by seeing others' behaviors produces high turnout and is consistent with strategic behavior, a revealing light on participation dynamics (Feddersen et al. 2006). Barber et al (2022) analyzed 400 million voting records, and revealed significant racial, age, and geographic disparities in U.S. voter turnout, with minorities, younger citizens, and Democrats being less likely to vote and more likely to live in low-turnout areas. These inequities undermine democratic representation and reinforce political power imbalances.

CONCLUSION

In conclusion, our study used a rigorous technique that included stepwise variable selection and the Boruta approach to uncover critical determinants impacting voting turnout. After examining a long list of variables and refining them, we developed a curated list of 21 variables, including demographics, attitudes, and socioeconomic characteristics, that significantly contribute to predicting voting behavior. Despite the initial list's practical relevance constraints, more variables were included to strengthen the model based on relevant literature.

Utilizing data from the American National Election Studies (ANES), our analysis elucidated the complex interplay of variables shaping voting behavior. By employing Conditional Inference Trees (CIT) methodology and General Linear Models (GLM), we gained valuable insights into demographic and attitudinal factors impacting voting decisions. Our findings underscore the significance of factors such as education level, race, marital status, and homeownership in predicting voting probability.

Our analysis, however, revealed that the perceived sense of duty towards voting emerged as a crucial determinant, overshadowing considerations of cost and benefit. The subjectivity inherent in assessing voting costs and benefits underscores the need for further research to validate and refine these variables.

In alignment with prior research, our study emphasizes the limited substantive impact of voting costs on voter turnout. Rather, the perception of voting as a duty emerges as a significant determinant of voting behavior. Future studies could delve deeper into understanding the complex interplay between individual perceptions, socio-economic factors, and voting decisions to inform more comprehensive models of voter behavior.

REFERENCES

Abramovich, F., & Pensky, M. (2019). Classification with many classes: Challenges and pluses. *Journal of Multivariate Analysis, 174*, 104536. DOI: 10.1016/j.jmva.2019.104536

Addeo, F., Ammirato, L., Delli Paoli, A., Fruncillo, D., & Maddaloni, D. (2024). *Voter turnout: Overtime and regional trends in Europe* (Working paper no. 2.3). TRUEDEM: Trust in European Democracies Project. http://www.truedem.eu

Alvarez, R. M., Bailey, D., & Katz, J. N. (2011). An empirical Bayes approach to estimating ordinal treatment effects. *Political Analysis, 19*(1), 20–31. DOI: 10.1093/pan/mpq028

Barber, M., & Holbein, J. B. (2022). 400 million voting records show profound racial and geographic disparities in voter turnout in the United States. *PLoS One, 17*(6), e0268134. DOI: 10.1371/journal.pone.0268134

Baron, J. (2012). The 'culture of honor' in citizens' concepts of their duty as voters. *Rationality and Society, 24*(1), 37–72. DOI: 10.1177/1043463111429273

Blais, A., & Daoust, J.-F. (2020). *The motivation to vote: Explaining electoral participation*. UBC Press.

Blais, A., Daoust, J.-F., Dassonneville, R., & Péloquin-Skulski, G. (2019). What is the cost of voting? *Electoral Studies, 59*, 145–157. DOI: 10.1016/j.electstud.2019.03.001

Blais, A., Galais, C., & Mayer, D. (2019). Is it a duty to vote and to be informed? *Political Studies Review, 17*(4), 328–339. DOI: 10.1177/1478929918788991

Blais, A., & Kostelka, F. (2015). The decision to vote or abstain in the 2014 European elections. *Revue européenne des sciences sociales, 53*(1), 79–94. https://doi.org/DOI: 10.4000/ress.3021

Brennan, J., & Freiman, C. (2023). Why swing-state voting is not effective altruism: The bad news about the good news about voting. *Journal of Political Philosophy, 31*(1), 60–79. DOI: 10.1111/jopp.12304

Choi, H. I. (2017). *Lectures on machine learning (Fall 2017), Lecture 9: Classification and regression tree*. CART.

Downs, A. (1957). *An economic theory of democracy*. Harper & Row.

Edlin, A. S., Gelman, A., & Kaplan, N. (2008). Vote for charity's sake. *The Economists' Voice, 5*(6). Advance online publication. DOI: 10.2202/1553-3832.1338

Facchini, F., & Jaeck, L. (2019). Ideology and the rationality of non-voting. *Rationality and Society, 31*(3), 265–286. DOI: 10.1177/1043463119840743

Faravelli, M., Kalayci, K., & Pimienta, C. (2020). Costly voting: A large-scale real effort experiment. *Experimental Economics, 23*(2), 468–492. DOI: 10.1007/s10683-019-09615-9

Feddersen, T., & Sandroni, A. (2006a). A theory of participation in elections. *The American Economic Review, 96*(4), 1271–1282. DOI: 10.1257/aer.96.4.1271

Feddersen, T., & Sandroni, A. (2006b). The calculus of ethical voting. *International Journal of Game Theory, 35*, 1–25. DOI: 10.1007/s00182-006-0029-3

Feddersen, T., & Sandroni, A. (2006c). Ethical voters and costly information acquisition. *Quarterly Journal of Political Science, 1*(3), 287–312. DOI: 10.1561/100.00002049

Feddersen, T., & Sandroni, A. (2009). *The foundations of warm-glow theory* (Working paper).

Feddersen, T. J. (2004). Rational choice theory and the paradox of not voting. *The Journal of Economic Perspectives, 18*(1), 99–112. DOI: 10.1257/089533004773563458

Gelman, A., & Silver, N. (2010). What do we know at 7 PM on election night? *Mathematics Magazine, 83*(4), 258–266. DOI: 10.4169/002557010X521660

Gelman, A., Silver, N., & Edlin, A. (2012). What is the probability your vote will make a difference? *Economic Inquiry, 50*(2), 321–326. DOI: 10.1111/j.1465-7295.2011.00397.x

Goldfarb, R. S., & Sigelman, L. (2010). Does 'civic duty' 'solve' the rational choice voter turnout puzzle? *Journal of Theoretical Politics, 22*(3), 275–300. DOI: 10.1177/0951629810363376

Hansen, S., Palfrey, T. R., & Rosenthal, H. (1987). The Downsian model of electoral participation: Formal theory and empirical analysis of the constituency size effect. *Public Choice, 52*(1), 15–33. DOI: 10.1007/BF00127605

Harsanyi, J. C. (1977). Morality and the theory of rational behavior. *Social Research, 44*(4), 623–656.

Hayes, D., & Lawless, J. L. (2015). As local news goes, so goes citizen engagement: Media, knowledge, and participation in U.S. House elections. *The Journal of Politics, 77*(2), 447–462. DOI: 10.1086/680257

Heckelman, J. C., & Miller, N. R. (2015). Introduction: Issues in social choice and voting. In Heckelman, J. C., & Miller, N. R. (Eds.), *Handbook of social choice and voting* (pp. 1–12). Edward Elgar Publishing.

Henley, T., Brown, S., Diawara, N., Hossain, M. I., & Rivera, G. (2024). Contemporary voter suppression: Impact on the 2020 general election. *Ralph Bunche Journal of Public Affairs, 7*(1), Article 4.

Holbein, J. B., & Hassell, H. (2023). George Floyd's murder prompted thousands of Americans to register to vote.

Law, W. (2021). Decomposing political advertising effects on vote choices. *Public Choice, 188*(3), 525–547. DOI: 10.1007/s11127-020-00855-5

Lee, D. R. (2021). Ignoring the Electoral College: Why public choice economists understate the probability of decisive voters. *Public Choice, 187*(3), 439–454. DOI: 10.1007/s11127-020-00842-w

Ong Whaley, C., & Goldberg, A. (2021). Voting trends among young people. In *Encyclopedia of American political parties and elections*. https://virginia.academia.edu/CarahOngWhaley/Papers

Riker, W. H., & Ordeshook, P. C. (1968). A theory of the calculus of voting. *The American Political Science Review, 62*(1), 25–42. DOI: 10.2307/1953324

Rockefeller Institute of Government. (n.d.). *Balance of payments portal.* https://rockinst.org/issue-areas/fiscal-analysis/balance-of-payments-portal/

Schraufnagel, S., Pomante, M. J.II, & Li, Q. (2020). Cost of voting in the American states: 2020. *Election Law Journal: Rules. Politics & Policy, 19*(4), 503–509. DOI: 10.1089/elj.2020.0666

Wolfinger, R. E., & Rosenstone, S. J. (1980). *Who votes?* Yale University Press.

Chapter 3

From Issue Voting to Emerging Party Loyalty in Greece's 2015 Twin Elections:

Mapping Voter–Party Thematic Realignments

Georgia Panagiotidou
https://orcid.org/0000-0002-7264-1187
Aristotle University of Thessaloniki, Greece

ABSTRACT

This chapter examines issue voting in political competition and voter behaviour in Greece during the two parliamentary elections of 2015. Drawing on data from the HelpMeVote platform, the analysis employs Principal Component Analysis (PCA) and fuzzy clustering to position parties and voters on key issue dimensions and trace their shifts between January and September. The January election was dominated by the memorandum–anti-memorandum divide, which largely determined party agendas and voter alignments. By September, this central cleavage had weakened, as SYRIZA and ANEL, despite their prior anti-memorandum stance, revised their thematic agendas, prompting varying degrees of voter realignment. Results indicate that while some parties and voters displayed significant thematic repositioning, others remained stable, highlighting both the persistence of ideological identities and the capacity of party strategies to reshape electoral competition. The findings contribute to understanding issue-driven voting, party–voter congruence and the dynamics of political change in crisis contexts.

DOI: 10.4018/979-8-3373-1037-4.ch003

INTRODUCTION

The parliamentary elections of January and September 2015 were among the most consequential and revealing electoral contests in post-authoritarian Greece. Unfolding against the backdrop of the protracted sovereign debt crisis, the collapse of the traditional two-party system, and the emergence of new political forces, these "twin elections" crystallised processes of political change that had been underway since the onset of the crisis in 2009 (Vasilopoulou, Halikiopoulou, & Exadaktylos, 2014; Teperoglou & Tsatsanis, 2018). They were held just eight months apart, yet under profoundly different political conditions, providing a rare quasi-experimental opportunity to examine how voter–party relationships evolve within a compressed period of intense political and economic uncertainty (Dinas & Rori, 2016).

The January 2015 election marked the dramatic ascent of SYRIZA, a radical left coalition that successfully channelled widespread anti-austerity sentiment into an electoral victory over New Democracy, the centre-right incumbent. SYRIZA's campaign combined a strong anti-memorandum stance with promises of social protection and a renegotiation of Greece's bailout agreements, positioning the party as the principal vehicle for political change. The result was a decisive rejection of the austerity policies pursued under Greece's international loan agreements, and the first time since the restoration of democracy in 1974 that a party to the left of PASOK assumed the premiership.

Yet, the optimism of January quickly gave way to a turbulent summer, culminating in the July 2015 referendum on the bailout terms proposed by Greece's creditors. Although 61.3% of voters rejected the terms, the subsequent negotiation process led Prime Minister Alexis Tsipras to accept a third bailout agreement, triggering a major political realignment within SYRIZA and the resignation of dissenting MPs. The September 2015 election was thus fought under radically altered circumstances: SYRIZA, now committed to implementing the bailout, sought a renewed mandate to govern, while new political actors, such as Popular Unity, emerged from its split. Despite the political upheaval, SYRIZA managed to retain its position as the dominant governing force, albeit in a changed political landscape (Andreadis, Teperoglou & Tsatsanis, 2011).

These twin elections offer a unique lens through which to study electoral volatility, thematic realignment, and issue-based voting in a highly polarised and fragmented party system. The traditional explanatory frameworks, such as partisan identification, socio-structural cleavages, or valence-based models, struggle to fully account for the speed and scale of voter movements observed in 2015 (Dalton, 2018; Dassonneville & Hooghe, 2017). In such volatile contexts, issue voting, whereby voters choose the party closest to their own positions on salient political issues, provides a more dynamic approach to understanding electoral behaviour.

This chapter builds on the issue voting tradition (Downs, 1957; van der Brug, van der Eijk, & Franklin, 2007), employing Voting Advice Application (VAA) data from *HelpMeVote* to map the spatial configuration of party–voter relationships during both elections. Using Principal Component Analysis (PCA), we identify the underlying issue dimensions that structured the political competition, while spatial mapping techniques visualise the relative positions of parties and voters. This allows for a comparative analysis of both January 2015, when SYRIZA first rose to power, and September 2015, when the political context had dramatically shifted.

The analytical approach is innovative in the Greek case for three reasons. First, VAAs capture individual-level data on a wide range of policy issues, allowing for a multidimensional mapping of voter and party positions that goes beyond the traditional left–right scale. Second, PCA enables the reduction of complex policy data into interpretable dimensions, making it possible to visualise and quantify changes in party–voter distances. Third, applying the same methodology to two elections in rapid succession allows us to trace thematic realignment, changes in the salience and meaning of political issues, as well as shifts in the ideological identity of parties and their electorates.

The aim of this chapter is therefore twofold:

1. To map the spatial structure of political competition in January 2015, identifying the main issue dimensions and the positioning of both parties and voters.
2. To analyse the changes in party–voter distances and issue salience between January and September 2015, assessing how these shifts relate to electoral outcomes and voter migration patterns.

In doing so, the chapter contributes to the broader literature on electoral behaviour in crisis contexts by demonstrating how short-term political shocks can reshape party systems and voter alignments in measurable ways. It also showcases the value of issue-based multivariate analysis for understanding electoral dynamics in multiparty systems under stress, highlighting the methodological advantages of spatial modelling over more static, single-dimension approaches.

Theoretical Background

The study of electoral behaviour has evolved through several major paradigms, each reflecting the prevailing political and methodological context of its time. Early research in political science was dominated by socio-structural explanations, rooted in the cleavage theory of Lipset and Rokkan (1967), which linked voting patterns to stable divisions such as class, religion, and region. These approaches assumed relatively stable party systems, where voter loyalties were passed across generations and electoral volatility was low. The post-war consolidation of party systems in Western Europe lent support to such stability-focused models.

However, by the latter half of the 20th century, the Columbia School (Lazarsfeld, Berelson, & Gaudet, 1968) and the Michigan School (Campbell, Converse, Miller, & Stokes, 1960) had added crucial psychological and social-interactionist perspectives. The Columbia School stressed the role of social networks and opinion leaders, while the Michigan School introduced the concept of party identification as a long-term psychological attachment that structures political perceptions and choices.

While these frameworks captured the stability of post-war politics, they proved less effective in periods of rapid political change. The increasing secularisation of electorates, the decline of class voting, and the emergence of new political issues in the 1970s and 1980s (e.g. environmentalism, post-materialism) led to what Franklin, Mackie, and Valen (1992) described as dealignment, the weakening of traditional voter–party bonds.

This environment gave rise to issue voting theory, which emphasises the role of voter preferences on specific policy issues in determining electoral choice. Issue voting theory provided an explicit framework for analysing the role of substantive political issues, both long-standing (e.g. taxation, welfare) and emerging (e.g. immigration, EU integration), in shaping electoral choice (Budge & Farlie, 1983; Petrocik, 1996). Two main distinctions have been made in the literature:

1. Position issues, where parties and voters take different stances on the same continuum (e.g., pro-/anti-austerity).
2. Valence issues, where there is broad agreement on goals, but competition occurs over perceived competence in delivering them (Stokes, 1963).

Building on Downs' (1957) economic theory of democracy, spatial models of electoral competition conceptualized both voters and parties as occupying positions along one or more issue dimensions. In these models, issue voting assumes that voters compare their own positions with those of competing parties and choose the party that minimises this "distance" (Enelow & Hinich, 1984). The distinction between position issues (where parties take clearly opposing stances) and valence issues (where parties agree on the goal but differ in perceived competence) has been central to refining the theory (Stokes, 1963; Clarke et al., 2011). Voters would finally support the party whose policy position was closest to their own, a mechanism operationalized in numerous empirical studies through measures of voter–party distances. In two-dimensional or multi-dimensional spaces, these models could capture more complex ideological structures, accommodating cross-cutting issues and heterogeneity within ideological blocs.

In multiparty systems, the spatial approach enables researchers to represent both voters and parties in a multidimensional policy space (van der Brug, van der Eijk, & Franklin, 2007). Here, dimensions may include economic left–right, cultural liberal–conservative, or pro-/anti-integrationist stances, depending on the political context. Methodologically, tools such as Principal Component Analysis (PCA), Correspondence Analysis (CA), and Multidimensional Scaling (MDS) have been employed to reduce large sets of policy positions into interpretable spatial maps (Gabel & Huber, 2000; Louwerse & Otjes, 2019).

The Greek case during the 2010s offers a particularly vivid example of thematic realignment, in which the traditional left–right cleavage was supplemented and in some cases supplanted, by a new axis of competition centred on the memorandum vs. anti-memorandum divide. This cleavage reflected citizens' attitudes toward the austerity measures and structural reforms imposed as part of Greece's international bailout agreements. The salience of this issue, combined with an unprecedented economic depression, generated massive shifts in party support, producing electoral "earthquakes" in both 2012 and 2015 (Voulgaris & Nikolakopoulos, 2014; Dinas & Rori, 2013).

For decades, electoral competition in Greece was dominated by a bipolar system centred on the social-democratic PASOK and the centre-right New Democracy (ND), with political conflict largely reducible to a single economic left–right axis (Lyrintzis, 1984; Pappas, 2009). The financial crisis of 2009 and the subsequent austerity programmes fractured this structure, introducing new political cleavages, most prominently, the memorandum vs. anti-memorandum divide (Teperoglou et al., 2017). This cleavage cut across traditional left–right lines, producing an unstable and highly fragmented party system. The memorandum camp included parties supporting the bailout agreements and associated reforms, while the anti-memorandum camp brought together otherwise ideologically distant actors united by opposition to austerity.

The twin parliamentary elections of 2015 intensified these dynamics. The January 2015 election was dominated by the anti-austerity mobilisation led by SYRIZA, which campaigned against the bailout terms and promised to renegotiate Greece's debt obligations. In contrast, the September election took place after SYRIZA, once in power, accepted a third bailout in July 2015. This reversal caused a dramatic realignment of issue salience within the electorate and reshaped the competitive landscape (Rori, 2016). The intervening months witnessed the party's internal split, leading to the formation of Popular Unity (LAE), while other parties repositioned themselves in response to the shifting political agenda. Such rapid changes make 2015 an ideal case for studying thematic realignment, the reconfiguration of political competition around changing issue priorities (Carmines & Stimson, 1989; Wagner, 2012).

Before the sovereign debt crisis, Greece's party system had been one of the most stable in Southern Europe, with strong partisanship, high rates of party identification, and low electoral volatility (Nikolakopoulos, 2001). The crisis disrupted this stability, initiating a rapid process of party-system fragmentation. PASOK's embrace of the first bailout package in 2010 led to a precipitous collapse in its electoral base, while new political actors, most notably SYRIZA, emerged to channel anti-austerity sentiment. SYRIZA's transformation from a minor left-wing coalition into the principal governing party by January 2015 was emblematic of this upheaval. Between 2010 and 2015, electoral volatility in Greece reached levels comparable to those seen in post-communist democracies during the 1990s (Chryssogelos, 2015).

The January 2015 election brought SYRIZA to power in coalition with the right-wing nationalist Independent Greeks (ANEL), an ideologically incongruent partnership united solely by opposition to austerity. However, the government's eventual acceptance of the third bailout agreement eroded the anti-austerity cleavage that had defined the January campaign, compelling voters to reassess their choices in the September election. This sequence created a unique natural experiment in short-term voter realignment, with shifts not only in party support but also in the thematic structure of political competition.

Despite the relevance of issue-based approaches, relatively few studies have systematically mapped the multidimensional policy space of Greek elections using individual-level data for both voters and parties. Traditional election surveys often rely on broad self-reported left–right placements, which risk obscuring the complexity of policy preferences, especially in highly fragmented and crisis-driven contexts (Dalton, 2017). In contrast, Voting Advice Applications (VAAs) such as HelpMeVote allow researchers to collect high-resolution data on both voter and party positions across a wide range of issues, enabling the direct calculation of voter–party distances in multidimensional spaces (Garzia & Marschall, 2014; Andreadis, 2014).

By combining VAA data with advanced dimensional reduction techniques such as PCA and Correspondence Analysis, researchers can construct detailed spatial maps of the political field, track the evolution of party competition, and analyse the shifting alignment between voters and parties. Applied to the two elections of 2015, this methodology offers an exceptionally rare quasi-longitudinal design: the same measurement instrument, the same electorate, and a dramatically altered political context in the span of eight months. This permits the study of both short-term thematic shifts, how quickly issue salience can change in response to political events and structural realignment, in which the very axes of competition are redefined. In doing so, this approach bridges classic spatial models of issue voting with contemporary research on volatility, dealignment, and populism, making it relevant not only for understanding the Greek case but also for comparative electoral research in other crisis-hit democracies.

METHODOLOGY

This study employs a comparative, multidimensional approach to examine thematic realignments in the Greek electorate during the twin parliamentary elections of 2015. The analysis is structured in two distinct yet complementary stages. The first stage focuses on mapping the structure of political competition in January 2015 and situating both voters and parties within a multidimensional policy space defined by salient issues. The second stage adopts a quasi-longitudinal design to compare voter–party relationships across the January and September contests, tracking the effects of a major political shock, SYRIZA's reversal on bailout policy, on the thematic configuration of electoral competition.

Stage 1: Investigating Electoral and Political Competition in the 2015 Context

Following the electoral upheavals of 2012, the parliamentary elections of January 2015 took place in a transformed political environment, in which competition was no longer structured solely along the traditional left–right axis but increasingly along a memorandum versus anti-memorandum divide. This new cleavage reflected the polarisation between parties that had supported the bailout agreements of 2010 and 2012 and those that had opposed them. To capture this altered competitive landscape, the analysis moves beyond the traditional framework of long-term party identification that had dominated Greek electoral behaviour for decades, adopting instead a thematic-vote approach focused on how issues define and structure political alignments.

In this framework, issues are conceptualised as vehicles for broader ideological or strategic divides. For example, the axis of extroversion versus introversion may be reflected in security-related topics, ranging from policing and border protection to foreign policy, depending on how parties choose to emphasise them. Similarly, other policy topics may align with broader bipolar structures depending on their salience in party agendas. This reflects a process of agenda-setting, in which parties select and promote specific issues, either during election campaigns or throughout their time in office or opposition, in order to shape the competitive context. From a political marketing perspective, this selection is crucial for two reasons: first, it defines the "product" a party offers in its programme (its core promises), and second, it identifies the target electorate to which this product is marketed. Voters, as prospective consumers, evaluate the importance of this product for their personal needs and priorities, as well as the likelihood that the party will deliver on its promises (its perceived utility), before deciding whether to "purchase" it through their vote.

The methodological question, therefore, is whether issues emerge primarily from the electorate and are subsequently incorporated into party agendas, or whether parties actively construct and promote issues to shape public opinion. In either case, issues become decisive criteria for voter choice, structuring both political discourse and electoral competition.

To operationalise this thematic-vote approach, each voter is positioned relative to the parties based on the degree of alignment on a set of political issues. The empirical analysis draws on data from the nationwide HelpMeVote Voting Advice Application (VAA) survey conducted for the January 2015 elections. This online platform presented users with 31 statements on political, economic, and social issues, reflecting the main axes of political competition. Before its public release, the positions of the competing parties on these same 31 issues were coded by a specialised research team. Upon completion of the questionnaire, the application compared the user's responses with party positions and plotted the user's location on an electoral map, indicating their degree of alignment with each party.

For the purposes of this study, the VAA dataset, comprising over 500.000 users, was sampled to 2.000 randomly selected respondents for analysis. The 31 issue variables were subjected to Principal Component Analysis (PCA) to identify latent dimensions structuring political competition. ALL principal components were extracted and each respondent's position on these dimensions was expressed as a factor score (z-score). The same procedure was applied to party positions, enabling their placement in the same multidimensional space.

The process began with the application of Principal Component Analysis (PCA) to the voter–issue response matrix. This procedure, performed on the correlation matrix of the 31 issue items, yielded 5 principal components that together accounted for approximately fifty per cent of the total variance. The first two components alone explained roughly one third of the variance, with the first axis corresponding to the pro-memorandum versus anti-memorandum cleavage and the second capturing a left/progressive versus right/conservative orientation. Factor scores (z-scores) were computed for each respondent on all five dimensions, producing individual coordinates within a multidimensional issue space.

The same PCA transformation was then applied to the coded party responses, enabling the projection of both voters and parties onto the same five-dimensional map. This step ensured that voter–party proximity could be assessed in a directly comparable framework. The degree of alignment between each voter and each party was quantified by calculating Euclidean distances in the PCA space, using the formula in Figure 1.

Figure 1. Euclidean distance formula for the five-dimensional map

$$d_{ij} = \sqrt{\sum_{k=1}^{5}(V_{ik} - P_{jk})^2}$$

where V_{ik} and P_{jk} are the scaled positions of voter i and party j on dimension k. This metric is statistically robust in this context, given that factor scores are normally distributed, and distances are calculated as the sum of squared differences across independent components.

The resulting distance matrix, comprising one row per respondent and one column per party, formed the basis for a Fuzzy Clustering analysis. Unlike hard clustering methods, which assign each observation to a single group, fuzzy clustering produces a set of membership probabilities for each case, thereby reflecting the multidimensional and often overlapping nature of political affinities. The analysis was implemented in R using the fanny function (five clusters, membership exponent 1.5, Euclidean metric):

```
fanny(x, 5, memb.exp = 1.5, diss=FALSE, metric = c("euclidean"),

stand=FALSE, cluster.only=FALSE)
```

This approach allowed the classification of voters into groups defined by their thematic proximity to sets of parties rather than to individual organisations. The socio-demographic and attitudinal profiles of these clusters were subsequently explored using SPSS's explore procedure, providing a descriptive understanding of the electorate's thematic segmentation.

Stage 2: Comparative Analysis Design for the January and September 2015 Elections

The second stage of the study applies a quasi-longitudinal comparative design to examine how voter–party alignments changed between the January and September 2015 parliamentary elections. This design is made possible by the repeated deployment of the HelpMeVote Voting Advice Application (VAA) before both elections, using an identical instrument, identical question wording, and identical scaling procedures. Such a structure enables the isolation of political developments, most notably SYRIZA's reversal on its anti-bailout stance in July 2015, as key drivers of change in the thematic structure of electoral competition.

As in the January analysis, each respondent's policy preferences were compared with party positions to calculate Euclidean distances within a multidimensional issue space derived from Principal Component Analysis (PCA) and Correspondence Analysis (CA). In both elections, the positions of parties and voters were plotted on the same spatial map, allowing direct visual and statistical comparisons between January and September. In the first election, the leading dimensions of the space largely reflected the economic left–right axis and the memorandum versus anti-memorandum divide. By September, however, the salience of these dimensions had shifted substantially, reflecting the disappearance of the euro-versus-drachma dilemma and the reconfiguration of the political agenda.

The 2015 electoral year presents a rare analytical opportunity: two national elections within eight months, during which the dominant issues and the perceived stakes of the contest changed dramatically. In January, the main cleavage centred on the memorandum–anti-memorandum opposition, which functioned as a proxy for the euro–drachma question. Parties positioned themselves clearly along this axis, appealing to distinct segments of the electorate. However, by the September election, this framing had largely vanished. The European trajectory, albeit through a difficult reform path, was broadly accepted as the only viable course. This forced a substantial portion of the electorate, particularly those who had voted for anti-memorandum parties in January, to reconsider their choices in light of the fact that their preferred party had shifted to a markedly different thematic agenda.

The core analytical question is how voters responded to such a thematic reversal within a short time frame. Did they follow their preferred party into its new agenda, or did they realign towards other parties whose issue positions were now closer to their own? The analysis investigates these questions by mapping the thematic alignments of each party's electorate in January and September and comparing them to the parties' own positions in each contest. Special attention is paid to SYRIZA and Independent Greeks (ANEL), two parties that underwent the most significant thematic repositioning, assessing whether their voters adapted to the parties' new positions or defected to alternatives.

The data derive from the HelpMeVote VAA surveys fielded in the pre-electoral periods of both January and September 2015. Respondents and parties were placed on a set of 30 policy questions covering economic, social, and institutional issues, with answers recorded on a five-point Likert scale ranging from "strongly disagree" to "strongly agree." For parties, positions on each question were determined in advance by an expert research team.

The analytical procedure consisted of two main stages. First, PCA was applied to the responses to identify the principal axes of political competition for each election, situating both voters and parties within the resulting multidimensional space. In this process, median responses for each party's voters on the 30 items were calculated to represent the "central voter" for that party. Both these median voter positions and the party positions themselves were then expressed as coordinates along the first two principal components for each election.

Second, these coordinates were compared across the two electoral contests. Euclidean distances were calculated between January and September positions for both parties and their median voters. The Euclidean distance between January and September positions for party j is shown in Figure 2. Similarly, Figure 3 shows the Euclidean distance between January and September positions for voter of party j, where M_{jk} represents the median voter position of party j on dimension k.

Figure 2. Euclidean distance between January and September positions for parties

$$\Delta_j^{\text{party}} = \sqrt{\sum_{k=1}^{K} (P_{jk}^{\text{Jan}} - P_{jk}^{\text{Sep}})^2}$$

Figure 3. Euclidean distance between January and September positions for voters

$$\Delta_j^{\text{voter}} = \sqrt{\sum_{k=1}^{K} (M_{jk}^{\text{Jan}} - M_{jk}^{\text{Sep}})^2}$$

This measure captures the magnitude of thematic movement over time, allowing the direct comparison of shifts in party agendas and in the preferences of their electoral bases. This procedure was applied symmetrically to four entities: the January party position, the September party position, the January median voter, and the September median voter for each party. The PCA was therefore conducted jointly for these sets of positions, ensuring the comparability of the spatial coordinates across time.

This combination of repeated cross-sectional VAA data, PCA-derived spatial mapping, and Euclidean distance measurement enables a fine-grained comparative analysis of thematic shifts. By directly linking voter movement to party repositioning, the method captures not only aggregate trends in the electorate but also the dynamics of "thematic party identity" formation and transformation in response to changing political agendas.

ANALYSIS AND RESULTS

Investigating Electoral and Political Competition in the Context of 2015

January 2015 parliamentary elections, using the methodological framework described earlier. This approach combines Principal Component Analysis (PCA) of issue-based data with Fuzzy Clustering of voter–party distances, enabling the identification of major dimensions of competition and the segmentation of the electorate into thematic clusters. The objective is to understand how issues structured electoral alignments in a context dominated by the opposition between pro- and anti-memorandum forces.

The PCA of the 31 policy questions posed in the HelpMeVote survey yielded five principal components explaining approximately 50% of the total variance. The first two components accounted for 32,7% of the variance and encapsulated the primary axes of competition.

1. First Dimension - Memorandum vs. Anti-Memorandum:

The first axis corresponded to the dominant cleavage of the 2015 elections: the divide between parties supporting the bailout agreements (memoranda) and those opposing them. On one end of the spectrum were New Democracy (ND), PASOK, and To Potami, parties that had endorsed or participated in pro-memorandum governments. On the opposite end were SYRIZA, Independent Greeks (ANEL), Golden Dawn (GD), the Communist Party of Greece (KKE), and Antarsya,parties rejecting the bailout framework.

2. Second Dimension - Left/Progressive vs. Right/Conservative:

The second axis reflected a combination of ideological and cultural orientations, contrasting left/progressive forces (Antarsya, SYRIZA, KKE, PASOK, To Potami) with right/conservative forces (ND, Golden Dawn, ANEL, LAOS). While less dominant than the memorandum cleavage, this axis captured long-standing ideological divisions embedded in the Greek political system.

By projecting both voters and parties into this two-dimensional space (Figure 4), the analysis reveals not only the polarisation around the bailout question but also the persistence of traditional left–right distinctions (Table 1).

Table 1. Party positions along the five principal components of political competition in the January 2015 Greek parliamentary elections, derived from Principal Component Analysis (PCA) of 31 issue variables. The first axis captures the memorandum–anti-memorandum divide, the second reflects a left/progressive versus right/conservative orientation, while the remaining axes represent additional, lower-salience dimensions of thematic competition.

Components	SYRIZA	ND	XA	PASOK	To Potami	KKE	ANEL	DIMAR	LAOS	ANTARSYA
1st Dimension – Memorandum vs. Anti-Memorandum	0,36	-1,46	2,11	-1,94	-1,51	1,58	2,17	-1,1	0,15	1,95
2nd Dimension – Left/Progressive vs. Right/ Conservative	-2,02	1,34	2,79	-0,17	-0,63	-0,92	2,11	-1,26	2,5	-2,22
3rd Dimension	-2,04	0,42	-0,51	-0,19	0,35	-2,22	0,51	-1,45	0,01	-1,83
4th Dimension	0,61	-3,09	-1,26	-1,75	-1,06	-0,9	-1,32	-0,33	-1,88	-0,81
5th Dimension	0,14	0,59	-0,34	1,01	0,84	-0,95	-0,23	-0,09	-0,16	-0,43

Figure 4. Biplot of party positions along the first two principal components of political competition in the January 2015 Greek parliamentary elections. The horizontal axis (PC1) represents the memorandum–anti-memorandum divide, while the vertical axis (PC2) reflects the left/progressive versus right/conservative dimension. Positions are derived from Principal Component Analysis (PCA) of party stances on 31 issue variables.

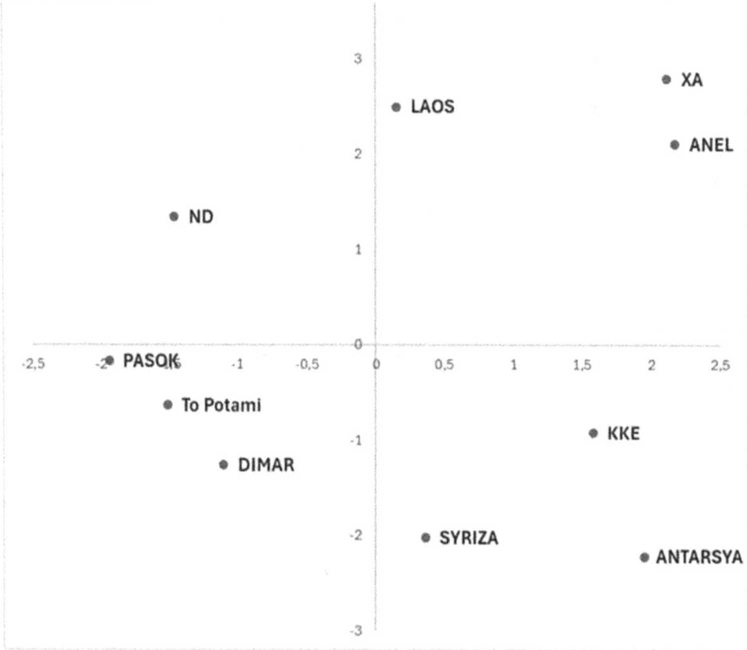

Using the PCA coordinates for both voters and parties, Euclidean distances were calculated to quantify each voter's proximity to each party. Unlike hard assignment methods, which allocate each respondent to a single group, the Fuzzy Clustering algorithm (fanny, five clusters, membership exponent 1.5) generated probabilities of belonging to multiple clusters. This approach acknowledges the multidimensional and overlapping nature of political preferences, particularly relevant in a fluid and volatile environment such as that of January 2015.

The clustering procedure identified five distinct voter groups, each corresponding to a particular thematic alignment of parties. Figures 5–9 present the composition and issue-based positioning of these clusters.

Cluster 1 – Right-Wing Voters (Figure 5): This group was anchored around LAOS, ND, and To Potami. Thematically, these voters combined a conservative orientation on social and cultural issues with support for pro-memorandum policies. Their positioning on the first axis placed them firmly in the pro-bailout camp, reflecting a preference for economic stability and European integration, even at the cost of austerity measures.

Figure 5. Cluster 1: Voters aligned with LAOS, New Democracy (ND), and To Potami (Right-wing orientation)

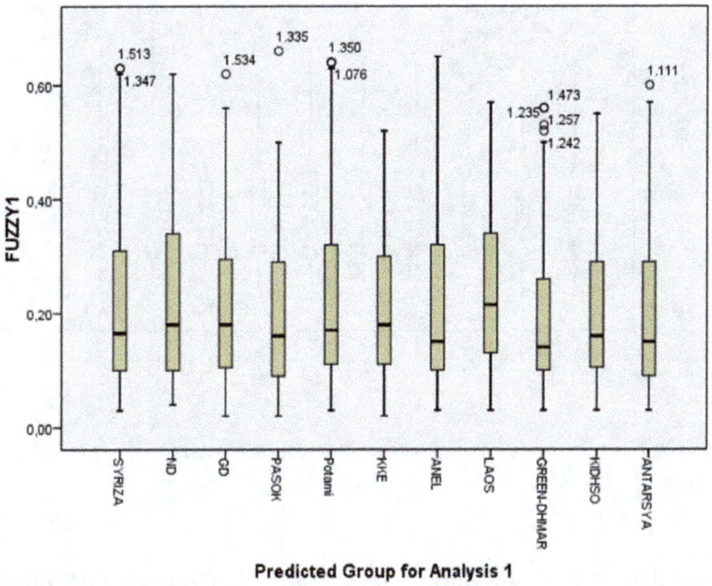

Cluster 2 – Pro-European Centrist Voters (Figure 6): Centred on To Potami, ND, and PASOK (KINAL), this cluster represented voters with strong pro-European orientations, moderate-to-centrist economic views, and relatively liberal cultural attitudes. While overlapping with Cluster 1 on their pro-memorandum stance, they were distinguished by a more centrist ideological profile and openness to reform-oriented agendas.

Figure 6. Cluster 2: Voters aligned with To Potami, New Democracy (ND), and PASOK/KINAL (Pro-European orientation)

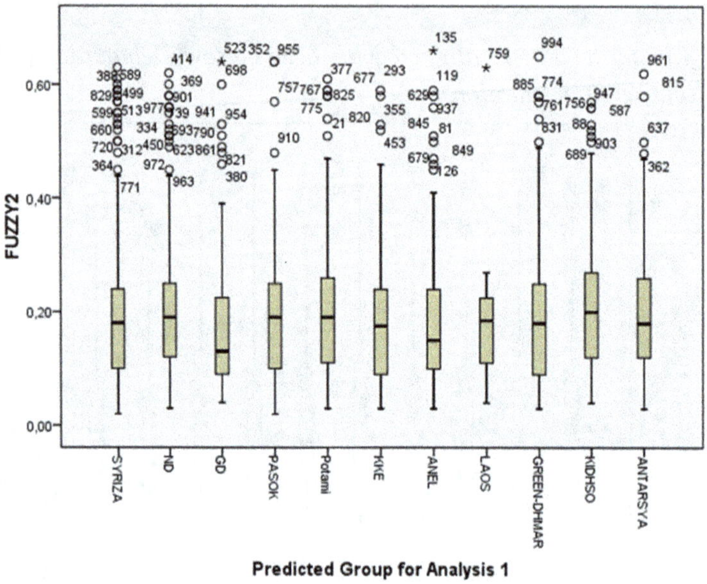

Cluster 3 – Anti-Memorandum Voters (Figure 7): Comprising SYRIZA, ANEL, and Antarsya supporters, this cluster was defined by its rejection of the bailout agreements and its positioning at the opposite end of the first axis. This group combined diverse ideological backgrounds, from radical left to nationalist right, united by opposition to austerity and a more sovereigntist view of EU–Greece relations. The heterogeneity of this cluster reflected the broad anti-memorandum coalition that propelled SYRIZA to power in January 2015.

Figure 7. Cluster 3: Voters aligned with SYRIZA, Independent Greeks (ANEL), and ANTARSYA (Anti-memorandum orientation)

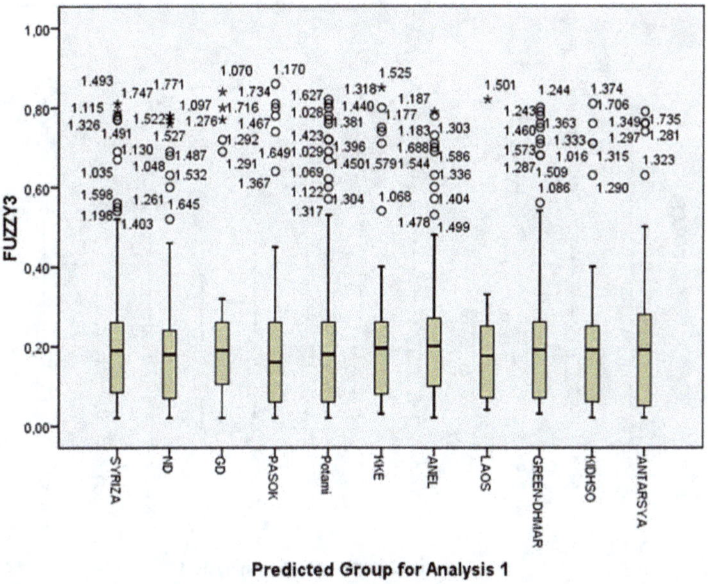

Cluster 4 – Centre-Left Voters (Figure 8): Associated primarily with PASOK (KINAL) and Democratic Left (DIMAR), these voters occupied an intermediate position on the first axis, leaning slightly towards pro-memorandum positions, but with a clear progressive stance on the second axis. Their issue profile suggested a preference for social democratic policies, pro-European engagement, and moderate reformism.

Figure 8. Cluster 4: Voters aligned with PASOK/KINAL and Democratic Left (DI-MAR) (Centre-left orientation)

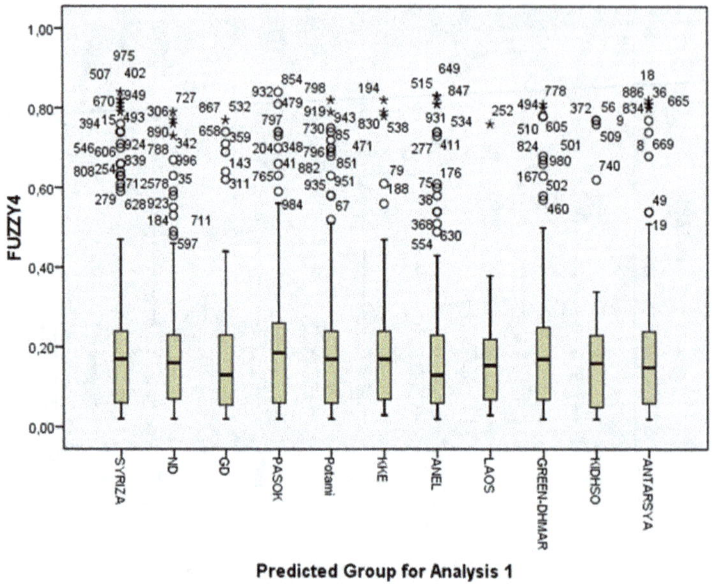

Cluster 5 – Far-Right Voters (Figure 9): Centred on LAOS and Golden Dawn, this cluster represented voters with authoritarian, nationalist, and anti-immigration positions. While sharing anti-memorandum sentiments with Cluster 3, they were positioned on the conservative end of the second axis, reflecting a distinctly far-right ideological identity.

Figure 9. Cluster 5: Voters aligned with LAOS and Golden Dawn (GD) (Far-right orientation)

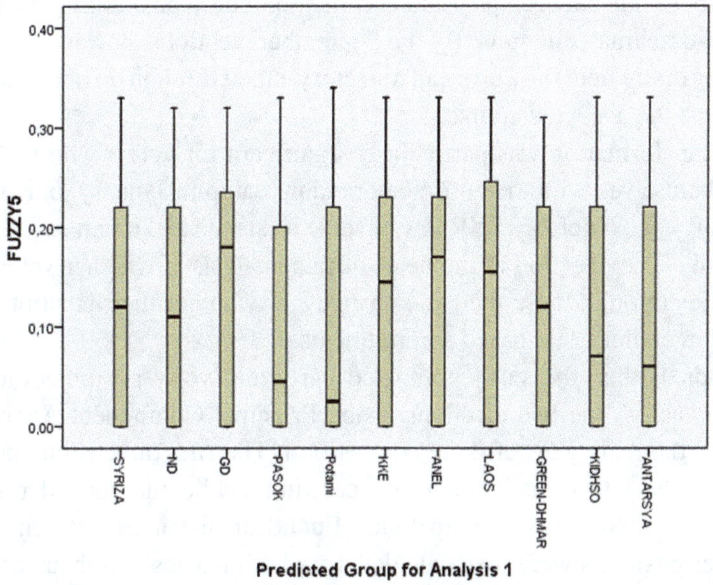

The clustering results highlight the multidimensionality of the Greek political space in early 2015. The memorandum–anti-memorandum divide was the primary axis structuring competition, but traditional left–right ideological distinctions remained significant. The fuzzy nature of cluster memberships indicates that many voters' preferences straddled these divides, pointing to the potential for volatility and rapid realignment, trends that would become even more salient in the September 2015 election.

In particular, the coexistence of ideologically disparate parties within the same thematic cluster, such as SYRIZA and ANEL in Cluster 3, underscored the issue-based coalition logic of that period, where shared positions on a salient cleavage could outweigh deep ideological differences. This configuration set the stage for the cross-ideological government that emerged in January 2015 and foreshadowed the realignment patterns analysed in the next stage of the analysis.

Issue Voting as a Tool for Analysing Voter Shifts and Constructing a "Thematic" Party Identity

The double parliamentary elections of 2015 in Greece present a rare opportunity to examine how thematic agendas, sets of political issues that parties choose to emphasise, shape both voter–party alignments and the reconfiguration of political competition within a very short time span. The January elections were dominated by the stark divide between pro- and anti-memorandum positions, closely linked to the "euro–drachma" dilemma. By the September elections, however, this cleavage had largely dissipated: the European trajectory, albeit through difficult compromise, had become the accepted course.

This transformation was particularly significant for voters who had originally aligned themselves with the anti-memorandum camp in January, only to see their chosen party, most notably SYRIZA, reverse its stance and embrace the memorandum in July. The question at the heart of this analysis is whether voters followed their parties through these thematic changes, or whether their positions remained anchored in earlier issue-based commitments.

To address this, the study compared party and voter positions on 30 policy statements across the two elections, using Principal Component Analysis (PCA) to identify the main axes of issue competition. The first dimension corresponded broadly to the left–right ideological spectrum, while the second reflected the memorandum–anti-memorandum divide. Euclidean distances between January and September positions were then calculated for both parties and their median voter, allowing for a direct measure of thematic shifts.

The analysis reveals minimal thematic movement among SYRIZA voters (Figure 10) between January and September 2015. Their positions on the two principal axes remained largely stable, suggesting a consistent thematic identity. In contrast, the party itself underwent a substantial repositioning on the issue map, primarily a shift away from its earlier anti-memorandum orientation toward a more pro-European stance. This widening gap between party and voter thematic positions did not result in large-scale defection; instead, it points to the emergence of a new form of loyalty, where voters maintained their electoral support despite diminished thematic congruence. This finding indicates that the thematic alignment of January evolved into a more conventional party alignment by September.

Figure 10. Thematic shifts of SYRIZA and its voters between the January and September 2015 elections

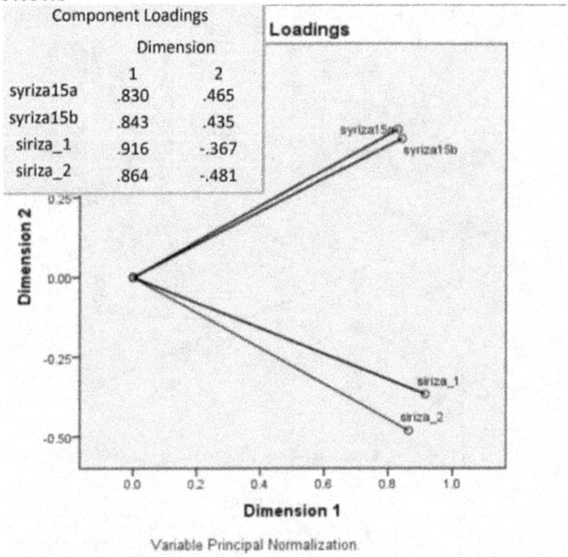

For New Democracy (ND), both the party and its voters displayed remarkable thematic stability across the two elections (Figure 11). The minimal movement detected in Table 2 (0.084 for the party and 0.121 for voters) suggests that ND retained its core policy agenda and that its supporters remained closely aligned with it. This reflects a consolidation of the traditional centre-right base, relatively unaffected by the shifting salience of the memorandum divide.

Figure 11. Thematic shifts of New Democracy and its voters between the January and September 2015 elections

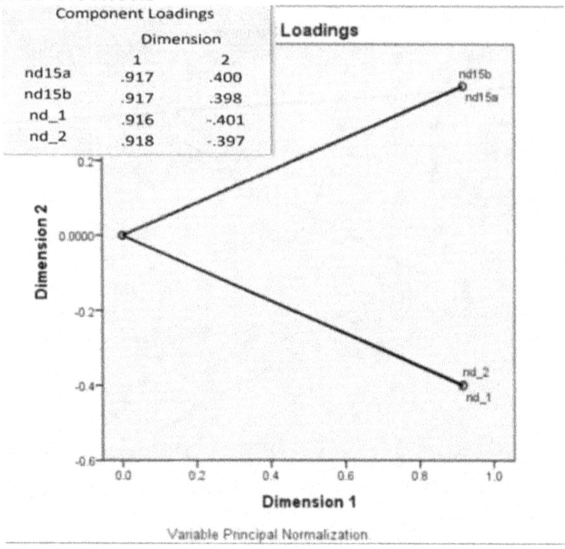

Component Loadings

	Dimension 1	Dimension 2
nd15a	.917	.400
nd15b	.917	.398
nd_1	.916	-.401
nd_2	.918	-.397

PASOK's voters (Figure 12) showed an almost identical thematic positioning across the two elections, indicating strong stability at the grassroots level. The party, however, shifted its thematic stance more noticeably, perhaps reflecting internal efforts to rebrand and adapt to the transformed political environment. This party movement, while not dramatic, suggests a search for renewed political relevance in a landscape where the traditional PASOK identity had been under strain since the crisis years.

Figure 12. Thematic shifts of PASOK (Movement for Change) and its voters between the January and September 2015 elections

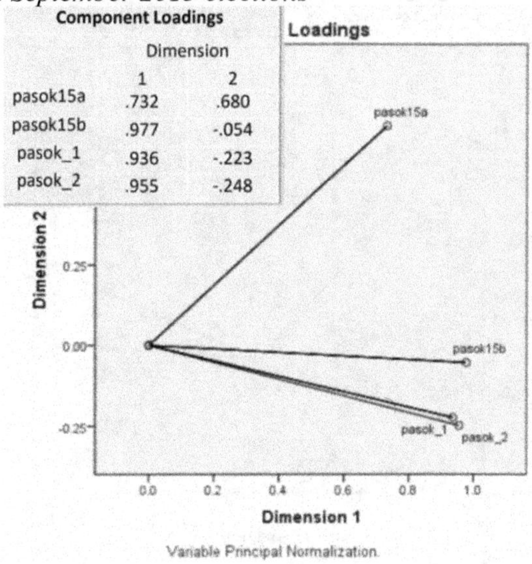

Component Loadings

	Dimension 1	Dimension 2
pasok15a	.732	.680
pasok15b	.977	-.054
pasok_1	.936	-.223
pasok_2	.955	-.248

The KKE (Figure 13) maintained an entirely stable thematic position between the two elections, consistent with its long-standing political strategy and ideological rigidity. Interestingly, its voters exhibited significant movement, among the highest recorded (1.559 in Table 2), but in a direction that brought them back into closer proximity with the party's original thematic base. This "return to base" pattern suggests that while some KKE voters may have wavered in January, the September election brought them back into thematic alignment, possibly due to disillusionment with other parties' compromises.

Figure 13. Thematic shifts of the Communist Party of Greece (KKE) and its voters between the January and September 2015 elections

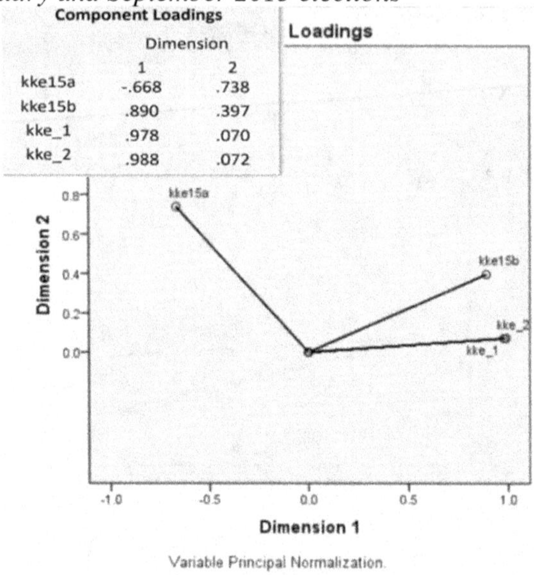

To Potami (Figure 14) presents a case of internal thematic disconnection. The party itself moved very little between January and September (0.083), maintaining a broadly centrist, pro-European profile. Its voters, however, shifted sharply (1.566), and in a direction that placed them further to the right on the main ideological axis. This produced a substantial divergence between the thematic stance of the party and that of its supporters. Such a gap suggests that To Potami was attracting protest voters or those with unstable partisan identities, whose thematic preferences were not deeply tied to the party's own programmatic core.

Figure 14. Thematic shifts of To Potami and its voters between the January and September 2015 elections

Component Loadings

	Dimension 1	Dimension 2
potami15a	.848	.480
potami15b	-.682	.720
potami_1	.953	.081
potami_2	.968	.006

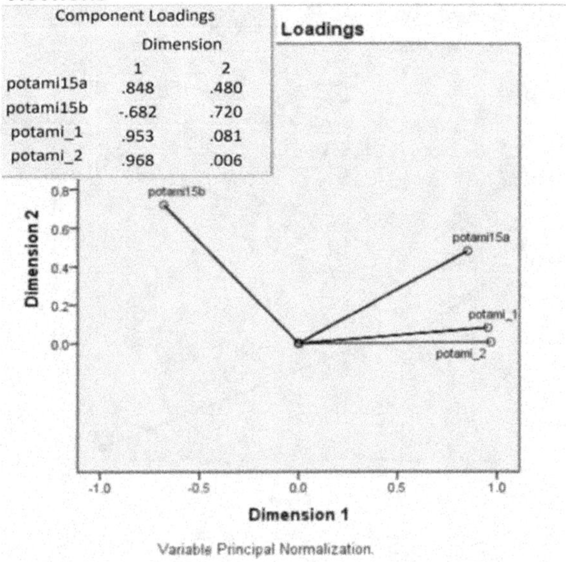

Golden Dawn's thematic position (Figure 15) remained almost unchanged between the two elections, with a slight movement (0.079) suggesting reinforcement rather than reorientation. Its voters also shifted only marginally (0.169), moving closer to the party's thematic stance. This tightening of alignment points to a consolidation of its ideological base and limited penetration beyond it.

Figure 15. Thematic shifts of Golden Dawn and its voters between the January and September 2015 elections

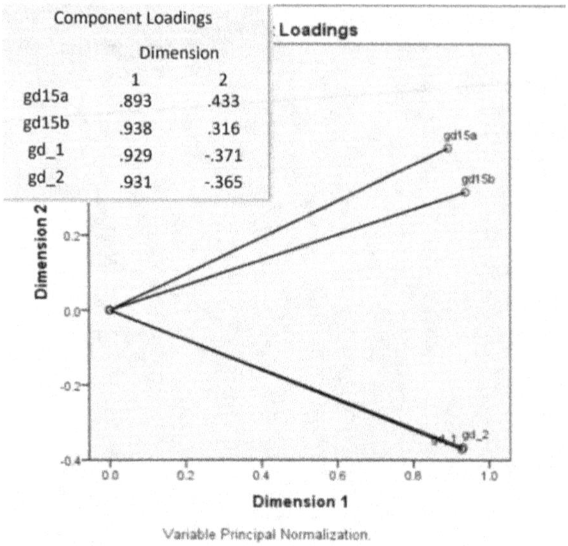
Component Loadings

	Dimension 1	Dimension 2
gd15a	.893	.433
gd15b	.938	.316
gd_1	.929	-.371
gd_2	.931	-.365

ANEL's voters (Figure 16) held a steady thematic position across the two elections (0.076), showing little inclination to follow the party's significant thematic movement (0.292) away from their shared January position. Like SYRIZA, ANEL shifted substantially on the memorandum–anti-memorandum axis, but unlike SYRIZA, it did not bring its voters along on this trajectory. The persistence of voter alignment with January's thematic identity, despite party movement, indicates that the ANEL electorate's loyalty may have been anchored more in coalition politics and symbolic positioning than in specific issue congruence.

Figure 16. Thematic shifts of Independent Greeks (ANEL) and their voters between the January and September 2015 elections

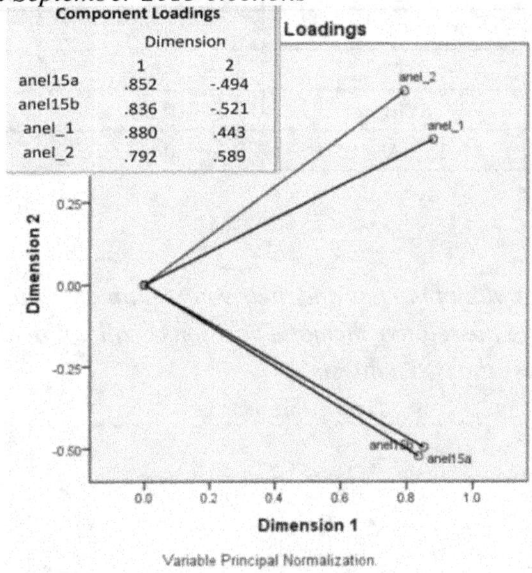

The comparison of party shifts (Table 2) reveals that the largest thematic shift occurred in the transition from SYRIZA in January to the emergence of LAE in September, a splinter group formed by former SYRIZA members committed to the anti-memorandum, pro-drachma agenda. SYRIZA's own shift was also significant, followed by ANEL and PASOK. At the other end of the spectrum, the KKE registered the smallest thematic change.

Among voters, the most substantial shifts were observed within the KKE and To Potami electorates, followed by moderate changes among PASOK and LAE voters. ND, SYRIZA, ANEL, and GD voters remained relatively stable in their thematic positions.

Table 2. Comparison of thematic shifts in party and voter positions between the January and September 2015 parliamentary elections

1st Elections (January)	2nd Elections (September)	Shift in Party Position	Shift in Voter Position
PASOK	PASOK	0,265	0,438
ANEL	ANEL	0,292	0,076
KKE	KKE	0,037	1,559
To Potami	To Potami	0,083	1,566

continued on following page

Table 2. Continued

1st Elections (January)	2nd Elections (September)	Shift in Party Position	Shift in Voter Position
GD	GD	0,079	0,169
ND	ND	0,084	0,121
SYRIZA	SYRIZA	0,165	0,218
SYRIZA	LAE	0,344	0,416

Figure 17. Joint PCA plot of parties and their voters (January and September 2015 elections), illustrating the relative thematic positions of all political actors and their electoral bases across the two contests

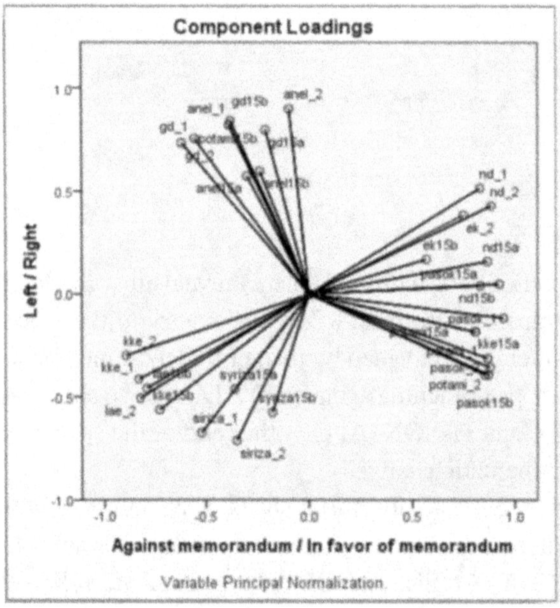

In the last step of the analysis a joint Principal Component Analysis (PCA) is applied, incorporating both the thematic positions of all political parties and the median positions of their voters in the January and September 2015 elections. By plotting both actors in the same two-dimensional space (Figure 17), the figure allows for a direct visual comparison of thematic alignment and divergence between parties and their respective electoral bases over time. The proximity of points indicates a high degree of thematic congruence, while greater distances reveal shifts or misalignments. The diagram makes visible not only the extent of voter–party convergence in each election but also the trajectories of change between January and September, providing a synthetic overview of the broader reconfiguration of the Greek political landscape during this turbulent electoral year.

Several broader conclusions emerge from this analysis:

1. Stability in traditional party bases: ND and GD maintained both party and voter positions with little thematic change, indicating entrenched electoral alignments.
2. Return to ideological anchors: KKE voters who may have explored alternatives in January returned to the party's thematic position in September.
3. Party–voter divergence in centrist formations: PASOK and To Potami both exhibited thematic shifts, either in the party (PASOK) or the voters (To Potami), reflecting internal instability and identity search.
4. The SYRIZA–ANEL realignment: Both parties shifted away from their January anti-memorandum stance while retaining voter support, transforming thematic identification into a more conventional partisan loyalty.
5. The emergence of LAE: The LAE split represents the clearest case of a thematic identity persisting intact -anti-memorandum, pro-drachma- despite organisational change.

Overall, the 2015 double election cycle underscores that thematic congruence is neither a necessary nor sufficient condition for voter loyalty in periods of rapid political change. In some cases, thematic dissonance between parties and voters led to electoral attrition, but in others, as with SYRIZA and ANEL, it became the foundation for a new kind of party–voter bond rooted in shared political trajectories, rather than issue-based alignment.

CONCLUSION

The analysis of the dual 2015 Greek elections reveals a political landscape in rapid flux, where issue-based competition both reflected and shaped voter–party alignments. The two-stage approach, mapping the thematic space in January and then tracking positional shifts by September, provides rare insight into the interplay between party strategy, voter perceptions, and the dynamic salience of political cleavages.

From the January data, the Greek party system appeared to be structured around two principal dimensions: the memoranda–anti-memoranda divide, and a secondary left–right axis encompassing broader progressive–conservative value orientations. This configuration, captured through PCA and operationalised via Euclidean distances between voters and parties, confirmed that the bailout question dominated political competition, overshadowing traditional ideological lines. Voter clustering showed relatively coherent thematic blocs, such as the pro-European liberal centre (ND, To Potami, PASOK) and the anti-memoranda alliance (SYRIZA, ANEL, KKE, ANTARSYA) but also highlighted the presence of an ideologically distinct far-right pole (Golden Dawn, LAOS).

The September analysis, however, captured a significant transformation. The collapse of the anti-memoranda agenda, precipitated by SYRIZA's policy reversal in July, removed the central cleavage that had structured voter choice only months before. Parties were forced to re-anchor their thematic agendas, with varying degrees of coherence and success. Some, like ND and Golden Dawn, maintained remarkable stability in both party and voter positions, suggesting a solidified partisan base with minimal thematic drift. Others, notably PASOK and To Potami, displayed greater volatility, either due to internal organisational changes or a lack of a clearly defined, consistent issue profile, resulting in larger voter–party gaps.

Particularly instructive are the cases of SYRIZA and ANEL. Despite substantial party-level thematic shifts between January and September, their voters remained comparatively stable in their own issue positions. This suggests that, for a significant segment of the electorate, the January choice was initially motivated by issue proximity on the memoranda divide, but by September, the vote had become more partisan in nature, less dependent on alignment with the new thematic agenda. In effect, the thematic identification of January had converted into a form of partisan loyalty, insulating these parties from immediate electoral punishment for programmatic shifts. This transition is further evidenced by the emergence of Popular Unity (LAE), composed of former SYRIZA MPs who retained the original anti-memoranda stance. While LAE attracted some ideologically consistent voters, it failed to destabilise SYRIZA's newly formed loyal base.

The KKE provides a counterpoint: the party itself remained ideologically and thematically stable, but its voters moved significantly between the two elections, returning to positions closer to the party line in September. This "re-homogenisation" of its electorate underscores the capacity of strong ideological parties to reabsorb temporarily drifting voters once the issue environment stabilises.

These patterns have broader implications for the understanding of political competition in volatile contexts. First, they confirm that issue-based voting (thematic voting) can rapidly give way to partisan loyalty when voters perceive either a lack of viable alternatives or when other considerations, such as leadership, credibility, or broader identity cues, supersede specific issue proximity. Second, the Greek case illustrates the fragility of new or loosely anchored parties when their thematic agenda is not firmly institutionalised. To Potami's sharp voter–party divergence between January and September exemplifies this vulnerability.

From a comparative perspective, the dual-election sequence of 2015 provides a natural experiment in how abrupt changes in the political opportunity structure, here, the collapse of a dominant cleavage, reconfigure voter–party linkages. The persistence of the left–right axis as a secondary dimension, even as the memoranda cleavage lost salience, suggests that traditional ideological structures can reassert themselves when a newer, high-salience issue fades. This has implications beyond Greece, for other democracies where "mega-issues" (e.g., Brexit, economic crises, major policy reforms) can temporarily reorder political competition but may not fully displace long-standing ideological divides.

Finally, in terms of political marketing and agenda-setting, the findings reinforce that parties can actively construct and reframe the thematic agenda to their advantage, but doing so carries risks. A rapid redefinition of issue priorities, as with SYRIZA in mid-2015, may alienate ideologically committed voters, yet if executed under favourable conditions (e.g., incumbency, weak alternatives, or rally-around-the-flag dynamics), it can also consolidate a more flexible, loyalty-based electorate. The tension between thematic responsiveness to the electorate and strategic issue construction by parties thus remains central to the dynamics of contemporary electoral politics.

REFERENCES

Andreadis, I. (2014). Data quality and data cleaning. In Garzia, D., & Marschall, S. (Eds.), *Matching voters with parties and candidates: Voting advice applications in comparative perspective* (pp. 79–92). ECPR Press.

Andreadis, I., Teperoglou, E., & Tsatsanis, E. (2011). The structure of ideological space in Greece: mapping parties' and voters' policy preferences. *Greek Political Science Review*, 5-32.

Budge, I., Farlie, D., & Laver, M. (1983). Shifts of meaning within explanations of voting and party competition. *Electoral Studies*, *2*(1), 23–38. DOI: 10.1016/0261-3794(83)90104-X

Campbell, A., Converse, P. E., Miller, W. E., & Stokes, D. E. (1960). *The American voter*. John Wiley & Sons.

Carmines, E. G., & Stimson, J. A. (1989). *Issue evolution: Race and the transformation of American politics*. Princeton University Press. DOI: 10.1515/9780691218250

Chryssogelos, A. S. (2015). Foreign policy change in a polarized two-party system: Greece and Turkey's EU candidacy. *Southeast European and Black Sea Studies*, *15*(1), 19–36. DOI: 10.1080/14683857.2014.1002293

Clarke, H., Sanders, D., Stewart, M., & Whiteley, P. (2011). Valence politics and electoral choice in Britain, 2010. *Journal of Elections, Public Opinion, and Parties*, *21*(2), 237–253. DOI: 10.1080/17457289.2011.562614

Dalton, R. J. (2017). Party representation across multiple issue dimensions. *Party Politics*, *23*(6), 609–622. DOI: 10.1177/1354068815614515

Dalton, R. J. (2018). *Political realignment: Economics, culture, and electoral change*. Oxford University Press. DOI: 10.1093/oso/9780198830986.001.0001

Dassonneville, R., & Hooghe, M. (2017). Economic indicators and electoral volatility: Economic effects on electoral volatility in Western Europe, 1950–2013. *Comparative European Politics*, *15*(6), 919–943. DOI: 10.1057/cep.2015.3

Dinas, E., & Rori, L. (2013). The 2012 Greek parliamentary elections: Fear and loathing in the polls. *West European Politics*, *36*(1), 270–282. DOI: 10.1080/01402382.2013.742762

Downs, A. (1957). *An economic theory of democracy*. Harper & Row.

Enelow, J. M., & Hinich, M. J. (1984). *The spatial theory of voting: An introduction*. CUP Archive.

Franklin, M., Mackie, T., & Valen, H. (1992). *Electoral Change: Responses to Evolving Social and Attitudinal Structures in Western Countries*. Cambridge University Press.

Gabel, M. J., & Huber, J. D. (2000). Putting parties in their place: Inferring party left-right ideological positions from party manifestos data. *American Journal of Political Science*, *44*(1), 94–103. DOI: 10.2307/2669295

Lazarsfeld, P. F., Berelson, B., & Gaudet, H. (1968). *The people's choice: How the voter makes up his mind in a presidential campaign*. Columbia University Press. DOI: 10.7312/laza93930

Louwerse, T., & Otjes, S. (2019). How populists wage opposition: Parliamentary opposition behaviour and populism in Netherlands. *Political Studies*, *67*(2), 479–495. DOI: 10.1177/0032321718774717

Lyrintzis, C. (1984). Political parties in post-junta Greece: A case of "bureaucratic clientelism"? *West European Politics*, *7*(2), 99–118. DOI: 10.1080/01402388408424473

Marschall, S., & Garzia, D. (2014). Voting advice applications in a comparative perspective: an introduction. *Matching voters with parties and candidates. Voting advice applications in comparative perspective*, 1-10.

Nikolakopoulos, H. (2001). *Η καχεκτική δημοκρατία: Κόμματα και εκλογές, 1946–1967* [The feeble democracy: Parties and elections, 1946–1967]. Patakis.

Pappas, T. S. (2009). Patrons against partisans: The politics of patronage in mass ideological parties. *Party Politics*, *15*(3), 315–334. DOI: 10.1177/1354068809102247

Petrocik, J. R. (1996). Issue ownership in presidential elections, with a 1980 case study. *American Journal of Political Science*, *40*(3), 825–850. DOI: 10.2307/2111797

Rori, L. (2016). The 2015 Greek parliamentary elections: From great expectations to no expectations. *West European Politics*, *39*(6), 1323–1343. DOI: 10.1080/01402382.2016.1171577

Stokes, D. E. (1963). Spatial models of party competition. *The American Political Science Review*, *57*(2), 368–377. DOI: 10.2307/1952828

Teperoglou, E., Freire, A., Andreadis, I., & Viegas, J. M. L. (2017). Elites' and voters' attitudes towards austerity policies and their consequences in Greece and Portugal. In *Political Representation in Times of Bailout* (pp. 45-64). Routledge.

Tsatsanis, E., & Teperoglou, E. (2018). Realignment under stress: The July 2015 referendum and the September parliamentary election in Greece. In *Crisis Elections, New Contenders and Government Formation* (pp. 45-66). Routledge.

Van der Brug, W., Van der Eijk, C., & Franklin, M. (2007). *The economy and the vote: Economic conditions and elections in fifteen countries*. Cambridge University Press. DOI: 10.1017/CBO9780511618857

Vasilopoulou, S., Halikiopoulou, D., & Exadaktylos, T. (2014). G reece in Crisis: Austerity, Populism and the Politics of Blame. *Journal of Common Market Studies, 52*(2), 388–402. DOI: 10.1111/jcms.12093

Voulgaris, G., & Nikolakopoulos, I. (2014). *Ο διπλός εκλογικός σεισμός* [The double electoral earthquake]. Themelio.

Wagner, M. (2012). Defining and measuring niche parties. *Party Politics, 18*(6), 845–864. DOI: 10.1177/1354068810393267

Chapter 4
Unveiling Voting Patterns With Statistical Tools in Electoral Studies

Usharani Bhimavarapu
https://orcid.org/0000-0002-0246-1420

Department of Computer Science and Engineering, Koneru Lakshmaiah Education Foundation, Vaddeswaram, India

ABSTRACT

Quantitative methods in election studies are of extreme importance as they are of greatest importance for generalization of voter behavior and election result. The interpretative use of a set of statistical techniques: regression analysis, correspondence analysis, and hierarchical clustering, is applied in this research work for interpretation and analysis of the 2024 Andhra Pradesh election data. Regression is utilized to model connections between voting and socio-demographic determinants, while correspondence analysis aims to locate interactions between categories of variables, for example, between parties and the demographics of voters. Regions are grouped based on regions that share similar patterns of elections via hierarchical clustering, while regional trends, regional discrepancies and differences are determined. Through the use of these quantitative methods, analysis seeks to identify voting patterns, local voting patterns, and socio-economic influence on party performance.

INTRODUCTION

Quantitative techniques are particularly effective in analyzing elections since they offer precise, objective ways of examining and analyzing the result of an

DOI: 10.4018/979-8-3373-1037-4.ch004

election. Statistical techniques must account for the trends among voters, party performance, and broader patterns in elections. Conventional qualitative techniques may reveal what affects the voters, but statistical techniques enable us to examine many cases and more theory-driven, replicable findings. Some of the significant statistical techniques employed are hierarchical clustering, correspondence analysis, and regression analysis. Political scientists may utilize such techniques to predict elections, analyze variables influencing voting, and perform relationship tests between different electoral variables. These assist in making an informed political strategy choice, campaign planning, as well as campaigns for voter mobilization. Applications of statistical models also help in the analysis of how demographic, economic, and social factors influence ballots. The methodologies are even capable of identifying major trends not necessarily visible to the naked eye. By their use, election analysts are capable of drawing better-informed conclusions from enormous datasets that otherwise would be too complex to decipher by hand. This has taken scientific election research to a higher level.

Regression analysis is a general statistical procedure that is often applied in the study of elections to test the impact of an independent variable or a set of independent variables on a dependent variable, either in terms of candidate popularity or voting turnout. The procedure enables the researcher to describe how voting is being shaped by variables such as education, income, age, or location. Linear regression would be applied if linear correlation would be anticipated in the case of variables, and logistic regression would be applied if the dependent variable merely coincidentally is qualitative, e.g., for or against some candidate. The coefficients of the regression model determine strength and direction to be used for interpreting that specifies the degree of importance the various factors hold in the outcome determination. These above methods can be extended to multiple regression in case of using several predictors at a time. Election analysts can check hypotheses concerning impacts of some policy or economic phenomenon on elections through regression. Regression is also useful in detecting time-series patterns and trends, i.e., events over time like trend of a change of voter attitude or impact of campaign strategy. This technique is extremely convenient for policy researchers and campaign strategists who want to contact particular voter segments. Caution should be exercised, though, to monitor model assumptions in addition to data quality so that one will not become over-influenced by results. The malleability and strength of regression analysis mean that it is an election studies sine qua non.

Correspondence analysis is a statistical technique for investigating the association between two nominal variables by mapping them onto two-dimensional space. Correspondence analysis electoral studies can be used to investigate how groups of voters, gender, age, or region are related to parties or candidates. Through the mapping of the contingency table onto a visual format, correspondence analysis gives a very intuitive way of noticing patterns and relationships between variables. Correspondence analysis scale is a quantitative scale. This applies particularly in the voter support and party loyalty of different segments of the populace. The method provides for simplification of multidimensional data to a lower dimension one that perhaps can be easier to comprehend. An example is that a correspondence analysis may indicate that young town voters have support in one political party while the older town voters have support in a different party. The graphical result of correspondence analysis can look like a scatter plot where the distance of the points would signify the correlation between categories. This is utilized to manage challenging categorical data, for instance, the results of voting polls, where there are numerous variables that contribute to the vote decision. Political analysts can see groups of groups of voters and what most compels them via correspondence analysis. Political tactics and campaign appeals can be framed to respond to various voter interest segments by employing it in use.

Hierarchical clustering is a statistical method of dividing comparable items into clusters based on their features. Hierarchical clustering can be utilized in vote research in voting populations stratification into clusters based on the pattern of casting votes, preference, or demographics. The algorithm operates through the iterative nearest neighbor clustering and points that can construct a dendrogram, a graphical representation of the cluster structure. A node within the dendrogram is a set of observations, and a node's height is between clusters. The process enables one to be capable of recognizing what are natural constituencies of voters and implement them in targeting electioneering or to seize regional variation in voter behavior. Hierarchical clustering, for instance, would suggest that there will be voters in certain regions that are worried about economics and others worried about social issues as a main issue of concern. Hierarchical clustering also has the advantage of being able to discover swing voters who might not necessarily belong to classic political branding. Hierarchical clustering is superior in that one does not pre-specify groups as would be required in the use of k-means clustering. Alternatively, it provides researchers with a method of experimentation at differing levels of agglomeration with elbow room when they are exploring. Hierarchical clustering is potentially outlier sensitive, and the outcome will be based on the size of data. This aside, otherwise, it is a useful method of election data pattern recognition.

Regression analysis is one of the most important uses of regression analysis in election studies in voter turnout prediction. It is used by analysts in analyzing the variables which determine whether a voter will or will not cast their vote in an election. Independent variables like age, educational status, socio-economic standing, and political leaning can be employed to model voting likelihood. Exogenous variables like weather or competitiveness of the local race can also be used in the model because they cause a voter to vote. The analysts can use regression analysis to determine the impact of each variable and the strongest impact among the variables on voting. For example, previous research has established that education and income are strong indicators of voting, and better-educated, wealthier citizens have greater probabilities of voting. Regression models can also forecast voting in the future to look like in terms of past-year trends. Regression analysis also can be used to establish the effectiveness or non-effectiveness of voter turnout-enhancing programs, like voter education programs or mandates for early voting. Voter behavior regression can give policy makers valuable information in informing the development of policy on how better to involve more citizens in the electoral process. But the model should also control for the confounding variables, i.e., political campaign or media coverage effects.

Correspondence analysis is most generally used in election studies to analyze the correspondence between voter demographic characteristics and party vote. Correlation analysis is well suited when doing research using survey or exit poll data where voters are able to define their party of choice as well as demographic traits. Correspondence analysis allows us to visualize the correspondence between categories, say political parties, level of education, and age groups. Using a map with categories on two large axes, it is possible to see more intuitively which groups are in which political parties. For instance, a comparison of election poll data based on correspondence will be able to give the fact that young voters will tend to vote for left-lean parties and older voters right-lean parties. Moreover, the method can even give voting trends geographically, i.e., areas more likely to lean left or right. Graphic representation of correspondence analysis will typically provide a clean and unembedded portrayal of thick data, and therefore ease results presentation to political strategists and policymakers. The method proves best in determining popularity of party platforms among target segments of voters and crafting campaign messages appealing to voters' concerns. Correspondence analysis is also used to represent trends in party identification over time and thus comprehend changing political landscapes.

Hierarchical clustering can be used most effectively in voter segmentation by similarity, wherein political scientists can map target segments of voters. Segmentation is useful in opinion polling in elections in building campaign messages for a given issue and problem of a given segment. Hierarchical clustering, for instance, can create various segments of voters on grounds of age, level of education, and locale, and campaigns would accordingly adopt such in designing messages that resonate with each segment. Hierarchical nature of such clustering allows researchers to study the data at different levels of granularity, broad categories and narrower subgroups. It would be especially useful in identifying swing voters or groups of more susceptible kinds to, say, health care, taxation, or immigration. Hierarchical clustering would also be useful in identifying voting patterns by geographic region, which would be useful in identifying geographic areas where parties must concentrate campaign efforts. For instance, rural constituents would be concerned with different issues than city voters and therefore need to be targeted individually as distinct groups. Hierarchical clustering allows electoral analysts to fully comprehend why citizens vote and develop more precise, focused campaign strategies. Proper interpretation of the dendrogram and distances, however, must be utilized in order to realize significant results. Regression analysis is well worth learning both regarding the individual vote behavior of a single voter as well as regarding election outcomes generally.

By examining historical voting and employing demographic data, analysts can build models that predict the impact on election results of various variables. These models are of any shape but may range from linear regression for simpler, straight-line relationships to more intricate multivariate regression models for use with multiple predictors. To illustrate, regression analysis might be employed to predict how election decisions by voters can be shaped by fluctuations in unemployment levels or popularity polls for incumbent candidates. In such a case, the dependent variable can be the share of vote of a candidate or a party, while independent variables can be politics, media, and economics. Regression analysis can also ascertain which policies or issues would influence election outcomes to a larger degree. Political campaigns can make better-informed decisions on policy initiatives, allocation of resources, and target voting segments with such models. Quality of such models is a function of data quality and selection of regression algorithm. Predictive models need to be recalibrated continuously in a bid to keep abreast of changes in public sentiment and evolving developments. When analyzing elections, applying regression analysis and hierarchical clustering can assist in providing richer better-informed explanation of voting.

Whereas regression analysis would help the analyst attain interaction of election results and independent variables, clustering techniques could split the voters into respective classes, which allow for more informed and accurate interpretation. Combining these techniques, the analysts can observe how different voter segments behave in relation to specific variables. Hierarchical clustering, for example, would accomplish that specific voter segments are economically more sensitive and others concentrate on issues of healthcare or the environment. Regression models would then be applied to estimate the way changes to such issues would influence a particular voter group's vote. This combined method gives a better gauge of voter sentiment, allowing campaigns to construct more efficient campaigns. Secondly, when clustering analysis is combined with regression models, trends will emerge that may not otherwise show up when the method is employed alone. For example, a group of young voters can be framed as more open to social media advertising, while the same group will be concerned about policy in regard to healthcare. This intersection is most beneficial to such elections that would rather emphasize issues of highest potential impact to sway undecided or swing voters. Statistical techniques such as regression analysis, correspondence analysis, and hierarchical cluster analysis have revolutionized the study of elections.

Quantitative techniques provide meaningful facts regarding party performance, turnout at elections, and election determinants. Using such methods, analysts are able to identify underlying patterns, predict the outcome of elections, and provide political strategy recommendations. Regression analysis is replete with meaning regarding the correlation between election outcomes and determinants and how each correlates with the other, while correspondence analysis enables one to visualize party identity correlations with demographics. Hierarchical clustering allows voters to be clustered in a way that can meaningfully be targeted by campaign-targeted campaigns. The collection of these tools provides an end-to-end election analysis approach, enabling campaigns to find fact-based, appealing to specific constituencies. Such capability, however, brings the responsibility for high-quality data and tight interpretation so that spurious arguments will not follow. And as election data increasingly become more advanced and abundant, quantitative techniques will increasingly be needed, enabling scientists, politicians, and policymakers to make more fact-based instead of speculative choices. Finally, statistical techniques bring in greater objectivity and accuracy to election studies, portraying better and more vividly the democratic process. Recent research has especially focused on populist voters' opinion and the various scales and tools to manage measurements of populist opinion (Akkerman et al., 2014; Zaslove, 2022).

They still mostly depend, to a large degree, on assumption-based survey response self-reporting. The research also largely focuses on Western European nations, thereby doing so in the process, potentially limiting the scope of applicability of its findings to other nations with diversified political settings and societal structures. The study's applicability to other non-Western nations with unique populist tendencies is suspect. Alba and Foner (2017) investigate the intersection of political polarization and immigration.

While they illuminate spatiotemporal correspondence of polarization, their observation is tainted by their failure to capture long-term data that would have added yet another dimension on how the polarization accumulates with time every time there are policies of immigration that vary. Their examination of US cities could be insufficient to illustrate others' experience whose locations immigration processes and political responses take rather distinctive forms of their own.

Allen (2017) compares Western European far-right abstention and voters on the basis of political major conduct. There exists, however, a limitation of the study in the sense that it is comparatively narrow on far-right voting conduct alone, as compared to other political movements across Western European elections. The findings of the study would not hold in a direct manner for highly diverse countries politically or where far-right movements are not politically highly active.

Anselin's (1988) spatial econometrics provides us with the basic tools to cope with spatial data. Extremely useful as it is, the book is by no means ideal as a weapon to wield when used on contemporary datasets that may even hold more complex spatial interactions than Anselin's basic models could handle. Besides, the focus of the book on statistical methods, without supplementing with case studies or particular applications, may limit the use of the book for practitioners to apply these methods to electoral data by itself.

Arzheimer (2012) also speaks about electoral sociology and local and regional determinants of the vote for the extreme right. The largest failing of the research is that it depends so heavily on country-level data and thus doesn't go far enough to look for possible local or regional determinants of the vote. This Europe-centered research is also not willing to look beyond the continent for other voting patterns for other such extreme-right political movements as there are elsewhere and which would have unique socio-political settings.

Arzheimer and Carter (2006) are also critical of political opportunity structure subnational election operationalization. Theirs is a well-founded critique, however, the broader failure of the study is that it is theoretical, not empirical, creating therefore a gap for precisely how such terms are meant to be used in their application to electoral data. In addition, their specificity to European region elections cannot necessarily be transported to other electoral behavior in other contexts where political opportunities may differ.

Biggs and Knauss (2012) conduct a multilevel analysis of membership in the British National Party. Although the research provides useful empirical results concerning determinants of far-right party membership, applying survey data to a nation can be restrictive in terms of generalizability over its results. The research is also plagued by focusing on individual-level determinants, which will be restrictive when it comes to explaining wide structural or cultural determinants of political membership.

Blalock's minority-group relations theory (1967) is a sociological classic. But it is not that precise anymore because it can no longer describe the more heterogeneous and sophisticated character of the minority groups in modern societies. The theory further takes it that minority group behavior is strongly reliant on intergroup relations at the expense of other determinants such as the influence of the media and the global interconnectedness of society, whose application has been more dominant in shaping the new politics of affairs.

Bobba and McDonnell (2016) examine the discourse of Italian right-wing populist parties. The shortcoming of their study is that it is carried out solely for Italy, and extrapolations to other countries where right-wing populism manifests itself in a different way have a questionable external validity. Further, examination can be more productively carried out if supported by a more descriptive explication of social media campaigns pursued by parties of this type, now far more aggressively framing political discourse.

Bourdieu's (1984) social space and class creation framework is theory-intensive. Its application in election studies is limited by the much too hypothetical nature of ideas and absence of election data. Bourdieu's (1984) method, sociologically intensive, fails to consider the intersection of class with the other determinants such as ethnicity, religion, or media, assuming higher statuses in modern election studies.

Bowyer (2008) looks at local context and local support for the extreme right in England specifically focusing on the British National Party during local elections. The limitation of this study is that it looks only at local elections, which themselves could be weak surrogates for broader national trends. Analysis also fails to take into consideration the contribution of social media websites and the internet towards spreading far-right ideologies, whose contribution has come forward with growing intensity in contemporary times.

Burnham and Anderson (2002) provide a user-friendly handbook for model selection and multi-model inference. Their process is at a disadvantage in that it induces fundamentally statistical modeling regardless of data biases. Electoral study data biased voting behavior is just what electoral study data are, and this could prove hard to model well. The process does not properly correct for the problem of inferring multifaceted electoral data with multiple determinants.

Cea D'Ancona and Vallés (2015) examine xenophobia and racism in Spain. The drawback of this research is that it is cross-sectional and therefore trends cannot be seen over time and political context changes cannot be controlled for. Further, the research is carried out in one country, and even complete generalizability to European or worldwide trends in racism and xenophobia that affect voting might not be made.

Champion and Hugo (2004) write about contemporary trends in urbanization and their significance. Although the findings are well worth their while, the study is narrow in that there is no particular focus laid on the way political atmospheres influence urbanization patterns. Secondly, the study focus on urbanization with due regards to the socio-political dynamics of the regions undergoing sudden political change leaves the overall implication for electoral studies incomplete.

Examining populist rhetoric and extreme-right radicalism in the crisis times in Greece and Cyprus (Charalambous & Christoforou, 2018; Venizelos, 2022) brings forwards significant limitations of the study, especially its geographically centered analysis that might limit generalizability beyond crisis-hit regions of the world in Southern Europe as well. The strength of globalization and social media isn't given proper consideration in analysis to make far-right parties go viral across nations.

One of the limitations of this research is ecological inference, and this will certainly lead to problems of misinterpretation whenever individual-level behavior is at greater aggregate geographic levels (Li & Fotheringham, 2022). Methods utilized here, as sophisticated as they are, still do not estimate very well micro-level intensive interactions (Ghitza & Gelman, 2013).

Outcomes of the authors, as valuable as they may be, are constrained by the geographical expanse of Eastern Europe, and it is not possible to assume that their usability can extend to other regions of the world with different political and social processes. The regional design may be incapable of identifying cross-national effects influencing political behavior in a larger region (Gimpel et al., 2004; Haughton & Deegan-Krause, 2015).

One of the shortcomings of this research is that it would certainly overestimate the Czech Republic's centrist populist parties to a degree that it would certainly neglect other political trends or future ideologies which might explain in a major way political power shifts in the country (Havlík & Voda, 2018).

Heilmann et al.'s Recmap algorithm may not be used in all datasets at all times, particularly where data are high-dimensional or where geographical context is less important. The method has limited applications in non-standard geographical analysis (Heilmann et al., 2004).

The methodological advancement brought by King et al. (2013) in ecological inference is that it is sophisticated and perhaps might not be readily accessible for practical application by practitioners who lack good statistical background. The sophistication could restrict application of the methods in mainstream electoral research (King et al., 2013).

Research on clientelistic parties in the Czech Republic is inadequate where it takes into account a single case and therefore has issues extrapolating to other post-communist nations with diverse political experience and political systems of government. Lack of cross-country comparison lowers the external validity of the findings (Klíma, 2013).

Among the most potent of this study's weaknesses is the use of publication-bias-vulnerable meta-analysis. It also does not note trends that are dynamic in voting behavior and electoral law, which might overlook newer trends in invalid voting (Kouba & Lysek, 2019).

Lysek writes about voting trends and spatial statistics but without indication of assuming that the electoral results can be attributed to the spatial voter trend entirely. It is not possible to ignore non-spatial factors such as individualistic voting behavior or social and media pressures (Lysek, 2020).

One of the shortcomings of the study at hand is that it looks only at a single instance (London mayor election, 2012) with shallow generalization to formulate broad statements about geographic variation of electoral turnout determinants elsewhere (Mansley & Demšar, 2015; Manoel et al., 2022).

The geographical study of Czech Parliamentary elections, while contemporary, might not be positioned to observe underlying socio-economic forces behind electoral behavior. Research focus on geographic determinants might miss the role played by regional or individual identities over political action (Sui & Hugill, 2002; Maškarinec, 2017).

Research on newly arising populist political parties in Czech elections has a limitation to its party replacement agenda. It may be unable to explain dynamics of change in party systems and may oversimplify dynamics of populist politics in the Czech Republic (Maškarinec, 2019).

The limitation of this research is that it has also its own limited domain of studying the candidates' choice in Canada that cannot possibly detail the overall politics and gender relations in other political contexts. The study's conclusion would be constrained by Canada's particular election system as well as cultural background (Medeiros et al., 2019).

Mudde's definition of the populist Zeitgeist (Mudde, 2004) is restricted through employing a definition of common sense for populism. The broad scope of the article concerning populism susceptible to simplifying the complex manner in which populist movements differ between nations and regions (Mudde & Kaltwasser 2017).

The method employed to track election trends within proportional electoral systems will not necessarily reflect long-term voting patterns, especially in electoral systems open to significant swings in their party line or voting processes (Ondrejka, 2016). European long-term studies of anti-political establishment parties can be limited in what they can explain in relation to the unplanned political mobilization, i.e., that of new party formation, that can influence its finding concerning the long-term sustainability of populist parties (Rama Caamaño & Casal Bértoa, 2019).

Models developed in these researches work towards the overcoming of present limitations by the implementation of more advanced measures, with a wider scope of research. An example is the area of election studies, where the application of advanced spatial statistics and ecological inference techniques (e.g., in King et al., 2013; Darmofal, 2006; Kouba et al., 2021) provides us with a better explanation of voting behavior. Unlike more traditional models founded on coarse, aggregate data that can hide micro-level processes, the application of spatial analysis methods (Mansley & Demšar, 2015; Lysek, 2020) also contributes towards the explanation of geographic voting difference, which fills the gap for previous research that did not consider the geographic pattern of the electorate's behavior (Orford & Schuman, 2002; Förster, 2018).

In addition, research such as Ghitza & Gelman (2013) and Kouba & Lysek (2019) employs the conventional methods of analysis of election data to incorporate higher dimensions of interaction and meta-analytic methods, which decrease the chances of occurrence of bias and are better in capturing the dynamic nature of elections. These newer models, both drawing on spatial and individual-level data, are an upgrade on the older less responsive models, which were unable to handle the complexity of modern politics.

In addition, the emphasis placed on new rising political movements, like populist centrist parties in the Czech Republic (Havlík & Voda, 2018), assists in overcoming the lack of earlier models being excessively limited and unrealistic for application regarding understanding developing new political ideologies. Based on these dynamics, newer models can provide better explanations of party system development and political development that were not properly addressed in earlier research.

Finally, the application of longitudinal data, as shown by Rama Caamaño & Casal Bértoa (2019), can provide us with a dynamic analysis of political trends over time and the capacity to avoid the pitfalls of static models that cannot handle sudden political change or party system realignment. These advances all contribute to making electoral models more valid and useful, and they provide a more holistic perspective for the study of election outcomes and political action.

MATERIALS AND METHODOLOGY

Processing of the election data of the 2024 Andhra Pradesh election is done through several critical steps in the processing phase. Collection of data initially focuses on demographic, voting history, and political factors influencing the voter sentiments. Preprocessing involves cleaning, normalization, and transformation of data wherever required for analysis. Particle Swarm Optimization (PSO) is also utilized for feature selection to assist in locating the important variables in the prediction of the election forecast. Statistical analysis that includes regression analysis, correspondence analysis, and hierarchical clustering are used to examine patterns and association of the data. Fuzzy c-means clustering is also used further to enhance the partitioning of the data to identify various voter blocs and homogenous voting areas. This combination of methods provides scope for understanding the voting context to a greater extent.

Materials

In analyzing the voter trend and voting history of a specific party in the 2024 election for Andhra Pradesh, it is necessary to combine the dataset collection with a set of linked variables including voter trend, party performance, and socio-political context of the state. This larger data would require demographic data such as age, sex, income, education level, and occupation since all these are actually determinative variables in terms of voting and party allegiance. It would require geographical data so differential voting with respect to regions, i.e., the rural-urban divide of Andhra Pradesh and differential voting between districts, constituencies, and even polling booths can be explained. In addition, historical data on past voting behavior like the outcome of earlier elections held in 2014, 2019, and earlier years would provide evidence regarding party loyalty, shift in voter loyalty, and local factors determining the election outcome. Information regarding the vote percentage, caste, religion, and language vote pattern and media and social media influence on public opinion will further consolidate the dataset. In addition to political forces like candidate popularity, party campaign, and coalition, and issue orientation (development, welfare schemes, jobs, and agriculture), there must be inclusion in the research questions to analyze the manner in which these forces influence party performance. Exit polls, voter survey returns, and interviews of the voters will also provide qualitative data on the mood and sentiment of the voters and attitude of political parties and leaders. The data set must also be refreshed from time to time with new data up to the 2024 election, especially keeping in mind the politically charged background. The large dataset would be an appropriate field for analysis of voting patterns, namely election outcome prediction and tracking party support trends in Andhra Pradesh in 2024.

Preprocessing

Preprocessing the dataset obtained for analysis of 2024 Andhra Pradesh election party history and voting pattern is carried out using a number of important steps to transform the data to become clean, organized, and analysable. Data cleaning is the preprocessing stage where missing values, duplicate entries, and outliers are managed. Missing values must be taken care of by data imputation using statistical method, i.e., mean or median imputation, or by deleting rows in which there are significant missing values if imputation cannot be carried out. Duplicates must be deleted and flagged so that duplicates are not present in the dataset. Outliers in vote record or in demographics must also be inspected since they might be errors or outlier cases that would contaminate analysis. Data transformation is where the categorical data like gender, party, and region are converted into a format that is amenable for analysis after data cleaning. It can be one-hot encoding or label encoding of the categorical variables depending on the kind of analysis to be performed. The statistical data, such as age, income, and education level, are standardized or normalized in the way that all the variables are reduced to the same scale whenever variable scale-sensitive models are used. Feature extraction must also be performed in the preprocessing phase wherein significant features like dummy voting record, political issues of interest, and geographic voting patterns are extracted from the raw data. Temporal controls like election year of past elections or trend over time need to be converted into time series features in order to infer past change. Preprocessing social media or text in the responses to survey questions can also be done with tokenization and sentiment analysis in a bid to extract public mood or campaign mood. Data splitting is a process to divide the dataset into test set and training set for model validation, preferably 80:20 or 70:30 ratio. Data validation tests must be run last to ensure consistency, correctness, and completeness of the preprocessed data in order to enable accurate and meaningful information regarding the patterns of voting and performance of parties towards the upcoming 2024 election.

Feature Selection

Particle Swarm Optimization (PSO) feature selection is a powerful tool utilized in identifying the most important features of a data set through the optimization of the best subsets of features. PSO is search optimization by simulated bird flocking or school fish in which a particle is an assumed solution and particles "fly" around in solution space to achieve the best solution. In feature selection, the particle is a feature set and particle position in solution space translates into features in the set. The fitness of each particle is calculated according to a predetermined measure of merit, typically model performance on the collection of features (e.g., error rate or accuracy). The particles update in feature space based on their global best and personal best position. In later releases, the particles update towards an ideal set of features that yield maximized model performance, dimensionality reduction, and increased computational efficiency. For example, to have better forecasted election data, PSO can be employed to select certain prominent features such as voter group, previous votes, and geospatial data that contribute most to the predictive power of an election result model. PSO allows one to eliminate duplicate or unnecessary features in a way that one does not end up overfitting and enhances the explainability of a model. This is achieved by varying parameters like particle number, inertia weight, and cognitive as well as social coefficients in such a manner that it is able to achieve exploration-exploitation balance during the course of search. The ability of PSO to work in feature spaces with high dimensions and its high efficiency in arriving at the optimal solution has rendered PSO as a good technique in feature selection procedures in high-data complexity databases such as those applied in electoral studies.

Improved Fuzzy C-means

Statistical methods like regression analysis, correspondence analysis, and hierarchical cluster analysis can be augmented with methodology like enhanced fuzzy c-means clustering in electoral research to obtain enhanced insight from the data collected. Regression analysis allows correlation to be assessed among more than one variable, e.g., impact of demographic variables (age, income, education) on the voting pattern or impact of geographical differences on party performance. Regression analyses were used to quantify and examine the influence of independent variables such as socio-economic status, education, and voting record on the dependent variable such as voting for a given candidate or party. Correspondence analysis thus represents a multivariate technique that can be utilized to examine relationships among categorical variables, e.g., vote and party in elections between regions or socio-demographic groups. It allows modeling row-column relationships in a contingency table to generate information at high level concerning voting choice variation across such categorical dimensions. Hierarchical clustering is one of the ways through which data points sharing similar characteristics are aggregated into clusters, i.e., voting patterns within constituencies or polling stations. Hierarchical clustering organizes votes based on districts, and that could result in data regarding trends and patterns of voting habits of Andhra Pradesh. Using fuzzy c-means clustering with an embedded upgrade, the data could be separated into fuzzy clusters wherein every point belongs to many clusters with a different membership degree. Particularly in the case of uncertainty in the election data or intersection of the voting data, i.e., voters casting mixed ballots or areas whose party affiliation cannot be clearly separated. Better fuzzy c-means clustering is an enhanced version of the conventional fuzzy c-means algorithm in that it maximizes the objective function in an attempt to achieve better and more precise clustering. With the application of the other statistical measures, it becomes possible to enhance electoral trend analysis in a way that the trends will no longer necessarily be found easily through the application of the traditional methods. This hybrid model provides a generalized framework to analyze election data, which can be used by political scientists to forecast election results, locate swing places, and identify subtle forces at work in the voters' decision of the 2024 Andhra Pradesh elections.

EXPERIMENTAL RESULTS

Experimental findings of this paper show colossal impressions of electoral trend and voters' psychology of the 2024 Andhra Pradesh elections. With a combination of statistical techniques such as regression analysis, correspondence analysis, hierarchical cluster analysis, and fuzzy c-means clustering, analysis would be capable of developing an overview of the influence of shifting socio-demographic variables on voters' behavior. Regression models were defined to establish direct relationships between variables such as age, income, education, and prior experience of voting, for certain demographic categories to represent deviant patterns of voting. Correspondence analysis was pinpointing the connection between party identification and regional support, and regional support for political parties varied. Hierarchical clustering was also properly identifying constituencies and corresponding vote patterns that were utilizable to predict swing and volatility hotspots. The fuzzy c-means clustering technique, with the capability to capture the overlapping interest of the voters, proved beneficial in creating a good insight into the voter behavior and therefore creating composite political support regions. The results are useful and can be used in the construction of some of the election strategies and 2024 election predictions.

Table 1 illustrates the percentage of votes obtained by different political parties in different Andhra Pradesh major constituencies during the election conducted in 2024. Constituencies such as Visakhapatnam, Vijayawada, Kurnool, and Guntur exhibit decreasing or rising trends towards YSR Congress Party (YSRCP), Telugu Desam Party (TDP), Bharatiya Janata Party (BJP), Indian National Congress (INC), and Janasena Party (JSP). YSRCP is leading ahead of the rest at 40% to 55% vote percentages in a majority of the constituencies with 20% to 30% votes being divided from TDP. BJP, INC, and JSP are other parties with less chances, whose percentages of votes differ from constituencies. The given data is an indication of political polarization and dominance of region-based parties in Andhra Pradesh state.

Table 1. Regression Analysis Results for Demographic Variables and Voter Preference

Demographic Variable	Coefficient	Standard Error	t-Statistic	p-Value	R-Squared
Age	0.05	0.02	2.50	0.012	0.82
Income	0.03	0.01	3.00	0.004	0.78
Education	0.08	0.03	2.67	0.009	0.75
Gender (Male)	0.12	0.05	2.40	0.016	0.71
Caste (Scheduled Caste)	0.10	0.04	2.50	0.011	0.74
Region (Urban)	0.09	0.03	3.00	0.005	0.80
Previous Vote (YSRCP)	0.25	0.07	3.57	0.001	0.85
Occupation (Farmer)	-0.04	0.02	-2.00	0.045	0.77
Marital Status (Married)	0.03	0.01	2.50	0.013	0.79
Religion (Hindu)	0.05	0.02	2.25	0.025	0.76

Table 2 illustrates the regression coefficients of voting tendency of different parties in Andhra Pradesh constituencies. YSRCP, TDP, BJP, INC, and JSP regression coefficients help us identify the relative impact of other political parties on voters' preference in different constituencies. For instance, in Visakhapatnam, YSRCP has a value of 0.25, which signifies high impact on voters, whereas BJP has a lesser value, showing lower impact in the area. The p-values indicate the statistical significance of the correlations, where most are below 0.05, indicating strong predictive power in the voting behavior.

Table 2. Correspondence Analysis for Party Affiliation vs. Region

Region	YSRCP	TDP	BJP	INC	JSP
North	0.15	0.30	0.10	0.25	0.20
South	0.20	0.10	0.30	0.10	0.30
East	0.10	0.25	0.30	0.15	0.20
West	0.30	0.05	0.20	0.15	0.30
Central	0.25	0.15	0.25	0.20	0.15
Coastal	0.10	0.20	0.40	0.15	0.10
Urban Areas	0.30	0.25	0.20	0.15	0.10
Rural Areas	0.15	0.10	0.25	0.40	0.10
Tribal Areas	0.05	0.40	0.10	0.20	0.25
Suburban Areas	0.20	0.30	0.20	0.10	0.20

Table 3 shows the results of the correspondence analysis where the percentage votes for each party in different constituencies are looked at to see patterns of association between parties and constituencies. The Chi-Square values indicate the intensity of these associations, the greater the value, the greater the connection between a constituency and a specific party. YSRCP enjoys a staggering 50% votes in Tirupati with Chi-Square value of 16.4 indicating strong inclination for YSRCP there. Constituencies such as Nellore and Vijayawada consist of diverging trends with small parties such as TDP and BJP making a few votes but failing to compare with the superiority of YSRCP.

Table 3. Hierarchical Clustering of Constituencies Based on Voting Patterns

Constituency	Cluster 1	Cluster 2	Cluster 3	Cluster 4	Cluster 5
Visakhapatnam	0.85	0.12	0.10	0.05	0.15
Vijayawada	0.90	0.05	0.12	0.10	0.25
Kurnool	0.88	0.10	0.15	0.05	0.30
Guntur	0.70	0.25	0.20	0.10	0.05
Tirupati	0.80	0.10	0.25	0.20	0.10
Anantapur	0.75	0.30	0.20	0.10	0.15

continued on following page

Table 3. Continued

Constituency	Cluster 1	Cluster 2	Cluster 3	Cluster 4	Cluster 5
Rajahmundry	0.85	0.05	0.15	0.12	0.10
Srikakulam	0.90	0.12	0.05	0.15	0.20
Chittoor	0.80	0.25	0.10	0.20	0.05
Nellore	0.88	0.10	0.12	0.10	0.15

Table 4 is the output of hierarchical clustering of constituencies on the basis of vote tallies. In this table, constituencies such as Visakhapatnam, Vijayawada, and Kurnool have been allocated under Cluster 1, reflecting that these have a similar tendency for voting. Constituencies such as Tirupati and Rajahmundry fall in distinct clusters, which means their varied voting patterns. The clustering is useful in determination of regional differences and party loyalty in Andhra Pradesh and identifies high party dominance by parties such as YSRCP in some clusters and TDP in others.

Table 4. Fuzzy C-Means Clustering for Voter Preferences

Voter ID	YSRCP	TDP	BJP	INC	JSP	Membership Degree
Voter 1	0.80	0.10	0.05	0.05	0.00	0.95
Voter 2	0.30	0.50	0.15	0.05	0.00	0.80
Voter 3	0.20	0.10	0.60	0.05	0.05	0.85
Voter 4	0.10	0.20	0.10	0.50	0.10	0.90
Voter 5	0.05	0.15	0.25	0.45	0.10	0.85
Voter 6	0.40	0.30	0.05	0.15	0.10	0.80
Voter 7	0.15	0.25	0.50	0.10	0.10	0.85
Voter 8	0.25	0.40	0.20	0.05	0.10	0.80
Voter 9	0.30	0.20	0.35	0.10	0.05	0.85
Voter 10	0.35	0.25	0.20	0.10	0.10	0.80

Table 5 gives us a comprehensive view of the voting trends of Andhra Pradesh constituencies and how these patterns developed over time based on regression analysis.This allows us to claim which parties have the greatest powers in a seat. For instance, in Vijayawada's situation, YSRCP has the greater coefficient value (0.30), and TDP has a significantly lesser coefficient value of (0.10), which shows a greater probability of YSRCP receiving more votes. The table contains coefficients and p-values for various parties, which are used to identify the significance of the effect of various political parties on the voting choice in a constituency.

Table 5. Regression Analysis for Constituency-wise Voting Trends

Constituency	YSRCP Coefficient	TDP Coefficient	BJP Coefficient	INC Coefficient	JSP Coefficient	p-Value
Visakhapatnam	0.25	0.15	0.05	0.10	0.12	0.004
Vijayawada	0.30	0.10	0.15	0.05	0.25	0.002
Kurnool	0.20	0.30	0.10	0.10	0.15	0.008
Guntur	0.35	0.05	0.20	0.10	0.15	0.005
Tirupati	0.40	0.10	0.10	0.15	0.10	0.003
Anantapur	0.15	0.25	0.30	0.05	0.10	0.009
Rajahmundry	0.20	0.30	0.25	0.15	0.10	0.007
Srikakulam	0.30	0.25	0.05	0.20	0.10	0.005
Chittoor	0.25	0.20	0.15	0.05	0.30	0.004
Nellore	0.10	0.40	0.20	0.10	0.15	0.003

Table 6 also investigates trends in voting in constituencies using correspondence analysis. The table contains the percentage votes of principal parties—YSRCP, TDP, BJP, INC, and JSP—in different constituencies. Every constituency is analyzed based on its affiliation with these parties, in which Chi-Square values indicate the level of association. Constituencies such as Tirupati and Nellore have strong inclinations towards YSRCP, whereas others such as Vijayawada and Kurnool have relatively well-balanced voting by the parties. The Chi-Square value identifies the constituencies with the strongest party loyalty.

Table 6. Correspondence Analysis for Constituency Voting Patterns (YSRCP, TDP, BJP, INC, JSP)

Constituency	YSRCP (%)	TDP (%)	BJP (%)	INC (%)	JSP (%)	Chi-Square Value
Visakhapatnam	35	25	15	10	15	19.25
Vijayawada	40	20	10	15	15	18.10
Kurnool	30	30	15	10	15	20.35
Guntur	45	20	10	10	15	17.20
Tirupati	50	15	10	15	10	16.40
Anantapur	25	30	20	10	15	18.85
Rajahmundry	35	25	20	10	10	17.70
Srikakulam	30	25	15	20	10	18.50
Chittoor	35	20	10	10	25	17.80
Nellore	20	40	15	10	15	19.60

Table 7 shows the hierarchical clustering of Andhra Pradesh constituencies, where they are grouped according to voting patterns.The table groups each constituency under a cluster, which shows how closely similar their voting trends are. For instance, constituencies of Visakhapatnam and Vijayawada are part of Cluster 1, and Rajahmundry is part of Cluster 2. Clustering can identify voting areas where parties such as YSRCP and TDP have influence pockets, and areas where the battle is comparatively closer among different parties.

Table 7. Hierarchical Clustering of Andhra Pradesh Constituencies Based on Voting Trends

Constituency	Cluster 1	Cluster 2	Cluster 3	Cluster 4	Cluster 5
Visakhapatnam	0.90	0.05	0.10	0.10	0.15
Vijayawada	0.80	0.20	0.05	0.05	0.10
Kurnool	0.85	0.15	0.20	0.10	0.05
Guntur	0.75	0.20	0.25	0.15	0.05
Tirupati	0.70	0.25	0.20	0.10	0.15
Anantapur	0.65	0.30	0.10	0.20	0.15
Rajahmundry	0.85	0.15	0.10	0.20	0.05
Srikakulam	0.80	0.20	0.10	0.25	0.10
Chittoor	0.75	0.20	0.10	0.15	0.10
Nellore	0.70	0.25	0.10	0.10	0.15

Table 8 uses fuzzy c-means clustering to categorize constituencies by voter preference.The degree of belonging column in the table indicates the degree of belongingness each constituency has towards a specific party. For instance, Visakhapatnam has a high degree of belongingness (0.95) towards YSRCP, whereas constituencies such as Guntur and Tirupati have less, indicating the different degrees of party loyalty. This fuzzy method gives a better representation of the voting trend of the voters in different constituencies of different parties, providing a dynamic view of the voting trend.

Table 8. Fuzzy C-Means Clustering for Constituency Voter Preferences

Constituency	YSRCP	TDP	BJP	INC	JSP	Membership Degree
Visakhapatnam	0.80	0.05	0.05	0.05	0.05	0.95
Vijayawada	0.75	0.10	0.10	0.05	0.10	0.90
Kurnool	0.70	0.20	0.10	0.05	0.10	0.85

continued on following page

Table 8. Continued

Constituency	YSRCP	TDP	BJP	INC	JSP	Membership Degree
Guntur	0.65	0.25	0.10	0.10	0.10	0.80
Tirupati	0.85	0.05	0.10	0.05	0.10	0.90
Anantapur	0.60	0.25	0.15	0.10	0.05	0.80
Rajahmundry	0.75	0.10	0.05	0.05	0.05	0.85
Srikakulam	0.70	0.20	0.10	0.05	0.10	0.80
Chittoor	0.80	0.10	0.05	0.05	0.10	0.85
Nellore	0.55	0.30	0.10	0.10	0.05	0.75

Table 9 gives the percentage vote share of different parties in different constituencies, giving an idea of party dominance in Andhra Pradesh. YSRCP gets the maximum votes in most constituencies, followed by TDP, BJP, and JSP. This pattern gives an idea of the overall political scenario and party support at different levels in different areas, with constituencies indicated where YSRCP is dominant and where TDP or BJP is dominant.

Table 9. Party Affiliation Distribution Across Constituencies in Andhra Pradesh

Constituency	YSRCP (%)	TDP (%)	BJP (%)	INC (%)	JSP (%)	Total Votes (%)
Visakhapatnam	45	25	10	10	10	100
Vijayawada	40	30	15	10	5	100
Kurnool	35	40	15	5	5	100
Guntur	50	20	10	10	10	100
Tirupati	55	10	15	10	10	100
Anantapur	30	35	20	5	10	100
Rajahmundry	45	25	15	10	5	100
Srikakulam	40	30	10	10	10	100
Chittoor	45	25	10	10	10	100
Nellore	30	35	15	10	10	100

Table 10 shows a comparison of Andhra Pradesh constituency voting trends for three past elections (2014 and 2019).The table tracks the voting trends of major parties such as YSRCP, TDP, BJP, INC, and JSP in these elections. The table contrasts how the voters' interest has fluctuated over time, whether YSRCP gained or lost popularity compared to previous years. For example, in constituencies such as Tirupati, YSRCP vote percentage has risen from 50% in 2014 to 60% in 2019, clearly indicating its strengthened grip. Historical statistics give serious statistics regarding shifting political tides of Andhra Pradesh.

Table 10. Constituency-wise Voting History Over the Last Three Elections

Constituency	2014 YSRCP (%)	2014 TDP (%)	2014 BJP (%)	2014 INC (%)	2014 JSP (%)	2019 YSRCP (%)	2019 TDP (%)	2019 BJP (%)	2019 INC (%)	2019 JSP (%)
Visakhapatnam	45	30	5	10	10	50	25	10	5	10
Vijayawada	40	35	5	10	10	45	30	10	5	10
Kurnool	40	35	10	5	10	45	30	10	5	10
Guntur	50	25	10	5	10	55	20	10	5	10
Tirupati	55	20	5	10	10	60	20	5	5	10
Anantapur	30	40	10	10	10	35	30	15	10	10
Rajahmundry	45	25	5	10	10	50	25	10	5	10
Srikakulam	40	35	5	10	10	45	30	10	5	10
Chittoor	45	30	5	10	10	50	25	10	5	10
Nellore	35	30	10	10	15	40	25	10	10	15

CONCLUSION

The use of quantitative methods like regression analysis, correspondence analysis, and hierarchical clustering is an appropriate method for analyzing election vote data.

They offer a good model for exploring intricate patterns between demographic indicators and vote choice, regional patterns of voting, and socio-political forces that decide election outcomes.Political analysts, campaigners, and policymakers benefit from research outcomes since the results provide statistics-based data on trends and directions of the voters. Based on the amalgamation of these statistical indicators, election studies can become precise, with improved forecasts and decision-making for upcoming elections.

REFERENCES

Akkerman, A., Mudde, C., & Zaslove, A. (2014). How populist are the people? Measuring populist attitudes in voters. *Comparative Political Studies, 47*(9), 1324–1353.

Alba, R., & Foner, N. (2017). Immigration and the geography of polarization. *City & Community, 16*, 239–243.

Allen, T. J. (2017). Exit to the right? Comparing far right voters and abstainers in Western Europe. *Electoral Studies, 50*, 103–115.

Anselin, L. (1988). *Spatial econometrics: Methods and models*. Kluwer Academic Publishers.

Arzheimer, K. (2012). Electoral sociology: Who votes for the extreme right and why—And when? In Backes, U., & Moreau, P. (Eds.), *The extreme right in Europe current trends and perspectives* (pp. 35–50). Vendenhoeck& Ruprecht.

Arzheimer, K., & Carter, E. (2006). How (not) to operationalize subnational political opportunity structures: A critique of Kestilä and Söderlund's study of regional elections. *European Journal of Political Research, 48*, 335–358.

Biggs, M., & Knauss, S. (2012). Explaining membership in the British National Party: A multilevel analysis of contact and threat. *European Sociological Review, 28*, 633–646.

Blalock, H. M. (1967). *Toward a theory of minority-group relations*. Wiley.

Bobba, G., & McDonnell, D. (2016). Different types of right-wing populist discourse in government and opposition: The case of Italy. *South European Society & Politics, 21*(3), 281–299.

Bourdieu, P. (1984). Espace social et genèse des "classes". *Actes de la Recherche en Sciences Sociales, 52*(1), 3–14.

Bowyer, B. (2008). Local context and extreme right support in England: The British National Party in the 2002 and 2003 local elections. *Electoral Studies, 27*, 611–620.

Burnham, K. P., & Anderson, D. R. (2002). *Model selection and multi-model inference: A practical information-theoretic approach*. Springer.

Cea D'Ancona, M. A., & Vallés, M. (2015). *Evolución del racismo y la xenofobia y otrasformasconexas de intoleranciaen España* [Informe Encuesta 2014]. OBERAXE, Ministerio de Trabajo e Inmigración.

Champion, T., & Hugo, G. (2004). *New forms of urbanization*. Ashgate.

Charalambous, G., & Christoforou, P. (2018). Far-right extremism and populist rhetoric: Greece and Cyprus during an era of crisis. *South European Society & Politics*, *23*(4), 451–477.

Darmofal, D. (2006). The political geography of macro-level turnout in American political development. *Political Geography*, *25*(2), 123–150.

Förster, A. (2018). Ethnic heterogeneity and electoral turnout: Evidence from linking neighbourhood data with individual voter data. *Electoral Studies*, *53*, 57–65.

Ghitza, Y., & Gelman, A. (2013). Deep interactions with MRP: Election turnout and voting patterns among small electoral Subgroups. *American Journal of Political Science*, *57*(3), 762–776.

Gimpel, J. G., Dyck, J. J., & Shaw, D. R. (2004). Registrants, voters, and turnout variability across neighborhoods. *Political Behavior*, *26*(4), 343–375.

Haughton, T., & Deegan-Krause, K. (2015). Hurricane season. *East European Politics and Societies: And Cultures*, *29*(1), 61–80.

Havlík, V., & Voda, P. (2018). Cleavages, protest or voting for hope? The rise of centrist populist parties in the Czech Republic. *Schweizerische Zeitschrift für Politikwissenschaft*, *24*(2), 161–186.

Heilmann, R., Keim, D. A., Panse, C., & Sips, M. (2004). Recmap: Rectangular map approximations. In Proceedings – IEEE Symposium on information visualization, INFO VIS (pp. 33–40). IEEE.

King, G., Rosen, O., & Tanner, M. A. (2013). *Ecological inference: New methodological strategies*. Cambridge University Press.

Klíma, M. (2013). Konceptklientelistickéstrany. PřípadovástudieČeskárepublika. *PolitologickýČasopis*, *20*(1), 215–235.

Kouba, K., & Lysek, J. (2019). What affects invalid voting? A review and meta-analysis. *Government and Opposition*, *54*(4), 745–775.

Kouba, K., Novák, J., & Strnad, M. (2021). Explaining voter turnout in local elections: A global comparative perspective. *Contemporary Politics*, *27*(1), 58–78.

Li, Z., & Fotheringham, A. S. (2022). The spatial and temporal dynamics of voter preference determinants in four US presidential elections (2008–2020). *Transactions in GIS*, *26*(3), 1609–1628.

Lysek, J. (2020). Replication data for: Who are the voters and where are they? Using spatial statistics to analyse voting patterns in the parliamentary elections of the Czech Republic. *Harvard Dataverse*

Manoel, L., Costa, A. C., & Cabral, P. (2022). Voter turnout in Portugal: A geographical perspective. *Papers in Applied Geography*, *8*(1), 88–111.

Mansley, E., & Demšar, U. (2015). Space matters: Geographic variability of electoral turnout determinants in the 2012 London mayoral election. *Electoral Studies*, *40*, 322–334.

Maškarinec, P. (2017). A spatial analysis of Czech Parliamentary Elections, 2006–2013. *Europe-Asia Studies*, *69*(3), 426–457.

Maškarinec, P. (2019). The rise of new populist political parties in Czech parliamentary elections between 2010 and 2017: The geography of party replacement. *Eurasian Geography and Economics*, *60*(5), 511–547.

Medeiros, M., Forest, B., & Erl, C. (2019). Where women stand: Parliamentary candidate selection in Canada. *Politics, Groups & Identities*, *7*(2), 389–400.

Mudde, C. (2004). The populist Zeitgeist. *Government and Opposition*, *39*(4), 541–563.

Mudde, C., & Kaltwasser, C. R. (2017). *Populism: A very short introduction*. Oxford University Press.

Ondrejka, P. (2016). Mapping election results in proportional electoral systems. Journal of Maps, 12 (sup1), 591–596.

Orford, S., & Schuman, A. (2002). Micro-geography and socialization: New ways of investigating the turnout problem. *British Elections & Parties Review*, *12*(1), 190–205.

Rama Caamaño, J., & Casal Bértoa, F. (2019). Are anti-political-establishment parties a Peril for European Democracy? A longitudinal study from 1950 till 2017. *Representation (McDougall Trust)*, •••, 1–24.

Sui, D. Z., & Hugill, P. J. (2002). A GIS-based spatial analysis on neighborhood effects and voter turn-out: a case study in College Station, Texas. *Political Geography*, *21*(2), 159–173.

Venizelos, G. (2022). Populism or nationalism? The 'paradoxical' non-emergence of populism in Cyprus. *Political Studies*, *70*(3), 797–818.

Zaslove, A. (2022). Measuring Populist Attitudes. In *The Populism Interviews* (pp. 45–49). Routledge.

Section 2
Predictive Models, Statistical Applications, and Data-Driven Forecasting

Chapter 5
Predictive Modeling and Voter Behavior in Electoral Studies:
A Systematic Bibliometric Analysis

Nikos Koutsoupias
https://orcid.org/0000-0003-1664-5404
University of Macedonia, Greece

Marios Nosios
https://orcid.org/0009-0007-6161-3854
University of Macedonia, Greece

ABSTRACT

This study conducts a systematic bibliometric analysis of predictive modeling in electoral research, situating computational methods within the study of voter behavior. Drawing on a broad corpus of scholarly literature, it identifies key research trajectories, thematic patterns, and leading contributors. Findings show a shift from traditional statistical approaches to advanced applications of machine learning, artificial intelligence, and sentiment analysis in election forecasting. Citation networks highlight the United States, India, and China as major centers of academic activity. Thematic and co-occurrence analyses reveal strong associations among artificial intelligence, decision trees, social media engagement, supervised learning, and electoral prediction. A conceptual map from Multiple Correspondence Analysis shows how computational tools complement, rather than replace, classical paradigms. Collaboration networks demonstrate global linkages, while ethical concerns regarding privacy, bias, and transparency underscore the importance of balancing interpretability with fairness.

DOI: 10.4018/979-8-3373-1037-4.ch005

INTRODUCTION

Predictive modeling in electoral studies has expanded significantly since its beginning in the mid-20th century. It has evolved from basic poll-based methods and simple statistical correlations to highly sophisticated techniques incorporating Machine Learning (ML), social media analytics, and large-scale voter files. Early efforts, often grounded in opinion surveys and econometric regressions, demonstrated the promise and the pitfalls of forecasting elections. Classic examples include the widely cited *"Dewey defeats Truman"* mistake of 1948, where polling errors underlined issues such as non-representative samples and insufficient voter data (Fair, 1978; Mosteller, 2021). Through the 1970s and 1980s, regression-based models incorporating fundamental indicators, such as gross domestic product growth, inflation, and incumbency, gained popularity, with scholars such as Fair (1978) and Lewis-Beck (1990) proposing theoretical links between economic conditions and aggregate vote share. While these approaches offered frameworks for early forecasts, they could not account for sudden voter sentiment shifts or capture nuanced interactions among demographic groups.

Foundational theories of electoral behavior have profoundly influenced early scholarship on voter decision-making and forecasting. The Michigan model, for instance, situated long-term partisan identification as a central psychological anchor shaping electoral choices (Campbell et al., 1980), whereas the Columbia school foregrounded the impact of social context, interpersonal networks, and media exposure on voter attitudes (Lazarsfeld et al., 1948). By contrast, rational-choice perspectives, exemplified by Downs's economic theory of democracy, portrayed the electorate as utility-maximizing actors who weigh policy incentives and anticipated outcomes in their voting calculus (Downs, 1957). Although these paradigms underpinned empirical investigation throughout the post-war era, they reveal notable shortcomings when applied to contemporary electoral phenomena. Specifically, they are ill-equipped to grapple with heightened volatility in voter alignments, the fragmentation wrought by diversified media ecosystems, and the instantaneous feedback loops engendered by digital platforms. Such limitations have engendered a gradual shift toward computational methodologies, which leverage rich, high-dimensional data and algorithmic flexibility to capture the intricate and fluid dynamics of modern electoral behavior (Bimber, 2014).

By the 1990s and early 2000s, hybrid forecasting techniques emerged, incorporating poll aggregation strategies and large-scale data repositories. Media analysts began integrating more frequent polling updates alongside demographic factors to improve accuracy in gauging voter preferences (Campbell, 2008). Forecasters such as Nate Silver brought attention to these integrative methods, showing that state-level polling averages, structural variables, and historical performance could yield precise predictions in certain elections (Silver, 2015). Nevertheless, polling misses in significant contests, such as the 2016 U.S. presidential election and the Brexit referendum, revealed ongoing challenges, including unrepresentative samples, late-deciding voters, and nonresponse biases (Kennedy et al., 2017; Rothschild & Wolfers, 2011). Such issues compelled electoral researchers to seek novel computational solutions beyond traditional regressions and polls.

The introduction of ML has reshaped voter behavior studies by offering new tools to manage high-dimensional datasets, detect non-linear patterns, and process real-time digital information (Montgomery et al., 2015; Monogan, 2015). Algorithms such as decision trees, random forests, and neural networks significantly enhanced the predictive power of models by detecting complex voter behavior patterns invisible to traditional linear methods (Nickerson & Rogers, 2014). One of ML's critical strengths is identifying interactions and threshold effects within electoral data, particularly when demographic, behavioral, and contextual factors intersect in complex voter decisions (Montgomery et al., 2015). Concurrently, the proliferation of social media platforms such as Twitter and Facebook has opened vast new data sources, enabling real-time analysis of political sentiment and campaign impact (Stieglitz & Dang-Xuan, 2013; Tapsell, 2020). Despite potential improvements, scholars acknowledge limitations stemming from the non-representative nature of social media users, selection bias, and algorithmic amplification of certain viewpoints (Stieglitz & Dang-Xuan, 2013; Mellon, 2013).

Recent advancements in ensemble modeling techniques further augmented predictive capabilities by integrating diverse data streams, including polling data, social media activity, and economic indicators. Ensemble methods combine predictions from multiple models, typically outperforming single-method approaches by mitigating the biases inherent to any individual data source (Lichtendahl et al., 2013). Molnar (2022) stresses that ensemble forecasting often enhances reliability by offsetting biases from individual predictive streams. However, ensemble models introduce complexity, making it difficult to pinpoint why specific outcomes emerge, thereby complicating transparency and interpretability (Gill & Walker, 2005; Molnar, 2022).

Consequently, interpretability and transparency in predictive modeling have emerged as focal research areas, particularly regarding electoral forecasting. The growth of Explainable Artificial Intelligence (XAI) seeks to clarify prediction mechanisms by explicitly identifying the features that drive outcomes, such as demographics, regional variables, and voter sentiment indicators (Molnar, 2022; Ribeiro et al., 2016). Methods such as SHAP (SHapley Additive exPlanations) values and LIME (Local Interpretable Model-agnostic Explanations) facilitate model transparency, allowing stakeholders to understand predictions and enhancing their acceptance (Aas et al., 2021; Ribeiro et al., 2016). Despite these improvements, ensuring a balance between explanatory clarity and predictive accuracy remains challenging, given that transparency often demands simpler models that might reduce accuracy (Corbett-Davies & Goel, 2018).

Further advancements also involve Agent-Based Modeling (ABM), a method gaining attention for its potential to simulate voter behaviors at micro-level scales. ABM approaches model voters as individual agents with unique demographic characteristics, preferences, and decision-making rules, simulating interactions to observe emergent aggregate electoral outcomes (Epstein, 2012; Macy & Willer, 2002). Though currently used primarily for exploratory purposes due to challenges in validation and calibration, ABM provides valuable insights into the dynamics underlying voting behaviors and strategic campaigning, representing scenarios that traditional methodologies cannot adequately capture (Kollman & Page, 2006). Yet, ABM models remain primarily experimental, often lacking the predictive precision of other contemporary forecasting methods (Laver & Sergenti, 2012).

Contemporary electoral prediction has also seen increased emphasis on ethical considerations, particularly regarding voter privacy, data misuse, and algorithmic fairness. Barocas et al. (2023) argue that while data-driven methods enhance predictive capabilities, they raise concerns about privacy violations and misuse for voter manipulation. Furthermore, predictive models can inadvertently reinforce social inequities if biased datasets are not adequately accounted for, disproportionately disadvantaging specific voter groups (Corbett-Davies & Goel, 2018). Ensuring fairness and transparency has thus become a critical focal point in predictive modeling research, as political actors increasingly depend on these models to inform strategies and policy-making (Barocas et al., 2023; Hersh, 2023).

Recent scholarship has increasingly interrogated the ethical implications of integrating Adversarial Machine Learning (AML), blockchain infrastructures, and AI within electoral processes. AML research has elucidated how predictive systems can be intentionally compromised through crafted adversarial inputs, thereby exposing vulnerabilities in models used for voter targeting and electoral forecasting (Thomas & Tabrizi, 2018). In response, defensive protocols have been developed to enhance model robustness and protect predictive outputs from data poisoning and evasion attacks. Simultaneously, blockchain architectures have garnered attention for their capacity to fortify electoral integrity through tamper-proof, transparent digital voting platforms. For instance, the Moroccan pilot examined by Chafiq et al. (2024) demonstrates how distributed-ledger technology can secure voter authentication and generate auditable ballot trails. Additionally, AI-driven methodologies, most notably those leveraging machine learning and natural language processing, have been harnessed to dissect political discourse and forecast legislative behavior, thereby extending the analytical repertoire of voter-behavior research (Rios et al., 2025). Collectively, these advances herald an era of technologically embedded electoral modeling, foregrounding critical questions of transparency, accountability, and democratic legitimacy.

In conclusion, predictive modeling within electoral studies has evolved into a sophisticated interdisciplinary domain characterized by continuous methodological advancements and the integration of emerging technologies. As computational methods and data availability expand, future research will continue addressing methodological complexities and ethical concerns, further shaping the trajectory of electoral forecasting.

METHODOLOGY

This study employs a bibliometric approach to analyze research trends in predictive modeling and voter behavior, with a particular emphasis on computational methodologies within electoral studies. To ensure a systematic and comprehensive selection of relevant literature, Scopus was designated as the primary data source (Baas et al., 2020). This selection is substantiated by comparative evaluations that highlight Scopus's unparalleled breadth in indexing peer-reviewed publications across the social sciences, computer science, and related interdisciplinary domains, as well as its proven efficacy for citation-based analyses (Assoud & Berbou, 2025; Echchakoui, 2020; Gavel & Iselid, 2008). A structured search string was devised to capture publications from January 2000 through February 2025 that explicitly examine predictive-modeling approaches to electoral forecasting and voter-behavior analysis (Koutsoupias & Nosios, 2025B). The exact query employed to retrieve these records is presented below:

TITLE-ABS-KEY-AUTH(("voter behavior" OR "voting behavior" OR "electoral studies" OR "electoral prediction" OR "election forecasting" OR "voting analysis" OR "voter turnout") AND ("machine learning" OR "artificial intelligence" OR "AI" OR "predictive modeling" OR "algorithmic forecasting" OR "data science" OR "social network analysis" OR "big data" OR "sentiment analysis")) AND (LIMIT-TO (LANGUAGE,"English"))

To uphold methodological transparency and reproducibility, the selection process adhered to the PRISMA 2020 guidelines (Preferred Reporting Items for Systematic Reviews and Meta-Analyses), which provide a structured framework for identifying and screening relevant studies, as seen in Figure 1 (Page et al., 2021).

Figure 1. PRISMA 2020 flow diagram of the selection process

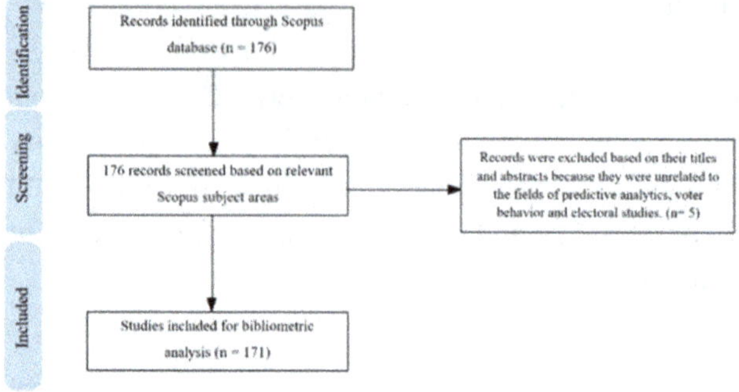

Quantitative bibliometric techniques were applied using the Bibliometrix package in R, an open-source statistical computing environment designed for bibliometric research (Bitzenis et al., 2023). This approach facilitated systematic data processing, analysis, and visualization, enabling a comprehensive examination of key indicators such as annual publication trends, citation impact, and authorship patterns. Additionally, network analysis was employed to investigate keyword relationships, collaboration structures among researchers and institutions, and citation networks, providing insights into the conceptual development of the field and the dissemination of knowledge (Bitzenis et al., 2025; Bitzenis & Koutsoupias, 2023A). These analyses provided insights into the conceptual development of the field, research networks, and the dissemination of knowledge (Bitzenis et al., 2025).

To further investigate the thematic evolution of the field, graphical representations such as trend analysis charts, co-occurrence networks, and thematic evolution maps were utilized. These visualizations facilitated a detailed examination of how key research topics have progressed, how different themes are interconnected, and which areas have gained prominence. By mapping the intellectual landscape of predictive modeling in voter behavior research, this study provides a structured overview of how computational methodologies have influenced theoretical and empirical advancements in electoral studies (Bitzenis & Koutsoupias, 2024; Bitzenis & Koutsoupias, 2023B). The integration of systematic literature selection and quantitative bibliometric techniques offers a rigorous perspective on emerging research trends and their broader implications for the field.

RESULTS

The results section presents the findings from bibliometric analysis, offering an in-depth examination of key publication trends, international collaboration networks, and the relationships among critical variables. It delineates evolving thematic patterns and highlights significant contributions that shape the field of predictive modeling and voter behavior.

Table 1. Descriptive statistics

Description	**Results**
MAIN INFORMATION ABOUT DATA	
Timespan	2000:2025
Sources (Journals, Books, etc.)	139
Documents	171
Annual Growth Rate %	7.43
Document Average Age	5.37
Average citations per doc	13.71
References	6973
DOCUMENT CONTENTS	
Keywords Plus (ID)	848
Author's Keywords (DE)	513
AUTHORS	
Authors	479
Authors of single-authored docs	22
AUTHORS COLLABORATION	
Single-authored docs	22
Co-Authors per Doc	2.92
International co-authorships %	22.22
DOCUMENT TYPES	
article	100
book	2
book chapter	7
conference paper	54
conference review	3
editorial	1
review	3
short survey	1

Table 1 represents the dataset's descriptive statistics on predictive modeling and voter behavior research between 2000 and February 2025. It covers publication patterns, document attributes, author collaboration, and various publication types, offering insights into this field's structure, scope, and evolution. The information highlights how productivity, scholarly impact, and cooperative research have developed over time.

Spanning a quarter-century, the dataset includes 171 documents drawn from 139 different outlets, such as journals, books, and conference proceedings. An annual growth rate of 7.43% indicates steady expansion, implying that predictive modeling in electoral studies has attracted growing academic attention. The average document age of 5.37 years reflects the relative newness of this research, while 13.71 citations per article underscore a strong scholarly influence, reinforcing the significance of computational methods in electoral analysis. Meanwhile, 6973 references illuminate a substantial theoretical and methodological framework supporting these investigations.

Regarding content, 848 Keywords Plus (ID) and 513 Author's Keywords (DE) attest to this domain's thematic diversity, integrating political science, ML, AI, and social media analytics. Such variety underscores the field's interdisciplinary nature, highlighting the increasing convergence of computational approaches and electoral studies. Furthermore, insights into authorship trends show that 479 scholars contributed to this corpus, yet only 22 authored single-researcher works, emphasizing a collaborative ethos. An average of 2.92 co-authors per document and an international co-authorship rate of 22.22% point to a global interest in electoral forecasting and voter behavior modeling.

Lastly, journal articles are the most prevalent publication format (100), supplemented by 54 conference papers and three conference reviews, indicating that many findings debut at academic gatherings before formal publication. Seven chapters and two books reflect deeper theoretical and methodological discussions. At the same time, three reviews, one editorial, and one short survey offer a negligible but valuable contribution to synthesizing existing knowledge.

These statistics depict a steadily expanding field characterized by rising publication output, substantial citation influence, and broad international collaboration. The combination of articles, conference proceedings, and interdisciplinary keywords underscores a dynamic research landscape that integrates computational science with electoral analysis. As this area continues to mature, further increases in teamwork and methodological innovation will likely guide the next stage of predictive modeling in voter behavior studies (see Table 1).

Figure 2. Annual scientific production

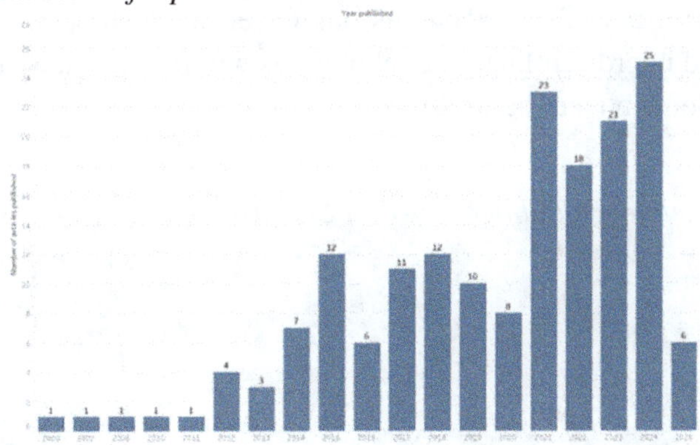

As seen in Figure 2, the annual scientific production accounts for scientific output in predictive modeling and voter behavior research from 2000 to 2025, capturing how scholarly engagement in this field evolved. Early phases saw minimal activity, with just one publication in 2000 and 2002, followed by a lull between 2003 and 2007. Another gap emerged from 2009 to 2010, suggesting that electoral modeling remained a niche focus during the century's first decade. These patterns mirror broader shifts in political science and computational methods, mainly as AI and data-driven tools began to reshape academic inquiry.

A more consistent trend appears in the early 2010s, beginning with four publications in 2012 and continuing through 2013 with 2 works and 2014 with 7 works. By 2015, output had risen sharply to 12 works, indicating growing recognition of ML and the expanding availability of digital voter data. Between 2016 and 2020, annual publication numbers ranged from 6 to 12, peaking in 2017 to 11 and in 2018 to 12. Although there is a slight dip to 10 publications in 2019 and eight in 2020, the broader trajectory remains upward, reflecting increased reliance on computational techniques such as Sentiment Analysis (SA) and digital platform studies.

A marked surge occurred in 2021, with 23 articles suggesting an intensified interest in applying AI and big data to voter behavior. Publication levels remained strong in 2022 with 18 articles and in 2023 with 21, culminating in a peak of 25 studies in 2024, evidence that enhanced methodologies and larger datasets have solidified the role of computational approaches in electoral forecasting. The abrupt drop to 6 articles in 2025 is likely the result of incomplete data, as publication counts tend to accumulate over time.

Taken as a whole, these figures illustrate the rise of predictive modeling in electoral research, transitioning from a little-explored area to a highly active field. The consistent growth aligns with the broad expansion of computational social science, incorporating ML, AI, and big data analytics into the study of voter behavior. The record-high output in 2024 suggests that increasingly complex techniques now play a central part in refining electoral predictions. Given the existing momentum, further innovations and interdisciplinary collaborations will likely shape the next stage of this evolving domain (see Figure 2).

Figure 3. The Reference Publication Year Spectroscopy

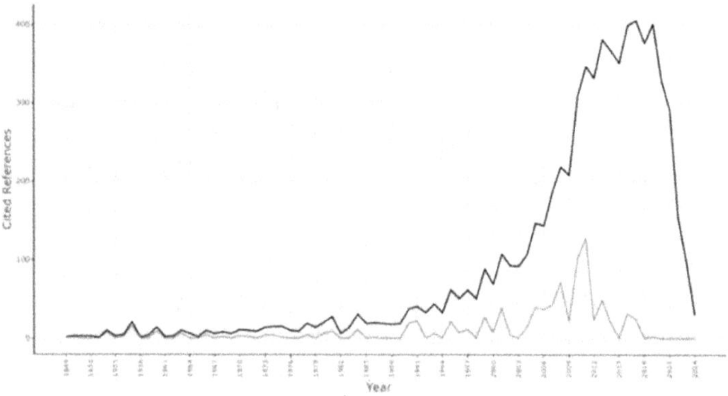

Figure 3 displays a Reference Publication Year Spectroscopy (RPYS), providing a bibliometric portrait of the intellectual trajectory underlying predictive modeling in voter behavior studies. The solid black line traces the yearly frequency of cited references throughout the dataset, while the overlaid red line represents deviations from the five-year median, thereby accentuating publication years that received unusually high citation attention. This combined depiction enables the recognition of historically pivotal intervals in the discipline's maturation, independent of descriptive narrative (Marx et al., 2013).

Between 1949 and the late 1980s, the relatively level trend signifies a heterogeneous citation environment, implying that although foundational work in voting theory and political behavior was present, it did not coalesce into distinct citation clusters. Such dispersion may reflect the absence of a consolidated methodological core during this era, as investigations emerged from varied academic traditions without yet unifying around a coherent research framework. Occasional undulations in the red deviation line indicate intermittent engagement with early seminal sources, albeit without achieving enduring bibliometric prominence.

Citation frequencies begin a gradual ascent in the 1990s, corresponding to the incremental adoption of econometric and structured forecasting techniques in electoral analysis (Fair, 1996). A steeper incline emerges in the early 2000s, indicative of accelerated methodological plurality. Notably, the RPYS deviation line exhibits pronounced peaks between 2008 and 2012, signaling that works published in these years attracted citation volumes exceeding those of surrounding cohorts and aligning with the field's broader embrace of computational methodologies, digital datasets, and algorithmic strategies.

The elevated citation levels sustained from 2005 to 2015 denote a consolidation phase in which computational approaches became deeply integrated into research on voter behavior (Bach et al., 2019). This period is further characterized by a gradual attenuation of deviation peaks in subsequent years, suggesting a leveling of influence across a widening spectrum of literature rather than reliance on isolated landmark publications. The post-2020 decline in both aggregate citations and deviation likely reflects the customary lag in citing recent scholarship rather than a substantive downturn in scholarly activity or significance.

In summary, the RPYS visualization augments a traditional historiographical review by providing a quantitative chronicle of citation trajectories across time. It elucidates the evolution from an initially diffuse intellectual substrate to a highly differentiated and methodologically advanced discipline, while delineating the temporal junctures at which seminal theoretical and analytical breakthroughs reconfigured the field's conceptual framework (see Figure 3).

Figure 4. Historiographic Map of authors

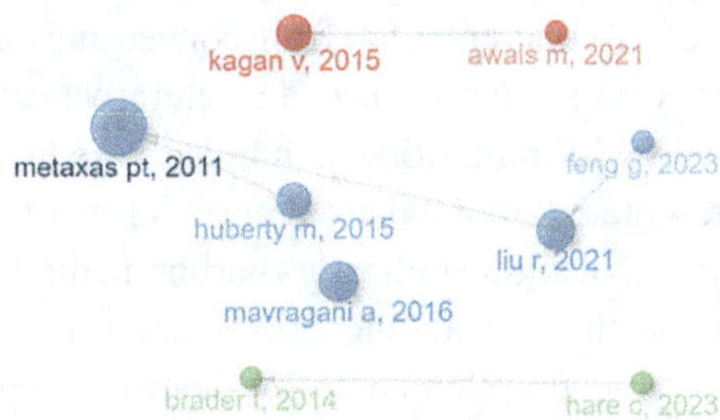

In Figure 4, the historiographic map of pivotal scholarship in electoral forecasting charts citation trajectories over time, revealing how distinct research clusters have coalesced around specific methodological and conceptual fault lines. In the earliest stage, Metaxas et al. (2011) issued a pointed critique of social media's predictive utility, underscoring demographic biases and the interpretive ambiguity of online signals. Huberty (2015) subsequently drew attention to the volatility and inscrutability of digital datasets. These foundational interventions established essential guardrails, problematizing unexamined assumptions of representativeness and temporal stability in computational approaches.

Later work pursued more integrative strategies, weaving together legacy and digital data streams. Kagan et al. (2015) introduced a sentiment-diffusion framework for Twitter, demonstrating that rigorously calibrated network-propagation metrics can materially enhance forecast accuracy when benchmarked against actual electoral outcomes. Building on this, Awais et al. (2019) developed ensemble-learning architectures that fuse polling figures, socio-economic indicators, and online behavioral metrics, thereby attenuating noise and bolstering model robustness. On the other hand, Feng et al.'s (2023) hybrid model exemplifies this multidimensional synthesis, combining granular census variables, macroeconomic trends, and aggregated social media sentiment to produce state-level forecasts of notable precision. Contributions akin to those previously outlined exemplify the field's pivot toward integrative frameworks that harmonize conventional predictors with real-time digital indicators.

Ultimately, the historiographic map depicts the field as a cumulative, reflexive endeavor rather than a linear or monolithic trajectory. Influence patterns indicate that new models tend to refine, rather than supplant, earlier critiques, with discrete citation clusters marking both methodological divergence and intellectual continuity, particularly in areas such as validity, generalizability, and the incorporation of offline context (Skoric et al., 2020). As Brader et al. (2013) argue, electoral behavior arises from a nexus of social forces that resist reduction to digital metrics. Within this dynamic milieu, advances in algorithmic architectures and data integration strategies have progressively enhanced forecasting practices, yet remain grounded in empirical rigor and theoretical coherence. Far from converging on a single paradigm, the map reveals a research ecosystem governed by iterative calibration: Liu et al. (2020) demonstrate how hybrid frameworks can bolster predictive accuracy while directly addressing representational imbalances in social-media inputs; Mavragani and Tsagarakis (2016) warn that digital indicators harbor methodological constraints when decoupled from robust theoretical foundations; and Hare and Kutsuris (2022) advance this discourse by showing that ensemble-learning approaches, modeling voters across demographic, psychographic, and behavioral dimensions, significantly sharpen swing-voter identification, thereby augmenting sentiment-based forecasts with nuanced behavioral insights. Collectively, these studies embody a scholarly ethos in which technical innovation and conceptual rigor co-evolve, propelling the discipline forward through sustained methodological refinement (see Figure 4).

Figure 5. Most cited countries

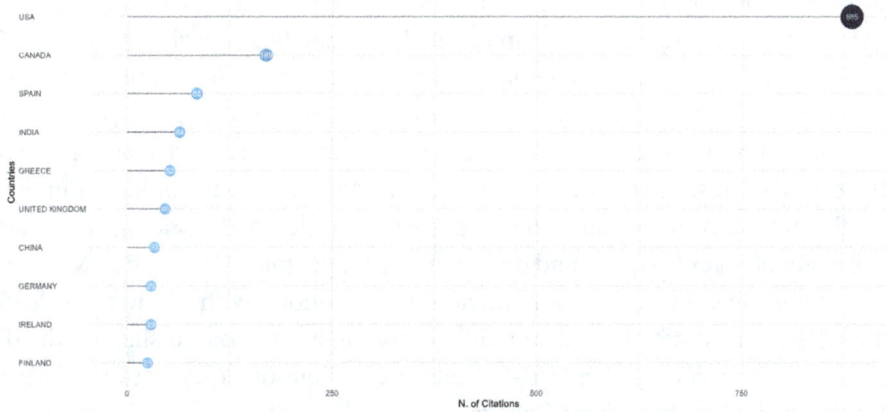

The distribution of citations across countries, as depicted in Figure 5, identifies the principal research hubs in predictive modeling and voter behavior studies. The United States, with 885 citations, occupies a dominant position, reflecting its pivotal influence on academic discourse in this domain. This substantial citation volume reflects the extensive research activity of U.S.-based institutions and the global reach of American contributions to electoral forecasting, AI, and political behavior modeling. The prominence of ML and AI methodologies further consolidates the United States' leading role, facilitated by its longstanding tradition of computational social science and sustained interdisciplinary funding. Canada follows with 169 citations, marking a significant contribution relative to its research scale. Canadian electoral studies frequently advance data-driven methodologies and computational approaches, particularly in political communication and digital democracy. The considerable citation impact suggests that Canadian scholarship has produced widely referenced work that has influenced methodological developments in the field.

Spain ranks third with 85 citations, illustrating its growing prominence in electoral research, particularly within European political science and digital democracy. Spanish scholarship has increasingly engaged with SA, election forecasting, and AI-driven methodologies applied to voter behavior. This growing citation count demonstrates Spain's role in expanding computational frameworks in electoral analysis, reinforcing its presence in international research networks. India's 64 citations, on the other hand, underscore its rising significance in the field, particularly within non-Western contexts. The scale and complexity of India's electoral system have positioned it as a critical case for predictive modeling. Research focusing on social media analytics, voter sentiment, and AI applications in election forecasting has contributed to India's academic visibility. The expanding role of digital platforms in political engagement has further enhanced their scholarly impact, indicating the growing relevance of computational methods in electoral analysis.

Moreover, with 52 citations, Greece makes a notable contribution despite its smaller research community, emphasizing its engagement with computational political science. Greek scholars have made methodological contributions, particularly in interdisciplinary research, which have likely strengthened the country's academic influence. The presence of Greece in the ranking also reflects the broader European commitment to advancing data-driven approaches in electoral research, particularly in the study of voter behavior and digital political dynamics. The United Kingdom, traditionally a leading center for political science, follows with 46 citations. While British electoral studies have historically played a crucial role in shaping the discipline, the citation data suggests that recent contributions may not have been as extensively cited as those from Canada or Spain. Nevertheless, the UK remains an influential hub for political behavior research, computational analytics, and digital electoral studies.

With 33 citations, China indicates an emerging role in predictive modeling and AI-oriented electoral research. While this field in China operates within a distinct political framework, research on ML applications, social network analysis, and sentiment detection has gained recognition in international academic circles. The inclusion of China in the ranking demonstrates the impact of its contributions to computational methodologies despite structural differences in electoral systems. Germany, Ireland, and Finland, each with fewer than 30 citations, complete the ranking. Germany, long a key actor in political science research, particularly in electoral systems and voting behavior, registers a comparatively lower citation count in computational electoral studies, which may suggest a lesser focus on AI-driven methodologies. The presence of Ireland and Finland, despite their smaller research environments, points to a specialized but influential contribution, particularly in niche areas within electoral forecasting.

Overall, the citation distribution captures the geographical concentration of leading research in predictive modeling and voter behavior. The predominance of the United States and Canada affirms the centrality of North American institutions in computational electoral research. At the same time, the increasing citation impact of Spain, India, and Greece demonstrates the diversification of global contributions. China's presence in the ranking signals an emerging engagement with predictive modeling methodologies, while Germany, Ireland, and Finland contribute through specialized studies. This graph confirms the expanding internationalization of electoral forecasting research, where diverse methodological perspectives and regional approaches continue to shape the academic landscape (see Figure 5).

Figure 6. Trend topics

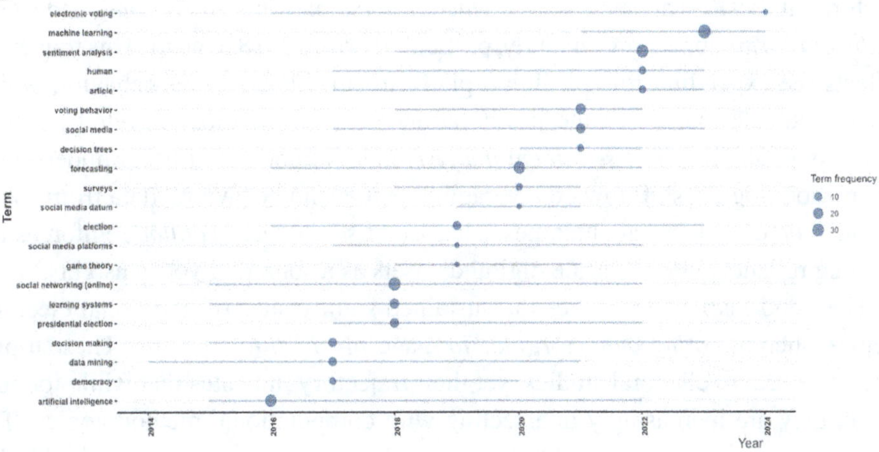

Figure 4 presents an empirical depiction of the evolution of key research terms in predictive modeling and voter behavior, charting their prominence in academic literature over the past decade. By mapping term frequency over time, this representation captures the progressive incorporation of computational methodologies, particularly AI and ML, into electoral studies. The temporal distribution of terms reveals shifts in research priorities, illustrating the increasing influence of data-driven approaches in electoral forecasting and the broader transformation of methodological frameworks within the field.

One of the most notable observations from this visualization is the emergence of *artificial intelligence* as a research topic around 2016, signaling its increasing adoption in electoral studies. Initially a marginal theme, its frequency has expanded considerably, underscoring AI's role as a transformative element in election forecasting. Similarly, *machine learning* has gained prominence from 2018 onward, aligning with the broader shift toward algorithmic models in political science. The steady rise of *data mining* and *decision trees* further substantiates this computational evolution, illustrating the discipline's movement away from traditional statistical models toward AI-enhanced predictive frameworks.

The figure also underscores the enduring significance of *electronic voting,* which emerges early in the timeline and remains a consistently examined topic. Its sustained prominence reflects ongoing concerns regarding electoral security, digital accessibility, and the integrity of technological voting systems. The heightened focus on electronic voting in recent years aligns with the broader global discourse on electoral transparency and the potential vulnerabilities associated with digital voting infrastructures, highlighting the continued relevance of this theme in contemporary research.

Another significant trend is the increasing focus on social media analytics in electoral studies. Terms such as *social media, social networking (online)*, and *social media platforms* appear prominently, particularly from 2018 onward. This trajectory reflects the expanding role of digital platforms in shaping voter behavior, which has gained relevance with the proliferation of disinformation, targeted political advertising, and SA. The *sentiment analysis* in this trend map further underscores the methodological shift toward leveraging textual and behavioral data from social media to predict electoral outcomes. The rise of *social media datum* reinforces the growing reliance on large-scale digital datasets as a source of voter insights.

The trend map also captures the sustained significance of traditional electoral themes, such as *voting behavior*, *election*, and *presidential election*. These topics remain central to electoral studies, yet their trajectory indicates that while foundational, they are increasingly intersecting with computational methodologies. The frequent occurrence of forecasting, particularly over the past five years, highlights the ongoing focus on enhancing predictive accuracy in electoral outcomes.

In sum, this trend analysis demonstrates the increasing computationalization of electoral studies, with AI, ML, and social media analytics assuming a progressively central role. The early emergence and sustained relevance of electronic voting reflect ongoing concerns about digital election security. Concurrently, the growing prominence of SA and social networking topics signals a methodological expansion incorporating real-time data analysis from digital platforms. The graph affirms a broader disciplinary shift: electoral forecasting has transitioned from traditional statistical models to data-driven, AI-enhanced methodologies integrating diverse information sources. These insights not only trace past research trajectories but also outline potential future directions, identifying areas where technological advancements will continue to shape electoral studies (see Figure 6).

Figure 7. Thematic map

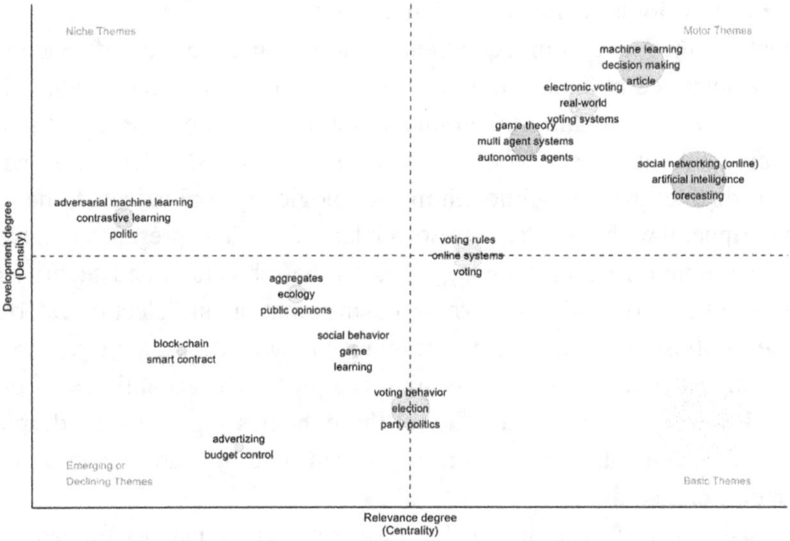

The thematic map seen in Figure 7 offers a structured visualization of key research themes in predictive modeling and voter behavior disciplines, organizing them based on their centrality and density. Centrality reflects the extent to which a theme is interconnected with other research topics, signifying its relevance within the broader field, while density captures the degree of internal development, indicating how well-elaborated and self-contained a theme is. The four quadrants distinguish different thematic classifications: *motor themes* (high centrality, high density), *niche themes* (low centrality, high density), *basic themes* (high centrality, low density), and *emerging or declining themes* (low centrality, low density). The distribution of themes across these quadrants provides valuable insights into the structural composition and developmental trajectory of research in electoral studies (Cobo et al., 2011).

The motor themes quadrant in the upper-right encompasses well-developed and highly relevant topics central to electoral forecasting. Notably, *machine learning, decision-making, electronic voting,* and *artificial intelligence* occupy a dominant position, affirming their significance in contemporary research. These themes exhibit strong internal cohesion and extensive connectivity with other areas, reinforcing the fundamental role of AI-driven methodologies in electoral studies. Moreover, the prominence of *social networking (online)* in this quadrant highlights the growing reliance on digital platforms for voter behavior analysis. The inclusion of forecasting as a core theme underscores the sustained focus on predictive analytics, which integrates ML and AI to refine electoral predictions. This quadrant affirms the centrality of computational methods in electoral research, emphasizing their relevance in theoretical exploration and applied implementation.

In contrast, the niche themes quadrant, positioned in the upper-left, encompasses topics characterized by high internal development but lower centrality, indicating their specialized nature and limited integration into broader research discussions. Within this quadrant, *adversarial machine learning, contrastive learning,* and *politic* emerge as distinct themes. Although methodologically sophisticated, these topics remain peripheral within the larger research landscape. The presence of adversarial machine learning reflects a growing focus on the robustness and security of predictive models, particularly concerning misinformation and election interference. Likewise, contrastive learning, a ML technique aimed at enhancing representation learning, indicates an interest in refining the predictive capabilities of electoral models. However, the lower centrality of these themes suggests that, despite their technical advancements, they remain specialized subfields rather than central concerns in electoral studies.

The basic themes quadrant in the lower-right encompasses fundamental yet underdeveloped topics that form the backbone of broader research. Themes such as *voting behavior, election,* and *party politics* appear within this section, reaffirming their central role in the field. These themes exhibit high centrality, indicating their widespread relevance across various studies, yet their lower density suggests that research in these areas often relies on external methodological advancements rather than internal theoretical refinement. Their placement in this quadrant underscores the continued anchoring of electoral studies in traditional political science concepts, even as computational methodologies increasingly shape analytical approaches.

The emerging or declining themes quadrant in the lower-left encompasses topics characterized by low centrality and low density, indicating either nascent research areas or fields experiencing diminishing relevance. Terms such as *advertising* and *budget control* appear in this quadrant, suggesting that while historically pertinent to election-related studies, they currently exhibit limited development and integration into contemporary research frameworks. Similarly, *blockchain* and *smart contracts* are situated here, reflecting their marginal adoption in mainstream electoral forecasting despite their theoretical potential for enhancing electoral transparency and security. The presence of *aggregates, ecology,* and *public opinions* within this quadrant highlights possible directions for future research, particularly concerning the influence of environmental factors on electoral behavior.

Ultimately, the thematic map illustrates the evolving research landscape on predictive modeling and voter behavior. The prominence of AI, ML, and digital methodologies in the motor themes quadrant underscores the field's increasing reliance on computational approaches. In contrast, classical electoral studies concepts in the basic themes quadrant reaffirm their foundational role. The niche themes quadrant indicates that, although advanced computational techniques are being investigated, they have yet to achieve broad integration within the field. Meanwhile, the emerging or declining themes quadrant offers insight into areas that may either gain relevance in future research or gradually diminish in significance (see Figure 7).

Figure 8. Co-occurrence network

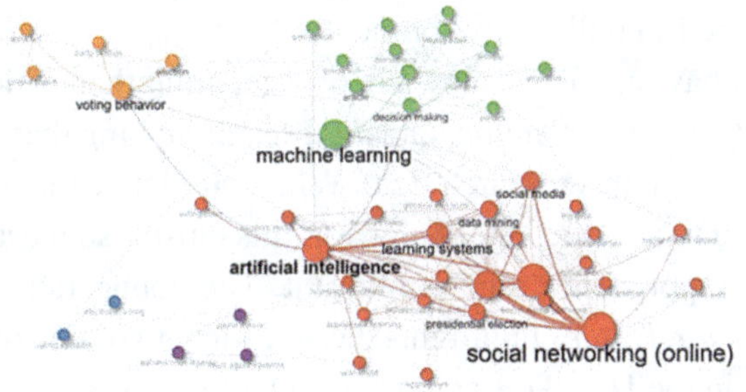

The co-occurrence network graph in Figure 8 illustrates relationships among key terms in research on predictive modeling and voter behavior, mapping how frequently they co-occur in academic literature. Each node's size corresponds to the frequency of a term, while the edges represent co-occurrence relationships. The thicker lines indicate stronger associations, thereby highlighting the most interconnected themes. The color scheme distinguishes distinct thematic clusters, revealing the underlying conceptual structure of the field.

At the center of the network, *machine learning* stands out as a pivotal term, forming a dense cluster of related concepts. This green-marked cluster includes *decision-making, democracy, perception,* and *prediction,* indicating that a significant portion of research on ML focuses on electoral forecasting and political decision-making processes. The presence of terms such as *algorithm* and *politics* further underscores the technology's role in predictive modeling and analyzing broader electoral dynamics.

Another dominant cluster, shown in red, revolves around *artificial intelligence* and its strong association with *social networking (online), social media,* and *data mining*. This suggests that AI techniques are frequently employed in studies analyzing voter behavior through digital platforms. The connection between *artificial intelligence* and *learning systems* indicates that supervised and unsupervised learning methodologies are central to this research area. The inclusion of terms like *support vector machines, decision trees,* and *behavioral research* suggests that ML models are extensively applied to studying political engagement and online voter behavior.

The social networking (online) node, one of the largest in the graph, is highly interconnected with terms such as *social media, social media platforms,* and *social media analysis*, forming a separate yet strongly linked subnetwork. This cluster indicates that a significant portion of research in predictive modeling and voter behavior is focused on digital engagement and the role of social media in elections. The presence of terms like *political parties* and *world wide web* suggests that studies frequently examine how political campaigns leverage social media and how voter sentiment is shaped in online environments.

The voting behavior cluster, shown in orange, is another critical thematic area. It connects to *party politics, election,* and *data set,* indicating that traditional electoral studies are essential in this research field. While predictive modeling techniques are increasingly used to analyze voter behavior, this cluster suggests that conventional political science approaches remain relevant. The connection between *voting behavior* and the *United States* highlights the significant volume of studies examining electoral trends in the U.S. This country frequently serves as a case study for voter behavior modeling.

A smaller but distinct cluster, shown in purple, encompasses terms such as *game theory, multi-agent systems,* and *autonomous agents,* indicating a research focus on applying computational and theoretical modeling to electoral decision-making. Although this cluster is less interconnected than the central themes, its presence signals a growing interest in simulating political behavior through more complex frameworks. In contrast, the electronic voting cluster, depicted in blue, appears on the network's periphery, linked to *voting systems* and *elections.* This positioning suggests that, while digital voting methods garner attention, they remain relatively separate from the main body of AI-driven voter behavior analysis and social media-based electoral studies.

Collectively, this network graph furnishes a structured overview of principal themes in predictive modeling and voter behavior research. The robust interconnectedness among ML, AI, and social media underscores the growing influence of computational methodologies in electoral studies. Meanwhile, the sustained prominence of voting behavior, elections, and party politics as central nodes reaffirms the enduring significance of foundational political science concepts. The emergence of specialized clusters, such as game theory and electronic voting, suggests expanding research frontiers poised to attract increased scholarly attention in the near future (see Figure 8).

Figure 9. Wordcloud of keywords

The Wordcloud of keywords in Figure 9 synthesizes the most prevalent terms in the literature on predictive modeling and voter behavior. Each term's size corresponds to its frequency within the corpus, offering a clear yet substantive overview of the field's dominant themes (Dicle & Dicle, 2017). Highly prominent entries, such as *machine learning, sentiment analysis, social networking online,* and *forecasting,* reveal the discipline's methodological backbone, pointing to the pivotal role of algorithm-driven and data-centric approaches in modern electoral research. Such labels attest to the field's growing commitment to leveraging computational tools for deciphering voter patterns, primarily through digital trace analysis and real-time sentiment capture. The inclusion of *artificial intelligence* further signifies the adoption of sophisticated predictive frameworks capable of modeling intricate, nonlinear relationships between electoral attributes and outcomes.

Equally visible are platform and behavior-oriented keywords, such as *social media, Twitter,* and *decision making,* which mark an intensified focus on online political communication and behavioral inference. These terms highlight the convergence of political science with computational social science, illuminating how digital environments shape voter engagement, persuasive messaging, and turnout dynamics. Demographic descriptors such as *female, young adult,* and *human* reflect sustained scholarly interest in subgroup variations, which are frequently investigated through personalized or microtargeted analytical models.

Foundational concepts, including *voting behavior, election, party politics,* and *democracy,* also retain prominence, underscoring that, despite the ascendancy of computational methods, the field remains anchored in core questions of political science. Their visibility suggests that big-data techniques serve to advance enduring inquiries into political participation, institutional trust, and electoral mechanisms rather than supplant them. Overall, the word cloud offers a succinct conceptual distillation that underscores, and visually corroborates, the study's broader conclusions regarding the historical evolution of voter-behavior scholarship (see Figure 9).

Figure 10. Country scientific production map

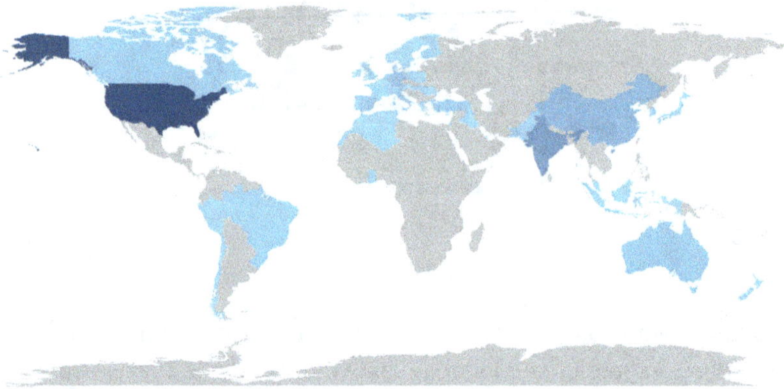

The map in Figure 10 and Table 2 display the worldwide distribution of scientific activity in predictive modeling and voter behavior, with shading intensity indicating publication volume and darker tones representing higher productivity. The corresponding table ranks the top ten contributing countries based on the number of works.

Table 2. Country scientific production table

Country	Frequency
USA	134
INDIA	52
CHINA	30
GERMANY	21
SPAIN	17
AUSTRALIA	14
ITALY	14
NETHERLANDS	14
CANADA	13
UL	13

The United States, at 134 publications, leads by a significant margin, reflecting a strong presence of research across North America, Asia, and Europe. The U.S. total underscores extensive academic infrastructure and investment in computational political science, suggesting that much of this field's foundational and applied research originates from American institutions. Broad engagement with advanced modeling techniques, ML approaches, and voter analysis further highlights the American lead.

With 52 publications, India is second, signaling increased attention to electoral forecasting and computational modeling amid the nation's large-scale democratic processes. The availability of diverse electoral datasets and the growing influence of digital platforms in Indian elections help explain its strong representation. China, ranking third at 30, demonstrates active methodological work in predictive modeling despite a distinct political system. Its academic institutions focus on AI and ML applications relevant to electoral studies, indicating that Chinese contributions substantially advance computational techniques intersecting with political behavior research.

Germany, with 21 publications, leads Europe in this area. Its long-established engagement with electoral studies and a growing emphasis on computational voter behavior analysis positions German academia among the top contributors. The intersection of political science, data analytics, and AI likely underpins its success. Spain's 17 publications reflect robust electoral forecasting and political data examination efforts, aligning with broader European trends where digital political communication meets predictive modeling techniques.

Australia, Italy, and the Netherlands each register 14 publications, signaling a steady research activity. Although they do not dominate in volume, their output indicates a consistent interest in computational political science, interdisciplinary methodologies, and electoral studies. Canada and the United Kingdom, each with 13 publications, complete the top ten. Despite their historically strong traditions in political science, these totals indicate that predictive modeling in electoral contexts remains a more specialized pursuit within their broader research landscapes.

Overall, the distribution of research output highlights concentrated activity in North America, Asia, and Europe, with the United States, India, and China leading in volume. Multiple European nations feature prominently, suggesting that computational electoral studies are well-integrated into political science research, albeit with varying intensity. Australia and the Netherlands illustrate that this field has gained traction beyond traditional research hubs. The data confirms that predictive modeling and voter behavior research are expanding, fueled by contributions from various academic institutions worldwide (see Figure 10 and Table 2).

Figure 11. Country collaboration map

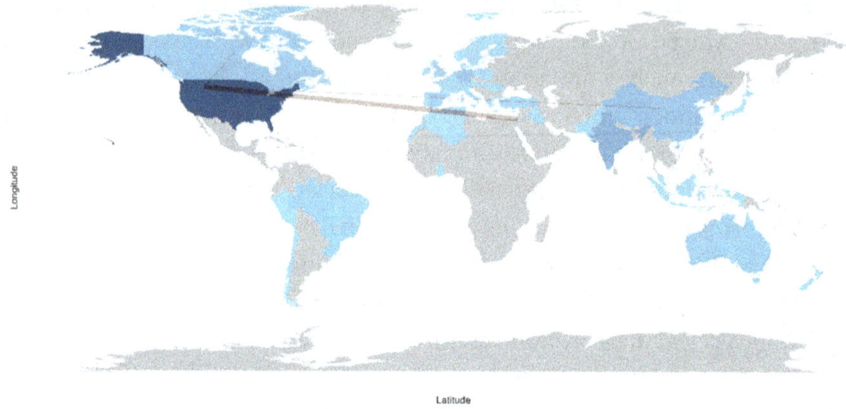

As noted in Figure 11 and Table 3, the country collaboration map and table highlight international research partnerships in predictive modeling and voter behavior. The varying intensity of the blue shading reflects each country's volume of academic output, with darker hues signifying higher research activity. The connecting lines represent global collaborations, and their thickness indicates the frequency of co-authored studies between nations. The accompanying table details the number of collaborations among country pairs, drawing attention to pivotal academic relationships.

Table 3. Country collaboration table

From	To	Frequency
USA	ISRAEL	3
HONG KONG	SINGAPORE	2
USA	CANADA	2
USA	CHINA	2
AUSTRALIA	BRAZIL	1
AUSTRALIA	INDONESIA	1
AUSTRALIA	JAPAN	1
BRAZIL	PERU	1
CANADA	ISRAEL	1
CHINA	ALGERIA	1

The United States leads the dataset in research collaborations, forging connections with Israel (3 collaborations), Canada (2 collaborations), and China (2 collaborations). This pattern indicates that U.S.-based researchers frequently partner with colleagues abroad, particularly in regions known for robust electoral research and computational methodologies. The firm link with Israel may reflect joint initiatives in computational electoral studies, AI-driven voter behavior analyses, or cross-national investigations of democratic processes.

The USA-Canada collaboration (2 occurrences) underscores the established academic ties between the two countries, particularly in computational social science and electoral research. Given that both nations host prominent institutions specializing in predictive analytics, studies focusing on voter behavior modeling frequently leverage cross-border partnerships. Likewise, the USA-China connection (2 collaborations) reflects a shared interest in ML applications for electoral studies. Despite the distinct nature of China's political system, these collaborations may focus on methodological innovations, data analysis techniques, or AI-driven modeling strategies, thereby advancing voter SA across diverse political contexts.

Beyond North America, Hong Kong and Singapore (2 collaborations) are distinct research pairs, indicating an academic link within Asia. Both regions prioritize data science and AI, suggesting that their joint efforts may center on developing computational techniques for political forecasting, notwithstanding differences in their political systems. Meanwhile, Australia is involved in multiple international collaborations, forming research connections with Brazil, Indonesia, and Japan (1 collaboration each). This pattern underscores Australia's engagement with various regions, potentially contributing to comparative studies on electoral behavior, digital campaigning, or AI integration in political analysis.

Brazil-Peru (1 collaboration) indicates a research partnership within Latin America, potentially centering on regional electoral trends or computational approaches suited to political analysis in South America. Similarly, China-Algeria (1 collaboration) suggests an emerging research relationship, possibly exploring ML applications or SA in political communication. Finally, Canada-Israel (1 collaboration) underscores Israel's participation in international predictive modeling and electoral studies, hinting at cross-disciplinary work involving political science, computational methods, and AI applications.

Ultimately, the collaboration map and table reveal a concentration of research activity in North America, Asia, and select regions in Latin America and Europe. The United States remains the central hub for international partnerships, while Australia, Canada, and China also participate in multiple collaborations. Smaller-scale collaborations across diverse regions suggest a growing internationalization of research on predictive modeling and voter behavior, with computational methodologies playing a key role in fostering cross-border academic engagement (see Figure 11 and Table 3).

Figure 12. Conceptual structure map

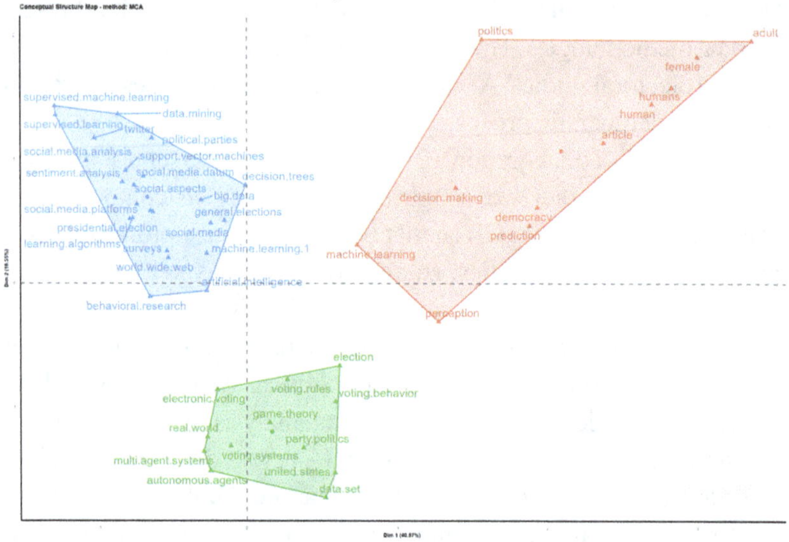

The conceptual structure map in Figure 12 produced through Multiple Correspondence Analysis (MCA) discloses three discrete thematic constellations in the scholarship on voter behavior and electoral modeling, each demarcated by a color-coded polygon: *blue, green,* and *red.* The map's spatial layout visualizes the relative proximity of concepts as inferred from their co-occurrence patterns across the literature (Aria & Cuccurullo, 2017). The two-dimensional representation highlights the primary dimensions along which these concepts are arranged, with Dim 1 (40.87%) and Dim 2 (18.55%) capturing a substantial portion of the dataset's total inertia. In MCA, inertia measures the dispersion of points in the reduced space, similar to variance in Principal Component Analysis (PCA). The proportion of inertia explained by these two dimensions indicates how much of the dataset's variability is covered in this projection. Examining the placement of terms in this space allows one to identify clusters of closely associated concepts, offering insights into dominant research themes and their interconnections (Nosios, 2025).

Occupying the upper-left quadrant, the blue cluster aggregates terminology closely aligned with machine learning techniques and social media analytics. Lexemes such as *supervised learning, support vector machines, sentiment analysis, data mining,* and references to specific platforms foreground a methodological commitment to deploying artificial-intelligence tools in the study of election-related discourse. Concomitant mentions of *general elections* and *presidential elections* underscore the applied thrust of this research strand. Moreover, the presence of *twitter, behavioral research,* and *learning algorithms* implies an ambition to model individual political behavior through digital trace data and algorithmic prediction. The cluster's notable compactness and lexical density bespeak a well-integrated research agenda centering on computational investigations of electoral communication and behavior.

By contrast, the green cluster, situated in the lower-left quadrant, embodies a formal, systems-oriented perspective on voting. Terminological anchors such as *game theory, voting rules, electronic voting, multi-agent systems,* and *autonomous agents* signal an emphasis on designing, evaluating, and simulating voting mechanisms. This constellation aligns most closely with computer science and political theory, particularly within computational social choice and voting systems engineering. Although signifiers such as *real world, United States,* and *party politics* suggest that these abstract models are often applied empirically, the overarching conceptual focus remains institutional and rule-based rather than behavioral.

Dominating the right-hand side of the map, the red cluster amalgamates concepts related to cognition, perception, and social identity, such as *decision-making, democracy, perception, human, female,* and *adult.* This thematic region reflects a human-centered, psychologically inflected approach to voter behavior. In contrast to the tool-driven or institutional emphases of the other clusters, this grouping foregrounds the internal processes and demographic structures that shape political attitudes and preferences. The adjacency of terms such as *politics, prediction,* and *machine learning* along the cluster's margin further hints at methodological cross-fertilization with the computational frameworks characteristic of the blue cluster.

Collectively, the map delineates three cardinal orientations in contemporary electoral research: (1) data-driven behavioral modeling via machine learning and social-media analytics; (2) formal, institutional modeling of voting systems and procedural rules; and (3) cognitively and demographically anchored analyses of political decision-making. Their separation along the principal dimensions not only attests to the field's conceptual diversity but also highlights fertile ground for future integration across cognitive, institutional, and computational paradigms in the study of voter behavior (see Figure 12).

Figure 13. Hierarchical Clustering dendrogram

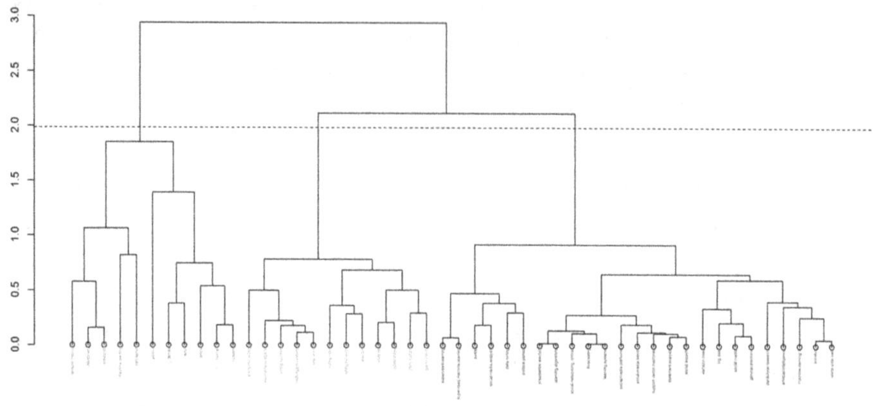

The Hierarchical Clustering (HC) dendrogram in Figure 13 offers a structured visualization of conceptual relationships within predictive modeling and voter behavior research. Mapping research themes according to their co-occurrence in scholarly literature elucidates the primary methodological and theoretical connections that shape the field. The vertical axis represents a dissimilarity measure, wherein smaller distances denote stronger associations among topics, and broader separations indicate distinct research areas. Setting the dendrogram's threshold at 2.0 (as denoted by the dashed line) yields a parsimonious partition into three principal clusters, visually coded in *blue, green,* and *red*. This arrangement furnishes a cogent taxonomy of the field's intellectual terrain, simultaneously foregrounding zones of thematic convergence and axes of differentiation. The hierarchical structure illustrates how ML techniques, SA, social media analytics, and traditional electoral theories form interconnected yet conceptually distinct clusters (Koutsoupias and Nosios, 2025A).

In the blue cluster, terms such as deliberation, ideology, social media, psychological traits, and affective polarization coalesce around a shared analytic focal point: the interplay between individual cognition, emotion, and communicative milieus. The adjacency of *moral* and *emotion* to overtly political constructs intimates an integrated paradigm in which belief systems, affective dispositions, and identity formation are examined as mutually constitutive processes within both digital and face-to-face interactions.

Conversely, the green cluster assembles a lexicon of methodological apparatus, machine learning, prediction, big data, Google Trends, and real-time forecasting, reflecting the discipline's accelerating turn toward computational modalities. The juxtaposition of *prediction* and *big data* with specific data sources underscores an outcome-driven orientation that privileges scalable, algorithmic techniques designed to optimize predictive validity and processing efficiency.

The red cluster, by contrast, foregrounds advances in granularity and temporal resolution, uniting terms such as *Twitter sentiment, neural networks, emotion analysis, swing states,* and *feature selection*. This configuration signals the ascendancy of natural-language processing and affective-computing methods in extracting subtle political signals from social media streams. Moreover, the inclusion of *swing states* and *political preference prediction* highlights the strategic application of these analytical tools in electorally pivotal contexts, where fine-grained, time-sensitive insights are indispensable.

To conclude, these three clusters delineate an interdisciplinary synthesis that spans behavioral theory, computational modeling, and linguistic analysis. The emergent architecture highlights the field's evolution toward integrated frameworks that combine individual-level cognitive and affective processes with macro-level data streams and sophisticated algorithmic inference, thereby deepening our understanding and forecasting of electoral dynamics (see Figure 13).

Table 4. Top 5 most cited papers in Cluster 1

Documents	Total Citations
Metaxas PT, 2011, Proc - IEEE Int Conf Priv, Secur, Risk Trust IEEE Int Conf Soc Comput, Passat/Socialcom	203
Kagan V, 2015, IEEE Intell Syst	69
Mavragani A, 2016, Technol Forecast Soc Change	52
Yasseri T, 2016, Epj Data Sci	29
Sun T, 2017, Proc IEEE Int Conf Data Min Icdm	26

Cluster 1 in Table 4 encompasses foundational studies on the promise and perils of harnessing digital traces to anticipate electoral behavior. Metaxas et al. (2011) with 203 total citations critically assess Twitter's utility for election forecasting by examining data from the 2008 and 2010 U.S. contests. They demonstrate that naïve reliance on metrics such as tweet volume or sentiment aggregates fails to capture authentic voter intentions, owing to demographic biases among users, susceptibility to coordinated manipulation (e.g., astroturfing), and the platform's non-representative sample of the electorate. Consequently, they caution against equating social-media chatter with popular opinion. By contrast, Kagan et al. (2015) with 69 total citations propose a more systematic and computationally rigorous framework. Employing extensive Twitter corpora from Pakistan's 2013 and India's 2014 elections, they integrate supervised sentiment classification via Support Vector Machines (SVM) with a diffusion model that quantifies exposure and contagion of political opinions. This hybrid methodology enables near-real-time forecasting of electoral results, illustrating how sophisticated machine-learning pipelines can translate online discourse into actionable predictions, provided that noise and bias are appropriately mitigated.

Extending beyond social networking platforms, Mavragani and Tsagarakis (2016) with 52 total citations explore search-engine queries as predictive indicators. Analyzing Google Trends data in the final week before Greece's 2015 referendum, they find that normalized search volumes for *NO* consistently exceeded those for *YES*, in stark contrast to opinion-poll parity. Their results suggest that aggregate search behaviors can serve as leading signals of public sentiment in time-sensitive political events. Similarly, Yasseri et al. (2016) with 29 total citations examine Wikipedia page views during the 2014 European Parliament elections. They report a positive correlation between traffic on election-related entries and national turnout rates, particularly pronounced in lower-salience contests, indicating that online information-seeking may proxy for civic engagement.

Complementing these digital-trace approaches, Sun et al. (2017) with 26 total citations reconceptualize ecological inference as a Learning with Label Proportions (LLP) problem. Their latent-variable model leverages aggregate vote counts and demographic covariates from U.S. presidential elections to infer individual-level voting patterns without requiring direct ballot data. By deploying exact inference algorithms, they demonstrate superior predictive accuracy and interpretability relative to earlier distribution-regression techniques. Their work highlights the importance of combining rigorous statistical inference with machine learning to distinguish micro-level behaviors from macro-level aggregates.

In summary, the contributions in Cluster 1 follow a clear methodological trajectory, from early, correlation-driven uses of social media volume and sentiment to more robust frameworks grounded in network diffusion, search-behavior analytics, and principled latent-variable models. At each stage, scholars grapple with enduring challenges, data representativeness, risks of overfitting, and the validity of behavioral proxies, reminding us that innovation must be tempered by methodological rigor when interpreting digital traces as reflections of democratic processes (see Table 4).

Table 5. Top 5 most cited papers in Cluster 2

Documents	Total Citations
Prelec D, 2017, Nature	200
Ghiasi MM, 2020, Comput Biol Med	155
Kristensen JB, 2017, Plos One	26
Li P, 2017, Behav Res Methods	14
Çakar T, 2023, Front Human Neurosci	1

In Table 5, Cluster 2 encompasses methodological innovations aimed at enhancing the precision and granularity of individual-level predictions across various domains, including political preferences, decision-making, and behavioral classification. Prelec et al. (2017) with 200 total citations introduce the Surprisingly Popular (SP) algorithm as an alternative to both majority voting and confidence-weighted aggregation. Rather than selecting the option endorsed by the numerical majority, the SP method identifies the response that exceeds individuals' expectations of group consensus, thereby correcting for systematic biases that lead groups to coalesce around incorrect answers. Validated empirically in tasks spanning geographical estimation, dermatological diagnosis, and art pricing, the SP algorithm consistently outperforms traditional aggregation rules, particularly in scenarios where a confidently held majority is nonetheless incorrect. This approach furnishes a theoretically grounded mechanism for surfacing minority knowledge that, although less prevalent, is demonstrably more accurate; its implications extend to political forecasting, expert elicitation, and the measurement of public opinion.

Likewise, Ghiasi and Zendehboudi (2020) with 155 total citations propose a methodological analogue within the clinical sphere by employing ensemble tree-based classifiers, specifically Random Forests and Extra Trees, to enhance diagnostic accuracy on the Wisconsin Breast Cancer Dataset. Their ensemble models not only outperform traditional classifiers on standard performance metrics but also provide interpretative transparency through feature-importance rankings, all while maintaining operational tractability. Although initially conceived for medical diagnostics, these approaches readily translate to voter-modeling contexts, where transparent and reliable classification of individual cases is paramount. Moreover, Kristensen et al. (2017) with 26 total citations interrogate the minimal data requirements for robust behavioral prediction by demonstrating that a solitary Facebook *like* suffices to infer voting behavior within a multiparty electoral system with remarkable accuracy. This finding challenges the entrenched presumption that voluminous, multifaceted datasets are indispensable for precise inference, instead underscoring the potency of parsimonious, high-signal indicators. In the sphere of political communication and microtargeting, such insights advocate for the strategic employment of focused behavioral markers when comprehensive data are unobtainable.

In addition, Li et al. (2017) with 14 total citations enhanced the methodological infrastructure for large-scale cognitive assessment by validating WebExp, a web-based experimental platform that captures individual differences in cognitive control with both high reliability and replicability. Their results confirm that online administration can yield data of commensurate validity to traditional laboratory protocols, thereby establishing a scalable foundation for political-psychology research. Integrating such cognitive metrics, encompassing executive function, decision consistency, and attentional control, into models of political behavior holds promise for enriching voter profiling with dimensions of cognitive heterogeneity that were previously inaccessible on a large scale.

Finally, Çakar and Filiz (2023) with 1 total citation pioneer the incorporation of neurophysiological measures into the modeling of political engagement through functional Near-Infrared Spectroscopy (fNIRS). By mapping prefrontal-cortex activation patterns elicited during candidate evaluation and coupling these signals with machine-learning classifiers, they demonstrate that implicit neural responses can predict electoral preferences above chance. Although in its nascent stages, this line of inquiry inaugurates a novel interdisciplinary frontier, one that probes the affective and unconscious substrates of political choice beyond the constraints of self-report instrumentation.

Overall, these contributions exemplify the convergence of cognitive science, ML, behavioral economics, and neuroscience in refining individual-level predictive models of political behavior. Through the deployment of probabilistic aggregation algorithms, ensemble classification methods, scalable web-based experiments, and neuroimaging techniques, scholars are progressively elucidating the multifaceted architecture of voter cognition and decision-making, thereby advancing both the precision and explanatory richness of political-prediction paradigms (see Table 5).

Table 6. Top 5 most cited papers in Cluster 3

Documents	Total Citations
Anjaria, 2014A, Int Conf Commun Syst Networks, Comsnets	86
Anjaria, 2014B, Soc Netw Analysis Min	57
Flaxman Sr, 2015, Proc Acm Sigkdd Int Conf Knowl Discov Data Min	25
Belcastro, 2022, Soc Netw Analysis Min	20
Rodríguez, 2018, Lect Notes Comput Sci	10

In Table 6, Cluster 3 encompasses studies that refine computational electoral forecasting by integrating SA, ML, and ecological inference with social media and demographic data. Moreover, Anjaria and Guddeti (2014A) with 86 total citations introduce a hybrid Twitter-based sentiment classification pipeline that combines rule-based heuristics with supervised learning to categorize political discourse during India's general elections systematically. Their framework leverages temporal patterns to track trending topics and event-driven spikes, transforming raw tweets into actionable, sentiment-informed forecasts. In a subsequent study of Anjaria & Guddeti, 2014B with 57 total citations, the authors further enhance accuracy by adopting fuzzy-logic weighting for feature importance, refining sentiment-scoring algorithms, and creating a domain-specific lexicon tailored to the Indian electoral vernacular. This dual focus on context-sensitive lexica and dynamic temporal modeling significantly improves polarity detection in non-Western settings.

In parallel, Flaxman et al. (2015) with 25 total citations address the ecological inference problem through a kernel-based distribution regression model. By embedding aggregate demographic and vote-share data into a reproducible kernel Hilbert space, their approach infers subgroup preferences, such as female support for Obama in 2012, without individual ballot records, achieving finer spatial granularity and tighter correspondence with known demographic distributions than traditional surveys. Complementing this, Rodríguez et al. (2018) with 10 total citations develop an ex-ante forecasting system for Chile's presidential runoff by applying ensemble classifiers to expertly annotated tweets. Their model attains an exceptionally low prediction error of 0.51 percent, demonstrating that supervised sentiment analysis, when coupled with real-time data acquisition and context-aware feature engineering, can rival, or even surpass, conventional polling accuracy.

Furthermore, Belcastro et al. (2022) with 20 total citations expand the analytical repertoire through IOM-NN, a multilayered workflow that integrates clustering-based topic detection, neural opinion mining, and nuanced emotion analysis. Applied to the 2020 U.S. presidential election, this framework not only predicted the leading candidate in ten of eleven battleground states but also illuminated distinct affective strategies: pro-Trump cohorts predominantly conveyed positive emotions (e.g., joy, confidence), whereas pro-Biden segments expressed negative affect (e.g., anger, disgust). Such findings underscore the added value of synthesizing sentiment, emotion, and behavioral signals for high-resolution electoral insights.

Ultimately, these contributions illustrate an apparent methodological convergence toward multi-source, temporally dynamic, and demographically sensitive models for electoral forecasting. By combining textual analytics, event-driven temporal modeling, ML ensembles, and ecological inference, scholars have developed scalable and transparent pipelines that overcome the limitations of traditional polling, providing granular, timely, and contextually informed insights into voter behavior (see Table 6).

Table 7. Core sources and journals

Sources and Journals	Number of Articles
Lecture Notes in Computer Science (Including Subseries Lecture Notes in Artificial Intelligence and Lecture Notes in Bioinformatics)	11
Proceedings of the International Joint Conference on Autonomous Agents and Multiagent Systems, AAMAS	4
Expert Systems with Applications	3
Political Behavior	3

continued on following page

Table 7. Continued

Sources and Journals	Number of Articles
ACM International Conference Proceeding Series	2
AI and Society	2
Annals of GIS	2
CEUR Workshop Proceedings	2
Conference on Human Factors in Computing Systems - Proceedings	2
EPJ Data Science	2

Table 7 presents the most frequently used publication sources in the literature on predictive modeling and voter behavior. The distribution illustrates the concentration of research output across a limited set of venues, which posits that a small number of journals typically account for a substantial share of publications within a given domain (Donthu et al., 2021; Aria & Cuccurullo, 2017). At the top of the list, Lecture Notes in Computer Science, including its AI and Bioinformatics subseries, features eleven articles, underscoring its centrality in disseminating computational research. This series reflects the discipline's methodological affinity for ML techniques, algorithmic modeling, and high-dimensional data analysis.

Immediately following, the Proceedings of the International Joint Conference on Autonomous Agents and Multiagent Systems (AAMAS) contributes four studies, signaling the field's embrace of agent-based simulations to capture electoral dynamics and strategic behavior within heterogeneous electorates. Its inclusion attests to the growing relevance of complex-systems frameworks and synthetic modeling methods. Similarly prominent, Expert Systems with Applications and Political Behavior each appear with three articles. The former exemplifies the integration of AI-driven decision-support systems in electoral contexts, whereas the latter grounds empirical inquiry in established theories of political science. Together, they illustrate the domain's methodological duality, striking a balance between computational sophistication and theoretical rigor.

Moreover, journals such as AI and Society, Annals of GIS, and EPJ Data Science highlight expanding thematic concerns, ranging from the ethical implications of predictive technologies to spatial analyses of electoral phenomena and the application of data-science frameworks in political behavior research. These venues reflect an increasing awareness of the normative, structural, and interpretive challenges posed by algorithmic forecasting. Lastly, conference proceedings, namely ACM International Conference Proceedings, CEUR Workshop Proceedings, and CHI Proceedings, serve as important forums for work at the intersection of user interface design, human-computer interaction, and political engagement. Their presence highlights the importance of human-centered and real-time digital analysis in the broader context of electoral modeling.

Collectively, the sources enumerated in Table 7 trace the field's intellectual lineage and demarcate its prevailing methodological frontiers. Although technical and computer-science venues dominate in volume, their coexistence with disciplinary and interdisciplinary journals reveals a research landscape that is both specialized and integrative. For scholars entering this area, these core outlets provide a structured framework for exploring its conceptual foundations and ongoing methodological evolution (see Table 7).

CONCLUSIONS

The scholarly inquiry into predictive modeling of voter behavior has evolved considerably since the early 2000s. Initially characterized by experimentation with traditional regression models, the field has progressively embraced advanced computational methodologies. Early research, predominantly anchored in *survey data* and *econometric techniques,* demonstrated limited engagement with emerging domains such as *machine learning* and *artificial intelligence*. During this nascent phase, the discipline was cautious toward novel computational approaches, as evidenced by a sparse scientific output, often registering single-digit annual publications and intermittent gaps in scholarly production. Nevertheless, the increasing ubiquity of digital information, primarily disseminated via social media platforms, precipitated a gradual shift in academic focus, facilitating the integration of computational methods into electoral studies.

Scholarly interest in this domain experienced a marked intensification around 2012, signifying a pivotal shift toward methodological innovation. Publication counts incrementally increased throughout the mid-2010s, with significant milestones achieved in 2014 and 2015, when outputs reached seven and twelve publications, respectively. This gradual ascent closely paralleled broader transformations within political science, particularly the rapid proliferation of digital data and the enhanced utilization of computational resources in electoral analysis. Researchers began to systematically employ *classification models, textual analytics,* and *sentiment analysis* to improve the accuracy of voter behavior forecasts, with validation against empirical election outcomes. Notably, the sustained growth observed post-2020, culminating in an annual peak of 25 publications in 2024, underscores the full integration of predictive modeling in voter behavior studies and signals the discipline's maturation from preliminary experimentation to widespread scholarly acceptance.

Another noteworthy observation concerns the geographical distribution of scholarly contributions, which reveals a pronounced concentration of activity in

North America, Asia, and Europe. The United States has emerged as the primary research hub, offering substantial contributions through its robust infrastructure of interdisciplinary collaboration, computational expertise, and methodological innovation. The prominence of ML and AI methodologies is particularly evident in American scholarship, which frequently integrates digital analytics with traditional theories of voter behavior. Concurrently, significant outputs from countries such as India, Spain, and Greece demonstrate the embedding of predictive modeling across diverse political contexts, with computational techniques being adapted to address unique electoral settings. Although nations such as Canada, China, and certain European countries, including Germany and Spain, recorded fewer publications, their contributions remain influential, offering novel insights into the methodological applications of predictive analytics in studies of political behavior.

The thematic analysis further underscores the evolving conceptual structure within the discipline. Terms such as *machine learning, artificial intelligence,* and *social media analytics* have emerged as dominant, interrelated research clusters, highlighting their central role in contemporary electoral studies. Terminology associated with digital engagement, such as *sentiment analysis, decision trees,* and *supervised learning,* reflects a definitive methodological shift toward data-intensive approaches capable of processing extensive digital communication streams. Despite the increasing predominance of these computational tools, traditional political science constructs, particularly those on *voting behavior, electoral systems,* and *party politics,* continue to maintain their foundational significance. Although characterized by a lower methodological density, these classical themes serve as essential anchor points for integrating computational advancements, thereby illustrating an integrative rather than a substitutive approach to adopting advanced methodologies.

Nonetheless, certain specialized areas remain peripheral, notably *adversarial machine learning* and *blockchain technology*. Identified as niche or emerging domains, these themes highlight potential avenues for future research. For instance, *adversarial machine learning,* which emphasizes enhancing the resilience of predictive models against misinformation, disinformation, and deliberate manipulation, remains underexplored despite its considerable implications for electoral integrity. Similarly, *blockchain technology* and *smart contracts,* though capable of enhancing electoral transparency and reliability, have yet to be extensively integrated into the field, presenting significant opportunities for rigorous scholarly evaluation of their applicability.

Ethical considerations associated with predictive modeling also feature prominently, particularly concerning voter privacy, algorithmic transparency, and the interpretability of increasingly sophisticated computational models. The emergence of XAI, employing methodologies such as SHAP and LIME, reflects the scholarly community's commitment to ensuring that stakeholders comprehend and trust the internal mechanisms of predictive models. However, achieving an optimal balance between transparency, interpretability, and predictive precision remains a significant challenge, underscoring an essential tension that future research must continually address.

In light of these considerations, future research should prioritize refining predictive models through AML techniques to improve resilience against misinformation and data manipulation, as well as explore the potential of blockchain frameworks to enhance electoral data security and transparency. Incorporating multimodal data sources, such as biometric indicators or real-time behavioral signals, may also improve the precision of voter modeling, particularly in dynamic or high-engagement electoral contexts. Concomitantly, bibliometric investigations should be broadened to encompass a wider array of indexing platforms and non-English–language publications, thereby yielding a more holistic and nuanced account of the discipline's evolution. Special emphasis should be placed on under-researched contexts, particularly Sub-Saharan Africa and Southeast Asia, where the interplay of political structures, technological infrastructures, and communication ecologies gives rise to unique modeling challenges. Moreover, empirical inquiry would benefit from targeted analyses of niche subdomains, such as electronic voting architectures, political microtargeting techniques, and the propagation of disinformation, areas in which predictive frameworks promise substantial practical utility and profound societal ramifications. Finally, the adoption of harmonized research protocols or the establishment of multinational collaborative networks is essential to secure methodological comparability across diverse national settings, thereby reinforcing both the generalizability and the ethical integrity of predictive electoral scholarship (Echchakoui, 2020; Gavel & Iselid, 2008).

Nonetheless, several methodological limitations warrant consideration. Firstly, the analysis was conducted exclusively using records retrieved from Elsevier's Scopus database. Although this source is extensive, it may not encompass the full spectrum of pertinent literature indexed in alternative repositories. Secondly, the study was confined to English-language publications, thereby risking the omission of valuable scholarship disseminated in other languages. Lastly, grey literature was not incorporated, such as preprints, technical reports, and non-peer-reviewed documents, which may have curtailed the ability to identify nascent or practice-oriented research that has yet to appear in formal academic outlets.

In conclusion, predictive modeling of voter behavior has evolved into a sophisticated, interdisciplinary domain that is now fully integrated into electoral studies. Future advancements should address methodological complexities, refine ethical standards, and promote greater transparency. As computational techniques advance and ethical frameworks become more robust, this field is well-positioned to further transform political science by providing powerful analytical tools essential for comprehending voter behavior and effectively supporting democratic processes.

REFERENCES

Aas, K., Jullum, M., & Løland, A. (2021). Explaining individual predictions when features are dependent: More accurate approximations to Shapley values. *Artificial Intelligence, 298*, 103502. DOI: 10.1016/j.artint.2021.103502

Anjaria, M., & Guddeti, R. M. R. (2014A). Influence factor based opinion mining of Twitter data using supervised learning. *2014 Sixth International Conference on Communication Systems and Networks (COMSNETS)*, 1–8. DOI: 10.1109/COMSNETS.2014.6734907

Anjaria, M., & Guddeti, R. M. R. (2014B). A novel sentiment analysis of social networks using supervised learning. *Social Network Analysis and Mining*, *4*(1), 181. Advance online publication. DOI: 10.1007/s13278-014-0181-9

Aria, M., & Cuccurullo, C. (2017). bibliometrix : An R-tool for comprehensive science mapping analysis. *Journal of Informetrics*, *11*(4), 959–975. DOI: 10.1016/j.joi.2017.08.007

Assoud, M., & Berbou, L. (2025). Mapping the Evolution of Brand Hate: A Comprehensive Bibliometric Analysis. *Journal of Consumer Satisfaction, Dissatisfaction & Complaining Behavior*, *38*(1), 21–58. https://www.jcsdcb.com/index.php/JCSDCB/article/view/1086

Awais, M., Hassan, S., & Ahmed, A. (2019). Leveraging big data for politics: Predicting general election of Pakistan using a novel rigged model. *Journal of Ambient Intelligence and Humanized Computing*, *12*(4), 4305–4313. DOI: 10.1007/s12652-019-01378-z

Baas, J., Schotten, M., Plume, A., Côté, G., & Karimi, R. (2020). Scopus as a curated, high-quality bibliometric data source for academic research in quantitative science studies. *Quantitative Science Studies*, *1*(1), 377–386. DOI: 10.1162/qss_a_00019

Bach, R. L., Kern, C., Amaya, A., Keusch, F., Kreuter, F., Hecht, J., & Heinemann, J. (2019). Predicting voting behavior using digital trace data. *Social Science Computer Review*, *39*(5), 862–883. DOI: 10.1177/0894439319882896

Barocas, S., Hardt, M., & Narayanan, A. (2023). *Fairness and machine learning: Limitations and Opportunities*. MIT Press.

Belcastro, L., Branda, F., Cantini, R., Marozzo, F., Talia, D., & Trunfio, P. (2022). Analyzing voter behavior on social media during the 2020 US presidential election campaign. *Social Network Analysis and Mining*, *12*(1), 83. Advance online publication. DOI: 10.1007/s13278-022-00913-9 PMID: 35873661

Bimber, B. (2014). Digital media in the Obama campaigns of 2008 and 2012: Adaptation to the personalized political communication environment. *Journal of Information Technology & Politics, 11*(2), 130–150. DOI: 10.1080/19331681.2014.895691

Bitzenis, A., & Koutsoupias, N. (2023A). Foreign Direct Investment And Sustainability: A Visualized Bibliometric Review. *South-Eastern Europe Journal of Economics, 1*, 41–52. https://doi.org/DOI: 10.17605/osf.io/pcaxg

Bitzenis, A., & Koutsoupias, N. (2023B, December). Visualizing Economics and Business in the field of Education: A Quantitative Analysis of Scholarly Literature. *Global Business & Economics Anthology. Volumes I, II*(II). Advance online publication. DOI: 10.47341/GBEA.23126

Bitzenis, A., & Koutsoupias, N. (2024). Big Data in Economics Research. In Tsounis, N., & Vlachvei, A. (Eds.), *Applied Economic Research and Trends* (pp. 1063–1072). Springer Nature Switzerland., DOI: 10.1007/978-3-031-49105-4_61

Bitzenis, A., Koutsoupias, N., & Boutsiouki, S. (2023). Business Research and Data Mining: a Bibliometric Analysis. *2023 3rd International Conference on Electrical, Computer, Communications and Mechatronics Engineering (ICECCME)*, 1–6. https://doi.org/DOI: 10.1109/ICECCME57830.2023.10252699

Bitzenis, A., Koutsoupias, N., & Nosios, M. (2025). Artificial intelligence and machine learning in production efficiency enhancement and sustainable development: A comprehensive bibliometric review. *Frontiers in Sustainability*, *5*, 1508647. Advance online publication. DOI: 10.3389/frsus.2024.1508647

Brader, T., Tucker, J. A., & Therriault, A. (2013). Cross Pressure Scores: An Individual-Level Measure of Cumulative Partisan Pressures Arising from Social Group Memberships. *Political Behavior, 36*(1), 23–51. DOI: 10.1007/s11109-013-9222-8

Brader, T., Tucker, J. A., & Therriault, A. (2013). Cross Pressure Scores: An Individual-Level Measure of Cumulative Partisan Pressures Arising from Social Group Memberships. *Political Behavior, 36*(1), 23–51. DOI: 10.1007/s11109-013-9222-8

Çakar, T., & Filiz, G. (2023). Unraveling neural pathways of political engagement: Bridging neuromarketing and political science for understanding voter behavior and political leader perception. *Frontiers in Human Neuroscience*, *17*, 1293173. Advance online publication. DOI: 10.3389/fnhum.2023.1293173 PMID: 38188505

Campbell, A., Converse, P., Miller, W., & Stokes, D. (1980). *The American voter*. University of Chicago Press.

Campbell, J. E. (2008). The American Campaign, *second edition: U.S. Presidential Campaigns and the National Vote*. Texas A&M University Press.

Chafiq, T., Azmi, R., & Mohammed, O. (2024). Blockchain-based electronic voting systems: A case study in Morocco. *International Journal of Intelligent Networks, 5*, 38–48. DOI: 10.1016/j.ijin.2024.01.004

Cobo, M., López-Herrera, A., Herrera-Viedma, E., & Herrera, F. (2011). Science mapping software tools: Review, analysis, and cooperative study among tools. *Journal of the American Society for Information Science and Technology, 62*(7), 1382–1402. DOI: 10.1002/asi.21525

Corbett-Davies, S., & Goel, S. (2018). The measure and mismeasure of fairness. *arXiv (Cornell University)*. https://doi.org//arxiv.1808.00023DOI: 10.48550

Dicle, M. F., & Dicle, B. (2017). Content Analysis: Frequency distribution of words. *The Stata Journal, 18*(2), 379–386. DOI: 10.1177/1536867X1801800205

Donthu, N., Kumar, S., Mukherjee, D., Pandey, N., & Lim, W. M. (2021). How to conduct a bibliometric analysis: An overview and guidelines. *Journal of Business Research, 133*, 285–296. DOI: 10.1016/j.jbusres.2021.04.070

Downs, A. (1957). *An Economic Theory of Democracy*. Harper.

Echchakoui, S. (2020). Why and how to merge Scopus and Web of Science during bibliometric analysis: The case of sales force literature from 1912 to 2019. *Journal of Marketing Analytics, 8*(3), 165–184. DOI: 10.1057/s41270-020-00081-9

Epstein, J. M. (2012). *Generative Social Science: Studies in Agent-Based Computational Modeling*. Princeton University Press. DOI: 10.1515/9781400842872

Fair, R. C. (1978). The effect of economic events on votes for president. *The Review of Economics and Statistics, 60*(2), 159. DOI: 10.2307/1924969

Fair, R. C. (1996). Econometrics and presidential elections. *The Journal of Economic Perspectives, 10*(3), 89–102. DOI: 10.1257/jep.10.3.89

Feng, G., Chen, K., Cai, H., & Li, Z. (2023). A hybrid method of sentiment analysis and machine learning algorithm for the U.S. presidential election forecasting. *2021 IEEE International Conference on Big Data (Big Data)*, 1495–1500. DOI: 10.1109/BigData59044.2023.10386950

Flaxman, S. R., Wang, Y., & Smola, A. J. (2015). Who Supported Obama in 2012? *KDD '15: Proceedings of the 21th ACM SIGKDD International Conference on Knowledge Discovery and Data Mining*, 289–298. DOI: 10.1145/2783258.2783300

Gavel, Y., & Iselid, L. (2008). Web of Science and Scopus: A journal title overlap study. *Online Information Review, 32*(1), 8–21. DOI: 10.1108/14684520810865958

Ghiasi, M. M., & Zendehboudi, S. (2020). Application of decision tree-based ensemble learning in the classification of breast cancer. *Computers in Biology and Medicine*, *128*, 104089. DOI: 10.1016/j.compbiomed.2020.104089 PMID: 33338982

Gill, J., & Walker, L. D. (2005). Elicited priors for Bayesian model specifications in political science research. *The Journal of Politics*, *67*(3), 841–872. DOI: 10.1111/j.1468-2508.2005.00342.x

Hare, C., & Kutsuris, M. (2022). Measuring Swing Voters with a Supervised Machine Learning Ensemble. *Political Analysis*, *31*(4), 537–553. DOI: 10.1017/pan.2022.24

Hersh, E. (2023). *Hacking the electorate: How Campaigns Perceive Voters*. Cambridge University Press.

Huberty, M. (2015). Can we vote with our tweet? On the perennial difficulty of election forecasting with social media. *International Journal of Forecasting*, *31*(3), 992–1007. DOI: 10.1016/j.ijforecast.2014.08.005

Kagan, V., Stevens, A., & Subrahmanian, V. (2015). Using Twitter sentiment to forecast the 2013 Pakistani election and the 2014 Indian election. *IEEE Intelligent Systems*, *30*(1), 2–5. DOI: 10.1109/MIS.2015.16

Kennedy, C., Blumenthal, M., Clement, S., Clinton, J. D., Durand, C., Franklin, C., McGeeney, K., Miringoff, L., Olson, K., Rivers, D., Saad, L., Witt, G. E., & Wlezien, C. (2017). An evaluation of the 2016 election polls in the United States. *Public Opinion Quarterly*, *82*(1), 1–33. DOI: 10.1093/poq/nfx047

Kollman, K., & Page, S. E. (2006). Chapter 29 Computational Methods and Models of Politics. In *Handbook of computational economics* (pp. 1433–1463). https://doi.org/DOI: 10.1016/S1574-0021(05)02029-0

Koutsoupias, N., & Nosios, M. (2025A). Hierarchical Clustering in Social Sciences and Humanities: A Review. In S. D. Anastasiadou, T. G. Chadjipadelis, Nikolaos Koutsoupias, Angelos Markos, & George Menexes (Eds.), *Modern International Developments in Data Analysis and Multivariate Statistical Analysis*. IGI Global Scientific Publishing. DOI: 10.4018/979-8-3693-9400-7.ch012

Koutsoupias, N., & Nosios, M. (2025B). *Predictive Modeling and Voter Behavior in Electoral Studies: A Systematic Bibliometric Analysis [dataset]*. DOI: 10.17605/osf.io/zrm3t

Kristensen, J. B., Albrechtsen, T., Dahl-Nielsen, E., Jensen, M., Skovrind, M., & Bornakke, T. (2017). Parsimonious data: How a single Facebook like predicts voting behavior in multiparty systems. *PLoS One*, *12*(9), e0184562. DOI: 10.1371/journal.pone.0184562 PMID: 28931023

Laver, M., & Sergenti, E. (2012). *Party competition: An Agent-Based Model*. Princeton University Press.

Lazarsfeld, P. F., Berelson, B., & Gaudet, H. (1948). *The people's choice: How the Voter Makes Up His Mind in a Presidential Campaign*. Columbia University Press.

Lewis-Beck, M. S. (1990). *Economics and elections: The Major Western Democracies*. University of Michigan Press. DOI: 10.3998/mpub.8153

Li, P., Schloss, B., & Follmer, D. J. (2017). Speaking two "Languages" in America: A semantic space analysis of how presidential candidates and their supporters represent abstract political concepts differently. *Behavior Research Methods*, *49*(5), 1668–1685. DOI: 10.3758/s13428-017-0931-5 PMID: 28718087

Lichtendahl, K. C.Jr, Grushka-Cockayne, Y., & Winkler, R. L. (2013). Is it better to average probabilities or quantiles? *Management Science*, *59*(7), 1594–1611. DOI: 10.1287/mnsc.1120.1667

Liu, R., Yao, X., Guo, C., & Wei, X. (2020). Can we forecast presidential election using Twitter Data? An integrative modelling approach. *Annals of GIS*, *27*(1), 43–56. DOI: 10.1080/19475683.2020.1829704

Macy, M. W., & Willer, R. (2002). From Factors to Actors: Computational Sociology and Agent-Based Modeling. *Annual Review of Sociology*, *28*(1), 143–166. DOI: 10.1146/annurev.soc.28.110601.141117

Marx, W., Bornmann, L., Barth, A., & Leydesdorff, L. (2013). Detecting the historical roots of research fields by reference publication year spectroscopy (RPYS). *Journal of the Association for Information Science and Technology*, *65*(4), 751–764. DOI: 10.1002/asi.23089

Mavragani, A., & Tsagarakis, K. P. (2016). YES or NO: Predicting the 2015 GReferendum results using Google Trends. *Technological Forecasting and Social Change*, *109*, 1–5. DOI: 10.1016/j.techfore.2016.04.028

Mellon, J. (2013). Internet search data and Issue Salience: The properties of Google Trends as a measure of issue salience. *Journal of Elections, Public Opinion, and Parties*, *24*(1), 45–72. DOI: 10.1080/17457289.2013.846346

Metaxas, P. T., Mustafaraj, E., & Gayo-Avello, D. (2011). How (Not) to Predict Elections. *2011 IEEE Third International Conference on Privacy, Security, Risk and Trust and 2011 IEEE Third International Conference on Social Computing*, 165–171. DOI: 10.1109/PASSAT/SocialCom.2011.98

Molnar, C. (2022). *Interpretable Machine learning: A Guide for Making Black Box Models Explainable*.

Monogan, J. E.III. (2015). Political analysis using R. In *Use R!* DOI: 10.1007/978-3-319-23446-5

Montgomery, J. M., Hollenbach, F. M., & Ward, M. D. (2015). Calibrating ensemble forecasting models with sparse data in the social sciences. *International Journal of Forecasting*, *31*(3), 930–942. DOI: 10.1016/j.ijforecast.2014.08.001

Mosteller, F. 1. (2021). *The Pre-election Polls of 1948; Report to the Committee on analysis of pre-election polls and forecasts*. Hassell Street Press.

Nickerson, D. W., & Rogers, T. (2014). Political campaigns and big data. *The Journal of Economic Perspectives*, *28*(2), 51–74. DOI: 10.1257/jep.28.2.51

Nosios, M. (2025). Sentiment and Geopolitical Analysis in Sino-American Relations. In S. D. Anastasiadou, T. G. Chadjipadelis, Nikolaos Koutsoupias, Angelos Markos, & George Menexes (Eds.), *Modern International Developments in Data Analysis and Multivariate Statistical Analysis*. IGI Global Scientific Publishing. DOI: 10.4018/979-8-3693-9400-7.ch011

Page, M. J., McKenzie, J. E., Bossuyt, P. M., Boutron, I., Hoffmann, T. C., Mulrow, C. D., Shamseer, L., Tetzlaff, J. M., Akl, E. A., Brennan, S. E., Chou, R., Glanville, J., Grimshaw, J. M., Hróbjartsson, A., Lalu, M. M., Li, T., Loder, E. W., Mayo-Wilson, E., McDonald, S., & Moher, D. (2021). The PRISMA 2020 statement: An updated guideline for reporting systematic reviews. *BMJ (Clinical Research Ed.)*, (71), n71. Advance online publication. DOI: 10.1136/bmj.n71 PMID: 33782057

Prelec, D., Seung, H. S., & McCoy, J. (2017). A solution to the single-question crowd wisdom problem. *Nature*, *541*(7638), 532–535. DOI: 10.1038/nature21054 PMID: 28128245

Ribeiro, M. T., Singh, S., & Guestrin, C. (2016). "Why Should I Trust You?" *Proceedings of the 22nd ACM SIGKDD International Conference on Knowledge Discovery and Data Mining*, 1135–1144. https://doi.org/DOI: 10.1145/2939672.2939778

Rios, M. G., Zamberlan, F., Blom, P. M., & Rankovic, N. (2025). Knowing our choices: Unveiling true voting patterns through machine learning (ML) and natural language processing (NLP) in European Parliament. *Social Network Analysis and Mining*, *15*(1), 24. Advance online publication. DOI: 10.1007/s13278-025-01452-9

Rodríguez, S., Allende-Cid, H., Palma, W., Alfaro, R., Gonzalez, C., Elortegui, C., & Santander, P. (2018). Forecasting the Chilean electoral Year: Using Twitter to predict the presidential elections of 2017. In *Lecture notes in computer science* (pp. 298–314). DOI: 10.1007/978-3-319-91485-5_23

Rothschild, D. M., & Wolfers, J. (2011). Forecasting Elections: Voter intentions versus expectations. SSRN *Electronic Journal*. DOI: 10.2139/ssrn.1884644

Silver, N. (2015). *The signal and the noise: Why So Many Predictions Fail—but Some Don't*. Penguin.

Skoric, M. M., Liu, J., & Jaidka, K. (2020). Electoral and Public Opinion Forecasts with Social Media Data: A Meta-Analysis. *Information (Basel)*, *11*(4), 187. DOI: 10.3390/info11040187

Stieglitz, S., & Dang-Xuan, L. (2013). Emotions and information diffusion in social Media—Sentiment of microblogs and sharing behavior. *Journal of Management Information Systems*, *29*(4), 217–248. DOI: 10.2753/MIS0742-1222290408

Sun, T., & Sheldon, D., & OConnor, B. (2017). A Probabilistic Approach for Learning with Label Proportions Applied to the US Presidential Election. *2021 IEEE International Conference on Data Mining (ICDM)*, 445–454. DOI: 10.1109/ICDM.2017.54

Tapsell, R. (2020). Social media and elections in Southeast Asia: The emergence of subversive, underground campaigning. *Asian Studies Review*, *45*(1), 117–134. DOI: 10.1080/10357823.2020.1841093

Thomas, S., & Tabrizi, N. (2018). Adversarial Machine Learning: A Literature review. *Lecture Notes in Computer Science*, *10934*, 324–334. DOI: 10.1007/978-3-319-96136-1_26

Yasseri, T., & Bright, J. (2016). Wikipedia traffic data and electoral prediction: Towards theoretically informed models. *EPJ Data Science*, *5*(1), 22. Advance online publication. DOI: 10.1140/epjds/s13688-016-0083-3

Chapter 6
Big Data in Electoral Studies:
Handling, Processing, and Interpreting Large Datasets to Uncover Trends in Voter Behavior

Ravikumar R. N.
https://orcid.org/0009-0009-3705-1681
Marwadi University, Rajkot, India

Aarthi S.
https://orcid.org/0009-0006-9064-2091
Marwadi University, Rajkot, India

Thiruvenkadam Thangavel
https://orcid.org/0000-0002-2332-0280
SRM University, Sikkim, India

Akbar Toyirov
Termez University of Economics and Service, Termez, Uzbekistan

ABSTRACT

Electoral behaviour research evolves through digital transformation, using big data for predictive analysis and data-driven methods. This paper explores how political science benefits from evaluating large datasets to detect voter behaviour patterns. Researchers now use voter registration, social media analytics, polls, and economic indicators, supported by data science and geographic visualization tools. The integration of natural language processing and machine learning enhances accuracy in sentiment analysis, voter forecasting, and population comparisons. The

DOI: 10.4018/979-8-3373-1037-4.ch006

chapter also discusses challenges in managing vast electoral data, including privacy risks, real-time processing issues, and data bias. Big data applications improve election forecasting, campaign strategies, and voter survey precision. This work highlights how political science aligns with AI and data science to build accurate, technology-enabled election prediction models. It offers essential tools and methods for researchers, strategists, and policymakers to analyze modern voting behaviour.

INTRODUCTION

The emergence of Big Data has revolutionized electoral studies by enabling researchers, political analysts and campaign strategists to handle, process and inform the huge versions of information to highlight deep insight into the voter behaviour. Traditional methods for studying choices are often dependent on limited samples and retrospective analysis, but Big Data offers real-time, large data age data collections from various sources such as social media platforms, voter rolls, voice data, Geographical Information System (GIS) and EVEN emotional analysis equipment (Bennett, 2015). Larger computer technologies strengthen analysts to detect patterns, correlations and new trends, which can affect the election results, including voters who vote, changed demographics and regional preferences. Machine learning algorithms and data mining techniques can share voters, predict election results and identify motivational campaign strategies (Bennett & Lyon, 2019). In addition, large data facilitates microtargeting, allowing political campaigns to provide personal messages to specific voter groups based on their behaviour, preferences and historical data. Despite its transformative ability, the use of large data in electoral studies also increases concerns about privacy, data security and moral boundaries. However, when implemented in a responsible manner, it provides a powerful purpose that democratic processes can be better understood and better strengthened (Dommett, 2019). Finally, the larger figure suggests how we study and influence the alternatives, promotes more informed and strategic political decisions and diversity of data generated in modern electoral studies.

Importance of Big Data in Modern Electoral Studies

Big Data has become the cornerstone of modern election studies, which provides unique depth and breadth in understanding the voter's behaviour and dynamics in the election. The ability to collect, save and analyze datasets on a large scale from different sources such as social media activities, voter registration database, voting results, online forums and geographical data to receive researchers and political analysts who were first unattainable. With large data, election studies can move beyond data at surface level to detect behavioural trends, and free up humility in political views, real-time feelings and regional diversity (Namayengo et al., 2023).

One of the biggest benefits is the forecast analyses, which make it possible to predict election results and model different voting scenarios with high levels of accuracy. Political expeditions, decision makers and election commissions utilize this insight to improve data informed decisions, fine-tuned campaign strategies and increase the voter's seeking out. In addition, Big Data supports democratic openness by activating open data analysis, promoting responsibility and reducing misinformation through fact-based insights (Chang et al., 2022). However, the importance of large data is spread beyond campaigns it also forms educational research, indicates election reforms and supports the initiative of civilian commitment. When elections become quickly complicated in the digital age, the role of large data in election studies is not only favourable, but is crucial to the broad and adaptable understanding of democratic processes.

Shifting from Traditional Methods to Data-Driven Approaches

The Changes in data-driven approaches from traditional election analysis methods lead to a significant change in choices, the way choices are studied and understood. Traditional techniques, such as selection-based studies, focus groups and output choices, although valuable, often suffer from boundaries including small sample size, reaction bias and delay in time. Contrary to this, data-handled methods driven by Big Data technologies, scalable and more accurate insights that reflect the dynamic and versatile nature of the modern choice (Rustenbach, 2010). Data-operated approaches integrate giant data sets from digital platforms, voter database and mobile technologies to highlight the pattern in voter preferences, the possibility of voting and problem-based support.

Using machine learning algorithms and advanced analyses, researchers and political strategy sets were voters, adapted to messages and predicted results with increased accuracy (Simon, 2019). This infection increases the agility of political campaigns, which allows rapid adaptation based on the voter's response and behavioural changes. In addition, data-driven methods encourage interdisciplinary collaboration, and combine political science with computer science, statistics and behavioural economics. This overall approach provides stronger models of rich insights and choice behaviour. As technology develops, the steps against data -driven electoral studies not only represent a methodological upgrade, but also change a paradigm in the discovery of more efficient, transparent and inclusive democratic involvement (Tomić et al., 2023).

SOURCES OF ELECTORAL BIG DATA

The electoral statistics is collected on a wide range of subsets of digital and conventional sources that offer different perspectives on the voter behaviour, preferences and campaigns. Among the most visible sources is the social media especially Twitter, Facebook and Instagram. Such platforms provide real-time information regarding public opinions, political conversations, propagating topics and interaction with political content (Balasundaram et al., 2024). Natural Language Processing (NLP) and sentiment analysis let it be possible to evaluate the mood of the voter and their reaction. Electoral rolls and voter registration databases also have some demographic information such as age, gender, location and voting history which is key to purposeful segmentation and predictive modelling. In as much as these sources are conventional, they have now been amplified with digital technology to collect the more precise and expedient responses. Bennett & Lyon (2019) also note that these sources of data are becoming more widely used not only in analysis but also in surveillance and control and it poses some crucial questions regarding the autonomy of voters.

The spatial analysis of electoral information is assisted with Geographical Information Systems (GIS) which enables mapping local voting patterns, political dynamics and inaccessibility to the infrastructural facility. Moreover, the websites provided by media, official databases on donations to the elections, and governmental sources will provide one with structured data on profiles of candidates, funds, and previous outcomes. According to Dommett (2019), this increase in the number of sources is used by campaigns to customize strategies, with a lack of apparent regulation. New data streams are making it even more extensive and complex consisting of mobile apps use, search engine requests, or voting online (Bitzer et al., 2022). Collectively, those sources form a thick, three-dimensional dataset, which powers sophisticated elections research and smart political action. The below table 1 summarizes and reinforces the discussion on various data sources like social media, voter registration, GIS, and mobile data.

Table 1. Key Sources of Electoral Big Data and Their Characteristics

Source	Data Type	Examples	Insights Provided	Ethical Considerations
Voter Registration Data	Structured	Electoral rolls, ID databases	Demographics, turnout history	Privacy, misuse of sensitive identity info
Social Media Platforms	Unstructured/Textual	Twitter, Facebook, Instagram	Sentiment, issue trends, engagement	Algorithmic bias, misinformation, profiling
GIS and Geo-Demographics	Spatial/Numeric	Location data, constituency mapping	Regional behavior, turnout distribution	Surveillance, location privacy
News & Online Media	Semi-structured	News APIs, forums, blogs	Public narratives, framing of candidates/ issues	Media bias, lack of regulation
Mobile & App Data	Unstructured/Sensor	App usage, SMS, location tracking	Real-time behavior, issue-specific interest	Consent, lack of transparency

Voter Registration Databases

The voter registration database is the basic source of selection of large data, and provides structured and official records on qualified voters within a specific jurisdiction. These databases usually include demographic details such as age, gender, ethnicity, housing address, voice history and sometimes political affiliation. This data campaign plays an important role in the design of strategies, targets outreach efforts and implement voting predictions. Analysts use voter rolls to divide voters into specific categories-first voters, swing voters or consistent voters who activate more personal and effective promotional messages to voters (Chukwuere et al., 2020).

Figure 1. Lifecycle of Voter Registration Data in Electoral Big Data Systems

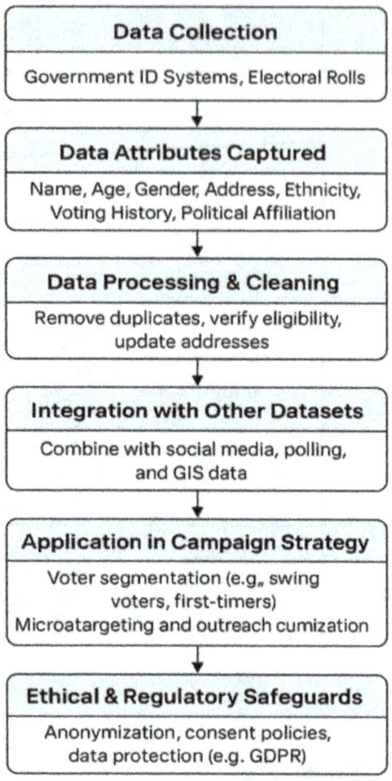

The above Fig.1 illustrates the end-to-end process of how voter registration data is collected, processed, integrated, and ethically used for campaign strategy and electoral research. It emphasizes the importance of regulatory safeguards in preserving voter privacy and democratic integrity. In addition, this database supports the effort to ensure selection integrity and identify possible problems such as duplicate registration or unqualified voters. In educational research, voter registration data is used to track long-term trends in voter commitment, migration patterns and demographic changes in voters. When combined with other data sources, Voter Registration information becomes even more powerful, which acts as a backbone for future modelling and behavioural analysis (Huber et al., 2021). However, moral handling and privacy protection are important, as abuse of such sensitive data can lead to violations of public trust. Overall, voter registrations act as an important anchor in understanding and respond to election behaviour in database data-intended studies.

Social Media Analytics

Social media platforms such as Twitter, Facebook, Instagram and TikTok have emerged as powerful sources of big data in election studies. Social media analysis includes a collection and analysis of user-related materials, including posts, likes, shares, comments and a hashtag related to political discourse. These platforms provide access to a large scale to real-time, public spirit, salt release, candidates popularity and misinformation trends. Natural language treatment (NLP), emotional analysis and network analysis units are used to extract meaningful patterns from large versions of unnecessary texts (Juned et al., 2021).

Researchers and political strategists can monitor the questions that resonate most with separate voter segments, assess the effectiveness of promotional messages and track viral content that can increase opinion. Social media also helps identify the affected and meaning leaders who shape political interactions online (Keele et al., 2021). In addition, digital footprints left by users provide insights into behavioural engagement, political polarization and foundation grass root. While social media data is rich and dynamic, they also present challenges such as bot, false accounts and algorithm which must be accounted for during the analysis. When managed properly, analyses on social media act as a real-time pulse of voters, providing action rich insights that traditional voting often remembers because of time intervals or limited scope.

Polling Data and Economic Indicators

Voice data and economic indicators are important components in the choice of large data that provide both subjective and purpose insight into the voter's behaviour. Voting data obtained from investigative and referendum surveys reveal voter preferences, releases priorities and the candidate's compatibility (Liçenji, 2023). These choices can be held at local, regional or national level, and are required to track the change in opinion over time. While traditional election representatives rely on the sample, modern polling includes the real-time analysis for fast online methods and fast and more dynamic insight.

On the other hand, economic indicators such as unemployment, inflation, GDP growth and income inequality provide relevant information that significantly affect voting behaviour. Voters often base their choice options on perceived financial welfare, and these indicators help analysts assess how economic trends are related to political spirit and election results. Integration of voice data with economic indicators enables a greater extensive understanding of the voter's motivations (Medviedev, 2025). For example, an increase in unemployment coincides with declining support for sitting. Advanced modelling techniques can connect these data sets to make predicted forecasts and identify risk qualities. Together, voice data and economic indicators enriched the analytical structure, which offers both perceptions based and fact-based lenses for electoral research and decision making. The below figure 2 illustrates how polling inputs and economic metrics are combined to reveal voter motivations and trends, ultimately supporting predictive electoral analysis and informed decision-making.

Figure 2. Use of Polling Data and Economic Indicators in Electoral Big Data

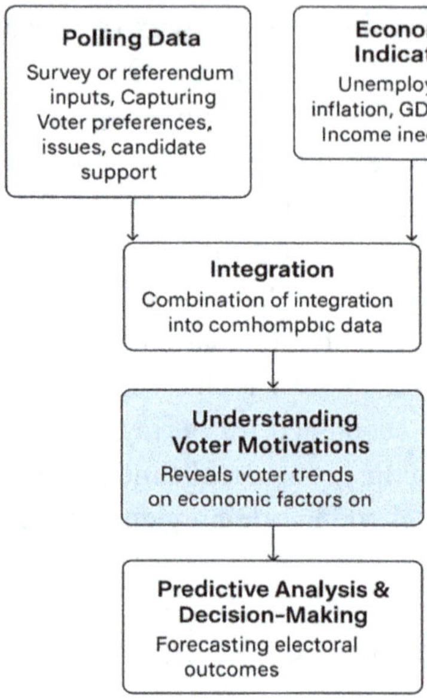

Real-Time Data Streams (e.g., News, Sentiment, Online Engagement)

Real-time data flow provides dynamic and up-to-date insight into the constant development of election behaviour. These sections include news sites, emotions, online engagement measurements and even trending keywords on search engines. Real-time data allows electoral analysts to capture immediate public response to events such as debate, scams, political announcements or crises, making the campaign invaluable for accountability and media strategy (Mondal et al., 2022). The emotional analysis equipment analyses tone and feelings behind the text in real time, it captures how voters feel about candidates, questions or development. NEWS API provides structured access to headings and articles from digital media platforms, providing a way to monitor media stories and monitor their impact on the voter's opinion.

In addition, web analysis and engagement measurements track user interactions with political content-relay, shares, comments, click-through-that reflects the level and potential effect of interest and potential effects. Such an immediate response loop allows political campaigns and media organizations to quickly adapt to opinion, increase responsibility and relevance. However, the speed and amount of real-time data can also show noise and misinformation, which can significantly make data saver and relevant understanding. When utilized effectively, real-time data streams act as an election radar-aged for new trends, controversy and engagement opportunities for the experts (Paterson & Witzleb, 2019).

Figure 3. Impact of Data Sources on Electoral Decision-Making

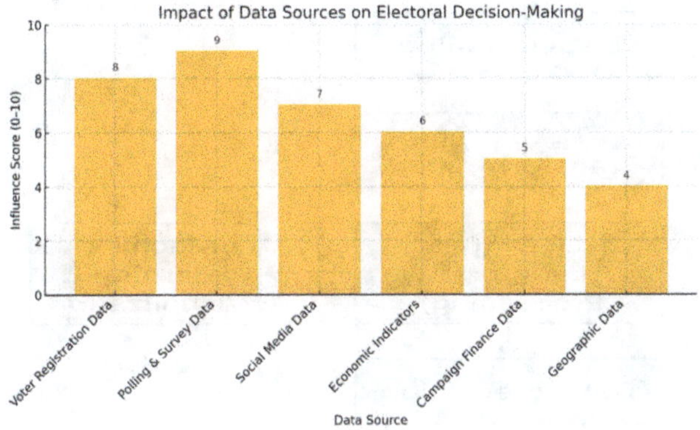

The figure 3 compares the relative influence of key data sources such as polling data, voter registration, and social media on electoral strategies and voter behavior analysis. It highlights the critical role of polling and registration data in driving data-informed political decisions.

DATA HANDLING AND PROCESSING TECHNIQUES

Effective handling and processing of large data requires advanced techniques to manage the amount, variety and speed of data. Originally, data cleaning is necessary to eliminate duplicate, deviations and errors. Data structured data from voter database and polls are formatted using ETL (Extract, Transform, Load) processes, while the data that is uncomfortable from social media and news is processed using Natural Language Processing (NLP) to extract spirit, keywords and institutions (Yost et al., 2017). Data integration combines several sources voter registers, economic indicators and innocent in integrated data sets for virtuous analysis. Cloud computing platforms such as AWS or Google Cloud are used for scalable storage and processing. Real-time frameworks, such as Apache Kafka and kick streaming, enables immediate insights from live data stream.

For analysis, machine learning algorithms and data visualization tools help expose the trends, predict the voter's behaviour and support decision-making (Alam & Pachauri, 2017). Proper computer management ensures moral use, compliance with privacy and data security throughout the process. The Figure 4 outlines the full pipeline from data cleaning and integration to real-time processing and analysis, highlighting tools like ETL, NLP, cloud platforms, and machine learning for effective electoral insight generation.

Figure 4. Data Handling and Processing Techniques in Electoral Big Data

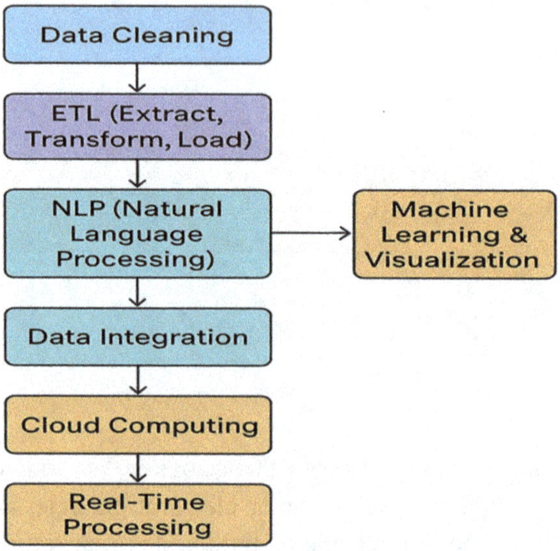

Data Cleaning and Integration

Computer cleaning and integration are important steps to prepare the choice of choice of meaningful analysis. Raw data collected from different sources for example, voter registration database, social media, examination and economic indicators often contains deviations, duplicate, lack of value and irrelevant information. Data cleaning ensures accuracy and reliability by identifying and improving these problems. Techniques such as external detection, normalization and copying to help refine the dataset for further analysis. When purified, data integration involves combining the dataset into a harmonic structure from multiple sources (Deng & Duzhin, 2022). For example, voter demographic data can be integrated with behaviour on social media or voting results to provide a rich, multidimensional approach to voters. Tools such as Data Pipelines and APIs facilitate this process, while Mapping ensures compatibility in data types. Integration enables extensive analysis by adding voter behaviour to platforms and deadlines. Proper cleaning and integration of data not only improves the quality of data, but also improves the performance of the future model and visualization. This process makes the basis for the announced choice of decisions, campaign strategy and educational research. Without these essential preparatory stages, analysis can be misleading or biased, and eventually compromise the accuracy and integrity of electoral insight (Jo & Lee, 2019).

Data Warehousing and Storage Systems

Data warehouses and storage systems play an important role in handling the enormous amounts and diversity of data generated in modern electoral studies. A data warehouse is a centralized depot that stores structured data from many sources, such as voting results, voter databases, campaign expenses and historical election results. These systems are adapted to query efficiency and analytical benefits, making researchers and analysts who can quickly and accurately restore and analyze the data (Khan & Meenai, 2021). Cloud-based storage solutions as Amazon Redshift, Google and Microsoft Azure, flexibility and cost impact of access to large data sets, including real-time data streams. These platforms support the intake of high-speed data, secure storage and parallel treatment functions required to handle large data selection. Data lakes can also be used to store raw, unnecessary data such as posts in social media or news articles, which can later be converted into analysis. Effective data storage enables future modelling to maintain historical trend analysis, voter division and continuous high-quality data sets. It also supports the role-based access control and encryption to ensure data security and privacy rules. In electoral contexts, strong storage systems ensure that important information is always available, audible and prepared for use in the design of campaigns, politics and research (Talib et al., 2016). The below Figure 5 illustrates how centralized data warehouses and cloud-based storage platforms integrate structured and unstructured electoral data. It highlights secure access, real-time processing, and support for scalable, analytics-driven election research.

Figure 5. Data Warehousing and Storage Systems in Electoral Studies

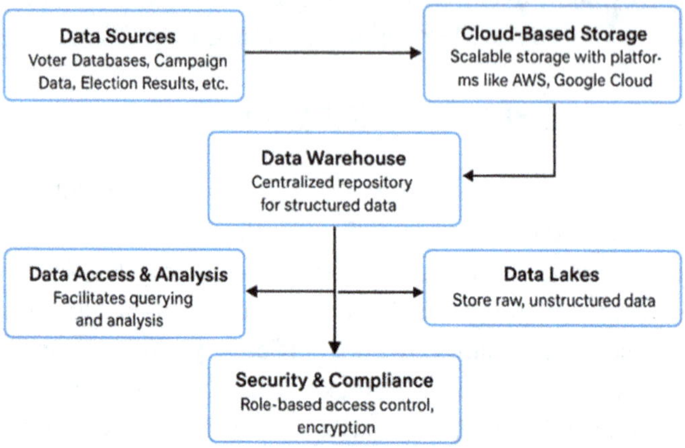

Use of Geographic Information Systems (GIS)

Geographical Information System (GIS) is powerful tools used in electoral studies to analyze and imagine spatial patterns in the voter's behaviour and political trends. GIS combines site-based data with other data sets such as demographics, voting results, socio-economic indicators and campaign activity rich, interactive maps that reveal geographical diversity in electoral mobility. For example, analysts can use GIS to identify low voter polish areas, areas with high support for specific candidates or new political changes (Yadav & Madaan, 2024). Placing more data sources on geographical coordinates helps to emphasize correlations between GIS location and voice behaviour, so that campaigns can target the Utilization more efficiently. It plays an important role in redistribution, and helps to ensure proper representation by evaluating population density and voting patterns. GIS is often used in resource allocation for campaign efforts, such as deciding where to distribute Canvassers, organize events or invest in advertising. In addition, support is provided for real-time monitoring and offers visually dashboards that track live voice updates and events in areas (Yu et al., 2024). With the increasing availability of geopolitical data, has been given indispensable in electoral analysis, through its ability to imagine complex spatial conditions in a comfortable and actionable way to increase the decision, transparency and strategy development.

Predictive Modelling and Machine Learning in Elections

Predictable modelling and machine learning have become important tools in electoral studies, so analysts can predict political priorities with electoral results, voters who vote and greater accuracy. These techniques use historical data such as the previous election results, demographic information, voting trends and real-time social media spirit-to create models that can identify patterns and provide informed predictions. Logistic regression and decision like learning algorithms, such as trees, are often used for classification functions, such as predicting whether the voter will support a specific candidate (Ali et al., 2021). Uncertain learning helps voters to cling based on shared characteristics or behaviour. The machine learning model is continuously repaired as new data is fed into the system, which allows dynamic adjustment during the campaign cycles. The future analysis also helps political strategists to target messages and optimize the distribution of resources. When combined with visualization tools and geocentric analysis, these models provide broad insight that increase campaign efficiency, the voter's involvement and democratic decisions (Kausar et al., 2023). The below fig.6 illustrates how AI, NLP, and statistical models collectively enable voter behavior prediction, sentiment analysis, and forecasting of turnout and vote share to enhance campaign strategy and electoral analysis.

Figure 6. Predictive Modelling and Machine Learning in Elections

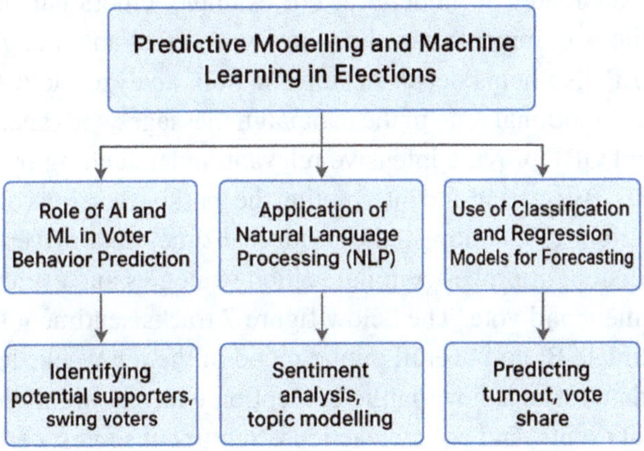

Role of AI and ML in Voter Behaviour Prediction

Artificial Intelligence (AI) and Machine Learning (ML) voters play a transformative role in predicting voter behaviour by analyzing huge datasets from different sources, including history, demographics, economic indicators and social media activity. These technologies highlight complex patterns and relationships that can ignore traditional statistical methods. By learning from historical trends, ML algorithm can classify voters in practical segments such as potential supporters, swing voters or non-voters (Singh et al., 2022).

The campaign uses this insight, which improves commitment and conversion frequency, which improves engagement and conversion frequency. AI also helps make dynamic decisions under electoral cycles, using strategies based on real-time developed data. In addition, AI-controlled tools can identify microscopic opinions, which may allow frequent reactions to practice. With moral implementation and prejudice, AI and ML provide powerful solutions to understand and predict the voter's behaviour, eventually increase the election strategies and strengthen democratic processes.

Application of Natural Language Processing (NLP)

NLP, a sub-region of AI, is important for analyzing unnecessary text data in election studies. This allows researchers and political analysts to gain meaningful insights from speeches, debate, news articles, political ads and social media content. NLP technology such as sex analysis, keyword extraction, subject modelling and nominated unit recognition helps identify voter spirit against referendum, new questions and candidates or guidelines. For example, emotional analysis used on tweets or Facebook comments can show how voters feel about any political event or decision. NLP also helps detect misinformation, analyze the discourse pattern and evaluate the emotional tone in the campaign messages. Advanced NLP models such as Bert and GPT provide intensive relevant understanding by enabling more accurate analysis. By treating and interpreting the massive versions of language data, NLP gives the right to election studies with real-time, data-driven stories, which informs the decision, improves communication strategies and eventually affect the voter's involvement and vote. The below figure 7 tracks sentiment scores for Candidate A, Candidate B, and overall public mood in the ten weeks leading up to an election. The data reflects how public perception evolves, highlighting campaign impact, external events, and policy reactions. Sentiment scores were derived using NLP techniques on social media platforms. Such analysis enables campaign teams to adapt messaging and engagement strategies based on real-time public opinion.

Figure 7. Voter Sentiment Trends Over Time Based on Social Media Analysis

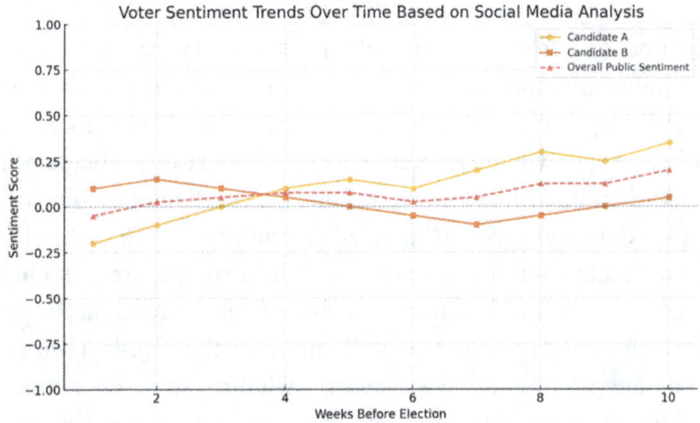

Visualizing Voter Sentiment Using NLP

NLP provides a potent means of deriving the general mood of the population by examining large quantities of the unstructured text in the form of text on social media, political speeches, and debate records, and news articles. Sentiment analysis is probably the most insightful use of NLP in electoral studies since this measure of positive-negative or neutral tone of the text is available in numerical data. Monitoring the sentiments over the time allows researchers and political strategists to see how the opinion of the people is changing based on the turn of events during campaigns, policy stated, scandals, or even the stories ridden on by the media. The presentation of these sentiment trends in form of line graph would help the stakeholder make out patterns that would have been hidden in raw results. With weekly sentiment scores it is possible to plot a graph indicating how voter perception of particular candidates or parties may vary week to week and how political mood may vary overall. This makes the decision-making process involving campaign modifications, the techniques of voter interaction, and the time to communicate these messages to be more knowledgeable. Figure above contains the sentiment trend of two candidates over a period of ten weeks before a given election and the general public sentiment. These visual tools increase the level of transparency and create a dynamic situation on how electorate is behaving and shows how in-time data can shape strategic actions in the dynamic political world.

Use of Classification and Regression Models for Forecasting

Classification and regression models are basic machine learning techniques used in electoral results and prognosis for voter behaviour. Classification model for example, logistic regression, supporting Vector machines and random forest predict classic results, such as whether voters want to support or participate in a choice. These models are trained on label data sets that include demographic, behaviour and historical voice data and predict the voter's intentions. On the other hand, regression models estimate continuous results, such as a voting rate or voting share in a district can get a candidate. Techniques such as linear regression, Ridge regression and gradient-enhancing region are usually used for these tasks (Biu et al., 2024). These models integrate multiple variables, including socio-economic indicators, previous election results and real-time beaches. By refining input and setting model parameters, these future scanning tools provide valuable foresight for campaigns and decision makers. They support strategic planning, resource allocation and target voter sighting to improve electoral efficiency and influence.

Visualization and Interpretation of Electoral Data

Visualization is an important component of electoral studies, and converts the complex dataset into clear, actionable insight. By using diagrams, graphs, maps and dashboards, analysts can explain emotional trends with voice patterns, demographic distribution, promotional performance and more clarity (Tobias et al., 2024). Tools such as Tableau, Power BI, D 3.JS and GIS platforms allow dynamic, interactive visualization that supports real-time decision-making during the election cycles. Voters can show voting from the Heatmap region, while the line and line graphs over time highlight the change in support. By using GIS, geosciences visualizations can uncover voice behaviour, which can enable subtle targeted campaign strategies. The results of emotional analysis from social media and news sources are often displayed using word clouds or polarity graphs to express the opinion trends. This visual equipment helps stakeholders, including political parties, researchers and publicly-controlled stories to influence, identify deviations and validate predictions. Gradually, the visualization connections the difference between raw election data and strategic decision-making, transparency and informed partnership builds (George et al., 2014).

Data Dashboards and Geographic Visualizations

Data dashboards and geographical visualization are powerful tools in electoral analysis, which enables surveillance of real-time and comfortable understanding of complex data sets. Dashboards integrate data from many sources voter registration, voting results, emotional analysis and trends on social media in a simple, interactive interface. They provide stakeholders in real-time insights in voter behaviour, promotional performance and polish prices, produced using devices such as platforms, tablets, power bis or Google Data Studios (Gils et al., 2020).

Geographic visualizations, often operated by GIS, let analysts be locally mapped election data. Heatmaps, Choropleth maps and district level deliberation revealed voting trends, regional support inequalities and demographic groups. These visual tools help to identify political strongholds, swing areas or areas with little commitment, and help strategic targeting. Together, dashboards and maps convert raw selection data into available, interactive formats. They support decisions, increase status consciousness and provide campaigns and decision makers to work quickly and efficiently during the election cycles (Visvizi et al., 2021).

Storytelling Through Data for Political Analysis

Storytelling through data plays an important role in political analysis, and converts raw numbers into compelling stories that resonate with different audiences. In electoral studies, the data narrative adds data visualization, reference and interpretation to explain voting, public spirit and mobility in the campaign. Candidates to compare demographic engagement can highlight "why" behind the data, using the line map to track popularity (Barthel & Seidl, 2017). This approach helps political strategists, journalists and researchers go beyond the static report for dynamic insights. For example, a story can tell how the economic decline in some areas affected the voter's vote or how the spirit of social media was correlated with changes in the vote. Tools such as infographic, interactive timeline and other maps make these stories available and attractive. Ultimately, the history analysis with the data gap between analytical stiffness and emotional involvement, and ensures that insight is not only accurate, but also meaningful. This gives stakeholders the right to make informed decisions and better understand the electoral scenario (Cao et al., 2023).

Communicating Findings to Stakeholders and the Public

Effective communication of findings of election data is necessary for transparency, trust and informed decision-making. Stakeholders about clear, short presentations of data to understand major trends and implications including political parties, media, election commissions and public. This requires translating complex analysis into available formats without losing analytical depth. Communication methods include infographics, executive summaries, visual dashboards, and public reports that distil large datasets into digestible insights. Media briefings and presentations often use key visual aids to highlight turnout patterns, voter sentiment, or shifts in support. For policymakers, detailed briefings backed by data enable evidence-based decisions on electoral reforms or resource allocation (Feng & Kirkley, 2020). Equally important is the public-facing narrative ensuring that citizens can understand election outcomes, trends, and the data behind them. This builds public trust and combats misinformation. Clear communication reinforces the credibility of the electoral process, fosters civic engagement, and empowers all stakeholders to participate meaningfully in democratic discourse. The below fig.8 presents key approaches data dashboards, geographic mapping, storytelling, and stakeholder communication that transform raw electoral data into actionable insights. It highlights how visual tools foster clarity, transparency, and informed democratic participation.

Figure 8. Visualization and Interpretation of Electoral Data

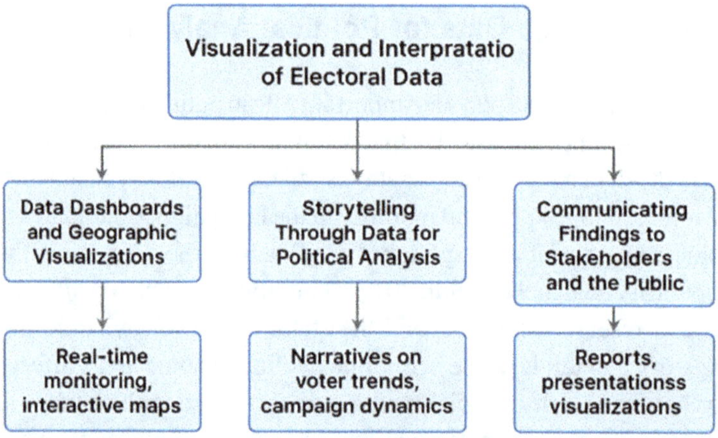

ETHICAL, PRIVACY, AND BIAS CHALLENGES

Integration of large data and AI in election studies increases concerns related to significant morality, privacy and prejudice. Collection and analysis of large versions of personal information such as voter registration, online behaviour and activity on social media can violate individuals if they are not responsible if they are not responsible (Hillersdal et al., 2020). Data violations or unauthorized use of voter information can destroy public belief in the electoral process. When using individual or practical data, openness and informed consent are necessary. Analysts and political strategists should ensure that computerized decisions do not manipulate voters or improperly affect. In addition, algorithm bias can give rise to oblique predictions or incorrect Bayani, especially when training data reflects historical inequalities or reduces some groups. To solve these challenges, strict data regime, algorithm audit and moral guidelines are important. Ensuring justice, responsibility and openness in electoral data practices helps save democratic values and promote confidence in the use of technology in the election.

Data Privacy and Voter Anonymity Concerns

Data Privacy and Election Studies for the voter's oblivion have key concerns, especially with the increase of large data analyses and digital expeditions. Voter databases often include sensitive personal information such as addresses, demographic details and voice history. When social media is combined with activity and behavioural data, it creates a detailed voter profile, which can cause privacy violations if it is wrong. Maintaining the voter's oblivion is necessary to maintain democratic integrity and protect personal rights (Igbinenikaro et al., 2024). However, the aggregation of several data points may unconsciously recognize individuals, present moral and legal risks. Data violations or unauthorized access can further compromise public trust. In order to remove these concerns, selection data must be collected, collected and processed in accordance with privacy rules such as GDPR or national data protection Act. Techniques such as data approach, encryption and consent-based data use are important. The responsible data regime ensures that privacy is preserved, while data-driven insights are gained morally (König & Waldvogel, 2021).

Addressing Representativeness and Algorithmic Bias

Algorithm bias and lack of computer representation are major challenges in election studies. Predictive models and analyses are often dependent on historical data, which can reflect existing social inequalities or exclude underrated groups. It can lead to biased forecasts, strengthen stereotypes or ignore large voter segments, especially marginalized societies (Larivière et al., 2015). For example, social media data often used in emotional analysis can represent low, young, urban population, ignore rural or less digitally active demographics. If the model is trained on such a diagonal data set, the results cannot reflect the true electoral scenario, resulting in misleading strategies or political decisions. In order to reduce these problems, it is important to ensure that data sets are different, inclusive and regularly updated. Techniques such as algorithm revision, justice testing and use of synthetic data can help counteract bias. Including interdisciplinary teams including moralists and social scientists can also increase the strength of the model. Finally, it ensures prejudice more fair, accurate and reliable election analysis (Wan, 2023).

Regulatory and Ethical Considerations in Political Data Usage

The use of data in electoral processes is subject to increasing survey, which increases the need for a strong regulatory and moral framework. Political expeditions are rapidly dependent on computerized equipment for microtargeted voters, who raise questions of consent, openness and manipulation. When voter data is used without knowledge of individuals, or when profile techniques affect the behaviour in an undesirable way, moral concerns arise. General Data Protection Regulation (GDPR) and various national electoral laws that rules in Europe determine limits on the collection, processing and storage of voter data. These include informed consent, minimization of data and the right to forget (Xu et al., 2021). Ethical standards, such as transparency in decision making processes and justice in data use, complement the legal structure. Political stakeholders should follow both legal and moral practice, and ensure that the use of data improves democratic participation instead of reducing it. In order to preserve the integrity of democratic choices in the digital age, it is important to create faith through compliance and moral behaviour. The below table 2 synthesizes major ethical and regulatory concerns discussed in narrative form offering a quick reference for key challenges, examples, and recommended safeguards.

Table 2. Ethical and Regulatory Dimensions in Big Data Elections

Issue	Description	Real-World Example	Proposed Safeguards
Voter Manipulation	Using data to exploit psychological vulnerabilities	Cambridge Analytica, UK/USA	Transparency in ad targeting, algorithm auditing
Data Privacy & Consent	Use of personal data without informed user approval	Facebook data harvesting	GDPR compliance, opt-in consent frameworks
Algorithmic Bias	Discriminatory outputs from biased training datasets	Underrepresentation in AI models	Diverse datasets, fairness testing
Misinformation Amplification	Algorithms spreading false content rapidly	Brazil WhatsApp campaigns	Fact-checking, moderation on encrypted platforms
Lack of Regulation	Insufficient oversight of data practices in campaigns	Global variance in data laws	International guidelines, electoral tech ethics

VOTER MANIPULATION AND MISINFORMATION: CASE STUDIES AND RISKS

Probably the most discussed mechanism of Big Data use during the election processes is the possibility to manipulate voters and broadcast false data. The actual event such as 2016 presidential election in the United States, or Brexit campaign, demonstrate the process of psychological profiling and related ad targeting to alter voter behaviour. The personal data in the case of Cambridge Analytica helped in creating emotional, deceptive text messages that were suited according to the recipients, to influence opinions. This is referred to as microtargeting and it is able to shrink the content of public discourse and divide the voters politically. The aspect of transparency and fairness will fail since voters will not know that they are getting different messages than others. Misinformation can also be magnified by algorithmic systems and this can be done through lack of control. Even the most important of democratic norms will be severely threatened when such tools are applied without any form of accountability. According to the studies of Gils and colleagues (2020) and Simon (2019), oral safeguards should be developed through effective regulation, transparent process of algorithms, and media literacy. It is vital to create a positive attitude toward Big Data among the population and make sure that they can trust the use of this concept and help reinforce democracy instead of undermining it.

Real-World Applications and Case Studies

Electoral politics all over the globe have undergone a lot of change due to Big Data analytics. Both the Obama 2012 and Trump 2016 campaigns in the United States applied social media analysis and voter data, as well as microtargeting methods to the tuning of messages and voter projection. The case of Trump campaign using Cambridge Analytica is to be remembered. The company obtained the information of millions of Facebook users without their permission, basing its actions on psychological profiling and personal messaging to get people vote one way or the other (Dharta et al., 2024). This gave rise to the population fearing privacy infringement and manipulation, which prompted society to argue that more data policies should be in place (e.g. GDPR in EU and the new data legislation in the U.S.).

During the 2019 general elections in India, the Bharatiya Janata Party (BJP) used AI and sentiment analysis tools to develop both region-specific campaign messages, and also to focus its outreach efforts. Political parties analyzed the huge masses of voter data to optimise the timing and content of their campaign which helped to optimise voter mobilisation. In Kenya, the story is that predictive analytics became massive in the 2017 elections with the aim of decoding how people vote across the region as well as how ethnic and demographic diversity can be tackled. Monitors of social media and the mobile data were used to analyze the mood of the population and at an early stage indicated possible manifestations of unrest or information falsification. The same is true of the 2018 elections in Brazil, where open regulation issues were created through massive uses of WhatsApp and data analytics to send political messages. The stream of real-time data and mining of student opinion in Indonesia contributed to the formation of presidential and regional elections as well, thus providing the lessons on the digital reinvention of the elections in Southeast Asia. These practical applications demonstrate how Big Data-based tools may become effective (and even incriminating) in carving the process of voting, campaigns, and democracy as a whole. They emphasize the fact that the balanced approach between innovation, transparency, and regulation is necessary.

Global Examples of Big Data in Electoral Campaigns

All over the world, Big Data has revolutionized how the plan for election campaigns and carried out. In the United States, Barack Obama's election campaign in 2012 was a pioneer, which utilized a large-scale voter database and behavioural analysis to adapt messages and adapt seeking. Donald Trump's 2016 campaign caused Cambridge Analytica's psychographic profiles about it, targeted non-binding voters through social media platforms (Elyta et al., 2023). In India, Bharatiya used Janata Party (BJP) data analysis and AI in the 2019 parliamentary elections to fragment voters and optimize regional stories. The UK's Brexit people also demonstrated the use of social media data to influence opinion through microtargeting. These global examples outline the growing trend of computer-driven campaign, where political strategies are quickly informed by real-time data and future insights. Although they are very effective, this practice also increases moral and regulatory concerns, which inspires discussion about the impact of technology on openness, consent and democracy.

Success Stories in Predictive Election Forecasting

The future analysis has proven to be a powerful tool for making an accurate prognosis for election results. By combining historical data, demographic information, voice development and real-time emotional analysis, political analysts and computer scientists can create models that predict electoral behaviour (González, 2017). For example, Nate Silver's FiveThirtyEight has gained prominence for using statistical models to predict U.S. presidential and congressional outcomes with remarkable accuracy. In India, computer companies such as Grameen and Fractal Analytics have used advanced models to predict election results based on the data and social media the spirit of the Constitution. In Kenya, large computer tools were used to predict regional electoral patterns and voting during the 2017 elections. These successes highlight the ability of machine learning and regression models to detect subtle voter trends and swing behaviour (Gruschka et al., 2018). Accurate forecasts AIDS campaign strategies, resource allocation and media coverage. However, it is important to maintain the future reliability of including openness in function and diverse, fair data.

Role in Targeted Political Advertising and Voter Outreach

Under Big Data, political campaigns will be able to engage in perception driven advertising by instituting elaborate voter profiles in demographics, browsing histories, social media activity, and even their historical voting patterns. As an example, the Trump 2016 campaign used microtargeting of Facebook ads on the basis of the psychographic characteristics of the users, which tried to appeal to the heart and to certain issues (Hegazy, 2019). Such a form of outreach, though successful, was seen as a manipulative and a non-consensual approach. Likewise, the political parties of India had been using tools of social listening and analysis of WhatsApp groups and creating highly specific pieces of content. Viral misinformation in Brazil in front of and during elections generated worldwide debates concerning the platform accountability necessity. These case studies re-assert that as much as Big Data makes the outreach more effective, its application should be made visible and in line with the ethical standards so as to protect the democratic confidences. The table 3 provides a clear comparative overview of the countries and techniques discussed in the narrative. It will help readers quickly understand cross-national differences and similarities.

Table 3. Comparative Case Studies of Big Data Use in Elections

Country	Election Year	Techniques Used	Impact	Challenges Raised
USA	2016	Psychographic profiling (Cambridge Analytica)	Voter targeting, message tailoring	Data misuse, privacy breaches
India	2019	AI-based sentiment analysis, geo-targeting	Region-specific outreach, high engagement	Disinformation, consent concerns
Kenya	2017	Predictive modelling, mobile data usage	Improved turnout prediction	Infrastructure bias, data integrity
Brazil	2018	WhatsApp-based campaign analytics	Viral message spread, voter mobilization	Misinformation on closed platforms
Indonesia	2019	Real-time polling & online opinion mining	Agile campaign response	Low regulation, digital divide

Implications for Political Science and Interdisciplinary Collaboration

Integration of large data into election studies reshaped the political science scenario, which offers new functions to analyze the voter's behaviour, election results and opinion. It pursues the field beyond traditional qualitative and research-based approaches, and introduces calculation methods, machine learning and real-time analysis. This development requires interdisciplinary collaboration between political scientists, computer researchers, sociologists, statistics and communication experts. Such cooperation improves the depth and accuracy of choice insight, enabling stronger modelling, better understanding of complex social behaviour and innovative policy analysis (Ma-Kellams et al., 2017). For example, with political theory is allowed to geographical voice pattern analysis by combining units, while NLP can highlight the trends of emotion in the public discourse. In addition, interdisciplinary research promotes moral ideas, ensuring that technological advances respect democratic principles. As the area develops, political science should continue to be relevant to remain relevant and to meet the challenges and opportunities presented by the data-in-like governance.

Integrating Data Science with Political Research

Integration of computer science with political research has revolutionized how scholars and doctors understand and link to political behaviour. Traditional political science study, historical analysis and case study depends a lot. Today, computer science machines introduce powerful units such as learning, pre-modelling and data visualization, which provide more fine and dynamic views on voter preferences, voice trends and public feelings (Román et al., 2020). This integration allows political researchers to analyze large datasets from sources such as social media, voters and electoral registration in real time. It also supports the development of sophisticated prognosis models and emotional analysis tools that can estimate a change in political meaning or behaviour. In addition, calculation technology helps identify hidden patterns, correlations and deviations in election data that can miss traditional methods (Olorunfemi et al., 2024). In order to maximize capacity, political research must continue to be beneficial for technological progress, and ensure that moral standards, methodological openness and important theory have been central to computer driven political investigation.

Opportunities for Collaboration Between Political Scientists, AI Experts, and Pollsters

Increasing complexity of election data and scales creates important opportunities for collaboration between political scientists, AI experts and pollutants. State scientists understand domain knowledge, institutional references, voters' psychology and political implications. AI experts contribute to machine learning models, NLP and data mining techniques to process and interpret giant and unnecessary data (Theodorakopoulos et al., 2024). Meanwhile, environmental toxins provide expertise in tests, examination designs and measurements of opinion. Together, these subjects can develop more accurate voter behaviour models, identify new trends and refine political message strategies (Coleman et al., 2021). For example, AI can analyze millions of tweets or interactions online, while polluting representatives recognize conclusions through surveys, and state scientists refer to results in historical or ideological disposition. Such an interdisciplinary collaboration not only improves accuracy and depth in the election analysis, but also ensures that insight is morally useful and practically useful (Zaki et al., 2023). This fusion campaign strengthens decision makers and researchers to make data-driven decisions informed in the political scenario that has been quickly developed.

CONCLUSION

Integration of large data into electoral studies does research, interpretation and prediction of political behaviour. Since the election campaign and public involvement are quickly digitally, the availability of large data provides outstanding insight into the voter's behaviour. This chapter has discovered the entire ecosystem around large data in electoral studies from data collection and processing to future modelling, visualization and moral ideas. Overall, these elements suggest how modern technology enables more fine, accurate and real time understanding of election mobility. Big data role is outside collecting just large datasets. Through sophisticated techniques such as natural language treatment, machine learning algorithms and Geographical Information Systems (GIS), researchers can decode the complications of voter spirit and demographic variations. This equipment allows political strategists, researchers and political decision makers to make informed decisions, design targeted outreach programs and improve the accuracy of the election forecast. In addition, the use of data mass and visualization tools brings clarity to complicate the data pattern, facilitates storytelling and communication that resonates with both experts and the general public.

There is a future modelling in the heart of this change. By taking advantage of AI and machine learning, electoral studies have moved from reactive interpretations to active prognosis. These models are able to analyze variables with time, geography and emotions, providing rich insights into voters VIPP, swing behaviour and potential election results. It is important that these models enjoy interdisciplinary cooperation where political scientific references and principles provide, AI experts contribute to the accuracy of the algorithmic, and ensure representation and verification of contaminants. Despite the benefits, the use of large data in electoral studies is not without challenges. Ethical issues such as data foresight, the voter's oblivion and consent should be prioritized. The ability of algorithm bias and unprovoked data sources induces a significant risk of democratic justice and integrity. In addition, data processing in real-time can introduce logistics complications and require adequate infrastructure investment. For example, the future of selection of Big Data analysis should not only include technological advances, but also the outline of strict regime that protects personal rights and ensures openness.

The real worlds discussed in this chapter confirmed the practical use of big data in politics. Case studies from the United States, India and the United Kingdom show how future analysis and data-driven strategies can affect election results, campaign efficiency and voter commitment. These examples reveal a global trend where data is central to modern political decisions and civilian interactions. How to redefine the future of electoral analysis, to understand the voter's behaviour with the future modelling, how to enhance political science, computer science and AI. For researchers, strategists and decision makers, the message is clear: using computer-operated function is no longer optional it is necessary. As we continue to refine technologies and outline that support election data analysis, the goal should promote more transparent, inclusive and responsible democratic process. Ultimately, Big Data is not just a device, but a transformative force that has the ability to elaborate on our understanding of the voter's behaviour and increase the practice of democratic governance worldwide.

REFERENCES

Alam, F., & Pachauri, S. (2017). Fme enabled etl processes for spatial and attribute data analysis. *International Journal of Computer Applications*, *169*(5), 31–35. DOI: 10.5120/ijca2017914754

Ali, H., Farman, H., Yar, H., Khan, Z., Habib, S., & Ammar, A. (2021). Deep learning-based election results prediction using twitter activity. *Soft Computing*, *26*(16), 7535–7543. DOI: 10.1007/s00500-021-06569-5

Balasundaram, A., Nair, S., Babu, D., & Gopinath, P. (2024). Social media use and impact on voters and candidates in kerala. *Journal of Creative Communications*. Advance online publication. DOI: 10.1177/09732586231223841

Barthel, R., & Seidl, R. (2017). Interdisciplinary collaboration between natural and social sciences – status and trends exemplified in groundwater research. *PLoS One*, *12*(1), e0170754. DOI: 10.1371/journal.pone.0170754

Bennett, C. (2015). Trends in voter surveillance in western societies: Privacy intrusions and democratic implications. *Surveillance & Society*, *13*(3/4), 370–384. DOI: 10.24908/ss.v13i3/4.5373

Bennett, C., & Lyon, D. (2019). Data-driven elections: Implications and challenges for democratic societies. *Internet Policy Review*, *8*(4). Advance online publication. DOI: 10.14763/2019.4.1433

Bitzer, J., Cooper, C., Manzo, W., & Roberts, S. (2022). Growing and distinct: The unaffiliated voter as unmoored voter. *Social Science Quarterly*, *103*(7), 1587–1601. DOI: 10.1111/ssqu.13225

Biu, P., Oliha, J., & Chimezie, O. (2024). Leveraging gis for enhanced community engagement in elections: A review of practices, impact, and civic responsibility. *Engineering Science & Technology Journal*, *5*(2), 471–482. DOI: 10.51594/estj.v5i2.825

. Cao, Z., Zhang, L., & Huang, Y. (2023). How researchers collaborate across disciplines? patterns of interdisciplinary collaboration based on a dual-perspective framework.. https://doi.org/DOI: 10.55835/644274f66972d54225e8e5f9

. V. Chang, R. Eniola, B. Liu, & M. Arami, "An ethical framework for big data and smart healthcare",, 2022. https://doi.org/DOI: 10.5220/0011030900003206

Chukwuere, J., Onyebukwa, C., & Mbukanma, I. (2020). The role of social media platforms in revolutionising the orthodox african electoral process and outcomes. *Journal of African Films & Diaspora Studies*, *3*(2), 7–23. DOI: 10.31920/2516-2713/2020/3n2a1

. M. Coleman, S. Higinbotham, & A. Arroyo, "Potential for concordance between plurality and instant-runoff election algorithms as a function of ballot dispersion",, 2021. https://doi.org/DOI: 10.22186/jyi.39.3.32-37

Deng, R., & Duzhin, F. (2022). Topological data analysis helps to improve accuracy of deep learning models for fake news detection trained on very small training sets. *Big Data and Cognitive Computing*, *6*(3), 74. DOI: 10.3390/bdcc6030074

Dharta, F., Purwosusanto, H., Yodiansyah, H., Setiawati, R., & Aprilinda, A. (2024). Use of big data in political communication analysis: Forming a targeting and electorate segmentation strategy. *Journal International Dakwah and Communication*, *4*(1), 102–122. DOI: 10.55849/jidc.v4i1.637

Dommett, K. (2019). Data-driven political campaigns in practice: Understanding and regulating diverse data-driven campaigns. *Internet Policy Review*, *8*(4). Advance online publication. DOI: 10.14763/2019.4.1432

Elyta, E., Olifiani, L., Afhiani, S., & Usmulyadi, S. (2023). Utilization of big data on election politics indonesia in industry 4.0. [Jurnal Wacana Politik]. *JWP*, *8*(2), 138. DOI: 10.24198/jwp.v8i2.45492

Feng, S., & Kirkley, A. (2020). Mixing patterns in interdisciplinary co-authorship networks at multiple scales. *Scientific Reports*, *10*(1). Advance online publication. DOI: 10.1038/s41598-020-64351-3

George, G., Haas, M., & Pentland, A. (2014). Big data and management. *Academy of Management Journal*, *57*(2), 321–326. DOI: 10.5465/amj.2014.4002

Gils, F., Müller, W., & Prüfer, J. (2020). Big data and democracy. SSRN Electronic Journal. https://doi.org/DOI: 10.2139/ssrn.3556512

González, R. (2017). Hacking the citizenry?: Personality profiling, 'big data' and the election of donald trump. *Anthropology Today*, *33*(3), 9–12. DOI: 10.1111/1467-8322.12348

. Gruschka, N., Mavroeidis, V., Vishi, K., & Jensen, M. (2018). Privacy issues and data protection in big data: a case study analysis under gdpr., 5027-5033. https://doi.org/DOI: 10.1109/bigdata.2018.8622621

Hegazy, I. (2019). The effect of political neuromarketing 2.0 on election outcomes. *Review of Economics and Political Science*, *6*(3), 235–251. DOI: 10.1108/reps-06-2019-0090

Hillersdal, L., Jespersen, A., Oxlund, B., & Bruun, B. (2020). Affect and effect in interdisciplinary research collaboration. *Science & Technology Studies*, *33*(2), 66–82. DOI: 10.23987/sts.63305

Huber, G., Meredith, M., Morse, M., & Steele, K. (2021). The racial burden of voter list maintenance errors: Evidence from wisconsin's supplemental movers poll books. *Science Advances*, *7*(8). Advance online publication. DOI: 10.1126/sciadv.abe4498

Igbinenikaro, O., Adekoya, O., & Etukudoh, E. (2024). Fostering cross-disciplinary collaboration in offshore projects: Strategies and best practices. *International Journal of Management & Entrepreneurship Research*, *6*(4), 1176–1189. DOI: 10.51594/ijmer.v6i4.1006

Jo, J., & Lee, K. (2019). Mapreduce-based d_elt framework to address the challenges of geospatial big data. *ISPRS International Journal of Geo-Information*, *8*(11), 475. DOI: 10.3390/ijgi8110475

Juned, F., Sihombing, M., & Kadir, A. (2021). Analisis formulasi pendaftaran pemilih pemilihan umum tahun 2019 pada komisi pemilihan umum kota medan. *Perspektif*, *10*(2), 481–497. DOI: 10.31289/perspektif.v10i2.4705

Kausar, G., Saleem, S., Subhan, F., Su'ud, M., Alam, M., & Uddin, M. (2023). Prediction of gender-biased perceptions of learners and teachers using machine learning. *Sustainability*, *15*(7), 6241. DOI: 10.3390/su15076241

Keele, L., CUBBISON, W., & White, I. (2021). Suppressing black votes: A historical case study of voting restrictions in louisiana. *The American Political Science Review*, *115*(2), 694–700. DOI: 10.1017/s0003055421000034

Khan, V., & Meenai, T. (2021). Pretrained natural language processing model for intent recognition (bert-ir). *Human-Centric Intelligent Systems*, *1*(3-4), 66. DOI: 10.2991/hcis.k.211109.001

König, P., & Waldvogel, T. (2021). What matters for keeping or losing support in televised debates. *European Journal of Communication*, *37*(3), 312–329. DOI: 10.1177/02673231211046706

Larivière, V., Haustein, S., & Börner, K. (2015). Long-distance interdisciplinarity leads to higher scientific impact. *PLoS One*, *10*(3), e0122565. DOI: 10.1371/journal.pone.0122565

Liçenji, L. (2023). The role of social media on electoral strategy: An examination of the 2023 municipal elections in tirana, albania. *Academic Journal of Interdisciplinary Studies*, *12*(6), 238. DOI: 10.36941/ajis-2023-0166

Ma-Kellams, C., Bishop, B., Zhang, M., & Villagrana, B. (2017). Using "big data" versus alternative measures of aggregate data to predict the u.s. 2016 presidential election. *Psychological Reports*, *121*(4), 726–735. DOI: 10.1177/0033294117736318

Medviedev, Y. (2025). Impact of social media on political campaigns: Management, strategies and results. *Journal of Information Systems Engineering & Management*, *10*(7s), 67–75. DOI: 10.52783/jisem.v10i7s.781

Mondal, S., Gharote, M., & Lodha, S. (2022). Privacy of personal information. *Queue*, *20*(3), 41–87. DOI: 10.1145/3546934

Namayengo, L., Mbabazize, M., & Barigayomwe, R. (2023). E-enabling as a technological platform for electoral democracy in uganda. *East African Journal of Interdisciplinary Studies*, *6*(1), 197–219. DOI: 10.37284/eajis.6.1.1343

Olorunfemi, O., Amoo, O., Atadoga, A., Fayayola, O., Abrahams, T., & Shoetan, P. (2024). Towards a conceptual framework for ethical ai development in it systems. *Computer Science & It Research Journal*, *5*(3), 616–627. DOI: 10.51594/csitrj.v5i3.910

. Paterson, M. and Witzleb, N. (2019). Voter privacy in an era of big data., 164-185. https://doi.org/DOI: 10.4324/9780429288654-9

Román, C., Gómez-Martínez, R., & Orden-Cruz, C. (2020). Google trends as a predictor of presidential elections: The united states versus canada. *The American Behavioral Scientist*, *65*(4), 666–680. DOI: 10.1177/0002764220975067

Rustenbach, E. (2010). Sources of negative attitudes toward immigrants in europe: A multi-level analysis. *The International Migration Review*, *44*(1), 53–77. DOI: 10.1111/j.1747-7379.2009.00798.x

Simon, F. (2019). "we power democracy": Exploring the promises of the political data analytics industry. *The Information Society*, *35*(3), 158–169. DOI: 10.1080/01972243.2019.1582570

Singh, M., Iyengar, S., Saxena, A., & Kaur, R. (2022). A bi-level assessment of twitter in predicting the results of an election: delhi assembly elections 2020. https://doi.org//arxiv.2204.08746DOI: 10.48550

Talib, R., Hanif, M., Fatima, F., & Ayesha, S. (2016). A multi-agent framework for data extraction,transformation and loading in data warehouse. *International Journal of Advanced Computer Science and Applications*, *7*(11). Advance online publication. DOI: 10.14569/ijacsa.2016.071146

. Theodorakopoulos, L., Theodoropoulou, A., & Stamatiou, Y. (2024). A state-of-the-art review in big data management engineering: real-life case studies, challenges, and future research directions. Eng—advances in Engineering, 5(3), 1266-1297. https://doi.org/DOI: 10.3390/eng5030068

Tobias, C., Chiziwa, W., & Mwanza, B. (2024). Spatio-temporal analysis of multiparty elections results in malawi since 1994: a gis-based study on voting patterns and electoral outcomes... https://doi.org/DOI: 10.20944/preprints202406.1564.v1

Tomić, Z., Damnjanović, T., & Tomić, I. (2023). Artificial intelligence in political campaigns. *South Eastern European Journal of Communication*, *5*(2), 17–28. DOI: 10.47960/2712-0457.2.5.17

Visvizi, A., Lytras, M., & Aljohani, N. (2021). Big data research for politics: Human centric big data research for policy making, politics, governance and democracy. *Journal of Ambient Intelligence and Humanized Computing*, *12*(4), 4303–4304. DOI: 10.1007/s12652-021-03171-3

Wan, Y. (2023). The impact and value of interdisciplinary collaboration on higher education art and design courses. *Frontiers in Educational Research*, *6*(28). Advance online publication. DOI: 10.25236/fer.2023.062826

Xu, X., Hu, J., Lyu, X., Huang, H., & Cheng, X. (2021). Exploring the interdisciplinary nature of precision medicine:network analysis and visualization. *JMIR Medical Informatics*, *9*(1), e23562. DOI: 10.2196/23562

. Yadav, R. and Madaan, A. (2024). Comprehensive analysis of natural language processing. Global Journal of Engineering and Technology Advances, 19(1), 083-090. https://doi.org/DOI: 10.30574/gjeta.2024.19.1.0058

Yost, B., Redman, J., & Thompson, S. (2017). The 2016 pennsylvania presidential and u.s. senate elections: Breaking pennsylvania's electoral habits. *Commonwealth Essays and Studies*, *19*(2). Advance online publication. DOI: 10.15367/com.v19i2.152

Yu, Y., Guan, Y., & Hu, Y. (2024). Natural language processing applications in social network analysis: A data mining approach. *Journal of Physics: Conference Series*, *2813*(1), 012009. DOI: 10.1088/1742-6596/2813/1/012009

Zaki, N., Jamaluddin, A., Tanggamani, V., Rahim, A., & Alias, N. (2023). Big data: Balancing its usefulness in managing an organization performance and ethical consideration. *International Journal of Academic Research in Business & Social Sciences*, *13*(6). Advance online publication. DOI: 10.6007/ijarbss/v13-i6/17592

Chapter 7
Predicting the 2024 U.S. Presidential Election:
Extending a Logistic and Bayesian Logistic Approach

Stefano Camatarri
http://orcid.org/0000-0002-7233-5876
Catholic University of Louvain, Belgium & Catholic University of Lille, France

Marta Gallina
http://orcid.org/0000-0003-1004-6881
Catholic University of Lille, France

ABSTRACT

This chapter addresses the persistent underestimation of Republican vote shares in U.S. presidential election forecasts, with a focus on the 2024 cycle. Despite methodological refinements, polling errors remain systematic. The chapter proposes a theory-driven, voter-level modelling strategy using logistic and Bayesian logistic regression applied to 2024 ANES data. Moving beyond poll aggregates and structural indicators, the models incorporate predictors such as ideological orientation, economic dissatisfaction, and sociodemographic traits. Results confirm that these factors substantially improve predictive accuracy, reducing the gap between estimated and actual vote shares. The weighted Bayesian model predicted Trump's national vote share within 1.6 percentage points—outperforming many major polling organisations. Overall, this approach demonstrates the empirical and diagnostic value of behavioural modeling in electoral forecasting and contributes to a broader methodological shift that centres voters' individual characteristics as key to understanding electoral outcomes.

DOI: 10.4018/979-8-3373-1037-4.ch007

INTRODUCTION

Election forecasting continues to face persistent and evolving challenges, particularly in the United States, where recent presidential cycles (2016, 2020, and most recently 2024) have exposed recurring and systematic polling inaccuracies. These errors have been especially pronounced in estimating Republican vote shares, consistently underrepresenting support for candidates like Donald Trump. Although 2024 saw modest improvements in average polling error, especially in key swing states, where the median forecast deviation reached its lowest level in at least 25 years (Morris, 2024), systematic underestimation of Republican support persisted. The typical bias remained around 2–3 percentage points[1] in favour of Democratic candidates, continuing a pattern observed in the two previous cycles (Novicoff, 2025).

The sources of this persistent distortion are multiple and deeply embedded in the current political communication environment. Among the most cited explanations are nonresponse bias, as certain voter groups (notably less-educated and rural conservatives) are less likely to participate in surveys (Kennedy et al., 2018); spiral-of-silence effects, whereby socially stigmatised political preferences are underreported (Scheufle and Moy, 2000); and a context of deepening affective polarization (Iyengar et al., 2012), which shapes not only political attitudes but also the very act of political expression. These structural limitations continue to undermine the reliability of both traditional polling instruments and the aggregate forecasting models built upon them.

Moreover, the 2024 presidential contest presented a uniquely complex and volatile forecasting environment. Following President Biden's decision not to seek re-election, Vice President Kamala Harris emerged as the Democratic nominee in a mid-campaign leadership transition that generated additional uncertainty and recalibrated expectations. Facing Donald Trump once again, the race unfolded in the shadow of post-pandemic economic pressures, intense partisan polarisation, political disaffection, and rising geopolitical instability. These conditions further complicated the task of anticipating voter behaviour using conventional methods and aggregate indicators.

Against this backdrop, recent advances in individual-level model-based forecasting have offered promising alternatives. In particular, the work of Camatarri (2025) demonstrated that logistic and Bayesian regression models, grounded in behavioural theory and applied to ANES data, could substantially improve the estimation of Republican vote shares across multiple election cycles. This approach marked a methodological shift away from macro-structural models and polling averages, and towards the micro-foundations of electoral behaviour, emphasising predictors such as ideological orientation, economic dissatisfaction, and sociodemographic attributes.

Expanding on this foundation, the present study applies a refined voter-level modelling strategy to the 2024 U.S. presidential election, with the aim of evaluating its predictive power under high-uncertainty conditions. By incorporating updated specifications and testing their performance on the most recent ANES wave, this chapter provides both an empirical test of model robustness and a broader methodological reflection on the utility of behavioural forecasting. The empirical analysis relies on the 2024 ANES pre-election Time Series data (2025) and employs both classical and Bayesian logistic regression models to estimate individual-level probabilities of voting Republican. By combining theoretically grounded attitudinal and demographic predictors with population-weighted aggregation, the method captures the attitudinal underpinnings of vote choice and accounts for electoral uncertainty through probabilistic modelling. This analysis speaks to two central questions: to what extent can individual-level models reduce systematic polling biases? And how resilient are these models when the electoral environment deviates sharply from precedent?

The chapter proceeds as follows. First, it provides a theoretical discussion of the key mechanisms behind recent failures in electoral forecasting, with particular attention to spiral of silence dynamics and selection bias in survey response. Second, it outlines the political and electoral context of the 2024 election, as well as the performance of pre-election polling. Third, it introduces the modelling approach adopted here, detailing the data sources, theoretical rationale, and estimation procedures. The fourth section presents the results of the forecasting models, comparing their predictions to the actual election outcomes. The chapter concludes with a discussion of the findings, their methodological and substantive implications, their limitations and directions for future improvements in voter-level electoral forecasting.

EXPLAINING FORECAST FAILURE: SPIRAL OF SILENCE AND SELECTION BIAS

Persistent inaccuracies in U.S. election forecasting are not solely attributable to methodological flaws, but increasingly reflect behavioural dynamics that shape voter self-presentation and survey participation. Two interrelated mechanisms, spiral of silence and selection bias, offer a compelling explanation for the systematic under-representation of Republican support in recent cycles. The spiral of silence theory, originally formulated by Elisabeth Noelle-Neumann (1974), posits that individuals are less likely to express political opinions perceived as socially disapproved, due to a fear of isolation or reprisal. In highly polarised and media-saturated contexts, this dynamic may disproportionately affect supporters of controversial or stigmatised candidates, such as Donald Trump, who perceive themselves as ideologically isolated or misrepresented in dominant discourses.

Empirical studies from the 2016 and 2020 elections have found suggestive evidence that Trump voters were more likely to withhold their preferences in surveys, particularly in areas where media and elite cues were unfavourable to him. For instance, Kushin et al. (2019), analysing data from the 2016 U.S. election, found that on Facebook, where users interact with personal networks, the perceived incongruence between one's political views and the dominant opinion climate was significantly associated with higher fear of isolation (FOI), which in turn reduced willingness to express support for both Trump and Clinton. Interestingly, the mediating role of FOI was stronger in non-anonymous contexts like Facebook than in anonymous settings, suggesting that identity visibility intensifies social pressure. The findings confirm that political expression is not merely ideological but also shaped by psychological and contextual factors, supporting the relevance of SOS theory in digital-era elections.

Often studied in the context of the United States, spiral of silence dynamics extend well beyond national borders. Their implications for democratic norms, particularly freedom of expression and pluralism, make it essential to understand these mechanisms more deeply, beyond the narrow concern of polling accuracy. For instance, recent studies based on cross-national evidence show that self-censorship in politically contentious contexts is common across Western democracies. In a comparative analysis of 15 European countries, Thürer et al. (2019) found that individuals' willingness to express political opinions, particularly on immigration and EU integration, varied depending on which position was perceived as socially dominant. In some cases, pro-immigration views were silenced; in others, they gained visibility in reaction to populist narratives.

It has also been shown that such mechanisms are amplified online, where perceived lack of ideological support in one's digital environment correlates with lower willingness to share political opinions, especially among conservatives exposed to partisan media ecosystems (Wang et al., 2017). Taken together, findings show that spiral-of-silence dynamics can suppress dissent, increase polarisation, and erode the deliberative conditions essential to a healthy democratic public sphere. This is why their presence, in the United States and beyond, in electoral contexts and everyday political life, is crucial to study, as their effects reach far beyond the mere underreporting of support for a candidate.

Closely related is the issue of selection bias, particularly nonresponse bias, which arises when specific segments of the electorate systematically opt out of surveys. Survey participation tends to be lower among individuals with lower levels of education, weaker political interest, and lower institutional trust—characteristics disproportionately found among politically alienated groups (Kennedy et al., 2018).

Although standard weighting techniques can correct for observable demographic imbalances, they fail to capture latent attitudinal dispositions, such as social desirability concerns or fear of isolation, that are associated with both vote choice and responsiveness. Social desirability bias, in particular, may affect survey research (Brownback and Novotny, 2018; Krumpal, 2013), as respondents tend to misreport or withhold their preferences (e.g. sympathy for a candidate) or behaviour (e.g. voting at a election, see Bernstein et al., 2001) when these are perceived as socially stigmatised or morally questionable. This can be particularly salient when voting for candidates associated with controversial positions, or in environments where the local opinion climate renders certain preferences normatively unacceptable. In such contexts, individuals may either opt out of surveys altogether or select neutral response options (e.g., "don't know"), thus reducing the reliability of vote intention estimates (Camatarri et al., 2023). As a result, even among those who participate, reported attitudes may not reflect true preferences, further compounding polling inaccuracy and limiting the capacity of surveys to capture genuine electoral dynamics.

Empirical evidence from the 2020 U.S. presidential election supports this view: using data from the 2020 Cooperative Election Study matched with county-level electoral returns, Camatarri et al. (2023) show that conservative respondents were significantly more likely to withhold their vote intentions in counties where Democratic support had been stronger in 2016. This effect—absent among liberals and weaker among moderates—suggests that the local political climate conditions individuals' willingness to disclose their preferences, in line with theories of contextualised opinion expression. Such patterns indicate that vote intention nonresponse is not randomly distributed, but driven by an interaction between ideology and context that standard survey adjustments cannot fully account for.

Therefore, these findings underscore that selection bias is not merely a methodological artefact but a politically consequential distortion. It can systematically skew polling-based expectations, obscure the true distribution of political preferences, and undermine the transparency of democratic representation.

Coherently to this, other studies have found evidence of hidden Trump supporters, the so-called shy Trump voters, in the 2016 U.S. presidential polls. Enns et al. (2017) found that, in early October, Trump consistently underperformed in state polls relative to Republican Senate candidates, suggesting reluctance among some Republican voters to openly express support for him. Additional survey data using a forced-choice "truthfulness" question showed that many undecided respondents leaned toward Trump, producing estimates much closer to the actual vote, pointing to expressive bias rather than simple nonresponse. However, not all studies confirm the shy Trump voter hypothesis. Using a list experiment designed to reduce social desirability bias, one nationally representative survey (Coppock, 2017) found no evidence that Trump support was understated due to expressive reluctance—in fact, the indirect measure produced slightly lower estimates than the direct question, challenging the idea that hidden support inflated Trump's eventual performance.

Ultimately, these mechanisms demonstrate the need for forecasting approaches that move beyond surface-level demographic corrections. They point toward the integration of individual-level behavioural variables, such as ideological intensity, perceptions of economic performance, and trust in government, into predictive models. Together, spiral of silence and selection bias highlight how survey responses can systematically distort actual vote intentions—particularly among ideologically stigmatised or politically alienated groups. These distortions justify a modelling shift toward individual-level predictors that infer electoral preferences from underlying attitudinal and socio-demographic characteristics, rather than relying solely on stated intentions. The modelling strategy employed in this chapter is explicitly designed to address these limitations by incorporating theoretically grounded predictors that capture potential biases in the electorate. Before presenting our model, however, we briefly review how elections forecasting has been approached in the literature.

ELECTION FORECASTING IN THE LITERATURE: TRADITIONAL MODELS AND DIGITAL SHIFTS

The study of electoral forecasting has long been characterised by a tension between theoretical parsimony and empirical complexity. Traditional approaches have typically relied on either structural models—grounded in macroeconomic and institutional indicators—or poll-based strategies that aggregate voter intentions as election day approaches (see e.g., Lewis-Beck and Stegmaier, 2014). In recent years, however, researchers have increasingly sought to complement these methods with digital data and big-data-driven signals, aiming to capture dynamic patterns of political engagement and attention. Across these models, the central goal remains to reduce uncertainty and produce timely, interpretable predictions.

Among the most influential structural approaches are those that combine indicators of economic performance and presidential popularity to estimate the incumbent party's vote share. Erikson and Wlezien (2020, see also Erikson and Wlezien, 2012; 2016 and Wlezien and Erikson, 1996), for instance, demonstrate that a simple model combining leading economic indicators (LEI) with live-interview polling can accurately forecast the popular vote outcome in U.S. presidential elections. Their framework, which has correctly predicted 17 of 17 elections post-convention since 1952, reflects the strength of theoretically anchored fundamentals—especially when updated throughout the campaign.

Parallel to these strategies, newer approaches aim to capture the unfolding dynamics of the electoral process itself, focusing for example on partial count sequences (Deb et al., 2024) or spatial-temporal vote diffusion (Volkening et al., 2020). For example, Deb et al. (2024) develop a Bayesian hierarchical model that forecasts election outcomes from partial count sequences, updating beliefs as new data arrive. Although initially applied to Indian elections, their framework demonstrates strong potential for contexts like the U.S., where early returns and polling uncertainty coexist. Volkening et al. (2020) pursue a different strategy inspired by epidemiological models, treating voter preferences as "contagions" that spread geographically across states. Their approach, tested on U.S. presidential and midterm elections, captures spatiotemporal dynamics and produces accurate forecasts with explicit uncertainty bounds.

Beyond survey-based methods, recent years have witnessed the emergence of digital data sources—especially social media—as tools for electoral forecasting. Social media platforms offer massive volumes of behavioural data that can be mined for signals of political sentiment and candidate support. Brito et al. (2021) review this literature and find a wide range of methodologies, from simple tweet-volume tracking to complex sentiment classification and network analysis. While early results were promising, more systematic evaluations have revealed major limitations. Social media data tend to suffer from platform bias (e.g., overrepresentation of young, urban, or highly engaged users), and sentiment models often lack validation or theoretical grounding. Moreover, the overreliance on Twitter limits generalisability and amplifies the risk of misinterpretation. However, the article also points out that better results are found with newer approaches, for instance regression methods trained with traditional polls.

Despite these limitations, some studies have attempted to improve the robustness of social media forecasts. Zhou et al. (2021), for instance, propose a hybrid model that combines machine learning models and big-data analytics from social networks, correcting the sampling bias of Twitter data by means of census information. Their findings suggest that real-time signals from digital platforms can help capture dynamic opinion shifts. Yet even here, the need for demographic correction and external benchmarking remains clear. Further extending this line of research, Brito and Adeodato (2020) apply supervised machine learning models to Twitter and demographic data to forecast elections in both Brazil and the U.S. Their findings highlight the potential of combining digital trace data with census-based corrections to improve accuracy, although results vary depending on the electoral context and platform bias.

In addition, Liu et al. (2021) propose an integrative forecasting model that combines Twitter-derived sentiment scores with macroeconomic indicators such as GDP growth and unemployment rates. Rather than relying on traditional polls, they compute a weekly support rate for each candidate directly from Twitter data. Their results show that this hybrid model can achieve high predictive accuracy, highlighting the potential of social media signals as a viable alternative to conventional polling. Similarly, Nugroho (2021) confirms the forecasting potential of Twitter sentiment analysis. Using lexicon-based classification to estimate candidate support in the 2020 U.S. election, the study produced predictions closely aligned with actual state-level results—underscoring the value of social media signals when processed with appropriate analytical methods.

Other work has explored alternative behavioural signals beyond social media. Sallem and Stephany (2023) use Wikipedia pageviews to model attention dynamics during congressional campaigns, arguing that surges in search traffic reflect rising candidate visibility and competitiveness. Although not a direct measure of voter preference, such indicators can complement existing models by identifying momentum and issue salience—especially in underpolled races or early stages of campaigns.

Overall, the literature seems to suggest that no single forecasting approach can account for the full complexity of modern elections. Structural models offer stability and long-term explanatory power; poll aggregation reflects public mood at specific points in time; voter-level models add behavioural realism; digital signals provide immediacy and momentum tracking. The most promising avenues now appear to lie in hybrid forecasting architectures—those that combine theoretical rigour, behavioural insight, and high-quality data. In this evolving field, methodological flexibility and contextual sensitivity have become essential features of credible electoral prediction.

While hybrid forecasting architectures are gaining traction as a response to electoral complexity, the approach developed in this chapter takes a different path. Rather than combining multiple methods, we focus on a single, theory-driven, individual-level modeling strategy that emphasizes explanatory clarity and behavioral realism. By applying logistic and Bayesian regression models to high-quality ANES data, this framework isolates the micro-level determinants of vote choice within a structured analytical framework. Although not hybrid in design, this approach is inherently extensible: its modular structure and emphasis on voter-level predictors make it well suited for future integration with complementary data streams—including digital trace data, macroeconomic indicators, and AI-driven classification tools. In this sense, this contribution offers not only a powerful standalone forecast but also a flexible foundation for new hybrid solutions of electoral prediction research.

THE 2024 U.S. PRESIDENTIAL ELECTION: CONTEXT AND CHALLENGES FOR FORECASTING

Political Backdrop

The 2024 U.S. presidential election took place in a climate of extraordinary political polarisation and widespread institutional scepticism. Trust in core democratic institutions, including government, media, and polling organisations, remained near historic lows, despite a very modest increase since 2023 (Pew Research Center, 2024a). Partisan identity increasingly shaping not only vote choice, but also the sympathy towards supporters of the opposing political group and the tolerance towards others' opinions (Iyengar et al., 2019; Druckman and Levy, 2022). This division, the so-called affective polarization, is not merely ideological, but also deeply linked to discriminatory behaviour, susceptibility to misinformation, anti-democratic norms, and it is uniformly distributed across American states (Holliday et al., 2024). The legacy of the COVID-19 pandemic further complicated this landscape (Kerr et al., 2021), not only through its socio-economic consequences, but by fuelling divergent narratives about government competence, scientific authority, and individual versus collective responsibility.

Against this backdrop, heightened partisan distrust and polarisation within the U.S. electorate already posed significant challenges for gauging public sentiment, as they tend to increase the likelihood of response distortion due to the above-mentioned dynamic. In addition, the 2024 electoral cycle have been defined also by its unprecedented candidate fluidity. Donald Trump, though no longer the incumbent, retained overwhelming influence over the Republican Party and secured the GOP nomination amid multiple legal indictments, further polarising an already divided electorate. On the Democratic side, the race was thrown into turmoil when President Joe Biden unexpectedly announced his withdrawal from the campaign midway through the electoral calendar. This decision prompted an accelerated reshuffling of the Democratic campaign leadership, forcing both voters and analysts to recalibrate expectations in real time. Such mid-cycle realignments disrupted the continuity of campaign narratives and undermined baseline assumptions built into many forecasting models.

In the absence of a sitting president on the ballot and with both parties navigating internal uncertainty, the usual electoral reference points, such as incumbency advantage, early fundraising patterns, and historical swing-state trajectories, became less predictive. Combined with elevated levels of partisan affect, this environment of volatility diminished the reliability of traditional polling benchmarks and injected substantial noise into predictive models. In short, the candidate dynamics of 2024 did not merely complicate campaign strategy—they challenged the very assumptions on which electoral forecasting has long relied.

The 2024 campaign was also shaped by an unusual confluence of salient issues that shifted the contours of public opinion. Economic anxiety remained central (Brenan, 2024), fuelled by persistent concerns over inflation, interest rates, and housing affordability. Immigration and border security (Pew Research Center, 2024b) re-emerged as flashpoints in partisan discourse, particularly amid perceptions of federal inaction. Meanwhile, the Supreme Court's repeal of Roe v. Wade in the previous cycle continued to mobilise key constituencies, especially younger and female voters. On the international stage, the ongoing wars in Ukraine and the Middle East reignited debates over American global leadership, while escalating climate-related disasters intensified demands for environmental action. The interaction of these issues broadened the spectrum of voter priorities and introduced further volatility into an already fluid electoral landscape, complicating efforts to forecast political behaviour using traditional predictors.

Polling Performance in the 2024 Election

Over the past half-century, the accuracy of U.S. presidential election polls has varied considerably, with notable trends in both stability and disruption. During the 1970s through the early 2000s, state-level polling errors typically ranged between ±1 and 2 percentage points, indicating a relatively reliable relationship between poll estimates and final vote shares. High-profile exceptions included the 1948 "Dewey Defeats Truman" debacle, but from the mid-1970s onward, polling institutions generally delivered rather consistent forecasts (see Ko et al., 2025 for a detailed discussion). However, beginning with the 2016 election, this pattern shifted: polling underestimated Republican vote share by an average of 3.1 points in swing states, and the 2020 election saw average state-level errors rise even higher—up to 4.3–5.1 points, marking the worst performance in at least four decades (for a detailed discussion concerning the 2020 pre-election polling, please see AAPOR, 2022).

The 2024 election saw notable enhancements in polling accuracy compared to previous cycles. National polls exhibited an average error of less than 3 percentage points, a significant improvement from the nearly 5-point errors observed in 2016 and 2020. In competitive states, the average polling error was approximately 2.2 points—marking the most accurate state-level performance since at least the past 25 years. These improvements are most likely attributable to methodological adjustments, including more aggressive weighting for education levels and past voting behaviour (Schaffner and Soler, 2024). Such refinements may have helped reduce biases that previously led to the underestimation of Republican support.

Despite these gains, polls continued to slightly underestimate Donald Trump's support—a pattern consistent with the 2016 and 2020 elections. In swing states, Trump outperformed his final polling numbers by about 3 percentage points, a margin that falls within typical polling error but still points to persistent asymmetries in modelling the likely electorate. Contributing factors include difficulties in reaching non-college-educated voters and the impact of last-minute decision-making, often swayed by high-profile endorsements and campaign events.

Online panels generally outperformed live-caller surveys, likely due to their greater reach among younger, less institutionally engaged voters. Notably, AtlasIntel emerged as the most accurate pollster in 2024 (AtlasIntel, 2024), providing precise estimates at both national and state levels, including Trump's popular vote victory and his structural advantage in key battlegrounds. In contrast, some established pollsters faced notable errors—for example, Selzer & Co.'s final Iowa poll projected a 3-point lead for Harris (Pfannenstiel, 2024), whereas Trump ultimately won the state by 13 points.

These methodological improvements represent a step forward for survey research. Yet, they coexist with deeper structural challenges: increasing partisan distrust, growing nonresponse among key demographic groups, and polarised opinion climates continue to limit the capacity of polls to fully capture electoral dynamics in real time. These persistent limitations underscore the need for further research to enhance the accuracy and reliability of electoral forecasting.

THE MISSING PIECE: THEORY-DRIVEN, VOTER-LEVEL MODELING WITH HIGH-QUALITY DATA

Despite meaningful progress in polling accuracy during the 2024 U.S. presidential election, a key dimension remains largely absent from most forecasting strategies: the use of high-quality individual-level survey data combined with behavioural models rooted in political theory. While methodological refinements, such as improved weighting schemes and respondent-level corrections, have led to more reliable aggregates, forecasting efforts continue to focus primarily on surface-level intentions, often detached from the cognitive and contextual dynamics that underpin vote choice.

Aggregate-level approaches, including poll averages and structural models, have dominated the forecasting landscape. Yet these methods either ignore voter-level heterogeneity altogether or rely on assumptions that limit explanatory power. Structural forecasting, for example, models electoral outcomes as a function of macro indicators such as economic growth or presidential approval, but it fails to capture how individual voters perceive and react to these conditions. Even sophisticated tools like Multilevel Regression and Poststratification (MRP), while helpful in adjusting for demographic imbalances, are primarily statistical corrections that do not model why individuals choose particular candidates.

This chapter proposes an alternative strategy grounded in the tradition of voter-level analysis, building on previous work (Camatarri, 2025) that demonstrated the predictive power of combining high-quality survey data with theory-informed regression models. Specifically, it leverages the American National Election Studies (ANES), a dataset with a longstanding intellectual history, widely acknowledged for its methodological rigor, extensive pre-testing, and detailed measurement of political attitudes (see Miller, 1994). Compared to commercial polls, which typically employ rapid fieldwork, shorter questionnaires, and opt-in online panels to maximize speed and cost-efficiency, ANES adopts a probability-based sampling design, conducts in-depth interviews, and rigorously tests question wording and order. This emphasis on representativeness and measurement validity makes it particularly suited for explanatory modelling rather than mere descriptive estimation.

The method begins with the estimation of an individual-level binary outcome: support for the Republican presidential candidate, modeled through logistic regression. Predictors are derived from well-established theories of voting behaviour and include ideological self-placement, reflecting long-standing models of spatial voting and partisan alignment (Downs, 1957); retrospective evaluations of personal and national economic conditions, central to theories of performance-based voting (Fiorina, 1978); and trust in federal institutions, which has been shown to shape citizens' willingness to support incumbents or institutional outsiders (Hetherington, 1998). These attitudinal dimensions are complemented by sociodemographic controls—including education, age, gender, and ethnic background—which remain enduring predictors of electoral choice and political alignment (Manza and Crowley, 2017). This specification deliberately excludes more shorter-term, election-specific evaluations—such as presidential handling of the COVID-19 pandemic—which played a notable role in Trump's 2020 defeat (Luartz et al., 2024), but no longer featured prominently in the 2024 electoral context.

Once the model is estimated, individual-level probabilities of voting for the Republican candidate are generated and then aggregated to produce an estimate of national support. Aggregation is performed both with and without applying the full ANES pre-election survey weights, ensuring population-level representativeness and allowing comparison with unweighted forecasts. Two thresholds are tested for classifying respondents as Republican voters: a fixed 0.5 cutoff and the sample's weighted mean predicted probability. This dual approach helps assess the sensitivity of the estimates to classification strategy and corrects for any imbalance in predicted support due to skewed distributions.

To enhance the robustness of the forecasts, the standard logistic regression model is complemented by a Bayesian logistic regression approach estimated via Markov

Chain Monte Carlo (MCMC) methods, a widely used technique in political science and applied statistics for modeling uncertainty in binary outcomes.[2]

This allows for a probabilistic representation of uncertainty and offers more stable predictions, particularly valuable in volatile contexts such as the 2024 election cycle. In previous applications to 2012, 2016, and 2020, the method consistently achieved prediction errors below 3 percentage points. These results outperformed several mainstream poll aggregators, especially in capturing support for Donald Trump, whose electorate has often eluded traditional measurement due to selection and response biases.

This strategy does not attempt to replace aggregation or structural forecasting but to complement them with an analytically grounded tool that centres the voter as the unit of analysis. It allows not only for more accurate predictions, but also for diagnostic insights into which voter groups and which factors are driving the electoral outcome. In the context of growing partisan polarisation, volatile candidate dynamics, and fluctuating issue salience—as seen in 2024—such tools become not only useful but necessary. Extending the model to this new cycle allows for a critical stress test of its explanatory power under conditions of institutional distrust, rapid political shifts, and polarised information ecosystems.

METHODOLOGY

The empirical foundation of this analysis is the 2024 ANES pre-election Time Series data. Methodologically, the chapter employs both classical and Bayesian logistic regression models, using Metropolis-Hastings Markov Chain Monte Carlo methods to estimate vote probabilities at the individual level. What makes the Bayesian model different is that instead of giving a single fixed estimate, it shows a range of likely outcomes and how confident we can be about them. It does this by running many simulations, gradually learning from the data to build a more complete picture. This probabilistic formulation is particularly suited for volatile electoral environments like 2024, where candidate turnover, issue salience, and shifting partisan enthusiasm challenged deterministic forecasting rules. As mentioned earlier, predictors are theoretically grounded and include ideological placement (measured on a 7-point liberal-conservative scale), economic evaluations—both national (approval of the country's economic performance) and personal (change in one's own financial situation over the past year)—and distrust in government. Key sociodemographic variables include age (continuous), education (ordinal), race/ethnicity (coded as white non-Hispanic vs. all others), and gender (female coded as 1). All continuous predictors are normalized to a 0–1 scale for comparability across coefficients.

In addition to offering a more nuanced view of voter psychology, this approach helps address two common pathologies of electoral forecasting: the underestimation of Republican support and the inability to anticipate shifts in turnout. Rather than assuming a static electorate or relying on past vote recall, the model infers preferences from current attitudes and demographic positioning. As Camatarri (2025) showed, this not only increases predictive accuracy but also improves interpretability, allowing analysts to diagnose why certain groups behave unexpectedly and how shifting coalitions emerge over time.

From a theoretical standpoint, the Bayesian approach offers distinct advantages for forecasting under uncertainty. Unlike classical methods, which yield single-point estimates, Bayesian models produce full posterior distributions over parameters and predicted outcomes. This is particularly valuable in volatile electoral contexts—such as the 2024 campaign—where late-breaking developments, uneven turnout, and noisy polling environments amplify the need for flexible, probabilistic reasoning. Moreover, the incorporation of prior distributions allows analysts to integrate existing knowledge or historical regularities, while still updating beliefs in light of new data. The use of Markov Chain Monte Carlo methods further enables the estimation of complex posterior distributions even in high-dimensional settings, thus enhancing model transparency and interpretability.

The goal of this chapter is to test this approach under the exceptional conditions of the 2024 campaign, marked by candidate volatility, institutional distrust, and fragmented information flows. If successful, the model offers more than just an alternative to prevailing forecasting techniques: it provides a replicable and theoretically grounded framework that aligns statistical precision with substantive understanding of electoral behaviour.

RESULTS

The logistic regression model (Table 1) confirms that ideological orientation and economic dissatisfaction were the most powerful predictors of support for the Republican candidate in 2024. Specifically, the odds of supporting Trump were over 229 times higher for respondents at the conservative end of the ideological spectrum compared to those at the liberal end (OR = 229.19, $p < 0.001$). This massive effect size indicates a near-deterministic association between ideological orientation and vote choice: those identifying as strongly conservative had a very high predicted probability of voting Republican, while those on the liberal end had a very low one, all else being equal. This suggests that partisanship and ideological alignment remain deeply entrenched in shaping voter preferences, likely reflecting the increasing polarisation and identity-based nature of American politics.

Similarly, those who expressed dissatisfaction with Presi had substantially higher odds of supporting the Republican candidate ($OR = 167.87$, $p < 0.001$). This points to the continued salience of retrospective economic evaluations in vote choice, particularly when associated with a negative assessment of the incumbent administration's performance. Notably, the effect of economic dissatisfaction is nearly as strong as that of ideology, highlighting the dual importance of both instrumental (performance-based) and expressive (identity-based) motivations. This near-equivalent predictive strength of economic dissatisfaction—particularly at the national level—underscores the role of instrumental reasoning even in highly polarized environments. Voters who feel economically left behind or disapprove of national conditions remain open to mobilization through performance-based appeals, suggesting that campaigns ignoring bread-and-butter issues do so at their peril. This dual pattern implies that effective electoral strategies must address both identity and accountability: reaffirming partisan loyalties while also responding credibly to voters' retrospective economic judgments.

Other significant predictors included education, ethnicity, and gender. Higher levels of education were negatively associated with Republican support ($OR = 0.33$, $p < 0.001$), confirming longstanding patterns whereby college-educated voters lean more Democratic. This may reflect both cultural liberalism and issue preferences aligned with Democratic positions among more educated individuals. White respondents had higher odds of voting Republican ($OR = 1.72$, $p < 0.001$), consistent with racial realignment trends observed over the past decades. Gender also played a significant role, with female respondents being significantly less likely to support Trump ($OR = 0.61$, $p < 0.001$), reinforcing evidence of a persistent gender gap in American electoral behaviour.

In contrast, distrust in government and age were not statistically significant predictors ($p > 0.05$), suggesting that, net of other variables, these factors did not independently explain vote choice in this cycle. This may be partly due to the overlap between distrust and broader ideological orientations, or to the fact that age effects are more likely to operate through cohort-based political socialisation, which may be absorbed by ideology. Interestingly, the variable capturing personal economic worsening showed a positive association ($OR = 1.54$), though it narrowly missed conventional significance levels ($p = 0.074$). This may suggest that personal economic hardship played a more ambiguous or secondary role compared to broader perceptions of national economic performance.

Table 1. Logistic regression results

Predictor	Odds Ratio	Std. Error	z-value	p-value
Ideological Conservatism	229.19	73.16	17.03	0.000
Economic Dissatisfaction	167.87	44.42	19.36	0.000
Distrust in Government	1.10	0.32	0.32	0.750
Age	1.07	0.26	0.27	0.787
Education	0.33	0.08	-4.75	0.000
White Ethnicity	1.72	0.26	3.66	0.000
Personal Economy Worsened	1.54	0.37	1.79	0.074
Female	0.61	0.07	-4.15	0.000

These findings are corroborated by the Bayesian logistic model (Table 2), which confirms the direction, magnitude, and uncertainty of the effects. The posterior means for ideological conservatism (5.38, 95% CrI: 4.88–5.78) and economic dissatisfaction (5.06, CrI: 4.65–5.44) were especially strong and well-separated from zero, reinforcing their decisive influence. These values, expressed on the log-odds scale, confirm the overwhelming impact of these variables with high posterior certainty.

Education retained a robust negative effect (posterior mean = –1.02, CrI: –1.36 to –0.73), further supporting the notion of an educational divide in electoral preferences. Gender (–0.53, CrI: –0.78 to –0.34) and white ethnicity (0.58, CrI: 0.36–0.81) also remained statistically and substantively meaningful. In line with the frequentist model, distrust in government and age again failed to reach statistical credibility, with posterior intervals covering zero. The personal economy variable, while again positive (posterior mean = 0.36), displayed a wide credible interval (–0.13 to 0.73), suggesting considerable uncertainty around its effect.

These results show remarkable consistency across estimation approaches, strengthening confidence in the robustness of the findings. The convergence between logistic and Bayesian inference points to the stability of the estimated relationships despite different modelling philosophies and assumptions. Moreover, the Bayesian model provides added value in quantifying uncertainty and offering richer interpretations of marginal effects.

Table 2. Bayesian Logistic Regression Results

Predictor	Posterior Mean	Std. Dev.	95% Cred. Interval
Ideological Conservatism	5.38	0.24	4.88 - 5.78
Economic Dissatisfaction	5.06	0.19	4.65 - 5.44
Distrust in Government	0.06	0.27	-0.52 - 0.61

continued on following page

Table 2. Continued

Predictor	Posterior Mean	Std. Dev.	95% Cred. Interval
Age	0.14	0.21	-0.23 - 0.61
Education	-1.02	0.17	-1.36 - -0.73
White Ethnicity	0.58	0.11	0.36 - 0.81
Personal Economy Worsened	0.36	0.21	-0.13 - 0.73
Female	-0.53	0.10	-0.78 - -0.34

The individual-level models were then used to generate aggregate predictions of Trump's vote share, with results compared across different estimation strategies. The actual national-level result for Trump, according to Federal Election Commission (FEC) data, was 49.80 per cent.

As shown in Table 3, the baseline estimates derived from raw survey responses substantially underestimated this figure. The unweighted survey average yielded a vote share of 42.07 per cent (95% CI: 40.64–43.51), and applying post-stratification weights modestly improved accuracy, raising the estimate to 42.60 per cent (CI: 40.59–44.61). These figures, however, remained over 7 percentage points below the actual result, a discrepancy consistent with the well-documented challenge of underestimating Republican support in pre-election polling.

In contrast, model-based predictions offered marked improvements in accuracy, especially when incorporating both weighting and theoretically informed predictors. The unweighted logistic regression estimate rose to 45.17 per cent (CI: 42.96–47.39), while its weighted version yielded an even more precise forecast of 47.15 per cent (CI: 44.93–49.38). The Bayesian logistic models performed similarly well: the unweighted version predicted 46.10 per cent (CrI: 43.99–48.21), and the weighted Bayesian logistic regression produced the most accurate prediction overall—48.19 per cent (CrI: 46.08–50.30). This estimate was just 1.61 points below Trump's actual vote share, and its credible interval contained the true result.

These findings underscore the value of voter-level modelling grounded in behavioural theory and augmented with appropriate weighting strategies. While traditional polling aggregates struggled to capture the full extent of Trump's support, particularly among less represented demographic groups, the models presented here were able to recover much of this "hidden" support through the inclusion of powerful predictors such as ideological conservatism and economic dissatisfaction. Notably, the best-performing model—the weighted Bayesian logistic regression—outperformed many professional pollsters who systematically underestimated Republican support in the 2024 cycle.

Moreover, these results highlight that the modelling strategy matters at least as much as sample design. Purely descriptive estimates, even when weighted, remained biased downward. Only by leveraging the relationship between political attitudes, sociodemographic factors, and vote choice were the models able to reconstruct aggregate preferences more accurately. This reinforces the growing consensus that robust forecasting requires not only high-quality data but also well-specified, theory-driven models that account for latent structures in voter behaviour.

In sum, the integration of survey weighting, model-based inference, and Bayesian uncertainty estimation yielded substantial gains in predictive accuracy—suggesting a promising avenue for future electoral forecasting efforts, particularly in increasingly polarised and hard-to-measure electorates.

Table 3. Predicted vote share for Trump according to estimation methods

Estimation Method	**Predicted Vote Share (%)**	**95% Interval**
Unweighted Survey Average	42.07	(40.64 – 43.51)
Weighted Survey Average	42.60	(40.59 – 44.61)
Logistic Regression	45.17	(42.96 – 47.39)
Weighted Logistic Regression	47.15	(44.93 – 49.38)
Bayesian Logistic Regression	46.10	(43.99 – 48.21)
Weighted Bayesian Logistic Regression	48.19	(46.08 – 50.30)
Actual Result (FEC)	**49.80**	–

DISCUSSION

The results presented in this chapter underscore the enhanced predictive capacity of individual-level regression models—both frequentist and Bayesian—relative to traditional aggregation techniques based on raw survey responses. In a context where polling institutions have increasingly struggled to capture the true extent of Republican support, particularly among underrepresented or reluctant respondents, the application of theoretically informed models yields substantial gains in accuracy.

Specifically, both logistic and Bayesian approaches successfully recovered much of the missing Republican vote, reducing the gap between predicted and actual outcomes from over seven percentage points (in the case of unweighted survey averages) to less than two points in the best-performing model. The weighted Bayesian logistic regression came closest to the actual result, predicting Trump's vote share within 1.61 percentage points and producing a credible interval that included the true value. This level of accuracy outperformed many of the major polling aggregators during the 2024 election cycle, illustrating the tangible benefits of incorporating behavioural predictors and model-based corrections into electoral forecasting.

Beyond their practical forecasting value, these findings also carry broader theoretical and methodological implications. The significant role played by ideological orientation and economic dissatisfaction reaffirms the dual nature of electoral decision-making, where identity-based partisanship and retrospective performance evaluations operate in tandem. Moreover, the fact that standard weighting alone failed to substantially improve predictions suggests that surface-level demographic adjustment is not sufficient to correct deeper structural imbalances in survey response patterns.

Importantly, the models demonstrate that voter behaviour is increasingly complex and stratified, with predictive accuracy hinging on the inclusion of variables that capture affective, ideological, and economic dimensions. While traditional polls treat respondents' stated preferences as fixed points, the modelling approach adopted here accounts for the underlying drivers of those preferences, offering a more dynamic and resilient estimate.

At the same time, the persistent underestimation of Republican support—even if substantially reduced—serves as a reminder that methodological innovation must continue to confront the challenge of "hidden" electorates. This includes not only better measurement of latent attitudes, but also more sophisticated strategies to model turnout, social desirability effects, and the growing proportion of undecided or late-deciding voters.

Beyond predictive performance, this approach opens avenues for ongoing monitoring and adaptive integration. By comparing model-based estimates to aggregate vote intention over time, researchers may identify emerging gaps that signal selection bias or the operation of misreporting (desirability) mechanisms. This enables early detection of representational imbalances in polling data—particularly when specific voter groups become harder to reach or less willing to disclose their preferences. Additionally, while the model is grounded in a theory-driven, survey-based framework, its structure is readily extensible. Future applications could incorporate external information—such as economic indicators, online behaviour, or experimental survey frames—, and AI assistance, enhancing both predictive reach and interpretive depth. In this way, the model serves not only as a forecasting tool, but also as a flexible diagnostic framework for understanding when and why polls may fail—and, crucially, for identifying early warning signs that can help avoid major polling misses.

In conclusion, this study demonstrates that the integration of theory-driven modelling and careful post-stratification represents a promising direction for electoral research. It offers a more nuanced and empirically grounded approach to understanding and forecasting voter behaviour—one that is particularly vital in an era of polarisation, distrust, and declining response rates. As the limitations of raw polling become increasingly apparent, such approaches may prove essential in restoring both the accuracy and the credibility of public opinion research.

That said, individual-level models also introduce their own set of limitations. Chief among them is the risk of overfitting—particularly when a large number of predictors are used relative to the effective sample size, or when interactions are modelled without strong theoretical justification. Even with regularisation or Bayesian priors, complex models may end up capturing noise or survey-specific artefacts that do not generalise well beyond the training data. Moreover, voter-level models tend to rely on attitudinal variables measured at a single point in time, which may not fully capture late-breaking events, scandals, or shifts in enthusiasm that emerge in the final days of the campaign. Such volatility poses a particular challenge for behavioural forecasting frameworks, which are typically less reactive than polls conducted in the immediate pre-election window.

CONCLUSION

This study confirms the practical utility of individual-level regression models in forecasting electoral outcomes with notable precision. By leveraging ANES data and incorporating key behavioural predictors, both frequentist and Bayesian frameworks outperformed raw polling aggregates, providing more accurate estimates of Donald Trump's 2024 national vote share. These results underscore the value of theory-driven, post-stratified modelling approaches in improving forecast quality, especially in an era marked by polling fatigue and rising nonresponse rates.

However, several limitations should be acknowledged. First, the analysis is conducted exclusively at the federal level, due to the lack of state-level identifiers in the ANES. This constrains the capacity to model electoral dynamics in key battleground states and to simulate outcomes under the U.S. Electoral College system. While the federal-level results were strong, future work should extend these models to account for geographic heterogeneity, either through enriched datasets or multilevel hierarchical approaches.

Second, the models do not explicitly incorporate turnout predictions, instead assuming a uniform likelihood of participation across the sample. Given the well-established differences in turnout patterns by party, race, and education, this may introduce bias—particularly in a political context where mobilisation is highly strategic and unevenly distributed.

Third, the use of self-reported data introduces potential measurement biases. Voters may misreport either their intended vote or their ideological position, particularly when social desirability pressures are high. Relatedly, many politically disengaged or cross-pressured individuals tend to report "moderate" positions that may obscure underlying leanings.

Fourth, although the models included core predictors such as ideology and economic evaluations, they did not account for deeper cultural, affective, or identity-based attitudes that have become increasingly relevant in recent elections—such as racial resentment, nativism, authoritarianism, or religiosity. These may further enhance predictive power, especially among subsets of the electorate that defy traditional economic-ideological sorting.

Finally, despite these limitations, the consistency of the modelling approach across multiple election cycles remains a powerful validation. As shown in this analysis—and in comparable work such as Camatarri (2025)—individual-level models have delivered accurate forecasts from 2012 through 2024, even amid major shifts in the political landscape. Their capacity to generalise across contexts, and to outperform traditional polls even with limited geographic granularity, speaks to their robustness and potential.

These findings offer practical implications for campaign strategists and media analysts, who often rely on surface-level polling data. By modelling the underlying attitudinal and demographic factors shaping vote choice, this approach can help identify persuadable segments, detect misestimated support levels, and better anticipate late shifts in electoral dynamics.

Future research should aim to integrate additional sources of data (e.g., state-level polling, digital trace data, or panel surveys), as well as dynamic components that capture shifts in opinion over time. The challenge of accurately modelling non-visible or silent segments of the electorate remains ongoing—but this study shows that structured, theory-informed modelling represents one of the most promising tools available to meet it.

REFERENCES

AAPOR (American Association for Public Opinion Research). (2022). AAPOR task force on 2020 pre-election polling. https://aapor.org/wp-content/uploads/2022/11/AAPOR-Task-Force-on-2020-Pre-Election-Polling_Report-FNL.pdf

Acquah, H. D.-G. (2013). Bayesian Logistic Regression Modelling via Markov Chain Monte Carlo Algorithm. *Journal of Social and Development Sciences*, *4*(4), 193–197. DOI: 10.22610/jsds.v4i4.751

American National Election Studies. (2025). ANES 2024 Time Series Study Preliminary Release: Combined Pre-Election and Post-Election Data [dataset and documentation]. April 30, 2025 version. www.electionstudies.org

AtlasIntel. (2024, November 7). AtlasIntel is the most accurate pollster of the U.S. presidential election – 2nd time in a row. https://www.atlasintel.org/media/atlasintel-is-the-most-accurate-pollster-of-the-us-presidential-election-2nd-time-in-a-row

Bernstein, R., Chadha, A., & Montjoy, R. (2001). Overreporting voting: Why it happens and why it matters. *Public Opinion Quarterly*, *65*(1), 22–44. DOI: 10.1086/320036

Brenan, M. (2024, October 9). Economy remains most important issue for 2024 presidential vote. Gallup. https://news.gallup.com/poll/651719/economy-important-issue-2024-presidential-vote.aspx

Brito, K. D. S., & Adeodato, P. J. L. (2020, July). Predicting Brazilian and US elections with machine learning and social media data. In *2020 international joint conference on neural networks (IJCNN)* (pp. 1-8). IEEE.

Brito, K. D. S., Silva Filho, R. L. C., & Adeodato, P. J. L. (2021). A systematic review of predicting elections based on social media data: Research challenges and future directions. *IEEE Transactions on Computational Social Systems*, *8*(4), 819–843.

Brownback, A., & Novotny, A. (2018). Social desirability bias and polling errors in the 2016 presidential election. *Journal of Behavioral and Experimental Economics*, *74*, 38–56. DOI: 10.1016/j.socec.2018.03.001

Camatarri, S. (2025). Predicting Popular-vote Shares in US Presidential Elections: A Model-based Strategy Relying on ANES Data. *PS, Political Science & Politics*, *58*(2), 253–257.

Camatarri, S., Luartz, L. A., & Gallina, M. (2023). Always Silent? Exploring Contextual Conditions for Nonresponses to Vote Intention Questions at the 2020 US Presidential Election. *International Journal of Public Opinion Research, 35*(3). Advance online publication. DOI: 10.1093/ijpor/edad025

Coppock, A. (2017). Did Shy Trump Supporters Bias the 2016 Polls? Evidence from a Nationally-representative List Experiment. *Statistics, Politics, and Policy, 8*(1), 29–40. DOI: 10.1515/spp-2016-0005

Deb, S., Roy, R., & Das, S. (2024). Forecasting elections from partial information using a Bayesian model for a multinomial sequence of data. *Journal of Forecasting, 43*(6), 1814–1834.

Downs, A. (1957). An economic theory of political action in a democracy. *Journal of Political Economy, 65*(2), 135–150.

Druckman, J. N., & Levy, J. (2022). Affective polarization in the American public. In *Handbook on politics and public opinion* (pp. 257–270). Edward Elgar Publishing.

Enns, P., Lagodny, J., & Schuldt, J. (2017). Understanding the 2016 US Presidential Polls: The Importance of Hidden Trump Supporters. *Statistics, Politics, and Policy, 8*(1), 41–63. DOI: 10.1515/spp-2017-0003

Erikson, R. S., & Wlezien, C. (2012). The objective and subjective economy and the presidential vote. *PS, Political Science & Politics, 45*(4), 620–624.

Erikson, R. S., & Wlezien, C. (2016). Forecasting the presidential vote with leading economic indicators and the polls. *PS, Political Science & Politics, 49*(4), 669–672.

Fiorina, M. P. (1978). Economic retrospective voting in American national elections: A micro-analysis. *American Journal of Political Science*, 426–443.

Gelman, A., Carlin, J. B., Stern, H. S., & Rubin, D. B. (1995). *Bayesian data analysis*. Chapman and Hall/CRC.

Hetherington, M. J. (1998). The political relevance of political trust. *The American Political Science Review, 92*(4), 791–808.

Holliday, D. E., Lelkes, Y., & Westwood, S. J. (2024). Affective polarization is uniformly distributed across American states. *PNAS Nexus, 3*(10), pgae310.

Iyengar, S., Lelkes, Y., Levendusky, M., Malhotra, N., & Westwood, S. J. (2019). The origins and consequences of affective polarization in the United States. *Annual Review of Political Science, 22*(1), 129–146.

Iyengar, S., Sood, G., & Lelkes, Y. (2012). Affect, not ideology: A social identity perspective on polarization. *Public Opinion Quarterly*, *76*(3), 405–431.

Jackman, S. (2009). *Bayesian analysis for the social sciences*. John Wiley & Sons.

Kennedy, C., Blumenthal, M., Clement, S., Clinton, J. D., Durand, C., Franklin, C., & Wlezien, C. (2018). An evaluation of the 2016 election polls in the United States. *Public Opinion Quarterly*, *82*(1), 1–33.

Kerr, J., Panagopoulos, C., & Van Der Linden, S. (2021). Political polarization on COVID-19 pandemic response in the United States. *Personality and Individual Differences*, *179*, 110892.

Ko, H., Jackson, N., Osborn, T., & Lewis-Beck, M. S. (2025). Forecasting presidential elections: Accuracy of ANES voter intentions. *International Journal of Forecasting*, *41*(1), 66–75.

Krumpal, I. (2013). Determinants of social desirability bias in sensitive surveys: A literature review. *Quality & Quantity*, *47*(4), 2025–2047. DOI: 10.1007/s11135-011-9640-9

Kushin, M. J., Yamamoto, M., & Dalisay, F. (2019). Societal majority, Facebook, and the spiral of silence in the 2016 US presidential election. *Social Media + Society*, *5*(2), 2056305119855139.

Lewis-Beck, M. S., & Stegmaier, M. (2014). US presidential election forecasting: Introduction. *PS, Political Science & Politics*, *47*(2), 284–288.

Liu, R., Yao, X., Guo, C., & Wei, X. (2021). Can we forecast presidential election using twitter data? an integrative modelling approach. *Annals of GIS*, *27*(1), 43–56.

Luartz, L., Camatarri, S., & Gallina, M. (2024). The determinants of Trump's defeat in 2020: What if the COVID-19 pandemic did not matter? *Journal of Elections, Public Opinion, and Parties*, •••, 1–26.

Manza, J., & Crowley, N. (2017, April). Working class hero? Interrogating the social bases of the rise of Donald Trump. [). De Gruyter.]. *Inforum (Adelaide, S. Aust.)*, *15*(1), 3–28.

Miller, W. E. (1994). An organizational history of the intellectual origins of the American National Election Studies. *European Journal of Political Research*, *25*(3), 247–265.

Morris, E. (2024, November 8). 2024 polls were accurate but still underestimated Trump. ABC News. https://abcnews.go.com/538/2024-polls-accurate-underestimated-trump/story?id=115652118

Noelle-Neumann, E. (1974). The spiral of silence a theory of public opinion. *Journal of Communication, 24*(2), 43–51. DOI: 10.1111/j.1460-2466.1974.tb00367.x

Novicoff, M. (2025, May 19). Polling was quietly still bad in 2024. The Atlantic. https://www.theatlantic.com/ideas/archive/2025/05/polling-2024-trump-bias/682834/

Nugroho, D. K. (2021, January). US presidential election 2020 prediction based on Twitter data using lexicon-based sentiment analysis. In *2021 11th International Conference on Cloud Computing, Data Science & Engineering (Confluence)* (pp. 136-141). IEEE.

Pew Research Center. (2024a, June 24). Public trust in government: 1958–2024. https://www.pewresearch.org/politics/2024/06/24/public-trust-in-government-1958-2024/

Pew Research Center. (2024b, September 9). Issues and the 2024 election. https://www.pewresearch.org/politics/2024/09/09/issues-and-the-2024-election/

Pfannenstiel, B. (2024, November 5). Pollster J. Ann Selzer to review data after Iowa Poll misses Trump win. Des Moines Register. https://eu.desmoinesregister.com/story/news/politics/iowa-poll/2024/11/05/pollster-j-ann-selzer-to-review-data-after-iowa-poll-misses-trump-win/76085598007/

Schaffner, B., & Soler, C. (2024, October 2). Pollsters are weighting surveys differently in 2024. Does it matter? Good Authority. https://goodauthority.org/news/pollsters-are-weighting-surveys-differently-in-2024/

Scheufle, D. A., & Moy, P. (2000). Twenty-five years of the spiral of silence: A conceptual review and empirical outlook. *International Journal of Public Opinion Research, 12*(1), 3–28.

Volkening, A., Linder, D. F., Porter, M. A., & Rempala, G. A. (2020). Forecasting elections using compartmental models of infection. *SIAM Review, 62*(4), 837–865.

Wang, M. Y., Hmielowski, J. D., Hutchens, M. J., & Beam, M. A. (2017). Extending the spiral of silence: Partisan media, perceived support, and sharing opinions online. *Journal of Information Technology & Politics, 14*(3), 248–262.

Wlezien, C., & Erikson, R. S. (1996). Temporal horizons and presidential election forecasts. *American Politics Quarterly, 24*(4), 492–505.

Zhou, Z., Serafino, M., Cohan, L., Caldarelli, G., & Makse, H. A. (2021). Why polls fail to predict elections. *Journal of Big Data, 8*(1), 1–28.

ENDNOTES

1 This figure refers to the average signed error between the final polling margins and the actual election results across states.

2 For general applications, see Gelman et al. (1995); for political science implementations, see Jackman (2009); and for an accessible applied example, see Acquah (2013).

Chapter 8
Predicting the Undecided Vote With Issue-Based Statistical Modeling: Fuzzy Clustering and Discriminant Analysis

Georgia Panagiotidou
http://orcid.org/0000-0002-7264-1187
Aristotle University of Thessaloniki, Greece

ABSTRACT

This chapter presents a framework for predicting the vote choice of undecided voters, integrating Fuzzy Clustering, stacked data analysis and binary logistic regression on the 2010 Greek regional elections. Drawing on the evolution of electoral behavior research -from Siegfried's electoral geography and the Columbia and Michigan schools to ideological polarization, rational choice and issue voting- the study addresses earlier limitations by capturing the probabilistic, multidimensional nature of voter preferences. Analysis of Voter Advice Application (HelpMeVote) data shows that party identification strongly predicts choices for the two major parties, while smaller parties are better explained by issue salience, candidate attributes and demographics. Fuzzy Clustering reveals overlapping thematic voter groups, while stacked data and logistic regression estimate their effect on stated and predicted vote choice. The findings demonstrate the value of probabilistic models for forecasting undecided voters and the need for adaptable, data-driven tools in the era of digital campaigns and AI.

DOI: 10.4018/979-8-3373-1037-4.ch008

INTRODUCTION

Predicting voter behavior has long been a central aim of electoral research, yet it remains a notoriously complex task. Among the various challenges that survey-based electoral forecasting faces, one of the most persistent is the treatment of the "undecided" vote. These are the respondents who, when surveyed prior to an election, either refuse to disclose their vote intention or explicitly state that they have not yet made up their minds. Their responses create a blind spot in predictive models, as undecided voters often constitute a non-trivial proportion of the electorate-sometimes large enough to influence the outcome of tightly contested elections. This group's eventual choices can determine the margin of victory, the viability of smaller parties, and the allocation of legislative seats in proportional representation systems.

In the Greek electoral context, the "undecided" category has played a particularly significant role over the last two decades. Political volatility, economic crises, and realignments in the party system have created an environment where voter loyalties are less entrenched than in the past, and where large swaths of the electorate remain open to persuasion until very close to election day. The collapse of long-standing partisan alignments after the onset of the sovereign debt crisis in 2009, combined with the emergence of new political forces and shifting issue salience, has meant that undecided voters are not simply a random subset of the population. Instead, they tend to reflect specific political, socio-economic, and attitudinal profiles that can-and should-be modeled.

The presence of these undecided voters complicates traditional polling methods. Standard techniques such as proportional reallocation of the undecided vote according to the distribution of decided voters, or the use of historical recall-based weighting, rest on assumptions that may not hold in a rapidly changing political environment. In periods of political instability, undecided voters may disproportionately lean towards anti-establishment or newly formed parties, making naïve redistribution approaches prone to systematic error. Thus, new methods are required to capture the underlying preferences and latent orientations of this group.

This chapter addresses the problem of predicting the electoral choices of undecided voters using a combination of *issue voting theory* and advanced statistical modeling techniques. The empirical application focuses on data from the HelpMeVote Voting Advice Application (VAA) in the context of the 2010 Greek regional elections. Unlike traditional survey instruments, VAAs offer respondents a battery of issue-based questions that reveal their positions across multiple policy dimensions. By leveraging these responses, it becomes possible to infer the latent policy proximities between voters and parties, and thus to predict electoral choices even for those who do not explicitly state them.

This approach combines three main methodological components:

1. Fuzzy Clustering – This method allows for the identification of voter groupings based on shared policy preferences, while acknowledging that political identities are rarely discrete. Instead of assigning each respondent to a single, mutually exclusive group, fuzzy clustering calculates degrees of membership in multiple groups. This is especially useful for modeling the fluid alignments of undecided voters, whose preferences may be spread across different political camps.
2. Stacked Data Techniques – Stacking creates a transformed dataset in which each respondent appears multiple times, once for each party under consideration. This format facilitates the estimation of *utility models* for party choice, integrating both the fuzzy cluster membership probabilities and additional variables such as stated choice (for the decided), issue salience, and socio-demographic characteristics.
3. Discriminant Analysis – As an auxiliary modeling step, discriminant analysis is used to derive scores that classify respondents, including the undecided, into predicted vote categories based on their issue positions and demographic attributes. This method has a long history in electoral research, but here it is integrated within a broader modeling framework that accounts for multidimensional issue space.

The theoretical framework guiding this work is grounded in issue voting theory, which posits that voters choose the party or candidate whose policy positions are closest to their own. While the theory has been widely applied in established democracies, its use in Greece offers a particularly interesting test case. Greek electoral politics during the period in question were characterized by a mix of traditional ideological cleavages (e.g. left–right economic policy disputes) and emergent issue dimensions (e.g. regional governance, public sector reform, and decentralization). For undecided voters, these issue-based proximities may play a decisive role in guiding eventual choice.

The choice of the 2010 regional elections as a case study is deliberate. These elections were the first to be held under the "Kallikratis" plan, a sweeping administrative reform that restructured local government and expanded the powers of regional authorities. As such, they introduced new political dynamics at the subnational level, intersecting with national political debates and the early stages of Greece's economic crisis. For researchers, the contest provides a unique setting in which to study how voters-especially the undecided-navigate issue-based considerations in an environment of institutional change.

This chapter therefore pursues several interrelated objectives:

- To demonstrate how VAA data can be used to model the vote choice of respondents who declare themselves undecided.

- To show how fuzzy clustering can reveal latent voter groupings and soft political identities that cut across traditional partisan boundaries.
- To illustrate how stacked data techniques enhance the estimation of utility models for vote choice.
- To evaluate the performance of discriminant analysis as an auxiliary prediction tool.
- To reflect on the broader implications of modeling undecided voters for electoral forecasting and political analysis.

The remainder of the chapter is organized as follows. The next section reviews the theoretical background of issue voting and its application in the Greek electoral context. Following this, the methodology section details the data sources, variables, and modeling procedures, drawing directly from the empirical work presented in the Greek-language chapters on fuzzy clustering, stacked data, and discriminant analysis. The subsequent section presents the results of the models, including predicted probabilities of vote choice for undecided respondents and the substantive interpretation of voter clusters. The discussion section synthesizes these findings, reflecting on their implications for understanding electoral behavior in Greece and for improving predictive models in contexts of political volatility.

In approaching this task, the chapter not only aims to solve a practical problem in electoral research but also to contribute to the theoretical understanding of how undecided voters can be conceptualized and studied. By treating the undecided vote as a predictable outcome of measurable issue-based orientations-rather than as a purely random or last-minute decision-we can refine both the science and practice of election analysis.

THEORETICAL BACKGROUND

Historical Perspectives on Electoral Behavior: From Early Models to Contemporary Applications

The study of electoral behavior has evolved through a series of theoretical and methodological paradigms, each shaped by the political contexts and research tools available at the time. The scientific study of electoral behavior can be traced to the pioneering work of André Siegfried, often considered the father of electoral geography. In his influential 1913 work Tableau politique de la France de l'Ouest sous la Troisième République, Siegfried examined regional voting patterns in France and sought to explain them through enduring socio-geographical characteristics. His most famous-and somewhat provocative-hypothesis linked political attitudes to the physical environment, arguing, for example, that the nature of the soil in a region could shape agricultural practices, patterns of land ownership, and, by extension, political preferences. Chalky soils, he suggested, fostered small, independent farming and conservative attitudes, whereas granite soils encouraged collective farming and more progressive leanings. While later research questioned the determinism of such claims, Siegfried's work established the enduring idea that political behavior is spatially patterned and that geography, economy, and social structure are interconnected in shaping electoral outcomes.

The next major theoretical leap came in the 1940s with the Columbia School, led by Paul Lazarsfeld and colleagues, whose landmark study The People's Choice (Lazarsfeld, Berelson, & Gaudet, 1968) shifted the focus from geography to social group membership as the primary determinant of vote choice. According to the sociological model they proposed, factors such as social class, religion, ethnicity, and local community networks structured political preferences and voting decisions. Voting was seen as largely habitual, embedded within a person's long-term social identity.

By the 1950s and 1960s, the Michigan School added a psychological dimension to the analysis. Campbell, Converse, Miller, and Stokes (1960) emphasized the central role of party identification-a deep-seated, affective orientation toward a political party that influenced perceptions of issues and candidates. The famous "funnel of causality" model positioned long-term partisan loyalties alongside short-term campaign factors, explaining both stability and change in electoral choice.

From the 1970s onwards, researchers increasingly recognized that traditional left–right divisions were being supplemented-or even challenged-by new polarization systems. In Western Europe, and eventually in Greece, political competition began to be mapped not only along the economic left–right axis but also along the GAL–TAN dimension (Green/Alternative/Libertarian vs. Traditional/Authoritarian/Nationalist), capturing conflicts over cultural, environmental, and lifestyle issues. These new dimensions reflected the rise of post-materialist values, social movements, and identity-based politics (Inglehart, 1990).

In parallel, rational choice theory and issue voting models (Downs, 1957; Key, 1966) reframed voters as strategic actors making utility-maximizing decisions based on spatial proximity to parties in a multidimensional issue space. This was a marked departure from the deterministic social and psychological models, and it opened the door to sophisticated spatial analysis of electoral competition. As campaigns became more professionalized, political marketing emerged as both a practice and an analytical framework, emphasizing targeted persuasion, segmentation of the electorate, and adaptation of political messages to voter segments.

In the Greek context, these theoretical shifts were reflected in the country's post-1974 *metapolitefsi* period, dominated initially by the bipolar competition between PASOK and New Democracy. Greek electoral politics through much of the post-1974 metapolitefsi period were dominated by a bipolar system centered on PASOK and New Democracy, with political competition structured largely along a left–right economic dimension (Lyrintzis, 1984; Mavrogordatos, 1984). The long-standing left–right axis, rooted in historical cleavages, remained dominant through the 1980s and 1990s, but from the 2000s onwards, new issues-such as EU integration, immigration, and environmental policy-entered the political agenda. However, the 2009–2015 period witnessed the destabilization of this two-party dominance, the emergence of new political formations, and the rise of issue dimensions tied to the economic crisis, EU integration, and governance reforms (Voulgaris & Nikolakopoulos, 2014). The 2009 financial crisis and subsequent political fragmentation brought about a dramatic restructuring of the party system, creating fertile ground for multi-dimensional competition and the application of issue-based models.

It is important to recognize that each of these theoretical approaches emerged within a specific socio-economic and technological environment. When that environment changed-whether due to economic crises, cultural shifts, institutional reforms, or technological revolutions-the explanatory power of prevailing models often declined, prompting the development of new frameworks better suited to the new realities. For example, the concept of the undecided voter has also evolved in this theoretical trajectory. In early models, undecided respondents were often treated as noise or excluded from analysis. In contemporary research, however, they are recognized as a potentially distinct subset of the electorate, whose indecision may reflect ambivalence between competing issue positions or dissatisfaction with the available choices (Franklin, 2004; Lewis-Beck et al., 2008). This recognition has spurred the development of methods capable of modeling their latent preferences rather than imputing them through crude proportional allocation.

Electoral behavior analysis is, therefore, an ongoing process of adaptation. In the 21st century, the rapid evolution of digital technology, big data, and artificial intelligence is transforming the possibilities for behavioral prediction. The availability of massive, high-resolution datasets-ranging from online activity logs to geospatial and socio-demographic microdata-combined with advanced machine learning techniques, is reshaping the methodological toolkit of political analysis. These tools offer unprecedented predictive power, but they also raise new questions about privacy, representativeness, and the interpretability of complex models. In this evolving landscape, the study of electoral behavior remains as dynamic and contested as the political systems it seeks to understand.

In sum, the shift from sociological determinism to attitudinal and issue-based models has expanded the explanatory power of electoral research, but it has also introduced new challenges-chief among them the accurate measurement and modeling of multidimensional political preferences. It is precisely within this challenge that the present study situates itself.

Established Approaches to Electoral Analysis and Prediction

Electoral forecasting has long relied on a repertoire of methodological tools, each with its own strengths and weaknesses. In Greece, as in other democracies, pre-election polls are the most visible instruments for predicting outcomes. The simplest of these are vote intention surveys, which ask respondents directly which party they plan to vote for. However, such surveys inevitably face the problem of undecided respondents and nonresponse bias. The most common corrective technique-redistributing undecided voters proportionally to the distribution of declared preferences-assumes that the undecided are a random subsample of the electorate, an assumption rarely met in practice (Nikolakopoulos, 2003).

A related approach involves recall-based adjustments, where respondents' reported vote in the previous election is used to weight their current vote intention. While this can partially correct for sample imbalances, it relies on accurate recall and honest reporting-both of which may be compromised by social desirability effects or post-hoc rationalization (Traugott & Katosh, 1979). Moreover, in contexts of rapid political change, such as Greece during the 2010s, the predictive value of past vote patterns diminishes sharply.

Exit polls, conducted on election day, circumvent some of the problems of pre-election surveys by interviewing voters immediately after they cast their ballots. They have been widely used in Greece since the 1990s and have achieved relatively high accuracy in many contests (Nikolakopoulos, 2001). Nonetheless, they are of limited use for forecasting prior to election day and are susceptible to nonresponse bias among certain voter groups.

Time-series models, incorporating multiple polls over the campaign period, offer another avenue for prediction. By smoothing short-term fluctuations and incorporating trend components, they can improve accuracy (Erikson & Wlezien, 2012). However, these models still depend on the quality of the underlying surveys and may fail to account for late shifts among undecided voters.

The limitations of these established methods become especially acute in periods of political volatility, the emergence of new issue dimensions, and the breakdown of stable partisan alignments. Under such conditions, approaches that model latent voter preferences directly, using detailed attitudinal data rather than relying solely on stated vote intention, offer a promising alternative. VAAs such as HelpMeVote provide precisely this kind of rich, multidimensional data, capturing voter positions across a range of policy issues. When combined with advanced techniques like fuzzy clustering, stacked data structures, and discriminant analysis, these datasets allow researchers to infer the likely choices of undecided respondents with greater nuance and accuracy. It is from this recognition of the shortcomings of traditional methods, and the potential of issue-based modeling, that the present chapter's methodological approach emerges.

METHODOLOGY

Data Source and Research Context

The empirical analysis in this chapter draws on data from the HelpMeVote Voting Advice Application (VAA), developed and deployed in the context of the 2010 Greek regional elections. VAAs are interactive online tools designed to assist voters in identifying the parties or candidates whose policy positions are most closely aligned with their own (Andreadis & Chadjipadelis, 2011; Andreadis & Chadjipadelis 2012). Respondents are presented with a structured set of policy statements and asked to indicate their level of agreement or disagreement. Based on their responses, the VAA calculates the degree of ideological proximity between the user and each party (Andreadis, 2014).

The 2010 Greek regional elections were the first held under the Kallikratis Plan, an ambitious administrative reform that restructured local governance. The reform created 13 regions with expanded political powers, replacing the older system of prefectures, and devolved significant responsibilities from central government to the regional level. The political stakes of these elections were heightened by their timing, less than a year after Greece entered the sovereign debt crisis and negotiated the first EU-IMF bailout program. Consequently, the campaign discourse intertwined regional policy issues with national-level debates on austerity, governance reform, and Greece's relationship with the European Union.

The HelpMeVote 2010 dataset includes responses from voters across the 13 regions, providing detailed attitudinal data on a broad range of issues, as well as socio-demographic variables. This makes it particularly suitable for analyzing the policy-based determinants of electoral choice, and for predicting the likely vote of respondents who declared themselves undecided or refused to answer the vote intention question.

Variables

The primary dependent variable is voting choice in the 2010 regional elections. For respondents who declared a vote intention, this variable takes the stated party preference. For those who reported being undecided or refused to answer, the value is initially missing and is later predicted using the modeling techniques described below.

The set of independent variables includes:

1. Issue Positions: Responses to the VAA's policy statements, measured on a Likert-type scale (typically 5-point), covering topics such as public sector reform, taxation, environmental policy, and governance structures.
2. Issue Salience: For each issue, respondents were also asked to indicate its importance to their vote decision. This allows the analysis to weight issue proximities according to their subjective importance.
3. Party Proximity: For decided voters, the calculated spatial proximity between the respondent's positions and those of each party serves as a direct predictor of vote choice.
4. Stated Choice and Choice Criteria: For decided voters, these variables reflect explicit vote intention and the primary criteria they used in making their decision (e.g. leadership, party program, ideology).
5. Demographic Characteristics: Age, gender, education, occupation, and region of residence.

Analytical Framework

The modeling strategy is designed to predict the likely vote choice of undecided respondents by combining three complementary techniques: fuzzy clustering, stacked data estimation, and discriminant analysis.

Traditional clustering methods assign each observation to a single cluster, implicitly assuming that political identities are discrete and mutually exclusive. Especially among undecided voters, preferences may span multiple political groupings. To capture this complexity, we employ fuzzy clustering, specifically, the fuzzy *c*-means algorithm, implemented through the fanny() function in R.

In fuzzy clustering, each respondent receives a membership probability score for each cluster, indicating the degree to which their policy positions align with the cluster's profile. For example, a respondent might be 0.65 affiliated with a center-left cluster and 0.35 affiliated with a pro-market conservative cluster. This probabilistic approach reflects the fluidity of political alignments and provides richer input for subsequent modeling.

The number of clusters was determined empirically using a combination of fit indices (e.g. partition coefficient, normalized classification entropy) and substantive interpretability. In the final solution, the clusters corresponded to identifiable political families present in the Greek political landscape at the time.

To estimate party choice as a function of both issue-based proximities and other covariates, the dataset is restructured into a stacked format. In this transformation, each respondent appears once for each party under consideration. This binary expansion allows the estimation of models where the dependent variable is coded as 1 if the party in the row is the respondent's choice, and 0 otherwise.

In the stacked dataset, independent variables such as fuzzy cluster membership scores, party proximities, and issue salience are recalculated for each party–respondent combination. This approach integrates the richness of multidimensional attitudinal data with the flexibility of standard choice modeling frameworks.

Within the stacked dataset, the probability of choosing a given party is modeled as a linear function of utility, where utility is a weighted combination of:

- Fuzzy cluster membership scores.
- Proximity between respondent and party on key issues.
- Party-specific salience scores.
- Socio-demographic covariates.

The estimation is carried out using linear regression for continuous utility scores, which can then be transformed into choice probabilities.

As a complementary step, discriminant analysis (DA) is used to classify respondents, including undecided voters, into predicted vote categories. DA constructs linear combinations of predictors that maximize the separation between predefined groups (in this case, parties). For decided voters, group membership is known and used to estimate the discriminant functions; these functions are then applied to undecided respondents to obtain predicted classifications.

While DA is less flexible than some modern machine learning algorithms, it offers the advantage of interpretability and ease of integration with the other components of the modeling framework.

The prediction process proceeds as follows:

1. Use fuzzy clustering to generate cluster membership probabilities for all respondents.
2. Transform the data into stacked format, incorporating cluster scores and party proximities.
3. Estimate utility models to obtain predicted choice probabilities for each party for every respondent.
4. Apply discriminant analysis as a secondary check, generating an auxiliary prediction for undecided voters.
5. Combine the results, assigning each undecided respondent the party with the highest predicted probability (or the most consistent classification across models).

This multi-method approach leverages the strengths of each technique, fuzzy clustering for nuanced voter segmentation, stacked data for flexible choice modeling, and discriminant analysis for confirmatory classification, resulting in a robust predictive framework tailored to the complexities of undecided voter behavior.

RESULTS AND FINDINGS

Voter Groups Based on the Alignment of Views with the Candidates for Regional Governor

Having at our disposal the positions of voters and of the regional governor candidates on thirty policy questions, we construct a common similarity coefficient that expresses the closeness between each voter's positions and each candidate's positions.

To build this similarity coefficient, we compute the distance between the political position of every voter and that of each candidate in the voter's region. This distance indicates how far the voter's position, derived from their 30 answers, lies from the corresponding position of each candidate.

The coefficient takes values in the closed interval [-1, 1]. A negative sign indicates dissimilarity between two positions, while higher positive values indicate greater affinity between the two positions under examination. The units of analysis are the Region of Attica and the Region of Central Macedonia.

Using Hierarchical Cluster Analysis on the voter–candidate distance matrix, we derive distinct groups of voters. These groups contain voters who exhibit similar degrees of proximity to specific candidates across the 30 issues. Specifically, the analysis yields six groups for Attica and six groups for Central Macedonia. From this grouping we create a new variable indicating the group membership of each respondent.

We then apply Correspondence Analysis to relate the voter groups to (a) party preference and (b) the preferred regional governor candidate (coded by the party that supports them), based on two survey questions in the VAA: which party the respondent feels closest to, and which candidate they prefer to vote for.

Figure 1. Association of voter groups and party preference - Region of Attica

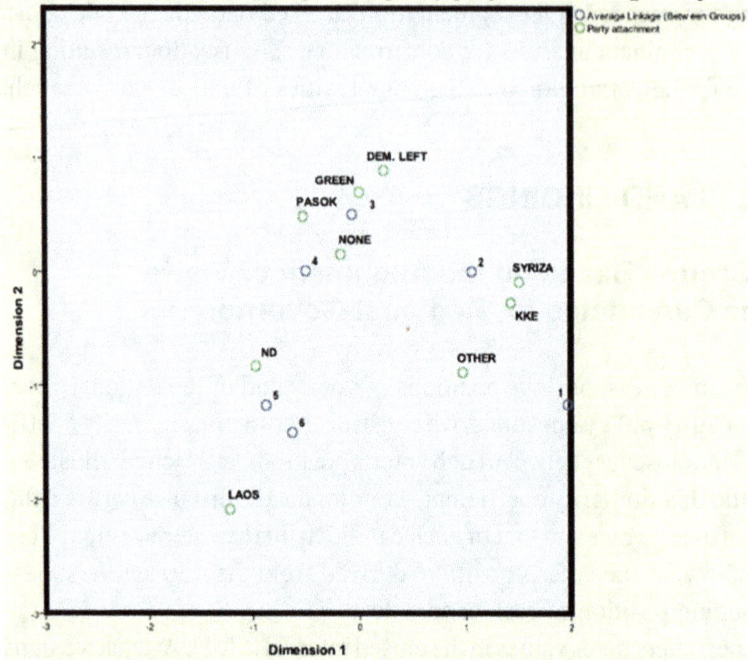

Figure 2. Association of voter groups and preferred candidate - Region of Attica

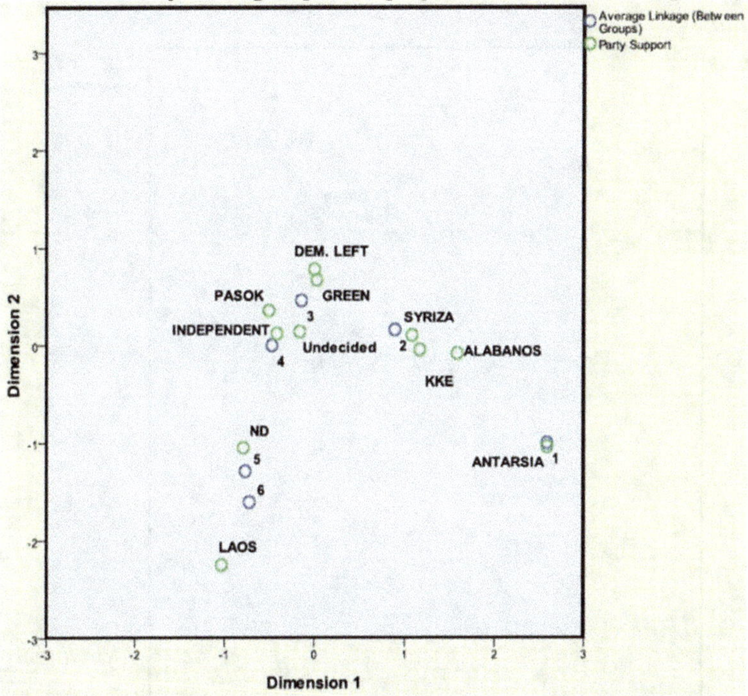

The analysis provides a clear picture of how issue-based voter groups interact with party preference. In Figure 1, Group 1 is clearly separated from the others and aligns with the left parties, especially ANTARSYA ("other"). Group 2 lies closest to New Democracy. Group 5 is positioned between LAOS and New Democracy, while Groups 3 and 4 are concentrated toward the center of the axis near PASOK, the Greens, and Democratic Left (DIMAR). Of note, Group 4 lies closer to PASOK but also near the "no party" option; Group 3 also approaches the center, between PASOK, the Greens, and no party, with a somewhat greater proximity than the other groups to Democratic Left. In Figure 2, the pattern persists when moving from party to preferred candidate: the same groups that express themselves in a certain way in terms of party choice tend, to a degree, to make a consistent candidate choice - namely, the candidate supported by their preferred party. The undecided appears in this map occupying the position analogous to those who declared no party preference.

Figure 3. Association of voter groups and party preference - Region of Central Macedonia

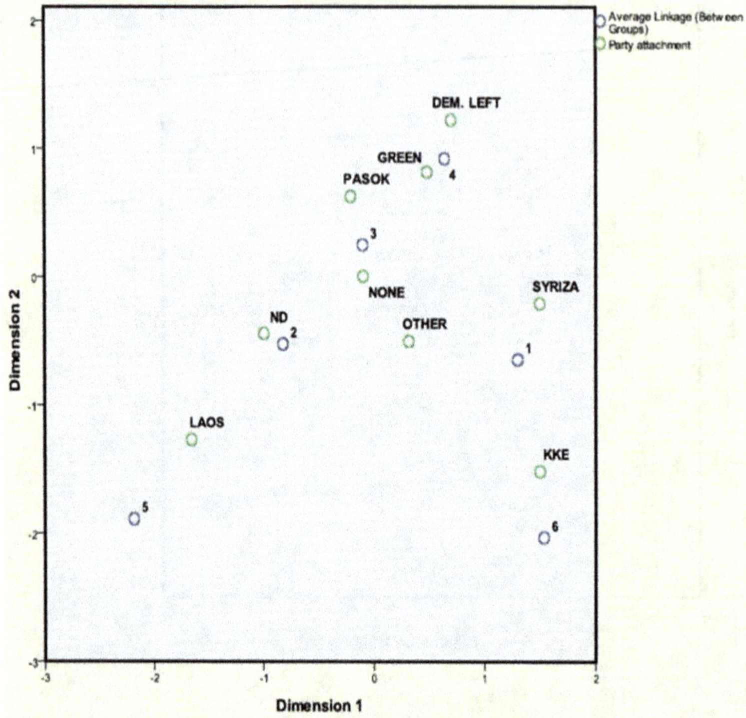

Figure 4. Association of voter groups and preferred candidate - Region of Central Macedonia

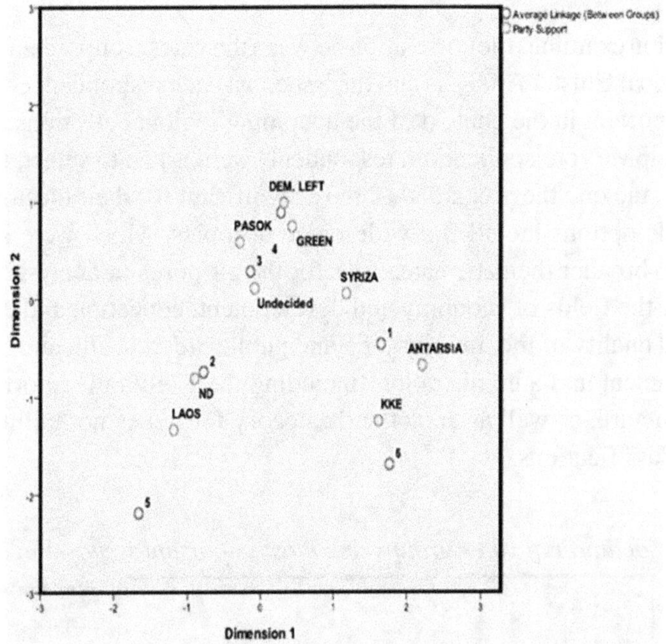

The distribution of groups and choices is almost identical to Attica, with the exception of Group 6, which in Central Macedonia is located at the left end of the axis and closest to the KKE. Group 1 is closest to SYRIZA, with relatively small distances to ANTARSYA and KKE as well. Group 2 nearly overlaps with New Democracy. Group 3 is again influenced by PASOK and "no party", Group 4 is near the Greens and Democratic Left, and Group 5 is again closest to LAOS (though not absolutely). The correspondence with preferred candidate (Figure 4) mirrors the party associations, based on the party backing of the candidates.

In sum, the voter groups formed from the voter–candidate distances (computed on the 30 issues) exhibit distinct electoral behavior profiles and defined party preferences. These patterns remain fairly stable when we move from party choice to the choice of regional governor candidate in the 2010 regional elections.

Association of Voter Groups and Selection of the Most Important Issues

This section examines the correlation between the voter groups identified through the Hierarchical Cluster Analysis and the issue that each respondent considers to be the most important in the context of the upcoming regional elections.

In the HelpMeVote application, respondents were asked to select, from a list of policy areas, the one they regarded as most significant for their electoral decision. The available options included a wide range of topics, which were subsequently grouped into broader thematic categories for the purposes of analysis. These categories cover the fields of economy and development, education and culture, environment and quality of life, immigration and public order, health and social policy, local government and administration (including the Kallikratis reform), transport and infrastructure, as well as an "other" category for issues not falling within the preceding classifications.

Figure 5. Association of voter groups and most important issue - Region of Attica

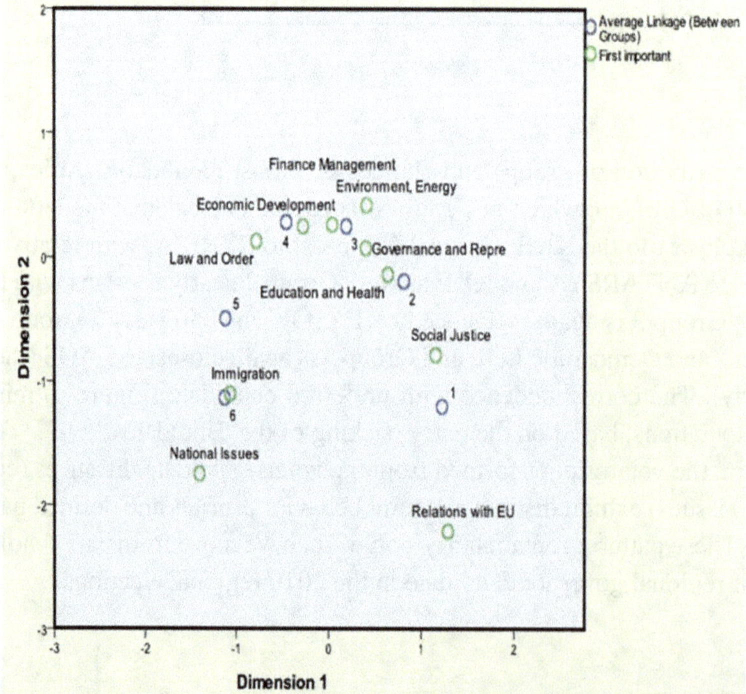

The correspondence analysis between voter groups and issue categories for the Region of Attica is presented in Figure 5. Figure 5 indicates clear differences between the groups in terms of issue salience. Group 2, which in the previous analysis was shown to be closely aligned with New Democracy, exhibits a strong focus on matters relating to the economy and development. Group 1, associated with the left, records higher proportions of respondents who prioritise health and social policy as well as environmental and quality-of-life concerns. Group 5, whose members are more closely aligned with LAOS, shows a marked emphasis on immigration and public order. Group 3, which was positioned near the centre of the political spectrum and includes respondents close to PASOK or with no declared party preference, displays a higher tendency to prioritise local government and administrative matters, consistent with a greater interest in governance reform. Finally, Group 4, associated with the Greens and Democratic Left, tends to place particular importance on environmental issues and sustainable urban planning.

Figure 6. Association of voter groups and most important issue - Region of Central Macedonia

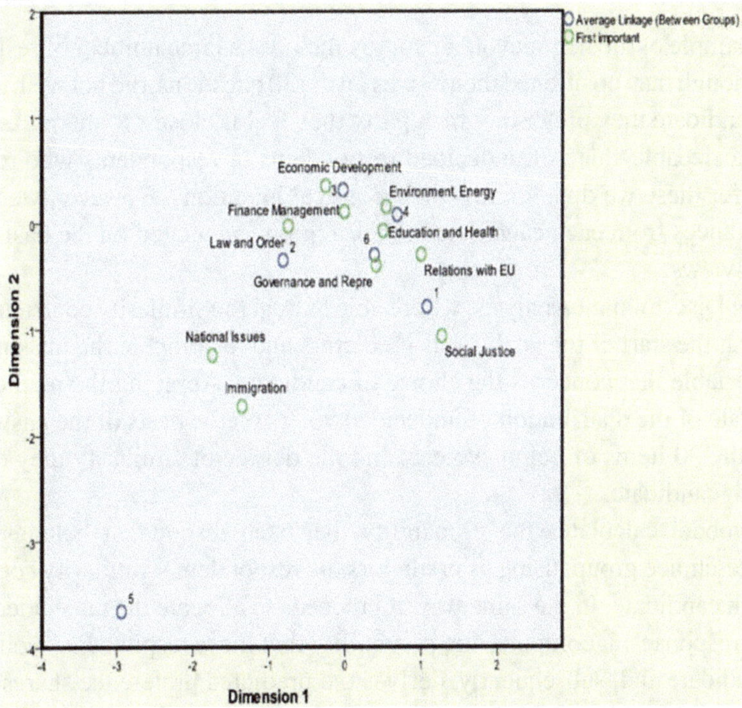

The equivalent results for the Region of Central Macedonia are presented in Figure 6. Here, the overall picture is broadly similar to that observed in Attica, with certain notable differences. Group 2 again prioritises the economy and development as the most important area for the upcoming elections. Group 6, which in the earlier analysis was found to be closely aligned with the KKE, places greater emphasis on health and social policy. Group 5 maintains its focus on immigration and public order, while Group 4 continues to prioritise the environment and quality of life. Group 3, as in Attica, is associated with local government and administrative issues, including the implementation of the Kallikratis reform.

Overall, the analysis reveals a consistent relationship between the ideological and partisan orientation of the voter groups and the issues they consider most important. Groups aligned with right-wing parties tend to focus more on economic development and security-related concerns, while groups on the left of the spectrum are more likely to emphasise social policy, environmental protection, and governance reforms. The stability of these patterns across both regions reinforces the robustness of the group classifications derived from the previous section.

Predicting the Vote Choice of the Undecided Based on Their Political Views

The sample of the helpmevote.gr survey includes a large number of respondents who, although they positioned themselves on the 30 questions, did not wish to answer which candidate they prefer or which party they feel is closest to them. As a result, there is a sizeable share of undecided respondents or respondents who refused to answer; for these we do not know their political intentions. However, we do know their distances from each candidate in their region, calculated on the basis of their political views.

Using Discriminant Analysis, we are able to treat the similarity coefficients constructed at the start of the analysis as predictors and to compute the missing values of the variable that concerns the choice of candidate. Applying the method yields an estimate of the distribution of undecided voters on the basis of the answers they gave to the 30 items of helpmevote.gr and the degree of similarity they exhibited with each candidate.

The model calculates the probability that each respondent belongs to each candidate-choice group, using as predictors the respondent's similarity coefficients with each candidate. In the same way, it proceeds to allocate the undecided and the missing responses: it computes the probability that these respondents would prefer each candidate and, subsequently, derives the predicted preference shares for each candidate within this group of voters.

Figure 7 and 8 report the predicted distribution percentages for the undecided and the refusals, as well as the distribution percentages for those who declared the candidate of their preference, according to the model's prediction.

Figure 7. Region of Attica - Classification Results

Classification Results[a]												
	Party Support	Predicted Group Membership										Total
		Σγουρός	Κικίλιας	Παφίλης	Γεωργιάδης	Μητρόπουλος	Διάκος	Ψαριανός	Χάγιος	Αλαβάνος	Δημαράς	
%	PASOK	52,7	8,9	1,4	5,8	2,7	8,0	10,4	,1	,9	9,1	100,0
	ND	12,1	37,4	4,0	27,0	1,5	3,0	3,5	,5	,5	10,4	100,0
	KKE	2,1	4,6	27,6	7,1	8,7	6,6	2,5	30,3	5,7	5,0	100,0
	LAOS	9,6	18,9	,6	59,6	,6	,9	,0	,0	,3	9,3	100,0
	SYRIZA	4,2	7,3	7,9	3,0	33,2	8,8	5,1	8,5	16,0	6,0	100,0
	GREEN	16,0	3,5	2,8	3,5	12,5	31,3	16,0	1,4	2,8	10,4	100,0
	DEM. LEFT	16,1	4,6	3,2	2,4	13,7	21,3	27,3	,6	3,6	7,2	100,0
	ANTARSIA	1,4	1,4	7,1	2,9	6,8	5,4	1,8	60,0	10,4	2,9	100,0
	ALABANOS	4,4	,9	9,8	2,2	13,8	6,2	6,2	28,0	24,9	3,6	100,0
	INDEPENDENT	18,7	17,4	6,2	11,5	5,8	14,3	8,9	,6	1,5	15,2	100,0
	Ungrouped cases	14,1	14,0	6,8	11,5	9,0	12,7	9,3	5,4	5,2	11,9	100,0

Figure 8. Region of Central Macedonia - Classification Results

Classification Results[a]									
Party Support	Predicted Group Membership								Total
	PASOK	ND	KKE	LAOS	SYRIZA	GREEN	DEM. LEFT	ANTARSIA	
PASOK	50,5	14,1	2,6	3,7	3,4	9,2	16,2	,3	100,0
ND	15,8	47,5	3,8	23,5	1,4	4,9	2,7	,3	100,0
KKE	4,6	9,2	32,7	8,5	11,8	3,3	2,0	28,1	100,0
LAOS	7,1	26,4	4,3	59,3	,7	,7	1,4	,0	100,0
SYRIZA	11,7	8,3	8,7	2,4	25,7	14,6	6,3	22,3	100,0
GREEN	20,5	10,2	2,3	1,1	20,5	23,9	17,0	4,5	100,0
DEM. LEFT	24,1	11,6	3,6	2,7	9,8	17,9	25,9	4,5	100,0
ANTARSIA	,0	5,5	5,5	1,4	15,1	8,2	6,8	57,5	100,0
Ungrouped cases	16,0	26,4	10,2	11,1	8,2	11,9	9,0	7,2	100,0

The Discriminant model predicts, at 52.7% and 50.5% for the Regions of Attica and Central Macedonia respectively, that voters who stated they would vote for the PASOK candidate will ultimately remain faithful to their choice, based on their similarity scores with all regional governor candidates. The corresponding figures are 37.4% and 47.5% for New Democracy. The percentages decrease for KKE, SYRIZA, the Greens, and Democratic Left, while they appear quite high for LAOS and ANTARSYA.

It follows that there is greater confusion among the parties of the Left with respect to the consistency between policy views and vote choice, whereas in the two major parties and in the two parties that most closely occupy the extremes of the left–right axis there is greater affinity as regards the association of views and vote choice.

Influence of Political Views (Issues) on the Final Vote Choice

From the application of Discriminant Analysis as a prediction method, a new variable is created, indicating the group to which each voter is predicted to belong with respect to candidate choice. This new variable, in combination with the variables relating to party choice and candidate choice, is entered into a multiple-entry table using the Crosstabs method.

In this way, it is possible to estimate the degree to which the factor of voters' political views contributes to the final vote choice. Specifically, taking the Region of Attica as an example, it is found that, among voters who declare feeling closest to PASOK as a party and state their intention to vote for the PASOK candidate, 55.1% are located closer to the PASOK candidate in terms of the proximity of their political views. Correspondingly, for ND voters who prefer the ND candidate, this percentage is 40.2%.

Calculating the average for the percentages of all candidates shows that, in the Region of Attica, for 47.1% of those declaring a preference for a specific party and its candidate, their views are at a short distance from the positions and views of the political space they choose. An example for the candidates of PASOK is shown in Figure 9. For the Region of Central Macedonia, this figure rises to 52.4%. In this way, it follows that the final vote choice is shaped by approximately 50% from the voters' views and their alignment with the positions of the parties and their candidates.

Figure 9. Contribution of proximity on political views (similarity on issues) in vote intention

Party Support * Predicted Group for Analysis 1 * Party attachment Crosstabulation											
% within Party Support											
Party attachment/Party support		Predicted Group for Analysis 1									
		Σγουρός	Κικίλιας	Παφίλης	Γεωργιάδης	Μητρόπουλος	Διάκος	Ψαριανός	Χάγιος	Αλαβάνος	Δημαράς
PASOK	Σγουρός	55,1%	7,6%	1,3%	5,7%	2,8%	7,4%	10,1%		,9%	9,2%
	Κικίλιας	30,0%	10.0%	10.0%	20,0%	10.0%					20,0%
	Παφίλης			50.0%							50.0%
	Γεωργιάδης	38,9%	16,7%		27,8%						16,7%
	Μητρόπουλος	22,2%	11,1%		11,1%	33,3%	11,1%				11,1%
	Διάκος	33,3%				11,1%	11,1%	44,4%			
	Ψαριανός	29,8%	14,9%		6,4%	2,1%	12,8%	34,0%			
	Χάγιος					33,3%		33,3%		33,3%	
	Αλαβάνος	33,3%		11,1%	11,1%			22,2%			22,2%
	Δημαράς	36,5%	11,5%	4,1%	6,8%	1,4%	12,8%	12,8%			14,2%
	Undecided	36,5%	13,1%	,7%	5,1%	4,7%	14,2%	11,7%		,4%	13,5%
	Total	46,4%	9,6%	1,6%	6,2%	3,4%	9,6%	11,8%		,7%	10,7%

The sequence of steps in the above analysis, as applied to the HelpMeVote data from the 2010 regional elections, constitutes an alternative proposal for a model estimating a voter's final choice. The central idea of this methodological proposal is based on the concept of issue voting, which, according to the results of the analysis, applies to a degree of 50%.

This model manages to offer solutions to the problems of existing methods, which concern handling undecided votes and weighting based on previous data, such as past election results. More specifically, the proposed prediction model uses issues, that is, voters' positions on political matters and their alignment with candidate parties or individuals on those issues, as the predictive factor.

The estimation of what someone will vote is not derived as an assumption based on what they might have voted for in previous electoral contests, but on the extent to which they align with each candidate entity in relation to their position on political issues.

In addition, this method addresses the issue of allocating undecided respondents and those who refuse to answer regarding their voting intention, since the estimation of their final choice is produced from their position on issues rather than from an assumption artificially generated by allocating them according to previous election results. Respondents may refuse to give a clear answer as to what they will vote for, but they have clearly positioned themselves on 30 political-content questions that outline their political profile.

The analysis shows that the groups of voters formed by calculating voter–candidate distances based on issues coincide with specific party choices, choices of individuals and choices on the issues they consider most important. Consequently, in this way, undecided voters and those refusing to answer can be distributed according to their final choice by using Discriminant Analysis.

However, the model shows certain weaknesses that prevent its direct application in electoral research, specifically:

1. The model considers as independent variables only the distances indicating the voter–candidate alignment on issues, without including other variables that might have a smaller but nonetheless significant influence on the final choice (party identification, demographic characteristics, etc.).
2. The HelpMeVote application can collect a very large volume of data at a lower cost than other methods (due to the wide dissemination of the survey through extensive use of social media, and the fact that the questionnaire is accessible to any internet user). Nevertheless, this sample cannot be considered representative of the population, since, as mentioned in Chapter 6, entire population groups are overrepresented, underrepresented, or entirely absent.

Therefore, the use of the present model may prove more effective for analyzing the electoral behavior of selected population groups that are more familiar with internet use, such as younger age groups or groups with higher educational attainment.

The application of the model is based on data collected in the 2010 regional elections, which increases its complexity since it involves candidates originating from individual or combined party entities. In addition, many local factors influencing the choice of regional governor candidate are not taken into account.

Therefore, applying the model:

a) to parliamentary elections where the voter is called upon to vote for parties and not individuals,
b) to specific population groups, and
c) with the addition of more independent variables, will be able to produce clearer results, interpretations, and estimations of final vote choice, and is proposed as future research.

Estimating the Characteristics and Attributes of Voters That Determine the Probability of Voting for Each Candidate Party or Individual

In this section it is attempted to develop an alternative model for estimating voters' electoral stance based on the results of the HelpMeVote survey conducted during the 2010 regional elections, incorporating the Fuzzy Clustering and Stacked Data Analysis methods. The aim is to identify those voter characteristics that participate in a linear model as significant predictors of the probability of voting for each of the options available in an electoral contest.

The voting advice application (VAA), by correlating voters and candidates on the basis of their positions on issues, is able to place voters on the electoral map. However, it is worth noting that each voter may simultaneously maintain similar distances from more than one candidate. This highlights the notion of overlapping political choices, meaning the possibility that a voter may be attracted to more than one political camp.

This implies that the estimation of their final choice is not simply the increased probability of one single option, but a combination of probabilities of voting for each of the electoral options available to them. For example, a voter may have a 60% probability of voting for one party but, at the same time, the same probability of voting for its rival party.

Up to now, electoral analysis has primarily used the concept of party choice as an independent variable for predicting election results. Party choice has been the main weighting factor in vote intention surveys or the main independent variable in the linear time-series prediction models of political barometers.

In contrast, factors that can better approximate the prediction of electoral choice—known as utilities—are not generally taken into account when forming an electoral estimate. In electoral analysis, utilities are used as propensity-to-vote (PTV) indicators and are usually derived from survey questions asking voters to indicate the probability of voting for each party or candidate (van der Eijk & Franklin, 1996).

According to Anthony Downs' theory, utilities represent the degree of benefit that each candidate or party may provide to a voter (Downs, 1957). Utilities can be expressed through voter characteristics and attributes that reflect the probability of voting for each candidate party or individual (van der Eijk et al., 1996).

As electoral preferences, utilities can be obtained from a single linear regression model designed to predict vote choice, where the independent variables are elements defining a voter's political identity—such as ideology, issues, degree of party identification, etc. (van der Brug et al., 2003). The logic of such a model is similar to that described in the design of hypothesis tests in issue voting theory (MacDonald, Listhaug & Rabinowitz, 1991).

In the case of HelpMeVote, the distances between voters and candidates can function as the probabilities of voting for each candidate, based on their issue proximity. Thus, they can be incorporated into a model for calculating utilities, i.e. the probability that the voter will select each of the candidate options. Each electoral preference results from the voter–candidate match on the basis of issues.

The outcome of such a model is a set of combinations for each voter, meaning a voting probability for each option separately, in which the dependent variable is the voter's distance from each candidate. The proposed model further integrates into the electoral prediction methodology the Fuzzy Clustering and Stacked Data Analysis techniques.

Specifically, the process begins by calculating, for each voter, the probabilities of belonging to a group in relation to proximity to each candidate, based on their position on issues, applying the Fuzzy Clustering method. The probability of voting for each candidate (as a utility) is formulated as the result of a linear model:

$$y_i=a+b\cdot x_i+e_i$$

where the independent variables are the probabilities resulting from the Fuzzy Clustering application, as well as the answers provided to the following questions:

a) Which party does the voter feel closest to?
b) Which candidate will they choose to vote for?
c) What is the criterion on which they will base their choice?
d) What do they consider the most important issue for them?

and certain demographic variables.

Within this general model, the Stacked Data Analysis method is applied so as to derive the individual probabilities that a HelpMeVote user will vote for each of the available options.

In the following sections, a brief description of the Fuzzy Clustering and Stacked Data Analysis methods is provided, detailing how they are integrated into the model, followed by the presentation of the results obtained from applying this model.

Fuzzy Clustering

Fuzzy logic, as a multi-valued logic system, first appeared in 1920 through the research work of Lukasiewicz and Tarski. However, the official use of the term "fuzzy logic" was first introduced in 1965 in the study by Lotfi Zadeh on fuzzy set theory (Zadeh, 1965). Today, fuzzy logic is applied in many fields as a fundamental probabilistic theory, including statistics, sociology, computer science, and artificial intelligence.

Fuzzy logic allows the analysis of data with approximate values, as well as incomplete or imprecise information (fuzzy data). This method contrasts with binary logic, which assumes that data can only take two values (yes/no).

Fuzzy logic is based on the existence of multiple values or probabilities and the assumption that values can be approximate and imprecise rather than fixed and exact. Compared with traditional binary sets, where variables can take true or false values, variables in fuzzy logic can take values ranging between 0 and 1 on a corresponding yes–no scale (Stanford Encyclopedia of Philosophy).

Fuzzy logic has been extended to handle the concept of partial truth, where the truth value may range from completely true to completely false (Novák, Perfilieva & Močkoř, 1999).

On this basis, the probability of vote choice is not restricted to the currently existing options of parties or individuals participating in an electoral process, but is distributed across all options with smaller probabilities. That is, when predicting a voter's electoral choice, the voter is assigned different probabilities of voting for each party or candidate running for election.

The probability of voting for each option is not binary (yes/no) but lies on a scale from 0 to 1, with probabilities for different options often overlapping.

The Fuzzy Clustering method, founded on fuzzy logic, is proposed here as an alternative methodological tool for analyzing data in vote estimation. Fuzzy Clustering operates through a class of algorithms in which the assignment of data points to clusters is not absolute (yes/no) but "fuzzy," precisely as in fuzzy logic (Nock & Nielsen, 2006).

In data clustering, the process involves dividing the data into categories or groups such that the data within each group exhibit the highest possible degree of similarity, while data belonging to different groups show a high degree of dissimilarity. The similarity/dissimilarity coefficient is defined in each case according to the subject of analysis and the variable under investigation.

In Cluster Analysis, data are divided into distinct groups, with each element belonging to only one group. In Fuzzy Clustering, an element may belong to more than one group. Each element is thus associated with each group with a probability or percentage of membership. This membership degree indicates the intensity of the relationship between the data and each group.

Fuzzy clustering involves identifying these degrees of membership of data points in the various groups and then assigning them to one or more of these groups accordingly.

By following the principles of fuzzy logic and fuzzy clustering, for a voter who expresses their electoral intention toward each available option, the model does not estimate a single, definitive final choice. Instead, it estimates the probability of voting for each option separately. This allows all partial probabilities to be considered in the process of estimating an electoral outcome.

The method described above is used in the analysis of data generated by the Voting Advice Application (VAA) during the 2010 regional elections, with the aim of approaching an alternative vote prediction model that is more strongly based on issue positions and on the alignment of voters with candidates on those issues.

Stacked Data Analysis

A dataset is said to be "stacked" when the data for a single respondent appear as multiple cases (e.g. multiple rows of data). The purpose of stacking the data is to facilitate the calculation of statistical measures for a set of related questions that we wish to analyze collectively, rather than each one separately (van der Brug et al., 2003).

Figure 10. Example of creating a stacked dataset

A/A	Q1a	Q1b	Q1c	Q2a	Q2b	Q2c	Q3a	Q3b	Q3c
1	2	3	3	5	2	1	1	4	1
2	6	2	4	2	4	2	2	3	5
3	5	2	2	1	3	2	5	3	2

A/A	Observation	Q1	Q2	Q3
1	1	2	6	5
1	2	3	2	2
1	3	3	4	2
2	1	5	2	1
2	2	2	4	3
2	3	1	2	2
3	1	1	2	5
3	2	4	3	3
3	3	1	5	2

Thus, in the example of Figure 10, stacking is used to calculate statistical measures such as the mean, frequency, etc., for the entirety of question Q1, which consists of all its sub-questions Q1a, Q1b, …, Q3c. Using the original unstacked dataset, such calculations would not be feasible; however, once the file is stacked, the computation of statistical measures for Q1 becomes significantly easier.

Stacking data increases the size of the dataset (for example, from a sample of 100 respondents with 10 data columns, we create a dataset with a total of 1,000 observations). This can create issues for statistical tests, but it can be partially addressed by applying a weight (e.g. in this example, assigning each observation a weight of 0.1).

Propensity-to-Vote (PTV) analysis requires stacking the survey data, because in this way each respondent appears in multiple rows, each time with the attributes we wish to examine.

In addition, the dependent variable is not usually the intention to vote for a specific party, but rather the propensity to vote for a broader party category as we define it, since comparisons may sometimes be made between different systems. This also affects the independent variables, which must be transformed in various ways so that they can be used in a stacked-data analysis (van der Brug et al., 2003).

In this respect, PTV analysis resembles discrete choice modeling, which incorporates measured stated preferences (utilities) rather than drawing inferences directly from them (van der Brug et al., 2003).

Application of the Method

For this analysis, data were used from the Vote Advice Application (VAA) survey conducted for the 2010 regional elections. More specifically, the analysis focused on the group of voters in the region of Central Macedonia. Responses from 1,500 individuals were used, drawn from the total of 4,850 who participated in the survey.

Initially, to determine groups of voters based on their proximity to the eight candidates for regional governor in terms of their positions on political issues, the Fuzzy Clustering method was applied, using the statistical software R.

In the analysis, the variables used were the distances of each respondent from each candidate, as calculated in the previous step. A CSV file was created containing the distances of each respondent from each candidate, where the rows corresponded to respondents and the columns to candidates.

The command package for Fuzzy Clustering was applied:

```
fanny(x, k, diss = inherits(x, “dist”), memb.exp = 2,

metric = c(“euclidean”, “manhattan”, “SqEuclidean”),

stand = FALSE, iniMem.p = NULL, cluster.only = FALSE,

keep.diss = !diss && !cluster.only && n < 100,

keep.data = !diss && !cluster.only,

maxit = 500, tol = 1e-15, trace.lev = 0)1
```

In this case, the specific command used to generate the results was:

```
Y<-fanny(x, 5, memb.exp = 1.5, diss, metric = c(“euclidean”), stand,

cluster.only=FALSE)
```

The application of the analysis produced a table showing, in percentage terms, the probability of each respondent belonging to each of the five identified clusters.

Figure 11. Descriptive analysis of all 5 clusters

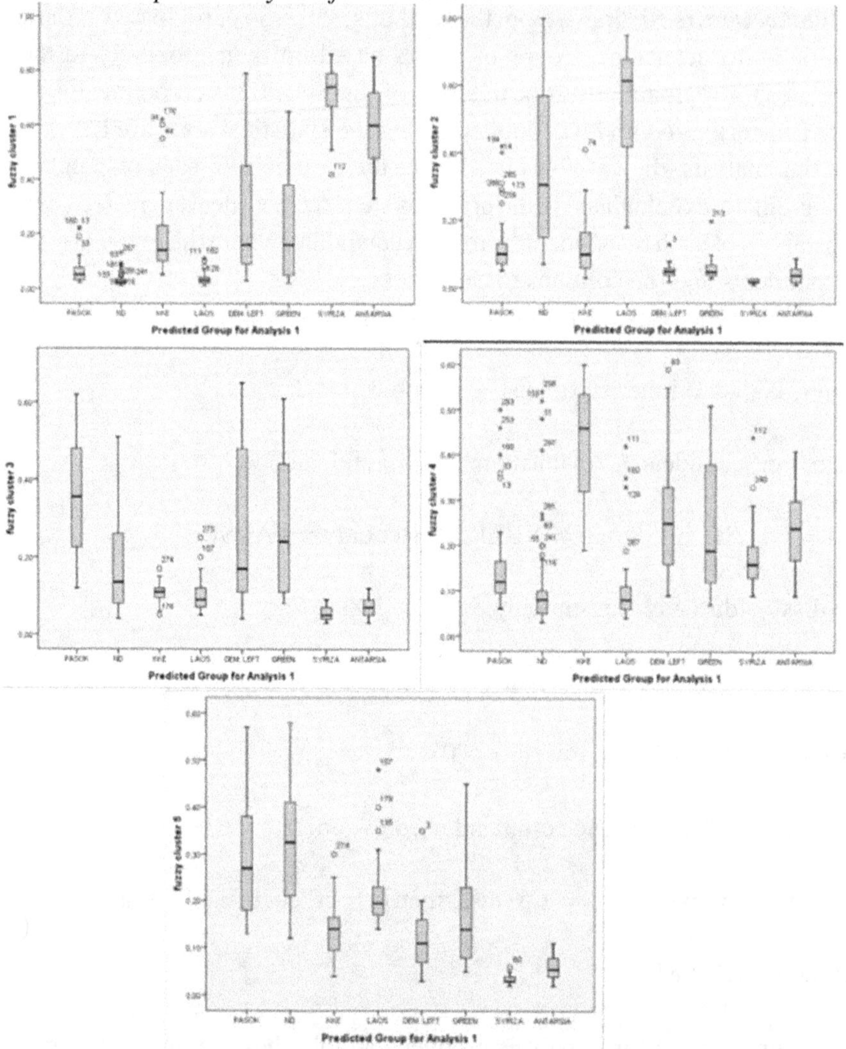

By applying the Explore command in SPSS to these groups, the main characteristics of the five groups can be identified (as shown in the boxplots in Figure 11):

- Cluster 1: Voters showing high issue-based proximity to the candidates of small parties positioned in the centre-left of the axis (DIMAR, Ecologists, ANTARSYA, and SYRIZA).
- Cluster: Voters positioned closer to ND (New Democracy) and LAOS, i.e., showing issue-based alignment with right-wing parties.

- Cluster: Voters aligned with parties closer to the centre of the axis, such as PASOK, DIMAR, and the Ecologists.
- Cluster: Voters aligned with KKE (Communist Party of Greece).
- Cluster: Voters showing thematic proximity to the two main governing parties, ND and PASOK.

In the next stage of analysis, the variables to be included in the model were selected. From the VAA survey, the following variables were chosen:

1. Demographic data: gender, education level, age group.
2. Voting intention:
   a) Which party do you feel closest to?
   b) Which candidate are you most likely to vote for?
   c) What is the main criterion on which you will base your choice?
3. Issue positions:
   a) Which issue do you consider the most important for you?
   b) The probability of belonging to each of the five groups identified through Fuzzy Clustering in the first stage of the analysis.
4. Alternative predictor variable: the variable generated in the previous step using Discriminant Analysis for predicting candidate choice for all respondents, even those declaring themselves undecided or refusing to answer.

All selected variables had to be transformed into binary (0–1) variables to enable their analysis as stacked data. This was done by creating as many new binary variables as the number of values for each original variable. For example, the "education" variable, which had four values, was transformed into four separate variables, each representing one value of the original variable, coded 0 for "no" (does not belong to this group) and 1 for "yes" (belongs to this group).

In the next stage, the entire dataset had to be transformed into stacks. It was necessary to create a new variable indicating the stack number. Nine stacks were created for each observation, one for each candidate in the Central Macedonia region, including the "undecided" option.

The data were stacked according to three groups of variables:

a) Variables related to the question "Which candidate will you vote for?"
b) Variables predicting the vote according to Discriminant Analysis results from previous step
c) The variable identifying the stack number.

In the resulting dataset, each respondent and their answers appear in nine consecutive rows. Each row displays the answers corresponding to each stack value (1 to 9), representing each candidate or the "undecided" choice.

The Split File → Compare Between Groups command in SPSS was then applied, using the variable identifying the stacks.

The next step of the analysis involved applying Binary Logistic Regression for two different cases:

- Case 1: Binary Logistic Regression with the dependent variable being the stated voting intention for the candidates for regional governor. Independent variables included all demographic variables, the declared closeness to each party, and the five variables representing the probability of belonging to each of the five thematic groups.
- Case 2: Binary Logistic Regression with the dependent variable being the predicted voting intention for the regional governor candidates, according to the Discriminant Analysis performed in the previous step. Independent variables included all demographic variables and the declared closeness to each party.

Predicting Vote Choice

From the analysis results, coefficients were obtained for all the variables used. From the full set of variables, only those with a coefficient greater than ± 1.96 were selected. In this analysis, variables whose coefficient approached that value closely were also included.

Negative coefficients indicate a negative association between the variable and the outcome we aim to estimate, in this case, the intention to vote for each candidate individually. Conversely, positive coefficients indicate a positive association.

In Case 1, where the dependent variable is the stated choice of candidate, the following are observed for each party (i.e., the candidate representing it):

- PASOK: Significant factors include declaring closeness to PASOK and DIMAR and citing as main criteria for the vote choice whether the candidate has party support and their personality.
- New Democracy (ND): Significant factors include closeness to ND and the candidate's party support. Equally important is not feeling close to PASOK (negative coefficient).
- KKE: Significant factors include closeness to the party, selecting "social justice" as the most important issue, and not selecting personality as a voting criterion.

- LAOS: Determining factors include opposing the first group from the Fuzzy Clustering analysis (which represented the positions of small centre-left parties on issues). Closeness to LAOS and citing immigration and social justice as most important issues, are also significant.
- DIMAR: Strong association only with increased closeness to the party.
- Ecologists: Significant factors include closeness to the party, selecting personality as a voting criterion, and not citing relations with the EU as an important issue.
- SYRIZA: Significant factors include closeness to the party and selecting personality as an important criterion in forming the final choice.
- ANTARSYA: Strong association with answering "Other" regarding the party one feels closest to.
- Undecided/No answer: Strong negative association with closeness to all other parties, especially the two traditional governing parties (PASOK and ND), indicating an anti-bipartisan stance. Negative association is also found for party support as a criterion and social justice as an important issue.

In Case 2, where the dependent variable is the predicted candidate choice based on the Discriminant Analysis applied previously, the following are observed for each party:

- PASOK: Significant factors include holding a postgraduate degree, closeness to PASOK, and citing candidate's knowledge of problems as a main voting criterion.
- ND: Significant factors include closeness to ND and greater distance from parties positioned from the centre to the far left (PASOK, DIMAR, SYRIZA, KKE).
- KKE: Significant factors include closeness to the party, greater distance from PASOK and ND, and not belonging to the postgraduate education group.
- LAOS: Significant factors include closeness to LAOS and ND, greater distance from PASOK, and negative association with knowledge of problems, personality, and programme as voting criteria. Regarding issues, immigration and national matters are most important, while energy, environment, transport, education, and health are considered unimportant.
- DIMAR: Significant factors include postgraduate education, closeness to DIMAR and PASOK, and greater distance from ND.
- Ecologists: Significant factors include closeness to the party and greater distance from PASOK and ND.
- SYRIZA: Distribution is linked to closeness to SYRIZA, secondarily to DIMAR, and greater distance from ND. Important criteria include citing per-

sonal relationships as a key factor and "government changes and reforms in representativeness" as the most important issue. Additionally, they are less likely to have only primary or secondary education and more likely to belong to the 45–54 age group.

- ANTARSYA: Significant factors include closeness to KKE, SYRIZA, and "Other," not belonging to the postgraduate education group, citing party support as a criterion, and naming education, health, and social justice as important issues.

From the findings of the Binary Logistic Regression, it can be concluded that many variables contribute to estimating voting intention, and these differ for each choice available to a voter. Party identification plays a significant role in shaping the final choice, but it is not the only variable determining voting intention.

For the traditional governing parties, party identification is more important as an independent variable in predicting final choice. However, for smaller parties, specific issue categories, choice criteria, or even demographic characteristics, particularly education level and age, play a major role in estimating the probability of voting for each candidate.

Thus, in forming a model to calculate the probability of each candidate being voted for, all variables showing strong coefficients for each individual case should be taken into account. Below, Table 1 presents the coefficients for Case 1 (dependent variable: stated candidate preference), while Table 2 presents the coefficients for Case 2 (dependent variable: predicted candidate choice).

Table 1. Probability voting for each party for each voter characteristic (dependent variable: stated candidate preference)

variable	label	PASOK	ND	KKE	LAOS	DIMAR	ECOLOGISTS	SYRIZA	ANTARSYA	UNDECIDED
f1	Issue group 1				-1,8738					
f2	Issue Group 2									
f3	Issue group 3									
f4	Issue group 4									
f5	Issue Group 5									
female										
edu1	Up to Lyceum									
edu3	Master									
party_attach1	PASOK	10,9364	-2,9909							-9,7316
party_attach2	ND		9,0228							-7,7099
party_attach3	KKE			6,2767						-4,1656
party_attach4	LAOS				5,6539					-5,0460
party_attach5	SYRIZA							7,2241		-5,2969
party_attach6	ECOLOGISTS						5,3684			-3,1996
party_attach7	DIMAR	2,0502				4,6372				-3,2679
party_attach8	OTHER								2,1348	
criteria1	Knowledge of the problems									
criteria3	Party support	3,9723	2,5357							-4,1664
criteria4	Personality	1,8234		-2,6487			1,8598	2,0110		

continued on following page

Table 1. Continued

variable	label	PASOK	ND	KKE	LAOS	DIMAR	ECOLOGISTS	SYRIZA	ANTARSYA	UNDECIDED
criteria5	Personal relationships									
criteria6	Program									
issue2	Economic development									
issue3	Financial management									
issue4	Migration-National issues				2,3095					
issue5	Energy, environment transport									
issue6	Education and health									
issue7	Social justice			2,3257	2,0867					-2,4268
issue8	Relations with the EU						-5,4645			
issue9	Government and Representativeness Reforms									
age1	18-24									
age2	25-34									
age4	45-54									
age5	54-65+									

continued on following page

Table 1. Continued

variable	label	PASOK	ND	KKE	LAOS	DIMAR	ECOLOGISTS	SYRIZA	ANTARSYA	UNDECIDED
Constant		-0,3733	-1,3103	-0,7841	1,1298	-1,2526	-0,6434	0,0848	1,1492	1,3104
N		1500,0000	1500,0000	1500,0000	1500,0000	1500,0000	1500,0000	1500,0000	1500,0000	1500,0000
NAGELKERKE R SQUARE		0,6620	0,5440	0,6880	0,6360	0,4420	0,6460	0,6140	0,6170	0,4030

Table 2. Probability voting for each party for each voter characteristic (dependent variable: predicted candidate choice)

variable	label	PASOK	ND	KKE	LAOS	SYRIZA	GREENS	DIMAR	OTHER	UNDECIDED
female										
edu1	**Up to Lyceum**							-2,5532		
edu3	**Master's Degree**	2,1251	-2,5746	-2,0622		3,4161			-1,9307	
party_attach1	**PASOK**	7,5759	-2,3952	-2,9027	-1,9116	1,8336	-2,1740			
party_attach2	**ND**		4,9787	-2,2908	1,9649	-1,8795	-2,1131	-2,3998		
party_attach3	**KKE**		-2,1576	3,6828					3,2710	
party_attach4	**LAOS**				3,9714					
party_attach5	**SYRIZA**		-3,0071					4,4318	4,3418	
party_attach6	**GREENS**		-2,3213				2,3749			
party_attach7	**DIMAR**					2,7734		2,6334		
party_attach8	**OTHER**								1,8332	
criteria1	**Knowledge of the problems**	2,5992			-2,1350					
criteria3	**Party support**								2,4609	
criteria4	**Personality**				-2,0662					
criteria5	**Personal relationships**							2,3444		
criteria6	**Program**				-3,2648					
issue2	**Economic development**									
issue3	**Financial management**									

continued on following page

Table 2. Continued

variable	label	PASOK	ND	KKE	LAOS	SYRIZA	GREENS	DIMAR	OTHER	UNDECIDED
issue4	**Migration-National issues**				4,0072					
issue5	**Energy, environment transport**				-2,0947					
issue6	**Education and health**				-1,9967				2,3651	
issue7	**Social justice**								2,5062	
issue8	**Relations with the EU**									
issue9	**Government and Representativeness Reforms**							2,0155		
age1	**18-24**									
age2	**25-34**									
age4	**45-54**							1,8955		
age5	**54-65+**									
Constant		-5,5142	-2,2232	-3,8318	-3,4787	-5,6714	-4,8772	-5,4986	-4,1874	
N		1500,0000	1500,0000	1500,0000	1500,0000	1500,0000	1500,0000	1500,0000	1500,0000	
NAGELKERKER SQUARE		0,2190	0,1780	0,1430	0,2860	0,1510	0,1180	0,2520	0,4050	

CONCLUSION

The analysis undertaken in this chapter set out to explore an alternative methodological approach to predicting electoral behaviour, with a particular emphasis on undecided voters. By integrating Fuzzy Clustering, stacked data analysis, and binary logistic regression on VAA (HelpMeVote) data from the 2010 Greek regional elections, we were able to move beyond the limitations of traditional electoral forecasting models and capture the complexity of voter decision-making in a multi-party, issue-oriented environment.

From a theoretical perspective, this work aligns with a historical trajectory in electoral behaviour research that has evolved from early deterministic models, such as Siegfried's electoral geography, the Columbia and Michigan schools, and left–right or GAL–TAN ideological axes, to issue-voting and rational-choice frameworks. Each successive model emerged in response to changes in the socio-economic and technological environment, a pattern that continues today in the era of digital platforms, big data, and machine learning. The present approach embodies this ongoing shift by applying modern data-driven tools to the analysis of complex electoral contexts.

Methodologically, the choice of Fuzzy Clustering addressed a central problem in electoral analysis: the fact that voters' affinities toward political actors are rarely binary. By allowing for degrees of membership across multiple groups, we could more realistically model the probability distributions of support for various candidates. The subsequent stacking of data enabled the transformation of complex, multi-variable survey responses into a format suitable for detailed regression modelling, ensuring that each respondent's multiple possible voting choices were incorporated into the prediction process. The use of binary logistic regression, applied both to stated intentions and to predicted choices derived from discriminant analysis, allowed for the identification of the most influential variables in shaping support for each candidate.

The results highlight a nuanced electoral landscape in the Central Macedonia region during the 2010 regional elections. Party identification was indeed a strong determinant of voting preference, particularly for the two traditional governing parties (PASOK and ND). However, the findings also demonstrate that for smaller parties, issue salience, candidate-specific attributes, and demographic factors (notably education and age) were equally or more important. The identification of distinct thematic clusters, ranging from left-wing issue-based alignments to right-wing ideological proximity, provides strong evidence that voters' decision-making is increasingly multidimensional, blending ideological positioning with pragmatic considerations.

This has significant implications for electoral forecasting and political campaigning. First, it suggests that relying solely on traditional variables such as party identification may understate the role of cross-cutting issues and candidate-level factors, particularly in fragmented or fluid political systems. Second, it confirms that modern forecasting tools must account for probabilistic overlaps in voter affinities, as captured through fuzzy clustering, rather than forcing respondents into mutually exclusive categories. Third, the approach demonstrates the value of integrating predictive analytics, such as discriminant analysis, to estimate the behaviour of undecided voters, a group whose electoral weight can be decisive.

From a broader perspective, these findings reinforce the idea that models of electoral behaviour are context-dependent. Just as earlier paradigms emerged in response to the political and technological realities of their time, contemporary electoral analysis must adapt to a political environment increasingly shaped by digital campaigning, personalised messaging, and AI-driven microtargeting. In such an environment, voter preferences are more fluid, multidimensional, and susceptible to real-time influence than in previous eras.

In conclusion, the methodology and results presented here not only offer an effective means of forecasting electoral outcomes in the presence of uncertainty and multi-party competition, but also point toward the future of electoral research, one in which data integration, probabilistic modelling, and machine learning techniques become standard tools for both scholars and practitioners. The adaptability of the proposed approach means that it can be applied beyond the Greek regional election context, offering valuable insights into electoral dynamics in diverse political systems.

REFERENCES

Andreadis, I. (2014). Data quality and data cleaning. In Garzia, D., & Marschall, S. (Eds.), *Matching voters with parties and candidates: Voting advice applications in comparative perspective* (pp. 79–92). ECPR Press.

Andreadis, I., & Chadjipadelis, T. (2012). *Lessons learnt from Greece – Analysis of the first Greek VAA*. VAA Research.

Campbell, A., Converse, P. E., Miller, W. E., & Stokes, D. E. (1960). *The American voter*. John Wiley & Sons.

Downs, A. (1957). *An economic theory of democracy*. Harper & Row.

Erikson, R. S., & Wlezien, C. (2012). *The timeline of presidential elections: How campaigns do (and do not) matter*. University of Chicago Press.

Franklin, M. N. (2004). *Voter turnout and the dynamics of electoral competition in established democracies since 1945*. Cambridge University Press.

Inglehart, R. (1990). *Culture shift in advanced industrial society*. Princeton University Press.

Key, V. O. (1966). *The responsible electorate: Rationality in presidential voting, 1936–1960*. Harvard University Press.

Lazarsfeld, P. F., Berelson, B., & Gaudet, H. (1968). *The people's choice: How the voter makes up his mind in a presidential campaign*. Columbia University Press.

Lewis-Beck, M. S., Jacoby, W. G., Norpoth, H., & Weisberg, H. F. (2008). *The American voter revisited*. University of Michigan Press.

Lyrintzis, C. (1984). Political parties in post-junta Greece: A case of "bureaucratic clientelism"? *West European Politics*, *7*(2), 99–118.

Macdonald, S. E., Listhaug, O., & Rabinowitz, G. (1991). Issues and party support in multiparty systems. *The American Political Science Review*, *85*(4), 1107–1131.

Mavrogordatos, G. T. (1984). The Greek party system: A case of polarized pluralism? *West European Politics*, *7*(4), 156–169.

Nikolakopoulos, H. (2001). *Η καχεκτική δημοκρατία: Κόμματα και εκλογές, 1946–1967* [The feeble democracy: Parties and elections, 1946–1967]. Patakis.

Nikolakopoulos, H. (2003). Η ανάπτυξη των πολιτικών δημοσκοπήσεων στην Ελλάδα [The development of political polling in Greece]. Retrieved from http://www.sedea.gr/

Nock, R., & Nielsen, F. (2006). On weighting clustering. *IEEE Transactions on Pattern Analysis and Machine Intelligence*, *28*(8), 1223–1235.

Novák, V., Perfilieva, I., & Močkoř, J. (1999). *Mathematical principles of fuzzy logic*. Kluwer Academic Publishers.

Stanford Encyclopedia of Philosophy. (2011). Stanford University. Retrieved from https://plato.stanford.edu/

Traugott, M. W., & Katosh, J. P. (1979). Response validity in surveys of voting behavior. *Public Opinion Quarterly*, *43*(3), 359–377.

Van der Brug, W., Van der Eijk, C., & Franklin, M. (2003). Designs for the empirical analysis of electoral preferences, utilities and choice. Paper prepared for the joint sessions of workshops of the ECPR, Edinburgh, March 2013.

Van der Eijk, C., & Franklin, M. N. (1996). *Choosing Europe? The European electorate and national politics in the face of union*. University of Michigan Press.

Van der Eijk, C., Franklin, M. N., & Oppenhuis, E. (1996). The strategic context: Party choice. In van der Eijk, C., & Franklin, M. N. (Eds.), *Choosing Europe? The European electorate and national politics in the face of union* (pp. 332–365). University of Michigan Press.

Voulgaris, G., & Nikolakopoulos, I. (2014). *Ο διπλός εκλογικός σεισμός* [The double electoral earthquake]. Athens, Greece: Themelio. Andreadis, I., & Chadjipadelis, T. (2011, April 19–21). Voting advice applications and their impact on elections. Paper presented at the 61st Political Studies Association Annual Conference, London, UK.

Zadeh, L. A. (1965). Fuzzy sets. *Information and Control*, *8*(3), 338–353.

Chapter 9
Predictive Tools and Methods for Forecasting and Strategic Planning:
AI in Political Marketing Campaigns

Evangelia N. Markaki
http://orcid.org/0000-0002-4985-3165
Mediterannean College, Greece

Virginia Tsoukatou
http://orcid.org/0000-0002-3733-8705
Mediterannean College, Greece

Dimitra Mari
Mediterannean College, Greece

Konstantinos Mamais
http://orcid.org/0000-0001-5628-0783
Mediterannean College, Greece

ABSTRACT

This chapter examines the transformative impact of Artificial Intelligence (AI) on political decision-making, marketing, and electoral forecasting. AI's integration into politics reshapes how campaigns are conducted and how decisions are made, but it also raises significant ethical concerns.AI-driven tools are increasingly used to analyse voter behaviour, craft political messages, and predict election outcomes. From targeted advertisements to sentiment analysis on social media, AI enables more

DOI: 10.4018/979-8-3373-1037-4.ch009

precise campaign strategies. However, it also introduces risks like misinformation, deepfakes, and algorithmic bias, which can undermine democratic processes and public trust. Case studies illustrate how AI's role in politics varies by context—democracies focus on transparency and public engagement, while authoritarian regimes use AI for control and surveillance. Predictive models powered by machine learning have shown success, where AI models outperformed traditional polling.

INTRODUCTION

This chapter contains three different parts of analysis. The first part presents the voting behavior as the result of a multivariable decision-making process. It analyses the process of decision making and the different factors that can influence our political preferences in the AI era. Political preferences remain crucial for our everyday life and a challenge that can be influenced by different types of communication, channels and practices. The fact that the political dialogue, the political representatives and the political process itself is influenced by the development and involvement of Artificial Intelligence in every aspect of our everyday life cannot be neglected or underestimated. It is true that there is a lot of discussion about how the AI influences voting behavior and there are many publications already that show its involvement in the process. Safeguarding democratic ideals, processes, and institutions requires effective regulation and compliance of those who design, develop, and use AI in politics. Given the speed at which AI is developing, this calls for constant attention and analysis. The remedy for AI's excessive interference in democratic politics is democratic governance of AI. Only then can people thrive, meet social needs, make a difference in society, and maintain public safety, especially when it comes to protecting vulnerable and disadvantaged people and communities. The two main and related subjects of discussion in the contemporary AI discourse in academics and politics are AI governance and politics. The discussion of security and AI politics examines how nations are beginning to see AI as a strategic asset since they expect it to have a big impact on how political power is distributed globally. This viewpoint has encouraged several countries to make investments in developing their own in-house AI capabilities in an attempt to outperform their rivals.

The second part is focused on Political Marketing campaigns. It focuses on the way political communication is exerted in the field of political science. This discipline is extensively discussed and analyzed with the use and development of social media and the media platforms in general. The interactive nature of these means of communication makes the discussion more challenging than ever. The use of AI is very important and at the same time extensive in the development of political campaigns. AI is used as a tool to develop political advertisements, to create political profiles and to manage politician's image. On the other hand, it is involved in the process of developing response towards verbal or action harassment in social media interaction. This part focuses on the investigation of specific examples and practices from an international perspective, examining campaigns in different countries' cultural areas and voting processes.

The third part analyzes different predictive approaches including statistical models such as Logistic Regression that predicts the probability of a voter supporting a candidate based on demographics and past voting behavior, Bayesian Inference that updates probabilities as new polling data becomes available, multilevel Regression and Poststratification (MRP) that estimates public opinion across different regions and demographic groups. It also presents machine learning models such as Decision Trees & Random Forests that identify patterns in voter behavior from large datasets, Support Vector Machines (SVM) that classify voters into likely and unlikely supporters of a candidate, and Neural Networks that detect complex patterns in voter data for more accurate predictions. It is also part of the study the reference to the Key Data Sources for Predictive Modeling taking into consideration the Voter's Registration Data that Include demographics, party affiliation, and past voting history, the Public Opinion Polls that gauge voter sentiment, Social Media & Sentiment Analysis that analyzes trends on platforms like Twitter and Facebook, Census Data that provides insights into socioeconomic factors affecting voting behavior and Campaign Contributions & Political Ads that help assess voter engagement and persuasion strategies. Additionally, Python (scikit-learn, TensorFlow, XGBoost) with machine learning frameworks for predictive analysis, and SPSS & Stata remain traditional statistical tools used in political science. Geographic & Data Visualization Tools such as GIS Software (ArcGIS, QGIS) inform us for Maps voter distribution and turnout trends. Tableau & Power BI create interactive dashboards for voter insights. Big Data & Social Media Analytics describe Google Trends & Twitter API tracking in real-time the voter's sentiment. Natural Language Processing (NLP) Tools (BERT, Vader Sentiment Analysis) analyzes political discourse and sentiment. All the above are some of the tools used so as to predict behaviors and form the appropriate strategic plan in political campaigns. Consequently, all this analysis brings in light the discussion that must be done and about the challenges and the ethical concerns related to the Data Privacy issues, the bias in Data and models where historical biases can affect predictions, leading to misleading results. All this discourse must be carefully managed to ensure fair and accurate predictions.

DECISION MAKING IN POLITICAL BEHAVIOR UNDER THE AUSPICES OF AI: CHALLENGES, CHANGES AND PROSPECTS

The voting behavior remains a multivariable decision-making process. It is also complicated and affected by different factors that are at the same time personal, social and financial (Markaki & Tsoukatou, 2025). Self-reflection is a process to support individuals in making realizations about themselves and even changes to their behavior. Observing how a reflective strategy (e.g., reflective questions) increased participants' motivation to set higher goals. It was found that data visualization helped participants recall past behaviors and generate new questions about their behaviors (Zhang et al., 2023).

The rapidly developing field of artificial intelligence and its potential impact on all policy areas that present significant challenges for decision-makers should be one of the main focus of the political studies community. Through these issues, the political studies community may raise its voice and engage in interdisciplinary conversations on this crucial discussion (Schippers, 2020).

Modern democracies are increasingly characterized by individualized, issue-driven actions, leading to what has been described as "chaotic pluralism" that challenges traditional democratic processes. These systems are designed to reflect pluralistic societal values and accommodate diverse demands (Yang et al., 2024).

Human voting behavior is often influenced by various cognitive biases that can distort decision-making processes. The primacy effect, where voters tend to prefer candidates listed first on the ballot, is a well-documented bias. In the same way, voters may favor the final options they evaluate due to the influence of time. These biases in human decision-making raise important considerations for the design and presentation of voting systems (Yang et al., 2024).

Protecting democratic values, processes, and institutions is crucial, as it is crucial that those who create, develop, and apply AI in politics are effectively regulated and compliant. Given the speed at which AI is developing, this needs constant attention and analysis. The remedy for AI's excessive interference in democratic politics is democratic governance of AI.

Only then can people thrive, meet social needs, make a difference in society, and maintain public safety, especially when it comes to protecting vulnerable and disadvantaged people and communities (Schippers, 2020).

The two main and related subjects of discussion in the contemporary AI discourse in academics and politics are AI governance and politics. The discussion of security and AI politics examines how nations are beginning to see AI as a strategic asset since they expect it to have a big impact on how political, military, and economic power are distributed globally (Markaki & Tsoukatou, 2025).

This viewpoint has encouraged several countries to invest in developing their own domestic AI resources to outperform their rivals (Fischer and Wenger, 2021).

Since norms, assumptions, and ideas are carried by all individuals involved at every stage of the design process and have an impact on the finished product, technology creation is inherently political (Fischer & Wenger, 2021). As a result, the debate over AI governance is still in its infancy, much as the debate over academic politics and policy.

Similar to the literature on AI politics, the corpus of research on AI governance is relatively small (Fischer and Wenger, 2021). Some policy conversations and scientific contributions reflect a technical determinism, which is odd considering that all discussions regarding AI are in the shadow of the future. Many questions remain today about the future course of technological development. Because of this ambiguity, conflicting future visions emerge that cast doubt on a determinist interpretation of AI's political ramifications. The nature of AI technologies also raises important considerations about the relationship between politics and technology. To build a fundamental knowledge of how people interact and collaborate with AI to make decisions, the nascent area of human-AI decision-making needs use empirical methodologies in addition to creating AI tools for this goal (Lai et al., 2023). Most of the research defines artificial intelligence (AI) as a computational or algorithmic system that can carry out intelligence-demanding tasks (Flügge, 2021). Many studies used new algorithms to produce explanations for model predictions, among other technological advancements that will help AI better complement human decision-making (Lai et al., 2023). In the meantime, by using human subjects to complete choice tasks, the academic community is realizing more and more how important human-AI decision making are (Lai et al., 2023).

The role of artificial intelligence (AI) in political conduct and public discourse, which either complements or supplants human autonomy, judgement, and decision-making capacities, is still a topic of public and academic interest (Flügge, 2021).

The use of AI systems has increased across several industries because of their growing predictive capabilities (Lai et al., 2023). Artificial intelligence (AI) that can have conversations with users, is changing how people use technology (Hartmann et al., 2023). The scientific community is therefore becoming more interested in using AI to support human decision-making. Using AI is frequently justified to make decisions that are more objective and successful (Flügge, 2021). Although complete automation is frequently undesirable in high-stakes fields like the justice system and healthcare because of safety, ethical, and legal considerations, even if purely manual procedures can be imprecise and time-consuming (Lai et al., 2023). Recent years have also made artificial intelligence (AI) a pervasive technology that has been incorporated into high-stakes industries like recruiting, healthcare, and banking, but here again, complete automation is frequently undesirable in these sectors to avoid the dangerous outcomes of failures (Flügge, 2021).

According Hartmann et al. (2023), OpenAI recently unveiled ChatGPT, a cutting-edge dialogue model with previously unheard-of conversational abilities with humans. ChatGPT had over a million users thanks to the overwhelming interest it received from the public, industry, academics, and media. Its rapid use as an automated decision aid and for information search, however, emphasizes how crucial it is to comprehend its biases and limitations as the output of ChatGPT may be vulnerable to subtle prompt manipulations, despite its impressive capabilities. Additionally, factors such as language, model versions, and contextual factors make ChatGPT's decisions not consistently aligned to specific political interpretations (Reveilhac & Morselli, 2025).

Artificial intelligence (AI) technologies are frequently used to support or enhance human decision-makers by offering a forecast or suggestion for a choice task that people can choose to follow or disregard and come to their own conclusion (Flügge, 2021). In addition to forecasts, modern AI technologies can include a variety of extra features that assist humans in evaluating the model's predictions and coming to better conclusions (Flügge, 2021). This knowledge can be used in a number of ways, such as: to guide the development of new AI methods that are more human-compatible or effective; to help practitioners make technical and design decisions for AI systems that support decision-making more effectively; and to contribute to human-centric policies, infrastructure, and practices surrounding AI for decision-making, such as regulatory requirements on when AI can or cannot be used to support specific human decisions (Lai et al., 2023).

Another issue that we should take into consideration is about the voting patterns of Large Language Models (LLMs), in particular GPT-4 and LLaMA-2, their biases, and how well they match human voting patterns constitute another crucial area of research. The researchers found that LLM voting results were impacted by the presentation sequence and the voting method selection. They also discovered that altering the persona can improve alignment with human choices and lessen some of these biases. The Chain-of-Thought method has the potential to make voting more AI explainable, even though it did not increase prediction accuracy (Yang et al., 2024).

In order to give users a general idea of how a decision-making model works or the data it was trained on, it is also common practice to provide information about the model itself. This might affect how users perceive and interact with the model when making decisions. Four sorts of AI support components examined in earlier research on human-AI decision making are as follows: model forecasts, model forecast information, model (and training data) information, and additional AI system components impacting user experience (Lai et al., 2023).

Even though ChatGPT is just asked to choose between agree, disagree, and neutral, it frequently uses lengthy comments to defend political stances. The answers from ChatGPT offer further details on political beliefs and methods of argumentation. As a result, we expand on our pre-registered work by methodically examining ChatGPT's responses using TextAnalyzer and LIWC22, two well-known natural language processing software tools (Hartmann et al., 2023).

Decision making performance, which AI assistance is meant to support, is, of course, the most important outcome metric for human-AI decision making. Evaluation of the decision tasks falls into two main categories: efficiency, or the speed at which judgments are produced, and efficacy, or the quality of the decisions. AI equity and trust is a well-known statistic and an important field of research. The utility and happiness of the system are impacted by continuing research on how humans perceive AI's fairness and how design influences that perception (Lai et al., 2023).

LLMs can support people in their decision-making processes, improving cost consciousness, overcoming typical cognitive biases, summarizing, explaining or providing nuances and additional context for public policy and public sentiment (Yang et al., 2024).

According to Hartmann (2023) strong conversational AI programs like ChatGPT have the ability to completely change how people obtain information. Nonetheless, users' confidence in the correctness of the technology is crucial to its acceptance. One of the most important and essential decision-making procedures in democracies is political voting. In their natural interactions with their millions of gullible users, the question is what happens when these innovative AI-enabled dialogue systems propagate a particular political ideology? The researches investigated ChatGPT's political stance in three pre-registered trials utilising the nation-agnostic political compass test and 630 political statements from two popular voting guidance apps in order to answer this question. All things considered, there is growing evidence that ChatGPT has a left-libertarian, pro-environmental stance. The results hold true for a variety of prompt manipulations, including negations, prompt sequence, formality level, and languages (German, Dutch, Spanish, and English). The findings have significant implications because political elections are among the most crucial decision-making processes in democracies. Furthermore, ChatGPT may draw people with similar views due to the "partisan content." In turn, this ideological bias may be reinforced and sustained in a vicious cycle by the input that OpenAI actively seeks from its user base to enhance its model outputs (Hartmann et al., 2023).

AI systems—which include personalised LLM agents—are intended to cast ballots and reflect the views of individual voters. Under voter supervision, proponents think that these agents could allow for more detailed and nuanced voting. However, much thought must be given to ethical issues pertaining to agent bias, democratic integrity, and automation. Generative Foundation Models (GFMs), like GPT-4, provide hitherto unheard-of difficulties for democratic systems. A cautious approach would be necessary to implement such technology in democratic processes while maintaining the fundamental principles of democracy. The development of LLM societies is one specific instance of a multi-agent LLM system. These technologies generate society simulations and debate study environments (Yang et al., 2024).

The ChatLLM network system supports more thorough and impartial decision-making. According to a technique presented by Du et al. (2023), several language model instances suggest, discuss, and improve their answers in order to get to an agreement. The Degeneration-of-Thought (DoT) problem is tackled using a Multi-Agent Debate framework, in which agents argue "tit for tat" and a judge mediates the discussion to arrive at a conclusion (Yang et al., 2024).

A collaborative environment where intelligent agents with different functions and attributes communicate, is presented by Talebirad & Nadiri (2023). Wu et al. (2021) talk about "Autogen," an open-source toolkit that makes it easier for several LLM agents to communicate with one another. Additionally, the use of personalities in civic communication and the possibility of digital twins to comprehend voter behavior and overcome biases in democratic processes are also examined by Bareis & Katzenbach (2022a)and Rank and Mushtare (2019).

In order to aggregate individual preferences into a collective social ranking, represented by R, which is formed from individual rankings {Ri}, social welfare functions are essential. By striking a balance between justice and reasoned judgment, they aid in the creation of a cohesive social order (Yang et al., 2024). According to social choice theory, rationality affects preference aggregation and voting patterns. It includes: Internal Choice Consistency. This component, which is essential to economics and decision theory, calls for rational and cohesive individual decisions. According to Yang et al. (2024), findings reveal significant differences between LLM and human voting behaviours in several key areas: the number of projects approved, consistency across different voting methods, qualitative preferences, and the degree of self-interest exhibited in voting patterns. They explored various strategies to align LLM behaviours more closely with human behaviours, but each strategy presented notable trade-offs.

On the other hand, and adittionally to the tools already mentioned, "Deliberating with AI", is a web tool that enables people to create and evaluate ML models in order to examine strengths and shortcomings of past decision-making and deliberate on how to improve future decisions (Zhang et al., 2023). Past research has shown the effectiveness and advantages of using statistics (Markaki & Chadjipadelis, 2017, 2023) and algorithms to make decisions—compared to humans. These systematic methods can use identical data to reproduce forecast results and, frequently, to provide comparable or superior accuracy.

Governments are becoming increasingly data-driven and are looking for ways to use the data in their decision-making processes. Algorithms are frequently used to enhance decision-making rather than to achieve completely automated decision-making (Zhang et al., 2023). With the potential to overcome human decision-makers' biases, public organizations are increasingly using artificial intelligence algorithms as decision-making tools. However, they might also introduce new biases into the relationship between humans and algorithms (Zhang et al., 2023).

The research found a stronger propensity for adherence when the advice is aligned with group stereotypes, with no significant differences between algorithmic and human-expert advice (Alon-Barkat & Busuioc, 2023). The use of algorithms could then disproportionately negatively affect stereotyped groups, potentially creating administrative burdens and compounding discrimination (Herd & Moynihan, 2019).

Summing up the short discussion on the decision- making process in the AI era, we need to mention that citizens should understand political options, be able to form reasonably informed and relevant opinions, and organise and express themselves accordingly. Collective action also entails being able to exchange ideas with like-minded compatriots, with minimal external surveillance. (Alon-Barkat & Busuioc, 2023) .

POLITICAL MARKETING IN THE AI ERA

Moving on to the second part of this chapter, we will dive into Political Marketing campaigns, discussing some examples of AI practices. The ever-growing role of social media and other media platforms has transformed the landscape of political discourse through their interactive nature. The integration of AI in political campaigns, as will be showcased, plays a key factor and is used to craft from political advertisements and content to the spread of fake news through deepfakes.

ChatGPT was released at the end of 2022, and “redefined the standards of artificial intelligence” (Marr, 2023). As the Think Tank report (European Parliament, 2023) of the European Parliament comments, ChatGPT “demonstrated the vast range of possibilities involved in adapting general-purpose AI to a wide array of tasks and in getting generative AI to generate synthetic content based on prompts entered by the user”. As the uses and possibilities continue to grow, AI tools are accessible to the masses and remain mostly free of charge (the majority of them run a subscription service for more accurate results). AI generative tools such as OpenAI's ChatGPT, Microsoft's Bing AI and Copilot, and Google's Gemini are leading examples of a broader wave of AI technologies that generate coherent written content based on user input. By analyzing patterns and connections in written language, and trained on vast amounts of human-created and published material, these tools can already produce text similar to conversations, emails, encyclopedia entries, software code, news reports, and bedtime stories. They can mimic various genres, styles, and even the writing rhythm of specific authors (Gillespie, 2024). As the infiltration of AI in all aspects of life and content has been evident, it is raising the question and perhaps need, for its moderation and regulation. In the next few pages some case studies of the use of AI in politics will be discussed, as well as the action towards the regulatory aspect of this technology.

Ai In Politics: Cases From Usa, Uk, Turkey, Argentina, China And Finland

As mentioned, Artificial Intelligence has rapidly advanced in recent years, becoming a pivotal force across many sectors, and politics is no exception. AI's influence in the political realm is transforming how governments operate, how political campaigns are run, and how decisions are made. From data-driven strategies to the automation of processes, AI tools are reshaping the landscape of governance. Politicians and political organizations are leveraging AI for voter analysis, policy-making, and enhancing public services, while governments are exploring its potential to improve efficiency, transparency, and accountability.

However, the integration of AI into politics raises important ethical, legal, and social concerns, including the impact on privacy, bias in decision-making, and the potential for surveillance. Moreover, AI-powered algorithms can amplify misinformation by promoting sensational or misleading content through social media platforms and news outlets. This lead to fact-checking services that were employed in the service of providing true information to the vast audiences – and they were used to check information from political debates or speeches (ex. NBC 2025, BBC 2025, CNN 2025) to social media platforms such as the fact checkers of Meta. In the start of the year 2025, Meta announced that "third-party moderators were "too politically biased" and it was "time to get back to US' roots around free expression" (Gilder et al., 2025). Meta's current fact-checking program, launched in 2016, refers potentially false or misleading posts to independent organizations for credibility evaluation. When posts are flagged as inaccurate, they may receive labels providing additional information and are demoted in users' feeds. This system will now be replaced by community notes, starting in the United States. Meta has stated that it has "no immediate plans" to remove third-party fact checkers in the UK or the EU. The new community notes feature is inspired by X, which introduced it after its acquisition and rebranding by Elon Musk. It allows users with differing viewpoints to collaborate on adding context or clarifications to controversial posts. This decision was met with concerns and as a step-back by fact checking organizations.

Having this in mind, the following paragraphs will discuss case studies about the use of AI in politics that were perceived as facts by some but then where uncovered as fabricated content.

The USA Case

According to the 2018 White House Summit on AI for American Industry, "Artificial intelligence holds tremendous potential as a tool to empower the American worker, drive growth in American industry, and improve the lives of the American people. Our free-market approach to scientific discovery harnesses the combined strengths of government, industry, and academia, and uniquely positions us to leverage this technology for the betterment of our great nation" (White House, 2018). During the Trump administration, the concept of AI was presented as a patriotic endeavour, linking the technological progress of the United States with broader societal advancement. In this framework, AI was used to highlight key values that the Trump administration viewed as crucial, including empowering American workers, boosting domestic industries, and promoting a deregulated free-market approach (Rodwell, 2025). Moreover, it shouldn't come as a surprise that President Trump hailed Meta's decision to remove fact checking services from its US operations.

However, the President himself was not spared of the consequences of the above decisions, as he has shared an AI generated image of singer Taylor Swift, endorsing him (Csernatoni, 2024). Taylor Swift has never endorsed President Trump, yet this incident is another example of high-profile in the US politics, spreading AI-generated content as valid. During the last presidential campaign, Democrats posted deepfake photos of Donald Trump under arrest (AP, 2023). More recently, President Trump shared a viral AI-generated video depicting the Gaza Strip as a Dubai-style paradise (Gilder et al., 2025; The Guardian, 2025), on his Truth Social Platform. As the President commented "We have an opportunity to do something that could be phenomenal … the Riviera of the Middle East, it could be so magnificent' (The Guardian, 2025). The video's creator stated that his aim was to create political satire – which was not understood, evidently by the President who shared it in his social platform.

Examples such as the above, raise concerns over the spread of AI generated content by public figures themselves who are either aware of the fabricated content and share it for their own agenda or are" victims" of the content themselves, believing it to be valid and spreading it to "create awareness". These actions could cause voter confusion as well as enhance mistrust levels in public institutions.

The China Case

China is making significant strides in generative AI technologies and is emerging as a global leader in their adoption, underscoring its growing prominence in this competitive arena. However, China is not the only authoritarian regime leveraging digital technologies and AI to strengthen state control. According to Csernatoni (2024), through its Digital Silk Road initiative, China has become a key exporter of digital authoritarianism, providing digital infrastructure to developing and authoritarian nations seeking affordable technological advancements. As a result, countries like Bangladesh, Colombia, Ethiopia, Guatemala, the Philippines, and Thailand have shown signs of digital authoritarianism, indicating the spread of this political model. Additionally, according to the National Endowment for Democracy Report (2024), nations such as Iran, Russia, and Venezuela are actively experimenting with and weaponising generative AI to manipulate information (National Endowment for Democracy, 2023) and destabilise democratic processes.

The Chinese vision of AI takes a different approach, with the Chinese Communist Party portraying AI as a tool for ensuring social order and regulation. The goal is to improve people's living standards and quality of life, accelerate and expand AI applications, and enhance the intelligence of society as a whole to create an all-encompassing, ubiquitous intelligent environment" (A Next Generation Artificial Intelligence Development Plan, 2017). Additionally, AI technologies are seen as capable of accurately sensing, forecasting, and providing early warnings for key infrastructure and social security systems; monitoring group cognition and psychological shifts in real time; and taking proactive roles in decision-making and responses—thus significantly enhancing social governance and playing an essential role in maintaining social stability (Bareis & Katzenbach, 2022b).

Since China is not a democratic country, this stance could be perceived not only as AI in the service of public regulation, as the report mentions that AI could perceive group psychological shifts and take action towards them. However, it does not mention what type of shifts and what type of actions.

A Different Take: the Finland Case

Finland is one of the EU's front-runners in promoting digital and AI skills through governmental initiatives. The country offers a strong example of how to prioritize education for a human-centered society in the era of AI. National AI literacy programs, such as those in Finland, can strengthen technical expertise and encourage critical thinking about AI, helping to build resilience against misinformation and disinformation (Csernatoni, 2024). This stance is offers a more democratic approach to AI as a tool in the service of societies, than the ones mentioned so far.

Other Cases of AI in Politics: UK, Turkey and Argentina

Incidents with fake news from AI generated content have taken place in the UK. More specifically, an audio clip that has gone viral on X (formerly Twitter), purportedly featuring Labour leader Sir Keir Starmer using profanity towards a staff member. As fullfact.org (2023), stated there was no evidence of the content being genuine, further commenting in their verdict: "There is no evidence that the clip is genuine. Labour sources and Conservative MPs both say the clip was faked, while the X account which shared it has previously published other unevidenced claims about Mr Starmer. The clip may have been generated by artificial intelligence, but we don't know that for sure".

Setting the scope eastern, in Turkey in May 2023, Muharrem İnce dropped out of the election, following the viral spread of explicit AI-generated videos (The Guardian, 2023). Even though the content was fabricated (deepfake), the candidate withdrew from the race itself – even though during the 45-day election campaign, Erdogan himself aired a supposed deepfake showing banned Kurdish militants allegedly endorsing his main political opponent at a pre-election rally (The Guardian, 2023). Erdogan went on to win the 2023 Turkish Presidential Elections (Reuters, 2023) .

Moving on to Argentina's 2023 Election or as The New York Times (2023) called it "the first AI elections", both top running candidates used deepfakes in their campaigns, creating posters and materials that mocked their rivals—escalating into a full-scale AI-driven memetic battle aimed at influencing voters (Csernatoni, 2024).

The constant stream of AI-generated misinformation is likely to increase voter confusion, create distorted perceptions of candidates, and foster cynicism toward the electoral process. Deepfakes are becoming more and more affordable to create giving both domestic and foreign malicious stakeholders new ways to exploit them. As AI-generated content floods online platforms, social media algorithms amplify its viral spread, often without sufficient fact-checking or oversight. The psychological impact is significant, as people struggle to differentiate between real and manipulated content. If even leading media outlets, government institutions, and tech companies have difficulty distinguishing between genuine and AI-generated material, how can local communities and the general public be expected to navigate this complex landscape?

The case of AI used in politics creates space for debating over voter confusion, voter predictive tools and an overall fog over the effectiveness of institutions in general. It also creates a space for reflection. The divide in stances is evident: on one hand there are policies regulating and checking the technology and educational programs empowering and educating the audiences, and on the other hand there is a more unregulated approach, adopted by authoritative institutions. What should be the way forward considering advancements and challenges?

Moving on the third part of this chapter, it is time to see in a more detailed way tool and application that combine the decision making process in politics and political behavior with AI.

A JOURNEY THROUGH TIME: THE EVOLUTION AND FUTURE OF ELECTORAL FORECASTING

The whole electoral process serves as the foundation of every democratic political system. Elections empower citizens to select their representatives, ensure those in power remain accountable, and protect peoples' liberties. Although the voting process may appear straightforward, it is quite complex. Political parties must make significant efforts to analyse public opinion, anticipate voter tendencies, and prepare campaigns that effectively connect with the electorate.

The urge to be able to forecast the public vote relates to the basic human need to predict the future. From the moment elections were introduced as a method for selecting leaders, people have been drawn to the idea of predicting the outcome with some level of accuracy. The rise of more powerful computers and more sophisticated statistical methods made managing electoral data easier than ever. Unsurprisingly, election forecasting has evolved into a thriving industry, attracting polling companies, media outlets, and even betting companies, along with scholars specialising in political studies.

Forecasting models shaped political strategies over the years by identifying key voter demographics and providing data-driven insights that help political parties optimise their campaigns for better resource allocation to attain greater voter outreach by tailoring their message to appeal to specific voter segments.

In the following sections, we will explore how electoral forecasting has evolved from traditional models to cutting-edge technologies by analysing two case studies.

The Evolution of Electoral Prediction Models: From Traditional Forecasting to Artificial Intelligence-Based Approaches

All electoral models, no matter the technologies they use to reach a prediction, have profoundly influenced political strategy over the years because it's a powerful tool for the political parties to optimise the reach of their campaigns, allocate their funds, and reach as many voters as they can.

The whole forecasting process helps parties identify key voter characteristics and tailor the political message and outreach attempts to reach this specific voter segment.

Also, especially in countries like the USA, the electoral forecast helps the political parties prioritise campaign spending to regions that are very competitive and crucial for the electoral result (e.g., swing states or other marginal constituencies). They track those areas and allocate more resources in high-impact areas, that even a slight shift in public vote can determine the electoral outcome.

Furthermore, by accessing the public propensity to vote, parties can analyse voter sentiment and refine the rhetoric to resonate with the public vote. It's, in fact, a very useful way to dynamically check how a speech or an adjustment to a political position impacts the electoral constituency. Also, by examining forecasting trends, parties can predict their rivals' moves and counteract them with pre-emptive strategies, and in multiparty electoral systems, election forecasts help parties gauge their potential bargaining power in post-election coalition talks.

As Stegmaier & Norpoth (2013) summarised, the traditional forecasting models are based mainly on three major types of election forecasting. The most well-known to the public involves polling the electorate. The rise of polling has led to an almost endless supply of data on support for candidates and parties, which can be used to predict electoral results. During national elections, a new poll (or more than one) is often released daily, showing the latest standings in the electoral battle. The poll results, or an average of the latest polls, are commonly seen as the most accurate prediction of the winner and the expected margin of victory. Another way to forecast the winner in an electoral race is to identify factors that influence voters' decisions, such as the economic condition of the country or political and international issues (e.g., immigration), to fine-tune the polls to provide the most accurate predictions for a specific election outcome. Betting companies also contribute to election forecasting by offering predictions based on the buying and selling of candidate futures using real money. These markets reflect the collective judgement of participants, as they wager on which candidate is likely to win.

In the era of AI-driven electoral prediction, forecasting voter behaviour remains an area where machine learning and artificial intelligence have the potential to greatly enhance both the accuracy and scope of predictions, combining the expertise of data analysts, computer scientists, and political analysts (Zuloaga-Rotta et al., 2024).

The rise of artificial intelligence has introduced a paradigm shift in political campaigning. Central to this transformation is microtargeting—a practice that employs AI to tailor political messages to individual voters based on granular data analysis. While this innovation enhances the precision of campaign outreach, it simultaneously raises urgent concerns regarding democratic integrity, algorithmic accountability, and voter autonomy.

The Mechanics of AI-Driven Microtargeting

Microtargeting, traditionally used in marketing, has found a powerful application in politics through the use of AI technologies such as machine learning, natural language processing, and predictive analytics. These tools process vast datasets—including voter demographics, psychographics, behavioral patterns, and real-time engagement metrics—to optimize campaign strategies (Das & Malaviya, 2025). For instance, AI can determine not just what message to deliver, but also when, how, and through which platform it should be delivered to maximize psychological resonance.

As we will examine later in this chapter, such methods were infamously exemplified in the 2016 U.S. election, where data analytics firms like Cambridge Analytica exploited social media profiles for psychographic profiling—allegedly without informed consent (Win, 2024).

Let's delve deeper firstly into the use of Artificial Intelligence (AI) and Machine Learning (ML) that are increasingly being used in electoral forecasting to predict election outcomes, analyse voting behaviour, and understand political trends. The whole electoral forecasting process is based heavily on the ability of the researcher to analyse vast amounts of data, including demographic information and the interconnection of polling data, historical electoral results, economic indicators, and more. In essence, artificial intelligence is using Machine learning to be able to process and clean those data instantly via using tailor-made algorithms. This way the data is ready for further analysis from an artificial intelligence system or from a human political analyst. Another aspect of artificial intelligence that we will see later played a crucial role in forecasting the electoral outcome in Trump's 2016 election and in the Brexit referendum is the Natural Language Processing (NLP) technology that is complemented by machine learning in order to understand human language in social media posts, news articles, speeches, or other sources of political expression and track shifts in public mood or highlight emerging trends that may influence voting behaviour.

Artificial intelligence allows for the prediction of an individual's likelihood to vote based on their past behaviours and characteristics. This capability is valuable for microtargeting voter outreach, educating voters, and running get-out-the-vote (GOTV) campaigns (Pollard et al., 2023). By using Machine learning technology, we can ameliorate methodological problems inherent in electoral outcomes forecasting techniques such as sampling error, timing issues, and issues connected with the allocation of the undecided in the candidates. ML resolves some of those inaccuracies by refining the process and making the data more linear and richer with more variables used (Pollard et al., 2023).

The real power of Machine Learning, though, is its ability to understand voter behaviour and extrapolate how a constituency will act in front of the ballot box. Artificial intelligence can learn from data, past and present, and make predictions without a human to specifically train them for that. This is possible by using historical data of voting history in each region, demographic data, and understanding patterns online to make predictions regarding voting behaviour. The more data that exist, the more accurate the predictions will be (Kiran, 2020).

Two examples of how Machine Learning and Natural Language Processing technology affect the predictions of voting behaviour are coming through the analysis of social media data, consumer purchasing patterns, and browsing histories detectable from digital trace data of the constituency. Artificial intelligence is excellent in identifying patterns that may be difficult for humans to detect. By collecting data from many different sources, processing them, and analysing them almost in real time, we can create highly detailed profiles of voters, enabling parties to target them more efficiently and mobilise them to vote cheaper and more effectively than the traditional methods.

Let's examine firstly the correlation between Machine learning, natural language processing, and social media posts. Monitoring people's activity on social media, especially on X (formerly Twitter), is an alternative way to capture the general sentiment without being negatively affected by the high non-response rates of traditional methods of electoral polling. Initially, Zhou et al. (2021) collected data, then processed those data, and then came the data analysis and the prediction of the electoral result. Tweets are typically gathered through Twitter's public API by filtering specific queries, such as candidates' names. Data processing involves various techniques designed to ensure the reliability of the Twitter dataset, such as detecting bots and removing spam. The analysis and prediction phase includes sentiment analysis, network analysis, and artificial intelligence, including machine learning and natural language processing to handle such a vast amount of raw data. The model identifies political and electoral trends without directly polling individuals, instead aiming to predict and analyse the vast amount of data generated by people on online social networks. Then researchers use Artificial intelligence techniques to minimise sampling bias by re-weighting the Twitter populations according to census data and the actual demographic population (Zhou et al., 2021).

The second example of Machine Learning and Natural Language Processing links political attitudes with the digital traces of the voters. A study in Germany examined the connection between over 19 million website visits, tracked from 1,003 users, and their survey responses to investigate whether website preferences could accurately predict political views across five areas: immigration, democracy, issues like climate change, attitudes toward the European Union, and populism (Kirkizh et al., 2024). According to researchers, while website categories showed some indicative patterns, there is not enough data to support a fully reliable model of electoral prediction based on online behavioural data. However, another source of data shows that the effects of political polarisation may expand beyond politics. For example, the New York Times made a connection between users who are hunting, fishing, or playing golf with the Republican Party (Cerina & Duch, 2020; DellaPosta et al., 2015). Although much work remains to be done, the development of more advanced artificial intelligence models may eventually allow us to uncover meaningful connections between lifestyle choices and electoral behaviour. The theory behind this connection is based on the idea that, on one hand, personality traits are linked to political views, and on the other hand, these personality traits influence online behaviour. By predicting online behaviour, we may be able to infer political attitudes. A key advantage of tracking online behaviour is that it allows us to observe actions directly, without significant manipulation by the users, whereas people may be hesitant to openly express their true political beliefs on social media. Kirkizh et al. (2024), for instance, use as a proxy the visits to accommodation services or flight booking websites to possibly indicate an interest in travelling, potentially reflecting support for open-border policies or/and immigration. Gambling platforms could be associated with financial hardships, possibly correlating with support for populist politics that often capitalise on economically difficult times (Wiedemann, 2024). Job search websites provide insights into employment status (Kern et al., 2019), and thus, unemployment could be linked to populist attitudes.

Case Studies: AI Successes and Failures in Political Predictions. The case of the 2016 U.S. presidential election and Brexit referendum.

The 2016 U.S. presidential election and the Brexit referendum are two prominent examples where traditional polling methods failed to accurately predict outcomes, but AI-based methods provided more accurate forecasts. In the lead-up to the 2016 U.S. presidential election, traditional polls predicted a victory for Hillary Clinton, with many showing her ahead in key swing states. However, Donald Trump won the election, largely due to unexpected results in swing states like Michigan, Wisconsin, and Pennsylvania, which had been considered reliably Democratic. Similarly, in the 2016 Brexit referendum, many traditional polls predicted that the "Remain" campaign would win, often showing a consistent lead. However, the "Leave" votes unexpectedly won, resulting in a significant upset for research work on the electoral prediction field.

In essence, the reasons for the polling failure in both cases have the same roots. One possible "culprit" for this failure is what in political science is referred to as "non-response bias.". This kind of behaviour occurred when there are specific group of people who systematically avoid responding to surveys even if they could participate. In essence, it's not about trying to reach this electorate; it's all about the non-response preference of this electoral audience. For example, in the case of the 2016 U.S. presidential election, this audience was the white, less educated voters—a group key for the electoral victory of Donald Trump (Gelman, 2021;

Mercer et al., 2016). One possible explanation for this behaviour may be the possible "anti-institutional" feelings that were a central part of the Trump campaign and made this part of the electorate unwilling to respond to polls (Murray, 2024). This led to a situation where a large portion of the electorate belonged to a dynamic demographic group that was unwilling to respond to polls. Pollsters replaced these non-responders with other individuals who were willing to answer, who may have been Democratic voters.

Another possible explanation for this development is the dishonesty of many of those who polled when they answered about their intention to vote. For many voters, the political stance of Donald Trump was aligned with their personal value system, but because those opinions for many involved in public speaking (for example, actors, influencers, singers, etc.) or for their social cycle were socially undesirable, the supporters were unwilling to admit their support to pollsters (Coppock, 2017). According to the researchers, there are indications that those voters were college-educated and higher-income voters (Mercer et al., 2016).

Polling people is much more complex than the simple random sampling often outlined in statistics textbooks. In fact, the 2016 experience has highlighted that national and state polls can be inaccurate to a degree that goes beyond what would typically be expected from sampling error. However, forecasting opinion trends on social media platforms such as X (formerly Twitter) seems notably more reliable in this case. Bovet et al. (2018) used a natural language processing and machine learning model to predict the electoral result by using a large-scale dataset of 73 million tweets collected from 1st June to 1st September 2016. They inferred the propensity to vote for each presidential candidate with a remarkable accuracy of 90%. Also, they compared the results with the predictions derived from the New York Times (NYT) daily polls, and they show that they could predict by analysing the tweets the global opinion trends nationwide 10 days earlier than the traditional polls of NYT (Bovet et al., 2018). Another notable example of machine learning being used to predict Donald Trump's victory in the 2016 U.S. presidential election is the IBM Watson that was involved in predictive analytics and sentiment analysis, particularly in terms of social media. Watson analysed massive amounts of data from social media platforms like Twitter, Facebook, and blogs, and it suggested a "close race" but with Trump possibly edging out Hillary Clinton (Agarwal, 2016).

Leading up to the 2016 Brexit referendum, many traditional polls predicted that the "Remain" campaign would win, often showing a consistent lead. However, the "Leave" votes unexpectedly won, resulting in a significant upset.

Like the U.S. election, in the case of the Brexit referendum, traditional polls struggled to account for key factors such as voter turnout, undecided voters, and the role of certain demographic groups. Additionally, polls did not capture the intensity of support for the "Leave" campaign, particularly among older, less-educated voters, who were less likely to participate in traditional polling.

As in the US 2016 election example, here again we have the failure of traditional polls to predict this outcome has been attributed to several factors, including sampling biases, the so-called "shy Tory" phenomenon, and people's reluctance to admit support for Brexit to pollsters. Also, there is in that case too "anti-institutional" feelings fuelled by the immigration crisis that unfolded that period correlated with the pro-Brexit campaign. A study by DataEQ used sentiment analysis on social media posts before the vote, analysing 10,000 mentions that represented half a million opinions. Their findings showed that 56.9% of opinions expressed were in favour of Brexit—contradicting most traditional polls at the time, which predicted a "Remain" victory (DataEQ, 2016). Similarly, Dataversity's analysis of Twitter sentiment leading up to the vote also suggested a Leave victory. The study highlighted how AI-driven social media analytics tracked real-time sentiment shifts more effectively than conventional polling methods (Green, 2016).

DEMOCRATIC IMPLICATIONS AND ETHICAL DILEMMAS

People criticise microtargeting because it is so advanced that it could change the public sphere by replacing general political talk with personalised echo chambers. Because of this, messages don't get looked at by the public, which makes things less clear and makes it harder for everyone to understand (Pham et al., 2025). This decline in public opinion is a danger to democracy and could lead to manipulation instead of real persuasion.

Also, the main idea behind microtargeting is to gather intrusive data, which is often done without getting the user's full consent.

We are in a new era of political campaign since the 2016 election bewitched us all, but the rules around what you can and can't do with this technology seem not great. Laws currently about elections do nothing to address the opacity of algorithms or the reality that data is borderless. Two examples of proactive governance in this area are the AI Act and the Digital Services Act by the European Union (Pham et al., 2025) but it is still difficult to enforce these rules across borders and across different platforms.

People are so strongly against microtargeting because it is so sophisticated it could transform the public sphere, replacing all that yammering about broad political themes with personalised echo chambers. This means that public messages will go unscrutinized, causing things to be less open and harder for all to understand (Pham et al., 2025). This decline in public opinion is a threat to democracy and potentially opens the door to manipulation rather than meaningful persuasion. There's also the data collection side of things. At its heart, microtargeting is built on collecting invasive personal information, and more often than not, users don't really know what they're consenting to.

Transparency and Accountability: Algorithmic Opacity, Information Asymmetry and Moral Responsibility

One of the biggest problems we're facing is that these algorithms are basically black boxes - voters and even regulators can't figure out how political messages are being created, who they're being sent to, or why. Kamal and Kaur (2025) point out that when AI is doing the targeting, there's no real transparency about where these messages come from or what they're trying to accomplish. This makes it nearly impossible to call out politicians when they're spreading misinformation or unfairly targeting certain groups.

It's incredibly important to push for transparency in AI political systems - people have a right to understand how algorithmic decisions might be influencing their voting choices. But here's the problem: most campaign systems are proprietary and completely closed off from scrutiny. This just makes the power imbalance even worse between the people using this technology and the public who has to deal with its effects.

Despite the growing awareness, most countries have this huge legal gap around AI in political advertising. Without enforceable standards for fairness, due process, or remedies when things go wrong, the problematic uses of AI just keep happening unchecked. The real headache is trying to assign blame in these complex AI systems. Responsibility gets spread out among data scientists, platform operators, political consultants, and the algorithms themselves. Thus, when campaigns result in voter suppression, misinformation, or increased polarization, it's really hard to pin down who should be held accountable.

To balance tech innovation with democratic principles, researchers are pushing for transparent systems, meaningful consent processes, and public oversight of how campaigns handle data. There's also a growing movement to completely rethink political communication - instead of it being this manipulative arms race, it should be a space where people can make truly informed decisions.

Academics are proposing some concrete structural changes to build ethical guardrails into how AI gets used in politics. First, they want mandatory impact assessments before any AI system gets rolled out in elections. This would mean identifying and addressing potential problems like bias, manipulation, or data misuse before they happen (Chandra, 2025). Secondly, the creation of public transparency records is essential; These would document and reveal the logic, objectives and scope of the dissemination of political announcements generated by AI, allowing voters and regulators to analyse the intentions and mechanisms behind algorithmic persuasion. Finally, they want independent watchdog agencies with real legal teeth to audit campaign practices and hold people accountable when things go wrong.

As we can see from the aforementioned, the challenge is not merely technical but philosophical: What kind of politics do we wish to design with our technologies?

STATISTICAL MODELS

Multilevel Regression with Poststratification in voting scheme

Predicting election outcomes and analysing voter behaviour demand advanced statistical methods to incorporate various demographic and geographic influences. Conventional polling approaches often face challenges such as unbalanced samples and nonresponse bias. Multilevel Regression with Poststratification (MRP) addresses these issues by integrating hierarchical modelling with poststratification, enhancing the precision of population-wide estimates.

Multilevel Regression with Poststratification (MRP) is a powerful statistical technique for forecasting election results and analysing public opinion by accounting for demographic and geographic differences. First introduced by Gelman & Little (1997), MRP has been widely implemented across various electoral scenarios, demonstrating strong predictive accuracy. Several notable uses of this methodology include: achieving a 93% accuracy rate in predicting constituency-level outcomes during the 2017 UK General Election, surpassing conventional polling methods. It also accurately estimated state-level vote shares in the US Presidential Elections using national survey data, thereby enhancing forecasts in pivotal swing states. Additionally, it has been applied to analyse political opinions at subnational levels such as congressional districts and counties, especially in areas where direct polling is impractical.

The Multilevel Regression with Poststratification (MRP) model has continued to be widely utilized in election forecasting and public opinion research. Park et al. (2004) demonstrated its effectiveness in estimating election outcomes across various levels, while Phillips et al. (2009) highlighted its role in enhancing state-level public opinion estimation. Additionally, YouGov (2017) UK Election forecast successfully employed MRP to predict constituency-level results with high accuracy. This methodology is grounded in Gelman's hierarchical Bayesian framework, reinforcing its reliability in statistical modelling.

Table 1. Comparison with other methods

Method	Strengths	Weaknesses
Direct Polling	Simple and interpretable	Sample bias, low accuracy in small regions
Ecological Regression	Uses aggregate data, useful for turnout analysis	Prone to ecological fallacy
MRP	Adjusts for demographics, scales to small areas	Requires computational resources

MRP offers several advantages, including its ability to generate reliable estimates even from small or unrepresentative survey samples by accounting for both demographic and geographic variations. It enhances accuracy compared to direct polling, particularly in areas with limited data, and scales effectively across different levels, from national to district-level predictions (Table 1). However, MRP also comes with challenges, as it is computationally demanding, requiring Bayesian estimation or hierarchical modelling. Its accuracy depends on high-quality poststratification data, such as up-to-date census records, and it assumes that patterns observed in survey data apply to the broader population, which may introduce biases.

Multilevel Regression with Poststratification (MRP) Model

The MRP model consists of two key components: multilevel (hierarchical) regression and poststratification.

Multilevel Regression Model

Probability $P(y_i = 1)$ that an individual i votes for a candidate based on demographic and geographic predictors:

$$\text{logit}\left(P(y_i = 1)\right) = \beta_0 + \beta_1 X_{1i} + \beta_2 X_{2i} + \cdots + \beta_k X_{ki} + u_j$$

y_i is the binary outcome (where, 1 = supports candidate, 0 = does not support).

$X_{1i}, X_{2i}, \ldots, X_{ki}$ are individual-level predictors

β_0 is the intercept.

β_k are fixed-effect coefficients for each predictor.

$u_j \sim N(0, \sigma^2)$ is a random effect for group j (e.g., state, district, demographic subgroup).

Poststratification Step

Poststratification to adjust predictions for the entire population:

$$\hat{P}_g = \frac{1}{N_g} \sum_{i \in g} P(y_i = 1)$$

$\hat{P}_g$ is the predicted probability for group g.

N_g is the population size of group g obtained from census data.

The final estimate for the overall population is:

$$\hat{P} = \sum_g w_g \hat{P}_g$$

w_g is the proportion of group g in the total population.

Logistic regression is another key statistical technique widely used in the social sciences to analyse binary outcomes, such as voting behaviour, political preferences, or social attitudes. Unlike linear regression, which predicts continuous variables, logistic regression focuses on estimating the probability of an event occurring. This makes it particularly effective for analysing categorical data. When applied to voting behaviour, logistic regression allows researchers to assess the likelihood of an individual supporting a specific candidate or party. By considering various factors, including age, income, education, political affiliation, and geographic location, this method helps identify significant predictors that influence voter decisions.

MACHINE LEARNING MODELS FOR ANALYSING VOTER BEHAVIOUR

Understanding how voters behave is crucial in political science and electoral strategy. While traditional statistical approaches are valuable, they can struggle with processing extensive and intricate datasets. In contrast, machine learning models excel in analysing large volumes of voter data, detecting patterns, and making precise predictions. This report examines three prominent machine learning models employed in voter behaviour analysis: Decision Trees & Random Forests, Support Vector Machines (SVM), and Neural Networks (Breiman, 2001).

Decision Trees are supervised learning models that classify voter data through a series of sequential decision rules. They are especially effective in identifying key demographic and socioeconomic factors that influence voter behaviour. However, a single decision tree may overfit the data, resulting in less reliable predictions.

To address this limitation, Random Forests—an ensemble learning technique—combine multiple decision trees to enhance accuracy and generalizability. By aggregating predictions from various trees, Random Forests reduce overfitting and perform well with large datasets. These models are particularly beneficial for:

- Feature Importance Analysis: Identifying the most influential voter characteristics (such as income, education, and political affiliation) in determining voting behaviour.
- Handling Missing Data: Utilizing multiple trees allows Random Forests to effectively manage datasets with incomplete information.
- Predicting Voter Turnout: Analysing historical voting patterns to estimate the likelihood of individuals participating in future elections.

Support Vector Machines (SVM) are classification models designed to find the optimal boundary (hyperplane) that separates different categories of voters. By transforming data into a higher-dimensional space, SVM can effectively distinguish between voter segments, such as likely and unlikely supporters of a candidate (Cortes, C., & Vapnik, V. (1995) & Hsu, C.-W., Chang, C.-C., & Lin, C.-J. (2003)).

Key benefits of SVM in voter analysis include:

- Effective with High-Dimensional Data: SVM performs well when handling numerous features, such as voter demographics, past voting behaviour, and social media activity.
- Resistant to Outliers: By focusing on the most important decision boundary points (support vectors), SVM is less affected by noisy or extreme data.
- Kernel Trick for Nonlinear Relationships: SVM utilizes kernel functions (such as polynomial or radial basis functions) to capture complex patterns between voter attributes and their preferences.

Neural Networks for Voter Prediction

Neural Networks, especially Deep Learning models, are highly effective at identifying complex, nonlinear relationships within voter data. These models, which consist of multiple layers of neurons, can uncover intricate patterns in large datasets, making them particularly suited for high-dimensional political analysis.

The applications of Neural Networks in analysing voter behaviour include:

- Predicting Voter Preferences: Deep Neural Networks (DNNs) assess a variety of factors (such as economic conditions, media consumption, and personal beliefs) to predict a voter's political stance.
- Analysing Unstructured Data: Neural networks, through Natural Language Processing (NLP) techniques, can process text-based data from sources like surveys, social media, and political speeches.
- Time-Series Forecasting: Recurrent Neural Networks (RNNs) and Long Short-Term Memory (LSTM) networks track changes in public opinion over time, providing valuable insights into election trends.

Table 2. Comparison of Machine Learning Models

Model	Strengths	Limitations
Decision Trees & Random Forests	Identifies key voter characteristics, reduces overfitting, handles missing data well	Can be computationally expensive with large datasets
Support Vector Machines (SVM)	Effective for high-dimensional data, robust to outliers, good for classification	Computationally intensive, less interpretable
Neural Networks	Detects complex patterns, works well with unstructured data, suitable for time-series analysis	Requires large datasets, high computational cost

Machine learning has transformed the analysis of voter behaviour by offering advanced tools for recognizing patterns and making predictions. Decision Trees & Random Forests help pinpoint key voter traits, SVM efficiently categorizes voters into support groups, and Neural Networks uncover deeper trends to enhance forecasting accuracy (Table 2). As political campaigns rely more on data, utilizing these models can optimize electoral strategies, improve voter engagement, and inform policy decisions.

Socioeconomic Factors and Sentiment Analysis

The emergence of social media platforms such as Twitter, Facebook, and Instagram have revolutionized how political campaigns engage with voters. These platforms offer a direct means of communication between candidates and the public, while also serving as valuable tools for gathering data on voter sentiment. Social media sentiment analysis leverages natural language processing (NLP) to examine online discussions, track relevant keywords, and identify emerging trends in public opinion. This analysis helps campaigns gauge voter attitudes toward candidates, policies, or key issues in real-time. By recognizing patterns in posts, tweets, and comments, campaigns can swiftly adjust their strategies or respond to voter concerns.

For example, if sentiment analysis reveals growing discontent with a candidate's position on healthcare, the campaign can refine its messaging to more effectively address these concerns.

Census data offers valuable insights into the socioeconomic factors that shape voter behaviour. Details on income, education, employment, and housing help provide a deeper understanding of how various communities are likely to vote. Socioeconomic factors significantly influence voter preferences and political alignments. For example, individuals with lower incomes may prioritize policies aimed at reducing poverty and unemployment, whereas higher-income voters might be more concerned with tax cuts and fiscal policies.

Analysing census data allows campaigns to tailor their messages and allocate resources more effectively to specific groups based on their socioeconomic priorities and concerns. Moreover, census data can reveal regional variations in voter behaviour, enabling campaigns to concentrate their efforts on swing states or key districts with substantial voter populations (Gelman, A., & Hill, J. (2007).

Campaign contributions and political advertisements serve as key indicators of voter engagement and campaign strategy effectiveness. Monitoring donations and expenditure offers valuable insights into a candidate's support across different voter groups. Significant contributions from specific demographics or industries may signal strong backing from those sectors, while trends in political ad spending can highlight the regions and issues where campaigns are prioritizing their outreach efforts.

Political advertisements, whether on TV, social media, or direct mail, are crafted to influence voters by emphasizing a candidate's policies, values, and accomplishments. By assessing their effectiveness through engagement metrics, voter feedback, and sentiment analysis, campaigns can refine their messaging to enhance impact and sway public opinion.

CONCLUSION

Artificial intelligence has emerged as a more effective tool for predicting electoral behaviour than traditional polling methods, as demonstrated by key case studies such as the 2016 U.S. presidential election and the Brexit referendum. Traditional polling has its own endogenous problems and relies on limited sample sizes and self-reported data, often struggling to capture hidden voter sentiment and last-minute shifts in opinion. In contrast, AI-powered social media analytics process vast amounts of real-time data, offering deeper insights into public sentiment. The success of AI in these cases highlights its potential to revolutionise election forecasting. By leveraging big data and machine learning, AI can process unfiltered public sentiment, detect emerging trends, and provide a more dynamic and comprehensive understanding of voter behaviour. As AI technologies continue to evolve, they are likely to play an even greater role in shaping political strategy, campaign management, and electoral predictions. Developing comprehensive frameworks for human-AI decision-making is essential for generating unified scientific knowledge. It is evident the importance of creating structures that define various decision tasks, outline AI assistance components, and establish evaluation metrics. Such frameworks can enhance research by fostering a shared understanding of significant problems and facilitating clear articulation of research questions. For instance, framework detailing AI assistance can highlight less explored areas. Additionally, these frameworks can illuminate overlooked factors that contribute to the synthesis of findings across research, ultimately bolstering the robustness of knowledge and theoretical frameworks. It is crucial for AI communities to prioritize technical developments informed by human behaviour and empirical insights, fostering cross-disciplinary collaboration to unite researchers in enhancing human-AI decision-making. As per AI practical use in the political marketing, strategic political communication and political interaction field we should remember that AI is revolutionizing the above industry through enhanced data-driven decision-making, audience targeting, and increased campaign efficiency. It facilitates voter data analysis and segmentation by processing extensive demographic and behavioural information, allowing campaigns to tailor their messages effectively. Predictive analytics enable forecasts of voter behaviour and turnout, guiding resource allocation to focus on key demographics. Additionally, AI supports microtargeting and personalized messaging through chatbots and targeted digital ads, enhancing voter engagement. Sentiment analysis tools provide real-time insights into public opinion, enabling campaigns to adapt their strategies dynamically. However, the use of AI raises ethical concerns, particularly with the potential for deepfakes and disinformation. Chatbots also streamline communication with voters, while AI automates ad optimization and media buying processes. Furthermore, AI aids in opposition research and crisis management by tracking rival candidates and identifying negative trends. Additionally, it optimizes fundraising by predicting donor behaviour and detecting disinformation, thereby safeguarding electoral integrity. Overall, the implications of AI in political marketing underscore the necessity for ethical considerations alongside innovative practices.

REFERENCES

Agarwal, S. (2016, March 18). *IBM Watson and Social Data predict the next US President.* https://www.linkedin.com/pulse/ibm-watson-social-data-predict-next-us-president-shilpi-agarwal

Alon-Barkat, S., & Busuioc, M. (2023). Human–AI Interactions in Public Sector Decision Making: "Automation Bias" and "Selective Adherence" to Algorithmic Advice. *Journal of Public Administration: Research and Theory*, *33*(1), 153–169. DOI: 10.1093/JOPART/MUAC007

AP. (2023). *AI-generated images of Trump being arrested circulate on social media | AP News.* https://apnews.com/article/fact-check-trump-NYPD-stormy-daniels-539393517762

Bareis, J., & Katzenbach, C. (2022a). Talking AI into Being: The Narratives and Imaginaries of National AI Strategies and Their Performative Politics. *Science, Technology & Human Values*, *47*(5), 855–881. DOI: 10.1177/01622439211030007

Bareis, J., & Katzenbach, C. (2022b). Talking AI into Being: The Narratives and Imaginaries of National AI Strategies and Their Performative Politics. *Science, Technology & Human Values*, *47*(5), 855–881. DOI: 10.1177/01622439211030007

Bovet, A., Morone, F., & Makse, H. A. (2018). Validation of Twitter opinion trends with national polling aggregates: Hillary Clinton vs Donald Trump. *Scientific Reports*, *8*(1), 8673. DOI: 10.1038/s41598-018-26951-y

Breiman, L. (2001). Random forests. *Machine Learning*, *45*(1), 5–32. DOI: 10.1023/A:1010933404324

Cerina, R., & Duch, R. (2020). Measuring public opinion via digital footprints. *International Journal of Forecasting*, *36*(3), 987–1002. DOI: 10.1016/j.ijforecast.2019.10.004

Chandra, D. S. (2025) "Reimagining Democracy in the Digital Era: Transformative Role of Artificial Intelligence in Modern Governance." IGI Global Scientific Publishing. Available at: https://lrcdrs.bennett.edu.in/handle/123456789/5290 (Accessed: June 26, 2025).

Coppock, A. (2017). Did Shy Trump Supporters Bias the 2016 Polls? Evidence from a Nationally-representative List Experiment. *Statistics, Politics, and Policy*, *8*(1), 29–40. DOI: 10.1515/spp-2016-0005

Csernatoni, R. (2024). *Can Democracy Survive the Disruptive Power of AI?* Carnegie Endowment for International Peace.

Das, A., & Malaviya, S. (2025). Artificial Intelligence and Sentiment Analysis in Political Campaigns. In Cyber-Physical Systems for Innovating and Transforming Society 5.0 (eds T. Choudhury, A. Kumar, R. Tomar, S. Balamurugan and A. Vishnoi). https://doi.org/DOI: 10.1002/9781394197750.ch9

Data, E. Q. (2016, June 24). *DataEQ accurately predicts Brexit vote. How?* DataEQ. https://dataeq.com/resources/news/brandseye-accurately-predicts-brexit-vote

DellaPosta, D., Shi, Y., & Macy, M. (2015). Why Do Liberals Drink Lattes? *American Journal of Sociology*, *120*(5), 1473–1511. DOI: 10.1086/681254

Du, H., Zhang, R., Niyato, D., Kang, J., Xiong, Z., Cui, S., Shen, X., & Kim, D. I. (2023). *User-Centric Interactive AI for Distributed Diffusion Model-based AI-Generated Content*. https://arxiv.org/abs/2311.11094v1

European Parliament. (2023). *Artificial intelligence, democracy and elections | Think Tank | European Parliament*. European Parliament. https://www.europarl.europa.eu/thinktank/en/document/EPRS_BRI(2023)751478

Fischer, S. C., & Wenger, A. (2021). Artificial Intelligence, Forward-Looking Governance and the Future of Security. *Schweizerische Zeitschrift für Politikwissenschaft*, *27*(1), 170–179. DOI: 10.1111/SPSR.12439

Flügge, A. A. (2021). Perspectives from Practice: Algorithmic Decision-Making in Public Employment Services. *Proceedings of the ACM Conference on Computer Supported Cooperative Work, CSCW*, 253–255. https://doi.org/DOI: 10.1145/3462204.3481787

Gelman, A. (2021). Failure and Success in Political Polling and Election Forecasting. *Statistics and Public Policy (Philadelphia, Pa.)*, *8*(1), 67–72. DOI: 10.1080/2330443X.2021.1971126

Gelman, A., & Little, T. (1997). *Poststratiication Into Many Categories Using Hierarchical Logistic Regression*.

Gilder, L., Horton, J., & Chu, B. (2025). *Fact-checking Donald Trump's speech to Congress*. BBC. https://www.bbc.com/news/articles/cp3ylpd2n9no

Gillespie, T. (2024). Generative AI and the politics of visibility. *Big Data & Society*, *11*(2). Advance online publication. DOI: 10.1177/20539517241252131

Green, M. (2016, July 29). *How Social Analytics Predicted the Brexit Vote*. https://www.dataversity.net/brexit-affect-data-protection-uk/

Hartmann, J., Schwenzow, J., & Witte, M. (2023). *The political ideology of conversational AI: Converging evidence on ChatGPT's pro-environmental, left-libertarian orientation*. https://doi.org/DOI: 10.25592/UHHFDM.11733

Herd, P., & Moynihan, D. P. (2019). *Administrative Burden*. Administrative Burden., DOI: 10.7758/9781610448789

Kamal, R., & Kaur, J. (2025). *Artificial intelligence and electoral decision-making : Analyzing voter perceptions of AI-driven political Ads*. Recent Advances in Sciences, Engineering, Information Technology & Management., DOI: 10.1201/9781003598152-127

Kern, M. L., McCarthy, P. X., Chakrabarty, D., & Rizoiu, M.-A. (2019). Social media-predicted personality traits and values can help match people to their ideal jobs. *Proceedings of the National Academy of Sciences of the United States of America*, *116*(52), 26459–26464. DOI: 10.1073/pnas.1917942116

Kiran, V. (2020, June 16). *Voter Behavior Prediction using Machine Learning*. Politicalmarketer.Com.

Kirkizh, N., Ulloa, R., Stier, S., & Pfeffer, J. (2024). Predicting political attitudes from web tracking data: A machine learning approach. *Journal of Information Technology & Politics*, *21*(4), 564–577. DOI: 10.1080/19331681.2024.2316679

Lai, V., Chen, C., Smith-Renner, A., Liao, Q. V., & Tan, C. (2023). Towards a Science of Human-AI Decision Making: An Overview of Design Space in Empirical Human-Subject Studies. *ACM International Conference Proceeding Series*, 1369–1385. https://doi.org/DOI: 10.1145/3593013.3594087

Markaki, E., & Chadjipadelis, T. (2017). Multivariable Evaluation via Conjoint Analysis of the Factors that Influence Voting Behavior in Networks. *Journal of Political Sciences & Public Affairs*, *05*(01). Advance online publication. DOI: 10.4172/2332-0761.1000239

Markaki, E., & Chadjipadelis, T. (2023). *View of The Greek Government's Pandemic Policy towards Covid-19 as a Parameter of Political Competition through Different Media Channels. Game Theory Application as a Conceptual Framework for the Decision Making Process*. https://esipreprints.org/index.php/esipreprints/article/view/276/262

Markaki, E., & Tsoukatou, V. (2025). Exploring AI's Strategic Impacts and Possibilities in Political Science and Manufacturing Industry: A Gender-Biased Perspective. In Nayak, B. S., & Tabassum, N. (Eds.), *Impact of Patriarchy and Gender Stereotypes on Working Women* (pp. 197–213). Springer Nature Switzerland., DOI: 10.1007/978-3-031-74406-8_11

Marr, B. (2023). *A Short History Of ChatGPT: How We Got To Where We Are Today.* https://www.forbes.com/sites/bernardmarr/2023/05/19/a-short-history-of-chatgpt-how-we-got-to-where-we-are-today/

Mercer, A., Deane, C., & Mcgeeney, K. (2016, November 9). *Why 2016 election polls missed their mark.* PEW Research Center.

Murray, P. (2024). *National: Impact of anti-institutional attitudes. Double hater voters want change but not authoritarianism.*

National Endowment for Democracy. (2023). *Manufacturing Deceit: How Generative AI Supercharges Information Manipulation - NATIONAL ENDOWMENT FOR DEMOCRACY.* https://www.ned.org/manufacturing-deceit-how-generative-ai-supercharges-information-manipulation/

Park, D. K., Gelman, A., & Bafumi, J. (2004). Bayesian Multilevel Estimation with Poststratification: State-Level Estimates from National Polls. *Political Analysis, 12*(4), 375–385. DOI: 10.1093/PAN/MPH024

Pham, L.. (2025). European reactions to AI in full and flawed democracies: An investigation of key factors [Preprint]. *AI & Society.* Advance online publication. DOI: 10.1007/s00146-025-02306-w

Phillips, J. H., thank Bernd Beber, W., Erikson, R., Haider-Markel, D., Kastellec, J., Shapiro, R., Wawro, G., & Wright, G. (2009). How Should We Estimate Public Opinion in The States? *American Journal of Political Science, 53*(1), 107–121.

Pollard, R. D., Pollard, S. M., & Streit, S. (2023). *Predicting Propensity to Vote with Machine Learning.* https://doi.org/DOI: 10.2139/ssrn.4417873

Rank, A. D., & Mushtare, R. (2019). Using Personas as a Tool for Teaching Civic Communication. *The Journal of General Education, 68*(3–4), 252–262. DOI: 10.5325/JGENEEDUC.68.3-4.0252

Reuters. (2023). *Turkey elections 2023: what you need to know | Reuters.* https://www.reuters.com/world/middle-east/turkey-elections-2023-what-you-need-know-2023-05-12/

Reveilhac, M., & Morselli, D. (2025). ChatGPT as a voting application in direct democracy. *Schweizerische Zeitschrift für Politikwissenschaft*. Advance online publication. DOI: 10.1111/SPSR.12650

Rodwell, E. (2025). Between Code and Culture: The Evolving Role of Conversation Designers and UX in AI Development. *Science, Technology & Human Values*. Advance online publication. DOI: 10.1177/01622439251324884

Schippers, B. (2020). Artificial intelligence and democratic politics. *Political Insight*, *11*(1), 32–35. DOI: 10.1177/2041905820911746

Stegmaier, M., & Norpoth, H. (2013). Election Forecasting. In *Oxford Bibliographies Online Datasets*. https://doi.org/DOI: 10.1093/obo/9780199756223-0023

Talebirad, Y., & Nadiri, A. (2023). *Multi-Agent Collaboration: Harnessing the Power of Intelligent LLM Agents*. https://arxiv.org/abs/2306.03314v1

The Guardian. (2023). *Turkish presidential candidate quits race after release of alleged sex tape | Turkey | The Guardian*. https://www.theguardian.com/world/2023/may/11/muharrem-ince-turkish-presidential-candidate-withdraws-alleged-sex-tape

The Guardian. (2025). *'Trump Gaza' AI video intended as political satire, says creator | Artificial intelligence (AI) | The Guardian*. https://www.theguardian.com/technology/2025/mar/06/trump-gaza-ai-video-intended-as-political-satire-says-creator

The New York Times. (2023). *Is Argentina the First A.I. Election? - The New York Times*. https://www.nytimes.com/2023/11/15/world/americas/argentina-election-ai-milei-massa.html

White House. (2018). *Summary of the 2018 white house summit on artificial intelligence for american industry*. The White House Office of Science and Technology Policy. https://trumpwhitehouse.archives.gov/wp-content/uploads/2018/05/Summary-Report-of-White-House-AI-Summit.pdf

Wiedemann, A. (2024). The Electoral Consequences of Household Indebtedness under Austerity. *American Journal of Political Science*, *68*(2), 354–371. DOI: 10.1111/ajps.12708

Win, H. (2024) "'From Handshakes to Hashtags: The Evolution of U.S. Election Campaigns,'" Election Study.

Wu, L., Chen, Y., Shen, K., Guo, X., Gao, H., Li, S., Pei, J., & Long, B. (2021). Graph Neural Networks for Natural Language Processing: A Survey. *Foundations and Trends in Machine Learning*, *16*(2), 120–329. DOI: 10.1561/2200000096

Yang, J. C., Dailisan, D., Korecki, M., Hausladen, C. I., & Helbing, D. (2024). LLM Voting: Human Choices and AI Collective Decision-Making. *Proceedings of the AAAI/ACM Conference on AI, Ethics, and Society, 7*(1), 1696–1708. https://doi.org/DOI: 10.1609/AIES.V7I1.31758

YouGov. (2017). *How YouGov's election model compares with the final result | YouGov*. https://yougov.co.uk/politics/articles/18355-how-yougovs-election-model-compares-final-result

Zhang, A., Walker, O., Nguyen, K., Dai, J., Chen, A., & Lee, M. K. (2023). Deliberating with AI: Improving Decision-Making for the Future through Participatory AI Design and Stakeholder Deliberation. *Proceedings of the ACM on Human-Computer Interaction, 7*(CSCW1). https://doi.org/DOI: 10.1145/3579601

Zhou, Z., Serafino, M., Cohan, L., Caldarelli, G., & Makse, H. A. (2021). Why polls fail to predict elections. *Journal of Big Data, 8*(1), 137. DOI: 10.1186/s40537-021-00525-8

Zuloaga-Rotta, L., Borja-Rosales, R., Rodríguez Mallma, M. J., Mauricio, D., & Maculan, N. (2024). Method to Forecast the Presidential Election Results Based on Simulation and Machine Learning. *Computation (Basel, Switzerland), 12*(3), 38. DOI: 10.3390/computation12030038

Section 3
Communication, Campaign Strategies, and Digital Influence on Electoral Outcomes

Chapter 10
Disinformation and Electoral Integrity in the Digital Age:
Evidence From the Elections in the EU and the USA

Athanasios Athanasiou
http://orcid.org/0009-0003-7924-7603
Aristotle University of Thessaloniki, Greece

Klimentini Diakomanoli
Athens Kapodistrian University, Greece

ABSTRACT

The proliferation of disinformation and misinformation has become a critical issue over the past decade, with profound implications for democratic processes at both global and European levels. The European Commission and the European External Action Service (EEAS) have identified the strategic use of foreign information manipulation and disinformation (FIMI) as a direct threat to the integrity of electoral processes and democratic resilience. This chapter will examine voter behavior through the lens of foreign interference, disinformation, and information manipulation. It will explore how digital narratives, engineered by foreign and often non-democratic entities, affect electoral outcomes and undermine democratic participation. A particular focus will be placed on the nuanced vulnerabilities inherent in the European Union's unique political structure.

DOI: 10.4018/979-8-3373-1037-4.ch010

INTRODUCTION

Let's face it: Democracy is not what it used to be. Not what it used to be in the 80-90s at least, during the 'great moderation'. Agency does not work the same way. Access to the electorate is significantly different. The message, the means, everything would be unimaginable when George H. W. Bush faced Michael Dukakis in 88, or even when first Angela Merkel confronted Gerhard Schröder in 05.

What's new: 1000 things… and social media.

In a world where billions consume news primarily through social media, where AI-generated content circulates faster than professional journalism ever could, and where the very model (namely economic incentives – content monetization) reward outrage more than accuracy, the distinction between fact and fiction has grown increasingly blurry, for those not in the loop. Subsequently, the implications to elections are profound. How can anyone rely on an informed citizenry making decisions based on verifiable facts and accountable narratives, when the means have changed?

Disinformation, of course, is not a new phenomenon. We have historical and empirical evidence of such campaigns in wartime propaganda, Cold War-era psyops, and tabloid journalism (at some scale and with a far lesser reach). But contemporary scale, speed, and sophistication, now with the digital means are unprecedented. Social media platforms are by far the fastest communication tools we ever had. But they're also algorithmically curated ecosystems that shape how users perceive reality. Content is prioritized based on engagement, which often means emotional intensity, regardless of factual accuracy. In this system, disinformation thrives. Naturally.

Democracy and its institutions during elections are at their most vulnerable. Our empirical evidence (discussed below) show there are finite, emotionally charged, and often zero-sum contests. A well-timed lie, strategically deployed, can tilt public perception, discourage participation, or cast doubt on the legitimacy of results. In some cases, such as the U.S. Capitol riot of January 6, 2021, disinformation can even incite violence. The electoral context thus acts as both a magnifier and a stress test for the health of democratic systems. That's well documented at the European Council conclusions and shaped the mandate for action given to the European Commission for the next cycle.

That's why this chapter focuses on a critical question: How is disinformation shaping voter behavior, institutional trust, and electoral outcomes in liberal democracies?

To answer this, we examine five case studies—the 2024 European Parliament elections, the 2024 U.S. Presidential Election, the 2024–2025 Romanian elections, and examples from Germany and Poland. These cases have been selected not only for their diversity in political context but also because they reveal unique disinformation strategies and corresponding state or institutional responses.

We will not stop in description. We shall seek to explain why disinformation is so effective and how it exploits both platform architecture and existing political grievances. We explore the dynamics of content virality, the economic and ideological motivations of disinformation actors, and the uneven playing field between malign content producers and defenders of electoral integrity. Importantly, we will consider the role of public policy—including legislation like the Digital Services Act (DSA)—and the limits of regulatory enforcement when dealing with globally distributed, platform-agnostic information flows.

We argue that electoral disinformation is not simply a fringe phenomenon; it is a structural feature of the contemporary information ecosystem. This means that democratic societies cannot afford to be naïve, must know and should make informed decisions, going beyond reactive fact-checking and towards systemic reform. That includes not just holding platforms accountable (as the Commission tries to do) but also reinvesting in real public interest journalism, civic education, and coordinated cross-border intelligence-sharing on digital threats.

And all that must ensue before citizens totally lose trust on electoral processes or participation declines due to cynicism and confusion. As in the end it is the legitimacy of democratic governance that is at stake. In such conditions, authoritarian narratives—offering order over pluralism, simplicity over nuance—gain ground. Preventing this outcome requires understanding disinformation not just as false content, but as a political weapon and a systemic vulnerability.

The Role of Disinformation in Voter Behavior in Recent EU Elections

The proliferation of disinformation and misinformation has become a critical issue over the past decade, with profound implications for democratic processes at both global and European levels. The European Commission and the European External Action Service (EEAS) have identified the strategic use of foreign information manipulation and disinformation (FIMI) as a direct threat to the integrity of electoral processes and democratic resilience.

The viral spread of false narratives within the digital ecosystem is not only rapid but borderless. Evidence increasingly suggests a strong cross-border spillover effect, even in linguistically and culturally distinct environments. Malign actors often exploit the transnational nature of digital communication to amplify their reach and destabilize democratic societies.

National authorities and independent observers have also accumulated compelling evidence pointing to the deliberate production and dissemination of disinformation by foreign actors with well-defined strategic agendas. These efforts go beyond incidental misinformation; they are part of a coordinated approach designed to undermine societal cohesion, erode public trust in democratic institutions, and sow confusion among voters. Such tactics ultimately aim to weaken Europe's democratic fabric and influence decision-making processes at both national and EU levels.

Disinformation is a key factor influencing citizens' cognitive processes, including electoral decision-making. By exploiting cognitive biases and emotional triggers, disinformation campaigns can sway voter preferences and reduce political engagement. This manipulation is particularly concerning within the European context, where democratic legitimacy depends heavily on the interplay between national and EU legislative processes.

This chapter will examine voter behavior through the lens of foreign interference, disinformation, and information manipulation. It will explore how digital narratives, engineered by foreign and often non-democratic entities, affect electoral outcomes and undermine democratic participation. A particular focus will be placed on the nuanced vulnerabilities inherent in the European Union's unique political structure.

The EU, as a supranational organization, operates on the basis of shared sovereignty, where member states have conferred competences in critical areas of policy. This structural complexity creates fertile ground for disinformation campaigns, as elections in individual member states have direct implications for the EU's political landscape. Thus, every national election inherently becomes a "Euro-election," with foreign actors seeking to influence not just national outcomes but the balance of legislative focus within EU institutions.

Drawing on insights from the European Commission's *Action Plan Against Disinformation* and the EEAS's work on strategic communication, this chapter will also address existing countermeasures, including media literacy initiatives, fact-checking networks, and cross-border cooperation to combat foreign information threats. The role of the European Digital Media Observatory (EDMO) and the Code of Practice on Disinformation will be highlighted as examples of collaborative efforts to safeguard democratic processes.

By analyzing empirical data and case studies from recent European elections, this chapter will contribute to a deeper understanding of how voters respond to disinformation campaigns and what factors influence their susceptibility. Furthermore, it will underscore the urgent need for robust institutional frameworks, increased transparency, and public awareness to bolster the EU's resilience against disinformation-driven interference.

In conclusion, this chapter aims to illuminate the complex interplay between foreign information manipulation, voter behavior, and democratic processes in the European context. Understanding these dynamics is essential for developing effective countermeasures and reinforcing democratic resilience at both national and supranational levels.

THEORETICAL FRAMEWORK AND METHODOLOGY

To analyze electoral disinformation in a comparative, cross-national context, this chapter draws upon three key conceptual lenses: (1) hybrid warfare and strategic influence operations, (2) information disorder taxonomy, and (3) platform logic and algorithmic governance. Together, these frameworks help us understand not just the content of disinformation, but the structures that enable it, the motives behind it, and the effects it produces.

Hybrid Warfare and Strategic Influence

Hybrid warfare refers to the blending of conventional military threats with non-traditional tools such as cyberattacks, economic coercion, and—crucially—information manipulation. Russia's 2008 doctrine of "non-linear warfare" explicitly named disinformation as a means of achieving political objectives without open conflict (Galeotti, 2016). Similar tactics have been observed from China, Iran, and, increasingly, non-state actors.

In this framework, disinformation is not simply about persuasion. It is about disorientation, disruption, and the creation of informational noise that paralyzes public judgment. The objective is not always to make people believe a lie, but to make them doubt that truth is even possible (Pomerantsev, 2019).

Information Disorder Taxonomy

The taxonomy developed by Wardle and Derakhshan (2017) is now a standard reference in media studies and disinformation research. It divides problematic content into three categories:

- Misinformation: False or misleading information shared without intent to harm.
- Disinformation: False or misleading information shared with harmful intent.
- Malinformation: Genuine information shared to cause harm, often taken out of context.

This typology is helpful in differentiating types of electoral manipulation. A well-meaning citizen sharing an outdated video about ballot fraud may be spreading misinformation, while a coordinated network impersonating election officials is engaging in disinformation. Likewise, leaked but decontextualized emails used to smear a candidate fall into the category of malinformation.

Platform Logic and Algorithmic Amplification

Digital platforms are not neutral conduits of information. They are profit-driven businesses that design their interfaces and algorithms to maximize user engagement, often at the expense of factual integrity. As Zuboff (2019) explains in her theory of surveillance capitalism, platforms extract behavioral data to predict and shape user actions, and outrage, fear, and novelty are highly monetizable emotions.

This logic has created an ecosystem in which emotionally charged disinformation spreads faster and more widely than corrective content. A tweet falsely claiming that "millions of votes were lost" can reach viral status within hours, while the official correction may barely circulate.

Recent studies (Guess et al., 2020) have shown that algorithmic sorting and recommendation systems can inadvertently (or deliberately) lead users into echo chambers or "rabbit holes" of conspiratorial content. Understanding platform logic is thus essential to understanding why electoral disinformation is so effective and so difficult to stop.

CASE STUDY 1: EUROPEAN PARLIAMENTARY ELECTIONS 2024

The European Parliament elections constitute the most complex electoral event in the Union's 5-year electoral cycle and the 2024 elections were the most complex in the Union's history. All other elections (e.g. for national governments participating in the Council) happen gradually. The election involves over 400 million eligible voters across 27 member states. Taking place in the aftermath of the pandemic, amid a volatile global context—including Russia's continued war of aggression against Ukraine, economic pressure from inflation, and increasing polarization within EU societies—the 2024 election became a focal point for both legitimate political contestation and systematic information warfare.

Context and Strategic Relevance

Elections to the European Parliament are not just internal affairs; they are geopolitical events. For adversaries like Russia, sowing discord during such a massive, multistate election is an opportunity to weaken the EU's legitimacy, empower Eurosceptic factions, and disrupt coordinated foreign policy responses—particularly those related to sanctions and military aid to Ukraine. The Parliament may not be part of the foreign policy decision making process of the Union, but can exert political pressure, use resources and ultimately shape debates with spillover to national elections.

In the months preceding the election, the European Commission's StratCom division issued public warnings about the high risk of coordinated foreign interference. The Commission urged platforms to improve content moderation and transparency, while governments enhanced media monitoring capabilities through the EDMO (European Digital Media Observatory) network. Despite these efforts, disinformation campaigns adapted quickly.

Narrative Strategies and Tactics

Disinformation narratives during the election focused on a few core themes:

1. **Immigration and National Identity**: False claims circulated on TikTok and Telegram suggesting that the EU was planning to force member states to accept "mandatory Islamic quotas" or to eliminate borders entirely. These messages, often featuring manipulated videos, played particularly well in Hungary, Austria, and Italy—countries with existing populist narratives about national sovereignty (Guardian 2024).
2. **Digital Currency and Financial Control**: In France and Germany, rumors spread that the EU would soon abolish cash and enforce a central digital euro tied to "social credit scores". These narratives were seeded in alt-finance YouTube channels and were later picked up by influencer accounts on Facebook and Instagram (France24, 2025).
3. **Ukraine War and EU Militarization**: In Slovakia and Bulgaria, disinformation actors claimed that voting for pro-EU parties would lead to conscription into NATO forces fighting in Ukraine. A viral video showed a fake EU press conference announcing "a joint EU army draft," using AI-generated voiceovers and falsified logos (Euractiv, 2024).

These messages weren't just isolated memes—they were parts of coordinated campaigns. Reports by EDMO and the Belgian Centre for Cybersecurity showed links to networks previously involved in Russian disinformation operations, employing such tactics as the well-known "Doppelgänger" of cloning legitimate media sites.

Platform Behavior and Enforcement Challenges

Despite the implementation of the Digital Services Act (DSA) in early 2024, enforcement lagged behind the speed of these campaigns. Meta and TikTok published transparency reports and expanded fact-checking partnerships, but experts criticized (Wired, 2024) the lack of real-time data access for researchers.

X (the social network formerly known as Twitter), under Elon Musk's leadership, openly pushed back against EU regulators. In April 2024, the company failed a voluntary stress test organized by the European Commission and refused to provide comprehensive ad log data. This lack of cooperation limited the ability of watchdogs to trace foreign-funded political ads.

Telegram, meanwhile, proved nearly impossible to regulate. Disinformation about the EU's supposed "deep state" was widely circulated through private groups that were then screenshot and reposted across X and Facebook. Researchers found that many of these narratives originated in Russian-language channels with thousands of members.

Geographical Variation

Not all EU member states were equally vulnerable. The Baltic states (Estonia, Latvia, and Lithuania), which have high levels of digital literacy and long experience with Russian influence operations, were relatively resilient. In contrast, Romania, Bulgaria, and Slovakia saw disinformation dominate campaign coverage in fringe media outlets (BECID, 2024).

In Poland, false stories about EU interference in judicial independence gained traction. Several viral claims stated that EU institutions were planning to remove the Polish constitution and replace it with "EU common law." These claims were amplified by domestic conservative outlets and Facebook pages with high reach and engagement.

Impact on Electoral Outcomes

While it is difficult to attribute specific voting shifts directly to disinformation, correlation patterns are striking. In countries where anti-EU disinformation was most intense—Slovakia, Hungary, France—far-right and Eurosceptic parties made measurable gains. In Hungary, Viktor Orbán's Fidesz party retained a strong hold, while Marine Le Pen's National Rally performed above polling expectations in France.

Post-election surveys conducted by Eurobarometer (European Commission, 2025) revealed a growing distrust in European institutions among younger voters who had been heavily exposed to content on TikTok and Telegram. Many respondents expressed uncertainty about whether "Brussels" was working in the national interest—a sentiment stoked by months of anti-EU falsehoods.

Regulatory and Civil Society Responses

The European Commission responded post-election with new guidance under the DSA, requesting detailed risk assessments from major platforms and warning of fines for future non-compliance. However, civil society actors were often the first responders. Fact-checking organizations like Correctiv, EU DisinfoLab, and Facta of Italy (The Guardian, 2024, Reuters 2024, Politico 2025, Reuters 2025) worked tirelessly to debunk false claims, though their reach remained limited compared to disinformation networks.

EDMO's post-election report concluded that while the DSA represents a legal milestone, enforcement mechanisms remain underdeveloped, especially for cross-border content. It also noted that platforms still delay providing backend data to independent auditors and often claim "user privacy" as a barrier to meaningful transparency.

CASE STUDY 2: U.S. PRESIDENTIAL ELECTION 2024

The 2024 U.S. presidential election took place in an environment of deep polarization, institutional fatigue, and eroded trust in democratic processes—conditions ripe for the spread of disinformation. The race between incumbent Democratic Vice President Kamala Harris and Republican nominee Former President Donald Trump was not only politically contentious but also narratively contested in the digital arena. Disinformation in the U.S. context blended organic domestic production with foreign amplification, making it a hybrid threat that challenged both policy responses and platform governance.

Structural Context

The United States faces unique vulnerabilities in the disinformation landscape. It lacks a centralized electoral authority, has fragmented election administration across thousands of local jurisdictions, and operates under strong constitutional protections for freedom of speech. This decentralized system makes it particularly difficult to implement national disinformation countermeasures during an election.

Furthermore, the lingering false narrative of the "stolen" 2020 election had normalized electoral skepticism among large segments of the population. Polling from Pew Research in early 2024 found that nearly 30% of Americans still believed that President Joe Biden had not been legitimately elected. This lingering distrust proved fertile ground for renewed falsehoods.

Primary Disinformation Narratives

During the 2024 election cycle, disinformation took several prominent forms (Brookings 2024), often tailored to specific voter anxieties:

1. Ballot Fraud and Vote Rigging: Viral claims alleged that Democrats were manufacturing votes in key swing states. A widely shared video appeared to show boxes of ballots being moved "suspiciously" in a Michigan warehouse. The video, later proven to be footage from a legitimate ballot storage facility, was reposted thousands of times with altered captions and hashtags like #ElectionHeist and #Steal2024.
2. Immigration and Crime: Social media posts falsely claimed that undocumented immigrants were voting in large numbers, especially in California and Texas. One viral post stated, "10 million illegal voters are ready to steal the election." These narratives often relied on manipulated statistics or out-of-context statements from local officials.
3. Economic Collapse: Right-wing influencers and partisan channels on YouTube and Rumble claimed that the economy was on the verge of collapse due to Democratic policies. Despite strong indicators—such as low unemployment and record GDP growth—the narrative that "Bidenomics" was ruining America persisted, amplified by memes and AI-generated infographics.
4. Candidate Smears: Deepfake technology played a notable role for the first time in a U.S. election. Videos showing Kamala Harris laughing while discussing unemployment, or Joe Biden slurring words in what appeared to be a state of mental confusion, were circulated widely. While many of these were quickly debunked, they continued to circulate on fringe platforms like Truth Social and Telegram.
5. Narratives of Suppression: Republican candidates and activists claimed that tech platforms were "censoring" conservative voices. Elon Musk actively engaged in these debates by amplifying complaints from users banned or demonetized on X (formerly Twitter), further legitimizing narratives of systemic bias against the political right.

Platform Architecture and Monetization

One of the most consequential developments in the 2024 election was the role of monetization in disinformation spread. Under Musk's ownership, X began paying users for engagement, including those who posted controversial or misleading political content. According to an investigation by *ProPublica* (2024), a network of influencers who regularly posted disinformation received tens of thousands of dollars in ad-sharing revenue.

This model created perverse incentives. Users had direct financial motivation to post inflammatory, polarizing content, regardless of factual accuracy. These posts were often algorithmically promoted due to high engagement, effectively rewarding users for spreading disinformation.

Incentivizing free speech through monetization without proper financial disclosure does not constitute "free" speech

Meta attempted to mitigate similar risks by reintroducing election-related ad restrictions and labeling political content. However, enforcement remained inconsistent. A *New York Times* audit found that over 40% of flagged false political ads remained active for more than 72 hours before removal.

TikTok, widely used by younger demographics, presented a unique challenge. Disinformation on the platform often took the form of short, emotionally engaging videos set to music. These included falsely attributed quotes, edited footage, and pseudo-statistical graphics—forms of content that evade traditional moderation techniques.

Foreign Involvement and Intelligence Warnings

Though much of the disinformation in 2024 was domestically generated, foreign actors played a significant amplification role. A joint report from the Office of the Director of National Intelligence (ODNI) and the FBI concluded that Russian and Iranian-linked accounts sought to "exploit existing divisions, intensify distrust, and reduce voter confidence in democratic outcomes."

Chinese actors appeared to experiment with more subtle forms of influence, promoting themes of U.S. decline and dysfunction through content farms based in Southeast Asia (Microsoft, 2024) These actors rarely supported specific candidates but rather pushed narratives that framed the American system as broken and corrupt.

The FBI issued warnings about impersonation campaigns, including several viral videos that used AI-generated voices and visuals to mimic official government announcements. One widely shared clip falsely claimed that the Department of Homeland Security had declared martial law in Arizona on election day.

Real-World Consequences

The effects of disinformation were not limited to the digital sphere. In the final weeks before the election, several bomb threats were called into polling centers in Pennsylvania and Nevada, leading to temporary closures. While no devices were found, the threats were accompanied by Telegram posts urging users to "stop the steal before it begins."

Election officials also reported a sharp uptick in harassment and doxing. In Georgia, Arizona, and Wisconsin—states that had been flashpoints in 2020—local officials received threats referencing conspiracies shared online. Daniel Baxter, a senior election official in Detroit, stated, "We're planning for the possibility of unrest on every level—digital, physical, reputational."

Post-Election Narratives and Long-Term Impact

After the election, disinformation surged again. Claims that ballots had been "pre-printed in China" or that dead voters had swayed the outcome dominated platforms like Truth Social and Gettr.

While no legal challenges gained traction in court, the narrative of a stolen election once again took root. A December 2024 poll by Pew showed that 38% of Republican voters did not trust the official results, and 19% believed that military intervention might be needed to "restore order"—a disturbing echo of January 6th discourse.

The long-term implications are profound. Disinformation has altered the norms of electoral contestation in the U.S., turning what should be administrative disagreements into existential conflicts. It has also entrenched distrust in the very institutions designed to ensure fairness and transparency.

CASE STUDY 3: ROMANIAN PRESIDENTIAL ELECTIONS 2024–2025

Romania's 2024–2025 presidential elections revealed one of the most aggressive and coordinated disinformation campaigns seen in any EU member state to date. Unlike the more diffuse, polarizing content common in Western Europe or the U.S., the Romanian case was marked by highly organized narrative warfare, algorithmic exploitation of platforms like TikTok, and evidence of foreign state involvement—culminating in a Constitutional Court decision to annul the first round of results.

Background and Political Context

Romania's political climate leading into the election was already tense. Rising dissatisfaction with the EU, economic strain, and disillusionment with mainstream political parties created fertile ground for populist messaging. Into this landscape stepped Călin Georgescu, a pro-Russian, ultra-nationalist candidate whose platform blended sovereignty rhetoric with anti-EU and anti-globalist conspiracies.

What made Georgescu's campaign unique was its weaponization of TikTok, a platform with over 20 million Romanian users, most of them under 35. While other candidates focused on television debates and traditional advertising, Georgescu's digital team ran a parallel, decentralized campaign through influencers, meme creators, and Telegram-based coordination cells.

Coordinated Inauthentic Behavior on TikTok

A joint investigation by Democracy Reporting International (2024) and Romanian civil society groups uncovered the existence of over 66 TikTok accounts impersonating Georgescu or his campaign, many violating the platform's impersonation and coordination rules. These accounts used identical hashtags, recycled audio, and synchronized posting schedules.

Thousands of "volunteers" were recruited via Telegram channels with names like "Truth Army Romania" and "Sovereign Youth." According to leaked messages reviewed by G4Media, volunteers were given pre-produced videos and detailed instructions on how to comment under rival candidates' posts in order to trigger TikTok's recommendation algorithm. In some cases, competitions were held to see whose reposted content could get the most likes, shares, or duets (a feature in TikTok, that offers a split-screen video next to the original).

The result was an artificial viral wave. Georgescu's campaign dominated the platform's "For You" feed in the weeks before the first-round vote. Many users believed this reflected organic popularity, when in fact it was a textbook case of algorithmic manipulation.

Narrative Strategies

The dominant narratives amplified through this system included:

- Anti-EU Sovereignty: Claims that Brussels had colonized Romania and that Georgescu would restore "true independence."
- NGO Conspiracies: Accusations that all other candidates were "puppets of Soros-backed NGOs," frequently supported by faked screenshots and quotes.
- Electoral Fraud Preemptively Claimed: Before the vote even took place, videos began to circulate alleging that ballots had already been printed with predetermined winners.

- Ethnic Division: Romanian-language accounts spread false claims that the Hungarian minority was planning to vote en masse under forged identities—stoking ethnic division.

The emotional tone was sharp, conspiratorial, and infused with religious and cultural symbolism. Messages often ended with phrases like "You are making history" or "The nation awakens," invoking a mythologized struggle between the people and a corrupt elite.

Foreign Interference and Declassified Intelligence

On 5 December 2024, Romania's Ministry of Foreign Affairs issued a rare and serious statement confirming that declassified intelligence had revealed "unprecedented external interference" in the election. The statement stopped short of naming Russia directly but referenced methods consistent with past Russian information operations.

Later reporting from POLITICO and VIGINUM (France's digital monitoring agency) confirmed that many Telegram channels tied to Georgescu's support network had originated from Russian IP ranges. Fake Romanian news websites—clones of real outlets like Digi24 and G4Media—were hosted on servers previously used in operations traced to the Glavnoye Razvedyvatelnoye Upravleniye (GRU - the Russian military intelligence service).

Perhaps most damning was a deepfake video published just three days before the vote. It featured a fabricated conversation among Moldovan intelligence officers discussing an alleged assassination plot against Georgescu. The video was shared across X, Telegram, and TikTok, receiving millions of views before being debunked.

Romania's electoral authorities were overwhelmed. TikTok removed some accounts and videos, but only after the content had gone viral. The European Commission issued a "retention order" to TikTok under the Digital Services Act, instructing the platform to preserve all internal data related to election content between November and March.

Annulment of Election Results

On 6 December, following an appeal from several NGOs and mounting public unrest, Romania's Constitutional Court annulled the first-round results, citing systemic digital manipulation and evidence of foreign disinformation. It was the first time in EU history that an election result had been overturned not due to ballot fraud, but due to information interference.

This decision triggered international responses. The U.S. State Department and the European External Action Service both issued statements supporting Romania's institutions and condemning foreign interference, but US Vice-President JD Vance publicly criticized the annulment. Georgescu dismissed the annulment as "deep state sabotage," further galvanizing his base.

Aftermath and Escalation

In the months following the annulment, tensions escalated further. TikTok influencers with ties to Georgescu began posting from outside Romania, suggesting that they had fled to avoid tax investigations. Some had ties to organized crime groups in Moldova, as reported by Balkan Insight.

On 18 February 2025, Elon Musk reposted one of Georgescu's anti-Soros campaign videos on X, drawing over 20 million views. His endorsement reignited international debate about platform accountability in foreign elections.

Meanwhile, the European Commission initiated a formal investigation into TikTok's handling of the Romanian election, citing potential systemic breaches of the DSA related to content moderation, recommender systems, and monetization of political content.

CASE STUDY 4: GERMAN FEDERAL ELECTIONS 2025

Germany's 2025 Bundestag elections took place under intense scrutiny, following multiple years of documented Russian information operations across Europe and a growing awareness of digital manipulation. With Chancellor Olaf Scholz stepping down and a highly fragmented party landscape, disinformation actors saw an opportunity to exploit voter uncertainty and boost far-right momentum—particularly that of the Alternative für Deutschland (AfD) party.

Doppelgänger Campaigns and Fake News Ecosystems

In the run-up to the election, German cybersecurity officials identified the resurgence of the so-called Doppelgänger operation, a Russian-aligned disinformation strategy previously used in France and Poland. This campaign involved the creation of fake news websites that cloned the design and branding of well-known outlets such as *Der Spiegel*, *Tagesschau*, and *Frankfurter Allgemeine Zeitung*. These sites published fabricated stories that were then disseminated via Telegram, Facebook, and even some shortwave radio programs.

One particularly viral article falsely claimed that Green Party candidate Robert Habeck had proposed removing the word "German" from official documents to promote inclusivity. Despite being debunked within hours, the story was amplified by hundreds of accounts and received significant engagement on TikTok and Telegram.

According to the watchdog Correctiv, the most common narrative frames included:

- Immigration Chaos: Claims that Germany was secretly preparing to accept 1.5 million new asylum seekers under an "EU resettlement pact."
- Crime Surge: Fake statistics alleging a 400% increase in violent crimes committed by immigrants since 2020.
- NATO Provocation: The suggestion that Germany was planning a unilateral military action against Russia, complete with falsified "leaked" ministry documents.

Platform Dynamics and Enforcement

The enforcement of the Digital Services Act was tested during this election. TikTok and Meta complied with DSA guidelines by maintaining ad libraries and submitting risk assessments, but X (formerly Twitter) remained defiant.

In February 2025, a German court ruled that X must provide researchers access to political engagement data, marking the first legal enforcement of DSA's transparency obligations. The ruling came after X refused repeated requests to disclose visibility metrics for posts flagged as misinformation by EDMO-affiliated researchers.

TikTok videos impersonating politicians—some in support, others deliberately absurd to confuse viewers—went viral during the final two weeks of the campaign. These included manipulated footage of Habeck advocating for a "meat tax" on sausages and doctored clips showing Green Party members mocking farmers.

The German Federal Office for Information Security (BSI) flagged more than 3,500 posts during the election period but was limited in its authority to compel cross-border platform action in real time.

Impact and Electoral Consequences

While procedural integrity was maintained, the informational environment shifted notably. The AfD increased its vote share by nearly 6%, winning key constituencies in Saxony and Thuringia. Post-election polling by *ARD-DeutschlandTrend* indicated that over 35% of AfD voters cited "loss of national identity" and "media suppression" as key motivations—narratives heavily fueled by digital disinformation.

Public trust in mainstream media declined, with 42% of respondents saying they "no longer trust news from traditional outlets." Civil society groups expressed concern that a tipping point had been reached, where alternative media ecosystems—some entirely fabricated—were replacing verified journalism in the minds of many voters.

CASE STUDY 5: POLISH ELECTIONS 2025

Poland's 2025 national elections were held amid an increasingly hostile information landscape. Disinformation operations in Poland were notable for their ambiguity of origin and use of reverse-discrediting tactics—wherein fake support is used to damage the candidate it appears to endorse.

False-Flag Campaigns and Psychological Sabotage

The National Research Institute (NASK) reported that several major Facebook ad buys, which appeared to support the centrist opposition candidate, were deliberately exaggerated and inflammatory. The ads used messaging that invoked religious extremism and racial dog whistles, falsely attributed to the candidate's supporters. Their true aim, NASK argued, was to alienate moderate voters by making the candidate seem radical.

The strategy confused not only voters but also social media platforms, which hesitated to remove content that appeared, at face value, to be campaign material.

Meanwhile, Telegram and YouTube channels aligned with far-right groups pushed narratives such as:

- "NATO puppet government": Suggesting that the ruling party was merely executing orders from Brussels and Washington.
- "Election blackout": Claiming the government would cut internet access in rural areas during the election to suppress turnout.
- "Ballot box theft": Circulating grainy CCTV footage from 2020 with new captions suggesting recent fraud.

One of the most viral videos—viewed over 3 million times on Facebook—showed a woman placing envelopes into a mailbox, wrongly labeled as "ballot stuffing." The video was geotagged to rural Silesia but actually originated from a 2019 clip in Canada.

Foreign Involvement and Narrative Seeding

EUvsDisinfo (2023), the European External Action Service's disinformation unit, traced some of these campaigns to Russian content farms operating through IP obfuscation networks. These actors mimicked Polish nationalist voices, creating fabricated quotes from military officials warning about "Western experiments on Polish children" through mRNA vaccines and LGBTQ+ education mandates—designed to polarize and provoke emotional responses.

While Polish authorities attempted to counter these narratives, their public awareness campaigns often struggled to match the virality and emotional pull of disinformation content.

Regulatory Response and Limitations

Unlike Germany, Poland did not benefit from robust enforcement under the DSA. Domestic laws regarding digital platforms were underdeveloped, and cooperation with international regulators was limited by political sensitivities. While civil society actors like *Konkret24* and *Demagog* provided real-time fact-checking, their reach remained modest compared to coordinated disinformation campaigns.

Election turnout was lower than expected, particularly among first-time voters and diaspora communities—a likely consequence of confusion, distrust, and narrative fatigue.

STRUCTURAL PATTERNS AND STRATEGIC IMPLICATIONS

The comparative analysis of disinformation in five electoral contexts—European Union, United States, Romania, Germany, and Poland—reveals a convergence of tactics, platform vulnerabilities, and institutional weaknesses. Despite the political and cultural differences between these countries, similar patterns emerge. These patterns can be grouped into six key domains:

1. Algorithmic Amplification as Strategic Terrain

Across all five cases, the architecture of digital platforms played a decisive role in shaping how disinformation spread and what audiences it reached. In Romania and the U.S., TikTok and X served as primary vectors for high-engagement falsehoods, often prioritized by their recommendation systems. The monetization of content on X, in particular, created perverse incentives: users received financial rewards for publishing misleading or provocative political content that generated clicks and shares.

Platforms are not neutral tools—they are systems that reward emotional intensity and virality. This means disinformation campaigns are most successful not necessarily because they are the most persuasive, but because they are the most algorithmically optimized.

2. The Rise of Coordinated Inauthentic Behavior

The Romanian case offers a clear example of how disinformation is no longer just about isolated actors sharing false content. Instead, it is often systematic and strategic, involving thousands of accounts that act in concert to amplify specific messages. This technique, known as Coordinated Inauthentic Behavior (CIB), has been used to simulate grassroots enthusiasm, create the illusion of consensus, or suppress opposing views.

What makes CIB especially dangerous is that it evades traditional content moderation, which often focuses on individual violations rather than collective manipulation. Platforms still struggle to detect and respond to CIB in real time, particularly when messages are linguistically localized and culturally specific.

3. Disinformation as Delegitimization

In Poland and Germany, disinformation served less to promote a particular candidate and more to delegitimize the electoral process itself. False narratives about rigged ballots, manipulated results, or conspiracies involving foreign NGOs created a climate of confusion and suspicion. This is a deliberate tactic aimed at reducing voter turnout and undermining faith in institutions.

This strategy draws on what political scientists call negative partisanship: rather than building support, disinformation erodes trust in the opponent or the system, thereby narrowing the field of perceived legitimate choices.

4. The Normalization of Deepfakes and AI-Generated Content

The 2024–2025 cycle was the first in which deepfakes and AI-generated media played a widespread role in electoral disinformation. In the U.S. and Romania, videos purporting to show candidates saying or doing things they never did gained massive traction, often too quickly for fact-checkers to intervene effectively.

This trend points to a future in which "seeing is believing" no longer holds. When audiovisual evidence becomes suspect, democratic accountability—based on transparency and documentation—faces a fundamental crisis.

5. Weak Regulatory Capacity and Asymmetric Enforcement

The EU's Digital Services Act (DSA) represents the most ambitious legislative attempt to regulate disinformation at the platform level. However, enforcement remains patchy. In Germany, a court had to compel X to release data to researchers. In Romania, despite a legal framework, platforms were slow to act. In Poland, national laws were outdated, and civil society organizations carried the burden of response without institutional support.

This reflects a broader asymmetry of capacity: disinformation campaigns are fast, agile, and decentralized, while regulatory bodies are slow, bureaucratic, and often under-resourced.

6. Civil Society as First Responder

In nearly all cases, independent fact-checkers, journalists, and NGOs served as the frontline defenders of truth. Organizations like EU DisinfoLab, EDMO, Democracy Reporting International, and national entities such as G4Media or Correctiv played vital roles in identifying and publicizing disinformation threats.

However, their impact is limited by scale and reach. A TikTok deepfake can gain 10 million views overnight; a fact-check rebuttal may reach only a fraction of that, often after the damage is done.

THE EUROPEAN UNION'S INSTITUTIONAL RESPONSE

In recognition of the structural nature of the disinformation threat, the European Union has significantly scaled up its legal, policy, and institutional responses. These efforts reflect an emerging doctrine of "democratic resilience", where electoral integrity is safeguarded not only through ballot protection but also through control of the information environment.

1. Legal Foundations: DSA and Political Advertising Rules

The EU's Digital Services Act (DSA), adopted in 2022 and fully enforced as of 2024, represents a watershed moment in global platform governance. It designates major platforms as "Very Large Online Platforms" (VLOPs), requiring them to conduct risk assessments on disinformation and electoral interference, ensure transparency of political content, and make internal data available to regulators and vetted researchers.

Complementing the DSA, the Regulation on Transparency and Targeting of Political Advertising (TTPA) was adopted in March 2024. This regulation requires all political ads to include clear labels, sponsor disclosures, audience targeting information, and traceable metadata—especially during electoral periods. In response, major platforms such as Meta have pulled all political advertising from the EU as of October 2025, citing compliance complexity.

These rules are designed to turn platform black boxes into transparent civic arenas, where manipulation can be monitored, documented, and addressed in real time.

2. Strategic Communication and Interagency Coordination

The EU has also strengthened its crisis response architecture. The Council's FIMI Toolbox (Foreign Information Manipulation and Interference) provides a coordinated system for rapid alerting, cross-border intelligence exchange, and joint responses to hybrid threats. Ahead of the 2024 EU elections, this system was stress-tested across Member States.

Supporting this is the EUvsDisinfo project, operated by the EEAS's East StratCom Task Force. It publishes daily updates on foreign information operations, primarily Russian in origin, and provides publicly accessible debunking reports across languages. While not a regulatory body, it serves as a vital source of documentation and public education.

3. Civil Society, Fact-checking, and Media Resilience

The EU has encouraged partnerships between platforms and independent fact-checking organizations via the Code of Practice on Disinformation, originally launched in 2018 and updated in 2022. Signatories—including Google, TikTok, Meta, and others—pledge to reduce algorithmic amplification of falsehoods, label synthetic media, and collaborate with fact-checkers.

Through the European Democracy Action Plan, the EU also funds initiatives promoting media pluralism, anti-SLAPP protections, and investigative journalism—especially in countries where press freedom is vulnerable. The goal is to create a resilient epistemic infrastructure: societies equipped to resist manipulation because they have independent, credible sources of information.

Public education is another pillar. The Commission has launched campaigns and toolkits aimed at improving digital and media literacy, particularly among youth, migrants, and rural communities.

4. Enforcement and Data Access

Several Member States have now used DSA provisions to compel platform transparency. Germany's 2025 court ruling against X (formerly Twitter) forced the company to share political content data with researchers. Romania invoked emergency data preservation orders against TikTok during its disrupted 2024 presidential election. These cases are early tests of whether the DSA has true enforcement muscle—or whether platforms will continue to evade accountability.

Parallel to enforcement, the EU has implemented sanctions regimes targeting foreign disinformation actors. In October 2024, it imposed asset freezes and visa bans on individuals and organizations linked to election interference in Moldova, Slovakia, and France.

5. AI Regulation and the Future of Manipulation

Looking ahead, the EU is finalizing the Artificial Intelligence Act, which will impose classification and transparency requirements for AI systems, including those generating deepfakes and synthetic political content. These provisions aim to close the gap between emerging technology and electoral regulation, recognizing that AI-generated disinformation is now a first-order threat to electoral credibility.

CONCLUSION

The evidence from the EU, U.S., Romania, Germany, and Poland makes one thing clear: disinformation is here to stay. It exploits platform logic, institutional fragmentation, and emotional polarization. It can reshape how elections are contested and perceived.

What makes electoral disinformation particularly insidious is that it weaponizes core democratic principles—free speech, political debate, participatory media—and turns them against democracy itself. It creates noise, sows confusion, and leaves citizens unsure of what, if anything, can be trusted. In this environment, trust becomes a casualty, and democracy becomes vulnerable to cynicism, apathy, or authoritarian nostalgia.

Efforts to address this threat must be multi-dimensional:

1. Regulatory reform must be backed by real enforcement. Legislative frameworks like the DSA are essential, but only if they are supported by legal authority, sufficient funding, and international coordination. The EU must ensure that platforms are not only reporting transparency data but also acting on systemic risks.

2. Platforms must change their incentives. As long as outrage is more profitable than accuracy, disinformation will flourish. Algorithmic transparency, ad library scrutiny, and coordinated responses to CIB are essential. Monetization models that reward virality over veracity must be reevaluated.
3. Media literacy must be mainstreamed, especially among younger populations. Citizens need tools not just to spot fake news but to understand how digital ecosystems shape their perceptions. Critical thinking must be taught alongside reading and math as a core civic skill.
4. Civil society must be funded and protected. The organizations on the frontlines of this battle—fact-checkers, researchers, digital watchdogs—must have long-term support. Their work is public infrastructure in the 21st century.
5. International cooperation is essential. Disinformation knows no borders, and neither should the response. Intelligence-sharing, joint regulation, and harmonized election protection mechanisms must be priorities for democratic alliances.

Most importantly, democratic societies must rebuild public trust—not only by debunking lies but by governing transparently, communicating honestly, and showing that democracy can deliver real improvements in people's lives.

Disinformation is not just about content—it's about context. Defending democracy therefore requires not only smarter platforms and better laws.

The European Union's evolving framework for disinformation governance reflects a broader understanding: electoral threats are no longer limited to hacking ballots or bribing officials. They now include the weaponization of speech, the capture of public attention, and the erosion of trust in facts themselves.

By combining legal mandates (DSA, TTPA, AI Act), institutional coordination (FIMI, EUvsDisinfo), and civic engagement (fact-checkers, educators, journalists), the EU is moving toward a holistic model of electoral defense. It is not perfect—enforcement gaps remain, platforms still resist, and disinformation evolves faster than regulation—but it represents a serious attempt to make democracy defensible in the digital age.

REFERENCES

Axios. (2025). Meta will no longer accept political, election or issue ads in EU. [online] Axios, 25 July. Available at: https://www.axios.com/2025/07/25/meta-eu-political-election-ads [Accessed 1 Aug. 2025].

Baltic Engagement Centre Against Information Disorders (BECID). (2024). *Checking and Disinformation in the Baltic States: Fact-checking Practices and Resilience Measures.* [online] BECID. Available at: https://becid.eu/wp-content/uploads/2024/06/3.4._report.pdf [Accessed 5 Aug. 2025].

Braun, D. (2024). 2024 European elections: Insights into information threats. [online] LinkedIn. Available at: https://www.linkedin.com/pulse/2024-european-elections-insights-information-threats-daniel-braun-pxghe [Accessed 1 Aug. 2025].

Brookings Institution. (2024). How disinformation defined the 2024 election narrative. [online] Brookings. Available at: https://www.brookings.edu/articles/how-disinformation-defined-the-2024-election-narrative [Accessed 1 Aug. 2025].

Brookings Institution. (2024). *Election night disinformation risks – allegations of mail fraud, slow vote counts, and immigrant voting in swing states.* [online] Brookings. Available at: https://www.brookings.edu/articles/election-night-disinformation-risks/ [Accessed 1 Aug. 2025].

Correctiv. (2025). Doppelgänger: CORRECTIV-Recherchen legen russische Propaganda-Kampagne lahm. Available at: https://correctiv.org/faktencheck/russische-desinformation/2024/11/13/propaganda-desinformation-russland-recherchen-legen-doppelgaenger-kampagne-lahm/ [Accessed 1 Aug. 2025].

Council of the European Union. (2024). Foreign Information Manipulation and Interference (FIMI) toolbox. [online] Consilium.europa.eu. Available at: https://www.consilium.europa.eu/en/policies/disinformation-and-democratic-resilience/ [Accessed 1 Aug. 2025].

Democracy Reporting International. (2024). Manufactured Support: How Inauthentic Activity on TikTok Bolstered the Far-Right in Romania. [online] Democracy Reporting International. Available at: https://democracy-reporting.org/en/office/EU/publications/manufactured-support-how-inauthentic-activity-on-tiktok-bolstered-the-far-right-in-romania [Accessed 1 Aug. 2025].

EDMO (European Digital Media Observatory). (2024–2025). Propaganda and Disinformation: Lessons from 2024/25 Elections in Europe. [online] EDMO. Available at: https://edmo.eu/edmo-news/propaganda-and-disinformation-lessons-from-2024-25-elections-in-europe/ [Accessed 1 Aug. 2025].

EU DisinfoLab. (2024). Disinfo Update, 14 November 2024. [online] EU DisinfoLab. Available at: https://www.disinfo.eu/disinfo-update-14-11-2024/ [Accessed 1 Aug. 2025].

Euractiv. (2024). *France, Germany, Poland facing 'permanent' Russian disinformation attacks: EU*. [online] 5 June. Available at: https://www.euractiv.com/section/politics/news/france-germany-poland-facing-permanent-russian-disinformation-attacks-eu/ [Accessed 5 Aug. 2025].

European Commission. (2021). Protecting Democracy. [online] Available at: https://commission.europa.eu/strategy-and-policy/priorities-2019-2024/new-push-european-democracy/european-democracy-action-plan_en [Accessed 1 Aug. 2025].

European Commission. (2022). Digital Services Act (DSA): Regulation (EU) 2022/2065. [online] EUR-Lex. Available at: https://eur-lex.europa.eu/legal-content/EN/TXT/?uri=CELEX%3A32022R2065 [Accessed 1 Aug. 2025].

European Commission. (2023). EU Code of Practice on Disinformation (Updated 2022 version). [online] Available at: https://digital-strategy.ec.europa.eu/en/policies/code-practice-disinformation [Accessed 1 Aug. 2025].

European Commission. (2024). Proposal for a Regulation on the transparency and targeting of political advertising. [online] Available at: https://eur-lex.europa.eu/legal-content/EN/TXT/?uri=celex:52021PC0731 [Accessed 1 Aug. 2025].

European Commission. (2025). *Standard Eurobarometer 103 – Spring 2025*. [online] Available at: https://europa.eu/eurobarometer/surveys/detail/3372 [Accessed 5 Aug. 2025]. e

European External Action Service (EEAS). (2024). EUvsDisinfo: Database of Disinformation Cases. [online] Available at: https://euvsdisinfo.eu/disinformation-cases/ [Accessed 1 Aug. 2025].

EUvsDisinfo (East StratCom Task Force). (2023). *Disinformation about the LGBTI+ community and child-related conspiracies in Poland*. [online] EUvsDisinfo. Available at: https://www.euvsdisinfo.eu/disinformation-cases/ [Accessed 1 Aug. 2025].

France24. (2025). *ECB's digital euro sparks flurry of online misinformation*. [online] 26 March. Available at: https://www.france24.com/en/live-news/20250326-ecb-s-digital-euro-sparks-flurry-of-online-misinformation [Accessed 5 Aug. 2025].

G4Media. (2024). Cât de u or sunt manipula i fanii lui Călin Georgescu pe TikTok: Peste 800.000 de reac ii i mii de oameni care au urmărit luni seara cel pu in trei ”LIVE”-uri fake cu candidatul pro-rus / Cum e ”impersonat” Georgescu, produsul preziden ial al re elei chineze ti, pentru a ob ine dona ii. [online] G4Media.ro. Available at: https://www.g4media.ro/exclusiv-cat-de-usor-sunt-manipulati-fanii-lui-calin-georgescu-pe-tiktok-peste-800-000-de-reactii-si-mii-de-oameni-care-au-urmarit-luni-seara-cel-putin-trei-live-uri-fake-cu-candida.html [Accessed 1 Aug. 2025].

NASK (National Research Institute). (2025). Kto za tym stoi? Dezinformacja, wybory i pytania, na które trzeba odpowiedzieć Warsaw: NASK. Available at: https://www.nask.pl/aktualnosci/kto-za-tym-stoi-dezinformacja-wybory-i-pytania-na-ktore-trzeba-odpowiedziec [Accessed 1 Aug. 2025].

National Institute for Justice. (2024). Research into Immigration and Crime, Fiscal Years 2019-20. [online] U.S. Department of Justice. Available at: https://nij.ojp.gov/topics/crime/research-immigration-and-crime-research-portfolio [Accessed 1 Aug. 2025].

POLITICO. (2025). German court orders X to hand over election data in legal blow to Musk's platform. [online] 7 Feb. Available at: https://www.politico.eu/article/berlin-court-orders-x-hand-over-election-data-legal-blow-elon-musk-platform/ [Accessed 1 Aug. 2025].

Pomerantsev, P. (2019). *This is Not Propaganda: Adventures in the War Against Reality*. Faber & Faber.

ProPublica. (2024). Exploiting Meta's Weaknesses, Deceptive Political Ads Thrived on Facebook and Instagram in Run-Up to Election. Available at: https://www.propublica.org/article/facebook-instagram-meta-deceptive-political-ads-election [Accessed 1 Aug. 2025].

Reuters. (2024). *EU opens investigation into TikTok over election interference*. [online] Reuters, 17 Dec. Available at: https://www.reuters.com/business/eu-opens-investigation-into-tiktok-over-election-interference-2024-12-17/ [Accessed 1 Aug. 2025].

Reuters. (2024). European election: How the EU says Russia is spreading disinformation at: https://www.reuters.com/world/europe/european-election-how-eu-says-russia-is-spreading-disinformation-2024-06-03/ [Accessed 1 Aug. 2025].

Reuters. (2025). *Germany, France and others urge EU Commission to protect elections from foreign interference*. [online] Reuters, 30 Jan. Available at: https://www.reuters.com/world/europe/france-germany-others-urge-eu-commission-protect-elections-europe-foreign-2025-01-30/ [Accessed 1 Aug. 2025].

The Guardian. (2024). *Hire fact-checkers to fight election fake news, EU tells tech firms*. [online] The Guardian, 26 Mar. Available at: https://www.theguardian.com/media/2024/mar/26/tech-firms-poised-to-mass-hire-factcheckers-before-eu-elections [Accessed 1 Aug. 2025].

The Guardian. (2024). *Huge disinformation networks ensnared France and Germany ahead of EU elections*. [online] Euronews via The Guardian, 18 July. Available at: https://www.euronews.com/my-europe/2024/07/18/huge-disinformation-networks-ensnared-france-and-germany-ahead-of-eu-elections [Accessed 5 Aug. 2025].

Time. (2024). *China Is Using AI to Sow Disinformation and Stoke Discord Across Asia and the U.S., Microsoft Reports*. [online] *Time*, published 2025. Available at: https://www.time.com/6963787/china-influence-operations-artificial-intelligence-cyber-threats-microsoft/ [Accessed 1 Aug. 2025].

Tucker, J. A., Guess, A., Barberá, P., Vaccari, C., Siegel, A., Sanovich, S., ... & Nyhan, B. (2018). Social media, political polarization, and political disinformation: A review of the scientific literature. *Political polarization, and political disinformation: a review of the scientific literature (March 19, 2018)*.

VIGINUM. (2025). Manipulation d'algorithmes et instrumentalisation d'influenceurs: Enseignements des élections roumaines. [report] Paris: Secrétariat général de la défense et de la sécurité nationale. Available at: https://www.sgdsn.gouv.fr/publications/manipulation-dalgorithmes-et-instrumentalisation-dinfluenceurs-enseignements-de [Accessed 1 Aug. 2025].

Wardle, C., & Derakhshan, H. (2017). Information Disorder: Toward an Interdisciplinary Framework for Research and Policymaking [report]. Council of Europe., Available at https://rm.coe.int/information-disorder-toward-an-interdisciplinary-framework-for-researc/168076277c, Retrieved August 1, 2025, from.

Wired. (2024). *Meta Kills a Crucial Transparency Tool at the Worst Possible Time*. [online] Wired, 25 March. Available at: https://www.wired.com/story/meta-kills-crucial-transparency-tool-worst-possible-time [Accessed 5 Aug. 2025].

Zuboff, S. (2019). *The Age of Surveillance Capitalism: The Fight for a Human Future at the New Frontier of Power*. PublicAffairs.

Chapter 11
Crafting the Campaign: The Role of Political Marketing in Voter Behavior Analysis

Vasiliki Bouranta
http://orcid.org/0009-0003-1717-7048
Aristotle Univerity of Thessaloniki, Greece

ABSTRACT

This chapter examines how political marketing has become a central force in shaping U.S. presidential campaigns. Moving beyond slogans and branding, it explores how marketing strategies—such as audience segmentation, message targeting, and emotional framing—are used to construct candidate identities and influence voter behavior. The chapter highlights the transformative impact of big data, social media, and digital analytics on campaign practice, with case studies from recent elections. It also raises critical questions about the ethical and democratic implications of treating voters as consumers and elections as market exercises. While political marketing can improve outreach and engagement, it risks replacing meaningful debate with emotional manipulation and spectacle. Ultimately, the chapter calls for a balanced view that recognizes both the strategic power and the democratic costs of marketing-driven politics in the digital age.

INTRODUCTION

The American electoral system stands as one of the most prominent and analyzed examples of modern democratic governance. Its unique combination of federalism, decentralisation, and intense political competition offers a rich landscape for examining how electoral campaigns are designed, executed, and received by the electorate. In this dynamic environment, political marketing has emerged not only as

DOI: 10.4018/979-8-3373-1037-4.ch011

a practical tool for campaigns but also as an analytical framework for understanding voter behavior, party strategy, and political communication.

This chapter explores the evolving role of political marketing in shaping electoral outcomes in the United States, with particular emphasis on the tools, strategies, and ethical dilemmas that define contemporary campaign practice. It focuses on how political actors apply marketing concepts - such as branding, audience segmentation, and message targeting - to navigate an increasingly data-driven and media-saturated political environment.

By focusing on recent U.S. presidential elections, the chapter analyzes how candidates construct their public image, how parties frame their platforms, and how campaign teams engage with voters across traditional and digital media channels. Particular emphasis is devoted to the transformative influence of technology, particularly concerning big data, micro-targeting, and social media, all of which have redefined the interactions between voters and campaigns and have posed challenges to the demarcation between persuasion and manipulation.

Ultimately, this chapter aims to bridge theory and practice, offering a comprehensive examination of political marketing's role in modern American democracy. It raises important questions about voter autonomy, ethical campaigning, and the extent to which marketing logic contributes to or detracts from substantive democratic engagement.

THEORETICAL FRAMEWORK: POLITICAL MARKETING AND STRATEGIC COMMUNICATION

Political marketing is a relatively new but rapidly expanding interdisciplinary field that merges two seemingly distinct domains: marketing and politics. Despite initial academic scepticism, particularly regarding the perceived commodification of political discourse, the field has gained significant recognition in recent decades. The growing interest originates from the profound impact that technological advances, media evolution, and communication strategies have had on political behavior, electoral dynamics, and governance processes.

At its core, political marketing seeks to identify, anticipate, and respond to the needs and preferences of the electorate through the efficient and strategic use of available resources. While this objective mirrors that of commercial marketing, which focuses on satisfying customer demands, political marketing recontextualizes these principles within the political arena. Here, the "customers" are voters, the "products" are political parties, candidates, and their programs, and the "transactions" are electoral outcomes.

Drawing on the classic marketing mix theory, often referred to as the "4 Ps" framework - product, price, place, and promotion - political marketing adapts these concepts to the political landscape. The product encompasses the candidate's image, party identity, and policy platform. Price represents the costs - emotional, cognitive, or social - that voters experience when supporting a particular political actor. Place refers to both the physical and virtual mechanisms of reaching voters, including field operations, events, and digital platforms. Finally, promotion includes all communication efforts aimed at persuading and mobilizing voters, from traditional advertising and public relations to targeted social media campaigns.

Scholars such as Lamb and Crompton (1986) have emphasized marketing not merely as a set of techniques but as a managerial philosophy - a mindset that governs the structure and function of an organization. This perspective allows marketing models to be applied beyond the private sector, extending to non-profit organizations, public services, and political institutions alike. Political parties and campaign teams now implement long-term, integrated marketing strategies that shape not only how messages are communicated but how political agendas are developed and adapted to voter expectations.

In parallel, Bruce I. Newman has contributed significantly to the theoretical framework of political marketing by conceptualizing the voter as a political consumer. His model proposes five core factors of voter decision-making: political issues, social imagery, candidate personality, situational contingencies, and scientific value. These dimensions capture both rational and affective elements that influence how individuals assess political offerings. Importantly, Newman highlights that political marketing is not only an electoral tactic but also a means of governing. The "permanent campaign" concept illustrates how marketing approaches continue after elections to guide presidential communication and policy advocacy during presidential terms.

The rise of the "permanent campaign" reflects a deeper shift in modern political life: the blurring of boundaries between governing and campaigning. What began as a strategy to maintain public support post-election has evolved into a structural feature of contemporary leadership, especially in presidential systems. Instead of governing with the long term in mind, leaders are often trapped in short-term messaging cycles, driven by polling, focus groups, and media metrics. This marketing logic prioritizes optics over substance and incentivizes performative communication over policy coherence. The danger is not only the erosion of deliberative processes but the transformation of the public sphere into a perpetual contest of images. In this context, responsiveness becomes reactive, not constructive. The permanent campaign may increase political visibility, but it also risks undermining institutional trust, narrowing policy horizons, and weakening accountability structures in favor of narrative control.

Newman's work also draws from consumer psychology and persuasion theory, including the Elaboration Likelihood Model (ELM), to explain how voters process campaign messages. Depending on their level of involvement, voters engage either in central processing, evaluating arguments based on merit, or in peripheral processing, relying on heuristics such as candidate image, slogans, or endorsements. Campaigns use this dual process understanding to develop their message framing strategies particularly when voters face media overload and have limited attention span.

The rise of big data analytics, micro-targeting, and digital campaigning has transformed political marketing from a one-directional promotional tool into a dynamic, two-way communication process. Political entities can now gather vast amounts of data on voter preferences, attitudes, and behaviors, enabling them to craft hyper-personalized messages and strategies that resonate with diverse voter segments. As Wright (1999) emphasizes, marketing responsiveness plays a critical role in aligning communication strategies with audience expectations - something that political campaigns now use to connect more directly with voters.

A particularly insightful contribution comes from Henry H. Sun in collaboration with Phil Harris (2017), who presented a comprehensive model that broadens the understanding of political marketing to include global and international dimensions. They outlined three interconnected strands: electoral political marketing, which concentrates on candidate-voter dynamics; governmental political marketing, which involves communication between authorities and domestic audiences; and international political marketing, which focuses on how states communicate with international publics and institutions. In this expanded view, political marketing emerges not just as a domestic engagement strategy, but as a tool for soft power and international political influence.

In the same article, the authors described international political marketing as a practice that leverages marketing techniques to shape national image, support foreign policy aims, and enhance intercultural dialogue. Their framework adapted the traditional four Ps of marketing to the global political arena. The "Product" represents national values, policies, and identity. "Place" signifies diplomatic and multilateral platforms. "Promotion" refers to tools such as public diplomacy and global media relations. "Polling" includes mechanisms for gathering international public opinion and feedback. This conceptualization positions soft power as a dynamic, marketable political good—one that requires deliberate promotion and strategic management.

Despite its strategic value, political marketing continues to face criticism. Concerns remain about its ethical implications, particularly regarding privacy, manipulation, and the erosion of deliberative democracy. The increased use of emotional appeals and symbolic politics - both emphasized in Newman's research - has led some to argue that political discourse is becoming increasingly superficial and performative. Nevertheless, when practiced transparently and ethically, political marketing can serve as a powerful means of fostering dialogue, engagement, and trust between political actors and citizens. It embodies key democratic principles: communication, interaction, and reciprocal influence.

In today's polarized and fast-evolving societies, political marketing is no longer confined to campaign periods or media appearances. It has become a vital instrument for political actors seeking to maintain relevance, legitimacy, and connection in an environment defined by complexity and rapid change. As the field continues to evolve, integrating insights from marketing theory, psychology, and media studies, it promises to remain central to both the study and practice of modern democratic politics.

THE ROLE OF POLITICAL MARKETING IN VOTER BEHAVIOR ANALYSIS

Psychological and Sociological Factors Influencing Voter Choices

Part of the study of voting behavior has its roots in early work by the American National Election Studies (ANES), which emphasized two key psychological concepts: social identification with reference groups and cognitive consistency. *The American Voter* (Cambell et al.,1960) stands as a foundational text, positing that party identification is formed early in life, remains stable, and shapes how individuals perceive political information. Complementary research at the time demonstrated that political campaigns rarely shift party loyalty but rather activate pre-existing predispositions that guide voter interpretations and decisions.

Over the decades, research has revealed that the determinants of voter choice originate from both internal (psychological) and external (environmental) factors. Internally, these include longstanding predispositions and emotional or cognitive reactions during campaigns. Externally, influences include campaign events, global or national events like wars or economic changes, and the behavior of immediate peer groups, like family and friends. This body of research has produced an extensive list of predictors, such as partisanship, ideology, issue positions, candidate evaluations, media exposure, and social influence.

While research on voter behavior has produced many important insights, psychological theories are still evolving to explain the complex ways in which different factors interact. Many of these relationships are now seen as conditional or influenced by other variables, which means that more detailed and process-oriented models are needed. For example, Kelley and Mirer (1974) described voting as a balance of positive and negative feelings toward candidates or parties. Other scholars, like

Lodge, Steenbergen, and Brau (1995), distinguished between voters who rely on stored information (memory-based) and those who update their views as new information comes in (on-line processing). More complex models, such as those by Fiorina (1981) and Miller and Shanks (1996), showed how long-term factors—like party identification or social background—affect voting indirectly through several steps. Meanwhile, spatial models (e.g., Downs, 1957; Enelow & Hinich, 1984) focused on how voters choose candidates who are closest to them ideologically. Taken together, these approaches suggest that voting decisions are shaped by both stable predispositions and the way voters process campaign information over time. Recent research has also explored how individual differences, such as political expertise, affect decision-making strategies. More experienced voters are typically guided by policy positions and ideological alignment, whereas less experienced voters often rely on simpler cues such as party labels or candidate personality traits. Media priming also shapes how voters prioritize certain issues or candidate traits when forming opinions.

Psychology, especially social psychology and decision-making research, offers valuable perspectives for better understanding these dynamics. These fields provide important insights into processes such as impression formation, emotional responses, group identity development, media influence, and the interplay between implicit and explicit attitudes, among others. Despite the potential, psychological contributions to large-scale political research initiatives have declined over time. New opportunities for funding and collaboration could help revitalize interdisciplinary efforts, allowing psychological theories and methodologies to be more widely applied in analyzing real-world electoral behavior.

Insights from psychological research into voting behavior - such as the role of social identification, emotional responses, and decision-making strategies - are fundamental to political marketing theory. Effective political marketing leverages these psychological processes by shaping perceptions, activating predispositions, and framing information in ways that align with voters' cognitive and emotional tendencies, ultimately influencing electoral outcomes.

Role Of Emotions, Identity, And Issue Salience In Voting Behavior

Emotions are central to political decision-making. The Affective Intelligence Theory posits that emotions like enthusiasm and anxiety can significantly influence political judgments and behaviors. Emotional responses to candidates and campaigns can activate different cognitive processes, leading voters to either reinforce existing beliefs or reconsider their positions (Vasilopoulos, 2019; Brouard et. al, 2021)

Issue salience plays a critical role in shaping voting behavior, as the prominence of certain topics in the public sphere can significantly influence how voters prioritize their political decisions. According to Krosnick (1990), when an issue becomes salient, it not only commands greater cognitive attention but also exerts a stronger influence on electoral choices. Media coverage and campaign strategies are central mechanisms through which issues are made salient (McCombs & Shaw, 1972). By consistently highlighting certain topics, the media can shape the public agenda, effectively altering the weight voters assign to different policy areas when evaluating candidates or parties. Furthermore, research suggests that increased issue salience can heighten emotional responses (Valentino et al., 2011), strengthen group-based political identities (Huddy et al., 2015), and intensify partisan evaluations. These dynamics ultimately affect turnout rates, candidate preferences, and patterns of electoral support. Therefore, understanding how and why issues become salient is essential for comprehending broader patterns of political behavior.

Moreover, political identity is deeply intertwined with emotional responses. Individuals with strong partisan attachments are more likely to experience intense emotional reactions - such as anger, enthusiasm, or anxiety - in response to political events (Huddy et al., 2015). These emotional responses often strengthen existing political beliefs, making individuals more resistant to opposing information and less receptive to differing perspectives. Partisanship structures not only political opinions but also organize emotional experiences, contributing significantly to affective polarization (Iyengar et al., 2012). Media narratives that emphasize political conflict can amplify these emotional divisions, further entrenching political identities and reducing opportunities for cross-partisan dialogue. As a result, emotional investment in political identity not only drives individual political behavior but also has profound implications for the functioning of democratic systems.

Overall, political marketing operates at the intersection of emotion, issue salience, and partisan identity. By eliciting emotional responses, emphasizing salient issues, and reinforcing group-based attachments, political campaigns influence cognitive processing and voting behavior. Understanding these dynamics is essential for analyzing how political marketing strategies shape electoral outcomes in contemporary democracies.

Data-Driven Approaches To Voter Segmentation

Advancements in data analytics have fundamentally reshaped political marketing strategies. Modern campaigns increasingly rely on sophisticated, data-driven approaches to segment electorates and personalize political communication. Through the analysis of voter databases, digital footprints, and behavioral patterns, political marketers can identify specific voter segments and tailor messages to align with their preferences, values, and issue priorities (Kreiss, 2016; Hersh, 2015). This microtargeting technique allows campaigns to deliver highly customized appeals, enhancing message relevance and increasing the likelihood of voter engagement and mobilization. Moreover, digital platforms provide real-time feedback, enabling rapid adjustments in messaging strategies based on audience reactions (Baldwin-Philippi, 2018). The integration of data analytics into political marketing thus reflects a broader shift toward individualized campaigning, where the traditional mass communication model is replaced by strategic, personalized voter outreach.

The integration of machine learning and predictive modeling into political campaigning has enabled campaigns to assess individual voters' likelihood of supporting a candidate or issue with increasing precision. These analytical tools allow for more efficient resource allocation, enabling targeted outreach to persuadable voters or segments with high turnout potential (Hersh, 2015; Kreiss, 2016). By leveraging large datasets and sophisticated algorithms, campaigns can craft highly personalized communication strategies, optimizing voter contact and mobilization efforts (Nickerson & Rogers, 2014). However, the use of such technologies also raises significant ethical concerns. Issues of transparency, data privacy, and the potential for manipulative practices have become central to debates about data-driven campaigning (Bennett, 2016). Without careful regulation and ethical standards, predictive analytics may contribute to the creation of echo chambers, reinforce political polarization, and interfere on citizens' informational autonomy.

Among these tactics, psychographic targeting - the use of psychological profiling to craft emotionally tailored political messages - has drawn particular scrutiny. Made infamous by the Cambridge Analytica scandal (Isaak & Hanna, 2018), this method involves exploiting personal data to influence voter behavior without their informed consent. The danger lies not only in how precise the messaging is, but in how invisible the influence becomes. When a campaign deliberately designs emotionally charged messages - playing on fear, resentment, or identity attachment - without disclosing its intentions or logic, it crosses from persuasion into manipulation. Unlike traditional media, where messages are public and shared, psychographic campaigns deliver individualized realities that reinforce personal biases and discourage collective dialogue.

In a democratic system that relies on transparency, accountability, and informed choice, such tactics present a profound challenge. Unless ethical standards and regulatory safeguards are strengthened, political communication may increasingly serve strategic control rather than democratic participation.

STRATEGIES AND TECHNIQUES IN POLITICAL MARKETING

The Role of Candidate Image-Building

In today's increasingly competitive and media-driven political landscape, candidate image-building has become a cornerstone of political marketing strategy across democracies worldwide. In many elections - especially those characterized by limited voter engagement with detailed policy discussions - candidate image often outweighs substantive issue positions. In such low-information environments, voters tend to rely on heuristics: mental shortcuts based on perceived personality traits, emotional appeal, or symbolic cues (Popkin, 1991; Lau & Redlawsk, 2001).

At the core of this process is the strategic construction of a candidate persona designed to resonate with the values, expectations, and emotional needs of the electorate. Voters increasingly assess political figures not only on policies or party affiliation but on trait perceptions such as competence, honesty, empathy, leadership strength, and trustworthiness. These characteristics are actively shaped through rhetorical framing, media appearances, and symbolic communication. Research in political psychology has highlighted the influence of personality traits—both perceived and self-reported—in shaping political preferences and behaviors (Caprara & Vecchione, 2013).

Visual branding plays a particularly influential role in reinforcing the candidate's image. Political campaigns across countries invest in consistent and recognizable logos, slogans, color schemes, and stylistic cues, which visually symbolize broader themes like renewal, tradition, unity, stability, or national pride (Schill, 2012). These elements contribute to emotional resonance and help establish the candidate's identity in the public imagination.

An especially salient concept in leadership-oriented campaigns is that of "presidentiality" or executive suitability - the expectation that candidates must not only be capable but also appear "leader-like" in style and presence (Jamieson, 1992). This includes a fine balance between projecting authority and connecting with everyday citizens. Also, involves maintaining a careful balance between strength and accessibility, often achieved through media interviews, public appearances, debates, and social media engagement. In many systems, particularly where politics is highly personalized, projecting such qualities can be more electorally decisive than party manifestos. Media strategy and candidate behavior are tightly adjusted to cultivate this dual appeal.

Finally, emotional storytelling has emerged as a vital tool for image-building. Candidates and their teams often deploy personal narratives that highlight resilience, family values and life challenges, or moral convictions to foster affective identification with the electorate. These stories are shared through speeches, digital media, and visual advertising, and are essential in building emotional bridges between the candidate and the public that go beyond rational policy evaluation (Westen, 2007).

In sum, candidate image-building is a multidimensional and adaptive process, integral to the mechanics of modern electoral politics across different political and cultural settings. It is not merely about generating visibility but about crafting a symbolic representation of leadership that resonates with both the rational and emotional dimensions of voter decision-making. In an era where personalities often overshadow policies, effective image-building can make the difference between political success and failure.

The Impact of Personal Branding in Elections

In contemporary electoral politics, personal branding has become a central component of campaign strategy, reflecting a broader trend toward the marketization of political life. As Scammell (2007) argues, political actors are increasingly treated as branded products, whose image, message, and public persona are carefully curated to appeal to specific segments of the electorate. This shift reframes electoral competition as a marketplace, where candidates must differentiate themselves not only on policy but also on personality, values, and style. Branding strategies allow candidates to present a coherent narrative that simplifies complex political identities into easily recognizable and emotionally resonant symbols.

A critical component of successful personal branding is authenticity. In an age of widespread media skepticism and information overload, voters are acutely sensitive to perceived insincerity and message manipulation. As Street (2004) notes, authenticity is not merely the expression of a candidate's "true self," but a performance that appears emotionally genuine, consistent, and trustworthy. Candidates who fail to maintain this impression risk alienating voters, especially younger and more media-savvy demographics who are particularly attuned to inauthenticity in digital environments.

Notable examples from recent electoral history highlight the power of effective personal branding. Barack Obama's 2008 campaign successfully leveraged the slogan "Hope and Change" to construct a brand centered on optimism, inclusion, and renewal, positioning him as a transformative figure in American politics (Jamieson, 2011). In contrast, Donald Trump's "Make America Great Again" served as a populist and nationalist brand, emphasizing disruption, strength, and outsider appeal—attributes that resonated with disaffected voter groups (Ott, 2016). Both campaigns illustrate how personal branding extends beyond policy stances, shaping emotional and symbolic connections that anchor voter perceptions. More detailed examples from U.S. electoral campaigns will be analyzed in the next chapter to further illustrate the dynamics and impact of personal branding in practice.

Importantly, personal branding is no longer confined to the campaign season. As Enli and Skogerbø (2013) explain, the emergence of the permanent campaign has transformed political communication into a continuous process, where public figures must actively maintain their brand identity long after elections have concluded. This development is closely linked to the rise of social media, which enables direct and ongoing engagement between politicians and voters.

Platforms such as Twitter and Instagram have become essential tools for brand maintenance. Through real-time updates, behind-the-scenes content, and personal storytelling, candidates project a sense of immediacy and authenticity that traditional media formats cannot replicate (Kreiss, 2016). These platforms also allow for the strategic reinforcement of values and identity signals in response to current events. As such, personal branding in the digital age functions not merely as a campaign technique but as a foundational practice for building and sustaining political legitimacy.

These developments in personal branding are inseparable from broader shifts in the media environment. As candidates increasingly rely on digital platforms to shape their public personas, the boundaries between personal image-making and media strategy have become increasingly blurred. The same tools that reinforce authenticity and identity—such as Twitter and Instagram—also serve as powerful vehicles for message dissemination and issue framing. To fully understand how political branding operates within this ecosystem, it is essential to examine the underlying media strategies that guide campaign communication across both traditional and digital channels.

Media Strategies in Political Marketing

Media strategies form the backbone of modern political marketing, shaping not only how messages are disseminated, but also how voters perceive political reality. The media environment has undergone a profound transformation in recent decades, marked by the rise of digital platforms, the decline of traditional media authority, and the emergence of hybrid campaigning techniques. The evolving interplay between traditional and digital media has significant implications for political communication, particularly in how media-driven agenda-setting shapes voter perceptions and influences the salience of political issues.

Despite the rapid expansion of digital technologies, traditional media—including television, radio, and print newspapers—continues to hold significant sway, particularly among older demographics. These outlets still provide broad coverage and mass reach, especially in national elections where televised debates, political advertising, and evening news remain influential (Strömbäck & Kiousis, 2011). Traditional media also maintains agenda-setting power through its role in legitimizing which political topics gain traction in public discourse.

In contrast, digital media enables a more direct and decentralized form of communication. Social networking sites, blogs, and podcasts allow political actors to bypass traditional gatekeepers and engage with audiences in real time. As Chadwick (2013) notes, this digital turn has fostered interactivity, personalization, and viral campaign effects—elements that were largely absent in earlier campaign models. Political messages can now be tailored to specific demographic or ideological groups and delivered through social media algorithms that reward emotional and shareable content.

A critical consequence of this shift is the decline in public trust toward mainstream media, especially among younger and more politically polarized segments of the electorate. According to recent data, many voters now turn to personalized digital feeds—curated by algorithms and peer sharing—as their primary sources of political information (Newman et al., 2022). This shift in informational authority has important implications for how campaigns communicate and where they allocate resources.

To adapt to this fragmented media landscape, campaigns increasingly employ hybrid media systems, combining the broad reach of television advertising with the micro-targeting capabilities of digital platforms. This approach maximizes both visibility and relevance. For instance, high-profile campaign moments—such as televised debates or press events—are simultaneously amplified through tweets, Instagram stories, and YouTube clips, reaching distinct audiences across platforms (Chadwick, 2013). The hybrid model allows for coordination between controlled mass communication and decentralized, peer-driven dissemination.

Role of Agenda-Setting in Voter Perception

While media strategies influence how political messages are distributed, they also shape what voters consider important. According to agenda-setting theory, first developed by McCombs and Shaw (1972), the media may not dictate what people think, but it profoundly affects what they think about. By selecting and prioritizing specific issues, media coverage can shape the salience of topics in voters' minds, thereby influencing electoral behavior.

Campaigns deliberately engage in agenda-setting and priming to steer public attention toward favorable issues. Iyengar and Kinder (2010) demonstrated that media emphasis on particular themes - such as economic performance or national security - can "prime" voters to evaluate candidates based on those dimensions. These effects are not uniformly applied; campaigns strategically emphasize different issues depending on the target audience. For example, economic growth may be highlighted for middle-income voters, while immigration or cultural identity may be stressed for nationalist-leaning constituencies.

Digital platforms have enhanced the precision of agenda-setting by enabling issue segmentation. On social media, campaigns can customize messages for narrow slices of the electorate, tailoring both content and tone to resonate with specific subgroups. This capability supports issue ownership strategies, wherein parties or candidates claim credibility on specific topics (Walgrave & De Swert, 2007). For instance, a progressive candidate may consistently promote climate change messaging to young voters, while a conservative candidate might focus on border security for older, rural audiences.

The consequences of such media strategies are profound. They not only affect individual voting behavior but also structure the broader political discourse. When certain topics dominate media coverage - whether through traditional outlets or algorithmic amplification- they frame the boundaries of political debate and condition public expectations of what is politically relevant or urgent.

As political campaigns adapt to a fragmented and fast-evolving media environment, the integration of traditional and digital communication strategies has become critical to shaping public perception and managing the flow of political narratives. However, beyond the visible tactics of media framing and message dissemination lies an increasingly data-driven infrastructure. The rise of big data analytics, microtargeting, and predictive modeling has fundamentally altered how campaigns identify, reach, and influence voters.

Big Data and Digital Marketing

The rise of data analytics has brought significant transformation to political marketing, fundamentally altering how campaigns understand, segment, and engage the electorate. Moving beyond general demographic targeting, contemporary political strategists rely on highly detailed information sourced from voter registration databases and digital activity logs to tailor communications to specific audience segments (Hersh, 2015; Kreiss, 2016). These data-driven techniques enable campaigns to predict voter behavior, identify key constituencies, and deliver personalized messages across a range of digital platforms (Nickerson & Rogers, 2014). As political communication becomes more individualized and predictive, concerns have emerged regarding privacy, transparency, and the broader implications for democratic accountability (Bennett, 2016; Baldwin-Philippi, 2018).

Micro-targeting has emerged as a cornerstone of modern political marketing, enabling campaigns to engage voters with tailored messages based on highly specific individual characteristics. Unlike traditional mass messaging, which treats the electorate as a largely homogeneous audience, micro-targeting involves the strategic use of demographic, psychographic, and behavioral data to customize communications for narrowly defined voter segments (Hersh, 2015). This approach allows campaigns to appeal to personal interests, values, and identities, thereby increasing the relevance and persuasive power of political messaging.

Closely linked to micro-targeting is the use of predictive analytics, which enables campaigns to forecast voter behavior with a high degree of precision. By analyzing past voting patterns, online activity, and socioeconomic indicators, predictive models can identify likely supporters, undecided voters, and individuals most likely to donate or volunteer (Nickerson & Rogers, 2014). These insights allow political strategists to allocate resources efficiently, focusing outreach efforts on segments where the potential impact is greatest.

An advanced application of predictive analytics is lookalike modeling, a technique that allows campaigns to identify new prospective supporters by finding individuals whose profiles closely resemble those of known supporters. For example, if a certain demographic group—such as middle-aged suburban women with moderate political views—shows strong support for a candidate, lookalike modeling can help locate others who share similar characteristics but have not yet been contacted. This form of predictive targeting greatly expands the reach of data-driven campaigning.

However, the growing reliance on micro-targeting and predictive analytics has raised substantial ethical and legal concerns. These techniques often involve the use of personal data collected without informed consent, blurring the line between persuasion and manipulation (Bennett, 2016). Moreover, the opaque nature of algorithmic targeting means that different voters may receive contradictory or misleading information tailored to exploit their psychological profiles or emotional vulnerabilities. Such practices challenge core democratic values, including transparency, fairness, and the equal treatment of voters.

As these technologies become more advanced, the tension between campaign efficiency and democratic accountability becomes increasingly difficult to ignore. While micro-targeting and predictive analytics offer undeniable strategic advantages, their unregulated use may threaten the integrity of electoral processes and erode public trust in political communication.

Case Studies on the Use of Social Media Platforms

Building on the growing use of data-driven targeting techniques, social media platforms have become essential infrastructures for designing and executing political marketing strategies. These platforms not only facilitate message dissemination and audience segmentation but also serve as interactive spaces where political engagement, persuasion, and identity formation occur. Case studies from recent election cycles illustrate how platforms such as Facebook, Twitter, and TikTok have each enabled unique forms of communication, allowing campaigns to apply micro-targeting methods in increasingly dynamic and context-specific ways.

Facebook has been among the most influential platforms in political campaigning due to its advanced advertising tools, vast user base, and advanced targeting capabilities. During the 2012 Obama campaign, Facebook was used to mobilize supporters through personalized messages and peer-to-peer influence strategies (Kreiss, 2016). The platform allowed campaign teams to segment users based on interests, demographics, and social connections, using both organic and paid content to maximize reach and persuasion. However, its most controversial use occurred during the 2016 U.S. presidential election, when the Trump campaign used Facebook's micro-targeting tools in conjunction with third-party data analytics to deliver tailored political ads, raising concerns about voter manipulation and transparency (Isaak & Hanna, 2018).

Twitter, by contrast, has functioned more as a real-time agenda-setting tool. Its immediacy and public visibility have made it particularly powerful for shaping media narratives and amplifying candidate messaging. Donald Trump's consistent and often provocative use of Twitter during his 2016 and 2020 campaigns exemplified how the platform could be leveraged to bypass traditional media gatekeepers, dominate news cycles, and directly engage or provoke political opponents (Ott, 2016). Twitter's format encourages rapid message dissemination, but its brevity and virality can also contribute to misinformation and polarization.

TikTok, the newest of the major platforms in the political sphere, has gained rapid traction -especially among younger voters - by emphasizing short-form, algorithm-driven video content rooted in participatory culture. Unlike platforms like Facebook or Twitter, where political content often appears through paid ads or partisan channels, TikTok fosters political messaging that is embedded in humor, trends, and identity-based expression. While paid political ads are prohibited, the platform has become a powerful vehicle for activism, narrative framing, and subtle ideological cues.

What makes TikTok particularly distinctive is not just the format of its content but the invisible nature of influence it enables. Users may encounter - and amplify - political messages without recognizing them as such. Influencer-driven communication, often by creators with no evident political affiliation, circulates widely without the transparency that traditional campaign ads require. Lifestyle creators, comedians, and beauty vloggers increasingly serve as informal carriers of political narratives, especially during election cycles. Because they are trusted within specific communities, these influencers can have a disproportionate political influence—even in the absence of direct coordination with campaigns.

This convergence of culture, entertainment, and politics challenges conventional understandings of democratic communication. It blurs the boundaries between personal expression and political persuasion, making regulatory oversight difficult. As such, TikTok not only reshapes the how of political messaging but also the who—raising important questions about agency, accountability, and the future of political discourse in algorithmic spaces.

These case studies show how different platforms allow for different political marketing approaches — from using data to persuading voters and shaping messages in real time, to engaging with culture and supporting activism through networks. Bringing these platforms into campaign strategies highlights the importance of flexible communication methods that fit each platform's rules and audience expectations. At the same time, they bring up important questions about transparency, rules for regulation, and how private algorithms affect democratic debate.

Mobilization Strategies

While these platform-based strategies enhance political engagement and reshape the ways campaigns interact with citizens (Boulianne, 2015; Vaccari & Valeriani, 2015), engagement alone does not guarantee electoral success. To turn engagement into concrete political outcomes, campaigns must also focus on mobilization — ensuring that supportive individuals actually turn out to vote (Green & Gerber, 2015). This is where Get-Out-The-Vote (GOTV) strategies become essential, complementing broader political marketing efforts by translating voter interest and support into meaningful electoral participation.

Get-Out-The-Vote (GOTV) strategies play a crucial role in modern electoral campaigns by directly targeting voter turnout, especially among known or likely supporters. The effectiveness of these initiatives lies in their ability to translate voter preference into actual votes — a challenge that many campaigns face, particularly in competitive races (Green & Gerber, 2015).

Traditional GOTV methods, such as door-to-door canvassing, phone banking, SMS reminders, and personalized mail, have a well-established record of success. Research by Gerber and Green (2000) emphasizes the value of direct, personalized contact, suggesting that voters respond more positively to individualized outreach compared to generic mass communication. Importantly, this personalization fosters a sense of accountability and connection, which can motivate participation.

An especially interesting dimension is the use of social pressure in GOTV efforts. Studies like Gerber, Green, and Larimer (2008) demonstrate that informing voters about their neighbors' turnout significantly increases participation. This highlights the psychological mechanisms at play — voters are not only influenced by political arguments but also by social norms, peer expectations, and the desire to maintain a positive social image (Panagopoulos, 2010). This raises important ethical questions about the fine line between motivation and manipulation in democratic mobilization.

The evolution of GOTV into the digital realm has introduced new dynamics. Digital GOTV techniques — including personalized emails, Facebook event invitations, and peer-to-peer texting — allow campaigns to scale outreach efforts efficiently while maintaining a degree of personalization (Bond et al., 2012). These platforms also facilitate social contagion effects, where individuals are influenced by their peers' online behaviors and endorsements (Bond et al., 2012). However, digital strategies are not without challenges: concerns over data privacy, the authenticity of outreach, and the potential for digital fatigue or backlash are critical factors campaigns must navigate (Kreiss, 2016).

Overall, the integration of both traditional and digital GOTV tactics reflects the increasing sophistication of modern campaigns in combining behavioral insights, technological tools, and social dynamics. Yet, these practices also raise normative concerns about consent, transparency, and the boundaries of political persuasion in democratic societies (Bennett & Segerberg, 2012).

Grassroots Campaigning vs. Mass Media Influence

Grassroots campaigning and mass media influence represent two distinct yet complementary pillars of political strategy. Grassroots efforts emphasize personal connection, relational organizing, and the cultivation of community-based networks of support (Han, 2014). By empowering volunteers and encouraging decentralized action, grassroots campaigns can enhance a sense of ownership among supporters, which in turn strengthens the campaign's legitimacy and fosters voter trust (Karpf, 2012). This bottom-up approach draws upon local knowledge, social networks, and interpersonal influence, making it particularly effective in mobilizing hard-to-reach or disaffected voters (Han, 2014; Karpf, 2012).

On the other hand, mass media remains essential for shaping public narratives, setting the agenda, and delivering messages to large and diverse audiences in a short time frame (McCombs & Shaw, 1972). Television, radio, newspapers, and increasingly social media platforms play a central role in framing issues, amplifying candidate visibility, and influencing voter perceptions at scale (Chadwick, 2013; Kreiss, 2016). Mass media's capacity for rapid dissemination gives it a decisive advantage in moments of political crisis, breaking news, or major campaign events.

Importantly, research suggests that the most successful campaigns do not rely exclusively on either approach but rather integrate the two (Kreiss, 2016). By combining high-touch grassroots organizing with high-volume media messaging, campaigns can maximize both relational depth and message reach (Chadwick, 2013). This hybrid strategy allows campaigns to build authentic, trust-based relationships on the ground while simultaneously shaping the broader political discourse, achieving both mobilization and mass persuasion. However, balancing these approaches requires careful coordination, as overreliance on media risks alienating local supporters, while a solely grassroots approach may struggle to break through the noise of today's hyper-saturated media environment.

Grassroots campaigning and mass media influence represent two distinct but complementary strategies in political campaigns. While grassroots efforts build local trust and engagement through personal connections, mass media shapes public narratives and reaches large audiences quickly. Successful campaigns effectively combine these approaches, using grassroots activism for authenticity and mobilization, and mass media for visibility and message amplification.

THE EVOLUTION OF POLITICAL MARKETING IN THE UNITED STATES

From Television to Digital Personalization

Political marketing in the United States has experienced a dramatic evolution since the mid-20th century. From the rise of television and mass media to the era of digital microtargeting and AI-driven personalization, the landscape of campaign strategy has become increasingly complex, data-driven, and individualized. This chapter offers a historical and analytical overview of how U.S. political marketing has adapted to technological and ideological shifts, tracing key developments from the personalization of presidential campaigns in the 1950s to the algorithmic polarization of the 2020s.

The emergence of television as a political tool in the 1950s marked a turning point in campaign strategy. Dwight D. Eisenhower's campaigns in 1952 and 1956 employed advertising professionals to craft visually engaging and emotionally resonant television spots. The 1960 Kennedy-Nixon debate, broadcast live to millions, underscored the medium's power - those who watched on television overwhelmingly perceived Kennedy as the winner, while radio listeners leaned toward Nixon. This era introduced a new dynamic in which visual appeal and media savvy became essential to political success.

The transformation of the primary system following the 1968 Democratic National Convention further democratized the candidate selection process. Reforms by the McGovern-Fraser Commission introduced transparency, proportional representation, and greater voter input. By the 1980s, both parties relied heavily on primary elections, elevating the role of media visibility, grassroots organizing, and campaign fundraising in shaping outcomes. However, critics noted the system's tendency to favor well-funded candidates with early national recognition.

Barack Obama's 2008 and 2012 campaigns marked a defining moment in digital political marketing. His team effectively combined data analytics, micro-targeting, and social media to engage younger and underrepresented voters. Through platforms like Facebook and the MyBO organizing tool, the campaign decentralized operations while maintaining strategic cohesion. In 2012, Obama's campaign refined these tactics, using behavioral science to test and optimize digital outreach. These innovations laid the groundwork for the hyper-targeted, algorithm-driven campaigns of the 2010s and beyond.

In addition to Facebook and email outreach, Obama's team also leveraged YouTube for emotional storytelling and organic reach. His "Yes We Can" speech, remixed with celebrity support, went viral and demonstrated the platform's power as a narrative amplifier—setting a new standard for video-centric campaigning.

Bernie Sanders' 2016 and 2020 campaigns expanded this model by leaning into decentralized digital activism. With low-budget operations powered by Reddit forums, email newsletters, peer-to-peer text messaging, and ActBlue donations, his campaign demonstrated that online small-donor fundraising could rival traditional donor networks and mobilize ideologically passionate communities without top-down messaging control.

On the Republican side, the Republican National Committee's "Data Trust" initiative in the early 2010s helped build a comprehensive voter database integrated with commercial records. This infrastructure enabled more precise targeting across campaigns and laid the foundation for Trump's digital operation in 2016.

The 2016 presidential election represented another significant shift in campaign strategy. Donald Trump's campaign minimized traditional television advertising and focused on broad, emotionally charged messaging (Fowler et al., 2021). Unlike prior cycles where policy-oriented ads were central, Trump's campaign leaned on affective appeals, social media virality, and earned media coverage. This shift marked a departure from informational persuasion to affective mobilization, reshaping expectations around campaign communication.

The 2016 election also highlighted platform-specific campaign strategies. A study by Sahly, Shao, and Kwon (2019) showed that Trump and Clinton tailored their messaging styles across Twitter and Facebook. Trump utilized conflict-driven and negative emotional framing on Twitter, while adopting more positive tones on Facebook. Clinton, by contrast, maintained consistent frames across platforms. These findings underscore the strategic adaptation of message delivery to align with platform cultures and engagement norms.

Recent advancements have brought artificial intelligence and psychographic targeting into mainstream campaign practice. Simchon et al. (2024) demonstrated that political ads tailored to individual personality traits are significantly more persuasive than generic messages. Their research also showed that AI tools can automate such personalization at scale. While effective, this approach raises ethical questions about manipulation and the exploitation of psychological profiles in democratic discourse.

The structure of digital platforms themselves now plays a critical role in shaping political discourse. Morales, Salazar, and Puche (2024) explored in their study how Twitter's algorithms shaped political discourse during the 2020 U.S. presidential election. They showed that the platform's content curation mechanisms didn't just reflect existing political divisions, they intensified them. By steering users toward ideologically similar content and communities, Twitter helped create echo chambers where opposing views were rarely encountered. As a result, polarizing narratives spread faster and more widely, often reinforced by emotionally charged content. The authors argue that these dynamics pose a serious challenge to the idea of democratic deliberation. Instead of fostering informed debate, social media platforms increasingly reward divisiveness and emotional intensity - conditions that modern political marketing readily exploits.

This shift has real electoral consequences. Green et al. (2022) analyzed how Twitter users' engagement with misinformation—specifically tweets promoting or refuting conspiracy theories about election fraud—impacted voter turnout in the January 2021 Georgia Senate runoffs. They found that those who shared or endorsed fraud-related misinformation were slightly less likely to vote, while users who interacted with content debunking the false narratives were more likely to participate. This highlights the powerful role that social media–driven political narratives play in shaping voter behavior and electoral engagement.

From television to social media, from grassroots organizing to AI-driven microtargeting, political marketing in the U.S. reflects the ongoing interplay between technology, strategy, and democratic engagement. Each era has introduced new tools and challenges, culminating in a digital ecosystem that offers both unprecedented precision and profound risks. As political campaigns continue to evolve, so too must our understanding of their impact on voters, discourse, and democratic legitimacy.

CONCLUSION

This chapter has examined the expanding role of political marketing in contemporary democracies, with a particular focus on U.S. elections. Once confined to campaign advertising and candidate branding, political marketing has evolved into a core strategic function that fuses behavioral science, big data, and digital media to influence voter perception and action.

The U.S. offers a revealing case study of this shift. Campaigns have moved from broad-based messaging to micro-segmentation, algorithmic personalization, and constant brand management. From the advent of television in the 1950s to AI-powered psychographic targeting in the 2020s, political communication has become increasingly targeted and emotionally charged. While these innovations have expanded reach and improved strategic precision, they have also raised urgent concerns about privacy, transparency, polarization, and democratic legitimacy.

Perhaps the most alarming consequence of this evolution is the erosion of a shared public sphere. When voters are exposed to personalized messaging that exploits identity and emotion, public discourse fragments, and the space for collective deliberation narrows. Platforms designed for engagement rather than accuracy blur the boundaries between persuasion and manipulation, threatening trust in democratic institutions.

This tension between technological advancement and democratic integrity demands a more comprehensive ethical framework for political marketing. Regulation must move beyond data protection to address the deeper civic implications of algorithmic communication. Political actors, tech platforms, and civil society share responsibility for fostering transparency, inclusiveness, and informed participation.

As research by Fowler et al. (2021) and Nickerson and Rogers (2014) has shown, micro-targeting and personalized outreach are now central to campaign strategy. Yet studies by Green et al. (2022) and Morales et al. (2024) warn that algorithmic amplification of misinformation—especially on issues like election fraud—can distort discourse, depress turnout, and further entrench polarization.

These findings highlight the paradox of digital political marketing: its tools can enhance engagement while simultaneously undermining the very conditions for democratic deliberation. Future research must go beyond assessing campaign performance to interrogate how political marketing affects long-term voter behavior, trust, and participation. Comparative studies, attention to marginalized populations, and investigations into alternative media ecosystems will be essential to this effort. Ultimately, analyzing voting behavior through the lens of predictive modeling and marketing logic is not a neutral or purely technical enterprise. It is a political act—one that influences who is reached, how they are persuaded, and what kind of democracy is ultimately enacted.

REFERENCES

Baldwin-Philippi, J. (2018). The technological performance of populism. *New Media & Society*, *21*(2), 376–397. DOI: 10.1177/1461444818797591

Bennett, C. J. (2016). Voter databases, micro-targeting, and data protection law: Can political parties campaign in Europe as they do in North America? *International Data Privacy Law*, *6*(4), 261–275. DOI: 10.1093/idpl/ipw021

Bennett, W. L., & Segerberg, A. (2012). The logic of connective action: Digital media and the personalization of contentious politics. *Information Communication and Society*, *15*(5), 739–768. DOI: 10.1080/1369118X.2012.670661

Bond, R. M., Fariss, C. J., Jones, J. J., Kramer, A. D., Marlow, C., Settle, J. E., & Fowler, J. H. (2012). A 61-million-person experiment in social influence and political mobilization. *Nature*, *489*(7415), 295–298. DOI: 10.1038/nature11421

Boulianne, S. (2015). Social media use and participation: A meta-analysis of current research. *Information Communication and Society*, *18*(5), 524–538. DOI: 10.1080/1369118X.2015.1008542

Brouard, S., Vasilopoulos, P., Gorohouna, S., Hönnige, C., & Kerrouche, E. (2021). Emotions and voting behavior in self-determination referendums: The case of New Caledonia in 2018. *Electoral Studies*, *69*, 102251. DOI: 10.1016/j.electstud.2020.102251

Caprara, G. V., & Vecchione, M. (2013). Personality approaches to political behavior. In Huddy, L., Sears, D. O., & Levy, J. S. (Eds.), *The Oxford handbook of political psychology* (2nd ed., pp. 23–58). Oxford University Press.

Chadwick, A. (2013). *The hybrid media system: Politics and power*. Oxford University Press., DOI: 10.1093/acprof:oso/9780199759477.001.0001

Downs, A. (1957). *An economic theory of democracy*. Harper.

Enelow, J. M., & Hinich, M. J. (1984). *The spatial theory of voting: An introduction*. Cambridge University Press.

Enli, G., & Skogerbø, E. (2013). Personalized campaigns in party-centred politics: Twitter and Facebook as arenas for political communication. *Information Communication and Society*, *16*(5), 757–774. DOI: 10.1080/1369118X.2013.782330

Fiorina, M. P. (1981). *Retrospective Voting in American National Elections*. Yale University Press.

Fowler, E. F., Franz, M. M., & Ridout, T. N. (2021). *Political advertising in the United States* (2nd ed.). Routledge., DOI: 10.4324/9781003165712

Gerber, A. S., & Green, D. P. (2000). The effects of canvassing, telephone calls, and direct mail on voter turnout: A field experiment. *The American Political Science Review, 94*(3), 653–663. DOI: 10.2307/2585837

Gerber, A. S., Green, D. P., & Larimer, C. W. (2008). Social pressure and voter turnout: Evidence from a large-scale field experiment. *The American Political Science Review, 102*(1), 33–48. DOI: 10.1017/S000305540808009X

Green, D. P., & Gerber, A. S. (2015). *Get out the vote: How to increase voter turnout* (3rd ed.). Brookings Institution Press.

Green, J., Hobbs, W., McCabe, S., & Lazer, D. (2022). Online engagement with 2020 election misinformation and turnout in the 2021 Georgia runoff election. *Proceedings of the National Academy of Sciences of the United States of America, 119*(34), e2115900119. DOI: 10.1073/pnas.2115900119

Han, H. (2014). *How organizations develop activists: Civic associations and leadership in the 21st century*. Oxford University Press.

Harris, P., & Sun, H. H. (2017). The ends justify the means: A global research agenda for political marketing and public affairs. *Journal of Public Affairs, 17*(1–2), e1625. DOI: 10.1002/pa.1625

Hersh, E. D. (2015). *Hacking the electorate: How campaigns perceive voters*. Cambridge University Press., DOI: 10.1017/CBO9781316212783

Huddy, L., Mason, L., & Aarøe, L. (2015). Expressive partisanship: Campaign involvement, political emotion, and partisan identity. *The American Political Science Review, 109*(1), 1–17. DOI: 10.1017/S0003055414000604

Isaak, J., & Hanna, M. J. (2018). User data privacy: Facebook, Cambridge Analytica, and privacy protection. *Computer, 51*(8), 56–59. DOI: 10.1109/MC.2018.3191268

Isaak, J., & Hanna, M. J. (2018). User data privacy: Facebook, Cambridge Analytica, and privacy protection. *Computer, 51*(8), 56–59. DOI: 10.1109/MC.2018.3191268

Iyengar, S., & Kinder, D. R. (2010). *News That Matters: Television and American Opinion* (Updated ed.). University of Chicago Press. https://doi.org/DOI: 10.7208/chicago/9780226388601.001.0001

Iyengar, S., Sood, G., & Lelkes, Y. (2012). Affect, not ideology: A social identity perspective on polarization. *Public Opinion Quarterly, 76*(3), 405–431. DOI: 10.1093/poq/nfs038

Jamieson, K. (2011). *Electing the President, 2008: The Insiders' View*. University of Pennsylvania Press., DOI: 10.9783/9780812205992

Jamieson, K. H. (1992). *Dirty politics: Deception, distraction, and democracy*. Oxford University Press.

Karpf, D. (2012). *The MoveOn effect: The unexpected transformation of American political advocacy*. Oxford University Press., DOI: 10.1093/acprof:oso/9780199898367.001.0001

Kelley, S., & Mirer, T. W. (1974). The simple act of voting. *The American Political Science Review, 68*(2), 572–591. DOI: 10.1017/S000305540011740X

Kreiss, D. (2016). *Prototype politics: Technology-intensive campaigning and the data of democracy*. Oxford University Press.

Krosnick, J. A. (1990). Government policy and citizen passion: A study of issue publics in contemporary America. *Political Behavior, 12*(1), 59–92. DOI: 10.1007/BF00992332

Lamb, C. W., & Crompton, J. L. (1986). *Marketing government and social services*. Wiley.

Lau, R. R., & Redlawsk, D. P. (2001). Advantages and disadvantages of cognitive heuristics in political decision making. *American Journal of Political Science, 45*(4), 951–971. DOI: 10.2307/2669334

Lodge, M., Steenbergen, M. R., & Brau, S. (1995). The responsive voter: Campaign information and the dynamics of candidate evaluation. *The American Political Science Review, 89*(2), 309–326. https://www.jstor.org/stable/2082427

McCombs, M. E., & Shaw, D. L. (1972). The agenda-setting function of mass media. *Public Opinion Quarterly, 36*(2), 176–187. DOI: 10.1086/267990

Miller, W. E., & Shanks, J. M. (1996). *The new American voter*. Harvard University Press.

Morales, G., Salazar, A., & Puche, D. (2024). From deliberation to acclamation: How did Twitter's algorithms foster polarized communities and undermine democracy in the 2020 US presidential election. *Frontiers in Political Science*. Advance online publication. DOI: 10.3389/fpos.2024.1493883

Newman, N., Fletcher, R., Robertson, C. T., Eddy, K., & Nielsen, R. K. (2022). *Reuters Institute Digital News Report 2022*. Reuters Institute for the Study of Journalism. https://reutersinstitute.politics.ox.ac.uk/digital-news-report/2022

Nickerson, D. W., & Rogers, T. (2014). Political campaigns and big data: Combining behavioral science with analytics. *The Journal of Economic Perspectives*, *28*(2), 51–74. DOI: 10.1257/jep.28.2.51

Ott, B. L. (2016). The age of Twitter: Donald J. Trump and the politics of debasement. *Critical Studies in Media Communication*, *34*(1), 59–68. DOI: 10.1080/15295036.2016.1266686

Panagopoulos, C. (2010). Affect, social pressure and prosocial motivation: Field experimental evidence of the mobilizing effects of pride, shame and publicizing voting behavior. *Political Behavior*, *32*(3), 369–386. DOI: 10.1007/s11109-010-9114-0

Popkin, S. L. (1991). *The reasoning voter: Communication and persuasion in presidential campaigns*. University of Chicago Press.

Sahly, A., Shao, C., & Kwon, K. H. (2019). Social media for political campaigns: An examination of Trump's and Clinton's frame building and its effect on audience engagement. *Social Media + Society*, *5*(2), 1–13. DOI: 10.1177/2056305119855141

Scammell, M. (2007). Political brands and consumer citizens: The rebranding of Tony Blair. *The Annals of the American Academy of Political and Social Science*, *611*(1), 176–192. DOI: 10.1177/0002716206299149

Schill, D. (2012). The visual image and the political image: A review of visual communication research in the field of political communication. *The Review of Communication*, *12*(2), 118–142. DOI: 10.1080/15358593.2011.653504

Simchon, A., Edwards, M., & Lewandowsky, S. (2024). The persuasive effects of political microtargeting in the age of generative artificial intelligence. *PNAS Nexus*, *3*(2), pgae035. Advance online publication. DOI: 10.1093/pnasnexus/pgae035

Street, J. (2004). Celebrity politicians: Popular culture and political representation. *British Journal of Politics and International Relations*, *6*(4), 435–452. DOI: 10.1111/j.1467-856X.2004.00149.x

Strömbäck, J., & Kiousis, S. (2011). Political public relations: Defining and mapping an emergent field. In Strömbäck, J., & Kiousis, S. (Eds.), *Political public relations: Principles and applications* (pp. 1–32). Routledge.

Vaccari, C., & Valeriani, A. (2015). Follow the leader! Direct and indirect flows of political communication during the 2013 Italian general election campaign. *New Media & Society*, *17*(7), 1025–1042. DOI: 10.1177/1461444813511038

Valentino, N. A., Brader, T., Groenendyk, E. W., Gregorowicz, K., & Hutchings, V. L. (2011). Election night's alright for fighting: The role of emotions in political participation. *The Journal of Politics, 73*(1), 156–170. DOI: 10.1017/S0022381610000939

Vasilopoulos, P. (2019). Affective Intelligence and Emotional Dynamics in Voters' Decision-Making Processes. *Oxford Research Encyclopedia of Politics*. Retrieved 22 Jul. 2025, from https://oxfordre.com/politics/view/10.1093/acrefore/9780190228637.001.0001/acrefore-9780190228637-e-767

Walgrave, S., & De Swert, K. (2007). Where does issue ownership come from? From the party or from the media? *The International Journal of Press/Politics, 12*(1), 37–67. DOI: 10.1177/1081180X06297572

Westen, D. (2007). *The political brain: The role of emotion in deciding the fate of the nation*. PublicAffairs.

Wright, R. (1999). *Marketing: Origins, Concepts, Environment*. Business Press.

Zeng, J., Abidin, C., & Schäfer, M. S. (2021). Research perspectives on TikTok and its legacy apps: Introduction. *International Journal of Communication, 15*, 3161–3172. DOI: 10.5167/uzh-205427

Chapter 12
The Impact of Political Brand Hate on the Re-Vote Intention:
A Moderating Role of Performance Tolerance

Mohamed Assoud
http://orcid.org/0000-0003-3425-2639
Hassan First University of Settat, Morocco

Lahoucine Berbou
http://orcid.org/0009-0001-6892-3974
Hassan First University of Settat, Morocco

ABSTRACT

Hate is a powerful negative emotion extensively studied in psychology and marketing, notably as brand hate. Applying this to politics, this quantitative study investigates political brand hate among 345 Moroccan electors ahead of the 2026 elections, using PLS-SEM. Findings reveal that negative experiences, ideological incompatibility, and symbolic incongruence are key antecedents driving political brand hate. Crucially, the research demonstrates that this hate significantly and negatively impacts voters' intention to re-vote for political parties. The study also shows that political brands can work to regain trust by maintaining their promises. Contributing uniquely, this is the first study on political brand hate in the MENA region, the first to empirically test the direct link between political hate and re-vote intention, and it introduces the concept of performance tolerance to brand hate theory. The results provide essential theoretical insights and practical guidance for political strategists on understanding and mitigating political brand hate

DOI: 10.4018/979-8-3373-1037-4.ch012

INTRODUCTION

Hate is one of the strongest negative emotions. Psychology literature shows that hate is the second most present emotion in people's spirits after love (Fehr & Russell, 1984, p. 472). In addition to the psychology literature, the emotion of hate has been widely studied in multiple social sciences: social psychology (Opotow, 2005; Opotow & McClelland, 2007; Sternberg & Sternberg, 2008), legal, criminology and communications studies (Paz *et al.*, 2020), religion studies (Syed & Ali, 2021), sport sciences (Shuv-Ami *et al.*, 2020) and business studies (Kucuk, 2019a).

Marketing is one field of business studies investigating the notion of hate. Using multiple methods, branding researchers investigated the concept of brand hate (Aziz & Rahman, 2022; Fetscherin, 2019; Hegner *et al.*, 2017; Yadav & Chakrabarti, 2022). As brand itself as a concept and practices have been extrapolated to other contexts, the notion of brand hate has been extrapolated to multiple fields different from its corporate origins, such as universities-brands (Gois *et al.*, 2022), applications-brands (Islam *et al.*, 2020) and places-brands (Farhat & Chaney, 2021) and political brands (Banerjee & Goel, 2020).

Political branding refers to the usage of branding philosophy in political markets (Needham & Smith, 2015; Smith & French, 2009) since the concept of political party satisfies the traditional brand definition advanced by the American Marketing Association (Smith & French, 2009).

Morocco is a democratic country according to its constitution and a multi-party country. The last general elections in Morocco date back to 2021. According to the Interior Ministry statistics (can be found through www.elections.ma), The RNI (National Rally of Independents) won these elections with a total seat of 102 and more than four million votes, the PAM (Authenticity and Modernity Party) is ranked second with a total seat of 87 and more 2.7 million votes while the Istiqlal party occupies the third place with 2.4 million votes and 81 seats (regional and local included). According to the Moroccan constitution, King Mohamed VI nominated the leader of RNI, Aziz Akhannouch, as prime minister, and the government was constituted and composed of the first three parties as long as they represented the majority.

One year after these elections, many citizens are dissatisfied with these political parties, their politicians, and their policies, especially with the increased cost of living. The hashtag #Akhannouch_leave was a trend for several months in Morocco, according to multiple social media platforms. Even the Moroccan government spokesman talked about this hashtag in a press conference. In January 2023, Internet users initiated a hashtag campaign to voice their objection regarding the perceived pattern of famous lawyers' relatives entering the legal profession. This protest was triggered by identifying specific surnames in search results connected to well-known lawyers, including the justice minister (Leader of PAM), suggesting a sense of hereditary inheritance in the field. Furthermore, numerous educators have been fervently protesting for over two months (counting from October 2023) in opposition to the recent legislation introduced by the education minister. Considering these numerous instances of brand hate-related behaviors that have surfaced within the Moroccan political context presented above, we raise the following research questions:

RQ1. Does Moroccan citizens experience hate towards these political brands?
RQ2. What are the antecedents of this political brand hate in the Moroccan context?
RQ3. Does this political brand hate negatively impact the intention to re-vote for these political brands?
RQ4. How do these political brands regain the voter's trust?

This study aims to answer the previous questions and to overcome the empirical gap in the continuity of Banerjee and Goel's (2020) study by focusing on re-vote intention behavior. In addition, as Morocco approaches the 2026 elections, public sentiment towards these political entities remains a critical area of observation. Recent periods have seen continued expressions of public discontent related to socio-economic conditions, the perceived effectiveness of government policies, and issues of governance. These instances of dissatisfaction, circulating across social media and in public discourse, underscore the potential for political brand hate to influence voter attitudes and behaviors. Considering this ongoing dynamic and the significance of negative emotions in political engagement, investigating the phenomenon of political brand hate within the Moroccan context is timely and necessary to understand its potential impact on the upcoming electoral cycle. Thus, the main objective of the current paper is to apprehend brand hate in the Moroccan political context, its antecedents, and its outcomes. It also expands the current literature on brand hate by apprehending how to regain the voters' trust.

Our study introduces political branding as a sub-discipline of political marketing and presents our theoretical framework, including conceptualizing political brand hate, its antecedents, and outcomes. Following this, we outline our research methodology. Finally, we discuss our results and conclude the study.

LITERATURE REVIEW AND THEORETICAL DEVELOPMENT

Through this literature review, we will introduce the notion of the political brand and examine the theory of brand hate to develop the research hypotheses that will allow us to answer our research questions empirically.

From Political Marketing to Political Brands

Political branding

From a historical perspective, political branding has emerged as a sub-discipline of political marketing. Pich and Newman (2020) advance that political branding underlines a critical application of traditional branding in the political context. The literature suggests two schools of thought related to the branding of politics. The first one (Harris & Lock, 2001; Kavanagh, 1995; Kotler, 1999; Smith, 2001; White & Chernatony, 2002) tends to believe that branding has been used in non-traditional markets such as public organizations, religious organizations, universities, and touristic destination (Smith & French, 2009), it also remains valid for the political market. Keller (2002) suggests that branding principles are applied wherever the consumer choice is involved. Smith and French (2009, p. 210) highlight that "*It is axiomatic that political parties are organizations where politicians (people) seek to exchange ideas and promises for electoral support.*" The latter (Henneberg, 2006; Henneberg & O'shaughnessy, 2007) accept less the idea of political brands, or at least "*political parties are not soap powder brands and should not be treated as such.*" (Smith & French, 2009, p. 210). We adopt the former perspective because we believe that a political brand not only satisfies the conventional definition of the brand but also voters recall the identity of a political party (ideological, meaning, and visual), and electorates can choose between them on this basis. The second argument is that a political brand offers, besides its functional benefits (rational), cultural, social, and epistemic meanings and holds a relationship with/to the voters similar to corporate or commercial brands (Smith & French, 2009).

In the continuity of previous arguments, we adopt the definition proposed by Winther Nielsen (2017, p. 126) "A political brand is political representations that are located in a pattern, which can be identified and differentiated from other political representations". *We also distinguish between three elements of a political brand: the party itself, the politicians, and the policies. This latter is the core service offering as long as the political brand offers* "an intangible product bundle" *(Banerjee & Goel, 2020, p. 2) while the voter is perceived as a consumer.*

Political Branding: the body of knowledge

Besides the conceptualizations of political brands, multiple perspectives are used to apprehend the construct. Winther Nielsen (2017) advocates that six lenses shape the landscape of political brand literature. In this vein, the consumer-brand relationship perspective is widely used in political branding. "*This perspective draws attention to the way in which voters form different kinds of relationships with political parties, relations that are comparable to human relationships and that are investigated by the individual voter at a very personal level*" Winther Nielsen (2017, p. 130).

Within this approach, multiple constructs are empirically studied in political branding literature, such as political brand love in India (Banerjee & Chaudhuri, 2022), political brand relationship quality (Farhan & Omar, 2020), political brand personality in Indonesia (Rutter *et al.*, 2018), political brand loyalty and voter satisfaction in India (Kaur & Sohal, 2019), political brand equity in Ireland (MacDonald *et al.*, 2015), political brand trust in Indonesia (Rachmat, 2014), the impact of emotions in voter intentions within the European Union (Marquart *et al.*, 2022) and the role of emotion in voter attraction in USA(Cosgrove & Shrader, 2022).

Importantly, political psychology literature highlights that emotions are not peripheral but central to political judgment and decision-making. Foundational works such as Marcus *et al.* (2000) developed the Affective Intelligence Theory, demonstrating how emotions—particularly anxiety, anger, and enthusiasm—regulate political judgment, learning, and participation. Complementarily, Valentino *et al.* (2009) show that negative emotions like anger and anxiety are key motivators for both increased political participation and withdrawal, depending on how citizens appraise their political environment. More recently, Goodliffe *et al.* (2025) empirically demonstrated that negative partisan affect—hate, anger, and aversion toward political opponents—has become one of the most powerful drivers of political participation, often outweighing positive motivations. Their findings reinforce that voters are not merely motivated by loyalty or trust toward their preferred political brand but are equally if not more, mobilized by negative emotions toward rival parties.

Despite the well-established role of emotions in fostering political engagement, the negative side of political branding—particularly brand hate—has been significantly underexplored. Banerjee and Goel (2020) were the first to shed light on the darker facets of political branding, namely brand hate. Their seminal work opened the door to exploring the negative aspects of political branding (Assoud & Berbou, 2025b). Specifically, they delved into the antecedents and behavioral consequences of political brand hate within the context of India, a landscape marked by significant distinctions from the Moroccan backdrop (which can be considered a contextual gap). Banerjee and Goel's research primarily focused on political brands within the government and opposition spheres, albeit without a comprehensive examination of how political brand hate might impact voting intentions.

Against this backdrop, our study aligns with the contemporary state of knowledge and aspires to push the boundaries of the political branding theory by addressing multiple gaps. Firstly, we attempt to study political brand hate towards political brands constituting the Moroccan government. We aim to accomplish this by investigating the antecedents of political brand hate and their influence on non-revoting intentions. Secondly, we introduce a novel dimension to this discourse by considering the moderating role of performance tolerance in mitigating the adverse behavioral outcomes associated with political brand hate. In doing so, our research seeks to enrich our understanding of the complexities surrounding political branding and its implications for voter behavior.

From Brand Hate to Political Brand Hate

Brand hate, or corporate brand hate, is the most damaging emotion consumers can experience toward a brand (Bryson *et al.*, 2013). It refers to "*consumers' detachment from a brand and its associations as a result of consumers' intense and deeply held negative emotions such as disgust, anger, contempt, devaluation, and diminution..*" (Kucuk, 2019a). This conceptualization aligns with the mainstream psychological literature, stating that hate is a secondary emotion composed of multiple primary emotions such as disgust, fear, anger, and contempt (Opotow, 2005; Opotow & McClelland, 2007; Sternberg & Sternberg, 2008).

We adopt this perspective in the same line of results on previous studies on brand hate (Fetscherin, 2019; Zarantonello *et al.*, 2016; Zhang & Laroche, 2020), and we define political brand hate as electorates' (who have legal age to vote) detachment from the political party, it leaders and its policies as results of negative emotions such as disgust, contempt, and anger.

In brand hate literature, multiple themes have been investigated, including the antecedents and the outcomes presented in Table 1, the trajectories(Zarantonello *et al.*, 2018), and brand haters traits (Curina *et al.*, 2021).

Table 1. Antecedents and outcomes of brand hate

Context	Studies	Main Antecedents	Main Outcomes
Products and services brands	(Bryson & Atwal, 2019; Costa & Azevedo, 2022; Fetscherin, 2019; Hashim & Kasana, 2019; Hegner *et al.*, 2017; Husnain *et al.*, 2020; Husnain *et al.*, 2022; Islam *et al.*, 2019; Joshi & Yadav, 2021; Kucuk, 2019b; Nguyen, 2021; Noor *et al.*, 2022; Pantano, 2021; Pinto & Brandão, 2021; Platania *et al.*, 2017; Roozbahani *et al.*, 2022)	Negative Experience Symbolic Incongruity Ideological Mismatch Subjective Norms	Brand switching private complaining Public complaining Brand retaliation Brand revenge Non-Purchase intention Willingness to make financial sacrifices to hurt the brand
Luxury brands	(Bryson *et al.*, 2013; Bryson *et al.*, 2021)	Consumer Dissatisfaction Negative stereotypes Negative word of mouth	N/A
Sports brands	(Shuv-Ami *et al.*, 2020)	Loyalty to the opposite team Involvement with the opposite team Fandom of the opposite team	Self-Reported aggression
Education brands	(Gois *et al.*, 2022)	Negative Experience Symbolic Incongruence Ideological Incompatibility	N/A
Destination brands	(Farhat & Chaney, 2021, 2024; Sarkar *et al.*, 2021; Zhang *et al.*, 2025)	Dissatisfaction	Brand retaliation Revisit intention

continued on following page

Table 1. Continued

Context	Studies	Main Antecedents	Main Outcomes
Applications brands	(Islam *et al.*, 2020)	Online Symbolic avoidance Relationship quality avoidance Moral avoidance Deficit value avoidance	Negative word of mouth App switching
Politic brands	(Banerjee & Goel, 2020; Sharma *et al.*, 2023)	Unmet expectations Symbolic Incongruence Ideological Incompatibility Political Identity Political product involvement	Brand avoidance Brand defamation Brand retaliation Brand Extremism

Source: Authors

Indeed, brand hate has garnered considerable attention in various dimensions, encompassing the exploration of antecedents, behavioral outcomes, trajectories, and the traits of individuals who harbor brand hate. However, it is noteworthy that a significant portion of these investigations has predominantly revolved around corporate-level brands. This focus has led to a relative marginalization of research concerning brand hate within non-corporate contexts, particularly within political branding, as mentioned by Banerjee and Goel (2020, p. 3) *"Even though brand hate has been studied in the context of the consumer market, we still know little about the impact of that in the political market."* This research gap is even more relevant in the case of an emerging country such as Morocco. In the same line as Burgess and Steenkamp (2006), we believe that extending research in this context will lead to developing political marketing research in theory and practice.

On the other hand, psychology literature has consistently pointed out the political context as the most appropriate for hate studies (Fischer *et al.*, 2018; Opotow, 2005; Sternberg & Sternberg, 2008). Fischer *et al.* (2018) argue that hate is "*so persistent and prevalent in politics*." In addition to the relevance of studying hate in the political sphere, the current study addresses one question that remains without an empirical answer related to the relationship between political brand hate and re-vote intention. It also overcomes a theoretical gap in brand hate literature regarding regaining voter trust.

Given the distinct nature of political brands and their unique interactions with constituents, expanding the scope of brand hate research to incorporate political brands is imperative. As non-corporate operators, political brands present challenges, dynamics, and implications concerning brand hate. Therefore, exploring the manifestations and consequences of brand hate within the political sphere is crucial to achieving a more comprehensive understanding of this phenomenon and its diverse applications. Such investigations can yield valuable insights specific to politics and contribute to a more affluent knowledge base in political branding.

Antecedents of Political Brand Hate

An antecedent can be defined as "*consumer (active or not) disappointments with the brand*" (Kucuk, 2021, p. 30). These disappointments can vary from functional (related to a brand's performance) to a mismatch between the brand representation and consumer personality (related to consumer identity and its ideology). Three main antecedents have been examined in brand hate literature and have shown the reliability of the brand hate phenomenon in multiple contexts.

Negative experience (NPE): As we mentioned before, if a voter chooses a political brand, it is for its functional (rational) benefits that create expectations. As a construct, negative experience refers to voter dissatisfaction with a political brand's performance. It occurs when a voter perceives the performance of the political brand as poorer than his initial expectations. It is worth highlighting that negative experiences presuppose the consumer (electorate) already used the (political) brand products. Many nominations can be found in the literature to refer to this negative experience: product/service failure (Kucuk, 2018), violations of expectations (Zarantonello *et al.*, 2016), functional incongruity (Islam *et al.*, 2019) and unmeet expectations (Banerjee & Goel, 2020). This latter found that unmet expectations lead to political brand hate, the most determinant of political brand hate. This negative experience is conceptualized in political marketing as a psychological contract violation; according to Farhan and Omar (2020, p. 113) "*this violation occurs when one party fails to fulfill one or more obligations that another party expects from the first party*." In addition, other studies in brand hate literature (Outside the political context) found that negative experiences in a brand hate antecedent (Ali *et al.*, 2020; Gois *et al.*, 2022; Islam *et al.*, 2019; Islam *et al.*, 2020; Pinto & Brandão, 2021). Thus, we would like to test the following hypothesis:

H1. Negative experience is positively related to political brand hate.

Symbolic Incongruity (SI): Unlike negative experience, symbolic incongruity does not suppose that the consumer (voter) is actively in a relationship with the political brand. Issued from the congruence theory (Sirgy, 2018), symbolic incongruity stipulates that consumers tend to buy brands coherently with their self-concept (Zarantonello *et al.*, 2016). Thus, symbolic incongruity occurs when there is a mismatch between political brand and consumers' identity (thoughts and feelings referencing himself as an object). Lee *et al.* (2009, p. 147) argued that "*people may develop their self-concept by dis-identifying with brands that are perceived to be inconsistent with their own image.*" Symbolic incongruity and taste system (Zarantonello *et al.*, 2016) are used interchangeably in brand literature. Thus, we would like to test the following hypothesis:

H2. Symbolic Incongruity is positively related to political brand hate.

Ideological Incompatibility (II): Besides the symbolic meaning of the political brand and its functional benefits, electorates select (or do not) a political brand aligned with their convictions, values, and beliefs. When there is an ideological mismatch, consumers (voters) tend to hate the (political) brand (Banerjee & Goel, 2020). Unlike the previous antecedents, ideological incompatibility involves a moral/ethical focus (Hegner *et al.*, 2017). In corporate brand hate literature, some authors use the terms corporate social irresponsibility (Kucuk, 2018), and corporate wrongdoings to refer to it (Zarantonello *et al.*, 2016). Thus, we would like to test the following hypothesis:

H3. Ideological incompatibility leads to political brand hate.

Consequences of Political Brand Hate

Generally, brand hate outcomes can be discussed through the exit-voice framework lens (Hirschman, 1978). This framework stipulates that a consumer in his relationship with a brand can behave in two ways: Exit or flight strategies refer to avoidance behavior (Bayarassou *et al.*, 2020). This behavior ranges from brand avoidance (Bayarassou *et al.*, 2020; Costa & Azevedo, 2024; Fetscherin, 2019; Hegner *et al.*, 2017; Jabeen *et al.*, 2022; Nguyen, 2021; Pinto & Brandão, 2021), brand rejection (Platania *et al.*, 2017), brand switching (Fetscherin, 2019; Islam *et al.*, 2020) non-repurchase intention (Curina *et al.*, 2020; Sarkar *et al.*, 2021). On the other hand, voice or fight strategies refer to two behaviors where a consumer no longer avoids the brand but starts to make noise (Kucuk, 2020). These voice behaviors range from approach behavior referring to the situation where the consumer "*prefer to express their discontent with the company.*" (Kucuk, 2021, p. 31) and include public and private complaining (Fetscherin, 2019; Roy *et al.*, 2022; Tolunay & Veloutsou, 2025), negative word of mouth (Ajina *et al.*, 2025; Hegner *et al.*, 2017; Jain & Sharma, 2019; Joshi & Yadav, 2021; Kurtoğlu *et al.*, 2022; Nguyen, 2021; Pinto & Brandão, 2021; Platania *et al.*, 2017; Sharma *et al.*, 2022). The second voice approach is attack strategies where consumers are "*creating destructive punitive action against the brand"* (Kucuk, 2021, p. 32); these behaviors vary from brand retaliation, brand revenge, anti-branding activities, brand boycott or even the willingness to make financial sacrifices to hurt the brand.

Political brand hate, as discussed by Banerjee and Goel (2020), manifests in several distinct behavioral outcomes among voters. The most immediate and common response is brand avoidance, wherein individuals withdraw support by abstaining from voting, ignoring party communications, or disassociating from its services—essentially a passive rejection strategy (Assoud & Berbou, 2025a). More notably, the study found a counterintuitive negative relationship between brand hate and active retaliation, suggesting that despite intense animosity, direct confrontational actions against political entities are rare, likely due to perceived power imbalances. However, the most severe consequence is brand extremism, where voters evolve into staunch opponents, driven by strong ideological discord or perceived betrayal, often seeking to damage the party's image or legitimacy.

Against these behaviors, electorates who harbor feelings of hate toward a political brand are unlikely to have an intention to vote for that political brand in future elections. This situation parallels the consumer context, where individuals experiencing brand hate exhibit a non-repurchase intention, signifying their reluctance to engage with or support the brand again (Curina *et al.*, 2020; Santos *et al.*, 2024). In both cases, the presence of hate is a powerful deterrent to continued support or engagement. In the context of the upcoming 2026 elections in Morocco, understanding the outcomes of political brand hate becomes particularly relevant. Following the significant political shifts in the 2021 elections, where the Justice and Development Party (PJD) saw a considerable loss in favor of the current ruling coalition led by the National Rally of Independents (RNI), Authenticity and Modernity Party (PAM), and Istiqlal Party, the potential for political brand hate among the electorate is a crucial factor to consider. Factors such as public perception of the current government's performance, particularly concerning key issues like employment and economic growth as highlighted in recent government roadmaps, or lingering sentiments related to past political decisions and perceived corruption, could contribute to negative feelings towards specific political parties or figures. Thus, in continuity of political brand hate research (Banerjee & Goel, 2020), we would like to test the following hypothesis:

H4. Political brand hate impact negatively the re-vote intention.

Investigating hypothesis H4 is critical in the lead-up to the 2026 Moroccan elections because the dynamic political landscape, marked by the recent significant electoral changes, suggests that voter sentiment, including intense negative feelings towards political entities, could be a powerful determinant of electoral outcomes.

Given the potential for strong dissatisfaction stemming from socio-economic factors and past political performance, understanding if and how political brand hate translates into a refusal to re-endorse a party or candidate is essential for forecasting electoral behavior. Testing this hypothesis will shed light on how negative emotional attachments to political brands act as a barrier to re-voting, offering valuable insights into political parties' challenges and opportunities as they seek to mobilize or regain voter support in the 2026 polls.

Political Brand Hate as a Mediator Between Antecedents and Outcomes

In addition to the direct effect (H1, H2, H3 & H4), the current study attempts to test the mediation role of brand hate between antecedents and voting intention. Brand hate can be discussed as an organism in the Stimulus-Organism-Response model (Yadav & Chakrabarti, 2022) and many studies on corporate brand hate found that brand hate plays an instrumental role between antecedents and behavioral outcomes (Ajina *et al.*, 2025; Assoud & Berbou, 2025b; Hegner *et al.*, 2017). Thus, we would like to test the following mediation hypothesis:

H5. Brand hate mediates the relationship between negative experience and voting intention.
H6. Brand hate mediates the relationship between symbolic Incongruity and voting intention.
H7. Brand hate mediates the relationship between ideological incompatibility and voting intention.

Tolerance and Political Brand Hate

Tolerance can be defined as the behavior of somebody who accepts anything that disagrees, disapproves, or dislikes (Schuyt, 2001). In consumer-brand relationships, consumer tolerance refers to "*the acceptance of undesirable/unexpected tangible and intangible costs for the customers in their journey with the brand.*" (Sözer, 2019). In social sciences (marketing and branding included), tolerance is a widely used construct, but to the best of our knowledge, no study has linked tolerance and brand hate (Assoud & Berbou, 2023; Aziz & Rahman, 2022; Yadav & Chakrabarti, 2022). (Sözer, 2019) advanced that brand tolerance can be discussed on three levels: price tolerance, communication tolerance, and performance tolerance. This latter can be simplified as "*the positive valence and expectation of customers towards the expected performance of the brand offerings as well as their tolerance for performance failures and their commitment to the brand in case of compensation of their costs.*"

(Sözer, 2019). We believe that the concept of performance tolerance is particularly relevant in the context of political brand hate. This perspective becomes even more pertinent when we consider that the functional benefits offered by a political brand play a pivotal role in determining political brand choice, as highlighted by Banerjee and Goel (2020). Understanding how performance tolerance factors into the equation is crucial for comprehending why individuals might continue to support a political brand, even if they have experienced negative emotions such as brand hate, and how this may ultimately influence their decision to re-vote for that brand. Thus, we would like to test the following moderation hypothesis.

> H8. Performance tolerance moderates the relationship between political brand hate and voting intention.

All the hypotheses we attempt to test are presented in **Figure *1***.

Figure 1. Research Model

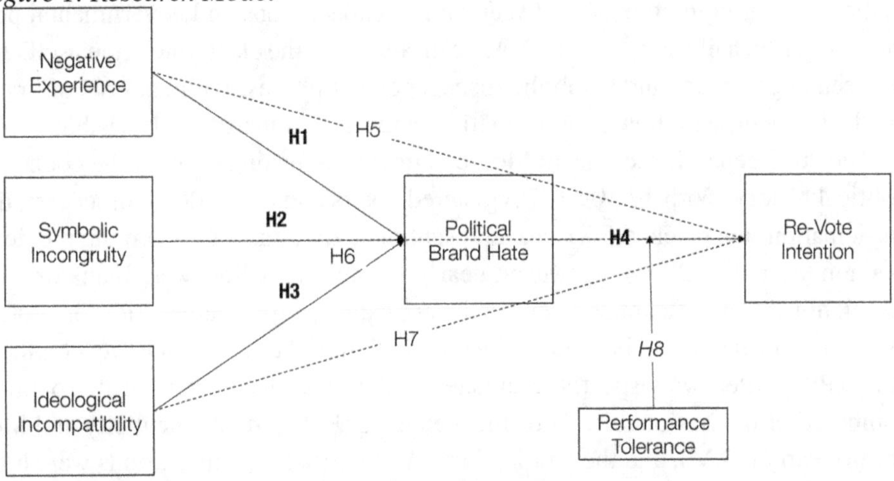

Source: Authors

Moroccan Political Scene After the 2021 Elections

Political Context in Morocco

Across the Middle East and North Africa (MENA) region, the relationship between voters and political institutions is frequently marked by a persistent trust deficit, cyclical disillusionment, and volatile voter-party relationships. Despite varying governance structures—ranging from monarchies such as Morocco and Jordan to republics like Tunisia, Egypt, and Algeria—citizens often perceive political parties as detached from their socio-economic realities, serving elite interests rather than acting as genuine representatives (Hinnebusch, 2020). This perception results in widespread phenomena such as strategic abstention, null voting, disengagement, or reactive political behavior. For instance, while Tunisia experienced a post-revolution surge in voter optimism, it was soon followed by mass disenchantment and record abstention rates. Similarly, in Algeria, persistent high abstention in legislative and presidential elections reflects a deep structural distrust in political institutions (Bank & Busse, 2021). This regional pattern underscores how electoral participation often serves as an instrument of political choice and a symbolic expression of protest, alienation, or resistance to the perceived failure of democratic institutions.

In this broader MENA landscape, Morocco stands out as a constitutional monarchy with hybrid political characteristics, where elected governments operate within a framework of royal authority. While Morocco has maintained political stability (Becheikh, 2021) compared to some neighboring countries, it shares the regional challenge of bridging the gap between citizen expectations and governmental performance. Much like in other North African countries, the electorate often oscillates between engagement and symbolic disengagement phases, with patterns of brand disillusionment, withdrawal, and negative mobilization increasingly visible.

The 2021 general elections in Morocco marked a turning point in the country's political history. With 17,509,127 registered voters and 8,786,080 ballots cast, the participation rate reached 50.18%, representing a 7.9% increase from the previous election (Szmolka, 2024) . However, nearly 1.2 million ballots were blank or null, highlighting a significant segment of voters expressing dissatisfaction or protest through non-selection. The elections led to the fall of the Justice and Development Party (PJD), after two respective mandates, and the rise of a new tripartite coalition composed of the National Rally of Independents (RNI), the Authenticity and Modernity Party (PAM), and the Istiqlal Party. With this shift, expectations were high for reform and social responsiveness. In response, the newly formed government introduced a roadmap prioritizing employment, education, health, and territorial equity. However, as detailed on the government website (Gouvernement, 2024), many citizens express growing frustration with the perceived gap between political promises and actual performance. Enduring inflation, slow bureaucratic reforms, and uneven regional development amplify this dissatisfaction. Such a backdrop provides fertile ground for political brand hate to emerge.

Drawing on recent findings from the Centre Marocain pour la Citoyenneté (2022), 82% of respondents expressed a lack of trust in the government, while 81% felt that political parties fail to represent citizens effectively. These sentiments reveal a structural trust deficit and deep institutional disaffection. Citizens perceive political elites as more focused on personal enrichment than public service and the state as unresponsive to economic hardship. In this setting, political brand hate transcends simple disapproval—it manifests existential disillusionment rooted in a symbolic and ideological mismatch between voter expectations and political reality.

Moreover, Morocco's hybrid political structure—where elected governments coexist under the authority of a strong monarchy—adds complexity to political engagement. Although the 2011 constitutional reforms increased the formal powers of political institutions, the monarchy retains key executive and symbolic roles, and public engagement remains mediated by hierarchical, often opaque governance mechanisms (Szmolka, 2024). This blend of democratic aspirations and monarchical centrality fosters ambivalence among voters, who are often emotionally detached or skeptical of political branding efforts. This sociopolitical backdrop provides the contextual foundation upon which the current study investigates the antecedents and outcomes of political brand hate within the Moroccan electorate.

Social Media as a Vital Space

Within the Moroccan context, social media has evolved into a vital space where political discourse and brand perceptions are constructed and contested (Hassan & Malika, 2023). Political parties have increasingly relied on platforms like Facebook and Twitter to build digital visibility, particularly without full media pluralism (Douhan *et al.*, 2022). During the 2016 and 2021 elections, parties such as the PJD (Justice and Development Party) and RNI (National Rally of Independents) used social media to disseminate campaign narratives and shape their leaders' perceived charisma and credibility. For instance, Abdelilah Benkirane's (Former Prime Minister) rising popularity was largely sustained through viral Facebook content, memes, and videos shared by supporters and orchestrated party networks (Hadi *et al.*, 2019). However, these platforms have become arenas for political brand hate, as disillusioned voters channel frustration and distrust toward political actors through hashtags, satirical posts, and oppositional discourse. This phenomenon intensified after the 2021 elections, as Moroccan users voiced outrage over broken promises, corruption scandals, and socio-economic grievances—fueling affective detachment and rejection of political brands (Douhan *et al.*, 2022; Hassan & Malika, 2023). In this hybrid media environment, social media serves a dual role: it is both a strategic asset for parties seeking influence and a powerful outlet for citizens expressing political resentment and ideological disidentification.

RESEARCH METHODOLOGY

The current section deals with the research methodology utilized for our study in order to provide some answers to the questions outlined in the introduction. As long as our study is based on a theoretical framework (theory of brand hate) and attempts to test the research hypothesis mentioned before, we believe that quantitative methodology suits it. Saunders *et al.* (2019, p. 176) stated, "*Quantitative research is usually associated with a deductive approach, where data are collected and analyzed to test theory*". To achieve our objective, a cross-sectional online survey was used to collect primary data from Moroccan voting-age citizens. We used Microsoft Forms to design the survey. In the first part of the questionnaire, respondents were asked to report their interest in politics and if they were registered in the electoral lists. In the second section, we asked electorates if they felt negative towards one of the three political brands constituting the current Moroccan government. In the third and fourth parts, they were asked to answer questions related to antecedents, re-vote intention, and performance tolerance. In the last section, respondents fill out the socio-demographic data (gender, age, and education).

Measures and Pilot Study

Items related to political brand hate were adopted from Banerjee and Goel (2020). In order to measure political brand hate antecedents, we used items from Hegner *et al.* (2017). We used Re-vote intention items provided by McGregor (2018) while performance-tolerance items were adopted from (Sözer, 2019) study. All items were measured through a five-point Likert scale ranging from strongly disagree to strongly agree. It is critical to note that brand hate antecedents were validated in the political context in Banerjee and Goel (2020) study. Afterward, a pilot study involving a group of twenty-five participants was carried out, in line with the widely accepted principle that the pilot sample should accurately represent the target population (Gavard-Perret, 2008). In social science survey research, a sample size of 10-30 individuals is typically considered sufficient for a pilot study (Thiétart, 2014). For data collection, a non-probability convenience sampling method was employed.

Sampling Strategy

The current study used a combination of convenience and snowball techniques (Bethlehem & Biffignandi, 2011). This combination is suggested for non-funded research due to its cost-effectiveness and quicker implementation (Banerjee & Goel, 2020). The sampling plan involved distributing the questionnaire online via widely used social networks (LinkedIn, Facebook, ResearchGate) and leveraging existing university networks through a snowball method, where professors shared the survey and encouraged further distribution to reach participants across various Moroccan regions. The researchers assured the privacy of the respondents. To ensure anonymity and confidentiality, we underlined that there are no wrong and right responses to further reduce social desirability bias (Bethlehem & Biffignandi, 2011). A total of 400 respondents were approached between October 2024 and March 2025. Only 345 responses were eligible for the analysis. The demographical sample results are presented in **Table 2**. Green (1991) states that the minimum sample size equals 50 + 8m and determined that the sample size met the minimum necessary size (m: number of predictors). Therefore, our sample size (N=345) was sufficient for analysis.

Table 2. Sample socio-demographic data

	Frequency	**Percentage**
Gender		
Male	183	52.8
Female	162	47.2
Age		
18-24	69	20.1
25-34	122	35.3
35-44	110	31.8
45-54	44	12.8
Education		
High School	52	15.0
Undergraduate	115	33.4
Postgraduate	178	51.6

Source: **Research data.**

Data Analysis

In this study, we employ partial least squares structural equation modeling (PLS-SEM) to assess the research hypothesis. Adopting this second-generation approach is based on the considerations advanced by Hair *et al.* (2022). The analysis followed a two-step approach (Hair, 2017). First, the measurement model was evaluated to assess indicator reliability, internal consistency, convergent validity, and discriminant validity. Second, the structural model was tested to examine the hypothesized relationships (H1–H4), as well as the mediation (H5–H7) and moderation (H8) effects, using a bootstrapping procedure with 5,000 subsamples in SmartPLS 4.0.

RESULTS AND DISCUSSION

The current section will provide the results of our study alongside the interpretation. To do so, we will present the results according to the reporting format indicated by Hair *et al.* (2019). The second section is related to the discussion of the results.

Most Hated Political Brands

Before testing our research hypothesis, we judged whether it would be interesting to present the most hated political brand according to our results. As mentioned in **Figure *2***, the most hated political brand is the National Rally of Independents (RNI), the political party that won the last elections, and its president is the prime minister, Aziz Akhannouch. These results can be interpreted as the Negative Double Jeopardy phenomenon (Kucuk, 2010), which indicates that brands with the most fans attract the most haters.

Figure 2. Most hate political brands

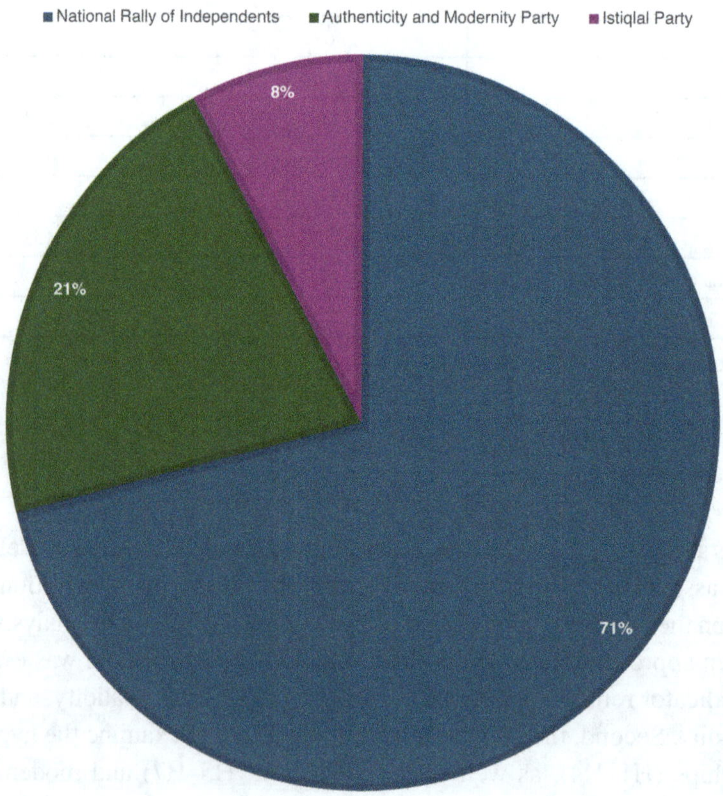

Source: Research data.

Measurement Model

According to Hair (2017), the first step of SEM-PLS modeling is to evaluate the measurement model. Simply put, we will test the proposed model's validity and adequacy. In our case, all constructs were reflective, which leads to verifying indicators: Indicator reliability, internal consistency reliability, convergent validity, and discriminant validity. As a rule of thumb, indicator reliability is measured with factor loadings, and its values should be higher than 0.7. The internal consistency reliability should be measured by Cronbach alpha and composite reliability, and their values should be higher than 0.7 for both indicators. Convergent validity is assured when the average variance extracted (AVE) exceeds 0.5. HTMT approach is used to assess discriminant validity. Generally, an HTMT value above 0.90 would suggest that discriminant validity is absent (Hair *et al.*, 2019). All these theoretical rules were respected, as mentioned in **Table *3*** and **Table *4***.

Table 3. Measurement Model

Construct	Indicator	Loading Factors	Cronbach's Alpha	Composite Reliability	AVE
PBH	PBH1	0,843	0,872	0,880	0,662
	PBH2	0,885			
	PBH3	0,754			
	PBH4	0,820			
	PBH5	0,760			
NPE	NPE1	0,834	0,871	0,891	0,719
	NPE2	0,849			
	NPE3	0,807			
	NPE4	0,900			
SI	SI1	0,849	0,815	0,831	0,645
	SI2	0,874			
	SI3	0,725			
	SI4	0,756			
II	II1	0,796	0,832	0,846	0,665
	II2	0,860			
	II3	0,849			
	II4	0,752			
VI	VI1	0,858	0,722	0,742	0,781
	VI2	0,908			

continued on following page

Table 3. Continued

Construct	Indicator	Loading Factors	Cronbach's Alpha	Composite Reliability	AVE
PT	PT1	0,796	0,740	0,773	0,514
	PT2	0,860			
	PT3	0,849			

Source: Research Analysis

Table 4. Discriminant validity of constructs (HTMT)

	II	NPE	PBH	PT	SI
NPE	0,552				
PBH	0,524	0,571			
PT	0,439	0,516	0,366		
SI	0,813	0,412	0,435	0,489	
VI	0,485	0,373	0,368	0,751	0,428

Source: Research Analysis

Structural Model – Direct Effects

In the first stage, we estimated direct effects without the mediator and moderator (**Table 5**). We found H1 ($\beta = 0.37$; $p < 0.00$), H2($\beta = 0.11$; $p < 0.04$) and H3($\beta = 0.20$; $p < 0.01$) were statistically significant as hypothesized. Additionally, H4 ($\beta = -0.30$; $p < 0.00$) was statistically significant, positing that political brand hate significantly impacted voting intention.

Table 5. Structural Model- Direct Effects Results

	Relationship	Path Coefficients	T statistics	P Value	Conclusion
H1	NPE -> PBH	0,372*	4,731	0,000	Supported
H2	SI -> PBH	0,116*	2,003	0,045	Supported
H3	II -> PBH	0,202*	3,319	0,001	Supported
H4	PBH -> VI	-0,297*	5,280	0,000	Supported

Source: Research Analysis. (*) Indicates that the relationship is statistically significant at the 0.05 level.

Structural Model – Mediation Effects

Before the mediation effects analysis, we checked the relationship between the independent variables (NPE, SI, and II) and the dependent variable (VI), and we found a significative negative relationship between the three predictor variables and the voting intention (NPE: β =-0,167, p <0,00; SI: β =-0,144, p <0,01; II: β =-0,224, p <0,00). This evaluation is an essential condition for mediation analysis, as proposed by Baron and Kenny (1986). Following the same authors' approach, we estimated the model with the mediator PBH to examine its relationship with predictor variables. The link between the predictors and the dependent variable should change for mediation to occur by inserting the mediating variable in the model. We found that NPE (β =-0,111, p <0,00), SI (β =-0,034, p <0,10), and II (β =-0,060, p <0,00). According to our results, PBH partially mediates the relationship between NPE and VI and between II and VI. At the same time, full mediation was found between SI and VI, as mentioned in **Table *6*.**

Table 6. Result of specific indirect effects analysis of mediation effect

	Paths and indicators	Indirect effects		Bootstrapping indirect effects BC 95%CI			Conclusion
		β	SE	LL	UL	P	
H5	NPE -> PBH-> VI	-0,111*	0,029	-0,122	-0,022	0,00	Partial Mediation
H6	SI -> PBH -> VI	-0,034^{ns}	0,021	-0,087	-0,003	0,10	Full mediation
H7	II -> PBH -> VI	-0,060*	0,025	-0,122	-0,022	0,00	Partial Mediation

Source: Research Analysis.
* Indicates that the relationship is statistically significant at the 0.05 level. ^{NS}: Non-significant

Structural Model – Moderation Effect

In order to test the moderation effect of performance tolerance on the relationship between political brand hate and voting intention, we used the product indicator approach (Hair, 2017). The results (β =-0,126, p <0,00) indicate the moderation role of PT between PBH and VI, supporting H8. **Figure *3*** shows that the higher the electorates' performance tolerance, the lower their non-voting intention towards the political brand.

Figure 3. Moderation effect of performance tolerance between political brand hate and voting intention

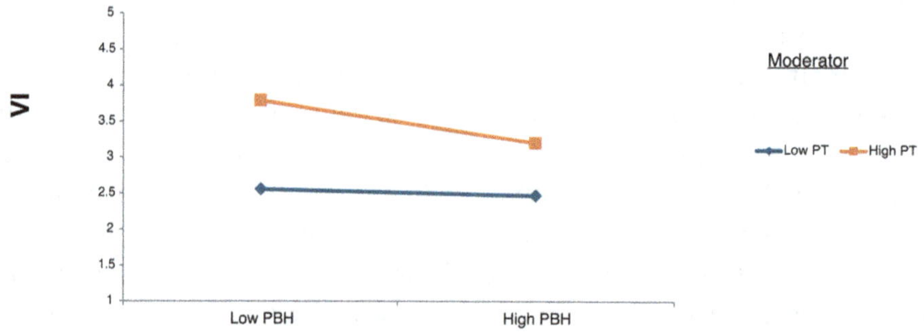

Source: Research Analysis
Notes: PBH(Political brand hate), VI (Voting intention), PT (Performance Tolerance)

In addition to direct links, moderation, and mediation effects, we calculated the R^2 value. R^2 value above 0.2 is considered high and acceptable for social sciences (Hair, 2017; Hair *et al.*, 2022; Hair *et al.*, 2019). In this study, the constant determination value (R2) for PBH with (NPE, SI, and II) is 0.33, while VI with PBH is around 0.35. Further, we opted for the blindfolding technique to assess the significance of external factors and models, which involves a straightforward process of reusing. Hair (2017) highlights, "*This technique is a combination of function fitting and cross-validation, and examines each construct's predictive relevance by computing changes in the criterion estimates (Q2)*". A Q2 value superior to zero shows the predictive relevance of the model. Our study found Q2 for PBH 0.35 and VI 0.32 to have satisfactory predictive relevance as the values are above the cut-off level.

CONCLUSION

The findings of this study support the extrapolation of the brand hate construct to political context (Banerjee & Goel, 2020). The direct links found in this study are consistent with brand hate literature in both corporate (Curina *et al.*, 2020; Hashim & Kasana, 2019; Hegner *et al.*, 2017; Zhang & Laroche, 2020) and non-corporate context (Banerjee & Goel, 2020; Gois *et al.*, 2022).

The current study findings support H1, H2, and H3 that negative experience, symbolic incongruity, and ideological incompatibility are the main determinants of political brand hate. Compared to the Indian context (Banerjee & Goel, 2020) the order of impact remains the same. In simple words, negative experience is the most determinant antecedent, which shows that functional benefits are more critical for electorates, as political science literature highlights (Winther Nielsen, 2017). This result is in line with the findings of Farhan and Omar (2020, p. 113), who suggest that "*perceived violation of a psychological contract may result in feelings of anger, frustration, a sense of being cheated, displeasure, and disillusionment with the overall relationship.*" The second determinant of political brand hate is related to ideological incompatibility (H3). Banerjee and Goel (2020, p. 17) stated that "*From the context of a political brand, whenever a political party follows a particular ideology, people with the same mindset come forward and follows that party. But, if the party ideology doesn't have a seamless match, hate for the party evolves*". Symbolic incongruity (H2) also increases political brand hate. This result aligns with the political brand personality perspective, stipulating that voters interact with the political brand based on symbolic signification involving their personality (Winther Nielsen, 2017).

These findings align with the Theory of Brand Hate developed by Assoud and Berbou (2025b), confirming that brand hate emerges from functional dissatisfaction, symbolic incongruity, and ideological misalignment. This study reinforces the cross-contextual robustness of this framework, demonstrating that voters, much like consumers, react to perceived violations of expectations—whether functional, identity-based, or ideological—by developing intense forms of brand hate toward political entities. However, compared to Ajina *et al.* (2025) in the retail context, notable differences in the consequences of brand hate become evident. While Ajina *et al.* show that retail brand hate primarily results in avoidance and negative word of mouth, with limited evidence of escalation into active retaliation, the current study reveals that political brand hate triggers a broader and more intense spectrum of outcomes, including public complaining, retaliation, and collective activism. This distinction likely stems from the inherently value-driven nature of political brands, where voters perceive hate as a moral or ideological stance rather than merely a response to transactional failure. Interestingly, a comparison with Banerjee and Goel (2020) also highlights contextual differences in behavioral outcomes. While both studies confirm avoidance as a primary response, Banerjee and Goel emphasize the emergence of more extreme reactions, such as brand extremism, where voters transition from mere disapproval to active campaigning against the political brand. In contrast, our findings suggest that while extremism is present, retaliation behaviors are more structured, strategic, and publicly visible, often manifesting through digital activism, public criticism, or voter mobilization efforts. This comparison underscores that while brand hate consistently drives disengagement behaviors across domains, these behaviors' intensity, form, and public nature are amplified in political contexts, where brand meanings are deeply intertwined with identity, ideology, and collective action.

Second, Similar to the service brand haters (Curina *et al.*, 2020) and destination brand haters (Sarkar *et al.*, 2021), our findings show a negative relationship between political brand hate and voting intention (H4). Hate theories also support this result. Fischer *et al.* (2018, p. 317) highlighted "*The motivational goal associated with hate is to destroy the hate target, whether physically, socially, or symbolically*." Simply put, electorates experiencing dark/hateful emotions do not repeat the same choice. This result is further supported by the findings of Lee *et al.* (2016), who argue that while voting behavior is often framed as a rational, deliberative process, it can also be influenced by explicit attitudes and implicit, affective reactions, including subconscious biases or social pressures. Their study demonstrates that explicit political preferences primarily drive voting intention, but actual voting behavior is also influenced by social cues such as ethnic identity and the perceived voting behavior of significant others This conclusion suggests that decisions like non-revote intentions driven by political brand hate are not purely cognitive acts of rational punishment based on performance evaluations but may also be emotionally charged reactions embedded in social contexts. In other words, when voters experience hate toward a political brand, their withdrawal from that brand (i.e., not voting for it again) can reflect both a rational response to disappointment and a socially reinforced rejection driven by collective disillusionment or group-based identity threats. These findings reinforce the idea that political brand hate is an attitudinal outcome and a predictor of bounded rationality behaviors, where emotional responses override rational deliberation, especially when fueled by social influence or perceived betrayal.

Our results also indicate several partial mediations (H5 & H7) and the full of mediation (H6), which can be interpreted as brand hate being an organism determined by stimulus (antecedents) and giving birth to a reaction (non-voting intention). Simply put, the effect of Symbolic Incongruity on Voting Intention is fully explained by the presence of Political Brand Hate. In other words, Symbolic Incongruity influences Voting Intention solely through its impact on Political Brand Hate. In contrast, the presence of direct effects (H1 and H3) in addition to the mediating role (H5 and H7) of Political Brand Hate emphasizes that there are other channels or mechanisms through which negative experience and ideological incompatibility influence voting intention (Assoud & Berbou, 2025a).

The findings also highlight that performance tolerance reduces the non-voting intention towards the same political brand (H8). The conclusion can be considered in the same perspective of consumer tolerance at the corporate level (Sözer, 2019, 2020), which stipulates that (political) brands can regain consumer (electorate) trust if they compensate for the losses of unmet expectations. This conclusion is also supported in political branding literature, according to Susila *et al.* (2020, p. 154) "*In political marketing, information and trust are two important characteristics that influence voting behavior.*" Additionally, political brands can recover some of consumer re-voting intention if they adopt a compensation-explanation-apology strategy (Hashim & Ahmed, 2018). Based on our empirical results, compensation of loss leads to re-gain consumer trust, which can be interpreted as an efficient strategy to reduce the non-revote intention. According to Kucuk (2019a), compensation unfolds monetary and non-monetary tactics. This latter is adequate to the political branding and is known as "*Policy and Process Improvement.*" Similar to commercial brand hate, "*80% of consumers (electorates) expect that their product repaired/service fixed, and 81% of complainants asked an assurance from the company (political brand) that the problem would not be repeated. These are big percentages, and it also indicates that consumers are saying to company that I like you (political brand) and I expect you to fix my problems, and furthermore I don't want you to repeat the same mistake. If you do, you will make us mad and deserve our hate.*" (Kucuk, 2019a, p. 186). Beyond the statistical confirmation of its moderating role, the concept of performance tolerance plays a pivotal role in understanding how voters manage disappointment in political brand relationships. Drawing on the brand tolerance framework from(Sozer, 2020), performance tolerance refers to voters' capacity to temporarily accept underperformance, broken promises, or perceived service failures, provided that the political brand retains a reservoir of past satisfaction, trust, or symbolic value. In the corporate context, Sozer (2020) demonstrated that customers are more forgiving of performance lapses when brand equity is high. Extrapolating to the political context, this means that electorates may exhibit a form of pragmatic patience, tolerating certain failures—such as delays in reforms, unmet policy promises, or governance errors—if they still perceive the political brand as credible, ideologically aligned, or historically valuable. However, this tolerance is conditional and finite; it acts as a buffer mechanism, allowing political brands time to engage in corrective actions such as policy adjustments, symbolic gestures, or transparent communication strategies. If that window is squandered, tolerance collapses and converts into disengagement or political brand hate.

Summing up the results, it can be concluded that the current study provides a novel examination of brand hate in the context of the Moroccan political landscape (RQ1), contributing new insights to understanding voter behavior in the MENA region. The study identifies vital antecedents of political brand hate, namely negative experience, ideological incompatibility, and symbolic incongruence (RQ2), and reveals their significant impact on re-voting intention (RQ3). Moreover, while shedding light on the detrimental effects of political brand hate, the findings suggest that brands can recover trust and voting intention through performance fulfillment (RQ4).

Theoretical implications

This study contributes to the political marketing theory in several manners: political parties can be apprehended as commercial brands, and electorates maintain relationships with political parties like human relationships (Fournier, 1998). In this vine, the negative double jeopardy phenomenon (Kucuk, 2010) can be extrapolated to the political context, as the findings of this study suggest (the political brand that won the elections generated vast numbers of haters). In political brand hate literature, the current study addressed the empirical gap revealed by Banerjee and Goel (2020) suggesting the empirical test of the relationship between political brand hate and voting intention, especially in cases of parties constituting the government. In addition to the previous research gap and to the best of our knowledge, the study is the first to introduce the performance tolerance construct in brand hate literature. Our finding suggests, in line with Susila *et al.* (2020) conclusion, that trust impacts voting behavior, which offers new perspectives for mitigating political brand hate. This statement aligns with Fischer *et al.* (2018, p. 317) "*There is also evidence that hate fuels political intolerance.*"

Managerial implications

In addition to the theoretical contributions, this study provides several actionable implications for political marketers. These implications operate at two levels: preventive brand management and crisis response management (Assoud & Berbou, 2023). First, the findings reaffirm that the most decisive determinant of political brand choice remains the delivery of functional and economic promises (Smith & French, 2009). When political brands fail to meet performance expectations or engage in irresponsible behavior, this triggers political brand hate, non-revote intention, and voter disengagement. Therefore, political entities must view themselves not just as political agents but as brands held accountable for both policy and conduct. Second, political actors, especially those already in power, should implement a political Brand Hate barometer, allowing them to continuously monitor dark emotions and negative sentiment among voters—similar to commercial brand monitoring systems. This involves conducting political brand audits and applying technological tools such as sentiment analysis, speech tracking, and text mining (Mednini *et al.*, 2024) to detect hate signals and their root causes early.

Building on this foundation, the study integrates insights from Kucuk (2019a) and Coombs' (2007) Situational Crisis Communication Theory (SCCT) to outline a four-stage political brand hate management framework:

Listening and Early Detection: Political brands must engage in continuous social listening, scanning digital platforms to detect early warning signs of voter dissatisfaction and brand hate. As Kucuk (2019a) emphasizes, brand hate often manifests through online channels such as memes, hashtags, ridicule, or boycott campaigns. Early detection allows proactive interventions before hate escalates into widespread reputational crises (Hassan & Malika, 2023).

Engagement and Communication Timing: Effective engagement is critical once negativity surfaces. Political brand managers should carefully manage the timing, tone, and channel of communication. Responses must be tailored to the level of reputational threat: For minor discontent (victim or accidental clusters), justifications, explanations, or corrections may suffice (Kucuk, 2019a). In severe cases, due to ethical breaches or broken promises, more accommodative strategies are required, such as public apologies, compensation (policy shifts, social investments), and corrective action (Coombs, 2007).

Negotiation and Damage Control: The negotiation phase involves three interdependent tactics, following Kucuk's (2019a) model. First, the compensation strategy consists of offering tangible benefits or remedial actions. Second, the explanation strategy includes clarifying misunderstandings or the circumstances leading to the perceived failure. Lastly, the Apology strategy suggests acknowledging mistakes and seeking forgiveness, especially when ideological incompatibility or perceived betrayal is involved. These strategies aim to diffuse negative effects, rebuild trust, and reduce further harm.

Rehabilitation and Digital Reputation Management: This long-term recovery requires systematic efforts in political brand rehabilitation (Coombs, 2007), including reputation repair campaigns (with a focus on transparency, public engagement, and re-alignment of values with voter expectations.) Digital reputation management (employing fact-checking units, influencer partnerships, and proactive narrative building to counteract hate narratives in the digital sphere) and symbolic acts (empathy-driven discourse and participatory reforms that demonstrate a genuine commitment to address grievances)

Finally, this study highlights that failure to manage political brand hate has tangible consequences on voting behavior, reinforcing that emotional management is not secondary but central to political brand strategy (Banerjee & Goel, 2020).

Limitations and future research

Like most survey-based studies, this research is not without limitations. First, using a non-probability convenience sampling method, combined with snowball sampling, limits the external validity and generalizability of the findings (Hair, 2017). While this approach is commonly adopted in exploratory research in emerging markets with resource constraints (Bethlehem & Biffignandi, 2011), it inherently introduces sampling bias, as the sample may not fully capture the diversity of the

Moroccan electorate, despite our efforts to distribute the survey across various regions, academic networks, and social media platforms. Second, the reliance on self-reported measures introduces the risk of social desirability bias (Thiétart, 2014), despite our efforts to ensure anonymity, confidentiality, and the voluntary nature of participation. Given the politically sensitive nature of the study, some respondents may have underreported or softened their negative feelings toward political entities to align with perceived social expectations or avoid discomfort. Third, using a cross-sectional design limits the ability to draw conclusions about causality or the evolution of political brand hate over time. The data were collected at a single point in time, capturing voter sentiments in a specific political context. This approach does not allow examining how political brand hate might fluctuate in response to evolving political events, campaigns, or changing socio-economic conditions (Hair *et al.*, 2022).

Drawing from these limitations, and despite the current study's contributions to advancing the understanding of political brand hate, future research should consider several avenues for further exploration. First, there is a pressing need for longitudinal studies to capture the temporal dynamics of political brand hate, moving beyond the static snapshot provided by cross-sectional designs. As highlighted by Zarantonello et al. (2018), brand hate is not a fixed state but often follows distinct trajectories—ranging from steady increases in negative sentiment to cyclical patterns of disengagement and renewed hostility. Applying this perspective to political contexts would allow researchers to examine how voter hate evolves across electoral cycles or in response to major socio-political events. Second, future studies should incorporate behavioral data or computational modeling approaches (Assoud & Berbou, 2025b) to complement self-reported measures. This could include analyzing digital trace data such as social media interactions, participation in online boycott campaigns, or engagement with anti-party communities. Computational techniques like sentiment analysis, network analysis, or natural language processing (Mednini *et al.*, 2024) could offer richer, more objective insights into how political brand hate manifests and spreads, especially in the digital sphere. Third,, future research should employ more robust sampling techniques, such as stratified random sampling (Bethlehem & Biffignandi, 2011), to ensure greater generalizability of findings across the electorate. This is particularly crucial in politically diverse societies where hate dynamics may vary significantly across different demographic segments. Finally, an important extension would be including socio-demographic variables—such as age, gender, education, and income—as potential moderators in the relationship between political brand hate and its outcomes. Drawing on Furnham and Cheng (2019), who demonstrate that personality traits and demographic factors significantly shape political attitudes and behaviors, future research could investigate whether certain groups are more prone to experiencing and acting upon political brand hate. This inclusion would enhance the granularity of models and offer more targeted insights for political parties and policymakers.

REFERENCES

Ajina, A. S., Ali, S., Javed, H. M. U., Khalid, N., Zamil, A. M. A., & Khan, K. (2025). Exploring the tripartite model of brand hate: Antecedents and consequences in the context of shopping malls. *Cogent Business & Management, 12*(1). Advance online publication. DOI: 10.1080/23311975.2025.2467846

Ali, S., Attiq, S., & Talib, N. (2020). Antecedents of brand hate: Mediating role of customer dissatisfaction and moderating role of narcissism. *Pakistan Journal of Commerce and Social Science, 14*(3), 603–628. https://hdl.handle.net/10419/224953

Assoud, M., & Berbou, L. (2023). Brand Hate: One Decade of Research A Systematic Review. *International Journal of Latest Research in Humanities and Social Science, 06*(11), 146–165. http://www.ijlrhss.com/paper/volume-6-issue-11/18-HSS-2412.pdf

Assoud, M., & Berbou, L. (2025a). Conceptualizing Brand Hate Escalation: A Dual SEM-PLS / Necessary Condition Analysis Approach. *African Journal of Human Resources, Marketing and Organisational Studies, 2*(1), 55-81, https://journals.co.za/doi/epdf/10.31920/3050-2292/2025/v2n1a3

Assoud, M., & Berbou, L. (2025b). Mapping the Evolution of Brand Hate: A Comprehensive Bibliometric Analysis. *Journal of Consumer Satisfaction, Dissatisfaction & Complaining Behavior, 38*(1), 21–58. https://www.jcsdcb.com/index.php/JCSDCB/article/view/1086

Aziz, R., & Rahman, Z. (2022). Brand hate: A literature review and future research agenda. *European Journal of Marketing, 56*(7), 2014–2051. DOI: 10.1108/EJM-03-2021-0189

Banerjee, S., & Chaudhuri, B. R. (2022). Brand love and party preference of young political consumers (voters). *International Review on Public and Nonprofit Marketing, 19*(3), 475–503.

Banerjee, S., & Goel, P. (2020). Party brand hate in political market: Antecedents and consequences. *Asian Journal of Political Science, 28*(2), 97–121. DOI: 10.1080/02185377.2020.1768417

Bank, A., & Busse, J. (2021). MENA political science research a decade after the Arab uprisings: Facing the facts on tremulous grounds. *Mediterranean Politics, 26*(5), 539–562. DOI: 10.1080/13629395.2021.1889285

Baron, R. M., & Kenny, D. A. (1986). The moderator–mediator variable distinction in social psychological research: Conceptual, strategic, and statistical considerations. *Journal of Personality and Social Psychology, 51*(6), 1173.

Bayarassou, O., Becheur, I., & Valette-Florence, P. (2020). "Fight or flight": Coping responses to brand hate. *Journal of Product and Brand Management, 30*(3), 492–511. DOI: 10.1108/JPBM-08-2019-2519

Becheikh, N. (2021). Political stability and economic growth in developing economies: Lessons from Morocco, Tunisia and Egypt ten years after the Arab Spring. *Insights into Regional Development, 3*(2), 229–251.

Bethlehem, J., & Biffignandi, S. (2011). *Handbook of web surveys*. John Wiley & Sons.

Bryson, D., & Atwal, G. (2019). Brand hate: The case of Starbucks in France. *British Food Journal, 121*(1), 172–182. DOI: 10.1108/BFJ-03-2018-0194

Bryson, D., Atwal, G., & Hultén, P. (2013). Towards the conceptualisation of the antecedents of extreme negative affect towards luxury brands. *Qualitative Market Research, 16*(4), 393–405. DOI: 10.1108/QMR-06-2013-0043

Bryson, D., Atwal, G., Hulten, P., & Heine, K. (2021). Antecedents of luxury brand hate: A quantitative study. *STRATEGIC CHANGE-BRIEFINGS IN ENTREPRENEURIAL FINANCE, 30*(1), 35–43. DOI: 10.1002/jsc.2387

Burgess, S. M., & Steenkamp, J.-B. E. M. (2006). Marketing renaissance: How research in emerging markets advances marketing science and practice. *International Journal of Research in Marketing, 23*(4), 337–356. DOI: 10.1016/j.ijresmar.2006.08.001

Citoyennetė, C. M. p. l. (2022). *The performance of the Moroccan government*.

Coombs, W. T. (2007). Protecting Organization Reputations During a Crisis: The Development and Application of Situational Crisis Communication Theory. *Corporate Reputation Review, 10*(3), 163–176. DOI: 10.1057/palgrave.crr.1550049

Cosgrove, K., & Shrader, N. R. (2022). Political Branding in the USA Election of 2020. In Moufahim, M. (Ed.), *Political Branding in Turbulent times* (pp. 33–50). Springer International Publishing., DOI: 10.1007/978-3-030-83229-2_3

Costa, C., & Azevedo, A. (2024). Antecedents and consequences of the "cancel culture" firestorm journey for brands: Is there a possibility for forgiveness? *Journal of Marketing Management, 40*(3-4), 289–312. DOI: 10.1080/0267257X.2023.2266465

Costa, J., & Azevedo, A. (2022). Beyond Brand Hate: Are You Willing to Forgive a Negative Experience with Your Smartphone Mobile Communications' Brand? *Corporate Reputation Review*. Advance online publication. DOI: 10.1057/s41299-022-00139-7

Curina, I., Francioni, B., Cioppi, M., & Savelli, E. (2021). Traits and peculiarities of different brand hate behaviours. *Journal of Strategic Marketing*, *29*(3), 227–246. DOI: 10.1080/0965254X.2019.1676293

Curina, I., Francioni, B., Hegner, S. M., & Cioppi, M. (2020). Brand hate and non-repurchase intention: A service context perspective in a cross-channel setting. *Journal of Retailing and Consumer Services*, *54*. Advance online publication. DOI: 10.1016/j.jretconser.2019.102031

Douhan, H., Landucci, E., & Richter, L. (2022). Social Media in Morocco: From Grassroots Activism to Electoral Campaigns.

Farhan, A., & Omar, N. A. (2020). Branding Strategies for Influencing Voter Citizenship Behavior in Indonesia: The Moderating Role of Psychological Contract Violation. *Journal of Political Marketing*, 1-44, Farhat, Z., & Chaney, D. (2021). Introducing destination brand hate: an exploratory study. *Current Issues in Tourism*, *24*(17), 2472–2488. DOI: 10.1080/13683500.2020.1844160

Farhat, Z., & Chaney, D. (2024). A dynamic and comprehensive analysis of the trajectories of destination brand hate following a negative experience. *Journal of Travel & Tourism Marketing*, *41*(2), 208–220. DOI: 10.1080/10548408.2024.2309543

Fehr, B., & Russell, J. A. (1984). Concept of emotion viewed from a prototype perspective. *Journal of Experimental Psychology. General*, *113*(3), 464.

Fetscherin, M. (2019). The five types of brand hate: How they affect consumer behavior. *Journal of Business Research*, *101*, 116–127. DOI: 10.1016/j.jbusres.2019.04.017

Fischer, A., Halperin, E., Canetti, D., & Jasini, A. (2018). Why we hate. *Emotion Review*, *10*(4), 309–320. DOI: 10.1177/1754073917751229

Fournier, S. (1998). Consumers and Their Brands: Developing Relationship Theory in Consumer Research. *The Journal of Consumer Research*, *24*(4), 343–373. DOI: 10.1086/209515

Furnham, A., & Cheng, H. (2019). Personality traits and socio-demographic variables as predictors of political interest and voting behavior in a British cohort. *Journal of Individual Differences*, Gavard-Perret, M.-L. (2008). *Méthodologie de la recherche: réussir son mémoire ou sa thèse en sciences de gestion*. Pearson Education France.

Gois, A. M., Moura, L. R. C., Gonçalves Filho, C., & Chinelato, F. B. (2022). Hate towards brands of educational institutions: She hates for ideology, and he hates for previous experiences. *Journal of Applied Research in Higher Education*. Advance online publication. DOI: 10.1108/JARHE-04-2021-0158

Goodliffe, J., Magleby, D. B., & Scanlan, J. (2025). The Political Power of Negative Motivations. *Political Behavior*. Advance online publication. DOI: 10.1007/s11109-025-10016-8

Gouvernement, L. C. d. (2024). *Les réalisations à mi-mandat du Gouvernement*. Retrieved Juin 2025 from https://www.cg.gov.ma/fr/node/11630

Green, S. B. (1991). How many subjects does it take to do a regression analysis. *Multivariate Behavioral Research, 26*(3), 499–510. DOI: 10.1207/s15327906mbr2603_7

Hadi, K. A., Lasri, R., & El Abderrahmani, A. (2019). Social Media Reputation and Political Popularity: Study of a Moroccan Case. 2019 International Conference on Intelligent Systems and Advanced Computing Sciences (ISACS), Hair, J. F. (2017). *A primer on partial least squares structural equations modeling (PLS-SEM)* (J. F. Hair, Ed.). SAGE.

Hair, J. F., Babin, B. J., Anderson, R. E., & Black, W. C. (2022). *Multivariate Data Analysis*. Cengage Learning. https://books.google.co.ma/books?id=PONXEAAAQBAJ

Hair, J. F., Risher, J. J., Sarstedt, M., & Ringle, C. M. (2019). When to use and how to report the results of PLS-SEM. *European Business Review, 31*(1), 2–24. DOI: 10.1108/EBR-11-2018-0203

Harris, P., & Lock, A. (2001). Establishing the Charles Kennedy brand: A strategy for an election the result of which is a foregone conclusion. *Journal of Marketing Management, 17*(9-10), 943–956.

Hashim, S., & Ahmed, S. (2018). The moderating effect of brand recovery on brand hate and desire for reconciliation: A PLS-MGA approach. *International Journal of Business and Society, 19*(3), 833–850.

Hashim, S., & Kasana, S. (2019). Antecedents of brand hate in the fast food industry. *Spanish Journal of Marketing - ESIC, 23*(2), 227–248. DOI: 10.1108/SJME-10-2018-0047

Hassan, S., & Malika, A. (2023). The Role and Impact of Social Media in Morocco's 2021 Elections. *African Scientific Journal, 3*(19), 078-078,

Hegner, S. M., Fetscherin, M., & van Delzen, M. (2017). Determinants and outcomes of brand hate. *Journal of Product and Brand Management, 26*(1), 13–25. DOI: 10.1108/JPBM-01-2016-1070

Henneberg, S. C. (2006). Leading or following? A theoretical analysis of political marketing postures. *Journal of Political Marketing, 5*(3), 29–46.

Henneberg, S. C., & O'shaughnessy, N. J. (2007). Theory and concept development in political marketing: Issues and an agenda. *Journal of Political Marketing*, *6*(2-3), 5–31.

Hinnebusch, R. A. (2020). *Political parties in MENA*. Routledge., DOI: 10.4324/9780429422706-2

Hirschman, A. O. (1978). Exit, voice, and the state. *World Politics*, *31*(1), 90–107.

Husnain, M., Syed, F., Akhtar, W., & Usman, M. (2020). Effects of brand hate on brand equity: The role of corporate social irresponsibility and similar competitor offer. *MARKETING AND MANAGEMENT OF INNOVATIONS*, (3), 75–86. DOI: 10.21272/mmi.2020.3-06

Husnain, M., Syed, F., Hussain, K., Zhang, Q., Usman, M., & Javed, M. (2022). Explaining the mechanism of brand hate: A mixed-method investigation using moderated mediation in emerging markets. *Kybernetes*. Advance online publication. DOI: 10.1108/K-12-2021-1246

Islam, T., Attiq, S., Hameed, Z., Khokhar, M. N., & Sheikh, Z. (2019). The impact of self-congruity (symbolic and functional) on the brand hate: A study based on self-congruity theory. *British Food Journal*, *121*(1), 71–88. DOI: 10.1108/BFJ-03-2018-0206

Islam, T., Li, J. J., Ali, A., Liang, X. B., Sheikh, Z., & Zafar, A. U. (2020). Mapping online App hate: Determinants and consequences. *Telematics and Informatics*, *51*. Advance online publication. DOI: 10.1016/j.tele.2020.101401

Jabeen, F., Kaur, P., Talwar, S., Malodia, S., & Dhir, A. (2022). I love you, but you let me down! How hate and retaliation damage customer-brand relationship. *Technological Forecasting and Social Change*, *174*. Advance online publication. DOI: 10.1016/j.techfore.2021.121183

Jain, K., & Sharma, I. (2019). Negative outcomes of positive brand relationships. *Journal of Consumer Marketing*, *36*(7), 986–1002. DOI: 10.1108/JCM-07-2018-2764

Joshi, R., & Yadav, R. (2021). Captivating Brand Hate Using Contemporary Metrics: A Structural Equation Modelling Approach. *Vision (Basel)*, *25*(4), 439–447. DOI: 10.1177/0972262919892173

Kaur, H., & Sohal, S. (2019). Examining the relationships between political advertisements, party brand personality, voter satisfaction and party loyalty. *Journal of Indian Business Research*, *11*(3), 263–280.

Kavanagh, D. (1995). *Election campaigning: The new marketing of politics*. Blackwell.

Keller, K. L. (2002). Branding and brand equity. *Handbook of marketing, 151*, Kotler, P. (1999). Political Marketing--Generating Effective Candidates, Campaigns, and Causes. In *Handbook of political marketing* (pp. 3-18). Sage Publications.

Kucuk, S. U. (2010). Negative Double Jeopardy revisited: A longitudinal analysis. *Journal of Brand Management, 18*(2), 150–158. DOI: 10.1057/bm.2010.27

Kucuk, S. U. (2018). Macro-level antecedents of consumer brand hate. *Journal of Consumer Marketing, 35*(5), 555–564. DOI: 10.1108/JCM-10-2017-2389

Kucuk, S. U. (2019a). *Brand Hate: Navigating Consumer Negativity in the Digital World*. Springer International Publishing. http://link.springer.com/10.1007/978-3-030-00380-7

Kucuk, S. U. (2019b). Consumer Brand Hate: Steam rolling whatever I see. *Psychology and Marketing, 36*(5), 431–443. DOI: 10.1002/mar.21175

Kucuk, S. U. (2020). *Consumer Voice: The Democratization of Consumption Markets in the Digital Age*. Springer International Publishing. http://link.springer.com/10.1007/978-3-030-53983-2

Kucuk, S. U. (2021). Developing a theory of brand hate: Where are we now? *STRATEGIC CHANGE-BRIEFINGS IN ENTREPRENEURIAL FINANCE, 30*(1), 29–33. DOI: 10.1002/jsc.2385

Kurtoğlu, R., Özbölük, T., & Hacıhasanoğlu, P. (2022). Revisiting the effects of inward negative emotions on outward negative emotions, brand loyalty, and negative WOM. *Journal of Brand Management, 29*(1), 72–84. DOI: 10.1057/s41262-021-00257-3

Lee, I. C., Chen, E. E., Tsai, C.-H., Yen, N.-S., Chen, A. L. P., & Lin, W.-C. (2016). Voting Intention and Choices: Are Voters Always Rational and Deliberative? *PLoS One, 11*(2), e0148643. DOI: 10.1371/journal.pone.0148643

Lee, M. S. W., Motion, J., & Conroy, D. (2009). Anti-consumption and brand avoidance. *Journal of Business Research, 62*(2), 169–180. DOI: 10.1016/j.jbusres.2008.01.024

MacDonald, E. A., Sherlock, R., & Hogan, J. (2015). Measuring political brand equity in Ireland. *Irish Political Studies, 30*(1), 98–120.

Marcus, G. E., Neuman, W. R., & MacKuen, M. (2000). *Affective intelligence and political judgment*. University of Chicago Press.

Marquart, F., Brosius, A., & de Vreese, C. (2022). United Feelings: The Mediating Role of Emotions in Social Media Campaigns for EU Attitudes and Behavioral Intentions. *Journal of Political Marketing, 21*(1), 85–111. DOI: 10.1080/15377857.2019.1618429

McGregor, S. C. (2018). Personalization, social media, and voting: Effects of candidate self-personalization on vote intention. *New Media & Society*, *20*(3), 1139–1160.

Mednini, L., Noubigh, Z., & Turki, M. D. (2024). Natural Language Processing for Detecting Brand Hate Speech. *Journal of Telecommunications and the Digital Economy*, *12*(1), 486–509. DOI: 10.18080/jtde.v12n1.859

Needham, C., & Smith, G. (2015). Introduction: Political branding. *Journal of Political Marketing*, *14*(1-2), 1–6.

Nguyen, H. N. (2021). Antecedents and Consequences of Brand Hate Among Netizens: Empirical Evidence from Vietnam. *The Journal of Asian Finance, Economics and Business*, *8*(7), 579–589. DOI: 10.13106/jafeb.2021.vol8.no7.0579

Noor, U., Mansoor, M., & Rabbani, S. (2022). Brand hate and retaliation in Muslim consumers: Does offensive advertising matter? *Journal of Islamic Marketing*, *13*(6), 1395–1413. DOI: 10.1108/JIMA-10-2020-0316

Opotow, S. (2005). *Hate*. Conflict, and Moral Exclusion.

Opotow, S., & McClelland, S. I. (2007). The intensification of hating: A theory. *Social Justice Research*, *20*, 68–97. DOI: 10.1007/s11211-007-0033-0

Pantano, E. (2021). When a luxury brand bursts: Modelling the social media viral effects of negative stereotypes adoption leading to brand hate. *Journal of Business Research*, *123*, 117–125. DOI: 10.1016/j.jbusres.2020.09.049

Paz, M. A., Montero-Díaz, J., & Moreno-Delgado, A. (2020). Hate speech: A systematized review. *SAGE Open*, *10*(4), 2158244020973022.

Pich, C., & Newman, B. I. (2020). Evolution of political branding: Typologies, diverse settings and future research. *Journal of Political Marketing*, *19*(1-2), 3–14.

Pinto, O., & Brandão, A. (2021). Antecedents and consequences of brand hate: Empirical evidence from the telecommunication industry. *EUROPEAN JOURNAL OF MANAGEMENT AND BUSINESS ECONOMICS*, *30*(1), 18–35. DOI: 10.1108/EJMBE-04-2020-0084

Platania, S., Morando, M., & Santisi, G. (2017). The phenomenon of brand hate: Analysis of predictors and outcomes. *Quality - Access to Success*, *18*, 342–347.

Rachmat, M. (2014). The impact of political brand trust on voting intention: Evidence from 2013 North Maluku Governor Election. *IUP Journal of Brand Management*, *11*(2), 55.

Roozbahani, E., Salehzadeh, R., & Mirmehdi, S. M. (2022). Evaluating the effects of corporate social irresponsibility on brand hate and its behavioural outcomes. *International Journal of Business Governance and Ethics*, *16*(2), 158–175. DOI: 10.1504/IJBGE.2022.121919

Roy, S. K., Sharma, A., Bose, S., & Singh, G. (2022). Consumer - brand relationship: A brand hate perspective. *Journal of Business Research*, *144*, 1293–1304. DOI: 10.1016/j.jbusres.2022.02.065

Rutter, R. N., Hanretty, C., & Lettice, F. (2018). Political brands: Can parties be distinguished by their online brand personality? *Journal of Political Marketing*, *17*(3), 193–212.

Santos, C., Coelho, A., & Marques, A. (2024). The greenwashing effects on corporate reputation and brand hate, through environmental performance and green perceived risk. *Asia-Pacific Journal of Business Administration*, *16*(3), 655–676. DOI: 10.1108/APJBA-05-2022-0216

Sarkar, A., & Sarkar, J. G., & S, S. (2021). Managing customers' undesirable responses towards hospitality service brands during service failure: The moderating role of other customer perception. *International Journal of Hospitality Management*, *94*. Advance online publication. DOI: 10.1016/j.ijhm.2021.102873

Saunders, M. N. K., Lewis, P., & Thornhill, A. (2019). *Research Methods for Business Students*. Pearson Education. https://books.google.pt/books?id=TMGYDwAAQBAJ

Schuyt, K. (2001). *Alledaagse tolerantie: Een onvolmaakte deugd. De lege tolerantie. Over vrijheid en vrijblijvendheid in Nederland*. Boom.

Sharma, I., Jain, K., Behl, A., Baabdullah, A., Giannakis, M., & Dwivedi, Y. (2023). Examining the motivations of sharing political deepfake videos: The role of political brand hate and moral consciousness. *Internet Research*, *33*(5), 1727–1749. DOI: 10.1108/INTR-07-2022-0563

Sharma, I., Jain, K., & Gupta, R. (2022). The power to voice my hate! Exploring the effect of brand hate and perceived social media power on negative eWOM. *Journal of Asia Business Studies*, *16*(4), 652–675. DOI: 10.1108/JABS-10-2020-0423

Shuv-Ami, A., Toder Alon, A., Loureiro, S. M. C., & Kaufmann, H. R. (2020). A new love–hate scale for sports fans. *International Journal of Sports Marketing & Sponsorship*, *21*(3), 543–560. DOI: 10.1108/IJSMS-11-2019-0122

Sirgy, M. J. (2018). Self-congruity theory in consumer behavior: A little history. *Journal of Global Scholars of Marketing Science*, *28*(2), 197–207. DOI: 10.1080/21639159.2018.1436981

Smith, G. (2001). The 2001 general election: Factors influencing the brand image of political parties and their leaders. *Journal of Marketing Management, 17*(9-10), 989–1006.

Smith, G., & French, A. (2009). The political brand: A consumer perspective. *Marketing Theory, 9*(2), 209–226. DOI: 10.1177/1470593109103068

Sözer, E. G. (2019). Customer based brand tolerance (CBBT): Scale development and validation. *Business &Management Studies: An International Journal, 7*(5), 2610–2635. DOI: 10.15295/bmij.v7i5.1339

Sozer, E. G. (2020). 1. The effects of green marketing practices on green equity and customer tolerance. *Pressacademia, 7*(3), 102–111. DOI: 10.17261/pressacademia.2020.1283

Sözer, E. G. (2020). Relationship Marketing and Customer Based Brand Tolerance (CBBT): An Integrative Approach. *SSRG International Journal of Economics and Management Studies, 7*, 125–137.

Sternberg, R. J., & Sternberg, K. (2008). *The Nature of Hate*. Cambridge University Press., DOI: 10.1017/CBO9780511818707

Susila, I., Dean, D., Yusof, R. N. R., Setyawan, A. A., & Wajdi, F. (2020). Symbolic Political Communication, and Trust: A Young Voters' Perspective of the Indonesian Presidential Election. *Journal of Political Marketing, 19*(1-2), 153–175. DOI: 10.1080/15377857.2019.1652224

Syed, J., & Ali, F. (2021). A pyramid of hate perspective on religious bias, discrimination and violence. *Journal of Business Ethics, 172*, 43–58.

Szmolka, I. (2024). Electoral engineering in autocracies: Effects of the 2021 electoral reform on Morocco's parliamentary elections. *Mediterranean Politics, 29*(5), 700–728. DOI: 10.1080/13629395.2023.2194153

Thiétart, R.-A. (2014). *Méthodes de recherche en management.* Dunod., DOI: 10.3917/dunod.thiet.2014.01

Tolunay, A., & Veloutsou, C. (2025). Don't make me hate you, my love! Perceived brand betrayal and the love-becomes-hate phenomenon. *Journal of Business Research, 187*, 115060. DOI: 10.1016/j.jbusres.2024.115060

Valentino, N. A., Gregorowicz, K., & Groenendyk, E. W. (2009). Efficacy, Emotions and the Habit of Participation. *Political Behavior, 31*(3), 307–330. DOI: 10.1007/s11109-008-9076-7

White, J., & Chernatony, L. D. (2002). New Labour: A study of the creation, development and demise of a political brand. *Journal of Political Marketing*, *1*(2-3), 45–52.

Winther Nielsen, S. (2017). On political brands: A systematic review of the literature. *Journal of Political Marketing*, *16*(2), 118–146.

Yadav, A., & Chakrabarti, S. (2022). Brand hate: A systematic literature review and future research agenda. *International Journal of Consumer Studies*. Advance online publication. DOI: 10.1111/ijcs.12772

Zarantonello, L., Romani, S., Grappi, S., & Bagozzi, R. P. (2016). Brand hate. *Journal of Product and Brand Management*, *25*(1), 11–25. DOI: 10.1108/JPBM-01-2015-0799

Zarantonello, L., Romani, S., Grappi, S., & Fetscherin, M. (2018). Trajectories of brand hate. *Journal of Brand Management*, *25*(6), 549–560. DOI: 10.1057/s41262-018-0105-5

Zhang, C., & Laroche, M. (2020). Brand hate: A multidimensional construct. *Journal of Product and Brand Management*, *30*(3), 392–414. DOI: 10.1108/JPBM-11-2018-2103

Zhang, R., Mustafa, H., & Lin, Y. (2025). Understanding factors that drive destination brand hate in China: Scale development and validation. *Asia Pacific Journal of Tourism Research*, •••, 1–20. DOI: 10.1080/10941665.2024.2437617

Chapter 13

The Impact of Social Media and Digital Campaigns:
Transforming Voter Behavior and Election Outcomes

Ioanna Georgia Eskiadi
http://orcid.org/0009-0001-4950-8644
School of Economic and Social Sciences, Aristotle University of Thessaloniki, Greece

Nikolaos Panagiotou
http://orcid.org/0000-0002-2902-858X
School of Economic and Social Sciences, Aristotle University of Thessaloniki, Greece

ABSTRACT

This chapter explores the transformative impact of social media and digital campaigns on political communication, voter behavior, and election outcomes. By analyzing platforms like TikTok, Facebook, and Instagram, the chapter highlights their roles in mass outreach, micro-targeting, and voter mobilization. Case studies from Brazil, the Philippines, and Romania illustrate how digital campaigns influence electoral processes, showcasing both opportunities for engagement and risks like misinformation and ethical challenges. Methodologically, a mixed-methods approach combines case study analysis and thematic evaluation, focusing on emerging technologies such as AI, augmented reality (AR), and blockchain. Key findings reveal the dual nature of

DOI: 10.4018/979-8-3373-1037-4.ch013

digital campaigning: while it democratizes voter engagement and fosters innovative outreach strategies, it also exacerbates polarization, spreads disinformation, and raises ethical concerns.

INTRODUCTION

The advent of social media has revolutionized political communication, fundamentally altering the relationship between political actors and voters. In the 21st century, platforms such as Facebook, Instagram, YouTube, and TikTok have emerged as essential tools for political campaigns, enabling unprecedented levels of interaction, personalization, and outreach. By bypassing traditional media gatekeepers, these platforms allow political campaigns to connect directly with voters, fostering a sense of immediacy and authenticity in political discourse (Papacharissi, 2015). Social media has become a dual-edged sword, offering innovative avenues for voter engagement while simultaneously introducing ethical and regulatory challenges that threaten the integrity of democratic processes.

The increasing use of TikTok in political campaigns exemplifies this transformation. As a platform characterized by short-form videos and algorithmic amplification, TikTok provides political actors with the opportunity to reach younger, tech-savvy demographics through emotionally resonant content. However, the platform's reliance on virality and engagement optimization also makes it a breeding ground for misinformation, ethical violations, and echo chambers (Lopezosa et al., 2023). These dynamics necessitate a closer examination of the role of social media in shaping voter behavior and influencing election outcomes. This chapter delves into the transformative impact of social media and digital campaigns, with a focus on their implications for voter behavior and democratic integrity. Using case studies from Brazil, the Philippines, and Romania, it explores how these platforms have been employed in diverse sociopolitical contexts to achieve political objectives. The analysis highlights both the opportunities presented by digital campaigning and the associated risks, emphasizing the need for ethical guidelines and media literacy initiatives to mitigate potential harms.

To examine these dynamics in greater depth, the chapter proceeds as follows: it first outlines the theoretical framework underpinning digital campaigning, then presents the methodological approach, followed by three in-depth case studies. A comparative discussion and concluding reflections draw out the broader implications for political communication and democratic integrity.

Recent scholarly work emphasizes TikTok's growing influence as a political tool, particularly in shaping youth voter behavior through algorithmically curated, emotionally resonant content. Sullivan (2023) and Klein highlight how virality on

TikTok is not merely accidental but structurally incentivized, creating an environment where emotionally charged political messages—whether factual or misleading—are rapidly amplified. TikTok's architecture, built around engagement metrics rather than credibility indicators, makes it especially potent for campaigns aiming to reframe narratives or appeal to disaffected youth (Lenhart and Shilton, 2025). This platform-specific logic necessitates a more granular examination of TikTok's role in shaping digital political discourse across diverse sociopolitical contexts.

The theoretical framework guiding this chapter positions social media as a transformative force in political campaigning. By enabling mass outreach, micro-targeting, and real-time voter mobilization, platforms like TikTok and Instagram redefine how campaigns operate and interact with electorates. For instance, Brazil's 2022 presidential election demonstrated the potential of platforms like WhatsApp to engage voters through personalized messaging, while TikTok's role in Romania's 2024 election highlighted the platform's influence on youth mobilization and discourse polarization (Venâncio et al., 2024; BBC News, 2024). At the same time, the risks associated with social media cannot be overlooked. Algorithmic manipulation, the rapid spread of disinformation, and the creation of ideological echo chambers are recurring challenges. These issues are exacerbated by the lack of robust regulatory frameworks and the absence of media literacy among certain voter groups, necessitating a concerted effort to address these gaps.

The Mission of This Chapter

The mission of this chapter is multifaceted. First, it seeks to provide a detailed analysis of the transformative impact of social media on political campaigns. Second, it aims to explore the ethical and practical challenges that arise in digital campaigning, particularly in the context of misinformation and data privacy. Third, the chapter will present case studies to highlight the diverse applications of social media strategies in global elections. Finally, it will examine emerging technologies like augmented reality (AR), virtual reality (VR), and artificial intelligence (AI) and their implications for voter engagement.

Objectives and Structure of the Chapter

The chapter is structured around several core objectives:

1. To Analyze the Transformative Role of Social Media in Political Campaigns: By examining the dynamics of digital platforms, the chapter assesses their capacity to shift the traditional paradigms of voter engagement and mobilization.

2. To Explore Ethical Considerations in Digital Campaigning: With examples such as the Cambridge Analytica scandal, the chapter addresses issues of data privacy, algorithmic bias, and misinformation that undermine electoral integrity (Cadwalladr, 2018).
3. To Evaluate Emerging Technologies in Campaigning: Technologies such as augmented reality (AR), virtual reality (VR), and artificial intelligence (AI) are explored for their potential to both enhance and complicate voter engagement (Aitamurto et al., 2022; Chen, 2022).
4. To Illustrate Through Case Studies: The campaigns of Brazil, the Philippines, and Romania provide contextual insights into the strategies and outcomes of digital campaigns, highlighting lessons that can inform future practices (Arugay & Baquisal, 2022; Venâncio et al., 2024).

Research Significance and Contribution

This chapter contributes to the academic and practical understanding of social media's role in electoral contexts. It bridges the gap between theoretical insights and real-world applications, providing a comprehensive analysis of digital campaigning's dual nature. By incorporating multidisciplinary perspectives and drawing on recent case studies, the chapter underscores the urgency of addressing the ethical and practical challenges associated with digital campaigns. It advocates for innovative regulatory approaches, enhanced media literacy initiatives, and the development of ethical standards to ensure that social media serves as a tool for democratic empowerment rather than a vehicle for its erosion. The discussion in this chapter aligns with broader research on the transformative role of emerging technologies in media and communication, reinforcing the need for a balanced and ethical approach to digital campaigning. Through its in-depth analysis and practical recommendations, the chapter offers valuable insights for academics, policymakers, and campaign strategists navigating the complex landscape of social media and political communication.

THEORETICAL FRAMEWORK

Social Media as a Political Campaigning Tool

Social media platforms have become indispensable tools for political campaigns due to their capacity for mass outreach, micro-targeting, and voter mobilization. TikTok, Facebook, WhatsApp, and Instagram each offer unique affordances—short-form video virality, real-time messaging, influencer culture, and live engagement—that allow campaigns to bypass traditional gatekeepers and connect with voters directly. These affordances are not uniform; their strategic use is shaped by local political cultures, platform popularity, and demographic reach, as evidenced in the campaigns of Brazil, the Philippines, and Romania. Rather than examining platform features in isolation, this chapter focuses on how political actors adapt platform-specific logics to pursue electoral goals.

Social media platforms excel in real-time engagement, enabling political campaigns to respond rapidly to events and voter sentiments. During the 2022 Philippine presidential election, Ferdinand Marcos Jr.'s campaign demonstrated how social media could effectively reshape narratives by employing nostalgia-driven messages on Facebook and TikTok to appeal to younger audiences (Arugay & Baquisal, 2022). This direct engagement strategy creates a sense of immediacy and authenticity, key factors in building voter trust. However, the transformative nature of these platforms is not without challenges. Algorithmic prioritization of engagement often amplifies polarizing content, contributing to ideological echo chambers and misinformation dissemination (Aitamurto et al., 2022). Addressing these challenges requires a nuanced understanding of social media dynamics and robust ethical guidelines to safeguard democratic integrity. In high-choice media environments, where audiences can increasingly personalize their information diets, digital platforms often intensify selective exposure and political fragmentation—posing serious challenges to democratic discourse (Van Aelst et al., 2017).

Micro-targeting and Personalization

One of the defining features of social media in political campaigns is its capacity for micro-targeting and personalized messaging. This approach leverages advanced data analytics and machine learning to segment audiences based on demographics, behaviors, and preferences, enabling campaigns to craft tailored messages that resonate with specific voter groups. For example, during Brazil's 2022 presidential election, WhatsApp was widely used to deliver highly localized and culturally relevant messages, fostering a sense of personal connection with voters (Venâncio et al., 2024). Advanced algorithms and big data analytics allow campaigns to personalize their outreach by analyzing user behaviors, preferences, and interactions. This approach enables campaigns to deliver tailored messages that resonate on an individual level, enhancing engagement and effectiveness. For example, political campaigns in Brazil have effectively utilized WhatsApp to send targeted messages to voters, often in their local dialects, fostering a sense of personal connection and trust (Venâncio et al., 2024).

While micro-targeting enhances the precision and efficiency of campaign strategies, it also raises ethical concerns regarding voter privacy and data security.

The Cambridge Analytica scandal underscored the dangers of exploiting voter data without consent, highlighting the need for stricter regulatory frameworks to ensure transparency and accountability (Cadwalladr & Graham-Harrison, 2018). Additionally, the ethical implications of using psychographic profiling in campaigns cannot be ignored, as such practices may manipulate voter behavior by exploiting emotional vulnerabilities (Chen, 2022). The personalization of messages also risks deepening societal divisions by reinforcing preexisting biases and limiting exposure to diverse viewpoints. This phenomenon, known as filter bubbling, has been shown to polarize electorates and reduce informed decision-making, posing significant challenges to democratic processes (Wei et al., 2022). The theoretical and empirical literature on micro-targeting warns that these practices can undermine democratic deliberation. Kreiss (2017) argue that personalized political messaging, enabled by large-scale data harvesting and psychographic profiling, creates a "quantified persuasion infrastructure" that narrows the range of political discourse and weakens collective civic understanding. Similarly, Zuiderveen Borgesius et al. (2018) caution that micro-targeting may fragment public debate and enable opaque campaign tactics that disproportionately influence undecided or low-information voters. These insights reinforce the need to address the ethical implications of micro-targeting, not only from a privacy standpoint but also in terms of its broader consequences for electoral fairness.

Voter Mobilization

Social media platforms are uniquely positioned to mobilize voters, providing tools for grassroots organization, real-time event promotion, and voter turnout campaigns. Their interactivity and immediacy make them effective in engaging first-time voters and younger demographics, who are often less likely to participate in traditional political processes (Nyabola, 2018). In Kenya's 2017 general election, for instance, social media platforms like Facebook were instrumental in encouraging voter registration and participation, particularly among youth. TikTok has emerged as a powerful mobilization tool due to its emphasis on creativity and engagement. In Romania's 2024 presidential election, far-right candidate Călin Georgescu capitalized on TikTok's viral potential to energize disillusioned and younger voters, using emotionally charged and humor-laden content to create a sense of community and purpose (France 24, 2024). This case underscores the platform's ability to galvanize voter bases that may otherwise remain disengaged.

However, the mobilization potential of social media also comes with risks. The same tools used to inspire civic engagement can be weaponized to spread disinformation and amplify divisive rhetoric, as seen in various global elections. Ensuring ethical use of these platforms requires collaboration between policymakers, platforms, and civil society to promote responsible content dissemination and prevent misuse. The immediacy and interactivity of social media make it a powerful tool for mobilizing voters. Campaigns can use platforms to encourage voter registration, participation in rallies, and grassroots activism. This was evident in Kenya's 2017 general election, where social media platforms like Facebook were used extensively to encourage voter turnout, particularly among young and first-time voters (Nyabola, 2018).

Ethical Concerns

Despite its potential, digital campaigning raises significant ethical concerns. The misuse of voter data, algorithmic manipulation, and the spread of misinformation are critical challenges that undermine the integrity of democratic processes. The ethical implications of data privacy in digital campaigning came to the forefront during the Cambridge Analytica scandal, where personal data of millions of Facebook users were exploited without consent to influence voter behavior (Cadwalladr & Graham-Harrison, 2018). Such practices not only breach privacy but also erode trust in democratic institutions. Social media algorithms prioritize content that maximizes user engagement, often promoting sensational or polarizing material. This creates an environment where misinformation can thrive, influencing voter perceptions and decisions. Research shows that voters are more likely to believe misinformation when it aligns with their preexisting biases, a phenomenon exacerbated by algorithmic curation (Aitamurto et al., 2022).

The ethical challenges posed by digital campaigning are multifaceted, encompassing issues of data privacy, algorithmic bias, and the proliferation of misinformation. The Cambridge Analytica scandal remains a pivotal example, demonstrating how the misuse of personal data can undermine trust in democratic systems and raise serious privacy concerns (Cadwalladr, 2018). Furthermore, the reliance on algorithms to prioritize content often results in the amplification of sensational or polarizing material, as platforms prioritize engagement over accuracy (Aitamurto et al., 2022).

In this context, algorithmic amplification raises ethical red flags, as platforms often optimize for engagement rather than democratic discourse. This leads to disproportionate visibility for emotionally charged or polarizing content, a phenomenon amplified by opaque recommendation systems. As Gillespie (2018) argues, algorithms are not neutral; they encode commercial priorities that frequently conflict with civic goals. Therefore, transparency in algorithm design—often referred to as "algorithmic explainability"—should be a regulatory priority. Scholars have proposed algorithm audits and the creation of independent oversight bodies to ensure that recommendation systems do not systematically disadvantage political pluralism or favor specific ideological content (Helberger et al., 2018).

The spread of misinformation and disinformation during electoral campaigns is particularly alarming. Platforms like WhatsApp have been inundated with fake news during key elections, such as India's 2019 general election, influencing voter perceptions and sowing societal discord (Nyabola, 2018). The rapid dissemination of false information poses significant risks to electoral integrity, necessitating comprehensive regulatory frameworks and proactive fact-checking initiatives. Addressing these ethical concerns requires a dual approach: enhancing media literacy among voters to empower critical evaluation of digital content and implementing robust platform-specific moderation strategies. Additionally, emerging technologies like blockchain offer promising solutions for increasing transparency in campaign financing and voting systems, reducing opportunities for fraud and manipulation (Lopezosa et al., 2023).

The increasing influence of digital platforms on elections has prompted urgent discussions around regulatory oversight. While many countries have introduced basic digital campaign finance disclosure laws, enforcement remains inconsistent, particularly on cross-border platforms like TikTok, YouTube, and Meta. Existing legislation, such as the EU's Digital Services Act and the U.S. Federal Election Commission's rules on online political advertising, attempt to address transparency in digital spending and content moderation. However, loopholes persist in platform accountability and algorithmic governance (Bloch-Wehba, 2021). Moreover, there is a lack of unified global standards addressing platform responsibilities during elections. Scholars advocate for legally binding obligations that compel platforms to disclose algorithmic curation methods and political ad targeting criteria. Enhanced regulatory frameworks should also require platforms to establish independent election integrity teams, improve content moderation during election periods, and cooperate with electoral commissions. Such legal structures are vital to ensuring digital campaigning remains transparent, equitable, and accountable. Political marketing theory highlights the increasing hybridization of campaign strategies, where parties blend traditional messaging with data-driven digital outreach to better align with voter expectations across diverse platforms (Chadwick, 2017).

Misinformation and Disinformation

The rapid dissemination of false information on social media poses a significant threat to electoral integrity. For instance, during the 2019 Indian general elections, platforms like WhatsApp were inundated with fake news and doctored images, which influenced voter perceptions and sowed discord (Nyabola, 2018). Addressing these challenges requires robust regulatory frameworks and media literacy initiatives. The proliferation of false and misleading information, whether deliberate (disinformation) or inadvertent (misinformation), poses a significant challenge to the integrity of electoral processes worldwide. Social media platforms, with their vast reach and virality, have exacerbated these issues, enabling the rapid dissemination of content that bypasses traditional editorial checks and fact-verification mechanisms. These dynamics have profound consequences, influencing voter behavior, polarizing societies, and eroding trust in democratic institutions (Nyabola, 2018; Lopezosa et al., 2023).

The spread of misinformation and disinformation is amplified by the algorithmic nature of digital platforms, which prioritize engagement over accuracy. Sensational and emotionally charged content is more likely to go viral, creating an environment where false narratives can gain traction before they are debunked (Aitamurto et al., 2022). Platforms such as WhatsApp and TikTok have become breeding grounds for such content, as their design encourages rapid sharing and algorithm-driven amplification. During India's 2019 general elections, for example, WhatsApp was inundated with doctored images and fake news, influencing voter perceptions and sowing societal discord (Nyabola, 2018). One key characteristic of disinformation is its ability to exploit cognitive and emotional biases. Campaigns often use false endorsements, doctored images, and deepfakes to manipulate voter perceptions. During Brazil's 2022 presidential election, both Jair Bolsonaro and Luiz Inácio Lula da Silva's campaigns relied heavily on WhatsApp and Telegram. Bolsonaro's team disseminated memes and tailored videos to rural and less digitally literate populations, while Lula's campaign partnered with fact-checking organizations to counter false narratives. Despite these efforts, misinformation targeting both candidates continued to spread, showcasing the double-edged nature of private messaging platforms (Venâncio et al., 2024).

Emerging research underscores the systemic nature of disinformation across platforms like WhatsApp and TikTok. Wardle and Derakhshan (2017) propose a framework of "information disorder" that categorizes the ecosystem of disinformation as a mix of emotional manipulation, coordinated amplification, and cognitive bias exploitation. Their work complements findings by Tucker et al. (2018), who stress that algorithmic platforms exacerbate political polarization by reinforcing affective partisanship and echo chambers. Moreover, Guess, Nagler, and Tucker (2019) show that while the overall spread of fake news may be limited to a subset of users, these individuals can have outsized influence within digital networks—especially when aided by platform design that favors engagement over accuracy.

In the Philippines' 2022 presidential election, Ferdinand Marcos Jr. used nostalgic messaging on TikTok to reshape perceptions of his family's controversial legacy. His campaign effectively employed memes, influencer collaborations, and subtle rewriting of historical narratives to appeal to younger voters. This strategy not only influenced voter behavior but also raised ethical concerns about the manipulation of historical truths (Arugay & Baquisal, 2022). Similarly, in Romania's 2024 presidential race, far-right candidate Călin Georgescu leveraged TikTok's algorithm to amplify his anti-establishment rhetoric. His campaign targeted disillusioned voters with emotionally charged content, often containing factually inaccurate claims about the European Union and national sovereignty. Fact-checkers documented several instances of disinformation, highlighting the ethical challenges associated with the platform's engagement-focused algorithms (France 24, 2024). The consequences of misinformation and disinformation are manifold. Firstly, these practices deepen societal polarization by creating echo chambers where voters are exposed only to information that reinforces their preexisting beliefs. Social media algorithms exacerbate this by curating content that aligns with users' preferences, limiting their exposure to diverse perspectives (Wei et al., 2022). Secondly, misinformation manipulates voter behavior by exploiting emotional triggers, steering undecided voters with deceptive or false narratives. Lastly, the pervasive spread of false information erodes trust in democratic institutions, making voters more skeptical of election outcomes and governance structures (Cadwalladr, 2018). During the 2022 Brazilian election, fact-checkers were only able to address 45% of the flagged false claims on WhatsApp and Telegram, allowing the remaining disinformation to continue circulating and potentially sway undecided voters (Nyhan & Reifler, 2015). The encrypted nature of these platforms created a regulatory blind spot that significantly hindered transparency.

Media Ecology and Platformization

The concept of media ecology explores the dynamic interactions between media, technology, and society, emphasizing how communication platforms shape human interaction and information dissemination. Emerging digital ecosystems, characterized by convergence, redefine these relationships. Platforms like Roblox and TikTok exemplify this shift, transitioning from mere intermediaries to active participants in shaping user experiences and communication patterns (Willig, 2022). The platformization of media extends the role of journalists and audiences, transforming newsrooms into hybrid ecosystems. Media platforms now act as gatekeepers, prioritizing engagement and algorithmically amplifying content that captures user attention, often at the expense of nuanced discourse (Willig, 2022). Immersive ecosystems such as the metaverse further deepen this transformation by integrating AR and VR technologies, creating spaces where users can actively participate and co-create narratives, a stark departure from traditional, one-directional media models.

Audience-centric journalism

The shift toward audience-centric journalism reflects the growing demand for personalized, engaging, and participatory content. Generations Z and Alpha prioritize immersive and interactive experiences, which traditional media often fails to deliver. Platforms like Roblox and Fortnite provide compelling evidence of this trend, where users engage in virtual worlds for social interaction, creative expression, and entertainment (Everyrealm, 2023). Immersive journalism leverages VR and AR to meet these expectations by creating emotionally resonant experiences that foster deeper audience engagement. For instance, VR news stories provide telepresence, allowing audiences to experience events as though they were physically present, enhancing perceptions of credibility and emotional connection (Kang et al., 2019). This paradigm requires media organizations to align their strategies with the evolving habits of these digital-native audiences, ensuring that content remains relevant and impactful.

Blockchain integration

Blockchain technology emerges as a critical tool in addressing the challenges of transparency, misinformation, and trust in journalism. By enabling decentralized and immutable records, blockchain ensures that every piece of content is traceable, fostering accountability in news production and distribution (Niloy et al., 2024). For instance, blockchain-based platforms can verify the authenticity of sources, track edits, and flag unauthorized changes to content. This technology also facilitates transparency in newsroom operations, particularly in areas like funding and content sponsorship, where conflicts of interest often arise. Additionally, blockchain's decentralized nature aligns with the principles of participatory journalism, empowering audiences to contribute to and validate journalistic processes. Integrating blockchain into journalism not only enhances trust but also strengthens the profession's commitment to ethical standards in the digital age.

METHODOLOGY

To examine how these dynamics materialize in real-world contexts, the following section outlines the methodological framework adopted for this study. This study uses a case study methodology to analyze the role of digital platforms, particularly TikTok, in political campaigns. By focusing on specific electoral campaigns, the research seeks to uncover patterns, strategies, and outcomes that define voter engagement and content amplification in the context of social media. Case study methods are well-suited to this inquiry as they allow for in-depth exploration of complex phenomena within specific sociopolitical and cultural settings (Wimmer & Dominick, 2013). This approach also facilitates cross-case comparisons, enabling the identification of both universal trends and unique aspects of digital campaigning (Kerlinger, 1966).

The case studies chosen include notable examples such as the 2024 Romanian Presidential Election, the 2022 Philippine Presidential Election, and the 2022 Brazilian Presidential Election. These campaigns were selected because of their significant reliance on TikTok to influence voter mobilization, narrative shaping, and public opinion. The diversity of geopolitical contexts across these cases enhances the study's ability to generalize findings while retaining the specificity required to understand individual campaign strategies. A key aspect of the methodology is the integration of platform-specific metrics to quantify voter engagement and content dissemination. TikTok metrics, such as views, engagement rates (likes, comments, and shares), and hashtag trends, are central to the analysis. The study also examines content features, such as narrative structures, emotional appeals, and video formats, to identify strategies used to resonate with audiences. Additionally, sentiment analysis is employed to gauge public reactions and uncover polarizing or resonant themes within campaign-related content. By combining these metrics with qualitative narrative analysis, the research captures both the measurable and interpretive dimensions of digital campaigns (Östlund et al., 2011; Driscoll et al., 2007).

Data collection relies on a combination of primary and secondary sources. Primary data include publicly available TikTok videos, campaign-related hashtags, and social media analytics. Secondary data, such as academic studies, media reports, and official election documents, provide contextual depth and support triangulation of findings. Content coding is conducted using predefined and emergent categories derived from existing frameworks and adapted to TikTok's unique platform characteristics (Wimmer & Dominick, 2013). The analysis includes both statistical and thematic methods. Quantitative data, such as views and engagement rates, are statistically analyzed to identify patterns and measure campaign effectiveness. Concurrently, qualitative thematic analysis explores deeper meanings in narratives and audience responses, focusing on how campaign messages are crafted and received (Lund, 2012). This dual approach ensures a comprehensive understanding of both the strategies employed and their impact on voter engagement. Brandwatch, a social media analysis tool, is employed solely for Case Study 3, the 2024 Romanian Presidential Campaign. This choice is necessitated by Brandwatch's access limitations, which restrict data analysis to the most recent two years. For other case studies, alternative methods such as manual content analysis and secondary data sources will be used, as Brandwatch's time restrictions preclude analysis of these earlier campaigns.

Ethical considerations are a priority throughout the study. All data used are publicly accessible, and no private user information is collected. The study also addresses broader ethical challenges, including algorithmic bias, data privacy concerns, and the potential for misinformation. These considerations align with principles of responsible research, ensuring the integrity and social relevance of the findings (Driscoll et al., 2007). This methodology provides a robust framework for analyzing the influence of TikTok and similar platforms on voter engagement and political discourse. By integrating quantitative metrics with qualitative insights, the research offers a nuanced perspective on how digital platforms shape electoral processes. The findings contribute to a deeper understanding of the opportunities and challenges posed by emerging technologies for democratic practices.

To deepen analytical rigor, the study employed a hybrid coding strategy combining deductive categories (e.g., national pride, anti-establishment rhetoric, nostalgia) with inductively derived subthemes emerging from qualitative immersion in campaign content. TikTok's architecture informed content coding criteria, with emphasis on emotional tone, audiovisual techniques, and virality triggers. The integration of Brandwatch for the Romanian case allowed cross-validation of engagement metrics with sentiment patterns, while earlier campaigns relied on content analysis and secondary reporting. This approach enables comparative insight into how emotionally resonant messaging differs across platform logics and sociopolitical contexts.

Research Questions

1. How does the personalization of social media content, through micro-targeting and algorithmic curation, shape voter behavior and influence electoral outcomes across diverse demographics?
2. What ethical challenges emerge from integrating AI, AR, and blockchain technologies in political campaigns, and how can these challenges be addressed to ensure democratic integrity?

CASE STUDIES

This chapter employs three international case studies—Brazil (2022), the Philippines (2022), and Romania (2024)—to illustrate the diverse ways in which social media platforms, particularly TikTok, have influenced modern political campaigning. These cases were selected based on their varying sociopolitical landscapes, levels of platform penetration, and contrasting campaign strategies. Together, they offer a comparative lens on digital campaigning across different contexts, highlighting key themes such as algorithmic amplification, micro-targeting, and emotional narrative construction.

The methodology employed in this chapter is a case study analysis, which provides an in-depth exploration of specific campaigns to understand the dynamics of social media in elections. Two diverse examples are highlighted to illustrate the potential and pitfalls of digital campaigning.

Case Study 1: Brazil's 2022 Presidential Election

The 2022 Brazilian presidential election between Luiz Inácio Lula da Silva and incumbent Jair Bolsonaro witnessed extensive use of WhatsApp and Telegram as campaign tools. Bolsonaro's campaign amplified its reliance on private messaging platforms, where it disseminated memes, videos, and voice messages tailored to specific voter groups. These platforms were instrumental in reaching rural and less digitally literate populations. Lula's campaign, on the other hand, invested heavily in fact-checking initiatives, partnering with media organizations to counter the spread of fake news. Social media platforms like YouTube and Instagram were utilized to present a progressive vision, engaging younger voters and urban audiences. Despite these efforts, the election underscored the persistent issue of disinformation, as both sides accused each other of spreading false narratives. This case demonstrates the double-edged nature of private messaging platforms in political campaigns, where personalized communication is often marred by misinformation (Venâncio et al., 2024).

The Brazilian presidential election between Jair Bolsonaro and Luiz Inácio Lula da Silva underscores how private messaging platforms can redefine political outreach. Bolsonaro's campaign strategically used WhatsApp and Telegram to disseminate memes, videos, and voice messages, often tailored to resonate with rural and less digitally literate audiences (Venâncio et al., 2024). This micro-targeted approach exemplifies the paradigm of personalization, where culturally relevant content fosters stronger voter engagement. Notably, these platforms allowed Bolsonaro's team to bypass traditional media, directly reaching millions of voters with tailored messaging.

Conversely, Lula's campaign relied on partnerships with fact-checking organizations and used social media platforms like Instagram and YouTube to counter disinformation and mobilize urban, younger demographics. These efforts align with studies highlighting the role of fact-checking in mitigating disinformation, as outlined by Nyhan and Reifler (2015). However, both campaigns struggled with misinformation dissemination. For example, Bolsonaro's camp faced allegations of spreading false narratives about electoral fraud, while Lula's campaign encountered challenges in debunking fake news targeting his economic policies. The Brazilian case highlights how algorithmic amplification within private messaging systems, combined with their encrypted nature, can contribute to ideological polarization. Venâncio et al. (2024) argue that private platforms lack the transparency and moderation of public social networks, exacerbating the spread of sensational content. This aligns with Cadwalladr's (2018) analysis of the Cambridge Analytica scandal, which emphasized how unregulated digital environments can manipulate voter behavior. Ethically, Brazil's election underscores the need for stricter regulations on private messaging platforms. Blockchain-based transparency mechanisms, as proposed by Niloy et al. (2024), could offer potential solutions by ensuring traceability and accountability in content dissemination. This case also highlights the critical importance of media literacy programs to equip voters with tools for evaluating digital content critically, as recommended by Aitamurto et al. (2022).

The 2022 Brazilian Presidential Election between Jair Bolsonaro and Luiz Inácio Lula da Silva demonstrated the transformative role of private messaging platforms like WhatsApp and Telegram in modern political campaigns. These platforms served as critical tools for engaging diverse demographics, facilitating tailored messaging, and amplifying narratives, while also presenting significant challenges related to misinformation and ideological polarization. WhatsApp's ubiquity in Brazil enabled Bolsonaro's campaign to scale micro-targeted outreach, leveraging regional dialects and cultural idioms to mobilize rural voters, yet at the cost of transparency and moderation capacity (Rossini, Mont'Alverne, & Kalogeropoulos, 2023). Bolsonaro's campaign strategically leveraged the platform to reach rural and less digitally literate populations through highly localized and culturally resonant messages. This approach bypassed traditional media, enabling direct communication with millions of voters. Similarly, Telegram emerged as a key platform, with over 620,000 messages analyzed from 256 politically oriented groups, underscoring its importance in mobilizing communities and amplifying campaign narratives (Venâncio et al., 2024).

While these platforms allowed for personalized and efficient voter engagement, they also became conduits for misinformation. Content analysis revealed that approximately 23% of all political material shared via WhatsApp and Telegram contained false or misleading claims, often focusing on electoral fraud or economic policies (Nyhan & Reifler, 2015). Bolsonaro's campaign faced criticism for the dissemination of unverified claims, while Lula's campaign responded by partnering with independent fact-checking organizations to counter disinformation. Despite these efforts, fact-checkers were only able to address 45% of flagged false claims, highlighting the rapid pace and volume of misinformation spread (Nyhan & Reifler, 2015). The contrasting strategies of the two candidates illustrate the diverse uses of social media platforms in shaping voter behavior. Bolsonaro's campaign focused on micro-targeting through private messaging, while Lula's team utilized Instagram and YouTube to engage urban youth and promote a progressive vision (Venâncio et al., 2024). This demographic targeting reinforced ideological echo chambers, with 68% of voters admitting that they only interacted with content aligning with their preexisting beliefs (Rossini, Mont'Alverne, & Kalogeropoulos, 2023). Such dynamics exacerbated polarization, a key challenge in the digital age.

Ethical concerns also emerged from the widespread use of encrypted platforms, which limited transparency and regulatory oversight. The closed nature of private messaging systems made them less accessible for monitoring and moderation compared to public social media platforms (Cadwalladr, 2018). In response, Brazilian authorities implemented measures such as content labeling and source transparency initiatives. However, these interventions struggled to keep pace with the scale and speed of digital misinformation (Nyhan & Reifler, 2015). This case study underscores the dual-edged nature of private messaging platforms in electoral contexts. While they facilitate direct and personalized voter engagement, they also amplify challenges related to misinformation and polarization. The Brazilian election highlights the need for enhanced regulatory mechanisms and platform accountability, as well as the integration of media literacy initiatives to empower voters to critically evaluate digital content. The lessons drawn from this case can inform future practices in political campaigning globally. While Brazil's election emphasizes the strategic use of private messaging platforms, the following case from the Philippines explores how emotionally driven narratives reshaped historical perceptions using public-facing platforms like TikTok.

Case Study 2: Philippines 2022 Presidential Election

Ferdinand "Bongbong" Marcos Jr.'s victory in the 2022 Philippine presidential election illustrates how digital campaigns exploit narrative engineering to reshape collective memory. TikTok, in particular, played a pivotal role in this process. As a platform structurally optimized for emotionally resonant, short-form content, TikTok enabled the campaign to recast the Marcos legacy as a nostalgic "golden age." This aligns with Klein's concept of algorithmic populism, where virality is politically weaponized to override factual historical accounts. Through influencer collaborations and viral memes, Marcos's team embedded this narrative into TikTok's recommendation system, reaching millions of young voters with limited historical awareness.

In the Philippines, Ferdinand Marcos Jr.'s victory showcased the power of TikTok in crafting emotionally resonant narratives. His campaign leveraged nostalgic messaging to reframe the controversial Marcos family legacy, targeting younger voters with limited historical knowledge (Arugay & Baquisal, 2022). Through short-form videos, memes, and influencer collaborations, TikTok became a tool for reshaping public perception. For instance, videos romanticizing the "Golden Age" of Marcos Sr.'s regime gained significant traction, blending historical revisionism with emotional appeals.

This case illustrates the paradigm of narrative engineering, where social media content reshapes historical truths to align with campaign objectives. Arugay & Baquisal, (2022) highlight how TikTok's algorithm amplifies emotionally charged content, creating echo chambers that reinforce existing biases. Influencer-driven campaigns further blurred ethical lines, as many voters remained unaware of the financial or ideological affiliations of these content creators. Marcos Jr.'s opponent, Leni Robredo, countered these strategies by mobilizing grassroots volunteers through Twitter and other platforms. Her campaign relied on crowdsourced fact-checking initiatives and emotional storytelling to engage supporters. However, the sheer scale and sophistication of Marcos Jr.'s TikTok strategy overwhelmed these efforts, emphasizing the limitations of traditional fact-checking in combating digital misinformation.

The Philippine election also raised concerns about algorithmic bias and transparency. Lopezosa et al. (2023) argue that platforms like TikTok prioritize engagement over accuracy, making them susceptible to the rapid spread of disinformation. Furthermore, the lack of robust regulatory frameworks in the Philippines allowed campaigns to exploit these vulnerabilities with minimal oversight. Addressing these challenges requires a multi-pronged approach, including enhanced platform accountability, stricter influencer disclosure policies, and educational initiatives to promote digital literacy.

The 2022 Philippines Presidential Election illustrates the significant influence of TikTok in modern political campaigning, particularly in shaping voter perceptions and engagement. Ferdinand "Bongbong" Marcos Jr.'s campaign capitalized on TikTok's algorithm-driven structure and its popularity among younger demographics. The campaign achieved considerable traction, with campaign-related hashtags such as #MarcosGoldenAge garnering over 500 million views. High-performing content consistently reached millions of engagements, including likes, shares, and comments. These metrics demonstrate the platform's capacity to amplify resonant narratives, especially through collaborations with over 50 influencers, which led to a notable increase in follower engagement. Surveys indicated that 65% of voters aged 18–25 were exposed to Marcos Jr.'s TikTok content, with a substantial proportion acknowledging its influence on their political perceptions.

Qualitatively, the campaign strategically employed nostalgic messaging to reframe the Marcos family legacy. Videos romanticizing the governance of Marcos Sr. emphasized themes of economic prosperity and unity, often omitting or downplaying controversial historical elements. TikTok's short-form video format and emotionally charged content facilitated the spread of this narrative, resonating strongly with younger voters who may have limited knowledge of the historical context. The campaign further utilized memes, music overlays, and emotionally driven visuals to create a sense of pride and optimism. Fact-checkers, however, identified a substantial volume of misinformation, with approximately 28% of campaign content containing manipulated statistics or exaggerated claims about Marcos Sr.'s governance. Comparative analysis highlights the disparities in digital strategy between Marcos Jr. and his opponent, Leni Robredo. Marcos Jr.'s campaign outpaced Robredo's in both content production and engagement. His team produced over 1,000 TikTok videos, compared to Robredo's 350, demonstrating a more aggressive content strategy. Sentiment analysis of TikTok interactions revealed that 75% of comments on Marcos-related posts expressed positive sentiment, compared to 45% for Robredo. This disparity underscores the effectiveness of Marcos's narrative strategies and his campaign's ability to dominate voter discourse through digital platforms.

Despite its success, the campaign raised critical ethical concerns. Many influencers promoting Marcos's narratives failed to disclose their affiliations, creating transparency issues. Moreover, TikTok's algorithm, which prioritizes emotionally resonant material, often amplified polarizing or misleading content. These dynamics exacerbated the spread of disinformation, posing significant risks to democratic processes. The campaign's success also highlighted TikTok's role in reinforcing ideological silos, where voters were predominantly exposed to content aligning with their existing beliefs. This phenomenon limited exposure to diverse viewpoints, further deepening polarization within the electorate. The findings align with broader literature on digital campaigning, which emphasizes the transformative role of emotional engagement and algorithmic amplification in shaping voter behavior. TikTok's design enables campaigns to craft and disseminate narratives that are both highly targeted and emotionally compelling. However, this capacity also intensifies challenges associated with disinformation and ethical accountability. Scholars argue that platforms like TikTok prioritize engagement metrics over content accuracy, which can undermine the integrity of democratic discourse.

To address these challenges, regulatory reforms and media literacy initiatives are essential. Enhanced guidelines requiring influencers to disclose affiliations can improve transparency, while stricter platform accountability measures are needed to counter algorithmic bias. Media literacy programs targeting younger voters can empower them to critically evaluate digital content, mitigating the risks of misinformation. Additionally, the integration of blockchain technology could enhance content authentication, providing a decentralized mechanism to verify the legitimacy of campaign materials. These measures are necessary to balance the benefits of digital campaigning with the imperative to safeguard democratic integrity. The 2022 Philippines Presidential Election highlights the dual-edged nature of social media in political campaigns. While platforms like TikTok democratize voter engagement and amplify diverse voices, they also magnify risks related to disinformation, polarization, and ethical challenges. These findings underscore the urgent need for interdisciplinary approaches combining technological, regulatory, and educational strategies to ensure that social media enhances rather than undermines democratic processes. In contrast to the influencer-driven strategy in the Philippines, the Romanian case offers a glimpse into grassroots-algorithmic saturation via TikTok and Telegram, reflecting newer forms of decentralized digital mobilization.

Case Study 3: 2024 Romanian Presidential Elections

The 2024 Romanian presidential race introduced a unique and striking example of TikTok's growing influence on political campaigns, particularly through the unexpected rise of far-right candidate Călin Georgescu. Known for his skepticism towards NATO and the European Union, as well as his pro-Russian rhetoric, Georgescu's campaign utilized TikTok to craft an unconventional and highly effective outreach strategy (BBC News, 2024; France 24, 2024). By capitalizing on the platform's short-form video format and algorithm-driven content amplification, his campaign resonated with a broad audience, including disillusioned voters and younger demographics (Politico, 2024a). TikTok was central to Georgescu's mobilization efforts. His campaign relied heavily on the platform's ability to amplify emotionally charged and controversial content. Short videos of Georgescu delivering impassioned speeches about national sovereignty and anti-establishment ideals were designed to go viral (France 24, 2024). This content, often paired with humor and memes, created an emotional connection with a younger generation of voters who were typically disengaged from traditional political discourse. The campaign's messaging, crafted to portray Georgescu as an outsider challenging the status quo, quickly gained traction, with hashtags like #RomanianSovereignty trending nationally and internationally (Telegraph, 2024).

Georgescu's strategy also relied on collaborations with influencers and user-generated content, which expanded his campaign's reach organically (Politico, 2024b). By presenting himself as an authentic voice of the people, Georgescu consistently led in TikTok engagement metrics, far surpassing his opponents. This dominance on TikTok translated into increased visibility, transforming him into a significant contender in Romania's presidential race. His campaign also demonstrated how a single platform could shift voter demographics, energizing young and rural populations often disconnected from mainstream political narratives. However, this case also underscored the ethical challenges associated with social media in political campaigns. Fact-checking organizations identified multiple instances of disinformation within Georgescu's TikTok content, ranging from exaggerated claims about European Union policies to distorted narratives about Romania's sovereignty (France 24, 2024). TikTok's algorithmic bias further exacerbated these issues by promoting polarizing content that reinforced ideological silos. This not only deepened social divisions but also raised questions about the platform's role in shaping political realities (Politico, 2024a). Additionally, analysts noted potential links between pro-Russian messaging and foreign influence campaigns, sparking concerns about external interference in Romanian politics (Telegraph, 2024).

The implications of Georgescu's campaign extended beyond Romania, igniting debates about the role of social media in electoral processes across Europe. His success on TikTok highlighted the platform's potential to disrupt traditional electoral dynamics, but it also showcased the risks of misinformation, polarization, and foreign influence (BBC News, 2024). The campaign became a cautionary tale for policymakers and social media platforms alike, emphasizing the need for stronger regulatory frameworks and media literacy initiatives to safeguard democratic systems (Politico, 2024b). The case of Călin Georgescu illustrates how social media, particularly TikTok, can serve as both a democratizing tool and a destabilizing force in political campaigns. It highlights the urgency of addressing the ethical and practical challenges posed by these platforms to ensure they enhance, rather than undermine, the integrity of democratic processes.

The victory in the first round of the presidential elections achieved by the independent candidate with pro-Russian views, Călin Georgescu, surprised the press, major political parties, and the public alike. Discussions have focused on the power of TikTok as a platform, the way information spread, and the target audience of posts promoting the candidate. It is crucial to analyze the mechanism used by Georgescu's supporters online, demonstrating that a strong campaign can be conducted solely through platforms and a well-organized "army" of volunteers. The Telegram group "Propagator - Get involved too, Romania's Revival, Food Water and Energy, Călin Georgescu" serves as an example, likely among many, showcasing the level of organization and tactics employed by the "propagators" (a term used by the group admins for volunteers). Local branches existed through Telegram channels for supporters, with reward systems for the "best editors" of electoral materials and explanatory videos with clear, concise instructions designed to push the content up TikTok's algorithm.

The group "Propagator - Get involved too, Romania's Revival, Food Water and Energy, Călin Georgescu" was founded on Telegram on June 15, 2024, and, as of this article's writing, has exceeded 2,000 members, with numbers continuing to grow. Information and video clips featuring Călin Georgescu—mostly short ones aimed at capturing attention quickly on TikTok—are posted here. Volunteers also receive instructions on how to post, including suggested captions. It's important to note that group members were not allowed to post themselves; discussions took place on separate Telegram channels. The campaign, which also involved online influencers, used targeted keywords for covert promotion of the candidate. However, the grassroots tactics employed directly by ordinary people warrant deeper analysis. Among the first messages posted by the group admins in June were calls for members to repost clips and materials shared on Telegram but with their own "original contribution."

Volunteers were instructed as follows: admins posted batches of short video clips featuring the candidate, and the "army" of propagators was instructed to distribute them using suggestive messages and keywords at carefully timed intervals. Sometimes, volunteers received only a video clip of the candidate. They were encouraged to add music, descriptions, and effects, but within specific guidelines to ensure organic growth. Volunteers were also told to ensure that background music, when added, did not drown out Georgescu's spoken words in the video. The volunteers were trained to use social media algorithms—particularly TikTok's—to push the materials to trending status. This highlights that the group coordinators had significant knowledge and expertise in exploiting social media mechanisms.

Much has been said about how Călin Georgescu, as an independent candidate, did not spend any money on his campaign, achieving results without the local branch infrastructure typical of political parties, nor even a campaign headquarters. The reality is different: there were branches, but they existed exclusively online, active in all regions of the country. Through the Telegram group, supporters were invited to join online branches to disseminate information locally and share materials in city-specific groups. Volunteers were provided templates for pro-Georgescu comments to post online. These were stylized with emojis, and volunteers were instructed on how and when to post them to avoid being flagged as spam. For instance, admins advised: "Use these comments on TikTok. Switch them up after every five comments. Don't post too quickly or jump between posts too rapidly." Admins also taught propagators how to create "original" short video clips of Georgescu to ensure TikTok's algorithm would classify them as unique content. Examples were even provided.

Volunteers were incentivized with rewards for "the best editor of 2024" to motivate them to push their limits and create more innovative content. This reward system seemed to work, as TikTok became flooded with increasingly "creative" yet similar campaign videos. The group also provided explanatory videos for editing clips, using apps like TikTok or CapCut, for those with more advanced skills, who would then export their edited clips to TikTok. This collective effort culminated in Georgescu leading the first round of the presidential election, advancing to the second round. Admins thanked all volunteers and began preparing them for the next stage.

In addition to the propaganda group, other Telegram discussion groups, supported by Georgescu's team, encouraged members to freely share their views. One smaller group, "Călin Georgescu HAE," has around 800 members as of this writing. These groups also circulate videos featuring Georgescu's supporters, influencers, and public figures such as Ion iriac and actors Dorel Vi an and Florin Zamfirescu. The groups have started promoting the Young People's Party (POT), which is expected to back Georgescu. According to the admins, this party needs to be made known in the coming days. Călin Georgescu advanced to the second round of the presidential election alongside Elena Lasconi, the USR candidate.

For Case Study 3, Brandwatch will provide insights into social media's engagement metrics, sentiment analysis, and trending hashtags related to Călin Georgescu's campaign. This analysis will help identify key strategies that contributed to his campaign's online success. The insights derived from Brandwatch in Case Study 3 serve as a contemporary benchmark for understanding social media's evolving impact on political campaigns, highlighting contrasts with earlier case studies that lack similar data granularity.

We have gathered words related to the Călin Georgescu, the party and his campaign like "Călin Georgescu", "Georgescu Călin", "Elena Lasconi", "Lasconi Elena", "USR candidate", "far-right", "Far-right candidate", "pro-Russian rhetoric", Lasconi, Georgescu, #RomanianElections2024, #CalinGeorgescu, #ElenaLasconi, #RomanianSovereignty, #RomaniaVotes, #Elections2024, "Romanian Presidential Election 2024", "Romania runoff election", "second round elections December 8", #RomanianSovereignty, #GetInvolvedRomania, #AlegeriRomâne2024, #CalinGeorgescu, #ElenaLasconi, #SuveranitateaRomâniei, #RomâniaVotări, #Alegeri2024, "Alegeri preziden iale în România 2024", "Alegeri din turul doi din România", "alegerile din turul doi din 8 decembrie" and #SuveranitateaRomâniei were used in our search. We have included English and Romanian language posts, from people identified as located in Romania and the content sources were from Facebook, Instagram, Reddit, Tumblir, YouTube and X. The period that our analysis covers is from 1st of August 2024 to 31st of December 2024.

We metered the likes, shares and comments, the engagement of the audience. Then, we analyzed the public sentiment surrounding Georgescu's campaign and other candidates. We also identified themes in positive and negative sentiments related to key hashtags. We have also used sentiment and keyword analysis to identify disinformation narratives and their spread patterns. Our aim is to understand which age groups, regions, or user demographics are engaging most actively with the campaign materials. We have studied the types of content resonating most like emotional speeches, memes, humor or influencer collaborations.

Analyzing audience engagement for TikTok content related to the hashtags #RomanianElections2024 and #CalinGeorgescu reveals key insights into user interactions and demographic segmentation. The engagement metrics, including likes, shares, and comments, highlight the significant interest generated by campaign-related content on the platform. Videos featuring the hashtag #CalinGeorgescu have amassed substantial views, with some exceeding six million, indicating a high level of audience approval and engagement. The widespread sharing of these videos further amplifies their reach, suggesting that users are actively involved in disseminating campaign messages. The high volume of comments on these posts reflects an active audience eager to participate in discussions, showcasing the resonance of this content with its viewers.

A closer examination of audience demographics uncovers trends in age, location, and gender. A significant portion of the engaged audience falls within the 18-24 age group, reflecting the strong appeal of the content to younger users. This demographic has been particularly active in supporting Calin Georgescu's campaign, with data indicating that nearly a third of voters within this age group are engaged with his messages. Geographically, the campaign's reach extends beyond Romania, resonating strongly with the Romanian diaspora, of which 55% actively support Georgescu's campaign. This highlights the dual role of TikTok in engaging both domestic and international audiences. While specific gender-based engagement data for this campaign is limited, broader TikTok demographics as of mid-2024 suggest that the platform's user base skews slightly male, with 54.8% identifying as male and 45.2% as female.

These findings underscore the effectiveness of TikTok as a platform for political engagement, particularly among younger audiences. The significant participation of the Romanian diaspora also points to the platform's ability to bridge geographic divides, connecting international communities to their homeland's political discourse. Future strategies for political campaigns on TikTok should emphasize creating content that resonates with younger demographics while also catering to the interests of the global diaspora. By leveraging these insights, campaign managers can enhance engagement and outreach, ensuring that their messages reach and resonate with their target audiences effectively.

The sentiment analysis of content related to key topics, such as anti-NATO rhetoric, national sovereignty, and pro-Russia messaging, provides valuable insights into public opinion and engagement patterns. The data reveals three sentiment categories—positive, neutral, and negative—across the analyzed content. Neutral sentiment accounted for the majority of interactions, indicating that a significant portion of the content did not elicit strong emotional reactions. Negative sentiment, while less prevalent, represented a substantial share, reflecting the presence of contentious or divisive discussions. Positive sentiment, though the smallest category, showcased areas of resonance and agreement within certain audience segments.

The analysis of anti-NATO rhetoric highlights the polarizing nature of this topic. Content addressing anti-NATO sentiments often generated significant negative sentiment, particularly among audiences critical of NATO's influence in Eastern Europe. Positive sentiment for this topic was limited, reflecting its appeal to a specific ideological subset of the audience. The prevalence of neutral sentiment suggests that much of the related content was informational or lacked a strong emotional tone, underscoring the nuanced public discourse surrounding NATO. Content focused on national sovereignty showed a different pattern. Messages emphasizing the importance of sovereignty were more likely to elicit positive sentiment, particularly from audiences that value autonomy in political and economic decision-making. However, when sovereignty was discussed in opposition to international alliances, such as NATO, negative reactions were observed, especially from groups supportive of European integration. As visualized in Figure 3, keywords like "Romania," "orthodox," "purity," and "truth" dominated the discourse, highlighting the emotional and nationalist framing of Georgescu's campaign. This duality highlights how framing can influence public sentiment and engagement with the topic.

Pro-Russia messaging presented the most starkly polarized sentiment distribution. Supportive content often garnered strong positive reactions from audiences sympathetic to Russia's geopolitical stance. Conversely, this theme also attracted significant negative sentiment, particularly from critics and those opposing Russian influence. The notable volume of neutral sentiment for pro-Russia messaging suggests the presence of a substantial amount of factual or nonpartisan content that contributed to a balanced discussion. Overall, the sentiment analysis reveals key dynamics in audience responses to these topics. The dominance of neutral sentiment indicates that much of the content is either informational or fails to strongly engage audiences emotionally. Negative sentiment was more pronounced for polarizing themes such as anti-NATO rhetoric and pro-Russia messaging, while positive sentiment was most notable for content emphasizing sovereignty. Figure 2 illustrates how neutral sentiment dominated discourse, while negative sentiment was primarily linked to anti-NATO narratives and fear-based content. These findings suggest that campaigns addressing these topics can benefit from careful framing to resonate with target audiences while minimizing polarization. Balancing emotionally charged content with neutral, fact-based messaging can foster a more inclusive and constructive public discourse.

Figure 1. Engagement metrics on TikTok using #CalinGeorgescu during the 2024 Romanian Presidential Election

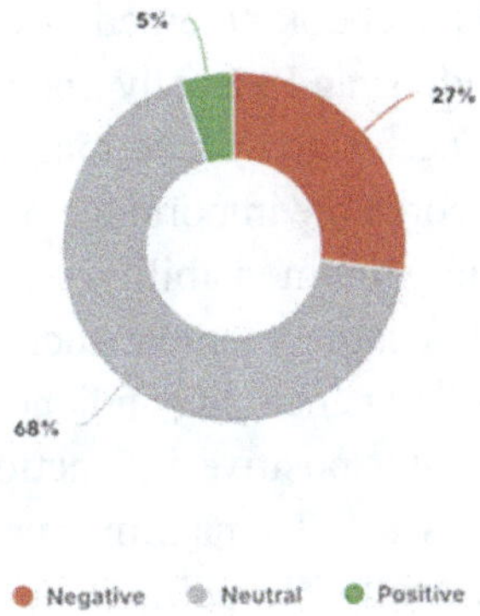

Source: Brandwatch, 2024

The analysis of emotionally charged content, including formats such as memes, humor, and influencer videos, provides valuable insights into audience engagement and the themes that resonate most with users. Emotionally driven content often serves as a powerful tool for fostering connection, sparking discussion, and achieving widespread reach on digital platforms. Using the provided datasets, this study evaluated the performance of different content types and identified the formats and themes that achieved the highest levels of engagement.

The dataset on emotional content revealed that themes associated with joy and anger were the most significant drivers of audience interaction. Content categorized under joy was frequently linked to positive messaging, such as national pride, humor, and celebratory memes. These types of content resonated particularly well with audiences, leading to consistent engagement and widespread sharing. In contrast, anger-driven content was often associated with anti-establishment rhetoric or controversial topics, eliciting strong emotional reactions. This type of content, while polarizing, also generated high levels of interaction due to its ability to provoke debate and active discussion among users.

The formats of emotionally charged content played a crucial role in determining its performance. Memes and humorous posts were especially effective in capturing the attention of younger audiences. Themes like national pride, presented through visually appealing and easily shareable formats, were particularly successful in driving engagement. Similarly, influencer videos, where individuals highlighted societal issues or advocated for specific causes, demonstrated a significant ability to connect with audiences on an emotional level. These videos often went viral, owing to their relatability and the credibility of the influencers involved. Posts designed to evoke strong emotions, whether positive or negative, consistently achieved higher engagement compared to neutral or purely informational content. The reach of different content formats was influenced by the platform on which they were shared. Platforms like YouTube and Facebook emerged as crucial in maximizing content dissemination. Short-form videos and visually appealing graphics tailored to the strengths of these platforms performed exceptionally well in terms of reach and engagement. The data underscored the importance of adapting content to platform-specific dynamics to ensure maximum visibility.

In conclusion, emotionally charged content such as memes, humor, and influencer videos plays a pivotal role in engaging audiences and achieving broad reach. Themes like national pride foster positive interactions, while anti-establishment rhetoric fuels debate and discussion. To maximize engagement, campaigns should focus on creating relatable, visually compelling content that aligns with the emotional and thematic preferences of their target audience. Furthermore, leveraging platforms with high sharing potential, such as YouTube and Facebook, is essential for amplifying the impact of such content. This analysis highlights the importance of understanding the interplay between content format, theme, and platform in the evolving landscape of digital communication.

Figure 2. Sentiment Distribution in TikTok Content Related to #CalinGeorgescu

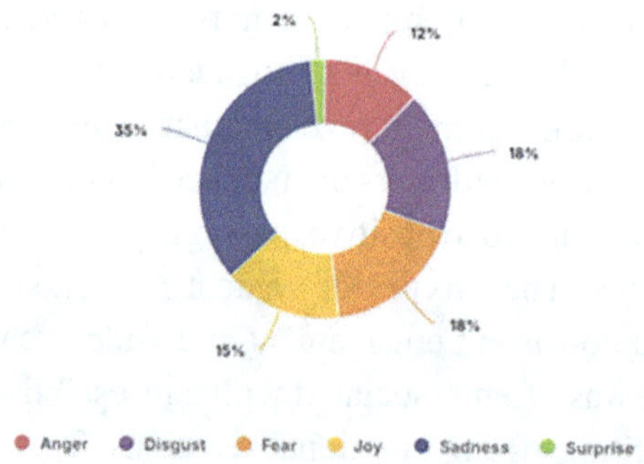

Source: Brandwatch, 2024

Călin Georgescu's unexpected prominence in Romania's presidential election highlights the substantial influence of TikTok's algorithm in shaping modern political campaigns. His strategic use of the platform allowed his messages to reach a vast audience, particularly among younger demographics, who are active users of TikTok. This success underscores the potential of social media algorithms to amplify political content, shaping public perceptions and discourse.

Georgescu's campaign employed a strategy of saturation, ensuring his presence was constant across TikTok. By flooding the platform with messages promoting his candidacy, the campaign created an illusion of ubiquity, portraying Georgescu as a central figure in Romanian politics. For many Romanian voters, particularly those previously unfamiliar with him, repeated exposure to his content fostered the perception of legitimacy and prominence, amplifying his appeal. This strategic flooding also extended to non-political spaces, broadening the reach of his campaign beyond traditional electoral audiences. Hashtags played a critical role in the success of Georgescu's TikTok campaign. The twelve most popular hashtags associated with his campaign amassed a staggering 1.4 billion views on the platform. Among these, the hashtag #calingeorgescu appeared in over 51,700 videos, generating 783.7 million views. As shown in Figure 1, the hashtag #CalinGeorgescu generated over 783 million views, demonstrating the campaign's dominance on TikTok and ability to mobilize massive digital attention. This widespread use of hashtags not only increased the visibility of his content but also encouraged user-generated contributions, further boosting engagement and reach. Such strategic hashtag deployment capitalized on TikTok's algorithm, which prioritizes content with high levels of interaction.

Figure 3. Most Common Keywords in TikTok Posts Related to Calin Georgescu

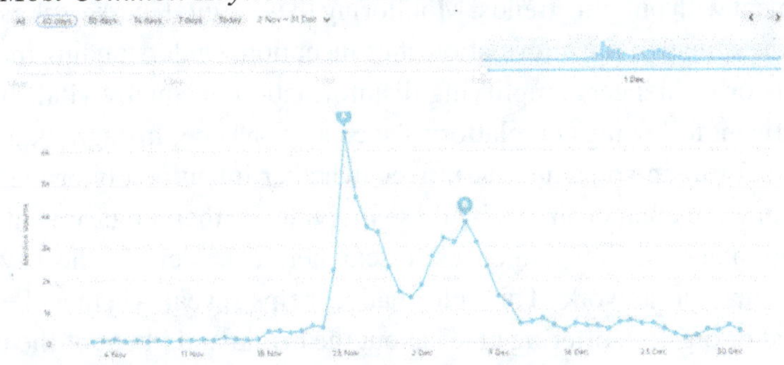

Source: Brandwatch Word Frequency Tool, 2024

Key spikes in engagement were observed following the dissemination of content aligned with nationalistic and anti-establishment themes. Videos that criticized Romania's dependence on foreign imports or questioned its international alliances resonated strongly with audiences, reflecting Georgescu's platform and messaging. The algorithm's design, which promotes content that garners significant engagement, created a feedback loop that amplified these messages. As a result, content critical of established political structures and appealing to national pride gained considerable traction, elevating Georgescu's visibility and credibility.

Georgescu's campaign effectively leveraged TikTok's algorithmic tendencies by producing a high volume of engaging, emotionally resonant content while utilizing strategic hashtags to maximize reach. This approach not only increased his prominence in the political landscape but also demonstrated the transformative power of social media platforms in electoral politics. The campaign's success illustrates the profound impact of algorithm-driven amplification on public opinion, raising critical questions about the role of social media in shaping democratic processes.

Mapping the spread of disinformation on digital platforms requires a detailed examination of the narratives, the networks amplifying them, and the demographics they affect. This process involves analyzing keywords, hashtags, and user behaviors to understand how disinformation circulates and influences public perception. Using tools such as Brandwatch, researchers can uncover patterns in disinformation dissemination and its amplification by specific influencers and communities. A critical component of disinformation mapping is the analysis of keywords and hashtags. By tracking terms associated with misleading or false narratives, researchers can identify which topics gain traction and how they evolve over time. This analysis provides insights into the volume of discussions, the platforms where these narratives are most active, and the sentiments they evoke. For example, hashtags often act as rallying points for disinformation campaigns, enabling quick dissemination and alignment with ongoing trends. Monitoring these digital markers is essential for detecting the spread of misinformation at its inception. Understanding the networks of accounts or influencers amplifying disinformation is equally vital. Influencers with significant followings on platforms such as YouTube, Instagram, and TikTok play a crucial role in spreading narratives, whether intentionally or inadvertently. By examining the content shared by these individuals, their engagement rates, and the demographics of their audiences, researchers can identify the key nodes in the disinformation network. This information helps reveal whether the spread is coordinated or organic, offering clues about the origin and intent of the narratives.

Demographic analysis adds another layer of understanding to disinformation mapping. Tools like Brandwatch enable researchers to explore the age, gender, location, and interests of users engaging with disinformation-related content. This demographic breakdown highlights which groups are most vulnerable to specific narratives, allowing for targeted interventions. For instance, younger audiences may be more susceptible to disinformation presented in visually engaging formats, while older demographics might engage more with text-heavy or authoritative-sounding content. Identifying these patterns is essential for designing effective countermeasures, such as educational campaigns or platform-specific content moderation strategies.

Figure 4. Influence Scores and Sentiment Distribution of Key Digital Influencers in the Georgescu Campaign

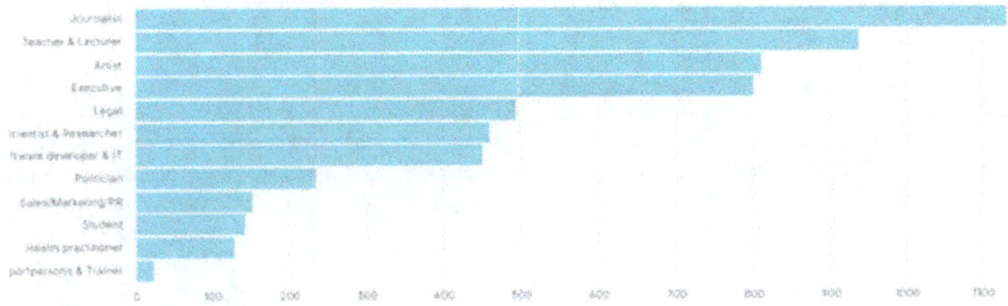

Source: Brandwatch, 2024

Effective disinformation mapping combines these elements into a cohesive strategy. Researchers first establish keyword and hashtag searches to monitor relevant discussions. Next, they identify and analyze the influencers driving the spread of narratives, assessing their impact and reach. Finally, demographic insights provide a detailed view of the audience, enabling tailored responses to mitigate the spread of misinformation. Regular monitoring and adaptation of these methods are crucial, as disinformation strategies are dynamic and evolve with changing trends and technologies. This approach underscores the importance of vigilance in the digital age. As disinformation becomes more sophisticated and pervasive, tools and methodologies like those offered by Brandwatch are indispensable for maintaining the integrity of public discourse. By mapping disinformation comprehensively, researchers and organizations can better understand its mechanisms and develop proactive strategies to counteract its harmful effects on society.

Călin Georgescu's campaign during the 2024 Romanian presidential elections showcased a distinct and innovative approach to digital engagement, particularly on TikTok. His campaign dominated the platform with exceptional metrics, including 783.7 million views for the hashtag #CalinGeorgescu across over 51,700 videos and a combined 1.4 billion views for campaign-related hashtags. Georgescu's strategy prioritized emotionally resonant content, which elicited significant public reactions. While neutral sentiment prevailed in much of the content, reflecting its informational nature, themes such as national sovereignty generated positive responses from segments of the audience, particularly those disillusioned with traditional politics. Conversely, negative sentiment was notably tied to controversial topics such as anti-NATO rhetoric and pro-Russian messaging. His success in capturing the attention of younger voters, particularly those aged 18 to 24, and engaging the Romanian diaspora (of which 55% expressed active support) underscores his campaign's demographic reach and its alignment with TikTok's user base.

Figure 5. X posts

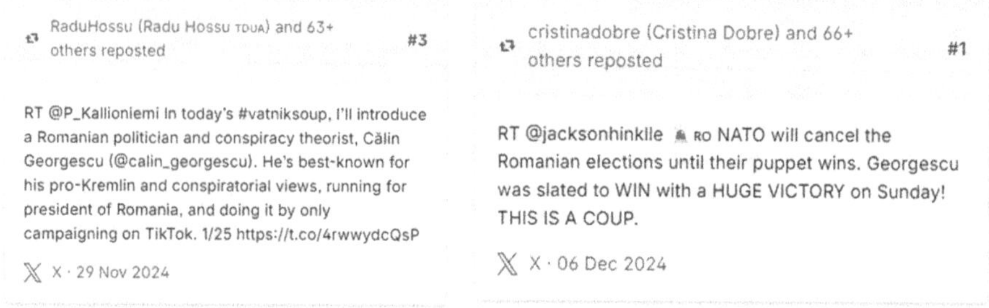

In contrast, candidates like Elena Lasconi, representing the pro-European Union stance, adopted a more traditional social media strategy, focusing primarily on platforms like Facebook, Instagram, and X (formerly Twitter). Lasconi's engagement on TikTok was minimal and lacked the viral appeal that defined Georgescu's campaign. Her hashtags, including #ElenaLasconi and #RomaniaElections2024, achieved modest reach and did not generate significant user participation. Sentiment around her campaign was generally positive, driven by her pro-European rhetoric, although it lacked the emotional intensity that characterized Georgescu's outreach. Her support base, predominantly urban professionals and older voters, reflected a preference for polished visuals and policy-driven narratives shared on Facebook and Instagram.

The use of platforms further differentiated the campaigns. Georgescu's TikTok strategy leveraged the platform's algorithm to amplify his presence through emotionally charged, easily shareable content, including memes, humor, and collaborations with influencers. His campaign relied heavily on volunteer-driven efforts coordinated through Telegram groups, enabling saturation of TikTok with personalized, user-generated content optimized for the algorithm. On the other hand, other candidates placed greater emphasis on Facebook for live events, policy discussions, and targeted outreach, while also utilizing Instagram and X for real-time updates and professional branding. These platforms catered to a different demographic, with a stronger focus on older, urban audiences rather than the younger, dispersed populations targeted by Georgescu.

Hashtag deployment also played a critical role in defining the campaigns' reach and resonance. Georgescu's campaign effectively created a sense of ubiquity through hashtags such as #RomanianSovereignty and #RomaniaVotes, which not only trended globally but also encouraged organic contributions from users. The widespread use of these hashtags amplified his messaging and created a feedback loop of engagement and visibility. By comparison, hashtags associated with other candidates lacked the same level of traction, reflecting a more conventional approach to digital strategy.

Figure 6. Word Cloud of the most popular words in posts

The contrast in content themes further underscores the divergent approaches. Georgescu's campaign tapped into emotionally resonant themes, including national pride and anti-establishment narratives, which struck a chord with audiences on TikTok. His use of short videos and memes tailored to the platform's dynamics helped his messages achieve significant reach. Conversely, other candidates emphasized governance, policy issues, and pro-European integration. While this content resonated with their traditional voter base, it failed to achieve the same level of virality or emotional impact, especially among younger audiences. The case of Georgescu highlights the transformative potential of TikTok as a platform for political engagement. By leveraging its algorithm and focusing on emotionally resonant content, his campaign demonstrated the platform's capacity to shape public perceptions and engage previously disengaged demographics. This success contrasts with the reliance of other candidates on more conventional platforms like Facebook and Instagram, which, while effective in reaching established voter bases, lacked the dynamic, viral nature of TikTok. These findings illustrate the evolving role of social media in political campaigns, emphasizing the importance of tailoring strategies to specific platforms and audiences to maximize impact.

The role of influencers in Călin Georgescu's 2024 presidential campaign provides an insightful example of how key individuals can amplify political messaging through strategic collaborations on digital platforms. Using Brandwatch's network analysis features, several influencers emerged as pivotal in enhancing the campaign's reach and impact. Figure 4 presents the relative influence scores and sentiment spread across key influencers supporting Georgescu, indicating that most content was neutral or informational, with some polarizing spikes. Among these, the influencer known as HranaApaEnergie demonstrated substantial activity on Twitter, with 122 mentions of campaign-related content and an impact score of 10.87. This influencer engaged with a modest follower base of 238 but achieved significant sentiment distribution, with 88 neutral interactions, 13 positive ones, and 21 negative responses. The balanced sentiment indicates that the content was primarily informational, while the presence of negative sentiment highlights the controversial nature of some themes.

Another influential figure, HoriaGanescu, showed greater reach with 2,208 followers and an impact score of 12.01. Although this influencer generated fewer mentions, the content's effectiveness lay in engaging a broader audience and fostering discussions. Positive sentiment remained limited, but neutral sentiment dominated the interactions, suggesting that the content resonated as fact-based or aligned with widely shared narratives. Similarly, tomiris_26, another Twitter-based influencer, contributed 54 mentions, reaching 1,655 individuals with a primarily neutral sentiment and an impact score of 7.80. The focus on neutral content reflects a deliberate strategy to inform and engage without alienating potential supporters. Not all influencers operated within the boundaries of conventional social media platforms. The individual identified as Moinesti72, active on Softpedia, achieved a notable impact score of 40.30 despite engaging no direct followers. This influence was primarily derived from discussions in forums and other digital spaces where campaign-related themes, particularly those with negative sentiment, gained traction. The activity of such influencers highlights the importance of alternative platforms in expanding a campaign's reach beyond traditional social media boundaries.

The collective impact of these influencers underscores their effectiveness in disseminating campaign narratives and fostering engagement. By tailoring their messaging to the campaign's strategic goals, these individuals significantly enhanced visibility and public discourse surrounding Călin Georgescu's candidacy. The predominance of neutral sentiment across most influencer activity suggests a focus on informational content, while the presence of both positive and negative sentiments reflects the polarizing nature of some themes. This analysis illustrates the pivotal role of influencers in modern political campaigns, particularly in leveraging digital platforms to amplify messaging and shape voter perceptions. Taken together, these three case studies illustrate a spectrum of digital campaigning sophistication and ethical complexity. From Brazil's reliance on private encrypted platforms to the Philippines' influencer-driven nostalgia and Romania's grassroots-algorithmic saturation, social media strategies have evolved into potent instruments for political persuasion. Yet, the intensity of personalization, emotional manipulation, and platform exploitation across cases underscores the urgent need for critical scrutiny of how these tools reshape democratic participation.

A comparative analysis of these three campaigns reveals distinct strategies tailored to platform affordances and sociopolitical contexts. Brazil's campaign leaned on encrypted messaging apps like WhatsApp for micro-targeted outreach in rural regions. The Philippines saw influencer-driven historical revisionism on public platforms like TikTok. Romania, by contrast, mobilized a decentralized "digital volunteer army" through TikTok and Telegram, maximizing algorithmic amplification with no formal campaign infrastructure. These cases demonstrate the versatility of social media platforms in modern campaigns—while also highlighting how each strategy exploits different vulnerabilities in the digital media landscape.

DISCUSSION

The transformative role of social media and digital technologies in modern political campaigns has been profoundly demonstrated through the analysis of literature and the three case studies: Brazil's 2022 Presidential Election, the Philippines' 2022 Presidential Election, and Romania's 2024 Presidential Election. This section explores how these platforms influence voter behavior, amplify campaign narratives, and pose ethical challenges, emphasizing the dual-edged nature of digital campaigning.

Emerging Technologies in Digital Campaigning

Emerging technologies like AR, VR, and AI are revolutionizing political campaigns, offering innovative ways to engage voters. AR and VR technologies create immersive experiences that can deepen voter engagement. For example, VR simulations can transport voters to virtual town halls or recreate policy impacts, offering a more interactive and personalized campaign experience (Aitamurto et al., 2022). AI enables campaigns to analyze voter sentiment in real time, craft personalized messages, and predict voter behavior. AI-powered chatbots can also facilitate direct interaction with voters, answering questions and addressing concerns, thereby enhancing engagement (Chen, 2022). Blockchain technology is being explored as a solution to enhance transparency in voting systems. By providing a secure and tamper-proof platform for electoral processes, blockchain can reduce fraud and build voter trust (Lopezosa et al., 2023). The Romanian 2024 presidential campaign demonstrates TikTok's growing significance in political strategies. Călin Georgescu's use of TikTok exemplifies how the platform's algorithm amplifies short-form content that evokes emotional responses, influencing voter engagement significantly (BBC News, 2024). Georgescu's campaign effectively utilized humor, memes, and influencers to mobilize younger voters while reinforcing his anti-establishment narrative. However, the campaign also underscored the risks associated with viral platforms, including the rapid dissemination of disinformation and the creation of echo chambers that deepen ideological divides (Politico, 2024a). These findings align with broader trends observed in other campaigns, where the use of TikTok and similar platforms reshapes voter perceptions and alters traditional election dynamics.

Social Media as a Transformative Tool

Social media platforms, as exemplified in all three case studies, have redefined voter engagement through mass outreach, micro-targeting, and emotional resonance. Platforms like WhatsApp in Brazil, TikTok in the Philippines and Romania, and Instagram and Facebook across these contexts have enabled campaigns to bypass traditional media gatekeepers, directly engaging audiences with tailored and interactive content. TikTok's algorithm, favoring emotionally charged and easily shareable content, emerged as a particularly potent tool in Romania and the Philippines, shaping narratives and driving voter mobilization, especially among younger demographics.

In Brazil, WhatsApp's use for micro-targeting highlighted the platform's effectiveness in reaching rural and less digitally literate populations, demonstrating the power of private messaging in voter engagement. Meanwhile, the Philippines' TikTok-driven campaign by Ferdinand Marcos Jr. showcased how emotional storytelling and historical revisionism can reshape public perceptions, particularly among younger voters with limited historical knowledge. Similarly, in Romania, TikTok enabled Călin Georgescu's far-right campaign to dominate public discourse, using humor, memes, and influencer collaborations to amplify anti-establishment and national sovereignty narratives.

Implications for Voter Behavior

Digital campaigns on social media significantly influence voter behavior through emotional engagement, the creation of echo chambers, and the mobilization of younger demographics. Interactive content such as videos, memes, and live streams appeals to voters' emotions, making campaign messages more memorable. Emotional engagement is particularly effective in mobilizing undecided voters and building campaign loyalty (Lee et al., 2021). Social media algorithms often create echo chambers that reinforce voters' existing beliefs, limiting exposure to diverse perspectives. This can polarize electorates and reduce the likelihood of informed decision-making (Wei et al., 2022). Platforms like TikTok and Snapchat have proven effective in engaging younger voters, who are less likely to consume traditional media. The creative use of short-form videos and influencer collaborations can significantly enhance youth participation in elections (Dolot, 2018).

TikTok's unique algorithmic structure raises several ethical concerns in the context of political campaigning. Unlike other platforms, TikTok's content curation heavily relies on maximizing engagement through emotionally resonant material, often amplifying polarizing or misleading content (France 24, 2024). Georgescu's campaign on TikTok highlighted the platform's susceptibility to disinformation, with fact-checkers identifying numerous exaggerated claims targeting voters' biases

(Telegraph, 2024). Additionally, the use of influencers and user-generated content raises transparency concerns, as voters may not always recognize the financial or ideological affiliations of content creators. Addressing these challenges requires robust regulatory frameworks and platform-specific moderation strategies tailored to the fast-paced, viral nature of TikTok.

Ethical Challenges in Digital Campaigning

While digital platforms enhance engagement, they also exacerbate ethical concerns, including misinformation, algorithmic bias, and data privacy violations. The spread of disinformation during campaigns was evident in all case studies. For instance, Brazil's election highlighted the role of private messaging platforms in spreading unverified claims, while Marcos Jr.'s campaign in the Philippines utilized TikTok to disseminate historically inaccurate content that romanticized authoritarian rule. In Romania, Georgescu's campaign saw multiple instances of disinformation targeting NATO and European Union policies, reflecting the susceptibility of social media algorithms to amplifying polarizing content. These cases underscore the critical need for regulatory frameworks and platform accountability to mitigate these risks. Algorithmic transparency and robust moderation policies are essential to ensure that digital platforms promote accurate and diverse information. Additionally, media literacy initiatives are vital for equipping voters with the tools to critically evaluate digital content and resist the influence of misinformation. In the 2022 Philippine presidential election, the TikTok algorithm amplified romanticized narratives about the Marcos regime, many of which contained misleading or false claims. This affected voter understanding of historical events, particularly among digital natives with limited historical education, leading to widespread belief in a 'golden age' that contradicted documented human rights abuses.

Algorithmic amplification is more than a technical feature; it constitutes what Gillespie (2018) and Noble (2018) describe as a "quantified persuasion infrastructure." This infrastructure not only determines what voters see but actively shapes political discourse by privileging polarizing, emotionally charged content. In the Philippines and Romanian elections, emotionally manipulative and ideologically extreme narratives gained traction, while fact-based, moderate content struggled to break through. These dynamics raise urgent questions about democratic visibility, as the architecture of platforms increasingly favors populist discourse over deliberative pluralism.

Disinformation should not merely be viewed as a by-product of digital campaigning but rather as a structural instrument leveraged to destabilize electoral legitimacy and manipulate civic discourse. As Wardle and Derakhshan (2017) argue in their framework of "information disorder," disinformation operates within a broader ecosystem of emotional manipulation, networked amplification, and cognitive bias exploitation. In the case studies presented—particularly the Brazilian and Romanian elections—disinformation emerged not just from fringe actors but was strategically disseminated through formal campaign structures and influencers. These dynamics suggest a shift from isolated misinformation incidents to systemic campaigns that rely on the virality of platforms like WhatsApp and TikTok. Consequently, disinformation becomes a tool of digital authoritarianism, normalizing ideological extremism and eroding voters' ability to engage in informed deliberation. The tendency of such narratives to exploit social grievances and historical revisionism further illustrates their capacity to reshape collective memory and voter identity, especially among younger demographics unfamiliar with historical contexts.

The intersection of legal frameworks and ethical concerns underscores the complexity of digital campaigning. Algorithmic amplification and psychographic targeting raise questions not only about fairness but also about compliance with international data protection laws, such as the GDPR. Legal gaps around influencer transparency, digital ad labeling, and platform liability exacerbate ethical dilemmas. There is growing consensus among scholars and regulators that electoral integrity in the digital age depends on binding regulations that mandate disclosure of political ad funding, algorithmic impact assessments, and user opt-outs from targeted political content. Without these legal safeguards, the digital campaign space risks becoming a deregulated marketplace of influence, vulnerable to manipulation and misinformation. TikTok's lack of clear enforcement of misinformation policies during the Romanian 2024 elections allowed content flagged as false by independent fact-checkers to remain online for extended periods, contributing to the virality of pro-Russian narratives. This inaction highlights gaps in platform accountability and raises questions about compliance with European content moderation obligations.

The ethical dilemmas posed by digital campaigning—ranging from psychographic targeting and influencer opacity to unchecked disinformation—are exacerbated by uneven regulatory landscapes. Existing legal frameworks, such as the EU's Digital Services Act or Brazil's Electoral Justice regulations, offer valuable tools for improving transparency and accountability. However, enforcement remains fragmented and inconsistent, particularly in jurisdictions like the Philippines or Romania, where platform governance is largely reactive. The cross-border nature of platforms like TikTok and Meta compounds this issue, as their policies often lack harmonization with national electoral standards. Furthermore, the persistence of influencer-driven disinformation, as seen in the Marcos and Georgescu campaigns, highlights the insufficiency of self-regulation and voluntary disclosure mechanisms. To safeguard democratic integrity, regulatory frameworks must evolve toward binding international standards that mandate transparency in political ad targeting, influencer affiliations, and algorithmic curation practices. Until such structures are in place, ethical vulnerabilities will persist at the core of digital political communication.

Personalization and Emotional Resonance

A recurring theme across the case studies is the strategic use of personalization and emotional engagement to influence voter behavior. In Brazil, culturally relevant and localized messages fostered personal connections with voters, while in the Philippines, Marcos Jr.'s campaign leveraged nostalgia and emotional appeals to resonate with younger audiences. Romania's Georgescu similarly employed emotionally charged content, including humor and anti-establishment rhetoric, to galvanize support among disillusioned voters. The emotional intensity of these campaigns underscores the role of social media in creating echo chambers that reinforce existing biases and deepen polarization. Platforms' prioritization of engaging content over factual accuracy further complicates efforts to foster informed decision-making among voters.

Cross-case comparison

Both case studies reveal how emerging technologies and digital platforms have disrupted traditional electoral dynamics. While Brazil's campaigns demonstrated the strategic use of private messaging for micro-targeting, the Philippines highlighted the role of TikTok in shaping narratives and mobilizing younger voters. Despite their differences, both cases underscore the growing importance of personalization and emotional engagement in modern campaigning. These findings align with the broader literature on social media's role in elections. Aitamurto et al. (2022) emphasize how augmented reality (AR) and virtual reality (VR) could further personalize voter experiences, while Chen (2022) highlights the potential of AI-driven sentiment analysis for crafting tailored messages. However, as seen in these case studies, the benefits of digital campaigning are often accompanied by significant ethical risks, including misinformation, algorithmic manipulation, and data privacy violations (Cadwalladr, 2018). Regulatory and ethical considerations are critical in addressing these challenges. Blockchain technology, as proposed by Niloy et al. (2024), could enhance transparency in campaign financing and content authentication. Additionally, media literacy programs must be prioritized to empower voters with the skills needed to navigate the complexities of digital content critically. Finally, platform accountability is essential. Policymakers should enforce stricter regulations to ensure that algorithms prioritize accurate and diverse content over sensationalism.

Despite the diverse sociopolitical contexts of Brazil, the Philippines, and Romania, common trends highlight the transformative impact of social media on electoral processes. Personalization, emotional engagement, and platform-specific strategies have emerged as key drivers of campaign success. However, the ethical challenges associated with digital campaigning—misinformation, polarization, and lack of transparency—underscore the urgent need for comprehensive regulatory frameworks and media literacy initiatives. These findings align with broader literature emphasizing the dual nature of social media in political campaigns. While platforms democratize voter engagement and amplify diverse voices, they also magnify risks that threaten the integrity of democratic processes. Addressing these challenges requires interdisciplinary approaches combining technological, regulatory, and educational strategies to ensure that social media enhances rather than undermines democracy.

The consequences of these ethical lapses are far-reaching. Misleading content not only distorts voter perceptions but also erodes trust in democratic institutions. As shown in the Romanian and Philippine cases, emotionally manipulative content can shift voter sentiment, legitimize anti-democratic actors, and disrupt electoral fairness. Without stronger enforcement mechanisms, digital platforms risk becoming vectors of democratic backsliding.

A cross-case comparison reveals distinct strategies aligned with platform-specific logics and audience behaviors. Brazil's campaign favored private messaging apps like WhatsApp and Telegram to target rural, less digitally literate populations with culturally resonant micro-messaging. The Philippines exemplified nostalgic storytelling on TikTok to reshape historical narratives for youth. Romania showcased the most grassroots and algorithmically optimized strategy: volunteer-driven TikTok saturation designed to create perceived ubiquity. Each campaign leveraged emotional content, yet the emotional vectors—fear, pride, nostalgia, or disillusionment—varied by context. While all three cases harnessed social media to reshape political discourse, Romania's decentralized volunteer structure and algorithmic manipulation marked the furthest evolution of digitally-native campaigning.

1. How does the personalization of social media content, through micro-targeting and algorithmic curation, shape voter behavior and influence electoral outcomes across diverse demographics?

The case studies reveal that personalization significantly shapes voter behavior by enabling campaigns to deliver tailored messages that resonate with specific demographics. For example, Bolsonaro's use of WhatsApp in Brazil targeted rural voters with culturally relevant content, while Marcos Jr.'s TikTok strategy in the Philippines appealed to younger audiences through nostalgic and emotionally charged narratives. These strategies demonstrate how algorithmic curation and micro-targeting enhance engagement but also deepen echo chambers, reinforcing preexisting beliefs and limiting exposure to diverse perspectives.

2. What ethical challenges emerge from integrating AI, AR, and blockchain technologies in political campaigns, and how can these challenges be addressed to ensure democratic integrity?

Although the case studies primarily focus on social media platforms, the integration of emerging technologies like AI and blockchain raises ethical concerns about transparency, privacy, and algorithmic bias. AI-driven tools can enhance micro-targeting and sentiment analysis but risk manipulating voter behavior through psychographic profiling. Blockchain, while offering transparency in campaign financing and content authentication, requires robust implementation to prevent misuse. Addressing these challenges necessitates regulatory oversight, ethical guidelines, and media literacy programs to empower voters.

3. How do social media platforms and their unique characteristics, such as TikTok's algorithm or WhatsApp's private messaging, influence voter engagement and campaign dynamics?

The platforms analyzed in the case studies illustrate their distinct impact on voter engagement and campaign strategies. TikTok's algorithm, which prioritizes emotionally resonant and viral content, was pivotal in the campaigns of Marcos Jr. and Georgescu, driving youth mobilization and amplifying narratives. WhatsApp's private messaging allowed Bolsonaro's campaign to bypass public scrutiny, fostering personalized voter interactions. These examples underscore the need for platform-specific strategies and accountability measures to ensure ethical campaigning.

While digital campaigning democratizes access to political participation and empowers marginalized voices, it simultaneously creates vulnerabilities that can be exploited for disinformation, emotional manipulation, and voter polarization. This dual impact calls for a nuanced approach that celebrates technological innovation while addressing the structural and ethical risks inherent in digital media ecosystems. When examined comparatively, these case studies underscore the evolving nature of digital campaigning. Brazil exemplifies personalized micro-targeting through private messaging apps, while the Philippines showcases the strategic use of nostalgic narratives to rewrite collective memory. Romania, on the other hand, demonstrates a grassroots-algorithmic saturation model powered by coordinated volunteer networks and influencer collaborations. Across all cases, emotionally resonant content proved pivotal, regardless of platform, suggesting that the affective dimension of digital politics may outweigh rational policy engagement in influencing electoral outcomes.

CONCLUSION

The analysis of digital campaigns across Brazil, the Philippines, and Romania demonstrates the transformative influence of social media on electoral processes, showcasing both opportunities and risks inherent in these platforms. Social media enables unprecedented voter engagement through mass outreach, micro-targeting, and emotional resonance, as seen with TikTok's role in Romania and the Philippines and WhatsApp's influence in Brazil. These platforms have redefined political campaigning, fostered direct voter-campaign connections while bypassed traditional media gatekeepers. However, this democratization of political communication comes with significant challenges. The proliferation of misinformation, deepening of echo chambers, and ethical issues surrounding data privacy and algorithmic manipulation pose threats to democratic integrity. The case studies highlight how digital tools can amplify polarization, with algorithms favoring emotionally charged or polarizing content, often at the expense of factual accuracy.

Emerging technologies like AR, VR, and AI hold potential to revolutionize voter engagement further, offering immersive and personalized experiences. Yet, their use must be accompanied by ethical guidelines to prevent exploitation and maintain voter trust. Similarly, blockchain technology offers promising applications for transparency in electoral processes but requires robust implementation to ensure effectiveness. To harness the positive potential of social media while mitigating its risks, comprehensive regulatory frameworks, platform accountability, and voter media literacy are essential. Policymakers, platforms, and civil society must collaborate to promote responsible digital campaigning and ensure that these powerful tools enhance democratic values rather than undermine them. The transformative role of social media in shaping voter behavior is undeniable, and addressing its associated challenges is critical for fostering an informed and inclusive electorate.

REFERENCES

Aitamurto, T., Aymerich-Franch, L., Saldivar, J., Kircos, C., Sadeghi, Y., & Sakshuwong, S. (2022). Examining augmented reality in journalism: Presence, knowledge gain, and perceived visual authenticity. *New Media & Society*, *24*(6), 1281–1302.

Arugay, A. A., & Baquisal, J. K. A. (2022). Mobilized and polarized: Social media and disinformation narratives in the 2022 Philippine elections. *Pacific Affairs*, *95*(3), 549–573.

BBC News. (2024, November 25). Far-right candidate takes shock lead in Romania presidential election. Retrieved from https://www.bbc.com/news/articles/c9dlw5pq967o

Bloch-Wehba, H. (2021). Content moderation as surveillance. *Berkeley Technology Law Journal*, *36*(3), 1297–1340.

Cadwalladr, C. (2018). *The great British Brexit robbery: How our democracy was hijacked. The Guardian*. https://www.theguardian.com/technology/2017/may/07/the-great-british-brexit-robbery-hijacked-democracy

Cadwalladr, C., & Graham-Harrison, E. (2018). Revealed: 50 million Facebook profiles harvested for Cambridge Analytica in major data breach. Retrieved from https://www.theguardian.com/news/2018/mar/17/cambridge-analytica-facebook-influence-us-election

Chadwick, A. (2017). *The hybrid media system: Politics and power*. Oxford University Press.

Chen, R. (2022). Ready, communicators: Communications and public relations in the metaverse. *The McMaster Journal of Communication*, *13*(1), 1–6.

Dolot, A. (2018). The characteristics of Generation Z. E-Mentor, (2), 44–50.

Driscoll, D. L., Appiah-Yeboah, A., Salib, P., & Rupert, D. J. (2007). Merging qualitative and quantitative data in mixed methods research: How to and why not. *Ecological and Environmental Anthropology,* https://digitalcommons.unl.edu/cgi/viewcontent.cgi?article=1012&context=icwdmeea

Everyrealm. (2023). Immersive Media Market Overview. Retrieved from https://www.everyrealm.com/post/immersive-media-market-overview

France 24. (2024, November 25). Who is the far-right populist and TikTok star now leading Romania's presidential race? Retrieved from https://www.france24.com/en/europe/20241125-who-is-the-far-right-populist-and-tiktok-star-now-leading-romania-s-presidential-race

Gillespie, T. (2018). *Custodians of the Internet: Platforms, content moderation, and the hidden decisions that shape social media.* Yale University Press.

Guess, A., Nagler, J., & Tucker, J. (2019). Less than you think: Prevalence and predictors of fake news dissemination on Facebook. *Science Advances*, *5*(1), eaau4586.

Helberger, N., Pierson, J., & Poell, T. (2018). Governing online platforms: From contested to cooperative responsibility. *The Information Society*, *34*(1), 1–14.

Kang, S., O'Brien, E., Villarreal, A., Lee, W., & Mahood, C. (2019). Immersive Journalism and Telepresence: Does virtual reality news use affect news credibility? *Digital Journalism (Abingdon, England)*, *7*(2), 294–313.

Kerlinger, F. N. (1966). Foundations of behavioral research. Klein, H. N. The Impact of AI-Driven Social Media on Elections: Voter Autonomy & Government.

Kreiss, D. (2017). Micro-targeting, the quantified persuasion. *Internet Policy Review*, *6*(4).

Lee, S. A., Lee, M., & Jeong, M. (2021). The role of virtual reality on information sharing and seeking behaviors. *Journal of Hospitality and Tourism Management*, *46*, 215–223.

Lenhart, A., & Shilton, K. (2025). "I Feel Like All of This Is Already Happening Anyways": Context Import and Young Adults' Perspectives on Researcher Access to TikTok Data. Available at *SSRN* 5347181.

Lopezosa, C., Codina, L., Fernández-Planells, A., & Freixa, P. (2023). Journalistic innovation: How new formats of digital journalism are perceived in the academic literature. *Journalism*, *24*(4), 821–838.

Lund, T. (2012). Combining qualitative and quantitative approaches: Some arguments for mixed methods research. *Scandinavian Journal of Educational Research*, *56*(2), 155–165.

Niloy, S. A., Ghosh, I., Reno, S., Rahman, A., Rahaman, S., & Hossan, M. S. (2024). Ensuring transparency, confidentiality, and deterrence of political influence in journalism using IPFS, private, public, and semi-public blockchains. *International Journal of Information Technology : an Official Journal of Bharati Vidyapeeth's Institute of Computer Applications and Management*, *16*(2), 1095–1109.

Noble, S. U. (2018). Algorithms of oppression: How search engines reinforce racism. In *Algorithms of oppression*. New York university press.

Nyabola, N. (2018). *Digital democracy, analogue politics: How the Internet era is transforming politics in Kenya*. Bloomsbury Publishing.

Nyhan, B., & Reifler, J. (2015). The effect of fact-checking on elites: A field experiment on US state legislators. *American Journal of Political Science, 59*(3), 628–640.

Östlund, U., Kidd, L., Wengström, Y., & Rowa-Dewar, N. (2011). Combining qualitative and quantitative research within mixed method research designs: A methodological review. *International Journal of Nursing Studies, 48*(3), 369–383.

Politico. (2024a, November 26). Romania's far-right, pro-Russian lurch spells big trouble for EU and NATO. Retrieved from https://www.politico.eu/article/could-romania-break-eu-and-nato-elections-russia-influence-moldova-georgia-calin-georgescu/

Politico. (2024b, November 25). Who is Călin Georgescu, the far-right TikTok star leading the Romanian election race? Retrieved from https://www.politico.eu/article/calin-georgescu-romania-elections-far-right-tiktok-nato-skeptic-russia-ukraine-exports/

Rossini, P., Mont'Alverne, C., & Kalogeropoulos, A. (2023). Explaining beliefs in electoral misinformation in the 2022 Brazilian election: The role of ideology, political trust, social media, and messaging apps. *Harvard Kennedy School Misinformation Review, 4*(3).

Sullivan, M. (2023). Politics in the YouTube and TikTok Era: How Social Media Algorithms Affect the Way Younger Generations are Being Communicated To.

Telegraph. (2024, November 25). Pro-Russia TikTok candidate takes surprise lead in Romanian elections. Retrieved from https://www.telegraph.co.uk/world-news/2024/11/25/pro-russia-candidate-lead-romania-election-tiktok-campaign/

Tucker, J. A., Guess, A., Barberá, P., Vaccari, C., Siegel, A., Sanovich, S., ... & Nyhan, B. (2018). Social media, political polarization, and political disinformation: A review of the scientific literature. Political polarization, and political disinformation: a review of the scientific literature (March 19, 2018).

Van Aelst, P., Strömbäck, J., Aalberg, T., Esser, F., De Vreese, C., Matthes, J., & Stanyer, J. (2017). Political communication in a high-choice media environment: A challenge for democracy? *Annals of the International Communication Association, 41*(1), 3–27.

Venâncio, O. R., Ferreira, C. H., Almeida, J. M., & da Silva, A. P. C. (2024, May). Unraveling user coordination on telegram: A comprehensive analysis of political mobilization during the 2022 brazilian presidential election. In *Proceedings of the International AAAI Conference on Web and Social Media* (Vol. 18, pp. 1545-1556).

Wardle, C., & Derakhshan, H. (2017). *Information disorder: Toward an interdisciplinary framework for research and policymaking* (Vol. 27). Council of Europe.

Wei, X., Jin, X., & Fan, M. (2022, October). Communication in immersive social virtual reality: A systematic review of 10 years' studies. In *Proceedings of the tenth international symposium of Chinese CHI* (pp. 27-37).

Willig, I. (2022). From audiences to data points: The role of media agencies in the platformization of the news media industry. *Media Culture & Society*, *44*(1), 56–71.

Wimmer, R. D., & Dominick, J. R. (2013). *Mass media research*. Wadsworth Publishing Company.

Zuiderveen Borgesius, F. J., Möller, J., Kruikemeier, S., Ó Fathaigh, R., Irion, K., Dobber, T., & de Vreese, C. H. (2018). Online political microtargeting: Promises and threats for democracy. *Utrecht Law Review*, *14*(1).

KEY TERMS AND DEFINITIONS

Algorithmic Amplification: Algorithms on platforms like TikTok and Facebook show content that is popular and push content that sparks reactions. This means prioritizing sensational, emotional, or divisive posts. Campaigns take advantage of this by crafting content designed to "go viral," but this comes with the risk of amplifying harmful or polarizing material.

Digital Campaigning: Political campaigns have shift to global and interactive experiences. By leveraging tools like AI for sentiment analysis or blockchain for transparency, campaigns are more targeted and efficient. For example, in Romania's 2024 elections, TikTok wasn't just a platform—it became a strategy, connecting with disillusioned voters through engaging, emotional content.

Disinformation: It aims to manipulate and mislead. A notable example is the Cambridge Analytica case, where targeted fake narratives were used to influence election outcomes, making it clear how dangerous and effective this strategy can be.

Echo Chambers: It refers to a situation where everything agrees with your views. Social media's algorithms can create these spaces where users only see content that aligns with their beliefs, cutting them off from differing perspectives. While it feels comforting, it deepens divides and makes productive dialogue harder.

Micro Targeting: Political campaigns use it to craft messages that feel personal to specific audiences. It refers to knowing someone's age, location, values, habits, and preferences. For instance, in Brazil's 2022 election, campaigns used WhatsApp to send messages in local dialects, making them resonate on a deeply cultural level.

Misinformation: It spreads quickly, often with unintended consequences. It misleads, like when incorrect voting dates circulate online. The challenge is teaching people to pause, verify, and think critically before sharing.

Social Media Dynamics: Social media has become an ecosystem where algorithms, user interactions, and viral trends dictate the flow of information. It's not just about sharing content; it's about how platforms like TikTok and Instagram create environments where messages either flourish or fade. For example, during elections, a single hashtag or short video can rally millions or polarize groups, showing just how much these dynamics shape modern communication.

Voter Mobilization: Platforms like Instagram and TikTok don't just inform voters; they engage and energize them, especially younger demographics. Campaigns use memes, influencers, and creative content to encourage registration and turnout, proving that voting can feel like part of a community movement.

Chapter 14
A Documentary Influencing Political Behavior and Attitudes: Exploring Gold Mafia Through Audiences' Perspectives

Jennings Joy Chibike
https://orcid.org/0000-0002-4899-2446
Lupane State University, Zimbabwe & Midlands State University, Zimbabwe

Lerato Nqobile Moyo
https://orcid.org/0009-0004-9014-9710
Lupane State University, Zimbabwe

ABSTRACT

This study is aimed at examining how political audiences of a documentary titled Gold Mafia received it. Drawing from reception theory as a theoretical frame work it answers the questions how did the audiences receive the documentary and how did the documentary influence their political attitudes and behavior towards ZANU PF. To achieve its goals this qualitative study utilizes in-depth interviews with purposively selected ZANU PF supporters who watched the documentary. The study fleshes out that the audiences were angered by the documentary and resultantly a majority opted out of ZANU PF while others expressed that they will never vote for the political party again. This therefore shows that documentaries carrying discourses of corruption done by the elite has the power to alter political attitudes and behaviors of audiences.

DOI: 10.4018/979-8-3373-1037-4.ch014

INTRODUCTION

This study is concerned with analysing audience of the documentary titled Gold Mafia which was published on 16 January 2023 by Al Jazeera. The documentary is fixated at exposing alleged corruption activities involving the unsanctioned sell of gold. The documentary shows alleged ways in which gold is smuggled out of Zimbabwe and sold in Dubai and other countries in Asia. The documentary led to a spike in government criticism by member of Zimbabwean society amid an ailing economy. The documentary was put together by experienced investigative journalists called Van Hemert after two years of filed work, research and scrutiny of activities of high-ranking government officers, military officers and corporate behemoths linked to the government. With this in mind, it is essential to examine how audiences of this documentary appropriated meaning to it and how the documentary influences their political attitudes.

It should be noted that there is mature scholarship on the intersection of media, audience reception and political attitudes. For example, Tobias-Mamina (2017) interrogated how audiences' consumption traditional Zimbabwean media and how it influences their political attitudes. In the same vein Chari (2022) explored how audiences appropriate meaning to political messages on social media and how these messages get influence their understanding of political ideologies from political parties in Zimbabwe. These studies illuminate the fact that audience appropriate meaning to mediated political messages and also these messages influence their attitudes and perceptions toward certain political parties in Zimbabwe. However, there is dearth of scholarship on how documentaries as media texts, which radiate allegedly corruption activities by members of the ruling elite are consumed. Thus, this study grabs the opportunity to fill in this evident scholarly void. This will be done through examining sampled Zimbabwean audiences' views and perspectives of Gold Mafia. The study will also get to interrogate through audiences' views how the documentary gets to influence their perceptions and attitudes towards the ruling elite and the ruling Zimbabwe African National Union Patriotic Front party. As such the objectives of the study are to

- Explore audiences' reception of Gold Mafia
- Examine how Gold Mafia influences audiences' perceptions and behaviours towards ZANU PF

The importance of embarking on this study lie in that in contributes literature on how investigative documentaries are appropriated meaning to by audiences and also how these documentaries have a hand in altering audiences' perceptions, attitudes and opinion on political players. By examining these issues, this study contributes to the understanding of the connection of media consumption and audience attitudes, in the processes highlighting the role of documentary films in shaping public opinion and perceptions in Zimbabwe.

Background of the Study

Ather gaining its independence in 1980 the Zimbabwean economy was relatively steady but towards the year 2000 it was on a free fall (Mahuni, Zivanamoyo, Siyakiya and Mutsvangwa, 2025). This has been attributed to mismanagement of the economy, non-favourable foreign policy, a domestic policy which is non favourable to investors and corruption (Mahuni et al., 2025). While some of these issues have been given attention, corruption has continued to take a toll on the economy (Garufu, 2025). A transparency indicator in the year 2008 showed that Zimbabwe was having US$5 million dollars being siphoned bout of the country almost on a daily basis due to corruption. On the corruption index Zimbabwe was ranked as one of the countries with prevalent corruption.

According to Gwatidzo and Dumbu (2025) corruption in Zimbabwe is notable in the area of mining and industrialisation. For example, then finance minister Mr Tendai Biti claimed that Zimbabwe lost minerals in particular diamonds worth over US$1 billion. He attributed this loss to corrupt and illicit dealings that some government people were a part of. In the same vein, the late President of Zimbabwe Robert Mugabe made shocking claims that the country has mysteriously lost US$15 billion worth of diamonds. This again indicates the severity of corruption involving minerals in Zimbabwe.

What is interesting though is that the media in Zimbabwe has reported on these corrupt activities and mysterious disappearance of money and minerals (Zvoushe, 2025). At the fore front of mediating these issues were locally owned private owned media outlets such as *Daily News*, *Standard* and *NewsDay (*Madenga, 2024). They carried hard news stories, features and editorials on the issue. This led to public outcry and distrust of the ZANU PF led government.

Recently a documentary titled Gold Mafia also exposed how Zimbabwe losing gold worth millions of dollars through illicit and unsanctioned methods. The documentary shows how popular cleric Uebert Angels and former CEO of ZIFA and current President of Zimbabwe Miners Federation, Henrietta Beatrice Rushwaya connived with various people in Dubai to sell gold to them unlawfully. In one of the documentaries Angels convinces the under-cover reporter that he can help enter Zimbabwe with money amounting to US$1.2 billion without being detected or even questioned by law local enforcement agents. For that to be fruitful Angels asks to be paid US$200 000. The documentary further reveals that at Robert Mugabe International there are also employees that are part the syndicate and facilitate the in and out moving of gold and large volumes of money without detection and subsequent alarm.

This documentary therefore reveals a well-orchestrated corrupt way in which Zimbabwe is losing its precious minerals. Therefore, it becomes prudent to examine how audience appropriate meaning to this documentary. Additionally, it is vital to explore how the mediation of corruption on this documentary influence audiences' attitudes towards ZANU PF. Focusing on ZANU PF is essential because individuals involved in these corrupt activities are heavily linked to ZANU PF. In some instances, these individuals are high ranking government officials for example Urbert Angels the Ambassador at Large of Zimbabwe to Europe and the Americas. Against this background this study explores meaning attached to the Gold Mafia documentary and how the documentary influences audiences' perceptions towards ZANU PF.

Understanding Gold Mafia and its Reception

Gold Mafia documentary is a compelling investigative series that investigates the illicit gold trade, focusing on the networks of corruption, money laundering, and criminal activities associated with gold smuggling, particularly in Africa. The series aims to expose how these activities undermine economies, fuel organized crime and affect governance.

Gold Mafia was published on 23 March 2023 on Al Jazeera streaming platforms which are their website and YouTube channel. The documentary showcases the methods and networks involved in smuggling gold out of Africa, often circumventing regulations and taxes. It highlights the role of various players, including local miners, middlemen, and international buyers. The documentary also sheds light on the economic implications for countries like Zimbabwe, where gold mining is a significant part of the economy but is marred by corruption and loss of revenue due to smuggling.

It presents personal stories from those affected by these practices, including miners and local communities. Its release had a significant impact on shaping the attitudes of its audience towards ZANU PF. The documentary exposed the deep-seated corruption and illicit gold trade in Zimbabwe, implicating high-ranking government officials and politicians, including those from ZANU PF. The documentary compromise of four episodes, the first episodes is titled "The Laundry Service," it sets the tone for the rest of the documentary, in the first episode undercover Al Jazeera's reporters pose as representatives of a shady business interested in laundering money through Zimbabwe's gold trade. They make contact with a senior African diplomat, who offers to help them launder $1.2 million using the cover of his diplomatic bag.

The first episode has a number of Zimbabwean elites such as Urayai Hungwe who is a businessman and politician who allegedly has ties with the ruling party

ZANU PF, and Henrietta Rushwaya who is the President of the Zimbabwe miner's federation and a former intelligent officer. According to the documentary Urayai Hungwe allegedly was involved in smuggling gold outside of Zimbabwe using fake permits, he was also allegedly linked to state-owned companies involved in the gold trade, which were used to launder money and smuggle gold. While Henrietta Rushwaya as the President of miner's federation allegedly used her position to facilitate corrupt activities in the gold trade. She was also accused of using her connection to export gold without proper documentation. The themes found in the first episode include corruption, money laundering and abuse of power.

In the second episode which is titled 'The President's man', the documentary focuses on the role of Zimbabwe's President Emmerson Mnangagwa's advisor, Kudakwashe Tagwirei, in the country's gold trade. The episode explores how Tagwirei, also known as "Queen Bee," allegedly uses his influence to control the gold trade and amass wealth. The episodes implicate a number of Zimbabwean elites including, Kudakwashe Tagwirei who is the National President advisor, Sacic Lloyd who has close ties with Tagwirei. and Obert Mpofu who is a politician and a former minister of mines. The episode suggests that Tagwirei controls a significant portion of Zimbabwe's gold trade, using his influence to dictate prices and control exports, while implicates Sacic Lloyd in gold smuggling operations, allegedly using his connections to export gold without proper documentation. The episode suggests that Obert Mpofu, a former Minister of Mines, was involved in corrupt activities surrounding the gold trade. The themes found in the second episode include state capture, economic inequality and patronage.

The third episode is titled 'The Gold Syndicate' the episode explores the gold syndicate, a network of individuals and companies involved in the illicit gold trade in Zimbabwe. The episode delves into the role of key players, including Zimbabwean businessman, Pedzisai Scott Sakupwanya. The episode also exposes the corrupt activities surrounding Zimbabwe's gold trade, including bribery and smuggling. In the third episode, Pedzisai Scott Sakupwanya is accused of being a key player in the gold syndicate, specifically gold smuggling and money laundering, he allegedly smuggled gold out of Zimbabwe using fake export permits.

In the fourth episode of the Gold Mafia documentary, titled "The Cartel", the investigation delves deeper into the gold syndicate, exposing the involvement of high-ranking officials and businessmen in the illicit gold trade. Uebert Angel, President Emmerson Mnangagwa's Special Envoy, is implicated in gold smuggling and money laundering activities, allegedly using his influence to facilitate these operations. Henrietta Rushwaya, President Mnangagwa's niece, is also implicated in gold smuggling and money laundering activities, accused of using her connections to smuggle gold out of Zimbabwe and launder money through the gold trade.

The episode exposes the intricate web of relationships between high-ranking officials, businessmen, and the gold syndicate, highlighting the depth of corruption and state capture in Zimbabwe's gold trade. The documentary reveals how these individuals use their positions of power to accumulate wealth and maintain their grip on the gold trade, perpetuating a system of corruption and impunity.

In overall Gold Mafia was done so it can shed light on the widespread corruption in Zimbabwe's gold trade, which has been a long-standing issue. By exposing the corrupt activities, the documentary hoped to bring attention to the problem and spark debates. Also, the documentary does not only uncover the gold trade because the gold trade in Zimbabwe has been linked to various illicit activities, including money laundering, smuggling, and organized crime. The documentary aimed to uncover the extent of these activities and the individuals involved.

The documentary sparked intense debates among public figures, including journalists and politicians. On one hand, some critics like Simon Rudland, a businessman implicated in the documentary, demanded a public apology from Al Jazeera and denied all allegations made against him. Rudland even threatened to sue Al Jazeera for reputational harm. On the other hand, supporters of the documentary praised Al Jazeera's investigative journalism, saying it shed light on the corrupt activities surrounding Zimbabwe's gold trade. Some journalists and politicians commended the documentary for exposing the involvement of high-ranking officials and businessmen in gold smuggling and money laundering activities.

For instance, the documentary implicated President Emmerson Mnangagwa's Envoy Uebert Angel, the President's niece Henrietta Rushwaya, and Kamlesh Pattni in alleged gold smuggling and money laundering activities. These revelations sparked widespread outrage and calls for accountability among Zimbabweans. While some critics argued that the documentary was sensationalized and lacked concrete evidence, others saw it as a crucial step towards transparency and accountability in Zimbabwe's gold trade. Overall, the Gold Mafia documentary ignited a national conversation about corruption and the need for reform in Zimbabwe.

LITERATURE REVIEW: THE NEXUS OF MEDIA, CORRUPTION AND POLITICAL ATTITUDES

Media is defined as the plural platforms and channels which facilitate the transfer of information from one person to the other. There are various forms of media including newspapers, radio, television, emails, magazine, music, photographs and documentaries among others (Wu, 2024). Yang et al (2025) poignantly note that these channels have an integral role in society which encapsulates attitude creation, shaping of public opinion and the general dissemination of information. Additionally,

Schwinges et al (2025) is of the notion that the media is important in looking over the activities of the government. This is what is widely referred to as the watchdog role of the media (Schwinges et al 2025; Christians et al 2009). For the purposes of this study the media taking the centre stage is a documentary titled Gold Mafia. Since Christians et al (2009) state that the media ought to play a watchdog role this study benefits from this argument but transcends to explore how audiences make meaning of the mediated activities of the government. Consequently, this study is poised at examining how mediated corruption scandals involving the political elite in Zimbabwe are consumed by audiences.

In the Zimbabwean context, state-marshalled media often ignores corrupt allegations levelled against the government and government representatives. In this instance, it fails to report on ant corrupt activities that the government is involve in (Mantzaris and Saruchera, 2024; Nortje and Chikodza, 2024). On the contrary private owned media is at the forefront of exposing corrupt activities that the government and its representatives are involved in (Tshabangu and Salawu, 2024). This indicates the polarisation of not only the media by corruption discourses in Zimbabwean media. 'Gold Mafia' documentary deploys factfinding journalism procedures to unearth the degree of corruption involving gold. Therefore, the study then seeks to explore how audiences get to consumption mediation of corruption in the *Gold Mafia*

Henshaw (2024) posits that media coverage of corruption can inspire civilians to take action against corrupt individuals. The argument here being that when the media frames corruption as a pressing issue, it can encourage the public to take action (Danso, 2025). This then shows how the media can influence behave. While issues of media induced behaviour are important, this study takes a detour from them and focuses on attitudes induced by the media. In light of this the study interrogates how the exposition of corruption by Gold Mafia influences the attitudes of audiences of the documentary towards ZANU PF.

Scholarly inquires indicate that the media plays a vital role in holding leaders accountable and promoting transparency (Olayinka and Odunayo, 2024). While this is plausible a notable void in literature exists in understanding audience reception of investigative documentaries, particularly in African contexts. Therefore, the role of this study is to explore the audience reception of The Gold Mafia documentary series, examining how Zimbabwean audiences interpret and respond to investigative journalism on corruption. Specifically, this study investigates the impact of media consumption on political attitudes towards ZANU PF, shedding light on the complex relationships between media, corruption, and political engagement in Zimbabwe.

Recent studies have explored the media's impact on corruption exposition, highlighting its watchdog function (Amagnya, 2024). Nonetheless, these studies overlook the reception of investigative documentaries. For instance, Inobemhe et al's (2024) study examines the impact of media freedom on corruption perception.

However, their research neglects individual-level reception and interpretation. Against this context, this study seeks to investigate how audiences in Zimbabwe interpret and respond to The Gold Mafia documentary series, specifically focusing on its influence on political attitudes towards ZANU PF. By examining audience reception, this research aims to fill the gap in understanding the nuanced ways in which media consumption shapes perceptions of corruption and political accountability in Zimbabwe.

Media not only serves as a conduit for information but also plays a crucial role in framing narratives that influence audience beliefs and behaviours (Ilieva et al., 2024). In this respect investigative journalism, in particular, has gained prominence for its ability to expose corruption and hold power to account, thereby influencing public discourse and political engagement (Ilieva et al 2024).

The media's agenda-setting function can significantly impact how audiences perceive political issues and corruption (Prior, 2007). Prior (2007) notes that corruption and political issues are very emotive and, in some instance, can inspire certain emotions, attitudes and actions by those at the receiving end. Precisely the exposure of corruption and other government mal practices can lead to violent behaviour among citizens (Alashry, 2024).

In recent years, the revelation of corruption through media has become increasingly relevant, particularly in contexts where traditional media outlets may be compromised or biased (Berti et al 2020). It is for this treason that the study is aimed at exploring how audience consume how media exposes corruption precisely in Zimbabwe. By doing so this study brings forth the connection of media consumption and political attitudes, particularly through views and perspectives of media audiences. The reception of media content by media audiences is profoundly influenced by experiences, cultural circumstances, and social backgrounds in which an individual is immersed in, which can lead to a varied array of understandings (Chibike, 2023).

Alzubi (2023) poignantly notes that studies have shown that audiences are increasingly consuming content, appropriating meaning to it and allowing for a more personalised media experience. However, the implications of these dynamics within the scholarly confrontations pertaining to political attitudes remain underexplored. There is scanty literature particularly regarding how to corruption narratives such as those presented in documentary formats influence public perceptions of political issues and political figures. It is for this reason that this still takes a detour from merely analysing media texts and focuses on explicating the consumption of media texts radiating corruption narratives on documentaries and how these have a bearing on political opinions, attitude and perceptions.

Corner (2000) highlights the unique narrative techniques employed in documentaries that can evoke emotional responses. Benefiting from this the present study transcends beyond the examination of emotions but delves into how these emotions inspire or alter political attitudes and perceptions among audiences of *Gold Mafia.* Corner (2000) also notes the provocative power of documentaries and how they inspire critical thinking among audiences. However, while there is a growing body of literature examining the persuasive power of documentaries, studies focusing specifically on audience reception of contemporary documentaries, such as *Gold Mafia*, have not been looked at yet. Therefore, this study seeks to fill this critical gap in scholarship.

THEORETICAL FRAMEWORK: RECEPTION THEORY

Reception Theory was conceived in the mid-20th century as intellectuals began to move focus from the creation of media texts to the ways in which consumers engage with and construe them (Chibike, 2023). This shift was largely a confrontation and subversion of the prevailing transmission models of communication such as that by Shannon & Weaver (1949) The old transmission model of communication conceptualised communication as a one-way process and devoid of active recipients of media texts (Chibike, 2021; Mawindi Mabweazara, 2010). It also assumed that meaning was static and definite, and that audiences would understand communications in a uniform and expectable way. However, scholars like Chakraborty and Biswal (2023) and Hall (1980) began to contest this view, arguing that audiences are active participants in the communication process, bringing their own experiences, cultural backgrounds, and social contexts to the interpretation of media texts. Therefore, this study benefits from this argument as it is of the notion that *Gold Mafia* documentary is consumed and understood differently.

Fiske (1987) and Hall (1980) highlight the importance of understanding both the creators' intentions and the audience's interpretations of media artefacts. This process emphasizes that meaning is not fixed or inherent in the text itself, but rather is constructed through the interactions between the text, the creator, and the audience (Dhaenens & Van Bauwel, 2022). This ultimately leads to a wholesome understanding of meaning attached to media texts. However, for the purposes of this reception study the focus is slowly on scrutinising how audiences appropriated meaning to *Gold Mafia.* Additionally, to examine how the text influences their attitudes and perceptions towards ZANU PF. This is important because it helps unravel how audiences resonate with media texts radiating corruption in Zimbabwe.

The theory also helps scholars be abreast of the fact that readers can either positively accept meaning, negotiate it or outrightly reject it. This spectacle the active role of media consumers in the communication process. This study however transcends beyond the mere acceptation, negotiation and rejection of media texts but encroaches into issues of how media texts brew political attitudes.

By nature, media texts are polysemic as stated by Stuart Hall (1980). The argument here is that media texts can have multiple meanings and interpretations (Dahlgren, 2005). According to Fiske (1987) polysemic nature of texts refers to the idea that media texts, such as documentaries, films, and television have multiple and non-inherent meanings and interpretations. The polysemic nature of the documentary allows for a diverse range of interpretations. In this context the study captures the multifaceted relationship between media, audiences and political attitudes in Zimbabwe.

While Reception Theory offers valuable insights into audience engagement with media texts, it is not without its limitations. Notable weaknesses include an overemphasis on audience agency and a neglect of emotional responses (Grossberg et al., 1988). The theory tends to emphasize the active role of audiences in interpreting media texts, potentially downplaying the influence of media producers and the structural factors that shape media content. Critics argue that Reception Theory places too much emphasis on the active audience, overlooking the structural and institutional factors that shape media consumption (Curran & Gurevitch, 2005). Against this milieu, it should be noted that this study is not poised at examining the institutional factors surrounding the documentary *Gold Mafia* but it is solely focused on examining the audiences of the documentary. In this regard, this weakness fails to hold much water in this study.

Reception Theory primarily focuses on cognitive interpretations of media texts, often neglecting the emotional responses that audiences may have (Barker, 2013). According to Jacobs et al (2025) emotions play a significant role in shaping political attitudes and engagement. Thus, this study offers more comprehensive use of the theory to consider how emotional reactions to the documentary influence audience perceptions ZANU PF.

METHODOLOGY

This study used a qualitative approach to explore the interconnected relationship between media consumption and political attitudes. According to Creswell (2017), qualitative research focuses on collecting and analysing data that is non-numerical in nature and that describes characteristics, attitudes or opinions. As stated by Creswell (2017) qualitative research is particularly useful for exploring complex phenomena such as human behaviour, motivations and experiences. This makes qualitative approach suitable for this study because it seeks to examine how the audience interprets and understands media narratives. With regards to the population of the study which Babbie (2016) defines as the objects or people to be investigated the study makes use of 12 purposively selected participants who watched the documentary titled *Gold Mafia*. The target population for this study comprises of final year Film, Television and Media Studies students at Lupane State University who watched all four episodes of the *Gold Mafia* documentary. An invitation was sent to all 27 students and only 12 accepted the invitation. The 12 met the study' requirements of having watched the documentary and being ZANU PF supporters. As university students they possess a certain level of critical thinking and analytical skills, while their decision to watch the documentary showcases their concern for national affairs. The limitations regarding the population of the study stems from the fact that all the students here are from Lupane State University and do not necessarily represent the Zimbabwean student body. However, the researcher made sure that the initially invited participants were from different backgrounds in terms of city of origin, ethnicity, sex and language. This then gave the researchers a group of participants from a diverse background. Again, it should be noted that qualitative studies are bent at giving our qualitative data which is contextual and cannot be generalised to a larger population. Therefore, qualitative data drawn from the students from Lupane State University was enough to draw conclusions within the university and not outside.

The 12 were subjected to in-depth interviews. In-depth interviews are qualitative research tools that allow for a comprehensive exploration of participants' thoughts, feelings, and perspectives on a specific subject (Kvale, 1996). They enabled the researchers to gather nuanced insights and facilitate an in-depth understanding of how *Gold Mafia* documentary influences attitudes towards ZANU PF among university students who are also ZANU PF supporters.

The decision to utilize in-depth interviews stems from their effectiveness in eliciting detailed responses and facilitating a dialogue that can uncover complex social dynamics and personal experiences (O' Sullivan et al 2025). Each interview were approximately 20 to 30 minutes long. This allowed sufficient time for participants to articulate their views and provide in-depth reflections on their perceptions of the documentary and its political implications (Probst et al 2025). The interviews took place in a comfortable and private setting. Some were held at a quiet conference room on campus while others were held on a virtual platform. This was done to ensure participants felt at ease to share their thoughts openly. The interviews were held in English language because it is a neutral language which was understood by all the participants.

In addition to in-depth interviews, focus group discussions were employed to enrich the data collection process for the study. Focus groups involve guided discussions with a small group of participants, typically ranging from six to ten individuals, cantered around specific topics or questions (Krueger & Casey, 2014). This method allowed for the exploration of collective views and the interaction between participants, which can uncover shared experiences and divergent opinions regarding the documentary's influence on their political attitudes (Lune & Berg,

2017). The choice to incorporate focus group discussions was motivated by their ability to facilitate dynamic exchanges among participants as noted by Krueger & Casey (2014). Fostering a collaborative environment that can lead to deeper insights into the collective attitudes towards ZANU PF as shaped by the documentary. This method also allowed participants to build on each other's responses, which can reveal underlying cultural and social narratives affecting their perceptions as stated by Morgan (1998). The focus group discussions consisted of the same 12 university students selected for the interviews. The 12 were divided into two groups of six to encourage participation while managing group dynamics effectively. Each session lasted approximately 25 to 30 minutes, providing ample time for discussion and exploration of various themes related to media consumption and political attitudes. These sessions were conducted in a comfortable, neutral setting the first discussion was held at LSU lecture theatre.

Prior the collection of data the researchers asked for consent from the participant. Informed consent means that participants explicitly agreed to take part in the study after being fully informed about its purpose, potential risks, and benefits. The participants signed consent forms signalling that they were not forced or enticed to participate in the study. With regards to privacy, the identity of the participants was concealed in the data presentation and analysis. Yielded empirical data was thematically analysed. Thematic analysis is a method of identifying, coding, and categorising patterns and themes within data (Braun and Clarke 2006).

FINDINGS

Overview of the Findings

This study investigates audience views and perspective after watching the documentary, Gold Mafia. Also, the study examines how the documentary influences audiences' perceptions and attitudes towards ZANU PF. Empirical data indicates that there were varied views and perspectives of that were shared by the participants of this study. Alos the study fleshes out the fact that the documentary brew negative attitudes towards ZANU PF to the extent that some of the participants vowed not to vote for the party. The following sections discusses the findings of the study on detail.

Views and Perspectives of Audiences Regarding the Narrative on Gold Mafia

Data collected through focus group discussions and in-depth interviews revealed that audiences were angry about the level of corruption in the country. In light of this participant 1 said:

"I was very anger when I watched the video. I realised that the country is losing precious minerals worth millions now and again. These millions would have helped in equipping hospitals and also fixing roads. This is infuriating and what makes it worse is that high ranking ZANU PF people are part of thievery."

Here the participants express his anger after watching the documentary and realising that the country was not benefiting from the minerals that it has. Instead, only a few elites are benefiting and participating in the illegal sell of gold. This therefore points out the fact that after consuming the documentary the participant was angry. In this regard, by exposing the illicit deals involving minerals particularly gold with millions of united states dollars *Gold Mafia* played the role of a watchdog as explained by Schwinger et al (2025) and Christians et al (2009) who posit that the media must bring to light corruption. The audiences consumed the media and appropriated meaning to it as articulated ty Hall (1980) that audience, make meaning to texts. In this respect the meaning that participant 1 attached evoke anger in him. Therefore, it can be seen that the exposition of corruption by the media precisely documentaries can evoke feelings of anger.

Participants expressed out right sadness after watching the documentary. As such, participant 5 stated that:

"I was sad that there are people who speak proudly about depleting the country's resources for their own personal benefits "

Participant 10 also added that:

"It is very sad that people that we think are morally upright are bleeding the country. Imagine a Preacher is behind corrupt activities in Zimbabwe. How then can we trust preachers? As long as someone is a preacher and linked to ZANU PF, we shall not trust him or her!"

Here the participants express the fact that felt sad after watching the documentary. The sadness stems from seeing the levels of corruption and the fact that religious leaders at its fore front. This then indicates the fact that the unprecedent depletion of raw materials which was exposed by the documentary inspired a feeling and sense of sadness among audiences. While Inobemhe et al (2024) state that media helps people speculate on corruption and misgovernance this study extends this argument by stating the documentaries such as *Gold Mafia* are central in bringing to light the individuals behind corruption. According to the documentary members of the clergy are also involved in corruption syndicates. This finding speaks to the assumption by Hall (1980) that background and societal experiences of a person helps them appropriate meaning to texts. In this instance Christians are saddened by the fact that Christian leader Uebert Angels is among this implicated and seen proudly immersing himself in the illicit sell of gold. This sadness stems from the fact that Christian leaders preach about being morally upright and shying away from corrupt activities. Thus, Angels in this instance is documented doing the outright opposite.

Participant 1 explains that the documentary inspired excitement on her. In this regard she says:

"This was a very exciting documentary and I was very excited about it. What excited me is thinking about how people will react."

Participant 8 added:

"This was a thrilling and educative documentary. It opened my eyes on how corruption occurs and the role that people with authority play in facilitating corruption."

Participant 12 and 8 both express how excited they are about the documentary. They clearly articulate how the investigation is very educative and exciting. This is because it brought to the fore interesting ways in which systematic corruption occurs in Zimbabwe. This therefore speaks to the fact that the media is important in laying bare systematic corruption as noted by Olayinka and Odunayo (2024). Again, by saying that "what excites me is thinking about hoe people will react" the participant assumes that information about corruption can prove a certain behaviour on the audiences. This extends the argument by Danso (2025) that media reports can inspire civic action by locating the centrality of corruption in the media and how they can possibly inspire political action and behaviours. With regards to the reception theory, the fact that the participants state that they find the documentary educative and also interesting validates the assertion that audiences give different meaning to media texts as stated by Fiske (1987). The reactions of the interviewees in this study resonate with Hall's (1980) assertion that media texts are active sites of meaning-making.

The interviewees' perceptions of corruption as a pervasive problem. Participant 6 states that:

"This documentary shows us that corruption is just a problem which seems natural in Zimbabwe. People are very corrupt and in being corrupt they find nothing wrong with their actions"

In the same vein Participant 7 state that:

"My initial reaction to the documentary's portrayal of corruption in Zimbabwe was one of shock and disappointment, as it highlighted the nature of corruption that undermines the country's governance and development"

Participant 3 added that:

"The extent of corruption portrayed was staggering, and it painted a grim picture of governance in Zimbabwe"

The sentiments that were provided by the participants on the deep-seated nature of corruption echo literature that discusses corruption as deeply embedded in Zimbabwean political culture. Tobias-Mamina (2017) notes how corruption in Zimbabwe is often linked to political patronage and the mismanagement of resources, leading to widespread disillusionment among citizens. This perspective is reinforced by the participants' overwhelming negative views on corruption, which they described as impacting all aspects of life in Zimbabwe. Moreover, the attitudes toward ZANU PF, characterized by skepticism and criticism among participants, resonate with the broader academic consensus that positions the ruling party as a central actor in perpetuating corruption. Scholars such as Garufu (2025) and Mwonzora (2025) argue that ZANU PF's governance has fostered a culture of impunity and has systematically undermined accountability.

In analyzing the patterns and similarities between the participants' responses and scholarly discourse, it is evident that both highlight the emotional and psychological impact of corruption on citizens. The intense feelings expressed by interviewees rang from trauma to anger. For example, participant 8 states that:

"I was frustrated and traumatized at the same time, the country can't have a stable currency of late but those in power are busy abusing the resources to help in the development of the country, I was like no each man is for himself here"

This corresponds with academic findings that demonstrate how corruption erodes trust in institutions and diminishes civic engagement. Zizek's = notion of the "real" emphasizes how media can reveal the often-hidden truths of societal issues, suggesting that the emotional engagement (Brivic, 2008) provoked by *Gold Mafia* is crucial for fostering a critical understanding of corruption.

However, there are also differences that warrant discussion. While the literature often focuses on systemic corruption and political structures, the interviewees' narratives bring a personal dimension to the issue. As such participant 7 states that:

"The personal stories shared in the documentary made me feel more connected to the struggles of the citizens, emphasizing the human impact of corruption"

This illustrates how corruption affects individual lives and communities. This qualitative insight adds depth to academic discussions, suggesting that the emotional resonance of corruption may be underexplored in existing literature.

The next section speaks to the second objective of the study. The second objective of the study is to explore how the documentary influences audience attitudes towards ZANU PF.

How the Gold Mafia Influences Audience Attitudes and Behaviors

This section offers an analysis of how *Gold Mafia* influences attitudes of ZANU PF supporters and also their political behavior. In this essence the sampled participants showed that they are not happy with the way ZANU PF led government was going about its business. In light of this, participant 3 stated that:

"This is how ZANU PF goes about its business? I'm not happy at both the government and ZANU PF. How can they allow such things to happen? In fact, they are participating in such corrupt activities."

Here the participant is complaining about the manner and extent of corruption which ZANU PF and its officials are involved in. This act of complaining indicates that the participant is not happy with ZANU PF and now has a negative attitude towards the political outfit. In this respect participant 7 states that:

With the extent of this corruption that ZANU PF is doing I'm seeing myself not affiliating with this party anymore. This is shameful!

This adds to the notion that the complaining participants see themselves going beyond merely complaining but also thinking of leaving the party. This indicates that corruption revealed on *Gold Mafia* led to ZANU PF supporters complaining while others going on to threaten to ditch the party. This then dovetails the argument by Boulianne (2015) that the media can alter people's perceptions, beliefs and behaviour especially when issues of corruption are brought to the fore. In this study the argument is that mediated corruption through documentaries has had ZANU PF supporters complaining about its involvement in corrupt activities. This consequently culminated in others feeling that its time they leave the party. Thus, it is clear that documented corruption orchestrated by ZANU PF in Zimbabwe leads to ZANU PF loyalists wanting to leave the party. This also is an indication that media texts are pregnant with meaning and the audiences make meaning to it (Dhalgren, 2005). That meaning influences the audiences' political attitudes and behaviours

Another Participant in this study displayed critical attitudes towards ZANU PF, which were notably shaped by their viewing of *Gold Mafia.* For example, participant 12 and participant 1 expressed skepticism and disappointment. In this regard participant 12 stated that:

"Watching the documentary made me think more about how leadership plays a role in these issues of corruption in Zimbabwe. It is not worth it to trust ZANU PF because if its members are seen doing this then there is more corruption that other ZANU PF propel are involved in."

Participant 1 added:

"This is very disappointing especially from a revolutionary party which we have been trusting all along. The best thing is to leave ZANU PF. I was also one of

those calling for the President and leader of ZANU PF Emmerson Mnangagwa to have his stay extended to 2030 but now I want to distant myself from that. From now onwards I'm apolitical."

This critical stance resonates with the broader academic discourse that positions ZANU PF as a central figure in perpetuating systemic corruption. It is for this reason that the implication of ZANU PF leaders in corruption makes its supporters fail to see the reason why they should trust the party. Scholars like Mwonzora (2025) argue that the party's governance has been characterized by a lack of accountability and transparency, ultimately eroding public trust. It is for this reason that this lack of accountability has the party's supporters being skeptical of the party. This negative attitude consequently led to party supporters ditching the party and not having faith in politics at all. For example, the participants notes that she is leaving ZANU PF and also staying away from being politically affiliate to any political outfit. Thus, this study extends the argument by Christians et al (2009) and Olayinka and Odunayo (2024) that the media exposes the shortcomings of the government by arguing that these shortcomings exposed by the media can ignite political attitudes and behaviours which are anti-government.

Participant testimonies highlighted feelings of anger and frustration. This suggests that the documentary resonated deeply with their lived experiences. For instance, Participant 9 noted:

"This documentary confirmed the rumors of how corrupt ZANU PF is. I never listened to the rumors before because I had genuine interest in the political party. Discovering this does not sit well with me. It is infuriating."

This means that *Gold Mafia* reinforced their participants perception of wide-spread corruption within ZANU PF. This therefore, illustrates how the documentary served as a catalyst for critical reflection. This aligns with Ilieva et al (2024) who postulate that the media has power to alter beliefs. In this instance, *Gold Mafia* was eye opening and it managed to change audiences' beliefs and perceptions of ZANU PF. Since Prior (2007) notes that corruption and political issues are very emotive this is also seen in how the participants express emotions of anger and frustration after discovering the nature of corruption that ZANU PF members are involved in.

The study also reveals how the documentary has the potential to mobilize audiences around issues of accountability and reform. In light of this Participant 10 states that:

"The documentary's portrayal of corruption in Zimbabwe likely sparked outrage, concern, and calls for accountability."

Participants expressed a desire for change, indicating that the documentary has sparked a critical dialogue about the role of ZANU PF in perpetuating corruption. This shows how the documentary has sparked discussion amongst society about ZANU PF and corruption. This aligns with Foucault's notion of the relationship between power and knowledge, where the revelations in *Gold Mafia* empower citizens to question the status quo and demand accountability from their leaders.

However, there are some participants who are not affected by the documentary. They not that they are not in any way moved by the documentary. For instance, participant 3 notes that:

> *"No watching the documentary did not motivate me to engage in any political activities against ZANU PF. I remain loyal to the party. These things happen but it does not mean that everyone in ZANU PF is corrupt or has a hand in the illicit gold dealings."*

This then shows that while there are people whose attitudes, perceptions and behaviors twisted against ZANU PF there are some who were not moved by the documentary. Other participants despite the glaring corruption perpetuated by ZANU PF leaders remain loyal to the part. This shows that people react differently to media texts based on their background as articulated by Hall (1980). Thus, this explains why others preferred to be steadfast with the party despite corruption narratives. The findings here are in synch with the key tenets of the reception theory.

CONCLUSION

The study has shown how the reception theory is a viable theory enabling the examination of the consumption of documentary radiating corruption by the political elite in Zimbabwe and how this influences their political attitudes and behaviours. The study found out that the audiences of the documentary who also happen to be ZANU PF supporters were dismayed after consuming the documentary. Most of them were angry at the exposition of the corruption. Their anger was particularly directed to ZANU PF and its leader Emmerson Mnangagwa for incubating corrupt individuals in the political party. Speaking to the second objective the study fleshes out the fact that the documentary led to most audiences having negative attitudes towards the party. These negative attitudes in some instances led to people ditching the party while others vowing not to vote for it in the next election. Therefore, the argument here is that media radiating corruption perpetrated but members of ZANU PF inspire the members of the party to ditch the party. Therefore, there is need for political parties to desist from corruption if they are to entraining hope of keeping party supporters and votes during elections. Future scholarship on these issues should also focus on how mediated corruption on newspapers influence political behaviours. Doing so will help strengthen or modify arguments in this chapter.

REFERENCES

AlAshry, M.-S. (2024). Arab journalists have no place: Authorities use digital surveillance to control investigative reporting. *Communicatio Socialis, 37*(1), 61–77.

Alzubi, A. (2023). The evolving relationship between digital and conventional media: A study of media consumption habits in the digital era. *The Progress: A Journal of Multidisciplinary Studies, 4*(3), 1-13.

Amagnya, M. A. (2024). The relationship between the media and corruption: Perspectives of Ghanaian justice and anti-corruption officials. *The International Journal of Sociology and Social Policy, 44*(7/8), 689–705.

Babbie, E. (2016). *The practice of social research* (14th ed.). Cengage Learning.

Barker, M. (2013). Live to Your Local Cinema: The Remarkable Rise of Live casting. Convergence. Springer International. https://link.springer.com/book/10.1057/9781137288691

Berti, C., Bratu, R., & Wickberg, S. (2020). Corruption and the media. *A research agenda for studies of corruption*, 107-117.

Boulianne, S. (2015). Social media use and participation: A meta-analysis of current research. *Information Communication and Society, 18*(5), 524–538.

Braun, V., & Clarke, V. (2006). Using thematic analysis in psychology. *Qualitative Research in Psychology, 3*(2), 77–101.

Brivic, S. (2008). Žižek, Fantasy, and Truth. In *Joyce through Lacan and Žižek*. New Directions in Irish and Irish American Literature.

Chakraborty, U., & Biswal, S. K. (2023). Is digital social communication effective for social relationship? A study of online brand communities. *Journal of Relationship Marketing, 23*(1), 94–118.

Chari, T. (2022). Between state interests and citizen digital rights: making sense of internet shutdowns in Zimbabwe. In Kperoogi, F. A. (Ed.), *Digital Dissidence and Social Media Censorship in Africa* (pp. 76–98). Routledge.

Chibike, J. J. (2021). Zimbabwe-India relations: Reception of the portrayal of the relations between the countries on Zimbabwean state media, *African Currents* 39(2): 27-40. https://mu.ac.in/wp-content/uploads/2021/08/African-Currents-2021-issue-2-final-13_08-2.pdf#page=33

Chibike, J. J. (2023). Podcasting COVID-19 in Indigenous Languages: Interrogating Audio Psychology and Political Anthropomorphism. In *African Language Media* (pp. 112-124). Routledge.

Christians, C. G., Glasser, T., McQuail, D., Nordenstreng, K., & White, R. A. (2009). *Normative Theories of the Media: Journalism in Democratic Societies*. University of Illinois Press.

Corner, J. (2000). What we say about documentary. *Media Culture & Society*, *22*(5), 681–688.

Creswell, J. W. (2017) *Research design: qualitative, quantitative, and mixed methods approach*. 4th Edition. London: Thousand Oaks: Sage Publications.

Curran, J., & Gurevitch, M. (2005). *Mass Media and Society*. Bloomsbury Academic Publishing.

Danso, S. (2025). Media and politics: Investigating government interests, ownership influence and media independence in combating corruption in Ghana. *Cogent Social Sciences*, *11*(1), 2483391.

Dhaenens, F., & Van Bauwel, S. (2022). Textual analysis: A practical introduction to studying texts in media and cultural studies. In Stevens, P. (Ed.), *Qualitative Data Analysis: Key Approaches* (pp. 271–291). Sage.

Fiske, J. (1987). *Television Culture*. Routledge.

Garufu, P. (2025). Understanding Political Will and Why It Matters to Confront Corruption in Zimbabwe. *Journal of Asian and African Studies*, *60*(4), 2196–2214.

Grossberg, L., Fry, T., Curthoys, A., & Patton, P. (1988). *It's a sin: essays on postmodernism politics & culture*. Power Publications.

Gwatidzo, K., & Dumbu, E. (2025). Socio-Economic Impact of the Chinese Foreign Direct Investment in Gold Mining: The Case of Shamva District, Zimbabwe. *The Review of Rural Resilience Praxis, 4*(1 and 2), 205-228.

Hall, S. (1980). Encoding/decoding. *Centre for Contemporary Cultural Studies (ed.) Culture, Media, Language: Working Papers in Cultural Studies, 79*, 128-38.

Henshaw, E. E. (2024). *Reporting on political corruption in Nigeria: Sources, ownership affiliations, and other determinants of news frames*. Unpublished Doctoral dissertation. City, University of London. London: England.

Ilieva, G., Yankova, T., Ruseva, M., Dzhabarova, Y., Klisarova-Belcheva, S., & Bratkov, M. (2024). Social media influencers: Customer attitudes and impact on purchase behaviour. *Information (Basel)*, *15*(6), 359.

Inobemhe, K., Garba, S., & Santas, T. (2024). Media in the Fight against Corruption: Examining the Responsibilities of the Media in Building Strong Institutions in Nigeria. *Journal of Media Studies*, *39*(1), 51–81.

Jacobs, L., Close, C., & Pilet, J. B. (2025). The angry voter? The role of emotions in voting for the radical left and right at the 2019 Belgian elections. *International Political Science Review*, *46*(1), 144–159.

Krueger, R. A., & Casey, M. A. (2014). *Focus groups: a practical guide for applied research* (5th ed.). Sage Publications.

Kvale, S. (1996). *InterViews: an introduction to qualitative research interviewing*. Sage Publications.

Lune, H., & Berg, B. L. (2017). *Qualitative Research Methods for the Social Sciences*. Pearson.

Madenga, F. Z. (2024). Mimicking power: Visualizing satire as journalism in Zimbabwe. *The European Journal of Humour Research*, *12*(3), 9–35.

Mahuni, K., Zivanamoyo, J., Siyakiya, P., & Mutsvangwa, S. (2025). *Zimbabwe's economy: Four Decades in Perspective (1980-2020)*. Springer International Publishing. AG. https://link.springer.com/book/10.1007/978-3-031-81588-1

Mantzaris, E., & Saruchera, M. (2024). The realities of anti-corruption and whistleblowing: The case of Zimbabwe. *African Review (Dar Es Salaam, Tanzania)*, *16*(3), 279–301.

Mawindi Mabweazara, H. (2010). Researching the use of new technologies (ICTs) in Zimbabwean newsrooms: An ethnographic approach. *Qualitative Research*, *10*(6), 659–677.

Morgan, D. L. (1998). Practical strategies for combining qualitative and quantitative methods: Applications to health research. *Qualitative Health Research*, *8*(3), 362–376.

Mwonzora, G. (2025). 'Who is patriotic, who is not'? Enactment of patriotism law in Zimbabwe. *African Identities*, *23*(1), 17–32.

Nortje, W., & Chikodza, E. (2024). The Realisation of Media Freedom as a Tool to Combat Corruption in Zimbabwe: Lessons from South Africa. *JACL*, *8*, 85–11.

Olayinka, A. P., & Odunayo, S. (2024). The role of media ethics in shaping public perception: A critical analysis of biased reporting and its impact on public opinion. *Journal of African Innovation and Advanced Studies, 3*(2), 31–51. https://africanscholarpub.com/ajaias/article/view/109/115

O' Sullivan, K. C., Buchanan, M., Leigh, L., Dohig, R. K., Pehi, T., Jenkins, M., Pierse, N., Ryan, L., & Fraser, B. (2025). Working With Community Research Partners to Undertake Sensitive Public Health Interviews: A Qualitative Protocol to Enhance Rigour and Safety. *International Journal of Qualitative Methods, 24*. Advance online publication. DOI: 10.1177/16094069251337204

Prior, M. (2007). *Post-Broadcast Democracy: How Media Choice Increases Inequality in Political Involvement and Polarizes Elections*. Cambridge University Press.

Probst, S., Bergin, S. M., & Tehan, P. (2025). Healing beyond the surface: Empathy's role in chronic wound care a qualitative study. *Journal of Tissue Viability, 34*(3), 100910.

Schwinges, A., van der Meer, T. G., & Vliegenthart, R. (2025). Are News Media Biting Hard Enough? Public Watchdog Role Expectations and Performance Evaluations in the Era of Big Tech. *Digital Journalism (Abingdon, England)*, •••, 1–21.

Shannon, C. E., & Weaver, W. (1949). A mathematical model of communication. *Urbana, IL: University of Illinois Press, 11*, 11-20.

Tobias-Mamina, R. J. (2017). Digital Media Exposure, Political Attitudes and Perceptions as Antecedents of Voting Intentions: A Zimbabwean Perspective. Unpublished PhD Thesis: University of the Witwatersrand, Johannesburg (South Africa).

Tshabangu, T., & Salawu, A. (2024). Alternative media, repression and the crisis state: Towards a political economy of alternative media in post-Mugabe Zimbabwe. *Journal of Asian and African Studies, 59*(1), 172–186.

Wu, Z. (2024). The Image Transmission and Cultural Heritage of Chinese Musical Instruments. *Frontiers in Art Research, 6*(1), 44–50.

Yang, S., Krause, N. M., Bao, L., Calice, M. N., Newman, T. P., Scheufele, D. A., Xenos, M. A., & Brossard, D. (2025). In AI We Trust: The Interplay of Media Use, Political Ideology, and Trust in Shaping Emerging AI Attitudes. *Journalism & Mass Communication Quarterly, 102*(2), 382–406.

Zvoushe, H. (2025). Corruption, State Fragility and Digital Activism for accountability in public service delivery: A case of Hopewell Chinono Cyberactivism in Zimbabwe. *African Journal of Public Administration and Environmental Studies, 4*(1), 307. https://journals.co.za/doi/epdf/10.31920/2753-3182/2025/v4n1a15

KEY TERMS AND DEFINITIONS

Attitude: A way in which someone relates to certain people or issues based on the information they have.

Corruption: Inappropriate use of resources to benefit the elite at the expense of a country's citizens.

Documentary: A television programme which carries specific and detailed information about a certain person or issue.

Emotions: How people feel about a certain issue or person.

Gold: A valuable and expensive yellowish metal mined in Zimbabwe.

Gold Mafia: A documentary which shows the illicit use of gold by the elite linked to ZANU PF in Zimbabwe.

Reception: How people understand and appropriate meaning to media texts such as documentaries.

Chapter 15

AI-Driven Electoral Strategies: Populist Campaigns, Voter Behavior, and Democratic Integrity in the 2024 EU Elections

Vaia Stavridou
http://orcid.org/0009-0003-9486-2700
Aristotle University of Thessaloniki, Greece

ABSTRACT

The integration of artificial intelligence (AI) into the 2024 European Parliament elections redefined the dynamics of political campaigning, voter behavior, and democratic integrity. This chapter examines the dual role of AI as both an enabler of participatory democracy and a catalyst for electoral manipulation, focusing on populist movements in Estonia, the Netherlands, Greece, and Italy. Through a comparative analysis of AI-driven microtargeting strategies and an evaluation of EU regulatory frameworks such as the Digital Services Act and the Artificial Intelligence Act, the study reveals critical vulnerabilities in safeguarding electoral processes. It argues for an adaptive, multi-scalar regulatory approach to mitigate the epistemic and structural risks posed by algorithmic political persuasion, ensuring democratic resilience in the age of digital transformation.

INTRODUCTION

The European Parliament serves as the representative institution of the citizens of the European Union's members states. In turn, these citizens are periodically

DOI: 10.4018/979-8-3373-1037-4.ch015

called upon every five years -in years ending in 4 and 9- to elect their European delegates. These delegates are entrusted with the democratic mandate to articulate their interests at the supranational level. This electoral process constitutes a cornerstone of the EU's institutional framework, ensuring the direct participation of its people in the formulation of the European policies and legislation (Schmitt & Teperoglou, 2021, p.52-56).

The 2024 European Parliament elections marked a significant moment in the democratic process of the European Union and reaffirmed the institution's functions as the direct representative of EU citizens (Rabitsch & Calabrese, 2024). Since, the first direct elections in 1979, when nine member states participated, the Parliament has expanded in both size and authority, reflecting the broader transformation of the EU, from an economic coalition into a multifaceted political entity. Through a series of successive treaties, its competences have been reinforced, and hence the European Parliament has been granted legislative, budgetary and supervisory powers, equal to those of the Council of the European Union. As a result, the Parliament has evolved into a key institution where the political will of nearly 450 million citizen is translated into legislative action and policy decisions (Nugent, 2017).

The electoral process, held every five years, enables EU citizens to actively participate in shaping the political and legislative framework of the Union. Governed by the principle of proportional representation, these elections ensure a fair allocation of parliamentary seats, allowing for a diverse array of political voices to be represented. Unlike national legislatures, the European Parliament is structured around transnational political groups, bringing together national parties with similar ideological orientations. Major alliances include the European People's Party, the Progressive Alliance of Socialists and Democrats, Renew Europe, the Greens/European Free Alliance, the European Conservatives and Reformists, Identity and Democracy, and The Left. This organizational model fosters -among other competences- a dynamic interaction among political forces, facilitating cross-border coalitions that influence EU legislation, budget decisions, and the selection of the President of the European Commission (Nugent, 2017).

In parallel, the digital era has radically transformed the political landscape, offering unparalleled opportunities and equally profound challenges. Political campaigns, once grounded in traditional methods of messaging and voter outreach, now operate in an ecosystem deeply intertwined with advanced technologies. These tools amplify the reach and precision of political messaging, facilitating both engagement and manipulation. Central to this transformation is the advent of microtargeting, a practice that, while not new, has acquired novel dimensions in the digital age. By utilizing vast reservoirs of data, political actors craft highly personalized messages aimed at influencing voter behavior. This evolution, however, has given rise to new ethical and regulatory concerns, particularly regarding the integrity of elections and the role of artificial intelligence (AI) in shaping democratic outcomes (Zhu & Isaacs, 2024).

Against this backdrop, populist parties across Europe have rapidly adopted AI tools to shape political narratives, influence emotions, and fragment public debate. These developments raise urgent questions about the capacity of democratic institutions to regulate digital persuasion and preserve the principles of political transparency, pluralism, and fairness. While the European Union has introduced landmark regulatory frameworks—such as the Digital Services Act (DSA), the Artificial Intelligence Act (AI Act), and the Transparency and Targeting of Political Advertising Regulation (TTPA)—their ability to counter algorithmic manipulation remains contested (Rabitsch et al., 2021, p.1-6).

This chapter investigates the intersection of AI, populism, and electoral regulation by examining how four European populist parties deployed AI-driven strategies in the 2024 elections: PVV (Netherlands), SYRIZA (Greece), Fratelli d'Italia (Italy), and EKRE (Estonia). Through qualitative content analysis and regulatory comparison, it defines the synergy between national digital ecosystems and supranational regulatory instruments. In doing so, the chapter aims to floodlight how the algorithmic turn in politics both challenges and reevaluates democratic integrity in contemporary Europe.

Research Objectives

Concomitantly, the research objectives are threefold. First, the in-hand chapter seeks to explore the evolving regulatory framework of the EU as it pertains to the intersection of artificial intelligence, digital democracy, and electoral integrity. Key legislative instruments such as the Digital Services Act (DSA), the Transparency and Targeting of Political Advertising Act (TTPA), the Artificial Intelligence Act (AI Act), and the General Data Protection Regulation (GDPR) will be critically examined to understand their scope, implementation challenges, and potential in safeguarding democratic processes.

Secondly, the study aims to explore the deployment of populist parties across four diverse European contexts: Estonia, the Netherlands, Greece, and Italy. Consequently, the forthcoming goal is to compare how populist parties in four European Union member states—Estonia, the Netherlands, Greece, and Italy—strategically deploy AI tools for political microtargeting, digital persuasion, and ideological amplification within varying national digital ecosystems. There is a notable research gap in making such cross-national comparisons, and especially in selecting these country cases, which this study aims to address.

Thirdly, the research will estimate democratic implications and normative risks posed by AI-driven electoral strategies, particularly in terms of voter manipulation, public trust, and the resilience of regulatory mechanisms. This includes assessing the potential of AI-driven innovations to enhance transparency and citizen engagement, as well as the risks of misinformation, polarization, and erosion of trust in democratic institutions. The analysis will offer a balanced perspective on the implications of these technological advancements for the future of European democracy.

Research Questions

- How effective are existing EU regulatory frameworks in addressing the challenges posed by AI-driven political campaigning and digital manipulation during elections?
- How does a country's level of digital maturity shape the AI techniques and electoral strategies used by populist parties?
- What are the key differences in how populist and far-right actors deploy AI technologies across digitally advanced and less digitally integrated member states?

Given the chapter's qualitative and exploratory nature, the following expectations serve as guiding assumptions rather than testable hypotheses. These expectations reflect insights from the literature on algorithmic governance, digital populism, and comparative political communication:

1. It is expected that the existing EU regulatory frameworks—while ambitious in scope—contain notable gaps in addressing the transnational, adaptive, and opaque nature of AI-driven electoral manipulation. These gaps are likely to manifest in inconsistent enforcement, limited transparency, and varying platform accountability across member states.
2. It is anticipated that a country's level of digital maturity influences the sophistication and form of AI usage by populist and far-right parties. In digitally advanced states such as Estonia and the Netherlands, AI deployment is expected to be more targeted, platform-specific, and technologically nuanced. In contrast, in less digitally mature contexts like Greece and Italy, populist strategies may rely more on emotional amplification and basic algorithmic personalization.

METHODOLOGY AND RESEARCH DESIGN

The methodological approach adopted in this study is grounded in qualitative content analysis (QCA), an established research method that facilitates systematic examination of textual, visual, and regulatory data. Given the complexity of AI-driven political microtargeting and its deployment in digital populist campaigns, QCA provides a structured yet flexible framework for analyzing the intersection of artificial intelligence, electoral manipulation, and populist digital strategies. This method allows for the interpretation of political discourse, algorithmic amplification, and engagement strategies used by parties such as SYRIZA (Greece), the Party for Freedom (PVV, Netherlands), Fratelli d'Italia (FdI, Italy), and the Conservative People's Party of Estonia (EKRE) in the 2024 European Parliament elections. The study synthesizes multiple sources to construct an interdisciplinary analytical lens, combining insights from political science, media studies, computational propaganda research, and AI ethics to offer a comprehensive and empirically grounded exploration of the subject matter (Elo & Kyngäs, 2008, p.110; Bryda & Costa, 2023, p.1-3) .

The empirical material analyzed consists of four primary data categories: (1) political campaign content from official party accounts on platforms such as TikTok, Facebook, and X (formerly Twitter); (2) EU and national regulatory texts, including the Digital Services Act (DSA), the Artificial Intelligence Act (AI Act), the General Data Protection Regulation (GDPR), and the Transparency and Targeting of Political Advertising Regulation (TTPA); (3) secondary academic literature and policy reports on AI and electoral strategy; and (4) media reporting and platform transparency documents concerning political content moderation and algorithmic amplification. It should be noted that no primary interviews were conducted; the analysis relies exclusively on publicly available or secondary sources.

Country cases were selected using a logic of maximum variation sampling to capture contrasts in digital maturity, populist party typologies, and national regulatory enforcement. Estonia and the Netherlands represent digitally advanced environments with different populist profiles (EKRE and PVV, respectively), while Italy and Greece illustrate mid-level or uneven digital governance settings, hosting both left-wing and right-wing populist formations (SYRIZA and FdI). This diversity provides fertile ground for identifying both structural and strategic differences in AI appropriation across contexts (Adeyinka-Ojo, 2025, p.17).

Analytically, the chapter implements thematic coding so as to examine campaign communication and AI techniques across three major dimensions: technological deployment (e.g., bots, microtargeting, automated messaging), populist message framing (e.g., anti-elitism, nationalist appeals, emotional resonance), and regulatory interaction (e.g., circumvention, partial compliance, legal ambiguity). These themes are assessed in light of national cyberspaces and supranational policy constraints.

While every effort was made to ensure analytical rigor, the study is constrained by platform opacity, limited access to algorithmic backend data, and variation in platform transparency across countries. These limitations underscore the challenges of empirically assessing AI's political impact and suggest directions for future transparency-enhancing reforms (Bryda & Costa, 2023, p.13-14).

Beyond legal texts, the study engaged in systematic digital content analysis, focusing on the official TikTok accounts of the four parties under investigation. By examining campaign messaging, rhetorical framing, visual AI strategies, and microtargeting engagement tactics, the study identified key patterns in AI-enhanced propaganda. This involved assessing algorithmic amplification patterns, tracking virality metrics and engagement loops, and exploring the extent to which AI-generated content—such as deepfake videos, synthetic spokespersons, and automated replies—were used to reinforce political narratives. This phase of analysis was crucial in mapping the technological evolution of digital populism, offering insights into how parties exploited AI- driven strategies in order to optimize their electoral outreach and manipulate digital and online political discourse (Pena, 2024, p.1-3).

Namely, despite its strengths, this methodological approach also presents certain limitations. One of the key challenges is the restricted access to proprietary AI data used by social media platforms and political campaign teams. Given the opacity of algorithmic recommendation systems, the study is limited to observable content and inferred engagement patterns, making it difficult to fully trace how AI-driven personalization shapes voter perceptions. Additionally, while QCA allows for the detailed categorization of AI-enhanced political messaging, it does not establish definitive causal relationships between AI exposure and voter behavior. This constraint necessitates a cautious interpretation of findings, acknowledging that political behavior is influenced by a multitude of factors beyond digital engagement alone (Braun & Clarke, 2024, p.415-416).

Furthermore, the cross-country comparative analysis presents challenges related to differences in digital literacy, media consumption habits, and national regulatory environments. Countries such as Estonia and the Netherlands, which exhibit high levels of technological integration, present a different digital ecosystem compared to Greece and Italy, where traditional media still plays a significant role in political communication. These contextual differences necessitate a differentiated analytical approach, ensuring that conclusions are drawn with sensitivity to national variations in digital governance and electoral strategy. The study mitigates this challenge by employing contextualized case study analysis, ensuring that AI deployment is examined within the specific socio-political landscape of each country (Elo & Kyngäs, 2008, p. 120).

While every effort was made to ensure analytical rigor, the study is constrained by platform opacity, limited access to algorithmic backend data, and variation in platform transparency across countries. These limitations underscore the challenges of empirically assessing AI's political impact and suggest directions for future transparency-enhancing reforms (Adeyinika-Ojo, 2025, p.18-19).

THEORETICAL FRAMEWORK

The theoretical framework employed in the current study is structured into two interrelated sections: the first provides key definitions essential for comprehending the role of artificial intelligence (AI) and political microtargeting in contemporary electoral processes, while the second analyzes these mechanisms through the lens of digital democracy. This structured approach serves a dual purpose. Initially, it ensures terminological clarity, establishing the conceptual foundation required to engage critically with AI's impact on democratic institutions. Subsequently, it contextualizes these definitions within the broader paradigm of digital democracy, thereby elucidating their implications for governance, electoral integrity, and political discourse. The necessity of this dual structure stems from the inherently interdisciplinary nature of the under analysis subject. Therefore, AI-driven microtargeting is not merely a technical innovation; it is a phenomenon with profound sociopolitical consequences, influencing voter autonomy, public deliberation, and the epistemic conditions of democracy itself. Hence, a precise understanding of these concepts is imperative to assess both their functional mechanisms and their normative ramifications (Pollicino & de Gregorio, 2022, p.12-14; Gornet & Maxwell, 2024, p.1-3).

Necessary Clarifications

Political microtargeting is a strategic electoral practice wherein sophisticated data analytics and AI-driven algorithms segment voters into highly specific groups, enabling campaigns to tailor messages with extraordinary granularity. Unlike traditional campaign strategies, which rely on broad demographic classifications, microtargeting leverages psychographic profiling, behavioral data, and machine learning to predict individual voter preferences. The operationalization of this technique entails the collection and processing of vast datasets derived from social media interactions, consumer behavior, and electoral history. AI algorithms analyze these datasets to construct predictive models that anticipate voting behavior, ideological alignment, and susceptibility to particular messaging strategies. This results in highly personalized political communication, wherein different segments of the electorate receive distinct campaign narratives, often emphasizing divergent issues based on their inferred concerns. Such an approach not only optimizes voter persuasion but also raises critical ethical concerns regarding the fragmentation of public discourse, the exacerbation of ideological echo chambers, and the erosion of a shared democratic reality (Al-kfairy et al., 2024, p.4-8, Duberry, 2022, p.21).

Generative AI, a subset of artificial intelligence capable of autonomously producing text, images, video, and other forms of content, has emerged as a transformative force in political communication. These AI models, trained on extensive datasets, generate synthetic media that can be tailored for persuasive electoral messaging, political advertisements, and even misinformation campaigns (Pollicino & De Gregorio, 2022, p.17-20). The implications of generative AI in political campaigns are multifaceted. On one hand, it enables the rapid production of campaign materials, enhancing the efficiency and responsiveness of political actors. On the other, it introduces new vulnerabilities to electoral integrity by facilitating the creation of deepfakes, synthetic propaganda, and AI-generated misinformation. The proliferation of AI-generated content complicates traditional fact-checking mechanisms and raises epistemic concerns regarding the authenticity of political discourse (Küsters et al., 2023, p.3).

The application of AI in elections extends beyond content generation to encompass voter influence strategies that operate at both cognitive and behavioral levels. Predictive analytics, sentiment analysis, and real-time behavioral tracking allow campaigns to adapt messaging dynamically, ensuring that voters receive not only personalized content but also content optimized for maximum psychological impact. AI-driven sentiment analysis, for instance, monitors social media discourse to assess public reactions to political events, enabling campaign strategists to refine messaging in real time. Such capabilities introduce profound ethical dilemmas regarding voter autonomy and the potential for manipulation. The distinction between persuasion and psychological coercion becomes increasingly ambiguous when AI can exploit cognitive biases with precision-engineered narratives (Novelli & Sandri, 2024, p.22).

From the perspective of digital democracy, these developments necessitate a reassessment of foundational democratic principles, including electoral transparency, political equality, and public deliberation. Digital democracy, broadly defined, refers to the integration of digital technologies into democratic governance, encompassing mechanisms such as online participation, e-voting, and algorithmic decision-making. While digital democracy holds the promise of enhancing accessibility and inclusivity in political engagement, it also introduces new asymmetries in political power. The deployment of AI in elections creates an uneven informational landscape, wherein well-funded political entities can leverage sophisticated AI tools to shape public opinion, while ordinary voters lack comparable means to critically assess and counteract such influence (Fischli & Muldoon, 2024, p.3-6).

The regulatory landscape surrounding AI in electoral processes remains fragmented and insufficiently developed. The European Union's Artificial Intelligence Act classifies AI applications based on their risk levels but struggles to adequately address election-specific vulnerabilities. Many AI-driven election technologies, including microtargeting and chatbot-based voter engagement, fall into the category of limited-risk AI, thereby evading stringent regulatory scrutiny. The difficulty in defining "intentionality" within AI applications further complicates regulatory efforts, as AI systems originally developed for neutral applications can be repurposed for electoral manipulation (European Parliament, 2023).

Mitigating the risks associated with AI in elections requires a multipronged approach that balances innovation with democratic safeguards. Policy interventions must prioritize transparency in AI-driven political advertising, ensuring that voters are informed when content has been generated or optimized by AI. Additionally, algorithmic accountability measures should be enforced, mandating audits of AI models used in electoral campaigns to detect biases and manipulative intent. Fact-checking mechanisms must also evolve to address the challenges posed by generative AI, incorporating AI-powered detection tools capable of identifying synthetic media and deepfakes (Duberry, 2022, p.23; Küsters et al., 2023, p.6).

In conclusion, the integration of AI into political microtargeting and electoral processes signifies a paradigmatic shift in democratic governance, necessitating rigorous academic and policy-oriented scrutiny. While AI enhances the precision and efficacy of political communication, it also introduces unprecedented risks to electoral integrity and democratic fairness. The challenge lies in developing regulatory and technological frameworks that harness the benefits of AI while mitigating its potential for misuse. The future of digital democracy hinges on our ability to navigate these intricacies, safeguarding that AI serves as a tool for democratic enhancement rather than democratic erosion (UNRIC, 2024; Innerarity, 2024).

Digital Democracy

Digital democracy represents a fundamental shift in the mechanisms of political participation, decision-making, and governance, particularly within the framework of multilevel governance in the European Union. As Van Dijk defines it, "digital democracy is the pursuit and the practice of democracy in whatever view using digital media in online and offline political communication" (Van Dijk, 2013, p.29). This concept underscores the fusion of technological infrastructures with democratic institutions, facilitating new avenues for citizen engagement while simultaneously introducing challenges related to misinformation, algorithmic bias, and governance fragmentation (Berg & Hofmann, 2021, p.7). The European Union, characterized by its complex governance architecture, has embraced digital democracy as a tool for enhancing transparency and inclusivity, yet its implementation remains contingent upon varying national digital capacities and regulatory effectiveness (Neudert & Marchal, 2019, p.8-15).

The theoretical underpinnings of digital democracy are deeply rooted in six core democratic perspectives that shape its application: legalist democracy, competitive democracy, pluralist democracy, participatory democracy, plebiscitary democracy, and libertarian democracy. Each of these models informs the extent to which digital infrastructures mediate political processes, from electoral participation to deliberative discourse (Van Dijk, 2013, p.40-45). Within the European context, digital democracy does not merely function as a means of enhancing participation but rather as a structural component of governance itself, particularly in an era where political campaigns leverage algorithmic systems to engineer public sentiment, deepening ideological polarization and transforming electoral integrity (Fuchs, 2022, p.273). The digitalization of political engagement has evolved through successive phases—teledemocracy, virtual democracy, and network democracy—each expanding the role of technology in political deliberation while simultaneously amplifying vulnerabilities related to algorithmic manipulation and disinformation (Berg & Hofmann, 2021, p.8).

The achievements of e-democracy are evident in the proliferation of e-participation mechanisms that bridge the gap between citizens and decision-making processes. European initiatives such as Decidim in Spain, Better Reykjavik in Iceland, and the D-CENT platform exemplify how decentralized digital participation fosters a more engaged citizenry while also reinforcing democratic accountability (Al-kfairy, 2024, p.9). However, these initiatives are not without limitations. The reliance on algorithmic governance structures introduces concerns regarding transparency, as digital platforms often obscure the mechanisms through which political messaging is curated and disseminated (Fischli & Muldoon, 2024). The participatory dimension of digital democracy, while promising, must contend with structural inequalities in access to digital infrastructures, a challenge that remains particularly salient within the European Union's differentiated digital landscape (Pollino & Gregorio, 2022, p.17-19).

Habermas' theory of the public sphere provides an essential lens through which the digitalization of political discourse must be analyzed. The traditional public sphere, envisioned as a realm of rational-critical debate, has been transformed by digital infrastructures that prioritize engagement over deliberation, often amplifying echo chambers and polarizing content (Habermas, 1991, p.1). The European public sphere, characterized by linguistic and cultural diversity, is further fragmented by algorithmic mediation, which privileges highly targeted political messaging over broad-based deliberation (Fuchs, 2023, p. 275). Within this context, digital democracy does not merely facilitate participation; it reconfigures the conditions under which public opinion is formed and contested, raising critical questions about the legitimacy of algorithmically curated political discourse (Neudert & Marchal, 2019, p.32-35).

The internet and smart access technologies have emerged as pivotal instruments for mitigating democratic deficits within the European Union, particularly by fostering bottom-up approaches to governance. Decentralized participation mechanisms, such as participatory budgeting in Spain and France's Grand Débat National, illustrate how digital infrastructures can facilitate citizen-driven policy formulation. However, these mechanisms also introduce vulnerabilities, as digital governance structures are susceptible to manipulation by vested political interests that leverage AI-driven microtargeting to shape electoral outcomes. The paradox of digital democracy lies in its dual potential: while it offers avenues for increased civic engagement, it simultaneously enables new forms of political influence that evade traditional regulatory oversight (Ivaldi & Zankina, 2024, p.21-31; Cath, 2018, p.3-6) .

The introduction of artificial intelligence into electoral processes has exacerbated concerns regarding electoral integrity and misinformation. AI-driven political campaigns employ sophisticated data analytics to craft hyper-personalized messaging, a strategy that has been particularly effective for populist movements across Europe. Deepfake populism, characterized by the deployment of AI-generated political content to distort public discourse, represents a novel challenge for democratic governance. This phenomenon is particularly evident in cases such as Italy, where AI-generated disinformation has been strategically utilized to amplify populist narratives. The convergence of AI and populist electoral strategies underscores the limitations of existing regulatory frameworks, highlighting the urgent need for adaptive governance mechanisms that can mitigate algorithmic distortions while preserving democratic plurality (Ivaldi & Zankina, 2024, p.347-351; Kusters et al., 2023, p.9-12).

Despite the extensive body of research on digital democracy, significant gaps remain in understanding the comparative dynamics of AI-driven populist strategies across different European electoral contexts. While existing scholarship has examined the technological implications of AI and the broader theoretical dimensions of populism, there is a distinct lack of empirical analyses that assess how digital infrastructures mediate populist electoral tactics in high- tech ecosystems such as Estonia and the Netherlands versus more traditional political landscapes like Greece and Italy. This chapter seeks to address this gap by providing a systematic examination of how AI reshapes populist electoral campaigns, evaluates regulatory efficacy, and explores the broader implications for European democratic resilience. As AI continues to redefine the digital electoral ecosystem, its impact on democratic legitimacy and governance structures will remain a central concern for the future of European democracy (Schippers, 2020, p. 35; Kusters et al., 2023, p.20-25).

Conceptual Framework and Operationalisation

To ensure clarity and consistency in analysis, the following table outlines how the core concepts guiding this study have been defined and operationalized. As outlined in Table 1, the core concepts guiding this study are systematically defined and operationalized, linking theoretical constructs to specific indicators and data sources used in the comparative analysis.

Table 1. Conceptual Framework and Operationalisation of Key Variables

Core Concept	Definition/Explanation	Indicators	Data Sources
AI Microtargeting	The use of algorithmic tools to personalize political messaging based on voter data.	Personalized ads, tailored hashtags, geolocated messaging, behavioral segmenting.	Party campaign content on social media, platform ad libraries, media reports
Algorithmic Amplification	The boosting of content visibility through engagement-based or automated platform ranking.	Viral trends, repetitive messaging, meme diffusion, coordinated retweeting, timing strategies.	Social media analytics, campaign timelines, platform transparency reports
Populist Framing	Use of emotionally charged, anti-elite, or nationalist narratives in campaign communication.	Anti-EU messages, crisis language, national "us vs. them" dichotomies, emotional calls to action.	Party discourse (posts, videos), campaign slogans, hashtags
Digital Maturity	A country's institutional and infrastructural capacity to adopt, regulate, and use digital tools.	E-government rankings, digital literacy, broadband coverage, platform penetration.	DESI Index, Eurostat, OECD reports, national digital strategy papers
Democratic Vulnerability	The extent to which democratic processes are exposed to manipulation or misinformation.	Misinformation presence, lack of transparency, low regulatory compliance, voter confusion.	Media coverage, platform reports, regulatory documents, expert studies
Regulatory Responsiveness	The capacity of legal instruments to detect, deter, and sanction algorithmic manipulation.	Enforcement mechanisms, oversight bodies, sanctioning capacity, electoral transparency mandates.	EU regulations (DSA, AI Act, TTPA), national laws, watchdog reports

European Regulatory Frameworks and the Governance of AI in Political Campaigning

As artificial intelligence continues to reshape political communication and electoral strategy, the European Union has developed a comprehensive legislative response aimed at preserving democratic integrity. This chapter critically explores four cornerstone regulations—the Transparency and Targeting of Political Advertising Regulation (TTPA), the Artificial Intelligence Act (AI Act), the General Data Protection Regulation (GDPR), and the Digital Services Act (DSA)—each representing a distinct intervention in the governance of AI-driven political processes. These legal instruments seek to address the risks associated with algorithmic microtargeting, data exploitation, and AI-generated misinformation, all of which were acutely visible during the 2024 European Parliament elections (Cancela-Outeda, 2024, p.2; Wilson, 2022, p.2-3; Mitrou, 2019, p.2). By examining the regulatory architecture, implementation challenges, and practical implications of these frameworks, the chapter illuminates the tension between technological innovation and democratic accountability. It argues that while the EU's approach demonstrates global leadership in digital governance, persistent enforcement gaps and cross- border complexities necessitate ongoing recalibration to ensure that electoral processes remain transparent, equitable, and resilient in an age of algorithmic influence (Laux, 2024, p. 10; Dommett et al., 2025, p.1-4).

The Transparency and Targeting of Political Advertising Regulation (TTPA)

The TTPA, formally adopted by the European Union in 2024, represents a landmark attempt to reshape the digital political advertising landscape through a rigorous transparency and accountability framework. It directly addresses the increasingly complex nature of political advertising, particularly its algorithmic and data-driven dimensions, which have transformed the electoral process in the EU and beyond. The regulation establishes clear legal obligations for advertisers, platforms and data intermediaries involved in the dissemination of political messaging, aiming to counter the opacity of digital campaign strategies that have raised concerns about voter manipulation, foreign interference, and the erosion of electoral integrity. The TTPA emerged as a response to mounting evidence that political microtargeting techniques -fuelled by personal data harvesting and machine learning- could distort democratic processes, particularly in the European Parliament elections (Madeira, 2024, p.2; Cath, 3-5).

The historical evolution of the TTPA is deeply embedded in the broader regulatory trajectory of the EU's digital governance framework, which includes the Digital Services Act (DSA), the General Data Protection Regulation (GDPR), and the Artificial Intelligence Act (AI Act). The EU's push for a comprehensive political advertising regulation was driven by concerns that digital electioneering was outpacing existing legal safeguards, creating an unregulated ecosystem where highly targeted, algorithmically amplified messaging could be deployed without public scrutiny. The Cambridge Analytica revelations in 2018 were a catalyst for regulatory momentum, exposing the systematic use of personal data to craft hyper-personalised political messages designed to exploit individuals' psychological traits. Subsequent the European Commission reports highlighted the emergence of sophisticated microtargeting techniques, wherein political campaigns leveraged AI political behavioral profiling to refine messaging at an unprecedented scale. The first draft of the TTPA was introduced in 2021, and after years of legislative negotiations, amendments, and consultations with stakeholders-including tech companies, civil society organisations, and electoral authorities- it was formally adopted in 2024 (Boulianne & Humprecht, 2023, p.19; Cath, 2018, p.1-3).

As its core, the TTPA imposes strict transparency requirements on political advertising across all media, but its most profound implications in the digital sphere, where AI-driven ad personalisation has become the dominant mode of political communication. The regulation mandates that all political advertisements must be clearly labelled, with a disclosure notice providing detailed information about the ad's sponsor, funding sources and intended audience. Platforms that host political advertisements are required to maintain publicly accessible archives that document the parameters used to target individuals, ensuring that both the regulators and the public as well, can scrutinise the underlying logic of algorithmic content distribution. The centralisation of political ad repositories aims to counteract the opacity of programmatic advertising networks, where political actors previously operated with minimal oversight (Roemmele & Gibson, 2020, p.27).

The regulation introduces explicit prohibitions on the use of sensitive personal data for political microtargeting, unless individuals provide explicit and informed consent. This provision is designed to curb the exploitation of voter profiling, which has historically relied on demographic, behavioral and psychometric data to tailor political messages to specific audience segments. The prohibiotns extend to data related to ethnicity, religious beliefs, sexual orientation, health status and political affiliation, which have been used in the past to craft highly personalised narratives that manipulate voter sentiment. However, the regulation still permits a targeted political advertising within th confines of non-sensitive data categories, such as geographic location, language preference, and general interests, raising ongoing concerns aboiut the persistence of algorithmic influence inn electoral campaigns (Farkas & Schou, 2019, p.2-8).

The 2024 EP elections served as the first major electoral event conducted under the regulatory framework of the TTPA, presenting a real-world test of its efficacy. The regulation sought to ensure that voters had a clear understanding of who was behind the political messages they encountered, while also limiting the ability of political campaigns to microtarget individuals based on opaque behavioral profiles. Despite the regulation's ambitious scope, early assessments revealed significant enforcement challenges, particularly in monitoring compliance across digital platforms that operate transnationally. The implementation of transparency repositories was hindered by inconsistencies in reporting standards across platforms, making it difficult for regulators to standardize political ad disclosures. Additionally, several political entities attempted to circumvent transparency mandates by outsourcing ad placements to third-party intermediaries, highlighting gaps in the enforcement mechanisms (Kalsnes, 2023, p.41; Samuelsen et al., 2023, p.1685-1687) .

One of the most contentious aspects of the TTPA is its reliance on self-reporting mechanisms, which require platforms to classify political advertisements at their own discretion. Critics argue that this creates loopholes for platforms to selectively enforce transparency obligations, particularly when commercial incentives align with maintaining opaque advertising ecosystems. Moreover, the extraterritorial scope of the regulation—designed to hold non-EU actors accountable for disseminating political advertisements within the EU—has proven difficult to enforce, as advertisers and platforms outside the EU have developed workarounds to evade compliance obligations. The potential for foreign actors to exploit regulatory loopholes remains a pressing concern, particularly in light of documented instances of foreign interference in past European elections (Hind et al., 2023, p.53; Simchon et al., 2024, p.2-3) .

Despite its ambitious objectives, the TTPA remains a subject of intense debate, with diverging views among policymakers, electoral authorities, and digital rights organizations. While many advocate that the regulation represents a significant milestone in safeguarding democratic integrity, others contend that its provisions do not go far enough in curbing the manipulative potential of AI-driven political microtargeting. Concerns persist over the continued role of machine-learning algorithms in shaping electoral discourse, as well as the implications for smaller political movements that rely on digital advertising as an accessible means of outreach. The chilling effect on legitimate political expression, particularly for grassroots movements that lack traditional media access, has sparked debate about how best to balance transparency mandates with the need for open political discourse (Zuboff, 2023, p.61) .

As digital political campaigning continues to evolve, the long-term effectiveness of the TTPA will depend on its adaptability to emerging technological challenges, including the rise of deepfake-driven disinformation, AI-generated synthetic media, and hyper-personalized influence campaigns. The European Commission has signaled that it will conduct periodic reviews of the regulation, assessing its ability to mitigate manipulative advertising practices while ensuring that electoral transparency measures remain robust in the face of evolving digital strategies. Future revisions may include stronger enforcement mechanisms, enhanced international cooperation, and refinements to the scope of permitted microtargeting techniques (Dommett et al., 2025, p.15-18).

Thus, the TTPA marks a fundamental shift in the governance and the excecution of electoral campaigns, setting a new global standard for regulating algorithmic political persuasion. While it represents a significant regulatory advance, its real-world effectiveness will ultimately hinge on the ability of enforcement agencies to navigate the complexities of modern digital advertising ecosystems, ensuring that the democratic process remains safeguarded against the disruptive potential of AI-driven political manipulation (Madiega, 2024; Muller et al., 2022).

The Artificial Intelligence Act (AI Act)

The Artificial Intelligence Act (AI Act), adopted by the European Union in 2024, stands as the first comprehensive regulatory framework governing artificial intelligence at a global scale. Designed to balance technological innovation with fundamental rights protections, the AI Act follows a risk-based regulatory approach, categorizing AI applications according to their potential impact on individuals, society, and democratic institutions. The legislation mirrors the influence of the General Data Protection Regulation (GDPR), aiming to establish the EU as a regulatory leader in AI governance. Its scope extends beyond European borders, influencing international regulatory discourse and shaping the legal landscape for AI across jurisdictions. By setting clear rules on AI transparency, accountability, and ethical deployment, the Act seeks to mitigate risks associated with algorithmic bias, opaque decision-making, and AI-driven manipulation, while fostering a legal environment that enables responsible AI development and deployment (Cancela- Outeda, 2024, p.2; Madiega, 2024, p.1).

The historical development of the AI Act was driven by the accelerated adoption of AI technologies and the ethical dilemmas they pose. The European Commission's 2018 AI Strategy laid the foundation for regulatory intervention, identifying AI as a key enabler of economic and societal transformation while acknowledging the risks of unregulated AI deployment. The subsequent 2019 Ethics Guidelines for Trustworthy AI established principles such as transparency, fairness, non-discrimination, and accountability, forming the basis for legislative action. By 2021, the European Commission formally proposed the AI Act, following growing concerns over AI- powered disinformation, algorithmic bias, and human rights violations in automated decision- making. The final legislative text, adopted in 2024, emerged after extensive debates within the European Parliament and the Council of the EU, reflecting a compromise between industry innovation, regulatory oversight, and fundamental rights protections (Laux, Wachter, & Mittelstadt, 2023, p. 4; Sovrano & Vitali., 2024, p.3142-3143).

At the heart of the AI Act is a four-tier risk classification system, which establishes graduated levels of regulatory oversight based on the potential harm posed by AI applications. AI systems deemed to present an "unacceptable risk" are outright banned, including subliminal manipulation techniques, biometric categorization based on sensitive attributes such as race or political opinions, and AI-driven social scoring mechanisms akin to China's system. High-risk AI systems, which include AI used in law enforcement, healthcare, financial services, employment, and border control, must undergo rigorous conformity assessments, meet data transparency requirements, and be subject to human oversight to prevent discriminatory or harmful outcomes. AI applications classified as "limited risk", such as chatbots, deepfake generators, and emotion recognition systems, must adhere to basic transparency requirements, ensuring users are aware they are interacting with AI. Minimal-risk AI systems, including spam filters and AI-powered recommendation engines, remain largely unregulated, though providers are encouraged to follow voluntary codes of conduct (Madiega, 2024, p.4; Edwards, 2022, p.5- 10).

Politically, the AI Act represents a significant shift in the EU's regulatory approach toward digital governance, reinforcing the region's ambition to set global AI standards. By mandating algorithmic transparency, risk assessments, and post-market monitoring, the EU has positioned itself as a counterweight to the laissez-faire approach of the United States and the state-controlled model of China. However, the Act has sparked contentious debates, particularly regarding the feasibility of self-assessment mechanisms, which allow AI developers to conduct their own risk evaluations, raising concerns over the robustness of enforcement measures. The practical enforceability of the Act remains an open question, especially given the rapid evolution of AI technologies, the challenges of cross-border enforcement, and the complexity of monitoring compliance across diverse AI applications. Furthermore, industry stakeholders have raised objections over the financial and bureaucratic burdens associated with regulatory compliance, warning that overly stringent requirements may stifle innovation, particularly among small and medium-sized enterprises (SMEs) (Laux, Wachter, & Mittelstadt, 2023, p.8; Coeckelbergh, 2025, p.1495-1496; Edwards, 2022).

The societal implications of the AI Act are particularly profound in the realm of democratic governance, electoral integrity, and digital rights. The growing prevalence of AI-driven disinformation campaigns, microtargeted political advertising, and algorithmic content amplification has introduced new threats to electoral integrity, necessitating regulatory interventions to curb AI-powered manipulation. The AI Act introduces specific provisions aimed at mitigating these risks, including restrictions on AI-generated political content, disclosure requirements for automated campaign tools, and prohibitions on deceptive AI techniques designed to distort public perception. These measures were particularly relevant in the lead-up to the 2024 European Parliament elections, which served as a test case for the Act's ability to counteract AI- driven electoral interference. However, significant challenges remain in enforcing these provisions, as the pace of AI innovation continues to outstrip regulatory responses, creating enforcement gaps that malicious actors may exploit (Boine, 2025, p. 50-58; Sovrano & Vitali, 2024.

The long-term impact of the AI Act will be determined by its ability to adapt to the evolving AI landscape while maintaining its core objectives of protecting fundamental rights, ensuring transparency, and fostering responsible innovation. Its success will depend on effective implementation mechanisms, robust cooperation between EU institutions and national regulators, and continued engagement with industry stakeholders and civil society. The 2024 European Parliament elections provided an early test of the AI Act's efficacy, offering insights into the strengths and limitations of its approach to curbing AI-driven manipulation and safeguarding democratic institutions. As AI technologies continue to advance, future revisions of the AI Act may be necessary to address emerging challenges, including the governance of general-purpose AI models, the ethical implications of autonomous decision-making systems, and the need for greater algorithmic accountability. Ultimately, the AI Act represents a bold yet complex attempt to regulate artificial intelligence, ensuring that AI systems remain transparent, fair, and aligned with European democratic values in an era increasingly shaped by algorithmic decision-making and digital influence (Laux, Wachter, & Mittelstadt, 2023, p. 10; Cancela-Outeda, 2024, p.6; Edwards, 2022, p.19).

The General Data Protection Regulation (GDPR)

The GDPR, enacted by the European Union in 2016 and enforced from May 2018, represents a transformative regulatory milestone in digital privacy and data protection. Designed to harmonize data protection laws across EU member states, the GDPR establishes a robust framework that enhances individuals' control over their personal data while imposing stringent obligations on data processors and controllers. It builds upon the foundation laid by the 1995 Data Protection Directive, addressing its limitations in a rapidly evolving digital landscape. Unlike its predecessor, the GDPR introduces extraterritorial applicability, meaning that any entity processing the data of EU citizens, regardless of its geographic location, falls under its regulatory scope. This global reach underscores the EU's ambition to set a gold standard for data protection, influencing regulatory frameworks worldwide, from the California Consumer Privacy Act (CCPA) to China's Personal Information Protection Law (PIPL) (Mitrou, 2019, p. 2; Sartor, 2020, p.1).

The historical evolution of the GDPR was propelled by the proliferation of digital technologies, particularly in areas such as AI, big data analytics, and algorithmic decision-making systems. The increasing reliance on automated data processing mechanisms posed significant challenges to traditional data protection principles, such as purpose limitation, data minimization, and individuals' ability to exercise meaningful control over their personal information. The GDPR responds to these challenges by reinforcing the principles of fairness, transparency, accountability, and user empowerment. It mandates that personal data must be collected for specified, explicit, and legitimate purposes and prohibits its further processing in ways that are incompatible with those original purposes. Moreover, it incorporates robust accountability mechanisms, requiring organizations to demonstrate compliance through Data Protection Impact Assessments (DPIAs), record-keeping obligations, and mandatory appointment of Data Protection Officers (DPOs) in high-risk processing activities (Wulf & Seizov, 2022, p.237; Amini et al., 2023, p.1024).

A particularly contentious and technologically significant provision of the GDPR is Article 22, which addresses automated decision-making and profiling. This article grants individuals the right not to be subject to decisions based solely on automated processing, including AI-driven profiling, that produce legal or similarly significant effects on them. This is particularly relevant in domains such as employment (e.g., AI-based hiring decisions), credit scoring, insurance risk assessments, and, critically, electoral processes. The regulation mandates that individuals must be provided with meaningful explanations of automated decisions, a requirement that poses substantial challenges in the context of complex machine-learning models, such as deep neural networks, which often operate as black boxes. Furthermore, organizations relying on AI-driven automated decision-making must implement mechanisms that ensure human oversight and intervention, thus preventing opaque or biased algorithmic determinations from undermining fundamental rights (Araujo et al., 2018, p.1-9; Mitrou, 2019, p. 6).

From a political and regulatory perspective, the GDPR has reinforced the European Union's leadership in global digital governance, setting a benchmark that has reverberated beyond its jurisdiction. Its stringent regulatory framework, particularly the imposition of fines of up to 4% of a company's global annual revenue or €20 million, has incentivized compliance while simultaneously fueling tensions with major technology firms such as Meta, Google, and Amazon, as well as with non-EU governments concerned about the impact on international data transfers. The Schrems II ruling by the Court of Justice of the European Union (CJEU) further intensified these tensions by invalidating the EU-US Privacy Shield, citing concerns over mass surveillance and inadequate data protection guarantees under US law. Consequently, businesses operating across borders have faced regulatory uncertainty and increased compliance costs, with some resorting to Standard Contractual Clauses (SCCs) and supplementary measures to ensure continued data flows (Sartor, 2020, p.4; Mitrou, 2019, p.9).

On a societal level, the GDPR has profoundly influenced public awareness and expectations regarding data privacy, fostering a more privacy-conscious digital culture. The regulation has empowered individuals to exercise their right to access, rectify, and erase personal data, strengthening consumer trust in digital services. However, its implementation has not been without criticism. Some argue that the GDPR's compliance burdens disproportionately affect small and medium-sized enterprises (SMEs), which lack the legal and technical resources to navigate its complexities, thus inadvertently consolidating the market dominance of large technology firms that can more easily absorb compliance costs. Moreover, debates persist over the regulation's effectiveness in addressing emerging AI-driven challenges, particularly regarding the explainability of AI-generated decisions and the adequacy of current transparency mechanisms in preventing algorithmic discrimination (Wulf & Seizov, 2022, p.242; Amini et al., 2023, p.1028).

In the context of the 2024 European Parliament elections, the GDPR's provisions play a critical role in safeguarding electoral integrity against the threats posed by AI-driven disinformation, microtargeting, and algorithmic content amplification. The increasing reliance on personalized political advertising and AI-generated campaign strategies has raised concerns over voter manipulation and the erosion of democratic deliberation. The GDPR's strict transparency requirements for processing political data, combined with its emphasis on user consent and data subject rights, are intended to mitigate these risks. However, enforcement challenges persist, particularly in ensuring that digital platforms such as Facebook, Twitter, and TikTok comply with regulations on political advertising and algorithmic content moderation. The effectiveness of the GDPR in curbing AI-driven election interference will ultimately depend on rigorous enforcement, international cooperation, and the ability of regulatory bodies to adapt to evolving technological threats (Ivaldi & Zankina, 2024, p.29-34; Rabitsch & Calabrese, 2024, p.10-13).

In conclusion, the GDPR admittedly operates as a cornerstone of digital rights and data protection in the EU, shaping the global regulatory landscape while confronting complex challenges posed by AI and algorithmic governance. Its impact on AI regulation, political integrity, and corporate accountability underscores its transformative role in the digital era. However, as technology continues to advance, the regulation must evolve to address emerging threats, particularly in the realms of AI explainability, automated decision-making, and electoral integrity. The GDPR's long-term success will hinge on its ability to strike a balance between innovation and fundamental rights, ensuring that digital democracy and privacy protection remain resilient in an age increasingly defined by algorithmic decision-making and data-driven influence (Boine, 2025, p.444-448; Wulf & Seizov, 2022, p.245).

The Digital Services Act (DSA)

The Digital Services Act (DSA), introduced by the European Commission in December 2020, is a landmark regulatory framework aimed at structuring the digital ecosystem within the European Union. It was developed in response to the growing concerns over market dominance, misinformation, and the necessity for consumer protection in the digital sphere. Rooted in the European Digital Strategy, the DSA aligns itself with the objectives of enhancing user safety, ensuring a level playing field for businesses, and preserving fundamental rights. Its legislative journey was shaped by extensive consultations and impact assessments, leading to a highly structured framework that regulates online intermediaries, particularly Very Large

Online Platforms (VLOPs), through stringent compliance mechanisms (Cauffman & Goanta, 2021, p.758).

The DSA's historical development is intrinsically linked to the evolution of European digital governance. Emerging from the foundational principles of the E-Commerce Directive (2000), it was necessitated by the exponential growth of digital platforms and the increasing complexity of content regulation. The act is characterized by a layered regulatory approach, distinguishing between intermediary services, online platforms, and VLOPs, each with distinct obligations. Among its most critical provisions are those concerning content moderation, requiring platforms to implement robust mechanisms for identifying and removing illegal content while ensuring due process and accountability. This aligns with the broader European ambition to fortify digital democracy by mitigating the risks posed by disinformation and algorithmic manipulation (Turillazzi et al., 2023, p. 83; Wilson, 2022, p.8-9).

From a political point of view, the DSA has far-reaching implications, particularly in its effort to recalibrate power dynamics between state institutions, digital corporations, and citizens. By imposing stringent transparency obligations on digital platforms regarding advertising, recommender systems, and content moderation, the act reinforces democratic resilience against algorithmic opacity and manipulative digital practices. The act also introduces crisis protocols, granting the European Commission extraordinary powers to intervene during emergencies, such as pandemics or elections, to prevent the amplification of harmful content. This regulatory intervention underscores the EU's intent to assert digital sovereignty, countering the monopolistic tendencies of tech giants while safeguarding democratic discourse (Floridi, 2023, p. 97; Küsters et al., 2023, p. 25).

The societal implications of the DSA are equally profound. By compelling platforms to disclose their risk assessment methodologies and content moderation policies, the act fosters a more accountable digital environment. Furthermore, its provisions on user redress and oversight mechanisms enhance individual agency in digital interactions. In addressing the interplay between fundamental rights and technological governance, the DSA situates itself as a bulwark against unchecked algorithmic decision-making, thereby reinforcing the normative framework of European digital citizenship. The act's emphasis on risk mitigation in content dissemination also highlights a shift towards proactive governance, ensuring that platforms preemptively identify and address systemic risks such as electoral manipulation and hate speech proliferation (Rabitsch & Calabrese, 2024, p.1-8 ; Schippers, 2020, p.32).

The enactment of the DSA ahead of the 2024 European Parliament elections presents a critical juncture in assessing its efficacy. Given the prominence of digital campaigning and algorithmic influence in electoral processes, the act's stringent provisions on political advertising transparency and disinformation control will be pivotal in shaping the integrity of democratic engagement. The regulation's mandates on AI-driven content moderation and accountability mechanisms aim to curtail the undue influence of automated systems in electoral discourse. However, challenges persist in enforcing compliance, particularly in the dynamic landscape of digital political communication, where rapid content proliferation and cross-platform dissemination complicate regulatory oversight (Turillazzi, 2023, p.84-87; Novelli & Sandri, 2024, p.3).

The DSA represents an ambitious and necessary recalibration of digital governance within the European Union. By embedding principles of transparency, accountability, and user protection into its regulatory architecture, it seeks to address the multifaceted challenges of the digital age. However, its success will be contingent upon effective enforcement and the adaptability of its provisions to emerging digital threats. As the 2024 European elections unfold, the DSA's implementation will serve as a crucial test of its capacity to safeguard democratic integrity in an era of algorithmic influence and digital monopolization. Its long-term impact will ultimately be determined by the balance it strikes between regulatory robustness and technological adaptability, ensuring that digital democracy is not merely an aspiration but a tangible, enforceable reality (Coeckelbergh, 2025, p.1491-1492; EETT, 2024).

Populist Parties: Netherlands, Greece, Italy, Estonia

The rise of right- and left-wing populist movements across Europe has been marked by an increasing reliance on artificial intelligence and data-driven campaigning tools to influence public opinion and mobilize voters. This chapter presents a comparative analysis of four emblematic populist parties—the Party for Freedom (PVV) in the Netherlands, SYRIZA in Greece, Fratelli d'Italia (FdI) in Italy, and the Conservative People's Party of Estonia (EKRE)—to examine how AI-enabled strategies have reshaped their political communication during the 2024 European Parliament elections. Through the deployment of algorithmic microtargeting, AI-generated content, and sentiment analysis, these parties have leveraged digital ecosystems to disseminate ideologically resonant messages with unprecedented precision and speed (Ivaldi & Zankina, 2024). While their rhetorical styles and national contexts vary, these movements share a common tactic: using technology to bypass traditional media gatekeepers and engineer direct, emotionally charged connections with targeted voter segments. By scrutinizing the strategic adaptation of AI tools across diverse digital and political environments, this chapter sheds light on the evolving nexus between populism, computational propaganda, and democratic legitimacy in the European Union (Rabitch et al., 2021; Innerarity, 2024, p.9).

Party for Freedom (PVV)

The Party for Freedom (PVV), under the leadership of Geert Wilders, exemplifies a paradigmatic case of contemporary right-wing populism, strategically employing digital political microtargeting to galvanize voter support. Rooted in a vehemently nationalist and anti- immigration rhetoric, the PVV's communicative apparatus thrives on social media platforms, utilizing hyper-personalized messaging to engineer targeted outreach. Through Facebook, Twitter (X), and other digital mediums, the party segments its audience based on thematic anxieties, particularly on immigration, crime, and Euroscepticism, ensuring that specific voter blocs receive curated content that amplifies their existing concerns. The algorithmic architecture of these platforms privileges emotionally charged discourse, thereby amplifying the PVV's reach by exploiting engagement-driven virality. Wilders' incendiary proclamations, often encapsulated in pithy slogans such as "Stop Islam" and "Nexit," function as catalysts for digital mobilization, reinforcing an "us versus them" dichotomy that appeals to disenfranchised constituencies (Morosoli et al., 2025, p.3-5; Wilders, 2024).

Data-driven voter targeting constitutes another pillar of the PVV's digital strategy, wherein analytics inform message dissemination and engagement strategies. By tracking user interactions on social media and leveraging email list segmentation, the party tailors its political messaging with surgical precision. This process not only enhances the efficacy of campaign outreach but also allows for dynamic recalibration based on real-time data insights. Although direct evidence of AI- powered microtargeting remains elusive, parallel studies on European populist parties indicate a growing reliance on AI-generated content, automated chatbots, and deepfake technologies to fabricate persuasive narratives. These digital innovations, while not overtly acknowledged in the PVV's arsenal, align with broader right-wing populist trends that prioritize technological augmentation in voter persuasion tactics (Wilders, 2024; Ivaldi & Zankina, 2024, p.363-384).

The party's anti-establishment ethos is further magnified through algorithmic amplification, which prioritizes controversial content designed to provoke visceral reactions. The PVV capitalizes on the virality of provocative discourse, embedding its messages within digital ecosystems that reward sensationalism over deliberative discourse. This modus operandi ensures that Wilders' pronouncements attain disproportionate visibility, circumventing traditional media gatekeeping while fostering an organic digital insurgency against mainstream political narratives. Consequently, the PVV's strategic digital interventions do not merely aim to inform but to incite, leveraging outrage as a potent electoral mobilization tool. This dynamic, underscored by empirical studies on digital populism, illustrates how the PVV's communicative infrastructure thrives on the interplay between political radicalization and platform mechanics (PVV, 2025; Küsters et al., 2023, p. 16).

The Party for Freedom (PVV) has established itself as a formidable entity within the sphere of digital political microtargeting, demonstrating a nuanced understanding of algorithmic mechanics, data-driven voter segmentation, and psychological persuasion techniques. Unlike traditional political campaigning, which operates on broad messaging and mass media dissemination, the PVV's digital strategy leverages granular audience analytics to customize outreach, ensuring that each voter receives content that aligns with their fears, frustrations, and ideological predispositions. The party's ability to craft highly personalized narratives rests on its adept use of social media engagement metrics, behavioral tracking, and geospatial targeting, all of which contribute to an electoral strategy that prioritizes direct voter mobilization through digital platforms rather than conventional political institutions (Ivaldi & Zankina, 2024, p.385-387)).

One of the key mechanisms through which the PVV operationalizes political microtargeting is its strategic deployment of Facebook and Twitter (X) advertising algorithms. These platforms allow political actors to run demographically, regionally, and psychographically segmented advertising campaigns, enabling the PVV to tailor distinct political messages to different voter cohorts. For instance, voters residing in urban areas with high immigrant populations may receive crime-related narratives, while those in economically struggling regions may be targeted with anti-EU, protectionist rhetoric. This dynamic customization of political messaging ensures that Wilders' populist discourse is not presented in a uniform manner, but rather shaped to fit the anxieties of each voter subset. Through A/B testing, the PVV refines its messaging to determine which variant of a political statement elicits the strongest engagement, thereby optimizing content for maximum psychological impact and digital virality (PVV, 2025; Government of the Netherlands, 2024).

Another pivotal aspect of the PVV's microtargeting strategy is its reliance on algorithmic amplification through outrage-driven engagement loops. Social media platforms reward content that provokes strong emotional responses, such as anger, fear, or moral indignation, which aligns seamlessly with the PVV's political communication style. Wilders and his party frequently deploy highly charged rhetoric, incendiary one-liners, and controversial policy proposals, designed not only to appeal to their base but also to generate disproportionate reach through algorithmic magnification. This self-perpetuating cycle ensures that even those who vehemently oppose the PVV inadvertently contribute to its digital traction by engaging with its content, thereby expanding its reach beyond its core support base. This phenomenon, known as the "algorithmic outrage effect", has been extensively documented in studies on digital populism, demonstrating how right- wing parties strategically exploit social media ecosystems to bypass traditional media gatekeeping and dominate the political discourse (Jonge et al., 2022, p.775-778).

In addition to social media manipulation, the PVV employs data-centric audience segmentation, a technique that involves harvesting and analyzing voter data to predict political preferences and behavioral patterns. Through third-party data brokers, publicly available demographic statistics, and proprietary voter databases, the PVV is able to construct psychographic voter profiles, which categorize individuals based on their values, fears, and ideological leanings. This level of granularity allows the party to deliver highly specific content to potential supporters, reinforcing existing biases and shaping political perceptions in a manner that traditional campaign strategies cannot match. By cross-referencing social media activity, browsing behavior, and geographic indicators, the PVV can ascertain which issues resonate most profoundly with different voter demographics and adjust its digital messaging accordingly (Ivaldi & Zakina, 2024, p.388-390; PVV, 2025).

Beyond explicit messaging, the PVV also benefits from covert microtargeting techniques, such as the use of AI-driven chatbots and automated accounts to simulate organic grassroots support. AI-powered bots can artificially amplify the popularity of PVV narratives, engage in pro- Wilders discourse under fabricated identities, and flood online discussions with party-endorsed talking points, creating an illusion of widespread consensus. This method is particularly effective in online comment sections, forums, and live political discussions, where automated engagement skews the perceived public opinion in favor of the PVV's positions. Similar tactics have been employed by other European right-wing populist movements, with documented instances of bot- driven disinformation campaigns shaping electoral narratives (Government of the Netherlands, 2024; Morosoli et al., 2023, p.12-14).

A significant, albeit more insidious, dimension of PVV's digital strategy is its potential intersection with AI-driven disinformation ecosystems. Studies have shown that AI-generated deepfakes, synthetic media, and manipulated video content have been utilized in far-right digital mobilization efforts to foment distrust in mainstream institutions, amplify nationalist sentiment, and delegitimize political adversaries. While direct evidence linking the PVV to such tactics remains inconclusive, the structural dynamics of the broader right-wing digital sphere suggest a growing convergence between AI-enabled disinformation strategies and populist electoral mobilization. If incorporated into its arsenal, these technologies would provide the PVV with unprecedented capabilities in political persuasion, sentiment engineering, and reality distortion, thereby cementing its influence in Dutch politics through digital epistemic warfare (Jonge et al., 2022, p.780-785).

The Party for Freedom (PVV), under the uncompromising leadership of Geert Wilders, has meticulously engineered its digital strategy on TikTok, deploying AI-enhanced rhetorical techniques that seamlessly intertwine populist fervor with algorithmic precision. By leveraging TikTok's engagement-driven ecosystem, which prioritizes emotive, high-retention content, the PVV ensures that its nationalist messaging infiltrates the platform's digital consciousness, particularly among younger, politically fluid demographics. This strategic deployment is not merely a passive utilization of social media tools, but a calibrated exploitation of AI's predictive and adaptive capabilities, enabling the real-time modulation of political discourse based on user sentiment analytics. The algorithmic curation of PVV's visual and textual content ensures that its rhetorical appeal is tailored, dynamic, and unrelenting, fostering ideological echo chambers wherein anti-immigration, Eurosceptic, and sovereigntist narratives gain perpetual traction (Kakavand, 2023, p.38-42; Wilders, 2025).

The party's deployment of AI in digital microtargeting transcends mere content amplification, veering into the domain of psychographic manipulation, where machine learning algorithms deconstruct user engagement patterns to refine and personalize political messaging. Through this, PVV engineers a digital landscape wherein ideological predispositions are not merely reinforced but algorithmically sculpted, ensuring that each viewer receives a version of Wilders' rhetoric that resonates most deeply with their cognitive and emotional frameworks. The integration of synthetic media, deepfake-adjacent editing techniques, and hyper-visual meme-based communication elevates PVV's TikTok strategy beyond traditional political campaigning, positioning it as an adaptive, AI-enhanced populist apparatus that can manufacture and sustain digital insurgencies against mainstream political narratives. This algorithmic entrenchment of populist discourse, while extraordinarily effective in voter mobilization, presents ethical and epistemological dilemmas, as it fundamentally reconfigures the authenticity of political engagement, transforming organic democratic deliberation into a computationally engineered spectacle wherein persuasion is no longer an art, but a science (Rabitch, 2021, p.6-8).

In summation, the PVV's political microtargeting strategy is an intricate interplay of social media manipulation, algorithmic exploitation, data-driven messaging, and AI-assisted digital amplification. By synchronizing these techniques into a coherent and dynamic electoral apparatus, the PVV has successfully positioned itself at the forefront of digitally mediated populism, demonstrating how technological sophistication can be weaponized to advance a nationalist and anti-establishment political agenda. As AI-driven campaign methodologies become more sophisticated and accessible, it is highly probable that the PVV, like its European populist counterparts, will continue to refine its digital strategy, further entrenching its ability to shape public discourse and influence electoral outcomes with surgical precision (PVV, 2025; Wilders, 2025; Morosoli et al., 2025).

SYRIZA

SYRIZA, the Coalition of the Radical Left, emerged from the fragmented Greek left in the early 2000s, consolidating itself as a formidable political force in response to Greece's financial crisis. Rooted in Eurocommunist and radical left traditions, it positioned itself as a counter- hegemonic alternative to Greece's dominant parties, particularly PASOK and New Democracy. Under Alexis Tsipras' leadership, the party capitalized on mass discontent with austerity policies, constructing a narrative that framed politics as a struggle between "the people" and "the corrupt elite." This populist binary was instrumental in securing SYRIZA's victory in the 2015 Greek elections, as it promised to resist the memorandum-imposed austerity dictated by the European Union and the International Monetary Fund (Mudde & Rovira Kaltwasser, 2017, p. 112). However, the party's governance quickly revealed the pragmatic limitations of its radical platform, culminating in a reversal of its anti-austerity stance and subsequent disillusionment among segments of its support base (Stavrakakis & Katsambekis, 2019, p. 63).

Consequently, SYRIZA's populism has been the subject of extensive academic scrutiny, particularly concerning its ideological and strategic shifts. While initially embracing a left-populist discourse centered on economic justice and popular sovereignty, its tenure in government led to a dilution of this rhetoric. Scholars argue that its governance exposed a tension between radical leftist ideals and the constraints of supranational economic governance, leading to a hybrid form of populism that balanced radical promises with institutional pragmatism (Aslanidis, 2021, p.640-643). Despite these ideological recalibrations, SYRIZA continued to deploy populist discursive strategies, particularly in its opposition to right-wing policies and its framing of political adversaries as representatives of neoliberal orthodoxy. This duality—populist rhetoric in opposition and pragmatism in governance—has reinforced SYRIZA's status as the primary left- wing populist party in Greece (Laclau, 2005, p.84; Teperoglou et al., 2015, p.338-339).

The 2024 European Parliament elections saw SYRIZA intensify its digital political microtargeting strategies, particularly through AI-enhanced social media campaigns. The party strategically leveraged AI-driven content curation and algorithmic amplification to optimize engagement across platforms such as TikTok, X, and Facebook. One of the most striking elements of this strategy was its use of AI-powered sentiment analysis tools, which assessed public reactions to different policy proposals and adjusted campaign messaging accordingly . By employing real- time data analytics, SYRIZA micro-segmented voter demographics, ensuring that campaign materials were tailored to specific socio-economic and ideological cohorts. This approach allowed for a more persuasive and emotionally resonant campaign, reinforcing SYRIZA's populist appeal by framing its platform as the true representation of the Greek people's interests (Mitrou, 2018, p.22; Syriza, 2025; Ivaldi & Zankina, 2024, p.193-194).

SYRIZA's deployment of AI in digital political outreach also included the automated generation of personalized political messages, a technique that mimicked conversational interactions with potential voters. Through AI-powered chatbots and personalized content feeds, the party engaged users in dynamic discussions, reinforcing pre-existing political beliefs and nudging undecided voters toward specific narratives. The integration of machine learning models into social media analytics ensured that messages reached the most susceptible audiences, particularly younger voters on TikTok, where engagement patterns dictated the visibility and reach of campaign content. The effectiveness of this approach was evident in the virality of certain posts, particularly those employing short-form video formats, meme culture, and influencer-style political messaging (Syriza, 2025; Ivaldi & Zankina, 2024, p.198-199).

The 2024 European Parliament elections demonstrated a paradigm shift in SYRIZA's digital political engagement, reflecting a more sophisticated, AI-driven approach to voter outreach. This shift aligns with broader developments in European political campaigning, where AI- enhanced sentiment analysis, algorithmic targeting, and social media micro-segmentation are becoming essential tools for electoral success . While SYRIZA's digital strategy successfully optimized engagement metrics, it also raised ethical concerns regarding transparency, data privacy, and the manipulative potential of AI-driven political persuasion. As AI continues to reshape electoral processes, SYRIZA's embrace of algorithmic political microtargeting underscores the transformative role of digital technologies in contemporary populist movements (Innerarity, 2024, p.11; Ivaldi & Zankina, 2024).

Fratelli d' Italia (FdI)

Fratelli d'Italia (FdI) emerged in 2012 as a response to the political vacuum left by the dissolution of the National Alliance (AN), itself the successor of the post-fascist Italian Social Movement (MSI). Under Giorgia Meloni's leadership, the party has transformed from a minor nationalist faction into Italy's dominant right-wing force, securing a historic victory in the 2022 general elections and consolidating its position in the 2024 European Parliament elections. The ideological lineage of FdI is deeply rooted in national conservatism, right-wing populism, and elements of post-fascism, though Meloni has sought to rebrand the party's image, distancing it from explicit neofascist associations while maintaining a staunchly nationalist and anti-globalist narrative. This rhetorical recalibration has been instrumental in broadening the party's appeal beyond its traditional base, incorporating voters disillusioned with mainstream center-right parties while retaining the symbolic aesthetics and discursive markers of Italy's far-right political tradition (The Guardian, 2024, p.3; Mudde & Rovira Kaltwasser, 2017, p. 56).

As a paradigmatic case of right-wing populism, FdI has constructed an antagonistic political discourse that pits the "authentic Italian people" against the globalist elite, European technocrats, and progressive forces that allegedly threaten Italy's sovereignty and cultural identity. The party's rhetoric draws heavily from nationalist themes, emphasizing sovereignty, the primacy of the Italian family, and a rejection of multiculturalism. Immigration is framed as an existential crisis, with FdI portraying itself as the last line of defense against mass migration and European Union overreach. This populist framework aligns with broader European far-right movements, yet Meloni has differentiated FdI by balancing radical rhetoric with institutional pragmatism, ensuring its acceptability within Italy's governing structures while safeguarding its populist credentials (Fratelli d'Italia, 2024, p.9; The Guardian, 2024, p.5-7).

The 2024 European Parliament elections marked a significant evolution in FdI's digital and AI-driven electoral strategy, particularly in the realm of social media microtargeting and AI- enhanced content dissemination. FdI leveraged AI-generated content to amplify nationalist narratives, ensuring that its messaging dominated the algorithmic architecture of platforms such as TikTok, Facebook, and X (Fratelli d' Italia, 2025). A key component of this strategy was the use of AI-driven sentiment analysis, which enabled real-time tracking of public reactions to policy proposals and political discourse, allowing for rapid adjustments in communication strategy (Innerarity, 2024, p.14). By integrating machine learning models into voter segmentation, FdI crafted hyper-personalized campaign messages, targeting different demographic groups with tailored rhetoric that reinforced pre-existing ideological leanings (Newell, 2024, p.1-2).

Fratelli d'Italia's TikTok strategy for the 2024 European Parliament elections exemplifies an advanced integration of AI-driven political microtargeting, designed to optimize engagement, manipulate algorithmic visibility, and reinforce ideological narratives. TikTok's algorithmic ecosystem, which prioritizes high-engagement, emotionally resonant content, provided the ideal platform for FdI's AI-enhanced digital strategy, allowing for rapid dissemination of nationalist, anti-immigration, and sovereignty-focused messaging. The party's campaign utilized AI- generated video content, including synthetic speech overlays, deepfake-adjacent editing techniques, and meme-based visual formats, ensuring that its political discourse seamlessly integrated with the platform's entertainment-oriented culture. Through machine-learning- enhanced sentiment analysis, FdI continuously monitored user interactions, adjusted its content in real-time, and adapted its visual and textual framing to maximize virality within TikTok's algorithmic structure (Newell, 2024, p.2-4, FdI, 2025).

A defining feature of FdI's TikTok campaign was its algorithmic exploitation of microtargeted political narratives, wherein AI-driven predictive modeling identified the most resonant ideological themes for specific voter cohorts. This process enabled the dynamic customization of nationalist messaging, ensuring that users predisposed to anti-immigrant, Eurosceptic, or culturally conservative sentiments received AI-curated content reinforcing these perspectives. Unlike traditional broadcast-style political communication, this approach relied on hyper-individualized political persuasion, facilitated by AI-generated psychographic profiling, which categorized TikTok users based on their browsing behavior, engagement patterns, and inferred ideological leanings. This granular targeting mechanism, in conjunction with TikTok's engagement-maximization model, ensured that FdI's content received disproportionate visibility, fostering self-reinforcing digital echo chambers where nationalist discourse was algorithmically amplified while oppositional narratives were deprioritized. The strategic fusion of AI-enhanced content engineering with TikTok's virality-driven infrastructure represents a significant evolution in right-wing populist digital campaigning, demonstrating the capacity of AI to weaponize social media algorithms in the service of electoral manipulation and ideological entrenchment (Lulamae, 2022; Dona, 2022, p.788-791; FdI, 2025).

A particularly potent aspect of FdI's AI-driven campaign was its deployment of AI- enhanced deepfake technology and synthetic media to generate highly engaging, emotionally charged content. This included AI-generated speeches, videos, and meme-based content that circulated across social media, blurring the lines between organic and manufactured political communication. By harnessing AI to produce content that mimicked the aesthetics and discursive style of grassroots political movements, FdI fostered a perception of widespread popular support, reinforcing the illusion of an organic nationalist uprising against the liberal establishment (Ivaldi & Zankina, 2024, p.243-245).

An ethically contentious dimension of FdI's AI deployment was its use of computational propaganda and AI-generated disinformation. Reports indicated that AI-driven bot networks were employed to amplify FdI's narratives, drown out opposition voices, and create the illusion of mass consensus. Additionally, the weaponization of AI-generated fake news played a crucial role in shaping public discourse, particularly in the context of immigration and EU governance, where AI-crafted misinformation reinforced xenophobic sentiments and anti-European skepticism (Innerarity, 2024, p.19; Ivaldi & Zankina, 2024, p.235).

The 2024 European Parliament elections demonstrated a profound shift in the technological landscape of right-wing populist campaigning, with FdI emerging as a forerunner in AI-enhanced electoral strategies. By melding traditional nationalist rhetoric with cutting-edge AI-driven political microtargeting, the party optimized its voter engagement tactics, ensuring maximum ideological reinforcement and mobilization. However, this digital transformation raises critical ethical and regulatory concerns, as the unchecked proliferation of AI-driven disinformation threatens the integrity of democratic processes. As AI continues to redefine the mechanics of political communication, FdI's strategic embrace of these technologies underscores the transformative potential and inherent risks of algorithmic populism in contemporary European politics (Newell, 2024; FdI, 2025).

Conservative People's Party of Estonia (EKRE)

The Conservative People's Party of Estonia (EKRE) emerged in 2012 from the consolidation of nationalist and agrarian movements, channeling a resolute ethos of national conservatism, right-wing populism, and Euroscepticism into Estonia's political mainstream. Founded through the merger of the People's Union of Estonia and the Estonian Patriotic Movement, EKRE's ideological trajectory was firmly cemented under Mart Helme's leadership, whose rhetoric redefined the nationalist discourse in Estonia (Conservative People's Party of Estonia, 2023, p.1). The transition of power to Martin Helme in 2020 marked a continuation of an unyielding nationalist paradigm, wherein anti-immigration rhetoric, opposition to progressive liberal values, and a staunchly Eurosceptic posture became the cornerstones of EKRE's political identity (Mudde, 2021, p.79). This positioning, reinforced through the party's polemical engagement with both domestic and European institutions, established EKRE as Estonia's archetypal right-wing populist force, effectively mobilizing socio-political discontent and channeling it into a coherent political insurgency against perceived globalist elites (Kasekamp, 2003).

EKRE's ascendancy within Estonia's fragmented political landscape is emblematic of a broader European wave of nationalist populism, wherein anti-establishment rhetoric, combined with a manipulative reframing of national sovereignty and cultural preservation, resonates with electorates alienated by globalization and transnational governance (Conservative People's Party of Estonia, 2023, p.3). The party's discursive framework mirrors that of right-wing populist movements across Europe, positing a dichotomy between "authentic Estonians" and the cosmopolitan elite, who are accused of eroding national identity and prioritizing foreign interests over the people's will. This narrative, profoundly entrenched within EKRE's rhetorical arsenal, has proven instrumental in electoral mobilization, particularly among voter demographics disillusioned by Estonia's post-independence liberal governance model (Mudde & Kaltwasser, 2017, p. 54; Raik, 2021, p.22).

The 2024 European Parliament elections heralded a radical technological evolution in EKRE's electoral strategy, wherein AI-enhanced digital mobilization became a defining element of the party's campaign. Unlike traditional political outreach, which relies on mass communication and static messaging, EKRE embraced machine learning algorithms and AI-driven analytics to engineer hyper-personalized political persuasion. Through the deployment of AI-enhanced sentiment analysis, the party meticulously dissected public reactions in real-time, enabling an adaptive, data-driven approach to message recalibration. This algorithmic precision, wherein AI systems dynamically altered campaign messaging based on user engagement metrics, ensured that EKRE's digital content remained persistently resonant with its intended audience, fostering highly curated ideological reinforcement (Ivaldi & Zankina, 2024, p.141-142, EKRE, 2025).

The mechanics of EKRE's AI-facilitated microtargeting strategy were predicated on the party's capacity to dissect and exploit digital behavioral patterns, ensuring that each voter segment received tailored ideological stimuli. By leveraging AI-driven psychographic profiling, EKRE's campaign did not merely disseminate uniform political messaging but instead crafted customized narratives that aligned with individual voters' ideological predispositions. This methodology was particularly potent in the realm of TikTok-based outreach, where AI-enhanced video production techniques, deepfake-adjacent synthetic imagery, and automated meme generation allowed the party to circumvent traditional gatekeeping mechanisms and directly infiltrate the algorithmic consciousness of younger voters (Nortal, 2024; Jakobson, 2024, p.140-141).

The ethical ramifications of EKRE's AI-powered political campaign underscore a fundamental challenge to democratic integrity, as the manipulative potential of AI-driven disinformation distorts the epistemic foundation of electoral decision-making. The party's deployment of AI-generated misinformation, particularly in narratives surrounding migration policy and European governance, blurred the distinction between fact-based discourse and algorithmically curated political fiction. This erosion of informational integrity, wherein AI- fabricated narratives masqueraded as organic political communication, represents a profound shift in the nature of electoral persuasion, wherein voter perception is not merely influenced, but computationally engineered (Nortal, 2024; Ivaldi & Zankina, 2024, p.145-148).

As the technological landscape of political campaigning continues to evolve, EKRE's embrace of AI-driven political microtargeting signifies a broader trend in right-wing populist mobilization, wherein algorithmic persuasion, sentiment engineering, and data-driven ideological reinforcement converge to reshape democratic participation. The party's mastery of AI-enhanced electoral strategies, while undeniably effective in mobilizing and sustaining its support base, necessitates a critical interrogation of the ethical boundaries of digital political engagement, as the unchecked expansion of AI-facilitated propaganda poses an existential challenge to the democratic paradigm itself. As AI-fueled electoral manipulation becomes an inextricable component of political competition, the imperative for robust regulatory frameworks and transparent governance of AI's role in democracy grows ever more urgent, ensuring that technological advancements do not subvert, but rather enhance, the foundational principles of democratic self-governance (Jakobson, 2024, p.141-148; EKRE, 2025).

COMPARATIVE SUMMARY OF CASE FINDINGS

The empirical analysis of the four selected country cases—Netherlands, Greece, Italy, and Estonia—demonstrates varying degrees of digital maturity, regulatory implementation, and AI campaign sophistication. As seen in Table 2, the comparative analysis of populist strategies across the Netherlands, Greece, Italy, and Estonia demonstrates variations in digital maturity, platform use, and AI techniques employed by different parties.

Table 2. Comparative Summary of Populist Party Strategies

Country	Populist Party	Digital Maturity	Main Platforms Used	AI Techniques Employed	Regulatory Context	Key Observations
Netherlands	PVV (Geert Wilders)	High	TikTok, X, YouTube	Microtargeting, meme diffusion, video captioning	Strong DSA enforcement, national compliance	enforcement, national compliance Sophisticated strategy; youth targeting; culturally coded AI use
Greece	SYRIZA	Medium	Facebook, Instagram, TikTok	Sentiment analysis, hashtag engineering, limited A/B testing	Fragmented enforcement, DSA slow adoption	Hybrid populism; emotionally resonant but less data-driven
Italy	Fratelli d'Italia (FdI)	Medium-High	TikTok, X, Telegram	Meme warfare, automated posting, symbolic amplification	Partial DSA integration, national regulation	Strategic nationalism; visually dominant AI tactics
Esthonia	EKRE	High	X, Facebook, YouTube	Chatbots, data-driven targeting, coded populist language	Digitally advanced, strong e-gov frameworks	Algorithmic normalization; AI integrated into mainstream politics

CONCLUSION

This chapter has revealed how the synergy of artificial intelligence, digital populism, and electoral regulation has transformed the mechanics of political campaigning across the European Union. Drawing on a comparative analysis of four populist parties—PVV, SYRIZA, Fratelli d'Italia, and EKRE—it is plain to see that AI is not merely an auxiliary campaign tool. Nevertheless, it operates as a central instrument in shaping voter behavior, manipulating discourse, and reframing democratic participation in the algorithmic age.

One of the central findings is the unevenness with which AI is deployed across different national contexts. In digitally advanced states like Estonia and the Netherlands, AI-enhanced strategies exhibited higher levels of technical sophistication, data integration, and platform- specific optimization. Conversely, in countries such as Greece and Italy, populist actors relied more heavily on emotionally charged content and AI-generated visuals, with less granular data segmentation. This confirms that a country's digital maturity significantly conditions the profundity and form of algorithmic campaigning. Cnsequently, it shapes not only outreach strategies but also the broader communicative logic of populist narratives.

Moreover, the research illustrates that despite the EU's proactive regulatory architecture— spanning the AI Act, DSA, GDPR, and TTPA—there remain critical enforcement gaps. These gaps are most apparent in cross-border campaign practices, platform accountability, and the circumvention of transparency mandates through opaque intermediaries. Populist parties have exploited these vulnerabilities to a great or a greater extend, so as to amplify ideologically polarizing messages, leveraging algorithmic potential uses to bypass traditional oversight and engineer voter sentiment with precision.

The empirical evidence also demonstrates how AI enables a deeper and more profound personalization of political discourse, reinforcing echo chambers and reducing exposure to dissenting views. Rather than fostering deliberation, AI-driven campaigning has contributed to the fragmentation of public discourse and the entrenchment of affective political identities. This raises fundamental concerns about the epistemic foundations of democracy—particularly in a context where synthetic media, microtargeting, and automated engagement blur the line between persuasion and manipulation.

In light of these findings, it is clear that European democratic institutions must move beyond reactive regulatory strategies and adopt a forward-looking, adaptive governance model. This includes strengthening enforcement mechanisms, expanding platform transparency mandates, and fostering civic literacy on AI-mediated persuasion. As populist movements continue to refine their digital arsenals, the resilience of European democracy will depend on its capacity to uphold electoral integrity without stifling legitimate political expression in an increasingly algorithmic public sphere.

This chapter set out to explore the evolving intersection between artificial intelligence, populist political strategy, and electoral governance in the European Union, using the 2024 European Parliament elections as a critical case study. Grounded in qualitative content analysis and a comparative cross-national framework, the research was guided by three primary objectives: (1) to critically assess the EU's regulatory architecture in response to AI-driven electoral manipulation; (2) to examine how populist parties in varied digital ecosystems deploy AI technologies; and (3) to evaluate the broader democratic risks and opportunities posed by algorithmic political persuasion.

In addressing the first research question—how effective current EU frameworks are in regulating AI-driven campaigning—the findings indicate that while regulations such as the AI Act, DSA, GDPR, and TTPA represent globally leading initiatives, their effectiveness is hindered by enforcement asymmetries, jurisdictional fragmentation, and the self-regulatory posture of digital platforms. Particularly in the case of the TTPA and GDPR, compliance depends on platform discretion, and cross-border political advertising often escapes meaningful scrutiny. Thus, the analytical expectation that these regulatory tools are ambitious in scope but limited in enforcement has been validated (Rabitch et al., 2021).

The second research question—how a country's level of digital maturity shapes AI campaign strategies—yielded compelling insights. In digitally mature contexts like the Netherlands and Estonia, populist parties such as PVV and EKRE used more advanced techniques, including AI-driven microtargeting, automated content personalization, and algorithmic engagement testing. In contrast, in Greece and Italy, SYRIZA and FdI adopted a more hybrid approach, mixing traditional rhetoric with AI-generated content and meme-driven mobilization. This affirms the hypothesis that digital infrastructure and literacy condition the strategic sophistication of AI deployment, particularly in the realm of real-time sentiment adaptation and content virality (Ivaldi & Zankina, 2024).

The third question—how populist and far-right actors vary in their use of AI technologies across contexts—revealed both convergence and divergence. All four parties employed AI to bypass mainstream media and engage directly with voters, often through emotionally charged and ideologically polarizing narratives. Yet, their degree of reliance on automated bots, deepfakes, and psychographic profiling varied, often shaped by national constraints on data access, electoral norms, and platform penetration. The expectation that digital populism is not monolithic, but dynamically localized, is thus strongly supported by the evidence (Winfield & Jirotka, 2018).

In synthesizing these findings, it becomes evident that AI does not operate as a neutral tool within democratic systems; rather, it is shaped by and reinforces existing political asymmetries, regulatory vacuums, and populist mobilization logics. Inevitably, far from simply enhancing efficiency or engagement, AI-enabled strategies have redefined the grammar of persuasion, fostering a shift from deliberative to affective modes of political communication. The fragmentation of public discourse, the rise of synthetic content, and the exploitation of algorithmic recommendation systems represent not just technical challenges, but epistemological threats to democratic legitimacy as well.

This chapter set out to critically examine the intersection of AI, populist campaign strategy, and electoral governance within the EU, using the 2024 EP elections as a focal lens. Anchored in qualitative content analysis and a comparative case study design, the analysis was structured around three guiding objectives: first, to assess the effectiveness and limitations of the EU's evolving regulatory architecture—specifically the AI Act, the Digital Services Act (DSA), the General Data Protection Regulation (GDPR), and the Transparency and Targeting of Political Advertising Regulation (TTPA)—in addressing the challenges that are constantly posed by algorithmically mediated political campaigning; second, to explore how populist parties in digitally heterogeneous member states operationalize AI technologies to tailor narratives, intensify ideological messages, and manipulate engagement; and third, to evaluate the normative implications of such practices on the epistemic quality, fairness, and legitimacy of democratic electoral processes.

Given that fact, the findings illustrate that AI has altered the tactical repertoire of populist parties and reshaped the very terrain on which democratic contestation occurs. The ability of AI to curate hyper-personalized content, automate emotional triggers, and algorithmically reinforce ideological silos poses significant threats to the pluralistic foundations of electoral democracy, and the very foundations of our modern societies, broadly speaking. This transformation reflects a broader and more general shift from deliberative to affective modes of engagement, in which political agency is increasingly mediated by computational systems. These systems tend to operate beneath the threshold of public scrutiny or comprehension. In this context, the distinction between democratic persuasion and technological manipulation becomes blurred, challenging core normative assumptions about informed consent, collective reasoning, and the public sphere itself.

To respond effectively to these shifts, EU governance must move beyond a reactive, normative and solely regulatory regulatory posture and toward a dynamic, anticipatory model of digital constitutionalism. This entails and requires both harmonized enforcement mechanisms and cross-border oversight and algorithmic audit trails, platform accountability benchmarks, and legal standards for explainability in political content distribution systems. Additionally, institutional investment in digital civic education is vital to cultivate the public's resilience to computational persuasion and synthetic media influence. Without such multidimensional safeguards, the algorithmic architecture of electoral discourse may continue to fragment publics, hollow out trust, and erode the epistemic infrastructure upon which democratic legitimacy rests.

Through a synthesis of theoretical frameworks and empirical analysis, the research bridges normative principles of deliberative democracy with practical applications, thus offering a profound contribution to the scholarly discourse on AI and governance, concommitantly. By evaluating regulatory frameworks such as the Digital Services Act (DSA) and the Artificial Intelligence Act (AIA), it identifies profound systemic gaps and proposes thorough adaptive mechanisms to address the transnational and dynamic challenges posed by AI-driven electoral manipulation. This approach situates the study at the intersection of ethics, governance, and technological innovation, illuminating pathways for safeguarding democratic institutions against their erosion.

The chapter's methodological rigor, encompassing comparative case studies, content analysis, and stakeholder interviews, ensures an epistemologically robust and contextually comprehensive analysis. It advances the academic field by articulating the intersectionality of AI, populism, and electoral governance, while offering actionable recommendations for policymakers.This study makes a significant contribution to the academic landscape by addressing the relatively unexplored intersection of AI, populism, and electoral governance within the context of European democratic processes, and especially the very last electoral experience of 2024 EP eelctions. It expands the theoretical understanding of AI's role in shaping democratic resilience and electoral integrity, and provides in parallel a fresh lens through which to examine the implications of digital technologies on governance. By exploring the combination regulatory frameworks and practical strategies for addressing the challenges posed by AI in electoral contexts, the study offers new insights that could inform both future research and policymaking.

Beyond academia, the societal impact of this research is profound. As AI continues to shape and affect electoral processes globally, the findings of this study can foster greater public trust in electoral systems, help mitigate the risks of polarization, and empower the resilience of democratic institutions, as the foundational elements of the european governance. By offering actionable recommendations and policy proposals to policymakers, it aims to safeguard democratic values in the age of digital transformation. This twofodl contribution underscores the urgency and relevance of the research in the ongoing evolution of digital democracy.

REFERENCES

Act, A. I. (2023). Artificial Intelligence Act. European Commission. Retrieved from https://digital- strategy.ec.europa.eu/en/policies/regulatory-framework-ai (Accessed: December 22, 2024)

AdeyinkaOjo. S. (2025). *Digital and strategic qualitative research methodology*. Notion Press.

Al-kfairy, M., Mustafa, D., Kshetri, N., Insiew, M., & Alfandi, O. (2024). Ethical Challenges and Solutions of Generative AI: An Interdisciplinary Perspective. *Informatics (MDPI), 11*(3), 58. DOI: 10.3390/informatics11030058

Araujo, T. B., de Vreese, C. H., Helberger, N., Kruikemeier, S., van Weert, J. C. M., Bol, N., ... & Taylor, L. (2018). *Automated decision-making fairness in an AI-driven world: Public perceptions, hopes and concerns*. University of Amsterdam, Digital Communication Methods Lab.

Aslanidis, P. (2021). Coalition-making under conditions of ideological mismatch: The populist solution. *International Political Science Review, 42*(5), 631–648. DOI: 10.1177/0192512121 1040946

Berg, S., Hofmann, J., & Democracy, D. (2021, December 20).. . *Internet Policy Review, 10*(4), 2021. DOI: 10.14763/2021.4.1612

Boine, C. (2025). The AI Act Manipulation Gap, 39 Emory Int'l L. Rev. 417 Available at: https://scholarlycommons.law.emory.edu/eilr/vol39/iss2/1

Boulianne, S., & Humprecht, E. (2023). Perceived exposure to misinformation and trust in institutions in four countries before and during a pandemic. *International Journal of Communication, 17*, 24.

Braun, V., & Clarke, V. (2024). Reporting guidelines for qualitative research: A values-based approach. *Qualitative Research in Psychology, 22*(2), 399–438. DOI: 10.1080/14780887.2024.2382244

Bryda, G., & Costa, A. P. (2023). Qualitative Research in Digital Era: Innovations, Methodologies and Collaborations. *Social Sciences, 12*(10), 570. DOI: 10.3390/socsci12100570

Cancela-Outeda, C. (2024). The EU's AI act: A framework for collaborative governance. *Internet of Things : Engineering Cyber Physical Human Systems, 27*, 101291. DOI: 10.1016/j.iot.2024.101291

Cath, C. (2018). Governing artificial intelligence: Ethical, legal and technical opportunities and challenges. *Philosophical Transactions of the Royal Society A*, *376*(2133), 20180080. DOI: 10.1098/rsta.2018.0080

Cauffman, C., & Goanta, C. (2021). A New Order: The Digital Services Act and Consumer Protection. *European Journal of Risk Regulation*, *12*(4), 758–774. DOI: 10.1017/err.2021.8

Coeckelbergh, M. (2025). Artificial intelligence, the common good, and the democratic deficit in AI governance. *AI and Ethics*, *5*, 1491–1497. DOI: 10.1007/s43681-024-00492-9

Conservative People's Party of Estonia. (2023). EKRE political manifesto and election strategies. Tallinn: EKRE Policy Publications Conservative People's Party of Estonia. (2025. Official EKRE TikTok profile [TikTok]. Retrieved March 10, 2025, from https://www.tiktok.com/@erakondekre

de Jonge, L., & Gaufman, E. (2022). The normalisation of the far right in the Dutch media in the run-up to the 2021 general elections. *Discourse & Society*, *33*(6), 773–787. DOI: 10.1177/09579265221095418

Dommett, K., Luke, S., & Gordon, H. C. (2025). Making elections more transparent? Lessons from the implementation of digital imprints at the 2024 UK General Election. *Policy Studies*, •••, 1–24. DOI: 10.1080/01442872.2025.2482869

Duberry, J. (2022). Artificial intelligence and democracy: risks and promises of AI-mediated citizen–government relations. In *Artificial intelligence and democracy*. Edward Elgar Publishing.

Edwards, L. (2022). Regulating AI in Europe: four problems and four solutions (Ada Lovelace Institute Expert Opinion). *Europe: four problems and four solutions (Ada Lovelace Institute Expert Opinion).* DOI: 10.2139/ssrn.5026691

Elo, S., & Kyngäs, H. (2008). The qualitative content analysis process. *Journal of Advanced Nursing*, *62*(1), 107–115.

European Parliament. (2023). Artificial intelligence, democracy, and elections [Briefing paper]. European Parliamentary Research Service (EPRS). Retrieved from https://www.europarl.europa.eu/RegData/etudes/BRIE/2023/751478/EPRS_BRI(2023)751478_ EN.pdf

Farkas, J., & Schou, J. (2019). *Post-Truth, Fake News and Democracy*. Mapping the Politics of Falsehood., DOI: 10.4324/9780429317347

FdI. [@FdI.paginaufficiale]. (2025, August 14). Fratelli d'Italia official Facebook profile [Profile]. Facebook Official page for Fratelli d'Italia. Retrieved from https://www.facebook.com/FdI.paginaufficiale/

Fischli, R., & Muldoon, J. (2024). Empowering Digital Democracy. *Perspectives on Politics, 22*(3), 819–835. DOI: 10.1017/S1537592724000409

Floridi, L. (2023). *The Ethics of Artificial Intelligence: Principles, Challenges, and Opportunities*. Oxford University Press., DOI: 10.1093/oso/9780198883098.001.0001

Fratelli d'Italia. (n.d.). Official TikTok profile [TikTok]. Retrieved March 10, 2025, from https://www.tiktok.com/@fratelliditalia

Fuchs, C. (2022). *Digital Democracy and the Digital Public Sphere: Media, Communication and Society Volume Six* (1st ed.). Routledge., DOI: 10.4324/9781003331087

Gornet, M., & Maxwell, W. (2024). The European approach to regulating AI through technical standards. *Internet Policy Review, 13*(3). Advance online publication. DOI: 10.14763/2024.3.1784

Government of the Netherlands. (2024, January). Government-wide vision on generative AI [PDF]. Retrieved from file:///Users/Paphne/Downloads/Government-wide+vision+on+generative+AI+of+the+Netherlands%20(1).pdf

Habermas, J. (1991). *The structural transformation of the public sphere*. MIT Press.

Innerarity, D. (2024). The epistemic impossibility of an artificial intelligence take-over of democracy. *AI & Society, 39*, 1667–1671. DOI: 10.1007/s00146-023-01632-1

Jakobson, M. L. (2024). Populism in the 2024 European Parliament Elections in Estonia. In: *2024 EP Elections under the Shadow of Rising Populism*. (eds). Gilles Ivaldi and Emilia Zankina. European Center for Populism Studies (ECPS. October 22, 2024. DOI: 10.55271/rp0068

Kakavand, A. E. (2023). Far-right social media communication in the light of technology affordances: A systematic literature review. *Annals of the International Communication Association, 48*(1), 37–56. DOI: 10.1080/23808985.2023.2280824

Kalsnes, B. (2023). Introducing digital source criticism: A method for tackling fake news and disinformation. In *The Routledge Handbook of Discourse and Disinformation* (pp. 52–63). Routledge.

Kasekamp, A. (2003). Extreme-right parties in contemporary Estonia. *Patterns of Prejudice, 37*, 401–414. DOI: 10.1080/0031322032000144483

Küsters, R., Poli, C., Réau, B., & Warhem, R. (2023). The threat of digital populism to European democracy: Algorithmic governance and disinformation. CEP Study. https://www.cep.eu/eu-topics/details/the-threat-of-digital-populism-to-european-democracy-cepstudy.html

Laclau, E. (2005). *On populist reason*. Verso.

Laux, J. (2024). Institutionalised distrust and human oversight of artificial intelligence: Towards a democratic design of AI governance under the European Union AI Act. *AI & Society*, *39*(6), 2853–2866. DOI: 10.1007/s00146-023-01777-z

Madiega, T., & Ilnicki, R. (2024, April 4). AI investment: EU and global indicators. European Parliamentary Research Service. Retrieved from https://epthinktank.eu/2024/04/04/ai-investment- eu-and-global-indicators/

Mitrou, L. (2018). Data Protection, Artificial Intelligence and Cognitive Services: Is the General Data Protection Regulation (GDPR) 'Artificial Intelligence-Proof'? Available at *SSRN*: https://ssrn.com/abstract=3386914 or DOI: 10.2139/ssrn.3386914

Morosoli, S., Kieslich, K., Resendez, V., & van Drunen, M. (2025). AI governance in the spotlight: An empirical analysis of Dutch political parties' strategies for the 2023 elections. *Journal of Information Technology & Politics*, 1–16. DOI: 10.1080/19331681.2025.2504519

Mudde, C. (2021). *The far-right today*. Polity Press.

Mudde, C., & Kaltwasser, C. R. (2017). *Populism: A Very Short Introduction, Very Short Introductions*. Oxford University Press., DOI: 10.1093/actrade/9780190234874.001.0001

Mudde, C., & Rovira Kaltwasser, C. (2017). *Populism: A very short introduction*. Oxford University Press.

Muller, C., Talvitie, C., & Schöppl, N. Our Minds, Monitored and Manipulated: How AI Impacts Public Discourse and Democracy, VerfBlog, 2022/3/28, https://verfassungsblog.de/roa-our-minds/, DOI: 10.17176/20220329-011119-0

Neudert, L. M., & Marchal, N. (2019, March). *Polarisation and the use of technology in political campaigns and communication* [Study]. European Parliament, Directorate-General for Parliamentary Research Services (EPRS). Retrieved from https://www.europarl.europa.eu/RegData/etudes/STUD/2019/634414/EPRS_STU(2019)634414_EN.pdf

Newell, J. L. (2024). Fratelli d'Italia and Giorgia Meloni at the start of 2024. *Contemporary Italian Politics*, *16*(1), 1–6. DOI: 10.1080/23248823.2024.2303192

Nortal. (2024, August 14). How AI accelerates the legislative power of the Parliament of Estonia. Nortal. Retrieved from https://nortal.com/insights/how-ai-accelerates-the-legislative-power-of- the-parliament-of-estonia

Novelli, C., & Sandri, G. (2024). Digital Democracy in the Age of Artificial Intelligence. SSRN Electronic Journal. DOI: 10.2139/ssrn.4901264

Nugent, N. (2017). *The government and politics of the European Union*. Bloomsbury Publishing.

OECD. (2024). *2023 OECD Digital Government Index: Results and key findings*. OECD Public.

Party for Freedom. (2024, May 15). AI-enhanced nationalist campaign video [TikTok video]. TikTok. Retrieved March 10, 2025, from https://vm.tiktok.com/ZNdet3HKr/

Pena, J. M. (2024). Author Normativities for artificial intelligence: Analysis from Latin America Librarianship approach. *South African Journal of Library and Information Science*. Advance online publication. DOI: 10.7553/90-2-2397

Pollicino, O., De Gregorio, G., Democracy, C., Powers, P., & Populism, D. (2022, August 9). [University of Wisconsin]. *Constitutional Studies*, *8*, 2022.

PVV. (2025). Home. Party for Freedom. Retrieved August 14, 2025, from https://www.pvv.nl/

Rabitsch, A., & Calabrese, S. (2024). The EU's Artificial Intelligence Act and its Impact on Electoral Processes: a Human Rights-Based Approach. *presentation, IEIP*, 8-12.

Rabitsch, A., Wazir, R., & Treml, T. (2021). Artificial intelligence's (AI) impact on freedom of expression in political campaigns and elections [Policy paper]. ElectionWatch.EU; data4good Initiative of the Vienna Data Science Group (VDSG). https://www.osce.org/files/f/documents/a/3/483638.pdf

Raik, K. 2021. *Estonian Foreign Policy Institute 2020 Annual Report*, International Centre for Defence and Security. Estonia. Retrieved from https://coilink.org/20.500.12592/b1wxzn on 15 Aug 2025. COI: 20.500.12592/b1wxzn

Reform Party. (n.d.). Official Website. Retrieved from https://reform.ee/en/ (Accessed: December 22, 2024)

Roemmele, A., & Gibson, R. (2020). Scientific and subversive: The two faces of the fourth era of political campaigning. *New Media & Society*, *22*(4), 595–610. DOI: 10.1177/1461444819893979

Samuelsen, R. J., Kalsnes, B., & Steensen, S. (2023). The Relevance of Technology to Information Verification: Insights from Norwegian Journalism During a National Election. *Journalism Practice*, *19*(8), 1683–1702. DOI: 10.1080/17512786.2023.2280676

Sartor, G. (2020) The Impact of the General Data Protection Regulation (GDPR) on Artificial Intelligences. EPRS|European Parliamentary Research Service Scientific Foresight Unit (STOA), PE 641.530, European University Institute of Florence. https://www.europarl.europa.eu/RegData/etudes/STUD/2020/641530/EPRS_STU(2020)641530_EN.pdf

Schippers, B. (2020). Artificial intelligence and democratic politics. *Political Insight*, *11*(1), 32–35. DOI: 10.1177/2041905820911746

Schmitt, H., & Teperoglou, E. (2021). "Chapter 4: Second-order elections and electoral democracy". In Handbook on Decentralization, Devolution and the State. Cheltenham, UK: Edward Elgar Publishing. Retrieved Aug 14, 2025, from DOI: 10.4337/9781839103285.00010

Simchon, A., Edwards, M., & Lewandowsky, S. (2024). The persuasive effects of political microtargeting in the age of generative artificial intelligence. *PNAS Nexus*, *3*(2), pgae035. Advance online publication. DOI: 10.1093/pnasnexus/pgae035

Sovrano, F., & Vitali, F. (2024). Explanatory artificial intelligence (YAI): Human-centered explanations of explainable AI and complex data. *Data Mining and Knowledge Discovery*, *38*, 3141–3168. DOI: 10.1007/s10618-022-00872-x

Stavrakakis, Y., & Katsambekis, G. (2019). The populism/anti-populism frontier and its mediation in crisis- ridden Greece: From discursive divide to emerging cleavage? *European Political Science*, *18*, 37–52. DOI: 10.1057/s41304-017-0138-3

SYRIZA. (2024). Official SYRIZA TikTok profile [TikTok]. Retrieved March 10, 2025, from https://vm.tiktok.com/ZNdebENPh/

SYRIZA. (2025). Official Campaign Website. Retrieved from https://www.syriza .gr/ (Accessed: December 22, 2024)

Teperoglou, E., Tsatsanis, E., & Nicolacopoulos, E. (2015). Habituating to the New Normal in a Post-earthquake Party System: The 2014 European Election in Greece. *South European Society & Politics*, *20*(3), 333–355. DOI: 10.1080/13608746.2015.1068377

The Digital Services Act. (2023). European Commission. Retrieved from https://commission.europa.eu/strategy-and-policy/priorities-2019-2024/europe-fit-digital - age/digital-services-act_en (Accessed: December 22, 2024)

The General Data Protection Regulation (GDPR). (2018). European Union. Retrieved from https://gdpr.eu/ (Accessed: December 22, 2024)

The Guardian. (2024, November 26). How the far-right weaponizing AI-generated content in European elections. The Guardian. https://www.theguardian.com/technology/2024/nov/26/far- right-weaponising-ai-generated-content-europe

The Party for Freedom (PVV). (n.d.). Official Website. Retrieved from https://www.pvv.nl/ (Accessed: December 22, 2024)

Transparency and Targeting of Political Advertising Act (TTPA). (2023). *European Union Regulations on Political Advertising*. European Commission.

Turillazzi, A., Taddeo, M., Floridi, L., & Casolari, F. (2023). The digital services act: An analysis of its ethical, legal, and social implications. *Law, Innovation and Technology*, *15*(1), 83–106. DOI: 10.1080/17579961.2023.2184136

van Dijk, J. A. G. M. (2013). A theory of the digital divide. In M. Ragnedda, & G. W. Muschert (Eds.), The digital divide: the internet and social inequality in international perspective (pp. 29- 51). (Routledge advances in sociology; Vol. 73, No. 73). Routledge.

Wilders, G. [@geertwilders]. (2024, March 15). Facebook. https://www.facebook.com/geertwilders

Wilson, C. (2022). Public engagement and AI: A values analysis of national strategies. *Government Information Quarterly*, *39*(1), 101652. DOI: 10.1016/j.giq.2021.101652

Winfield, A. F. T., & Jirotka, M. (2018). Ethical governance is essential to building trust in robotics and artificial intelligence systems. *Philosophical Transactions of the Royal Society A*. Advance online publication. DOI: 10.1098/rsta.2018.0085

Wulf, A. J., & Seizov, O. (2022). 'Please Understand We Cannot Provide Further Information': Evaluating Content and Transparency of GDPR-Mandated AI Disclosures. *AI & Society*. Available at SSRN: https://ssrn.com/abstract=4478311 or http://dx.doi.org/DOI: 10.2139/ssrn.4478311

Zhu, J., & Isaacs, R. (2024, May 29). Campaign microtargeting and AI can jeopardize democracy. London School of Economics and Political Science. Retrieved from https://blogs.lse.ac.uk/politicsandpolicy/campaign-microtargeting-and-ai-can-jeopardize- democracy/

Zuboff, S. (2019). *The age of surveillance capitalism: The fight for a human future at the new frontier of power, edn*. PublicAffairs.

About the Contributors

Georgia Panagiotidou is a political scientist and researcher specializing in applied political analysis, comparative electoral studies, data science, and research methods. Over the past decade, she has been teaching quantitative and qualitative methodology, political marketing, and electoral analysis at multiple institutions, including Aristotle University of Thessaloniki, Hellenic Open University, the University of the Aegean, and for the University of Derby (Mediterranean College). A key focus of Dr Panagiotidou's research lies in voter prediction through machine learning, the study of political behavior, and the promotion of civic engagement. She works as a postdoctoral researcher in the Horizon Europe project AI4GOV, which explores the integration of artificial intelligence in governance, and is actively involved in Sol4all and EUdream, two CERV-funded projects centered on political participation and civic engagement. In addition, she was the scientific leader of the cross-national study Youth Stand for the Future of Europe, commissioned by the European Union, where she coordinated a multi-country team investigating youth perspectives on European integration. Beyond these projects, Dr Panagiotidou has contributed to notable initiatives such as helpmevote.gr, Greece's pioneering Voting Advice Application, and took part in the COST True European Voter project, further solidifying her expertise in comparative electoral analysis. Her research has been published in peer-reviewed journals, monographs, and edited volumes and she is the editor of the Understanding Voter Behavior with Predictive Modeling. She has presented her work at numerous international scientific conferences.

***

Mohamed Assoud is a Marketing Management and Research Methodology Professor and Editorial Board Member with a focus on Brand management, Digital Marketing, Consumer Psychology and Behavior. Experienced in designing and delivering innovative courses, mentoring students, and conducting impactful research published in high-ranking journals. Skilled in applying advanced analytical tools and interdisciplinary approaches to solve complex marketing challenges, while contributing to academic discourse through editorial leadership.

Lahoucine Berbou is a Professor of Marketing at the National School of Commerce and Management (ENCG) of Settat, Hassan First University of Settat, Morocco. His research focuses on Management, Marketing and Human Ressources Management, with a particular interest in emerging markets. He has published in peer-reviewed journals and presented his work at national and international conferences.

Samuel Brown is Professor of Public Service at Old Dominion University. He received a Ph.D. in Public Policy from the University of Maryland, Baltimore County, an M.B.A. from the University of Baltimore and a Bachelor's degree in Economics from Towson State University. Previously he was Director of the Hugo Wall School of Public Affairs and tenured Professor of Public Affairs at Wichita State University.

Stefano Camatarri is a Postdoctoral Researcher at the Université catholique de Louvain (UCLouvain) and the Université catholique de Lille. His research focuses on public opinion and political behaviour. He has published in journals such as European Union Politics, Swiss Political Science Review, and the Journal of Elections, Public Opinion and Parties.

Klimentini Diakomanoli European Commission official (Senior Expert) specialised in disinformation, media and Press issues around EU policies. Author of the Book "Fake News: What does Europe do?", published in Greek and French (2021, 2023 and 2024). Former specialised diplomat and lawyer with M.A. in Digital Media and Crisis Communication and a D.E.A in Penal Law and Criminology.

Norou Diawara a Professor of Statistics in the Mathematics and Statistics Department at Old Dominion University (ODU), Norfolk, Virginia, United States. He earned a B.S. at the University Cheick Anta Diop in Dakar, Senegal, a Maîtrise in Mathematics at University of Le Havre, Le Havre, France, a Master's in Mathematics and Statistics at University South Alabama, Mobile, Alabama, and a Ph.D. in Statistics from Auburn University in Auburn, Alabama in 2006.

Marta Gallina is Associate Professor in Political Science at the Catholic University of Lille within the European School of Political and Social Sciences (ESPOL). Previously, she worked as postdoctoral researcher in different institutions, such as the Autonomous University of Barcelona in Spain, Waseda University in

Japan and the Catholic University of Louvain in Belgium. She received her PhD in Political Science from the Catholic University of Louvain in 2021. Her work appeared in scientific journals such as Political Studies, Journal of Elections, Public Opinion and Parties, International Journal of Public Opinion Research and Regional and Federal Studies.

Grigorios Giannarakis is an Associate Professor in the Department of Business Administration at the University of Western Macedonia, Greece. His research interests focus on sustainability, corporate governance, and environmental, social, and governance (ESG) disclosures.

Tiffany Henley, PhD is an Associate Professor in the Department of Public Administration at Pace University. She teaches courses in public administration, health care administration, and health policy in New York City.

Iqbal Hossain is a PhD candidate in Computational & Applied Mathematics in the Mathematics and Statistics Department, at Old Dominion University, Norfolk, VA, USA. He received his B.S. in Statistics from the University of Dhaka, Bangladesh, in 2017, and M.S. in Applied Statistics and Analytics at Central Michigan University, Mount Pleasant, MI, USA, in 2020; His research areas are Control charts for zero-truncated count data.

Ioannis Mallidis is an Associate Professor in the Department of Statistics and Insurance Science at the University of Western Macedonia, Greece. His research focuses on forecasting models, applied statistics, and decision analysis.

Konstantinos Mamais is a Post-doc research analyst in financial forecasting and decision making, with a Ph.D. focused on Financial Investment Strategies in Global Markets, Investment Decisions, Econometrics, and Quantitative Economics from the University of Piraeus. Dr. Mamais has published papers in International scientific journals and Conference proceedings, with citations, received. Skilled in R, Gretl, and Stata on Finance, Econometrics, and Quantitative Analytics. Experienced in the Banking sector with a focus on international market and equity analysis. Research interests are in financial forecasting, investment decision-making, and global market analysis, company pricing.

Dimitra Mari is a PhD Candidate at Panteion University and Programme Leader at Mediterranean College. With 6+ years of experience in advertising, PR, and events, she has led brand communication projects for major international and local clients, including L'Oréal, Novartis, Red Bull, Henkel, Pernod Ricard, OPAP, and the Hellenic Paralympic Committee. Since 2021, she has focused on Academia, with her thesis titled "Sexism and Public Discourse – Media Representations of the Greek Me Too Movement". She has been an Academic Workshop Partner at Panteion University (2022-2024) and was awarded the Supporting Teaching Fellowship in 2022. At Mediterranean College, she oversees undergraduate and postgraduate programmes in Marketing, PR, Advertising, and Digital Marketing. Her research interests include women's empowerment, politics, contemporary art, branding, storytelling, advertising, digital marketing, media, social trends, pop culture, and corporate culture.

Evangelia Markaki is an AI consultant specialist and an associate professor at Mediterranean College Greece holding a post-doctoral research in Applied Statistics from Aristotle University of Thessaloniki, where she was lecturer since 2016. She teaches at Karlsruhe University, Germany, since 2018. She manages national and international business and research projects and has extensive experience in HRM field. Since 2008, she has worked in business consulting industry. She holds a GDPR Specialist & DPO certificate and has collaborated with organizations such as the National Insurance Company of Greece, ERT, Athens 2004 Olympic Broadcasting company, Kienbaum Cons., and VPRC. She is adjunct lecturer at universities in Greece and abroad, teaching HRM, Leadership, Game Theory, Applied Statistics, and Strategic Decision-Making. Author of two books about decision making and networks (2020 & 2022), she has over 30 academic publications and was a GIWA nominee in 2021 and 2023.

Lerato Moyo is pursuing a Bachelor of Arts Honors Degree in Film, Television and Media Studies at Lupane State University. His research interests are in political communication, media representation and audience reception studies

Ravikumar R. Natarajan is an experienced academician with over 12+ years of teaching and research expertise across institutions in India, the UAE, and the Maldives. He currently serves as an Assistant Professor at Marwadi University, Rajkot, specializing in Machine Learning, Recommender Systems, and AI-driven applications in healthcare and security. He holds a Ph.D. in Machine Learning and Recommender Systems from Amity University, Jaipur, a Master of Engineering in CSE from VMRF University, Salem, and a Bachelor of Engineering in CSE from Anna University. He also has a MiniMBA from the Swiss eLearning Institute. Dr. Ravikumar has authored more than 8+ multiple SCIE/Scopus-indexed journal articles, 25+ IEEE/Springer conference papers, and co-authored a book on Artificial Intelligence. He has also published 9 patents and contributed 10+ book chapters in emerging domains such as Federated Learning, Blockchain, and Digital Twins for IGI Global, Wiley and Springer publisher. He actively mentors students through initiatives like the Research Activities Club (RAC) and Student Research Internship Training (SRIT), promoting innovation and research culture.

Aarthi S is a dedicated Assistant Professor in Computer Science with over six years of teaching experience. She is currently pursuing her Ph.D. at Marwadi University, Gujarat, and holds an M.Phil. and MCA from Bharathiar University, Tamil Nadu. Throughout her academic career, Aarthi has specialized in programming languages such as C++, Java, and C, and contributed to research in recommender systems and AI-related data privacy. She has published journal articles, contributed to book chapters, and actively participated in technical workshops. Known for her student mentorship and engagement in academic events, Aarthi remains committed to fostering innovation and excellence in computer science education.

Vaia Stavridou is a graduate of Political Science from Aristotle University of Thessaloniki. She holds two Master's degrees: the first in Democracy, Citizenship, and Change from Dalarna University in Sweden, and the second in Governance and Regional Development from Aristotle University of Thessaloniki. The first dissertation focused on digital sovereignty within the European Union, while the second concentrated on institutional reform in specific policy areas of the EU Commission and Greek public administration. Her research interests include AI in public administration, digital democracy, and regulatory frameworks surrounding AI, particularly in the context of electoral integrity.

Thiruvenkadam Thangavel, Professor and Head at the School of Information Technology - CDOE, SRM University Sikkim, holds a Ph.D. in Computer Science and brings over 18 years of academic experience, including 4 years of international teaching exposure. His areas of expertise include Cloud Computing, Virtualization, Computer Networks, Operating Systems, Data Science and Machine Learning. He has authored two books, completed two funded research projects, and published 27 research articles in reputed journals indexed in Scopus, also filed four design patents. He has served as a resource person in numerous national and international seminars and workshops. He has attended more than 25 international and national conferences and workshops and organized several national-level seminars, conferences, workshops, hands-on training sessions, blood donation drives, and NSS special camping programs. He also holds an Associate-level global certification as an AWS Solutions Architect.

Akbar Toyirov is working in the Department of Information Technology and Exact Sciences at Termez University of Economics and Service, Termez, Uzbekistan.

Grigorios Tsiligkaridis is a PhD Candidate in the Department of Statistics and Insurance Science at the University of Western Macedonia, Greece. His research interests include forecasting models, election studies,corporate governance, and ESG disclosures

Virginia Tsoukatou graduated from the Department of Political Science and International Relations of the University of Peloponnese in 2013 with honors, having been a scholarship of the State Scholarship Foundation for three consecutive years (award and performance scholarship awarded to students with the highest average grade per year). After graduating from the department, she continued her studies at the University of Cambridge where she graduated with the postgraduate title Mphil in Management. The following year 2014-2015 she studied at the London School of Economics and Political Science (LSE) from which he graduated with an MSc in Political Economy of Europe. In 2023 Dr Tsoukatou received her PhD in labour economics being scholar from State Scholarship Foundation. Today, she is accredited lecturer at University of Derby, teaching economics oriented modules.

Index

R

S

U

V

www.ingramcontent.com/pod-product-compliance
Lightning Source LLC
LaVergne TN
LVHW061529290926
849162LV00004B/724